Handbook of
ADOLESCENTS
and
FAMILY THERAPY

EDITED BY

Marsha Pravder Mirkin, Ph.D.
AND *Stuart L. Koman, Ph.D.*

FOREWORD BY CARLOS E. SLUZKI, M.D.

Allyn and Bacon
Boston   London   Sydney   Toronto

Copyright © 1985 by Allyn and Bacon
A Division of Simon & Schuster
160 Gould Street
Needham Heights, MA 02194

Library of Congress Cataloging in Publication Data
Main entry under title:

Adolescents and family therapy

Includes index.
1. Adolescent psychotherapy. 2. Family psychotherapy.
I. Mirkin, Marsha Pravder, 1953- . II. Koman, Stuart, 1954-
III. Title [DNLM: 1. Reproduction—In adolescence.
2. Sex behavior—In adolescence. 3. Contraception—in
adolescence. 4. Family planning. HQ 763.5 S65a]
RJ503.A328 1985   616.89'1'pr088055   83-16519

ISBN: 0-205-12448-8

Printed in the United States of America
10 9 8 7 6 5 4 3 2   94 93 92 91 90 89

Dedicated to our families:
past, present, and future

Foreword

A baby is born. Mysterious as his/her experiences may be to us observers from the world of the grown-ups, everything seems to indicate that the baby's experiences are a-temporal, that time dimensions have no internal representation for the newborn. From that assumption derives the attractive construct of psychodynamic origin that proposes that any deprivation suffered by the newborn is instantaneously experienced by him/her as an imminent catastrophy or death: there is no sense, however minuscule, of any future from which any hope of relief can be expected. What stage unfolds in the germinal development of the notion of time? The progressive incorporation of an image of future as a dimension distinct from the present is preceded by a spacial rather than temporal device, namely, the baby may generate an hallucinatory image of the needed object/experience in order to calm the anxiety created by its absence, until the need is met. Thus, the experience of waiting begins to lose its catastrophic quality as it transforms itself slowly into the more tolerable one of uncertitude. The experience of temporality grants instrumental quality to the hallucination but makes it unnecessary. Space becomes time; the world of hallucinations is progressively replaced by the world of thought, riding on the wave of the existentially apprehended notion of prospective. Hypothetic as all these elegant constructs may be, the fact is that, from its very inception, the experience of our own mind, of our own body, and our old-world ties in a common destiny with the *experience of prospection*, that is, the image that we have about our own future in which we are included as a figure.

Throughout infancy and childhood, prospective seems to be subdivided into two realms: an immediate one, which is apprehended and incorporated by the child as an instrumentable time-span in reference to different daily behaviors; and a mediate realm, which remains for the child as a nebulous intuition, a semi-intellectual acknowledgment over which the child does not claim ownership. (At age five, for instance, the promise of an ice cream this afternoon is more real and more motivating than that of a magnificent vacation six months from now.)

In adolescence, associated to the fireworks of abstract language and thought, the prospective dimension emerges in all its magnitude. The adolescent grasps it and feasts on it following a process with enormous individual variation but with a common pattern. We are witnessing the birth of the notion of "a future of his own," an experience that could be described as the subject being in the center of a circular or spherical field which has such an indefinite extension that its edge defies perception. Two types of emotions are attached in an intertwined fashion to this discovery/experience: the omnipotence derived from being able to project into the field of the future, limited only by the reach of the subject's imagination/fantasy; and the abysmal anxiety of knowing that this field, indefinite as it may look and be experienced, has a boundary. Thus the co-presence in the adolescents of the sensation of possessing all the time in the world and all the potential options, and the prediction of the subject's own death, for the first time as real as life.

One way or another, the storms of adolescence place the subject in the center of the vortex of his/her prospective. Even though, as occurs with any change, it takes place not as a curve but as a spiral, the transition between adolescence and early adulthood is expressed in this area with maximal clarity: the subject projects his presence in the future, and implements this projection, stacks the space/temporal field in which he will evolve, states, by word or action, "I will be/do this activity/role/ profession/person in my life, and not all the other possible alternatives." The width of the territory and the length of its radius will be, without doubt, affected by social determinants (the socio-economic and cultural feasibility of reaching those goals), by the amount of obstacles or facilitation in the road toward the goals, by familial styles, histories and patterns, and by individual skills and aptitudes. To choose a field will mean unavoidably to abandon, lose, or sacrifice other fields/projects, as any option implies exclusions, even in the case of the most passionate vocations. Not infrequently, as a prelude to this period, there will be a shifting back-and-forth between alternative fields of choice, perhaps as an interpersonal test, perhaps as an attempt to avoid the mourning of lost projects. In some cases, we witness a freeze, an incapacity to choose; in others, precipitous choices that may lead, years later, to changes in career, or to hobbies, or to a melancholic self-reproach.

The image of the extension of the subject's prospective field, i.e., the "depth" of his/her personal future, tends to shrink in proportion to the progression of aging, aided by the real presence of death, appearing habitually first in members of the preceding generation and then in the generation of the subject, reinforcing the universal awareness that people, in the long run, grow old and die. This process of reduction in prospection, far from being uniform, is also extremely discontinuous and occurs by jumps, habitually matching the random but relentless occurrence of "real" evidences of the passage of time (physical or psychic involution, death of parents, relatives and friends, the completion or failure to complete projects, the capacity or lack of it to initiate new projects, etc.) and other powerful indicators (such as becoming the target of biased social attitudes toward older people, e.g., discrimination against aging people in employment, etc). These jumps or jolts will appear as crisis in the life cycle of the adult and aging person. The subjective vicissitudes that accompany the shrinking of the prospective field will reflect the adaptive and creative capacity of the subject as well as the availability of alternative resources in his/her network. The subjective impact of the passage of time will be, in the long run, inversely proportioned to the capacity of the subject and his/her network to transform, in this area, quantity into quality. This transformation is not a process that takes place in old age (even though on some occasions it appears just then) but it occurs throughout the course of life. It is the overall product of individual and network resources, knowledge and experience; it is, to a good point, a project which requires collective participation. The result is a qualitative expansion of the boundaries of the prospective field, as it fuses itself with that of other people and other generations and makes of life a collective, rather than individual, experience.

These brief notes about the prospective field as an existential dimension throughout life convey some of the many lines of thought triggered in me by this book. A family evolves as a system or as a gestalt, while family members who belong to a different generation, simply by the fact that they are in a different moment of their development, *cannot* share many of their values, parameters and experiences both of time and of space, regardless of how much they want

and try. These members were in fact raised in different families and in different cultures—as most cultures evolve at present by leaps and bounds and have a direct access to individuals without the mediation of the family. Thus, with the exception of magic moments that visit, with greater or lesser frequency, most relationships, the generation gap may be meant to be bridged only in a minority of cases, when members of different generations happen to reach a period in which they share values and a common prospective territory, as may be the case with some not-too-old parents and some grownup offsprings.

Families, we should note, do not have any developmental tasks, they simply are, they simply evolve. Families have been described, however, as the main socializing agent, as the mediator in the transmission of norms from the culture into the individual being socialized. But, of course, this task lies on the shoulders of one subsystem, the parental one (and occasionally in the parentified component of any other subsystem). Which is, in that context, if any, the reciprocal task of the adolescent offsprings? In addition to the inevitable (albeit frequently questioned) task of being socialized, the task of the offspring could be defined as one of socializing the parents, at least in terms of the adolescents being intermediaries between the evolving new cultural norms and mores to which they are exposed at school and in other contexts, and their parents. However, needless to say, the process of parental evolution, of (re) socialization by their adolescent offspring is undermined not only by the difficulty of all members to shift family rules about roles (not to mention the fact that the socialization of parents is a task for which society bears no recognition) but by the fact that adolescents and grownups bring with them their respective views of prospective. Two sets of potential areas of familial conflict derive from these observations. One stems from the fact that change occurs through evolution and not through instruction. Putting it other ways, the passage from, e.g., the sense of owning a field with a total width and an indefinite length to the active choice of one slice of the pie of life occurs by a lengthy and complex individual evolution that cannot be replaced at all by no matter how many statements of wisdom by the wisest of the parental figures (which is probably the origin of that adult-centered statement "adolescence is a disease that only time can cure"). Thus the reiterated experience of frustration of parents who fail to teach their offspring on the bases of their own prior errors and the despair of adolescents who sense that these parents interfere with their life. Another source of conflict derives from the fact that these struggles and this idiosyncratic management of present and future by adolescents may reactivate in the parents their own unavoidably unresolved issues about prior life choices which they may or may not want to re-examine (as complicated as the fact that the future is uncertain, is the fact that the past is irretrievable!). Thus, an interesting equation frequently occurs between parents and adolescents by which the more the parents adhere to their values and defend their prior choices, the more the adolescent will question them and vice-versa. Educating the parents is probably as difficult a task for the adolescent as it is for the former to educate the latter. However, that reciprocal task is carried on faithfully, generation after generation. A curious, stubborn species is ours!

The editors and authors of this remarkable *Handbook of Adolescents and Family Therapy* have chosen the uneasy endeavor of exploring the many dimensions of the family as it evolves during a specific period in which one of its members display physiological, epigenetic and culturally-determined attributes and behaviors of being an adolescent, and other members display complementary attributes and behaviors. The authors define a normative period in the family life cycle, and, catching observables with a systemic net, explore generic and specific problems frequently noticed during that period, as well as attempt solutions, both those that contribute to perpetuate problems and those that contribute to their resolution—family strengths and resources as well as therapeutic contexts and interventions.

The contributions to this *Handbook* cover a vast territory. The prior paucity of the literature in the field of families and family therapy with adolescents is such that it increases even further the merit of this book as it breaks ground, plows and seeds. It is for us readers to harvest, process and gratefully nourish from this major, most welcome intellectual effort. And also to plow again, and seed again, and so on.

Carlos E. Sluzki, M.D.

Contents

PART I. THEORETICAL BACKGROUND

PART II. PRACTICE AND SETTINGS

PART III. ISSUES IN TREATMENT

Contributors

Cynthia G. Adrian, Ph.D.
   Psychology Intern
   Charles River Hospital
   Wellesley, Massachusetts

Larry G. Brown, M.S.W.
   Northeast Parent and Child Society
   Schenectady, New York

Marc D. Cohen, M.S.W.
   Coordinator of Planning and Research
   Charles River Hospital
   Wellesley, Massachusetts

Kenneth W. Covelman, Ph.D.
   Senior Faculty
   Family Therapy Training Center
   Philadelphia Child Guidance Clinic
   Philadelphia, Pennsylvania

Joseph Crumbley, D.S.W.
   Program Director
   Inpatient Adolescent Psychiatric Unit
   Fairmont Institute
   Philadelphia, Pennsylvania

A. Michael DeSisto
   Director
   DeSisto Schools
   West Stockbridge, Massachusetts

Barbara J. Green, Ph.D.
   Private Practice
   Hingham, Massachusetts
   (and)
   Senior Clinical Consultant
   Charles River Hospital
   Wellesley, Massachusetts

Edward Kaufman, M.D.
   Associate Professor
   Department of Psychiatry and Human
      Behavior
   College of Medicine
   University of California, Irvine
   Orange, California

Jamie Kelem Keshet, M.S.W.
   Assistant Director
   Institute for Remarriage and
      Stepfamilies
   Riverside Family Counseling
   Newtonville, Massachusetts

Newton Koltz
   Editor and Writer
   Newton Koltz & Associates
   Brooklyn, New York

Stuart L. Koman, Ph.D.
   Unit Administrator and
   Director of Ancillary Services
   Charles River Hospital
   Wellesley, Massachusetts
   (and)
   Assistant Clinical Professor
   Department of Psychiatry
   School of Medicine
   Boston University
   Boston, Massachusetts

Judith Landau-Stanton, M.D.
   Associate Professor of Psychiatry;
   Director and Chief Psychiatrist, Family
      and Marriage Clinic;
   Director of Family Therapy Training,
      Division of Family Programs
   Department of Psychiatry
   University of Rochester Medical Center
   Rochester, New York

Jay Lappin, M.S.W., A.C.S.W.
   Senior Faculty
   Family Therapy Training Center
   Philadelphia Child Guidance Center
   Philadelphia, Pennsylvania

Judith A. Libow, Ph.D.
   Clinical Psychologist
   Family Guidance Services
   Children's Hospital and Medical
      Center
   Oakland, California

Cloé Madanes, Lic.
  Co-Director
  Family Therapy Institute of Washington,
    D.C.
  Rockville, Maryland

Marsha Pravder Mirkin, Ph.D.
  Director of Adolescent Internship
    Training
  Charles River Hospital
  Wellesley, Massachusetts
  (and)
  Assistant Clinical Professor
  Department of Psychiatry
  School of Medicine
  Boston University
  Boston, Massachusetts

William Mitchell, Ed.D.
  Staff Psychologist
  Developmental Evaluation Clinic
  The Children's Hospital
  Boston, Massachusetts

Jess Morris, M.D.
  Staff Psychiatrist
  Westwood Lodge Hospital
  Westwood, Massachusetts

Thomas H. Neilans, Ph.D.
  Associate Director
  Family and Marriage Clinic
  University of Rochester Medical Center
  Rochester, New York

Betty Byfield Paul, L.I.C.S.W.
  Private Practice
  Counseling Associates
  Lexington, Massachusetts

Norman L. Paul, M.D.
  Associate Clinical Professor
  Department of Neurology
  School of Medicine
  Boston University
  (and)
  Private Practice
  Counseling Associates
  Lexington, Massachusetts

Nydia Garcia Preto, A.C.S.W
  Director
  Family Training Program
  (and) Director of Family Mediation
    Services
  University of Medicine and Dentistry of
    New Jersey

Community Mental Health Center of
  Rutgers Medical School
Piscataway, New Jersey

Russell J. Ricci, M.D.
  Chairman and Medical Director
  Behavioral Medical Care
  Wellesley, Massachusetts

Salvatore J. Rizzo, Ph.D.
  Clinical Director
  Boston Center for Family Health
  Brookline, Massachusetts

Michael Rohrbaugh, Ph.D.
  College of William and Mary
  Williamsburg, Virginia

Carlos E. Sluzki, M.D.
  Department of Psychiatry
  Berkshire Medical Center
  Pittsfield, Massachusetts

Joan L. Speck, M.S.W.
  Supervisor
  Family Institute of Philadelphia
  Philadelphia, Pennsylvania

Ross V. Speck, M.D.
  Clinical Professor
  Department of Psychiatry and Human
    Behavior
  Thomas Jefferson University
  Philadelphia, Pennsylvania

M. Duncan Stanton, Ph.D.
  Professor and Director
  Division of Family Programs
  Department of Psychiatry
  University of Rochester School of
    Medicine
  Rochester, New York

Gerald Stechler, Ph.D.
  Director of Child and Adolescent
    Services
  Charles River Hospital
  Wellesley, Massachusetts
  (and)
  Professor
  Department of Psychiatry
  School of Medicine
  Boston University
  Boston, Massachusetts

Martha Tavantzis, M.S.W.
  Clinical Supervisor

Northeast Parent and Child Society
Schenectady, New York

Thomas N. Tavantzis, Ed.D.
Associate Executive Director
Northeast Parent and Child Society
Schenectady, New York

Thomas C. Todd, Ph.D.
Director
Marriage & Family Therapy Training
Program
Bristol Hospital
Bristol, Connecticut

Norman Travis, Ph.D.
Clinical & Administrative Coordinator
Child Day Hospital
University of Medicine and Dentistry of
New Jersey
Community Mental Health Center of
Rutgers Medical School
Piscataway, New Jersey

John S. Weltner, M.D.
Director
North Shore Family Resource Center
Marblehead, Massachusetts

Preface

The *Handbook of Adolescents and Family Therapy* is a unique book. We know this, because as teachers and supervisors of a group of—at that time—novice family therapists working in a private hospital setting, we attempted and failed several times to find a book that would meet our needs in providing a framework for the comprehensive instruction of students in the application of systems theory to the various problems and settings encountered with adolescents. Each year as we searched for material to use in our seminar, we complained to each other about the lack of material in three specific areas. In reflecting on what we thought was missing in the literature, we recognized that each of these areas reflected an underlying perspective that we, as therapists and teachers, were deeply committed to. The three sections in this book are statements about these beliefs—beliefs that we have developed, in large part, through our training and through our experience with families. Specifically, the book attempts to focus on three elements: theory that integrates and organizes the many perspectives put forth in the field of family therapy over the last twenty years; the importance of the professional context in which one works and the various ways in which systems theory is applied, given the challenges of that particular environment; and the special problems that adolescents, families, and ultimately therapists face in understanding and intervening in adolescent symptomatology.

The first section, *Theoretical Background*, is composed of three chapters which share in their broad view of families and family therapy. In attempting to integrate various theoretical perspectives, this section of the book reflects a new stage in the evolution of theory regarding families and intervention in families. If, indeed, adolescence is the time when families must integrate perspectives from outside of the earlier, more protective unit consisting of parents and young children, then this stage in the evolution of family therapy may be seen as itself an adolescence of sorts. By enlarging the focus in each of their respective areas, the chapters present previously stated ideas in such a way as to enable anyone with knowledge in a sub-area to immediately grasp the larger theoretical context in which it exists. The chapters have been written in everyday language with useful case examples and metaphors so that the information presented clarifies rather than confuses. We believe that these chapters are good examples of systems thinking applied to the areas of family development, family therapist training, and the use of family therapy techniques, thus, sharing with the other two sections of the book, the ability to find application in one's everyday work.

We are proud to be associated with the achievements reflected in the chapters in Part II, *Practice and Settings*. Each chapter represents a great deal of hard work and commitment in the development of systems-based programs in widely different contexts. Chapters such as these are occasionally found in enlightened journals, but rarely in book format, and often go unrecognized. Yet, it is the direct application of family therapy in the various settings that demonstrates the inherent strength and effectiveness of the theory. It is also within the context of the application of theory to various settings that old ideas are re-thought and/or applied in new ways. This interaction between theory and practice in different settings creates a pool of perspectives that continually revive the life force of family therapy.

Indeed, much of the motivation for the undertaking of this book is due to the setting in which we operate. As clinicians and teachers in a private, inpatient psychiatric hospital, we have been confronted, like many of our colleagues, with the challenges of the particular context in which we work. The by-no-means exclusive list of challenges that we have confronted include the seemingly paradoxical task of creating a family program in a setting that hospitalizes only one member of the family; gaining acceptance for the ideas and techniques that support our work in a context that traditionally operated in a different way; organizing the therapy system so that one part would not undermine the other (e.g., family therapy vs. milieu therapy vs. medication); interacting with the community (police, welfare agencies, schools, etc.) to involve them in supporting responsible family functioning; and, last but not least, effectively treating the special problems presented by adolescents and their families. All of the practitioners represented in Part II had, and continue to have, an analogous set of problems to overcome in their daily work. We're certain that our readers are as interested in the challenge of applying family therapy techniques in the various settings as we are.

Part III, *Issues in Treatment*, is really a book within a book. Our intention in organizing this section was to provide a practical reference for clinicians on the specific types of problems and issues that adolescents present in treatment. This section includes articles devoted to adolescent eating-disorders, adolescents with special needs, physical and sexual abuse, drug and alcohol abuse, runaways, suicidality, and psychosis. There are also chapters on intervention in reconstituted families, on the special problems of adolescents in cultural transition, and on adolescents returning from hospitalization. In all cases, the chapters provide practical, how-to advice with supporting case material and/or new research to verify the effectiveness of the author's method of treatment.

We hope that the *Handbook of Adolescents and Family Therapy* becomes one of those books that you finally decide to leave on your desk because of the frequency with which you take it from the bookshelf. It should serve as an ideal reference for clinicians working with adolescents in any setting—clinicians who either need to review a specific area or who are looking for an alternative treatment strategy in a particularly difficult case. It should also provide program developers with new ideas about applying general systems theory and family therapy technique to new treatment settings. The theoretical section alone may serve many uses: provide a review of general systems theory as a basis for the field of family-therapy, provide an overview of adolescence as a family experience, organize treatment techniques in accordance with the type of problem being presented in therapy and, in general, encourage the practitioner to question and develop his/her own theory of change in order to contribute to the general effectiveness and responsiveness of our profession. Finally, we have included a selected, annotated bibliography to augment the chapter references found throughout. This should make the task of locating resources easier and, especially for busy practitioners, less time-consuming.

Wellesley, Massachusetts   MPM
                                              SLK

Acknowledgments

We are grateful to many of our friends and colleagues at Charles River Hospital for their support and enthusiasm at this time. We would like to thank our hospital administrators and supervisors: Peter Morris, Russell Ricci, Ethan S. Rofman, Gerald Stechler and Cloe Swidler for supporting our efforts.

Special thanks to Leonard Rosen for his editorial suggestions. We are most grateful to Judith Landau-Stanton and M. Duncan Stanton for guiding us through each step of this process with much patience and good humor.

We appreciate the support the text has been given by many at Gardner Press. In particular we would like to thank Gardner Spungin, publisher; Marilyn Moorcroft, copy editor; Sidney Solomon, production manager and designer; and Marsh Ross, publishing assistant, for their enthusiastic and conscientious work. Thanks are also extended to Janet Lee and Nancy Albaneze for typing the many drafts of the book, often with little advance notice.

We would like to acknowledge *Family Process* for allowing us to reprint Cloe Madanes' article and several of John Weltner's case examples; Seymour Weingarten Guilford Press for his permission to use some of the ideas in Judith Landau-Stanton's chapter.

A special thank-you must go to the psychology interns, psychiatry fellows, and therapists who provided the seed from which this cook blossomed.

Finally, our deepest gratitude is extended to our families: our spouses, Aleta Koman, and Mitch Mirkin; our parents, Ann and Sid Pravder, Toby Koman and Bernard Koman; and our most recent additions, Jason Koman and Allison Mirkin. It is our experience within our own families which gave us both the confidence to tackle this undertaking and also made us realize that even the most complete text does not begin to touch the complexity, love and uniqueness of family life.

—Marsha Mirkin
—Stuart Koman

Handbook of
ADOLESCENTS
and
FAMILY THERAPY

PART I

Theoretical Background

INTRODUCTION

*E*ach of the following three chapters is unique in focus, yet, in many ways, cut from the same cloth. Differing somewhat in their approach from that used in other volumes, none focuses on a particular school of thought or way of "doing" family therapy. All three chapters are integrative, each in its own way attempting to make sense of a broad spectrum of ideas now having currency in the field.

Chapter One, "Making the Jump to Systems," discusses the professional and personal transformations that take place when one applies a systemic understanding to the field of family therapy. Stuart Koman and Gerald Stechler argue here that the systemic world-view serves as a meta-theory from which the schools of family therapy derive their varying viewpoints. They review the basic properties of systems, paying special attention to their conception of how systems change. Change is also discussed in relation to the therapist's evolution into a systems thinker. These authors view the development of a humanistic attitude and a scientific method as central to the therapist's effective use of systems thinking in family therapy.

In Chapter Two, Nydia Preto and Norman Travis construct a bridge from theory and research in individual adolescent development to theory and research in the family life cycle. In "The Adolescent Phase of the Family Life Cycle," the authors reconcile the individual developmental perspectives of Erik Erikson and Peter Blos with the family life cycle theory developed by Elizabeth Carter and Monica McGoldrick; they do so by carefully delineating both the individual and the family tasks that must be accomplished during adolescence. Since most parents are approaching middle age as their children reach adolescence, Preto and Travis argue that it is common to see both generations confronting similar concerns. Case examples highlight the changes that must be made by parents and adolescents alike in the areas of identity clarification, sexuality, and separation. The second half of the chapter discusses the ways in which adolescents and their families are uniquely affected by differences in geographic location, socioeconomic status, educational level, gender, migration, and ethnicity. The chapter concludes with some initial thoughts about the psychological effect of the possibility of nuclear war on adolescents.

The final chapter of the theoretical section is virtually unique in its outlook on the world of family therapy. In "Matchmaking," John Weltner tackles the very difficult practical issues of selecting the best treatment for the problem presented. Rather than viewing the various schools of family therapy as competitive, Weltner proposes a model of integration whereby different therapeutic techniques are matched to different types of family problems. Having matched strategy and technique with problem or issue presented, Weltner arranges the matches into a hierarchy of treatment levels and states his basic therapeutic beliefs that intervention must address the level of the most basic problems before moving onto higher levels. Through discussion, case examples, and the metaphor of housebuilding, the author specifies the types of strategies and intervention techniques that effectively match the problem presented at each level. This chapter should prove to be compelling reading for experienced and novice family therapists alike.

This section is offered both as a general orientation to the methods of therapy and types of problems emphasized in later chapters and as an attempt to promote further organization or, in some cases, reorganization in the theoretical foundations of family therapy.

1

Making the Jump to Systems

STUART L. KOMAN, Ph.D.,
and GERALD STECHLER, Ph.D.

Students of family therapy are often confused by the vast array of theories and techniques promulgated by various schools of thought all claiming to be methods of "family therapy." It is not hard to understand why this is so, given the divergent appearances in therapy of the different schools and the—at times—extreme assertions of major figures differentiating their type of therapy from others. Understandably, the tasks of organizing one's thinking and of subsequent performance in conducting therapy can be overwhelming. However, experienced family therapists know that, numerous approaches notwithstanding, the essence of family therapy can be distilled to a set of basic principles, referred to in this chapter, simply as "systems." The systems approach has profound implications for the ways in which one views, thinks about, and intervenes in human social phenomena. It is *not* yet another theory existing side by side with the various schools of thought (e.g., structural, strategic, Bowenian, contextual, communications) but is rather a "meta-theory" (Hoffman, 1981; Watzlawick, Weakland, & Fisch, 1974; Keeney, 1983)—a theory which encompasses all of the other ideas put forth by various schools of family therapy. This meta-theory does not manifest itself directly in technique but rather in other theories, each theory focusing on some aspect of system functioning and, in turn, manifesting itself in a technique or techniques of intervention (e.g., genogram, sculpting, doubling, etc.).

This chapter is intended as a practical device, or tool, which will make the practitioner's transformation or jump from conceptual models of individual psychotherapy to a systems perspective more complete. The word "jump" is intentionally used to describe the process in which the practitioner's experience of what has traditionally been known as psychopathology (and has been more recently referred to as "problems-in-living") changes dramatically. "Jump" suggests a non-continuous process; that is, one jumps up to, or over to, something else. In this case, the change affects everything that a therapist does and, most importantly, how one thinks about oneself, one's profession, and one's professional encounters with other people. For the sake of clarity we will emphasize the discontinuity between conceptual models of individual therapy and the systems perspective. We recognize, also, points of similarity and, in a few places, discuss these as well.

A SYSTEMS PERSPECTIVE

In the one-to-one situation of individual therapy a unique view of the patient and of the patient's world is established through the patient's eyes, mind, and memory. The therapist's empathic connection with the patient's affects, fantasies, and behaviors allows the therapist to step into the patient's shoes while simultaneously maintaining the distance necessary to place that patient within the wider "map" contained in the therapist's mind.

Picture now a much more complex configuration. In the room are not only the patient and therapist, but also a number of other people who figure most centrally in the patient's life. Each in turn presents his/her own view of "self" and "other" and the relationships that connect them. A single incident is seen through many eyes and is barely recognizable as the same episode. Who is right, who is wrong, who is sane, and who is not?

This scenario is even more complex than that of the famed movie, *Rashomon*, in which a rape is seen from four individual perspectives; for in family therapy, all are in the room together and each is addressing the others as successive views of the story are told. Innuendoes and slight postural or facial cues which may be too subtle or swift even to be noted by the therapist, who is at best a novice within a newly encountered family system, are powerful enough to ignite stormy affects in the other family members. Thus, the recognizably difficult task of establishing an empathic connection with a single patient is, in one sense, increased by orders of magnitude when trying to accomplish this connection simultaneously with a roomful of people who have spent major portions of their life together.

Yet, as the family therapist's skill and experience grow, a transformation takes place within the therapist. Multiple perspectives begin to clarify rather than to confuse. One waits for a divergent point of view as a way of making sense of the whole. Single perspectives, however insightful or comprehensive, no longer seem adequate, once one comes to expect and in fact welcome the multiplicity of viewpoints.

Multiplicity in turn is itself just a step toward a further integration. One does not remain at the level of multiple simultaneous viewpoints. The family therapist at this point should take the discontinuous step, and construct, at a new level of organization, a model of the family system as a whole. The surface phenomena may recede, and a construction as counter-intuitive as the heliocentric model of the solar system may emerge. It took thousands of years of observing the sun, moon, and planets before the revolutionary idea was introduced that despite all appearances to the contrary, it is the earth that goes around the sun. Now we may truly be said to have conceptualized the family as an organizational system, not just as a collection of interacting forces. Once this organizational viewpoint is established, the individual phenomena may take on new and different meanings.

For instance, the family may have lived with a decades-old viewpoint about the loci of power within the family, but this may be a convenient myth in which all collude in order not to force a reorganization. Relationships change their meaning; intrusion is protection, and protection is intrusion; children are parents and parents, children. (Psychodynamically oriented individual therapists are familiar with the equivalence of opposites and therefore should not be surprised by this paradox.)

One last point before turning to a clinical example should also be familiar to the psychodynamic therapists: the position of participant-observer. Empathy, as stated above, clearly implies the concept of participant-observer. There is a process by which we interact with the patient in which he feels and fantasizes us and we feel and fantasize him. Training should make some difference in those respective feelings and fantasies. Picture now the much more complex situation in which we as therapists are returned not only to our own historic dyadic (one-to-one) relationships, but also are to some extent reimmersed in the turbulence of the family constellation. Framo (1965) recounts in some detail the reawakening of old patterns and conflicts as the family therapist enters this realm. Again, training and experience turn this turbulent sea into navigable waters.

Let us turn to a hypothetical case illustration.

> Mr. and Mrs. Everso Gracious come to therapy with their oldest son, Chip, and their daughter, Ami Gracious, with the presenting problem of Ami's rebellious behavior and deteriorating performance in school. Mr. Gracious, a well-to-do businessman in a small community where his family has lived for three generations, is embarrassed by his daughter's behavior in public and in school and wants it "fixed." Mrs. Elizabeth Gracious, 43, an experienced nurse who just returned to teaching full time, thinks that her daughter is just going through an "adolescent stage." Chip Gracious, 17, thinks that his sister is a spoiled brat who cannot stand not having her mother around to take care of her. Ami Gracious, 14, thinks that her parents are making a big deal out of nothing, but is angry at her father because of his "ridiculous" rules, which only she has to follow at home. Each family member has a different perspective as does the therapist who initially observes that a) the rest of the family essentially ignores the father when he speaks, b) that Mrs. Gracious has to continually tell her two children to stop inciting each other during the meeting and, c) that Chip and Ami alternate between fighting like little children, and exchanging knowing glances while their parents are talking.

In this example, each person in the family has a different perception of what the problem is. The therapist is responsible for both appreciating each person's perspective and supplying another, radically different perspective from which to begin the process of change. The particular perspective that family therapy or systems thinking brings to the process of change is one that views the family as a single functional unit that is both uniquely organized and irreducible. Understanding the family organization requires (1) getting the proper vantage point (described above) and (2) knowing what to look for (described below).

FAMILIES AS SYSTEMS

Basic Properties

Ludwig von Bertalanffy, the generally acknowledged founder of General Systems Theory, defines the system as "the totality of objects together with their mutual interactions (1956)." In reviewing other theorists' definitions, Baker (1969) concluded that . . . "in essence (these definitions) agree that a system is a set of units or elements which are actively interrelated and operate in some sense as a bounded unit." Thus, the notion of systems is eventually defined by two properties, the importance of interaction among elements, and the appreciation for the boundary which binds these elements together. It is hard to conceive of any practitioner in the mental health field having difficulty in seeing the connection between a family and the first property of systems. It is self-evident that members of families interact with each other. However, the second proposition is somewhat more difficult to accept as it implies a special meaning to the interactions among family members. The special meaning, which is defined in the acceptance of a family boundary, is one which produces a change at the level of organization such that the practitioner focuses on the family as a whole and each person as an integral part. In this organization, the family members are not merely interacting but are interrelated or interdependent, accruing definition and changing fluidly in response to each other.

While the property of interconnectedness of elements in a system may not be immediately obvious, it was just these types of observations about families that prompted the early researchers in family dynamics to begin to look outside the traditional psychodynamic formulations for models or paradigms of human social phenomenon. In the late 1950s and early 1960s, Jackson and Weakland (1959), Bowen (1960), and others began publishing papers which reported their observations on the interconnectedness of members in family systems. Specifically, Jackson, et al, noted that as schizophrenic members of families began to improve, some other member of the family would frequently show a major dysfunction. Focusing on the emotional level, Bowen began to trace the roots of dysfunction through a three-generational matrix. The important distinction to be made in view of these observations is that the term "systems" does not apply to the sum of the individual personalities in any family but rather to the interactions that occur between them. Systems theorists often refer to the geometric axiom, "the whole is greater than the sum of its parts," to underscore the point. Thus, to understand the family system, one must study the connections between individuals in the system and see how they interact.

The family therapist is concerned with the form or structure of interactions. Before intervention is possible, the therapist must construct a map or learn the rules by which interaction in a particular family takes place. This is accomplished by observing the sequence of interactions which occur repeatedly and form relatively enduring patterns. The observation of such patterns is the key to inducing change in a system regardless of the content of an interaction. It is assumed that the process of interaction, the way that members of a family system interact with each other, remains stable regardless of changes in content. Thus, a discussion of family chores will be structurally the same as a fireside chat or an explanation of supply-demand economic theory as long as the same elements of the system (i.e., the same people) are involved. The implication here is that a structural change in the process of interaction in any of these content areas will change the structure of the interaction in any other content area. Closely related to this idea is that no matter where one picks

up a particular sequence, the conclusion is always the same in terms of systems consequence.

Returning to the example of the Gracious family, the therapist began to construct a structural map of the family by noting the following sequence:

1. Long-winded speeches by the father during which the adolescent children bickered and were repeatedly implored by their mother to stop,
2. followed by father's scolding of mother for not being able to control the children,
3. followed by a discussion between the parents about who does what for whom in the family,
4. accompanied by the exchange of knowing glances between the adolescents.

Although a discussion in the original case presentation concerned the daughter's behavior, the subject of the discussion could just as easily have been the importance of green vegetables in the family diet with no change in the interaction between the four members of the family. That is, father would still give long-winded speeches, the children would still bicker, father would still admonish mother, and so on.

Families as Open Systems

Families are assumed to be *open* rather than *closed* because of the necessary interplay between them and their environments. Whereas closed systems have impermeable boundaries which allow no interaction with the environment, open systems exchange energy and/or information continually. This exchange with the environment can be both helpful and/or dangerous depending upon how the family system operates in response to the outside environment. Maintaining a balance between openness to the environment and shelter from it is a crucial aspect of family functioning which has vast practical implications for the family therapist. Too little exchange with the environment will result in what we will term a "stuck" family system (discussed later), while too much interaction with the environment will result in the loss of family identity and security. The family reaching the adolescent stage of its development is especially concerned with this balance since it is at this point that interaction with the outside world increases most.

While it is assumed that all people are members of different systems simultaneously, they do not maintain the same allegiance to each system. There are varying degrees of relative importance which the different systems occupy in a given person's life. The most important system is assumed to be the family system because this is the place where the individual learns to interact. The family system is irrevocably changed by the arrival of a new member and the new member is imprinted by that particular family's history, structure, style, etc. This process of imprinting on and being imprinted by one's family, and then carrying this template for interaction into other systems, is what might be called the "output" of a family system. A similar but opposite process, the input to a family system, occurs when a family member confronts a different reality outside of the family and brings this information back to the family system.

The importance of interaction with the outside world is demonstrated in the case example of the Gracious family. Specifically, Mr. Gracious has been embarrassed by his daughter's behavior in public. We might assume that being a long-time member of his community, Mr. Gracious is invested in maintaining an image as a competent father, husband, and businessman. His daughter's behavior is an affront to the code of behavior established by his family over the course of many years and possibly a threat to his success in the community. It is questionable whether his wife shares this view. In returning to school, Mrs. Gracious has taken a somewhat unusual course for this small community. Having interacted with the academic community, she finds her daughter's behavior mildly problematic. Finally, it is likely that Ami, the daughter, has been heavily influenced by her peers in developing her attitudes about her father's rules. Based on her associations with her schoolmates, she believes that they are overly restrictive.

Developmental Processes in Family Systems

Family systems can be thought of as having a life of their own. In a fashion similar to the way in which an individual develops, family systems pass through predictable life stages, evolving new methods of taking care of themselves and coping with the demands of the external world (Carter & McGoldrick, 1980). However, the process of its evolution does not often proceed in a smooth, linear fashion but rather in an uneven, sometimes halting, sometimes rapid progression through life. One pictures a train with a steam engine pumping its way up a hill, straining for the top, running smoothly for a while once it reaches a plateau, and racing down the other side.

A family's pace at any given moment will vary. Different stages will be handled differently by different families. For instance, one family may adjust quite easily to the birth of children but have extreme difficulty when it is time for these same children to go to college, whereas another family may have had difficulty in adjusting to the presence of adolescents in the family but move rapidly through the phase of launching children into their own lives. It is also possible for a system to become "stuck" at any time, but these times usually occur around a point of transition from one stage to another. It is at these times that family systems will invite outside intervention to help them get "back on track." This theoretical framework allows the family therapist to view the problems which are present in the family as "breakdowns" in the family's evolutionary quest (Haley, 1980; Hoffman, 1981; Carter & McGoldrick, 1980).

Demands on family function vary according to several different factors, including the stage that the family is in, the family structure, the family's emotional history, and pressure from the outside world. To meet the ever-changing demands that are placed on family systems requires a sometimes delicate balance between stability and flexibility. At times, the emphasis is on stability. During these times the system functions in such a way as to permit a fairly standard set of deviations as part of its normal routine. This pattern of homeostasis —the regulation of a system's interactional range—is produced through negative feedback loops which "inform" the system when it is in danger of going beyond the system's prescribed boundaries and thereby destabilizing the entire system. A commonly used analogy to this process is the thermostat on a heating system. When a room warms up to a pre-set temperature, the thermostat automatically shuts off the heat source. When the room gets too cold, the heat source automatically turns on. (Stabilizing and destabilizing processes are discussed in the next section.) Periods of homeostasis in the life of a family system occur between transitions from one stage to another, generally follow and precede more radical spurts in the structure of the system, and, in the absence of "pathological symptoms" in any individual member, generally connote a period of individual growth. On the other hand, a homeostatic pattern can be problematic, especially when some member of the family is symptomatic. At these times, the homeostatic pattern operates at the expense of some family member, locking that symptom into place and reflecting the family's difficulty in moving from one stage to another.

In our example of the Gracious family, there are several clues as to what is happening to the system in terms of its development. For instance, we know that Mrs. Gracious has just returned to teaching full-time after having been involved primarily in taking care of children and the home for some period of time. We also know that son, Chip, is seventeen years old, a time when adolescents generally will be making moves toward a more distinct separation from the family. We know also that Chip believes that the problem his younger sister is having is that she is having difficulty adjusting to a lack of attention from her mother. And finally, we know that Mr. Gracious has created a rather rigid set of rules for his daughter unlike anything that previously existed for other family members. Taking all this into account, a systems therapist might view the problem as being one in which the family is having difficulty with the adolescent phase of the life cycle, particularly in adjusting to age-appropriate separation and development for each individual member. These issues are reflected in everyone's behavior. An extensive though not exhaustive list of behaviors that reflect the system's present difficulty is as follows:

1. the daughter's rebellious behavior, which has brought attention to herself and demanded a more intensive involvement from her parents
2. the father's overly restrictive rules, which deny his daughter's age, and the lack of seriousness accorded the father by the rest of the family
3. the childlike bickering and teasing that takes place between the two children while the parents are talking
4. Mrs. Gracious's attempts to muffle the family conflict and soothe the "injured" parties.

In this list, the distinctly different developmental patterns for each individual within the family, as well as the developmental problem which the family is presently confronting, are demonstrated. The family is in transition, moving from a time in its history when the rearing of children was the primary focus and family roles were clearly defined. The present situation, which suggests a movement into another stage, is reflected in the mother's return to work full-time and her daughter's quest for autonomy. It could be said that the females in the Gracious family are moving at a rapid pace in their development at present, while the males seem to demonstrate a slower or even regressive trend marked by the father's active interventions suited more to an earlier age and the brother's greater-than-usual concern for the internal affairs of the family. This view of the family, however, is misleading. Other explanations for why the system functions as it does are equally possible, including an explanation that is opposite of the first! It could be strongly argued that the daughter's rebellious behavior in public is a sure sign of her lack of maturity and inability to accept more independence, that the mother's return to work is premature and reflective of a responsibility not completed, that the brother's involvement in the family is not meddling, but appropriate responsibility-taking for a mature adolescent, and that the father's rule-setting will provide the necessary structure to teach his daughter to behave in a more mature and responsible manner.

Causality in Family Systems

Demonstrated in the above example and explanation is a central concept in the understanding of systems. What we are saying here is that no explanation of why the system is the way it is, is "right." Both of the explanations described, as well as others which have not been described are "right." We are not, however, talking merely about different perceptions of the family, which could be accorded to any family member, but rather about an underlying conceptual understanding that is different from the way we normally view things. Specifically, in a system where people mutually effect each other, there is no specific cause of any behavior. Rather, the focus is on the way that the elements relate to each other, their interaction and mutual impact. In this view, each event (i.e., each interaction) that occurs is multiply determined by all of the forces operating within the system. No individual or interaction can be blamed. This concept is variously referred to in family therapy literature as equi-causality, circular causality, recursive thinking, or systems logic (Foley, 1974; Hoffman, 1981; Keeney, 1983).

The above points are further illustrated by the metaphor of the playground seesaw. Although we observe that one end of the seesaw is up while the other is down, do we say that one end is up *because* the other is down? Or, do we say that one end is up *when* the other is down? The difference between using the term "because," a term that implies that one thing caused

the other, and using the term "when" —which implies that two things happen in a particular sequence, in this case simultaneously—is a key to understanding the operation of and, hence, intervening in the system. It is far more accurate to say, in regard to the seesaw, that one end is down and the other end is up because it's a "seesaw." That is, explaining the position of either end is less important than recognizing and understanding the way that the seesaw operates. Similarly, in a system, we view the elements as being in a particular relationship with each other, less because of their individual qualities than because they are engaged in a particular type of system.

While the metaphor may help to simplify the concept of circular causality, it is extremely difficult to break the habit of thinking about events in the usual linear manner. Nor should one try to do this completely, since linear thinking is often the most direct method of solving a problem. We will now look further at the differences between linear and circular causality.

Linear thinking or linear causality describes the process in which an event, Y, is caused directly by a preceding event, X. This sets up the equation, if X then Y, or more simply stated, Y is caused by X. Many problems in everyday living are solved through the process of linear thinking. For example, if the car won't start, one generally works through a process of eliminating various possibilities for malfunction starting with the simplest and then working toward a more complex explanation. It is common to 1) first put the car in gear, then 2) check to make sure there is gas in the tank, then 3) determine other possible trouble sources depending upon what sound the car makes when one tries to turn it on, and 4) finally check out each possible cause until the problem is found. A similar problem is found with the newborn infant who is crying. One goes through a process of eliminating all possible causes for distress, including checking to see if the baby is hungry or wet or cold or warm, etc.

Linear thinking is effective for many types of family problems also. Take, for example, the frequent and not-so-simple problem of who gets to use the bathroom when. This problem may be solvable by increasing the family's organization, taking into account the schedules of all the family members. On the other hand, this problem can become a major point of conflict, which suggests other problems in the family structure. When problems cannot be solved by the direct process of eliminating various possible solutions until the right one is found, a different type of problem-solving is necessary. When all of the possible options for a solution to a particular problem are exhausted or when one gives up hope of trying to solve a problem in this fashion, a non-linear, systemic view is necessary. Such is probably the case with respect to the nuclear arms race where no simple cause for the current state of relationships between countries can be identified. Rather, the complex relationships of countries—each wrestling with the problem of survival; each maintaining a legitimate need for defense, yet faced with the problem of extinction—necessitates a systemic view. In short, linear thinking and systemic thinking should be viewed as complementary; each is extremely important in maintaining an individual's or family's flexibility to adjust to the various demands on their lives.

Systemic problem-solving will not necessarily eventuate in an unusual solution. Rather, systemic solutions often look very similar to solutions that are the product of linear thinking. However, there is often a difference in the timing of the solution (when a particular solution is used), in the perception of the solution by other family members, and in the method, or process, and logic that enables one to develop this particular solution. Returning to the case example, Mr. Gracious's response to his daughter's behavior via the set of behavior mandates could be seen as either a linear or systemic solution. However, each entails a different understanding of the problem and the solution for it, as well as the family's perception of the problem-solving attempt. If Mr. Gracious were thinking in a linear fashion, his new rules would be seen as a direct response to his daughter's "bad" behavior. The simple equation, "if you act 'bad,' you will be punished," de-

fines this situation; thus, his set of rules is seen by the rest of the family as a simple, direct response to his daughter's behavior.

The same solution could have evolved from a systemic understanding of the problem, but the type of logic needed to arrive at such a solution would be quite different. One such route is as follows: Mr. Gracious's attention is drawn by his daughter's unusual behavior in public. Mr. Gracious understands that many changes have taken place in the family. Now that his wife has returned to school, there is less attention paid to his daughter at home. His wife would prefer to minimize the problem, fearing that she will be required to do something about her daughter's behavior, possibly to relinquish her current plans. The brother, desiring more independence in the home, is angry at his sister's behavior as well. The last thing he wants to do at this time is to have to be more involved with her. Mr. Gracious concludes he must become more involved with his daughter and begins this process by constructing a set of limits which, though arbitrary, will give his daughter the message that he cares and will be there to help her feel secure. He communicates his intention to his daughter, to be more involved and to provide flexibly for her protection through rules which can be altered as she feels more comfortable with greater individual responsibility. This brings him into closer contact with his daughter and relieves her sense of insecurity which came at the time of her mother's return to school. Mrs. Gracious and her son, Chip, are then free to pursue their own development.

How Family Systems Change

Now that there is some picture of how family sytems function, the next question is how do family systems change? Specifically, how does a therapist operate to create change in a family system?

Development and change, in balance with homeostatic equilibrium, is a hallmark of a healthily functioning family system. Through its homeostatic mechanisms, some stability is maintained in the face of the inevitable disturbances and perturbations of everyday life. However, for each member of the family as well as for the family as a whole, the central issues of life-span changes as well as other stresses pose novel challenges, for which the healthy response is growth and development. Healthy adaptations tend to be multi-potential, allowing themselves to be used as foundations for further adaptations and integrations.

In contrast, one may say that the very definition of a pathological adaptation is that it has a "stuck" quality and does not lend itself to further transformation. These pathological adaptations also gain stability at the expense of loss of resilience. A well-adapted system in an ecological sense can be very specialized and highly stable if the environment is supportive and stable. Few human beings now live under such conditions. We are very complex and we live in very complex and changing societies. Thus, one state of being, no matter how highly adapted to a particular circumstance, will not suffice. Resiliency, that is the capacity to alter states as conditions change, must be balanced against the capacity to maintain a state in the face of minor external alterations.

The reasons for a strong investment in maintaining the status quo may be quite complex and variable from one system to another. But the reality of that investment is all too obvious as one attempts to introduce a new solution to a long-standing problem by using some simple rational suggestion. One or another reason is introduced to negate the suggestion. Or, the suggestion is accepted and then promptly sabotaged.

Knowing what we do about family systems and individual defensive structures, certain principles which govern system change can be explicated and then acted upon:

1. An individual and a family system is semi-open. Information is exchanged back and forth between the system and its surroundings.
2. Psychological and family system mechanisms serve to dampen out the disequilibria created by such exchanges.

3. For a new state of adaptation to emerge, the old state must be at least partially dismantled.
4. In pathological systems which maintain stability, at the expense of resilience, established ways of operating may have to become highly dysfunctional before they can be relinquished and replaced by new ways of operating.
5. Under certain conditions, either occurring normally in everyday life, or specifically introduced into therapeutic situations, the individual or family system does not homeostatically damp out the impact of new information, but rather uses that information to transform itself and create a new adaptation.

At this point, we may ask how does one conceptualize the changes that can be brought about in family systems through the process of family therapy?

While acknowledging the stability of many patterns (both adaptive and pathological) that characterize family functioning, it is important to try to differentiate between the stability of a pattern and its presumed immutability. For most people, when the image of a stable structure is conjured up in their minds, what appears is some permanent edifice like a fortress or the Eiffel Tower. It is this particular view of structure which tends to permeate our thinking. Modern theory in the natural and social sciences, however, alerts us to a different conception of structure, comprised not of bricks and of steel girders, but of self-sustaining loops. That is to say, a pattern exists in a uniform way not because it is frozen but because it constantly renews itself through a rehearsal of specific functions. Thus, in a particular family the adolescent child may test certain limits with the parents who then react with more restrictive proscriptions, to which the child responds with increased provocations and rebellion, until a typical, ritualized fight erupts. This may be understood in a number of ways but for us the most useful is that each member of the family and the system as a whole has, through a process of self-reinforcement, perpetuated a long-standing pattern.

If structure is viewed as a self-sustaining loop, then the possibilities for alteration seem much more realizable than if one maintains the fortress image. Under the loop model what needs to be analyzed are the various repetitive links which keep the loop in place and which prevent it from exiting and moving onto some more perhaps appropriate developmental form. The systems-oriented therapist will examine that loop and if clinically skilled, will examine many other loops that are peripherally involved with the maintenance of this pattern as well. Rarely, if ever, is it a single process that maintains itself stably over time. However, for the moment, let's regard the maintenance of stability as a single-loop process. Once the dominant pattern is discussed, we can entertain supporting patterns.

Examined more closely, one of the prevalent features of pathological, self-sustaining loops is that all of the parties seem to be locked into mutually defeating behaviors. Each person in the room feels powerless, feels dominated and controlled by the other, and reacts with self-defensive maneuvers which tend not to extricate this system from that loop, but rather to ensure to its members continuing defeat. It is as if each person in the room has only that amount of power which can ensure the defeat of the other but not enough to create a more constructive solution to the conflict or dilemma. The family may well be locked into a self-perpetuating pathological pattern, but it is logically and conceptually erroneous to then make the assumption that there is an investment by that family in maintaining the pathology. The concept of a need to be sick or a need to stay sick is, in fact, part of the linear thinking that family-systems schools of thought are trying to reject. However, this particular disturbing aspect of linear thinking has, at times, crept into family systems work.

The therapist should avoid inputing intent into the pathological loop but view it rather as a lock-in that is useful to the parties only insofar as it defeats the other. In the long run, the painful status quo is dissatisfying to all and is a situation from which they would be pleased to exit if there were some possibility of a safe exit. Given this view, the task of the therapist is de-finable and do-able. Now we are dealing with neither a fortress nor a self-perpetuating loop that somehow each person is invested in maintaining. Rather, it is a loop that all members are stuck in but that would quickly alter if a safe and profitable exit were provided simultaneously for all parties. What is probably intolerable for the family system as a whole is to see one member of the family exit from this lock-in while the others remain stuck in it.

It is the creativity and clinical skill of the therapist combined with the family's move toward health that leads to the new solutions. The aforementioned problem of other loops that surround the central one and block the attainment of new solutions now becomes more relevant. For example, parent-child role reversal or the double binding of children by ordering them to grow up could constitute such secondary loops. Thus, the therapist who has a broader understanding of the multiple configurations within the family is likely to be more successful in altering the pathological loop than is one who tends to disregard the ancillary processes.

Another feature that speaks perhaps more to the individual interpsychic features rather than to the family system as a whole also forms the basis for the change processes that can be instituted within the family system. We are here referring to the ubiquitous phenomenon of ambivalence. It is virtually beyond dispute in modern dynamic or structural psychology to acknowledge that every powerful feeling, every dominant behavior pattern, and every interpersonal style is the outcome of an internal struggle with the polar opposite of that particular manifestation. When, for instance, we see an individual extend extremely tight behavioral control over himself and over others, our understanding of ambivalence allows us to view this as the surface of an inner struggle which includes an almost equally powerful force toward uncontrolled, disruptive behavior. Paradoxical intervention or other methods of "going with the resistance" are based on the appreciation that one is in fact speaking a powerful truth to the less-conscious pole of the ambivalent pattern. If the therapist tries to overcome the resistance through persuasion or interpretation, the individual and the whole family system may indeed dig in and further strengthen their allegiance to the existing pattern. One of the most effective ways of altering the apparently stable pattern is to ally oneself unexpectedly with the less obvious side. For example, when parents bring an adolescent child into a psychiatric hospital, it is very common for these parents to feel, in addition to the sense of anguish and anger toward the child for being so sick, a profound sense of guilt and shame, based on the idea that they have failed as parents. Their encounters with other members of society tend to reinforce this view because the commonly accepted but primitive belief is that if something has gone wrong there must be somebody to blame for it. However much the parents might cover it, they come to the hospital with the expectation that in subtle, or in not so subtle ways, the hospital staff will find them at fault and will blame them for their child's difficulty. The process of change can begin immediately when the staff reacts in unexpected ways and says to them that they have been good parents, they have tried all of the reasonable solutions, and for reasons that are still unclear to everybody, the process did not work as expected. In making this kind of statement the staff breaks into old, long established loops, sides with the other part of the parental ambivalence about their own self-worth, and immediately establishes a therapeutic alliance. Thus, integrating the ideas of self-sustaining loops and the primacy of ambivalence gives one an immediate entree into changing a long established pattern.

An important caveat must be interjected at this time: conceptualizing the process as abstractly as we have just done may incorrectly lead to the idea of a technique-oriented therapy pattern. While it is true that the systems approach does provide the clinician with an array of techniques that are not necessarily evident in other forms of psychological treatment, we believe that the techniques are ethical and effective only if embedded within a thorough understanding of the complexities of individual and family development.

Take again, for example, the Gracious family. The systemic, multi-causal, view of the disturbing interactions within the family allows for the inclusion of developmental and intra-psychic viewpoints. The therapist does not necessarily need to bring intra-psychic interpretations into the family meeting. But it is extremely useful, and perhaps essential, for him/her to know that a likely developmental-psychic issue that has brought the pot to a boiling point at this time is the age-old struggle between fathers and adolescent daughters to maintain an appropriate distance. Now the system starts to vascillate between the attraction the two have for each other and the complex defenses they erect against that attraction.

Our position is that there is no specific viewpoint that is excluded from the systemic approach. Intra-psychic, developmental, family structural, cultural, biomedical, etc., approaches, when integrated by an informed therapist, enrich and substantiate the treatment. We may exclude elements here for purposes of simplification and clarity, but that is an expedient rather than a desideratum.

The family seen as a self-organizing system is ready and will seek a new pattern of organization when the process described above has been effective in disrupting the established pathological patterns. The period of transition from the old pattern to the new one is often filled with turmoil, conflict, a tendency to return to the old, perhaps comfortable, but dysfunctional pattern, and a fear of uneasiness that either anything could change and/or that none of the changes would be beneficial. It is in the nature of the organization of complex systems that the changes tend to be discontinuous. Particularly where pathological loops have been locked in for a long time it is very unlikely that a smooth, finely graded set of steps can lead from one position to another. Rather, it is something like stepping into a dark pool without any firm knowledge about where a solid bottom will be found. This is a point at which the skill and experience of the family therapist may be tested to the utmost. It is important that the therapeutic alliance be used to allow the family to endure the disruption, to endure the dysphoric affects that are aroused when old, albeit pathological, patterns start to be relinquished and when anxiety about the unknown reaches its maximum. The maneuvers to nullify the change will be numerous. On the other side is the possible trap of wishing to offer too rapid and too complete a resolution that reflects something more in the therapist's head than in the developmental position of the family. The change clearly will be most effective and have the greatest possibility of becoming the new self-sustaining pattern if it is something that is a creation of the family as a system.

The conceptual model of the family system, then, is one that does organize itself and that does at times get locked into dysfunctional patterns, remaining in these because the information, the affective investment, and the trust in a new solution are not present. Nevertheless, clinical experience in using this systems approach with families has taught many practitioners that old patterns can be relinquished, sometimes with startling alacrity, if the proper conditions are established.

THE THERAPIST AND THE FAMILY SYSTEM

The family therapist must be both humanist and scientist. As a humanist, the family therapist strains to achieve an effective attitude that enables the family/therapist system to work together. As a scientist, the family therapist works at achieving a systemic viewpoint, refines his/her ability to construct models of family organization and process, and constantly evaluates the effect of his/her input. The two go hand-in-hand, mutually influencing each other as new levels of understanding are achieved professionally and personally. Our experience suggests that family therapists evolve in treatment effectiveness as they become more comfortable with themselves and the way that they interact with others on a personal level and

become less invested in specific outcomes for their patient families.

The Family Therapist as Humanist

The humanistic attitude of the family therapist is partially defined by the scientific assumptions that are made in general systems theory, but the attitude must be nurtured and developed through one's experience with people, especially with one's own family. It is one thing to know intellectually what these assumptions are and to believe them intellectually, but it is quite another to feel and act in a manner consistent with them. Regarding the development of an effective clinical attitude, some have argued that "you either have it or you don't," while others might believe this discussion of the therapist's attitude as "philosophy," irrelevant to the task of therapy. We will take the position that all people, especially therapists, have "belief systems" about other people, primarily based on their experiences within their own families, and that these beliefs have an irresistible though not always apparent impact on what one does as a family therapist.

Humanism in family therapy comes about from two sources: (1) theoretical assumptions of circular causality and family competency, and (2) personal efforts to reconcile one's own history with these same assumptions. General systems theory views the existence of any type of interaction in a system as being multiply determined. In a world where all people mutually influence each other and organize themselves in relation to one another, there can be no simple tracing of "blame" to any particular individual or group of individuals for a particular systemic outcome. The goal of the family therapist is to aid families in delineating and understanding the types of problematic interactions that occur (and have occurred) and to co-construct with them a new reality—one in which interactions are changed so that the system works more effectively at meeting each member's needs (Watzlawick, 1984; Papp, 1984). Another source of the humanistic attitude in family therapy is found in the assumption of family competency. Many theorists in the field of family therapy (Haley, 1976; Hoffman, 1981) have suggested that problems in families appear or are exacerbated during times of transition from one stage of the family life cycle to another. In this view, the presence of symptoms or problematic interactions reflects a breakdown in the family's attempts to reorganize as it evolves during life-cycle transitions. Thus, the existence of symptoms or problematic interactions is time-specific, a sign akin to the temperature gauge in a car, indicating difficulty in the system's response to changing internal and external demands. The family therapist who accepts this view of symptoms or problems in families demonstrates an attitude of increased respect for a given family's ability to function autonomously up to the present point in its life; the therapist is also optimistic regarding the family's ability to function once a necessary systemic reorganization takes place. One uses intervention to help the family get "unstuck" but does not attempt to define the existing problem as a fixed pathology, some intrinsic weakness of the system, nor does one attempt to define the ultimate form of family reorganization, how the family will change to meet the current pressures. (It is often the case, however, that prescriptions for specific types of change are given in order to "prime the pump" or get the process of change started.) The focus of therapy is on change—that is, on promoting some changes in the ways in which system members interact so that the interactive problem is relieved.

A therapist who assumes that no one is individually responsible for the problems in a family and that the family is able to change in such a way as to relieve the current problem is one who begins therapy from a more respectful, more open, and less judgmental position than the therapist who, in assessment or treatment, attempts to categorize and define pathology in individual members of systems. Assumptions of competency and circular causality, however, will not in and of themselves suffice when one actually gets into the business of doing therapy. As is the case with many things in life, there's a big difference between accepting something intellectually and actually feeling, believing, and using it. This is very much the case in family therapy since one's personal experience of oneself and family is continually brought into the therapeutic equation. The second major source of humanism in family therapy emanates from this dilemma: the therapist's attitude about families-in-general continually butts up against the therapist's attitude about his own family. It is this struggle to achieve a sense of resolution and acceptance in regard to this dilemma which brings the family therapist into empathic synchronicity with his "patient family." Thus, the therapist is actually better prepared to work with families when he/she is struggling with personal issues (as long as he/she is aware of what those issues are) than when he/she assumes that all personal issues have been resolved. Respect for one's patient families emanates partly from recognition of similarities to oneself in relation to the process of living, that is, the humanistic idea that we are all struggling in one way or another.

Much more could be said about the therapist's multiple dilemmas in balancing professional and personal responsibilities. For the purpose of this chapter, we will be brief in simply outlining some of the most basic ones. The first, already described, is the idea that to achieve a truly professional attitude in family therapy—one that appreciates the nature of circular causality and human variability, both positive and negative—one must experience it at the most personal level as well. That is, to be professional, one must be personal and vice versa.

Navigating the professional/personal boundary is the essential dilemma for all types of therapists, but it is particularly heightened in the context of interaction with a family system rather than with a single individual. At the practical level, the family therapist's dilemma is how to get "in" the family to create change. Just as the professional attitude of the family therapist coevolves with the personal acceptance of one's own self and family, the therapist's position in relation to a patient family coevolves with the demands of the clinical situation. At those times when therapy is needed and the therapist joins the family in the endeavor of change, the therapist's involvement, the therapist's being "in," is guided by the questions: How far in? in what way? with what goal? at what phase of treatment?

The therapist should be aware, however, that the family will have different ideas, whether they be spoken or not, about where the therapist's position should be in relation to their family. To some degree, the family's comfort with the therapist will depend on how closely the therapist's position matches the family's ideas about where the therapist should be. The family's comfort, however, is not the ultimate goal of the therapist's intervention. Rather, the family therapist takes the family's communication about the therapist's position as a reflection of the family's organization based on its own history and patterns of interaction. In almost all cases, the therapist will want to defeat the family's attempts to align the therapist in a manner that is consistent and comfortable to their particular system. One major exception to this rule is that in the initial stages of therapy, a family therapist may knowingly align him- or herself in a manner consistent with what the family desires, in order to learn about the family culture and reduce the family's resistance to change.

There are two major issues for the family therapist to consider in establishing his/her position in relation to a patient family and to the family's attempt to align the therapist in a manner consistent with its typical style. The first issue is attitudinal. It is necessary for the therapist to be somewhat wary of the family's expectation of the therapist, but it is problematic for the therapist to assume that the family's interactions with him are malicious or intentionally controlling. Rather, the most effective attitude that a therapist can have would be to place a great deal of value on the power of systems to maintain themselves in the face of outside influences, a necessary and adaptive property for families in an ever-changing world. If a therapist assumes that there is some kind of nefarious plot to con-

trol him/her, there will follow an impulse to locate the source of control and to blame some family member.

The other side of this issue is what the therapist brings to each encounter with the patient family based on the therapist's history and style of interaction developed in his/her own family of origin. Family therapists do not assume that they are a neutral stimulus. Rather, each therapist's own interactional style is factored into the clinical situation. Therapists will show preferences for various types of interventions and treatment models based on what they find comfortable within their own personalities and even show preferences toward the kinds of families and problems that they confront in their work. These preferences are both positive and negative. On the one hand, a therapist may become particularly adept at treating a specific problem or specific type of family and will handle these cases effectively. On the other hand, the match between therapist and family or problem is far more random than the preceding suggests, since (1) therapists often do not have the flexibility to select their patients, and (2) it is difficult to determine a priori what problems the families will present. It is, therefore, necessary for clinicians to develop their skills in the model of the generalist and to pursue their personal development by interacting with families of varying interactional styles.

In relation to this last issue, the therapist should be suspicious of becoming either very comfortable or very uncomfortable with the patient family. Extremes in either direction should be viewed as a sign that the therapist has relinquished an effective therapeutic position. Framo (1965), among others, has viewed the tendency of the therapist to become comfortable within a patient family as an attempt to avoid the patient family's central dilemma because of its all too similar implications for unresolved issues in the therapist's own life. In this sense, the therapist's comfortable position insulates him/her and the family from the pain and stress that underlies the current problem in the family and the therapist becomes part of the "problem-maintaining solution" (Watzlawick, et al., 1974). A similar problem may exist when the therapist is extremely uncomfortable in the therapeutic interaction. In the situation where the therapist is extremely uncomfortable, it is likely that part of this discomfort is due to what the therapist has not worked out in his own family and life. This kind of discomfort will usually result in a lack of therapeutic empathy, a blaming posture, or an attempt to avoid the family altogether.

In concluding this section, there is one basic point that must be understood above all others: it is not the expectation of, nor is it possible for, the therapist to have resolved all of his/her own individual and family issues to do family therapy. But the therapist must be keenly aware of what is occurring between him/her and the family system. Novice family therapists attempting to make the jump to systems can easily become mired in the overwhelming amounts of information that the family presents, or "stuck" in attempting to understand a particular family from a particular point of reference. However, understanding the countertransference that the therapist develops in relation to the family—the typical way in which the therapist interacts with the family—is often the most crucial piece of information, for it clues the therapist into the system's point of stuckness. Once the therapist observes his/her recurrent pattern of interaction with the family, he/she can resume the process of change simply by changing his/her own interactional patterns. Regardless of one's confusion about a particular family, a change in therapist's reactions will result in a change in the family's patterns. In the case where the therapist is aware of his/her typical interactional style with a particular family and cannot change that style, there is often an unresolved personal issue which handcuffs the therapist. Therefore some type of therapy for the therapist is often necessary to determine his/her personal dilemmas and professional blindspots.

The Family Therapist as Scientist

The application of general systems theory to family therapy requires that the therapist develop a particular scientific attitude toward families and a scientific method for achieving and evaluating change. The scientific attitude is defined by the relative absence of moral judgment toward the family culture and its behavioral manifestations, and an absence of personal investment or commitment in the outcome of therapy other than such changes in the family's pattern of interaction that relieve the problems that it initially came into therapy with. The scientific method that accompanies this view of the family therapist is defined by a process of model construction, hypothesis-testing, and outcome evaluation.

The Scientific Attitude.

As stated, the scientific attitude is actually defined by omission—by the absence of a personal investment in, and judgment of, the family on the part of the therapist. This is not to say that the therapist is not personally committed to helping the family, just that the eventual form or product of the therapy is more the construction of the family based on their unique patterns rather than some predetermined construction of the therapist. This is, also, not to say that the therapist has no role in determining the direction of change in therapy. Of course, it is the therapist's responsibility to provide a means of change and, of course, every intervention implies a judgment and provides a direction. However, in systems thinking, the basis for intervention is not whether a behavior is "good" or "bad", "right" or "wrong," but useful and effective, or not. Since all family systems reside in larger systems and since all societies maintain standards of conduct that imply judgment, no therapy is free from moral considerations. The distinction that we are making here is one of type or kind rather than of degree. In this sense, the intention of the family therapist is akin to the intention of the cancer researcher. The goal is to find a "cure" that works for the family and can be tolerated by the society at large. This is a quite different attitude than one that starts out with the assumption that all families *should* conform to the style and organization of the Ideal Family.

THE SCIENTIFIC METHOD IN FAMILY THERAPY

In applying general systems theory to family therapy, the therapist attempts to use his/her understanding of the general theory to (1) construct a specific model of the patient family, (2) test out this model *in vivo*, (3) intervene and promote change, (4) evaluate the effect of the intervention and (5) refine the model, if necessary. We believe that this process occurs whether one is aware of it or not and that it begins with the first contact of any sort with the patient family. We are also of the opinion that this process does not flow smoothly over the course of therapy but rather proceeds unevenly. For instance, it is likely that in initial sessions the entire five-step procedure is recycled many times while in later sessions steps three and four are predominant. We further assume that the numbering of the elements of the therapeutic sequence is artificial, that the sequence could start with any of the elements, and that each element influences the others.

The obvious question at this point would be how does one construct a specific model of a family. This is where consideration of the various schools of family therapy arises. It is not the intent of this chapter to review that body of knowledge. Each school of family therapy provides a method for model construction complete with its unique language and techniques of intervention. However, what is often not specifically discussed in the various writings are steps two and four, testing the model and evaluating the intervention of the above model. These will now be considered.

The initial construction of a model of a specific family provides an overview of the system, which can then be refined to allow for greater understanding of the system as well as more effective intervention. Each school of family therapy emphasizes a different aspect of family functioning and creates its model of the family around that focus. Some schools of family therapy focus on internal structure or subsystems in families, others on affective connections between family members, others on power distribution in the family, and so on. Many of the models overlap in theory and, especially, in technique, since the object being described, the family, is the same for the various observers. We view the various theories and techniques as complementary, each describing a different aspect of family functioning, and recommend that each practitioner develop his/her own model and style based on personal experience with the various treatment issues. Having a repertoire of perspectives available makes good sense, since it allows for greater flexibility in the therapist's approach. We regard no particular view of families as being "truer" than any other. Instead, we view each as a tool, some fitting some families better than others, to promote change.

How does one know when one is using the right tool? Regardless of what school or combination of schools of family therapy a therapist subscribes to, the process of evaluating both the model of the specific family and the intervention strategies is central to the success of the therapy. Every model of a specific family defines a set of family rules or patterns which can be operationalized and observed if, in fact, it is a useful description of the family in an actual session. The therapist's understanding of the way the family works increases as he/she confirms or refutes predictions about how the system will function. This process of hypothesis construction and verification has many applications.* Every time a therapist makes a prediction about the way a family functions and has it confirmed or refuted, the model of the family becomes more accurate. When the therapist can predict reasonably well what the family will do in various situations, he/she is ready to go to the next level, the level of intervention. In cases where the model fails to accurately predict the unfolding process of a system, the model should be refined.

It is important to understand that the evaluation of predictions about a specific family provides a bridge between the theories of families in general and an understanding of the family that one is working

*The first author gratefully acknowledges the instruction of Dr. Irving Alexander, Psychology Department, Duke University.

with. This is an active process. In fact, many experienced therapists intervene rapidly, often within the first session, and co-evolve their models of the specific families along with their intervention strategies. The use of intervention and evaluation, interchangeably, demonstrates an understanding on the part of the experienced therapist that he/she is part of a new, therapeutic system that is changed by his/her very presence. However, it may be simpler to think of this scientific method as a two-step process: the first step is to build and verify a model of the family, the second step is to determine what effect the therapist's presence and intervention will have on the family. Thus, the eventual goal of the therapist is to appreciate, understand, and predict with some degree of accuracy what his/her impact will be under certain conditions with varying techniques of intervention. The therapist is then poised to promote change.

vidual practitioner and the field of family therapy with the potential for greater effectiveness. This is precisely the same point which unifies all family therapists; that is, that one must truly appreciate the context of interaction among family members to promote change in it. Changes in the theory of systems should be sought after just as we seek changes in the families that we treat. Changes have already occurred in regard to the application of general systems theory to family therapy, a major one being the change in the emphasis on homeostatic mechanisms in families to its evolutionary processes (Hoffman, 1981). In short, we believe that family therapists must practice what they preach. Though the outcome is uncertain and each reorganization holds the seeds of further upheaval, we are, like the family we treat, bound to change or fail to be useful.

CONCLUSION

Clinical experience tells us that families rarely change in exactly the way that is prescribed by a therapist. From this easily observable fact, we might then argue that all systems representations, all models, of families are inexact. Taken yet another step further, one might then question the wisdom of applying general systems theory to human social phenomena. We strongly support this type of questioning since we believe that therapists who continually question their models will ultimately achieve a more complete theory and better clinical outcomes. What disturbs us far more is the recent trend in family therapy to mass-produce or convert adherents to the various schools of thought, each with its own unique way of viewing and changing the patient family's world. Our concern is not with the various schools of thought in family therapy per se, but rather with the lack of instruction in understanding the context in which they exist. The appreciation of multiple views of family functioning and change processes provides both the indi-

REFERENCES

Baker, F. Review of general systems concepts and their relevance for medical care. *Systematics*, 1969, **7**(3), 209–229.

Bateson, G., Jackson, D., Haley, J., & Weakland, J. Toward a theory of schizophrenia. In D. Jackson (Ed.), *Communication, family and marriage*. Palo Alto: Science & Behavior Books, 1968.

Bertalanffy, L. von. General systems theory. *General Systems Yearbook*, 1956, **1**, 1–10.

Bowen, M. A family concept of schizophrenia. In D. Jackson (Ed.), *The etiology of schizophrenia*. New York: Basic Books, 1960.

Bowen, M. The use of family theory in clinical practice. In J. Haley, (Ed.), *Changing Families*. New York: Grune & Stratton, 1971.

Carter, E., & McGoldrick, M. Family therapy with one person and the family therapist's own family. In P. J. Guerin (Ed.), *Family therapy: Theory and practice*. New York: Gardner Press, 1976.

Carter, E., & McGoldrick, M. *The Family Life Cycle*. New York: Gardner Press, 1980.

Dell, P., & Goolishian, H. *Order through fluctuation: An evolutionary paradigm for human systems*. Presented at the Annual Scientific Meeting of the A. K. Rice Institute, Houston, Texas, 1979.

Foley, V. D. *An introduction to family therapy*. New York: Grune & Stratton, 1974.

Framo, J. L. Rationale and techniques of intensive family therapy. In I. Boszormenyi-Nagy & J. Framo (Eds.), *Intensive Family Therapy*. New York: Hoeber, 1965.

Group for the Advancement of Psychiatry. *The Field of Family Therapy* (monograph), No. 78, 1970.

Haley, J. Family therapy: A radical change. In J. Haley (Ed.), *Changing families*. New York: Grune & Stratton, 1971.

Haley, J. *Problem-solving therapy*. New York: Harper (Colophon Books), 1976.

Haley, J. *Leaving home*. New York: McGraw-Hill, 1980.

Hoffman, L. Deviation-amplifying processes in natural groups. In J. Haley (Ed.), *Changing Families*. New York: Grune & Stratton, 1971.

Hoffman, L. *Foundations of family therapy*. New York: Basic Books, 1981.

Jackson, D. The question of family homeostasis. In D. Jackson (Ed.), *Communication, family and marriage*. Palo Alto: Science & Behavior Books, 1968.

Jackson, D., & Weakland, J. Schizophrenic symptoms and family interaction. *Archives of General Psychiatry*, 1959, **1**, 618–621.

Keeney, B. *Aesthetics of change*. New York: Guilford, 1983.

Minuchin, S. *Families and Family Therapy*. Cambridge: Harvard University Press, 1974.

Papp, T. The creative leap. *The Family Theory Networker*, 1984, **8**(5), 20–29.

Ruesch, J., & Bateson, G. *Communication: The social matrix of psychiatry*. New York: Norton, 1951.

Watzlawick, P. *The invented reality*. New York: Norton, 1984.

Watzlawick, P., Beavin, J., & Jackson, D. *Pragmatics of human communication*. New York: Norton, 1967.

Watzlawick, P., Weakland, J., & Fisch, R. *Change: Principles of problem formation and problem resolution*. New York: Norton, 1974.

2

The Adolescent Phase of the Family Life Cycle

NYDIA GARCIA PRETO, A.C.S.W.,
and NORMAN TRAVIS, Ph.D.

*A*dolescence is a creative, exciting, and tumultuous stage in the life cycle of the family. The tasks of adolescence challenge the stability of the family system by posing new expectations and demands. Family patterns experience sudden and abrupt disturbances as adolescents reject and question values and defy rules while attempting to individuate. They move out of the home to explore the outside world and test their independence. Yet the need to be protected and nurtured is as authentic and strong as the need to be independent. It is this constant struggle for dependence and independence that confuses and challenges adolescents and their families. This period of turmoil allows for creative renegotiations of relationships across generations; it may also lead to prolonged stress and unresolved conflicts.

The goal of this chapter will be to analyze the changes that take place in the family system, as processes of individual development and family development interact with each other during the adolescent phase of the life cycle. The focus will be on the different tasks required of adolescents and parents during the stage of adolescence. Consideration will be given to some of the variables and factors that affect the family's ability to master those tasks. Case examples will be used to elaborate on clinical implications. Our viewpoint here of adolescence and family life is through the narrow lenses of middle America in the 1970s and '80s. To largely ignore the social, cultural, and historical contexts of these events, not to mention the dynamically fluid quality of society, will seem simplistic, but is necessary for our purposes, although an attempt is made to take some of these factors into account and to cite appropriate studies.

ADOLESCENCE AND FAMILY LIFE CYCLE THEORY

Adolescence, as generally known today in the United States, did not exist until the last two decades of the nineteenth century

21

(Aries, 1962). Prior to the Industrial Revolution and the move toward urbanization in this country, the family functioned more as a comprehensive economic unit. Most work took place in and around the home. Children often shared adult tasks and had a significant economic function. Childhood could be viewed as an apprenticeship period terminating with full responsibilities for work even before puberty.

With industrialization and urbanization the family's role changed. Its economic activities became primarily directed towards consumption and child-care (Hareven, 1982). The roles of children and parents became more separate as different economic expectations, such as child labor laws, created a discontinuity between childhood and adulthood (Keniston, 1962). As a result, the passage from childhood to adulthood became ambiguous and prolonged. To a large extent, young people coped with this ambiguity by creating their own rituals and culture. The invention of the concept of adolescence as chiefly developed by G. Stanley Hall (1904) was in part a response to this phenomenon as well as an attempt to understand the tasks, transitions, and experiences encountered by youth—no longer children but not yet adults—and their families.

During the twentieth century, views about adolescence in the United States have mainly been shaped from developmental and social perspectives (Elder, 1974). Physical and cognitive development has also been studied and considered essential in understanding and defining adolescence. Others have examined social influences such as parental and peer demands. More comprehensive theorists have focused on the interaction between internal developmental forces and environmental experiences. They also considered the impact of historical events on the adolescent process. In particular, the work of Blos (1962) and Erikson (1968) represent this attempt at theoretical integration.

Blos (1962) defines adolescence as the psychological process and adaptation to the condition of pubescence. He states that adolescents are deeply affected by the physical changes that take place in their bodies, but that on a more subtle and unconscious level, puberty affects the development of their interests, their social behavior, and the quality of their affective life. He views adolescence as a complex phenomenon which is highly dependent on the individual's life history and on the milieu in which the adolescent grows up. He begins by defining adolescence from an intrapsychic developmental perspective but moves toward a more integrative formulation that considers social and historical factors.

Erikson describes adolescence as a normative crisis. It is a normal phase of increased conflict characterized by what seems to be a fluctuation in ego strength. During adolescence there is a high potential for growth which can contribute to the process of identity formation. He links adolescence to the concept of the life cycle, the notion that human development involves sequential stages throughout life, each with its own tasks and requirements. Erikson views adolescence as a process involving psychosocial demands that are imposed whether or not there is an internal push. Adolescence, as Erikson conceptualizes it, is a time and source of strain and tension between self and society. His ideas constantly interweave individual developmental issues and social tasks with a superimposed notion of historical time as represented by the life cycle.

In terms of life cycle theory, adolescence is a period of identity formation involving the basic tasks of separation and individuation, but holding no more unique claim to identity formation than any other life stage (Toews, et al., 1981). The process of identity formation starts at infancy, when the newborn begins to differentiate from mother, and continues through old age. What seems unique about the formation of identity during adolescence is that, for the first time, physical development, cognitive development, and social expectations coincide to enable young persons to review their childhood identifications and anticipate a pathway toward the future (Marcia, 1980).

As the study of adolescence has progressed, specialists have come to realize that it is necessary, especially in the field of mental health, to look at that stage of development in the context of the family. It would be next to impossible to work effectively with adolescents in crisis without having knowledge about their families' developmental processes.

The family is the primary group in which most individuals learn the basic norms of human behavior and social expectations. Within that context, values and attitudes are passed down through generations, giving individuals a sense of history and continuity. The family also supports developmental growth by providing individuals with emotional nurturance. In the 1950s, perhaps as a result of this function, the concept of the family as the basic unit of human development evolved (Duvall, 1977; Carter & McGoldrick, 1980).

Sociologists first began to visualize the family as a unit composed of individuals having their own life cycle tasks. Later the observation was made that family members depend on each other to complete their own individual tasks. Finally, the family was seen as a unit having its own developmental tasks. This view led to the theory that the family had its own life cycle with predictable and identifiable transitions (Carter & McGoldrick, 1980; Haley, 1973; Solomon, 1973).

Family life cycle theory addresses the normal developmental processes experienced by most people as they move from one stage to another. The assumption is that there are tasks at each stage that need to be accomplished, and that the transition from one stage to another is always accompanied by a normal degree of crisis. How the family accomplishes these tasks and copes with the crises will have a tremendous effect on individual development. An important point to consider when using this framework is that differences in class and culture as well as changes in society will influence the life cycle of a family.

In the field of family therapy, family-life-cycle theory has been used as a framework for understanding some of the problems that individuals and families present in treatment (Haley, 1973, 1980; Minuchin, 1974; Watzlawick, 1974; Palazzoli, et al.,

1978; Carter & McGoldrick, 1980). Symptoms or problems are viewed as a signal that the family is having difficulty moving on to the next stage in its life cycle. The goal of the therapy is then to help the family move past a crisis and to the next stage of family life (Haley, 1973).

This framework is especially useful for understanding the experiences of adolescents and their families in today's society. It provides guidelines for examining the tasks and transformations required of the family having adolescents. The therapist can use this approach to make a clearer assessment of how the family is coping with that stage of development. Sharing this perspective with families can be an extremely effective method of intervention. For instance, the generational conflicts and power struggles that most of these families present as problems in therapy can be reframed as, or seen in the context of, normal developmental processes characteristic of adolescence. This may allow the family to view the situation as temporary rather than permanent and hopelessly out of control. By focusing on the tasks that need to be accomplished during that stage, the family can be helped to negotiate new roles and patterns of interaction for its members that may lead to developmental growth.

THE ADOLESCENT PHASE OF THE FAMILY LIFE CYCLE

The adolescent phase of the family's life cycle extends from the oldest child's entry into adolescence through the last adolescent's initiation into adulthood. For some families a child's entry into adolescence heralds the most significant change since the birth of their youngest child. Adolescence involves such significant shifts in the experience, identity and structure of the family that the family itself is transformed.

As role and identity experimentation by the young adolescent increases, neither s/he nor the family can ever be quite the same. At the very least, the sights, smells, and sounds in the home are markedly altered. Changes in space, energy level, and time schedule of the household usually occur. Parents may also find themselves reassessing their own values, belief systems, and personal styles, partly in response to their adolescent and partly as a result of their own developmental crises.

In most families when children reach adolescence parents are approaching middle age. At this stage of development, adults often realize that their dreams may, after all, remain dreams and that they have only a measured amount of time left to make them real. Often people at this age experience an acute dissatisfaction with themselves and their lives and feel compelled to make changes. Situations that have been tolerated for years become unbearable with the realization that time is limited. Marital separations and divorces are common during these middle years, and new families are often started, possibly in an attempt to recapture youth and the satisfaction and productivity of parenthood. Career changes are also common at this stage of the life cycle. For many women in the United States, returning to a career or to school has almost become an expectation. Consequently, it is common to see parents and adolescents confronting similar concerns. Both may be struggling with personal goals and relationships as well as grappling with issues of autonomy and individuation (Prosen, et al., 1981). Frequently, both may be embarking on significantly new pathways. In their respective attempts to achieve ambitions and/or as a result of viewing time as running short, both may act impulsively.

The impact of adolescence is felt across generations. As parents and adolescents become engaged in the tasks of this stage, unresolved conflicts between parents and grandparents may resurface. For instance, as in the following example, children attempting to differentiate may cause parents to reexperience unresolved conflicts about their own separation.

At fourteen, Clara began to withdraw from her mother, with whom she had been extremely close. She began to let her mother know that she didn't like some of her traits

and did not want to be like her. Her mother became extremely hurt, angry, and confused, since she had tried very hard to be the mother she had never had. Her daughter's reaction stirred and brought to the surface feelings about her mother that she thought had been buried. She had felt rejected by her own mother throughout childhood and especially during adolescence. As an adult had tried to forgive her, but feeling rejected by her own daughter had reactivated the hurt and resentment. This was exacerbated by Clara's disbelief that her grandmother had been rejecting.

It is also common for parents to try to avoid making the same "mistakes" they feel their own parents made. Yet, after raising their children "differently," they may be surprised to observe similarities in personality between their children and their parents. The following caption from a cartoon by Jules Feiffer illustrates this well.

"I hated the way I turned out. . . . So everything my mother did with me I tried to do different with my Jennifer. Mother was possessive. I encouraged independence. Mother was manipulative. I have been direct. Mother was secretive. I have been open. Mother was evasive. I have been decisive. Now my work is done. Jennifer is grown. The exact image of my mother." (Heller, 1982)

It is often that the child of an underfunctioning parent, for example, rears an underfunctioning child.

Ackerman (1980) describes other multigenerational shifts that he has observed in the organization of families with adolescents. He sees relationships in the nuclear family as mirroring relationships in the extended family. For instance, when an adolescent makes demands of a parent, a reciprocal change can be observed in the parent-grandparent relationship. As a result of this, the relationship between the grandparents may also be affected. Conversely, the retirement, illness, migration, or death of a grandparent will usually affect the adolescent and the child-parent relationship, and also the marital relationship.

By the time the family arrives at the adolescent stage of development its structural organization is well defined. Generally the family at this phase of the life cycle has reached a stable level of functioning. Family members may have learned to set limits on each other, demarking differences in roles and power status. Patterns of interaction for meeting needs and resolving conflicts have usually been established. During adolescence these patterns may come to be ineffective. With children shifting from childhood to young adulthood and parents reassessing their life goals, the balance in relationships among family members is shaken. Stability is disrupted, and some turmoil may ensue until a new equilibrium is established. This can occur both at the beginning and end of the adolescent phase of the life cycle.

An awareness of parallels in developmental issues for parents and children may help them gain understanding and appreciation of each other's tasks as they move through the life cycle. Both may be able to see more clearly how they complement each other and how their attempts at solving their own life stage problems create conflicts (Prosen, et al., 1981).

TASKS OF ADOLESCENCE

Terkelsen (1980) defines the basic purpose of the family as the provision of a supportive context for need attainment by its individual members. While survival needs may remain basically unchanged, clearly the developmental needs of the adolescent are substantially distinct from those of the younger child. Although the processes of identity formation and separation are really lifelong, puberty is a time of their acceleration. For example, the rapid physical growth and sexual development of an early adolescent challenges and changes his or her body image and concept of self. The adolescent's struggle to gain a new, clear, positive self-image and to venture forth into the world is enhanced when parents are able to experience the changes positively and communicate their acceptance to the child.

Prior to adolescence, in the period called *latency*, the span from ages six to twelve,

children are able to attain a sense of self-worth that is separate from their parents by achieving independently of them in the outside world. The development of cognitive skills, moral values, and a social conscience, as well as of physical growth are strengths that help them gain self-esteem. These achievements prepare children for coping with the increased demands of adolescence.

Concurrently, during these childhood years, parents are gaining a sense of competence as parents. Satisfaction can be gained as children grow and develop. Parents will also experience disappointment in their children and have the opportunity to learn to continue to love and accept them. Disobedience and defiance will be coped with, usually without chronic conflict characterizing the relationship. Parenting involves a continual process of loving and letting go. Leaving children with baby-sitters and allowing them to leave home to attend school are valuable experiences that prepare parents for coping with adolescents. As children develop their own interests, make friends, and join groups, increasing portions of their lives unfold without direct observation by, and with minimal knowledge of, their parents. Parents will come to grips with the hurts that children encounter while outside the family fold.

As adolescence approaches, the child again struggles with trying to resolve issues of trust vs. mistrust, autonomy vs. shame, initiative vs. guilt, and industry vs. inferiority, in preparation for the next crisis-identity vs. identity confusion (Erikson, 1968). The family must continue to provide a safe environment in which the child is able to test these conflicts. Structure and limits are necessary for protecting and challenging the pre-adolescent who needs to risk moving on to the next developmental stage. The family at this stage must learn to renegotiate rules of authority and begin to accept greater individuality (Rhodes, 1977). Successful negotiation at this stage of family life provides a strong basis for accomplishing the major tasks of the adolescent phase: identity clarification, coping with sexuality, and separation.

Identity Clarification

The physiological and psychological changes experienced by young people entering adolescence challenge their self-concept. Changes such as rapid physical growth and pubertal maturation have an implicit effect on how adolescents describe and evaluate themselves. These changes, although following biological developmental processes, are highly influenced by external stimuli. For instance, as the result of sexual maturation new social expectations about sexual roles and norms of behavior are imposed by the family, school, peers, and the media. On the other hand social changes such as improved nutrition, better housing, health care, and social conditions are a logical explanation for the acceleration in the rate of physical growth and faster sexual maturation that has been observed during childhood and adolescence in the past hundred years (Eveleth & Tanner, 1977).

Therefore, adolescents must learn to adjust to a new interplay between internal and external stimuli. Their ability to differentiate from others and clarify an identity will depend on how well they learn the expected social behaviors for expressing the emotions and impulses that are precipitated by puberty. This process is facilitated by the development of intellectual skills which allow adolescents to take an analytical perspective of their experiences and a broader view of reality (Inhelder & Piaget, 1958).

As adolescents begin to develop their own ideas and theories about the world, they also begin to perceive more sharply their parents' faults and virtues. They integrate into their own personalities parental attributes that will help them on the road to adulthood, and attempt to discard those they view as negative. Generally adolescents look for adults and ideas to have faith in and to model. Simultaneously, they may fear losing their sense of self if they totally accept someone else's beliefs or life style. Adolescents also avoid committing themselves to any specific belief that might go against the peer culture (Erikson, 1968).

As adolescents begin to clarify their identities, the family also struggles to maintain its own identity. Physiological and personality changes in the adolescent can have an unsettling effect on the family. As parental authority is relaxed, and the family's boundaries become more permeable, the family's sense of integrity may be compromised. In the midst of massive transformation, a reasonable degree of stability is necessary if the family is to be the protective haven the adolescent will periodically require. It is obviously difficult and confusing for the family to be both the target of rebellion and a sanctuary.

A sense of safety and acceptance within the family contributes to the emergence of a strong sense of self. As identity formation accelerates, new experiences in the world may subject adolescents to anxiety, disappointment, rebuff, and failure. The family that meets most of their needs for protection, nurturance, and guidance will provide strength by enabling them to refuel with sufficient supplies of self-esteem. Much of the family's energy must be devoted to this endeavor. Yet, if the family is too successful, is too ideal, the adolescent will prefer the security of home, and individuation will be discouraged. Thus, the very qualities that are essential for successful individuation and separation can unwittingly retard the process.

While such stagnation is possible, change and greater independence are more typical. For both adolescents and their families, identity experimentation may suddenly seem to increase dramatically and become a potential source of excitement and energy as well as confusion and immobilization. As with clothes and hair styles, roles may be tried on, prized briefly and then discarded, or clung to in an attempt to anchor a sense of self. While some of these roles are consistent with family values, they frequently challenge, if not assault, the mores of the family.

Therefore, for individuation to take place the family must be both strong and flexible. It must constantly strive for a balance of power that allows for experimentation and yet provides protection. Modulating parental authority is essential to successfully cope with this task. For instance, parents can respond to the adolescent's dependency needs by setting clear limits and expectations, and, at the same time, respect the adolescent's struggle for independence by being flexible and willing to change rules in the family.

If parental guidance and control becomes too lax, the risk for self-harm resulting from ill-informed, adolescent decision-making increases. By contrast, excessive, domineering parenting may impede development by inhibiting sufficient contact with peers and other external role models.

The need for flexibility and change also applies to the boundary that separates the family from the outside world. The adolescent who is now coping with more extensive ventures into the outside world needs a more fluid boundary to allow him/her to leave freely and return to the protection of the family fold. Increased permeability of that boundary permits the adolescent to form more significant relationships outside the family, while basically retaining family membership. In addition, it allows for other family members to be influenced by the adolescent's changing behavior, mode of self-expression, values, and beliefs.

However, if boundaries are weak and overly permeable, the family may not be able to successfully protect the adolescent from potentially avoidable self-destructive choices. Neither will the family be able to protect itself from excessive intrusion and domination resulting from the adolescent's introduction of life-style elements antithetical to the family's way of life. Weak boundaries may imply the lack of a clear family identity. This is usually manifested by the absence of clear values, expectations, and rules. In this type of family, adolescents are left with little to integrate, react to, accept, or reject in their struggle to establish their own sense of identity.

Sexuality

Coping with sexuality is another major task for adolescents and parents. The upsurge in sexual thoughts, feelings, and behavior is a developmental factor which not only transforms the self-concept of adolescents but also radically alters how they are perceived by other members of the family. When parents are comfortable with their own sexuality and the home has been a place where information has been shared, the family is more likely to accept the heightened sexuality of an adolescent and to convey their acceptance of it. Realistic, sensitive limits on behavior can be set, and minor transgressions tolerated if not condoned. This provides adolescents with an accepting framework within which to express, and experiment with, this new and important aspect of their lives.

When the adolescent's growing sexuality is denied, ignored, or rejected by the parents, the possibilities for the development of a positive sexual self-concept are diminished. In these families the probability of increased feelings of alienation between adolescents and their parents is greater. The risks for severe sexual inhibitions, or premature, excessive, or self-endangering sexual activity are also greater.

Incestuous impulses between the adolescent and opposite-sex parent are likely to increase with the adolescent's emerging sexuality. The energy and unacceptability of these urges can easily be transformed into heightened conflict. A previously special and loving relationship between father and daughter may rapidly evolve into a mutually hostile one, with the father being possessive and punitive and the daughter being provocative. In such a case, the family is clearly not able to adequately provide for the developmental needs of either child or parent. In fact, its capacity to provide for the developmental needs of any of its members is likely to be drastically reduced. Stepfamilies are probably especially vulnerable to these stresses since their boundaries tend to be less clear (Visher & Visher, 1979; Sager, et al., 1983).

Parents and children of the same sex often experience conflict and confusion when parents begin to experience their children as adults (Haley, 1973). When daughters mature into competing females, mothers may be unable to relate to them in any consistent way. Fathers may find

themselves caught in the middle and perplexed by this inconsistency. A similar pattern may also be observed between fathers
and sons. As sons mature, fathers must
relate to them not only as their children
but also as adult males. Often this is a difficult process.

Separation

Separation always involves some elements of grieving. As children enter adolescence, their membership status in the
family alters radically. As they increase and
strengthen their alliances outside, their
participation at home is often experienced
by other family members as decreasing.
The transition from childhood to adolescence marks a loss for the family—the loss
of the child. As adolescents move toward
greater independence, parents often feel
a void. They are no longer needed in the
same way. The nature of their care-taking
needs to change. Sometimes parents unable to cope with these transitions experience serious depression. Likewise,
adolescents experience feelings of loss as
they no longer enjoy the security and self-
assuredness of (childhood) latency.

Dependency and counter-dependency
between adolescent and family represents
an oscillating dynamic. Blos (1979) claims
that regression during this stage is necessary in order that individuals advance to
higher levels of differentiation. Furthermore, he states that the avoidance or exaggeration of regression is dangerous and
may lead to dysfunctional personalities.

The constant struggle between dependence and independence that adolescents
undergo generates a state of confusion for
themselves and their families. They need
a safe environment that allows for the
expression of an array of conflicting emotions. The family must be ready to cope
with sudden outbursts of hate and love,
rationality and irrationality, anger and
fear. Fears of abandonment especially are
aroused at this time.

Parental limits and guidance can help
adolescents feel safe during this period of
differentiation. They can also provide pa-

rameters for maintaining control. However, a continual conflict for parents is
adequately protecting their children while,
at the same time, encouraging them toward independence.

During adolescence, this conflict emerges
in full force. Certainly from an adult perspective, the adolescent's decisions in this
rapidly expanding area of choice, often
leave much to be desired. Yet distinguishing those behavioral choices that are merely
unwise and self-defeating from those that
are self-destructive, even life-threatening,
is often difficult. Uncertainty concerning
when to act as well as how to act is common
for parents of adolescents. The following
example describes how decisions about
discipline and/or protection become more
difficult while the stakes, for all concerned,
escalate.

> The Prousts are becoming increasingly
> anxious and indecisive about how to parent
> Wendy, who at fifteen is their oldest child.
> Should she have a curfew? If so, what time?
> Should they continue monitoring her school
> work? Should they insist she attend "family"
> events? And what about parties? Didn't sev-
> eral of her friends get quite drunk at one two
> weeks ago? And what about birth control?
> The rumor of her friend Olivia's recent abor-
> tion increases the Prousts' fears. And there
> is the example of Joe, down the block, a
> seemingly healthy, friendly child. Now, at
> 17, he is always stoned and increasingly in-
> volved in serious delinquency.
>
> Wendy's mother can resentfully recall the
> restrictions of her own teenage years.
> Shouldn't Wendy have an opportunity for
> the fun that she was deprived of? True,
> Wendy sometimes has made some unwise
> decisions, but isn't that what growing up is
> about? Perhaps she'd do best if she knew her
> parents trusted her, but do they dare? Her
> father agonizes over the possibility of his
> daughter being sexually assaulted or other-
> wise mistreated. But what should he do?

Retaining control while being objective
and supportive may be next to impossible
for parents who are the target of open rebellion. While adolescent rebellion is not
a universal experience, adolescent-parent
conflict is certainly common. It can reflect
the heightened emotionality of adolescents; it can also be a response to the rapid

changes that induce anxiety in both adolescents and parents. Conflict can serve a positive developmental function, assisting the process of redefining rules, roles, and relationships. Yet, for the family lacking skills in problem-solving and conflict-resolution, conflict can escalate dangerously or become a way of life. Constant conflict may be a symptom of a developmental impasse. As sometimes with a divorcing couple, conflict can serve to enmesh a relationship still further and interfere with growth and change.

Therefore, some degree of generational conflict is necessary for developmental growth to take place during this stage. Although the family's ability to be flexible is essential in providing a safe environment in which to resolve this struggle, it is not an easy task for most parents to accomplish when they feel judged and criticized by their own children. Parental toleration will tend to be low if self-acceptance and self-esteem are issues for them. Also, if parents have unresolved conflicts with each other, their ability to accept the adolescent's perceptions of them becomes impaired. The adolescent may then be triangled into power struggles which will complicate the process by increasing tension, dissatisfaction, misunderstanding, and conflict for all. Behavior that would otherwise represent individuation may be experienced as a collusive alliance with one parent against the other. The following example illustrates this point.

John's high school performance deteriorated rapidly. Within a year he had dropped out and helped form a punk rock group. John's father, despite his conservative life style, championed John's "independence" and repeatedly undercut his wife's desperate attempts to redirect their son's behavior. The parents had an openly hostile relationship. John's father felt chronically controlled and criticized by others. In many ways John's behavior continued a long pattern of an unhealthy father-son alliance against his mother. Aside from a younger brother, no one in the family was aware of the pattern.

The difficulties inherent in the task of separation are greater when the parental support system is not working or unavailable and there are no other adults who can provide assistance. Under such conditions, parents are likely to become overwhelmed and to respond by either attempting to control their adolescents arbitrarily or by giving up control completely.

Attempting to control adolescents at random and without reason may lead to serious symptomatic behavior. This type of control is often seen in families where, as Stierlin (1979) suggests, centripetal forces operate to keep members from leaving the system. Separation is experienced as dangerous, and efforts are made to protect the children from outside threats. Control may be exerted by reinforcing excessive infantile behavior, through mystification, or by demanding such strong loyalty ties that extreme guilt is induced when separation is considered. The case of Virginia Cooper illustrates this pattern.

At sixteen, Virginia was admitted to an adolescent psychiatric hospital. Her symptomatology consisted of somatic complaints, compulsive behavior, and fears about not being able to control her thoughts. The symptoms had started three years prior to hospitalization. They became progressively worse until she had stopped going to school. When asked about friends, activities, and her relationship with her family, she showed extreme anxiety. She claimed to have no close friends and that due to her present condition she was unable to participate in any activities. She said very little about her family except to complain that her parents worried too much about her.

After becoming more trusting at the hospital, Virginia expressed some of her frustration about living at home. She felt that her parents were too strict and their expectations excessive. Friendships were closely monitored and dating was not allowed. She was expected to be a high achiever at school and was enrolled in a Catholic high school. Contact with boys was only through school activities and under supervision. When this issue was raised with the family in therapy, her parents expressed their fear that she was immature and that without their strict limits she would have difficulty choosing friends and making decisions. They were afraid that going out with boys unsupervised would lead to problems, since they thought she couldn't protect herself sexually. Virginia confided that she panicked and felt she was betraying her parents on the rare occasions she felt attracted to a boy.

Virginia provided a sense of family for her parents. Their two children, a son, twenty-four, and a daughter, twenty, had left home early. The Coopers were anxious about their future. Financial pressures, job insecurity, and failing health exacerbated their fears. Most of all they feared being alone, childless. There was certainly a secondary gain for them in having an incompetent daughter to worry about and take care of. And there was a secondary gain for Virginia in not having to grow up. None of them was aware of these dynamics.

Adolescents who become entrenched by family boundaries may never grow up, perhaps never leaving home or achieving any semblance of adult independence. A similar but less severe outcome are the "emotionally bound" young adults described by Rashkis and Rashkis (1981). These individuals were inadequately equipped to understand and cope with their adult world. They persisted in perceiving the world through the eyes of their family as they had not been encouraged to transcend this limited perspective on life. In any case, an absence of conflict and discordance between parent and child during this stage may very well be cause for concern. The absence of conflict implies that the adolescent and family have become developmentally stuck.

Some families find themselves caught in ongoing struggles that only seem to reach resolution with a premature separation. Thus, parents, feeling overwhelmed by the tasks of adolescence, may give up all responsibility and call outside authorities to take control. In some cases, adolescents marry precipitously, without parental consent, or go to live with friends or lovers in an attempt to escape the conflicts at home. At the other extreme, some adolescents are essentially expelled from their families.

The expulsion of adolescents, also called extrusion (Sager, et al., 1983), may lead, in some cases, to a permanent family rift. Stierlin (1979) suggests that in these families centrifugal forces seem to impel the adolescent from the system. He has found that parents in these families are neglectful and rejecting, and tend to push adoles-

cents out by reinforcing in them a premature autonomy. In any case, this type of separation, while less intense than that following death, has significant and traumatic ramifications. For the adolescent cast-out or runaway, the casualty rate due to other inflicted or self-inflicted violence, including drug overdose, is high. Vulnerability to exploitation is also high; unemployment, underemployment, prostitution, and involvement with an abusive partner are more likely outcomes for the adolescent without family supports.

While the consequences may be less lethal for the remaining members of the evicting or deserted family, they are likely to confront heightened guilt, mutual blame, self-reproach, bitterness, continued anger, depression, and unresolved feelings of loss. The family's capacity to move ahead along its own life-cycle course may also be severely compromised. Both parents and other adolescents, or soon-to-be adolescents in the family, will be significantly affected by the experience as they attempt to negotiate their own transitions. Rashkis and Rashkis (1981) describe some of the adjustment difficulties of young adults who were "forced out, unprepared," i.e., launched with inadequate preparation. Their most salient limitation appeared to be an avoidance of intimacy.

FACTORS AFFECTING ADOLESCENCE

The family's evolution through the life cycle is influenced by different factors which affect the way individuals cope with specific stage tasks. For instance, geographic location, socioeconomic status, educational level, migration, and ethnocultural issues are all contributors to a family's level of functioning. The structure of the family—whether it is nuclear or extended, or includes a single or remarried parent—has significant implications. Family composition—i.e., the number of persons in the household and their age, rank, and sex—is another important element affecting individual development and relationship patterns within the family.

It is also important to consider the effect on family functioning of both predictable and unpredictable life stresses, such as death, birth, illness, retirement and divorce (Beal, 1980). Carter and McGoldrick (1980) view these stresses as having a continuing impact on family development over a long period of time. A number of studies have found life cycle connections between early loss or life cycle disruption and later symptom development (Orfanidis, 1977, and Walsh, 1978). Orfanidis (1977) and Walsh (1978) found a correlation between the death of a grandparent taking place at the time of the birth of a grandchild and that child's patterns of symptom development during adolescence. The timing of divorce or remarriage has also been found to be quite significant in the family's ability to manage the tasks of adolescence (Wallerstein and Kelly, 1980; Visher and Visher, 1979; Sager, et al., 1983).

Changes in Family Structure

Children are affected differently by changes in family structure, depending on their age at the time that the change takes place. Adolescents, unlike younger children, are more capable of intellectually understanding the reasons for the change and better equipped to maintain emotional distance from parental conflicts. Unfortunately they are still often unable to cope effectively, especially when they have been the focus of problems prior to the change.

Beal (1980) describes some of the patterns that emerge in families where adolescents are unable to maintain appropriate emotional distance from parental conflicts after a divorce or separation. The change in family structure may cause a blurring of generational boundaries and an intensification of bonds between parents and adolescent. Adolescents may assume adult roles in an effort to replace the missing spouse and support the single parent. Parents may regress emotionally and lean inappropriately on the adolescent. These patterns can lead to the family's inability to master developmental tasks. Generally, in single-parent families, adolescents assume more adult responsibilities than in two-parent families. However, the results are not always negative, especially if generational boundaries are reasonably maintained between parents and children.

In general, it has been found that adolescents recover from divorce and separation faster and better than latency-age children (Wallerstein and Kelly, 1980). However, in remarried families, they seem to have more difficulty adjusting than younger children (Sager, et al., 1983). At a time when they are trying to separate and individuate, adolescents can find negotiating membership in a new family extremely disconcerting. The closer that the divorce and remarriage are to the adolescent phase, the more difficulty the new family is likely to have in coalescing as a unit.

Unresolved conflicts and negative feelings between parents may interfere with their ability to co-parent, adding to the confusion of everyone involved. Conflicts between new spouses and ex-spouses can also add to the problems in the new households. Loyalty ties to a now-excluded parent are likely to deter the adolescent from building relationships in the new systems. Stepparents who have not experienced raising adolescents or who have not had enough time to establish bonds with their stepchildren prior to adolescence will probably feel more threatened by normal expressions of anger, hostility, and rebellion.

Another reality to consider is that the lack of blood ties results in blurred generational boundaries and tends to release incestuous impulses within the family, thus increasing the possibility for sexual attraction during this stage of heightened sexuality. As Sager and his associates state, these difficulties can be eased when the adults in the household accept the adolescent with understanding and flexibility (Sager et al., 1983). Also as noted earlier, the clear definition of rules and expectations and the availability of adult role models can provide a safe environment in which the adolescent can feel secure.

Another factor to consider is the considerable impact that the lack of extended family or other support group may have on how families manage adolescence. Some ethnic groups such as Puerto Ricans rely heavily on extended family members to help with the discipline of adolescents and the clarification of boundaries. It is common for Puerto Rican parents to send a rebellious adolescent to live with an uncle or godparent who can be more objective about setting limits. This move also serves to provide time for parents and adolescents to obtain enough emotional distance from each other to regain control and reestablish a more balanced relationship. Relying solely on the nuclear family, especially when it is a single-parent family, to provide control, support, and guidance for adolescents can overload the circuits and escalate the conflicts.

Sex Differences

Apart from the obvious physical characteristics that distinguish males from females there are basic differences in the way that both sexes structure their sense of self. Females rely more on the relationships and connections they make and maintain, while males place the emphasis on separation and individuation (Chodorow, 1974; Gilligan, 1982). These different approaches indicate that females may resolve the crisis of identity later in the life cycle than males, while males may resolve the crisis of intimacy later than females.

However, since most developmental theories have been based on studies about men, the assumption made has been that male patterns are the norm. Consequently when females don't conform to male standards of behavior, the tendency has been to view their behavior as problematic. This perception has been reinforced by the roles that males and females play in society. For instance, in this society females are implicitly undervalued when autonomy is equated with individuation and individual achievement, rather than with the ability to connect and form relationships.

Although recent changes in society have fostered some flexibility in roles and gender expectations, the economic position of

females and their access to power are still not equitable to males. The women's movement has helped raise social consciousness but options available to men in this society continue to exceed those available to women. Females may be more visible than ever on college campuses and in most areas of work; however, to obtain equality they still have to compete in a context where the rules are made mostly by men and for men. The answer for women who want equality has been to play like the men, creating a paradox since the rules of the game are often antithetical to their values.

Social values and attitudes about sex differences and gender expectations are reflected in the way that families cope with adolescence. For instance, although to a lesser degree than in previous generations, the tendency continues for families to protect females more than males. One reason for adhering to this pattern may be that in this society females are at higher risk for exploitation. For example, the incidence of sexual and physical abuse, inside and outside the family, is much higher for females.

In contrast, the belief that prevails regarding males is that they are less vulnerable and more able to protect themselves in the outside world. Males continue to be encouraged more towards independence. It is still more acceptable for females than for males to ask for support and to stay connected to family and friends during this transition. As a result males may run the risk of not receiving enough emotional support to cope with the conflicts of adolescence.

The patterns for launching adolescents into adulthood have also been changing. Traditionally families gave males greater encouragement for educational and occupational advancement, independent living, and financial self-sufficiency. Females, on the other hand, were primarily launched into adulthood through marriage. However, recently females have been demanding the same opportunities as males which implies that families need to reexamine their expectations and patterns of launching. The greater range of options present, especially for female adolescents, may require families to make choices that challenge the values held by previous generations. When there are no prototypes to provide role models, the conflict and confusion normally experienced during this phase may increase dramatically for families with female adolescents.

Family Composition

The number of children in a family, their ages and their rank are variables that influence the way in which families manage adolescence. Families having only one child will tend to handle adolescence very differently from the way families with several children do. For instance, parents who have only one child tend to be more egalitarian when they relate to their young (Carter & McGoldrick, 1980). Usually in these families power is equally distributed between parents and child, and the decision-making process is more democratic. Therefore, the transition from childhood to adolescence may not be as traumatic for the family if the child has had an equal relationship with the parents all along. Not having siblings with whom to compete or share may allow children to devote more energy to developing their own interests and achievements (Peck, 1977). However, the lack of generational conflict involving siblings and parents, as well as the lack of experience with competition and sharing, may leave the child less equipped for some adolescent struggles. In contrast, families with more than one child experience sharing, cooperation, and rivalry among siblings. Egalitarianism is not effective in families with children of different ages, needs and expectations (Carter & McGoldrick, 1980), because it doesn't address the uniqueness of each child. Acknowledging differences among children validates their self-perception. Adolescents, especially, need to experience their position in the family as changing. They need to have responsibilities and privileges that differentiate them from the other children in the family.

Generally, a family that experiences the adolescence of the first child and survives will be better prepared to launch the next child in line. Not only will the second child have the first as an example, but parents will feel less anxious about what to expect and more confident about coping with unpredictable changes. However, if the first child is unable to make that transition successfully, the family may be apprehensive when other children reach that stage. Also, the youngest, or last, child is likely to have more difficulty and require more time to enter adulthood since this transition will more profoundly redefine the family. For similar reasons, an only child might have difficulty gaining permission and support to grow up and leave home.

The experience of adolescence will also differ among children in the same family for other reasons. Parental attitudes will vary from child to child, depending not only on the child's rank and sex, but on alliances that parents form with certain children. Parents may identify more with a child having the same birth-order position as themselves (Toman, 1976). Or they may have stronger feelings, negative or positive, for a child who reminds them of someone in the extended family (Bradt, 1980).

If a child is unable to master the tasks of adolescence, the parents' explanation for this failure profoundly affects their expectations and reactions. The reaction caused by a mentally retarded or otherwise physically handicapped child's difficulty with this stage will be different than that caused by a juvenile delinquent, a drug or alcohol addict, or a psychotic child. A physical or organic handicap can be more easily understood and accepted by some families than problems of delinquency, addiction, or mental illness.

Coping with a disabled child may strengthen some families. On the other hand, the process of growth may be curtailed when families distressed by resentments, feelings of guilt, and profound sorrow are unable to accept having a limited child. Feelings of responsibility and guilt may interfere with the parent's ability to provide adequate guidance and support to any of their children. They may become overprotective or neglectful as a result of feeling inadequate. Other children in the family may also feel responsible and guilty and be afraid to venture into the outside world. These patterns may create a closed or overly isolated family system.

Delinquency and substance abuse tend to produce different reactions in families. Families may feel that these behaviors —unlike mental retardation, organic illness, and mental illness—can be learned from peers. They may experience themselves as victims of society. At times, they join the adolescent in a fight against institutions, such as schools and courts, and against other adults they perceive as persecutors. They may also react by giving up controls and asking outside authorities, such as police or public agencies, to take control of their child. Other children in the family may band together in an attempt to protect the one in trouble or may form alliances against the adolescent. Extended family, or friends, may become involved in trying to help the family through this difficult period. However, the family's alienation from society may be so extreme that they may react defensively by tightening their boundaries further in an attempt to ensure protection.

Geographic Factors

Another factor influencing adolescents and their families is the kind of community in which they reside. For example, the pressures and expectations experienced by families in rural areas are different than those experienced by families in urban areas. Adolescents who grow up in cities tend to be less dependent on their families for recreation. With public transportation and a greater concentration of recreational options, their potential for independent activity increases. Generally they are exposed to a greater diversity of life styles and role models, both positive and negative. This may increase the distance between parents and adolescents and escalate the normal conflicts of that stage. Parents may be less able to keep track of their children's friends and whereabouts and less concerned about doing so than their sub-

urban and rural counterparts. By contrast, adolescents in suburban rural areas may find themselves isolated from peer groups and dependent on the family for transportation and social stimulation. Greater dependence on the family may intensify the normal adolescent struggle for independence or slow down the growth process altogether. The acquisition of a driver's license and the availability of a car represent a transitional event permitting a major increase in independent actions by the adolescent.

Ethnicity and Migration

In recent years more attention has been given to the significant role that ethnicity and culture play in the lives of families. Relationship patterns are deeply influenced by ethnic values and attitudes passed down through the generations. Ethnic groups differ remarkably in the rituals used to demarcate life cycle stages (McGoldrick, 1982). The family's reaction to its tasks during the adolescence phase varies distinctly among ethnic groups.

For instance, British-Americans tend to promote the early separation of adolescents and their transition into adulthood (McGill & Pearce, 1982). Unlike most Italian, Hispanic, and Jewish families, they do not struggle to keep their adolescents close to home. McGill and Pearce observe that British-Americans are good at promoting separation but may provide insufficient guidance and support for adolescents. The result could be a premature separation that leads to a false adult identity and the establishment of immature relationships in an attempt to replace the family.

Portuguese families, while also expecting adolescents to make an early transition into adulthood, handle separation very differently. Adolescents are encouraged to find employment early and to make financial contributions to home just like adults. However, socially and emotionally, they are expected to remain loyal and under the supervision of their parents (Moitoza, 1982). They are expected to live at home until they marry. When these expectations are challenged, serious conflicts between parents and adolescents can occur. Leaving home before marriage involves the risk of being ostracized by the family. Parent-adolescent interaction and contact may substantially diminish or cease. If the adolescent is cut off, it will interfere with a healthy transition into adulthood.

Other ethnic groups—such as Puerto Ricans, Italians and Jews—also manage the separation and individuation of adolescents in ways that are quite distinct. Puerto Ricans, for example, expect adolescents to be as respectful and obedient of adults in the home as when they were younger children. Yet, they are often given adult responsibilities as caretakers of the young. These mixed messages with regard to behavioral expectations often lead to generational conflicts (Garcia-Preto, 1982).

Migration is another important variable affecting the life cycle of families. The stresses of adjusting to a new country are amplified by the generational conflicts between adolescents and parents. Such families who migrate may experience difficulty coping simultaneously with culture shock and the transitions of adolescence. They will have less time together as a unit before the children begin to leave home to resolve the issues of this stage (McGoldrick, 1982). During adolescence children may reject the ethnic values of their parents in an attempt to become more acculturated and assimilated. There are also long-range effects of migration and resettlement. Sluzki (1979) has found that the impact of migration in families is sometimes not felt until subsequent generations.

Difficulties may also arise when either the parents or the child migrate separately, leaving the other behind; as a result, adolescence is not experienced by the family as a unit. This is illustrated by the following case:

> Lee came to the United States at age thirteen to live with his older brother, who was attending college in New York. His parents remained in Hong Kong. They came to this country thirteen years later, when Lee was twenty-three years old and a graduate student. Because he was still single, they established a household with him. Six months

later Lee began to experience extreme anxiety and was unable to concentrate in school. He had to leave the university and, without funds, was forced to ask for welfare. He was encouraged to seek therapy. In therapy, it became clear that he and his parents were engaged in the adolescent process which had stopped when they had separated. Lee who had been functioning as an independent adult found this experience paralyzing and confusing. He and his parents needed to resolve the conflicts of an earlier stage in order for him to renegotiate the transition into adulthood.

Socioeconomic Factors

The socioeconomic status and educational level of families are factors that influence the availability of resources and opportunities for growth. The family's position in society can significantly affect its life cycle. Upper-class and middle-class families may experience acute pressure to achieve educational and professional goals, resulting in the postponement of marriage and childbearing until these goals are achieved. Having children later in life may have implications for parent-child relationships during adolescence. For instance, a greater age difference between adolescents and parents may lead to increased misunderstanding between the two generations. Parents who are coping with their own limitations—such as the failure to realize their dreams, and their own mortality—may try, excessively, to live through their children, or may have difficulty dealing with the expansiveness of adolescence. On the other hand, if they have attained their goals, parents may feel fulfilled and thus more capable of dealing with the demands and struggles of their adolescents.

For poor families, such pressures as unemployment or underemployment, substandard housing, limited educational opportunities, and poor health facilities have a tremendous impact on their lives. According to Colon (1980) the life cycle of poor families tends to be shorter than that of middle-class families; members seem to leave home, marry, have children, become grandparents, get old, and die earlier. Because of the shortened life cycle, there is less time to master the tasks of different stages. For instance, the shifts from childhood to adolescence to adulthood may be premature, and as a result, the boundaries between generations are often blurred.

The stresses of poverty contribute to family underorganization. The underorganized family is less able to cope with its needs and is less differentiated (Aponte, 1974, 1976). Parents in these families often have difficulty with their own role definitions and are not able to provide the guidance and controls needed to assist their children in mastering adolescence.

Adolescents in poor families represent a potential source of income. Since educational goals and opportunities are so limited, the tendency is for adolescents to drop out of school and find a job. Unfortunately their lack of basic and trade skills makes it difficult to succeed. Resultant frustration, combined with the pressures of living in a home with limited resources, may lead them to leave precipitously or the family to throw them out. Under these circumstances the possibility of their becoming involved in crime, prostitution, drug addiction, and/or alcoholism is very high.

The Nuclear Age

The massive transformation caused by advances in our modern technological world affects all aspects of our lives, including adolescence. Biologically and chemically we are in the process of radically modifying the environment in which we live, and, both deliberately and as an uninterrupted by-product of progress, rapidly altering our basic conceptions of life. Our capacity for rational thought and technical skill has enabled us to explore the universe, unlock secrets of atomic structure, computerize society, and decode the language of genetics. Unfortunately included among these advances are the panoply of nuclear weapons and their sophisticated delivery systems to haunt us.

Schwebel (1982) and Zeitlin (1983) have demonstrated the widespread concern over nuclear war among adolescents. Schwebel suggests that excessive anxiety and other disorders in adolescence may be related to this awareness of the nuclear threat. He also speculates that the fear of possible nuclear attack contributes to such phenomena as family instability, behavioral deterioration (including drug-abuse), and deteriorating academic performance. If nothing else, living under a nuclear threat encourages living for the moment without regard for future implications, accentuating an already common adolescent view of the world.

Perhaps society as we know it, at our moment in history, is undergoing an adolescence of sorts. Nuclear power is certainly a powerful, somewhat mysterious force, both wondrous and fearful. A parallel can easily be drawn to pubescent sexual urges. (The erotic element of nuclear war was captured in the film *Dr. Strangelove.*) Our society is in the midst of struggling to redefine how we live and what we value; these are typical adolescent concerns. The threat posed by nuclear weapons compels the question, "Will we live?" Collectively we are engaged in a struggle "to be or not to be," without the benefit of a family to assist us.

CONCLUSION

As we have noted, for the adolescent the functional family provides both anchor and springboard for the redefinition of self. The family hopefully remains a protective and stable social entity for the adolescent even as the family itself is transformed and destabilized during this phase of its life cycle. In the past, the family's tasks were supported by the relatively stable social framework provided by larger organizations or society as a whole. Today's pace of societal change and dislocation increasingly deprives families of this needed source of support. The specter of nuclear disaster presents, in a profound manner, a new limit on the family's capacity to protect itself and its children. It places in question the very future toward which so much of the energy of adolescence and of the family is directed. Adolescents and their families must today struggle through their developmental tasks under this external threat of extinction. The threat might never be realized, but because of it, the adolescent phase of the family life cycle is now even more complex and stressful for us all.

REFERENCES

Ackerman, N. J. The family with adolescents. In E. A. Carter & M. McGoldrick (Eds.), *The family life cycle: A framework for family therapy*. New York: Gardner Press, 1980.

Adelson, J. *Handbook of adolescent psychology*. New York: Wiley, 1980.

Aponte, H. Psychotherapy for the poor: An ecostructural approach to treatment. *Delaware Medical Journal*, March 1974, 1–7.

Aponte, H. Underorganization in the poor family. In P. J. Guerin, Jr. (Ed.), *Family therapy: theory and practice*. New York: Gardner Press, 1976.

Aries, P. *Centuries of childhood: A social history of family life*. New York: Vintage, 1962.

Beal, E. W. Separation, divorce, and single parent families. In E. A. Carter & M. McGoldrick (Eds.), *The family life cycle: A framework for family therapy*. New York: Gardner Press, 1980.

Blos, P. *On adolescence: A psychoanalytic interpretation*. New York: MacMillan, 1962.

Blos, P. *The adolescent passage: Developmental issues*. New York: International Universities Press, 1979.

Bradt, J. O. The family with young children. In E. A. Carter & M. McGoldrick (Eds.), *The family life cycle: A framework for family therapy*. New York: Gardner Press, 1980.

Carter, E. A. & McGoldrick, M. The family life cycle and family therapy: An overview. In E. A. Carter & M. McGoldrick (Eds.), *The family life cycle: A framework for family therapy*. New York: Gardner Press, 1980.

Chodorow, N. Family structure and feminine personality. In M. Z. Rosaldo & L. Lamphere (Eds.), *Woman, Culture, and Society*. Stanford: Stanford University Press, 1974.

Colon, F. The family life cycle of the multiproblem poor family. In E. A. Carter & M. McGoldrick (Eds.), *The family life cycle: A framework for family therapy*. New York: Gardner Press, 1980.

Duvall, E. *Marriage and Family Development* (5th ed.). Philadelphia: Lippincott, 1977.

Elder, G. H., Jr. Adolescence in the life cycle. In S. Dragasten & G. H. Elder, Jr. (Eds.), *Adolescence in the life cycle*. Washington, D. C.: Hemisphere, 1975.

Erikson, E. H. *Identity: Youth and crisis*. New York: Norton, 1968.

Eveleth, P., & Tanner, J. *Worldwide variation in human growth*. Cambridge: Cambridge University Press, 1977.

Garcia-Preto, N. Puerto Rican families. In M. McGoldrick, J. K. Pearce, & J. Giordano (Eds.), *Ethnicity and family therapy*. New York: Guilford, 1982.

Gilligan, C. *In a different voice: Psychological theory and women's development*. Cambridge: Harvard University Press, 1982.

Haley, J. *Uncommon therapy: The psychiatric techniques of Milton H. Erickson, M.D.* New York: Norton, 1973.

Haley, J. *Leaving Home*. New York: McGraw-Hill, 1980.

Hall, G. *Adolescence*. New York: Appleton, 1904.

Hareven, T. K. American families in transition. In F. Walsh (Ed.), *Normal family processes*. New York: Guilford, 1982.

Heller, S. *Jules Feiffer's America: From Eisenhower to Reagan*. New York: Knopf, 1982.

Inhelder, B., & Piaget, J. *The growth of logical thinking*. New York: Basic Books, 1958.

Keniston, K. Social change and youth in America. *Daedalus*, 1962, **91**, 145–171.

Marcia, J. E. Identity of adolescence. In J. Adelson (Ed.), *Handbook of adolescent psychology*. New York: Wiley, 1980.

McGill, D., & Pearce, J. K. British families. In M. McGoldrick, J. K. Pearce, & J. Giordano (Eds.), *Ethnicity and family therapy*. New York: Guilford, 1982.

McGoldrick, M. Ethnicity and family therapy: An overview. In M. McGoldrick, J. K. Pearce, & J. Giordano (Eds.), *Ethnicity and family therapy*. New York: Guilford, 1982.

Moitoza, E. Portuguese families. In M. McGoldrick, J. K. Pearce, & J. Giordano (Eds.), *Ethnicity and family therapy*. New York: Guilford, 1982.

Minuchin, S. *Families in Family Therapy*. Cambridge: Harvard University Press, 1974.

Orfanidis, M. *Some data on death and cancer in schizophrenia families*; paper presented at the Pre-Symposium Meeting of the Georgetown Symposium, Washington, D.C., 1977.

Palazzoli, M. D., Boscolo, L., Cecchin, G., & Prata, G. *Paradox and counterparadox*. New York: Jason Aronson, 1978.

Peck, E. *The joy of the only child*. New York: Delacorte, 1977.

Prosen, H., Martin, R., & Prosen, M. The remembered mother and the fantasized mother. *Archives of General Psychiatry*, 1972, **27**, 791–794.

Prosen, H., Toews, J., & Martin, M. The life cycle of the family: Parental midlife crisis and adolescent rebellion. In S. C. Feinstein, J. C. Looney, A. Z. Schwartzberg, & A. D.

Sorosky (Eds.), *Adolescent psychiatry: Developmental and clinical studies* (Vol. 9). Chicago: University of Chicago Press, 1981.

Rashkis, H. A., & Rashkis, S. R. Parental communication, readiness of adolescents to leave home, and the course of treatment. In S. C. Feinstein, J. C. Looney, A. Z. Schwartzberg, & A. D. Sorosky (Eds.), *Adolescent Psychiatry: Developmental and Clinical Studies* (Vol. 9). Chicago: University of Chicago Press, 1981.

Rhodes, S. L. A developmental approach to the life cycle of the family. *Social Casework*, 1977, **58**, 301–311.

Sager, C. J., Brown, H. S., Crohn, H., Engel, T., Bodstein, E., & Walker, L. *Treating the remarried family*. New York: Brunner/Mazel, 1983.

Schwebel, M. Effects of the nuclear war threat on children and teenagers: Implications for professionals. *American Journal of Orthopsychiatry*, 1982, **54**, 608–618.

Solomon, M. A. A developmental premise for family therapy. *Family Process*, 1973, **12**, 179–188.

Sluzki, C. E. Migration and family conflict. *Family Process*, 1979, **18**, 379–390.

Stierlin, H. *Separating parents and adolescents: A perspective on running away, schizophrenia and waywardness*. New York: Quadrangle, 1979.

Terkelsen, J. G. Toward a theory of the family life cycle. In E. A. Carter & M. McGoldrick (Eds.), *The family life cycle: A framework for family therapy*. New York: Gardner Press, 1980.

Toews, J., Prosen, H., & Martin, R. The life cycle of the family: The adolescent's sense of time. In S. C. Feinstein, J. C. Looney, A. Z. Schwartzberg, & A. D. Sorosky (Eds.), *Adolescent psychiatry: Developmental and clinical studies* (Vol. 9). Chicago: University of Chicago Press, 1981.

Toman, W. *Family constellation: Its effect on personality and social behavior* (3rd ed.). New York: Springer, 1976.

Visher, E. B., & Visher, J. S. *Stepfamilies: A guide to working with step-parents and stepchildren*. New York: Brunner/Mazel, 1979.

Wallerstein, J. S., & Kelly, J. B. The effects of parental divorce: The adolescent experience. In A. Koupernek (Ed.), *The child in his family*. New York: Wiley, 1974.

Wallerstein, J. S. & Kelly, J. B. *Surviving the breakup: How children and parents cope with divorce*. New York: Basic Books, 1980.

Walsh, F. Concurrent grandparent death and the birth of a schizophrenic offspring: An intriguing finding. *Family Process*, 1973, **12**, 179–188.

Watzlawick, P., Weakland, J. H., & Fisch, R. *Change: Principles of problem formulation and problem resolution*. New York: Norton, 1974.

Zeitlin, S. The nuclear threat and adolescents. In H. Hicks (Moderator), *Dealing with plans for the annihilation of life on earth: The reality of nuclear arms—changing fear, denial, ignorance and helplessness into action for life*. Session presented at the meeting of the American Orthopsychiatric Association, Boston, 1983.

3

Matchmaking: Choosing the Appropriate Therapy for Families at Various Levels of Pathology

JOHN S. WELTNER, M.D.

This handbook is concerned with the treatment of adolescents and their families. This chapter lays some groundwork by describing the world of family therapies and some of the broad characteristics of families in general. I will not focus in on specific issues of adolescents and their treatments, but rather on a more general issue: how to make a fit between therapeutic style and family style. Especially in the 1980s, when we have such a bewildering abundance of therapeutic approaches, matchmaking is a major therapeutic issue. It is less pressing for those whose diagnostic and treatment posture is fairly uniform regardless of the family's situation. But for most therapists, three central issues emerge in the early phase of intervention:

1. What is the most useful definition of the problem?

2. What needs to change so that this family can move to a higher level of functioning?

3. What techniques—structural, paradoxical, interpretational, etc.—are most suited to facilitating this kind of change?

These decisions often seem to flow intuitively, or perhaps from a case-by-case analysis that bypasses the question of general guidelines. Rarely do we commit ourselves to a specificity that states: In type x family, my usual intervention goal is y, and my techniques will probably include z.

One carefully developed attempt at such guidelines in the area of individual psychotherapy pairs three short-term therapy approaches with three developmental crises (Burke, White, & Havens, 1979). Burke et al. looked at the style and techniques of James Mann (the "existential" approach), Peter Sifneos (the "interpretive" approach), and Franz Alexander (the "corrective" approach). Examining issues of treatment focus and therapeutic style, they concluded that "each of the schools is best suited to patients whose problems characterize particular points along a developmental continuum" (p. 185).

The first developmental step considered by Burke et al. is the adolescent task of separation and leaving home. The authors here recommend James Mann's short-term model, with its emphasis on the issue of termination. Mann divides his twelve-session treatment into two phases, the second of which focuses on the fact that the therapy is time-limited and soon to end. Thus, he brings to the surface and works through the issue of loss and the development of autonomy.

Peter Sifneos forcefully attends to oedipal material. In unraveling the complex feelings involved in the family triangle, he seeks to free his patients from repeating the unhappy patterns that they bring into each current relationship. Thus, his short-term model seems ideal for people struggling with issues of intimacy—a later developmental issue.

Finally, Franz Alexander's emphasis on corrective behavior—action rather than awareness—makes it well suited for midlife transitions where the problems generally require new decisions and new behaviors.

One similar attempt in the domain of family therapy is Grunebaum and Chasin's (1982) integration of several family therapy approaches. They contrast two therapeutic modes: the "involved" or straightforward mode, and the "ingenious" or covert mode. In a final chart, they list characteristics of cases which invite one or the other mode. For example, out-of-control or impulsive families invite ingenious interventions; gentle, inhibited families suggest an involved therapeutic approach.

In this chapter, we attempt a different categorization. First, the major schools of family therapy are contrasted and some speculations are offered concerning characteristics of those families for which each school is often uniquely appropriate. The second part of the chapter presents a

framework by which families can be categorized by their level of functioning. Each level invites a specific overall intervention strategy. Along with the discussion, these are set out in chart form with specific intervention techniques appropriate to each level and to each overall strategy.

THE SCHOOLS OF FAMILY THERAPY

For purposes of simplicity, the many schools of family therapy are here divided into four groups (see Table 3.1):

1. The existential psychodynamic therapies
2. Structural therapy
3. Family systems therapy
4. Communications or strategic therapy

Briefly, the *existential psychodynamic therapies* (Ackerman, 1970; Kantor, 1975; Napier & Whitaker, 1978) focus on the inner experience of family members. They involve concepts like "emotional conflicts," "historical trauma," "critical image"—that image which captures the central family interaction that characterizes a person's childhood experience (Kantor, 1975). In short, this school focuses on the content of each person's emotional reality and the shared images of the family. Therapeutic goals involve clarification of these images, development of empathy and understanding between members, and the negotiation of mutually supportive decisions. Personal and spiritual growth are often explicit aims in this type of therapy.

Structural therapy (Minuchin, 1974; Aponte, 1976), by contrast, ignores the inner world. Interactions between people are studied and form the basis for mapping out the organization of the family. This mapping focuses on distance and closeness, hierarchy (the pecking order), family boundaries (who is in and who is out), and family subsystems (who is included in the separate alliances that exist inside the family). The structural theory of causality centers on problems of distance or closeness:

if a child is too close to either parent, or too distant from both of them, he or she may become symptomatic. Therapy modifies these excesses. By rebalancing triangles—for example, by involving a child more closely with his distant father, thus lessening his dependence on his overclose mother—or by shifting alliances, or by firming up or loosening boundaries, the therapist moves the family toward more functional structures. As these structural changes are achieved, symptoms disappear and the conditions for healthy functioning emerge.

Family systems therapy (Fogarty, 1976; Guerin, 1976; Bowen, 1978) honors the entirety of the multigenerational matrix in which symptoms develop. As in the psychodynamic school, family history is carefully noted. Genograms and time lines help identify the critical (nodal) family experiences which modify and mold the personalities of each generation. But much attention is also focused on the resulting structural elements. Fusion, the inability to separate fully from parent or from family of origin, is a key concept. This can be manifested by continued intense involvement (enmeshment), or by cutoffs in which enmeshment is avoided by total absence of contact. Both extremes testify to a person's inability to relate without losing a sense of self. Typical goals of systems interventions involve confronting interpersonal conflicts so that fusion yields to clearer definition of each person's wishes, interests, and viewpoints. This differentiation of family members, not the resolution of inner conflict, is the guiding principle of family system work.

The communications or strategic school (Watzlawick, Weakland, & Fisch, 1974; Haley, 1976; Papp, 1978; Palazzoli-Selvini, Boscolo, Cecchin, & Prata, 1978) is based on assumptions that were most clearly stated by Weakland, Fisch, and Watzlawick (1974):

> Our fundamental premise is that regardless of their basic origins and etiology—if, indeed, these can even be reliably determined—the kinds of problems people bring to psychotherapists *persist* only if they are maintained by ongoing, current behavior of the patient, and others with whom he interacts. Correspondingly, if such problem-maintaining behavior is appropriately changed or eliminated, the problem will be resolved or vanish, regardless of its nature, origin or duration. [p. 144]

Therapy, then, begins by clearly defining the sequence of interactions that precede, accompany, and follow symptomatic behavior. The therapist then intervenes to alter one or more of these contributions to the sequence. This alteration encourages or allows more adaptive behavior to emerge. The desired changes are defined in advance with the family. Small changes—a step in the right direction—are often chosen, owing to an assumption that the family will use this momentum to finish the change process without relying further on the therapist.

Each of these schools has its unique style, and each is well suited to specific goals and family characteristics. The existential psychodynamic school, by virtue of its unique goals (personal or spiritual growth) and its focus on awareness, is well suited to families who can tolerate its slower pace, higher cost, and lack of powerful shaping interventions on the part of the therapist. The therapy is geared more toward creating a deep and warm experience of human contact than toward symptom removal.

Structural therapy, at least in theory, does not focus on this dimension. It aims at the creation of adaptive family organization. Therefore, its most fertile culture is disorganized or pathologically organized families. Aponte (1976), who has worked extensively with such families, has used the term "underorganized." These families do not actively choose the few organizational patterns that they use. Rather, because of limited exposure, and often a long history of hostile social and economic influences, they have never been exposed to broader and more adaptive options. When these are offered or demonstrated by a therapist, they are eagerly accepted. These structural modifications take effect very quickly. In general, families presenting a symptomatic child in the context of disordered generational boundaries can expect relief of symptoms and overall improvement of family functioning within eight to twelve sessions of work on their structural imbalances. Of course, better-organized, motivated families will also respond to structural interventions; such families respond to *all* intervention strategies. The purpose here is to note which families are likely to respond to this type of intervention when other interventions are likely to fail.

Family systems therapy, because of its interest in three-generational patterns, asks more of the family. Most adults resist modifying their customary patterns of relating to their family of origin. Higher motivation and compliance are therefore required. Such an approach is particularly appropriate when a genogram can demonstrate linkage between onset of symptoms and precipitating events outside the nuclear family itself. It is also especially useful where the extended family exerts a chronically destabilizing influence on the nuclear family.

The communications school, presenting itself as the least ambitious therapeutically, has elaborated the most powerful technology for inducing change. It is ideally suited to families who request only symptomatic relief. But, in addition, it offers an approach to the resistant family—those characterized by previous treatment failure or by unwillingness to follow therapeutic directives. In such cases, "paradoxical interventions" are often used. A simple form of paradox might be the suggestion that a symptomatic child continue acting up, as his or her behavior will deflect the parents' attention away from the father's low-level depression. Often, put in this way, parents will protest, demonstrate that they can handle their own business, and thus release their child from this pressure to act out.

These schools are presented separately and, in a sense, each represents a discrete body of theory and practice. To view them as mutually exclusive, however, misses the enormous additive power they offer the therapist who will mix and match, for they merely represent separate views of a mul-

tifaceted family reality. Therapists need not be limited to one scenic vista. Therapeutic freedom varies with our willingness to choose from many diagnostic perspectives and to muster our therapeutic attack from the most strategically useful vantage point.

Interventions that merge schools offer a power any single school lacks. An oedipal diagnosis, in psychodynamic terms, is more easily treated if insight in the child is combined with a structural approach, which rebalances the triangle of parents and child. Or a structural diagnosis emphasizing the need for strengthening the cohesion and power of the parental subsystem may lead to therapeutic techniques borrowed from the strategic school—perhaps "reframing," suggesting to parents that their son suffers not from a sense of deprivation, but rather from a feeling that he is getting away with murder. This redefinition may enable parents to act together forcefully around limits, accomplishing the structural goal.

MATCHING THERAPEUTIC STYLE TO FAMILY

Therapeutic power is enhanced as the therapist masters a broader range of diagnostic and treatment strategies. But we also enhance the basic quandary about choice of intervention. The more flexible we are as therapists, the more we need a set of guidelines to inform our decisions.

First, from the bewildering array of diagnostic information, which diagnostic lens is most useful? Is this a family where evaluation of psychodynamic history and a careful psychological assessment of the symptomatic member are an appropriate first step? Or should we survey the resources of extended family and community involvements and overlook obvious intrapsychic pathology?

Treatment presents similar choices. A strategic, symptom-oriented approach is highly appropriate to a certain family but would be unacceptable to another where feelings of spiritual emptiness and a quest for meaning are palpable issues.

Table 3.2 is one highly simplified organizational matrix which pairs family typology with diagnostic and intervention strategy and some likely intervention techniques. It begins with a series of functional levels. It implies a basic therapeutic belief that intervention must address the level of the most basic fault before moving on to higher-level interventions. A house-building analogy comes to mind: the basement must be strong and secure before the framing can be set in place.

Level I

Level I, the basement, refers to life and death issues. Is there sufficient "executive capacity" (parenting) available to nurture and protect this family? If yes, go on to Level II. If no, then the intervention needs to address this deficiency. The suggested Level I strategy centers on mobilizing support for the ineffective executive system—often a single parent, or the strongest member in a family beset by illness, alcoholism, or pervasive life stresses. This strategy begins with a survey of potential resources (genograms are helpful) and strengths (the weaknesses are all too apparent and offer little useful information). We need to identify our best available resources. A good resource is defined as someone who is: (1) close to home, a member of the household or close relative, and (2) concerned and at least reasonably competent.

Our strategy is to add such resources to the executive system and to mold that system into a competently functioning unit. Note that on our list of resources or "troops" (see Table 3.2, Level I), family comes first, and a therapist, while better than no one, comes last. Our time is too scarce, our offices too distant, and our training too ethereal to offer the very real and concrete assistance that such families require. The following case illustrates a typical Level I intervention (Weltner, 1982):

Mrs. Pigpile presided over her eight children in a four-bedroom apartment in a racially mixed housing project. Problems were extensive at the time of referral, but the most

acute situation was 15-year-old Mike's truancy and delinquency. Each child had school problems, and almost all were frightened by the violence that surrounded them in the project.

Mrs. Pigpile was immobilized by both depression and fearfulness. She rarely went out, and then only with a friend or a child for security. Though she exaggerated the dangers of the outside world, she created a warm, stimulating environment at home. Good food was always available, but the family lacked designated mealtimes, bedtimes, and off-to-school times. Few rooms had doors. Her bed was a haven for a different child, c᷈ group of children, each night. The favorite family game was pigpile—one child lay on the floor, and each child jumped on top, creating a happy, writhing mass—a fine metaphor for this family's organization. The lack of boundaries did not end at the front door. That door was never locked and rarely knocked upon. Neighbors wandered in and out, as did a series of the homeless to whom Mrs. Pigpile offered shelter for days or weeks. [p. 206]

Our search for support began at home. Diana, 16, had quit school, so she was always available. Mike was an expert on life in the project. If asked, he could offer security and guidance to his mother and siblings. Margaret, age 14, the family obsessive, kept her room neat and her door closed. She became our gatekeeper, keeping the younger children out of the kitchen where we met with Mrs. Pigpile and her three teenagers.

In biweekly home visits, therapist, mother and "cabinet" ran through a series of concerns: (1) getting each child up and off to school on time and safely; (2) helping Timmy in his fight with the three boys who were out to get him; and (3) repairing the bathroom doors and creating a "men's room" and a "lady's room." The crises continued, but each one only served to consolidate the family's new organizational pattern. Working together, mother and "cabinet" could in fact provide sufficient leadership for each situation. By the end of a year, Mrs. Pigpile's depression had lifted, she became socially active, and had a boyfriend who visited frequently. The home was still random in style, but not fearful or crisis-ridden.

The intervention was most helpful to the

five younger children. All were attending school regularly and getting on well in the project. Mike continued toward a career as a charming conman. Diana got a job and never returned to school. Mrs. Pigpile declined the offer of individual therapy at the clinic.

A year after termination, Mrs. Pigpile called with a new crisis. Little Johnny had been attacked and was afraid to go out. Questioning revealed that her teenagers were rarely home and had not been consulted. We suggested that she gather her "cabinet" three times that week and then call back. She did, and reported that the crisis had been handled.

A somewhat different problem was presented by Mrs. Failing, a 31-year-old married woman who, eight years previously, had her first confirmed episode of multiple sclerosis. Accustomed since childhood to dealing with adversity, she continued her life as a preschool teacher with her usual enthusiasm and creativity. Three years ago, she married Mr. Failing, the youngest of a large, warm, loving, Italian family. Mr. Failing's family nickname was "baby." True to his name, he was loving but passive, expecting his wife to take up where his mother left off.

Mrs. Failing applied for individual treatment at a family service agency because of increasing marital stress and anxiety. Six months previously she had had to quit her job; although she could still walk, her energy was no longer sufficient to permit her to work. Her increasing demands on her husband put that relationship at some risk, and both were emotionally regressing.

Although her request was for individual therapy to help her cope better, the natural history of her illness predicted more and more demands on a husband unaccustomed to responsibility. Clearly, this executive system was under stress and would soon be overtaxed, regardless of how well Mrs. Failing coped emotionally. Within the next few years, some broadening of that system could be needed. A survey of potential strengths ruled out her family, beset by alcoholism and distance. His family, however, presented vast nurturant possibilities. In fact, early in their marriage, the Failings had lived in the large apartment building that housed his extended family.

Their move out to independence had put some strain on an otherwise good relationship with his family.

Therapeutic planning, then, had several components:

1. Helping Mrs. Failing discuss her illness, her feelings, and her need for outside support.
2. Involving Mr. and Mrs. Failing and his family in a discussion of Mrs. Failing's illness and her increasing needs.
3. A long-term plan which envisioned support for the couple's independence at first, with a periodic reevaluation as they moved further into dependency on—and physical proximity to—his family.[1]

Both these examples involve blurring of generational boundaries, often a part of Level I and II interventions. Should a family improve sufficiently, then its overall strength may permit the more demanding interventions that yield generational clarity, usually appropriate to Level III.

Level II

If Level I is the foundation, then Level II is the roof and the framing: containment. In Level II families, authority and limits, rather than nurturance and safety, are the prominent issues. The executive system is unable to maintain sufficient control over one or several family members, and this threatens the stability of the entire family system. The defect can be in the area of clarity—a lack of clear expectations—or it may represent insufficient power in the executive system such that expectations are not enforced. Once again, interventions begin with a survey of strengths and resources and the welding of a coalition strong enough to offer sufficient authority. This can require minimal adjustment, as in the following example:

Cathy Struggler, age 13, was an irregular school attendee. Her mornings began with physical complaints, building to a crescendo

[1] I am indebted to the staff of the Greater Lawrence Family Service Agency for assisting me in formulating this treatment plan.

as the time to leave for school approached. Mrs. Struggler, anxious, annoyed, helpless, joined the battle, angrily yelling at Cathy that she couldn't get away with this again. Mr. Struggler, volatile and eager for relief, generally glared at his wife and drove off in a huff midway through this scene. As in so many areas of family life, Cathy's persistence and cleverness undermined her parents' efforts at stewardship. They were habitually walking on "eggshells" to avoid another tantrum or well-targeted thrust into an area of parental conflict. And most significantly, the continual stress on their relationship led to very real threats of divorce. These threats increased Cathy's uneasiness and her efforts to control the entire family. The Strugglers were very close to dissolving as a family unit.

Taking the morning ritual as a primary intervention target, the therapist advised the following:

> 1. School would not be mentioned until 8:15—five minutes before it was time to leave. Cathy's complaints were to be ignored.
> 2. Father would stay home until 8:20, when he would stand next to his wife and pronounce in unison with her, "Cathy, you are to get in the car."
> 3. If Cathy protested, each parent would take her by one arm and help carry her to the car.

The first day, Cathy struggled slightly. After that, she went off without protest. Within several months, control was no longer a major family issue.

Here we were dealing with an executive system that was too divided to cope with a manipulative, strong-willed, and frightened child. The therapist guessed, however, that if the parents acted together, they could provide sufficient power without recruiting any outside source of authority. With sufficient encouragement and clarity of plan, they could confront and contain Cathy.

A more complicated but essentially similar intervention follows (Weltner, 1982):

> Ken Friendless was referred at 13 for school failure, lack of friends, and bizarre behavior including shooting at a neighbor's window with his shotgun. He was seclusive, awake until 3:00 A.M. reading science fiction, then sleeping past school time. His mother, drained by the stormy adolescences of three older girls, struggled to maintain herself and her job, upon which the family depended. She had no reserves to marshal on behalf of Ken, her last child.
>
> When it became clear that she could not single-handedly confront her determinedly eccentric son, two meetings were called with mother and her three daughters, two of whom were living at college, the third working in the same community. They ran through their concerns about Ken's lack of discipline and his sarcastic, withdrawn style. All agreed on the need for a bedtime, study times, school attendance, chores around the house, and regular mealtimes.
>
> In a third meeting, all four confronted him and laid down the law. Ken accepted with surprising ease. A long period of treatment of mother and son ensued, but the basic restructuring begun in this meeting was critical to Ken's emergence as an enjoyable, and now popular human being. [p. 207]

The use of a "cabinet" of teenagers presents certain problems, so do many Level I and II interventions: they so often blur, rather than clarify, generational boundaries. This can easily compromise teenagers' efforts at independence and their freedom to engage in age-appropriate experimentation. However, it is important to emphasize the adverse effect on their development of continued family chaos. Even if relatively independent, they are generally preoccupied by concern for their parents, and they often try vainly to intervene on behalf of younger siblings. Encouraging them to play a defined role in the therapy legitimizes and strengthens their position. It also avoids episodic overinvolvement, which is so common in such cases. From the standpoint of the overwhelmed parent(s), such assistance is especially useful: being members of the nuclear family, they are available in a more predictable and informed way than any extended family member or any outsider. As the chaos decreases, teenagers can gradually move out of their helping roles, and on into an age-appropriate stance.

While a wide variety of techniques may be used, both Level I and Level II interventions are essentially structural. They aim at modifying the organizational patterns of the family. In Level I, we are concerned only with increasing the capacity of the executive system. Level II interventions test or tax the system's strength. It is very important not to overestimate executive capacity in Level II interventions. Had Cathy or Ken resisted sufficiently and overwhelmed the executive coalition, then therapy would have been set back significantly. It is important to remember, however, the readiness to fall in line that such children have. They are often aware of how much their own—and their family's—lives suffer as a result of their lack of discipline and control.

Level III

Level I and II interventions are generally straightforward. They are usually gratefully accepted—a drowning man will grab any rope. When we get to Level III families, the situation is somewhat more complicated. A Level III family has a structure and a style that is often perceived as working. It usually represents an expression of a three-generational legacy, not a set of inherited deficiencies. As Aponte (1976) has stressed, "underorganized" families (Level I and II) generally do not transmit adequate patterns of coping. By contrast, Level III and IV families have a rich mixture of coping mechanisms—their characteristic defenses, their culture—to which they are committed and which they attempt to pass on through their children. If our work with such families involves changing ingrained patterns, we can anticipate some struggle. So, our techniques need to encompass and adapt to resistance.

Maria Fireworks was a 16-year-old whose unending episodes of drinking and defiance locked her into an endless struggle with her father. Coming from generations of Italian patriarchs, he would not step away from her daily provocations. He responded with increasing verbal and physical abuse, and with groundings which Maria ignored. Given the roar of this battle, Mrs. Fireworks was not audible. She had submissively adapted to her husband's control years ago. Her daughter also easily overwhelmed her feeble attempts at parental authority.

The central issue in this case was an overinvolved sexualized father-daughter relationship. The therapist saw immediately that if father could disengage, Maria would quiet down. In fact, in individual sessions, she was likable and quite sensible, but determined not to let father bully her as he bullied her mother.

This family presents issues typically seen at Level III. First, we recognize powerful resistance to change, or to put it more aptly, a powerful commitment to problematic behavior. Maria is not a passive victim of an ineffective system. She is fighting her mother's battle against tyranny, and her loyalty to this struggle gives it a frightening intensity. Father is also carrying out a multigenerational and cultural mandate to maintain control in his castle. Backing off would seem shameful and dangerous.

The generation issue centers on mother's childlike (and Maria's thunderous) status. They have reversed hierarchical roles. Mr. Fireworks is head tyrant, but this may be in conformity with his and his wife's cultural expectations. Perhaps an ideal structure for this family would leave father higher in authority, but help mother to be his right-hand woman, and allow Maria the freedom and distance of adolescence.

Despite her temptation to tackle father and quiet him down, the therapist instead sympathized with his plight and with the lack of respect showed him by Maria. She admired his persistence and offered to help in bringing Maria under control. However, she defined control of teenage girls as a mother's responsibility and requested that Mr. Fireworks help the therapist to teach his wife to deal with such a difficult teenager. Tasks like keeping track of her hours, checking her room for drugs, and calling the school were now delegated to mother, who reported to father. Mr. Fireworks, an "expert in confrontation," was asked to coach his wife in this fine art. Her manner became more assertive. The therapist praised father for this growth in his second-in-command. And, as a consequence, Maria's acting up diminished.[2]

[2]I would like to express my gratitude to Dr. Marsha Pravder Mirkin for allowing me to use this case as an illustration.

Typical of Level III, the therapist is able to aim for an "ideal" family structure. Level I and II interventions often include children, extended family, and even strangers in the executive system. By Level III, therapy is generally able to achieve the generational boundaries that allow appropriate parent-child differentiation.

One final aspect of this intervention: for the first time, our focus has been on problems and pathology. Within the three main characters there was sufficient strength and health to allow for resolution; surveying for additional executive resources was simply not needed. If we return to our home-building analogy, then, Level III is concerned with the inner architecture. It assumes foundation, walls, and roof. What it notices is that the inner space, the placement of walls and doors, is not functional. Maria seems to have invaded the parental areas of the family. Mother has vacated the master bedroom. Level III therapy is the process of reshaping this internal architecture until everyone has an appropriate space and appropriate amounts of access and privacy.

Level IV

At Level IV, therapy is concerned for the first time with the fine art of living. Decoration, pictures, rugs, lamps—the richness and quality of family and individual life—slip into focus. Correspondingly, thoughts, feelings, memories—the inner landscape—become a focus of our work. While we may also focus on issues of the inner world at earlier levels, it is primarily in order to inform our interventions toward change. For example, we might ask for Mr. Fireworks' recollections of his relationship with his mother and father. But if we do, it is primarily to determine whether the new hierarchy we are setting up in his family will conform to his inner expectations. At Level III, we would not expect to focus on and explore the ramifications of these expectations on his past and present relationships.

At Level IV, therapy focuses on such material for its own sake. Although we may still be treating symptomatic people, our goals have to do with the development of an inner "richness"—insight, more sensitive awareness of the relational world, an understanding of legacies and heritage. The techniques vary from psychotherapy and psychoanalysis to more evocative techniques such as family sculpture or critical image work. In all cases, we hope to deepen awareness of the inner world and to improve understanding of history, style, and unmet yearnings. A final step on this continuum is the spiritual therapies, such as psychosynthesis, which help patients discover the transcendent aspects of their beings.

A word about matchmaking: Level IV interventions are well suited to those who have reached Level IV adjustment. Their lives are in sufficient order that this kind of finishing experience makes sense, and they are living in a stable enough way to benefit. But pity the Level II client trying to do Level IV work. Appointments will have to defer to the periodic crises occurring in his life. And when he does keep an appointment, exploration of his feeling life is of little value against the larger issues of an alcoholic wife or the latest expulsion of a child from school. Although many of our most prized interventions are appropriate to Level IV, many of our families are not.

By contrast, therapists who have not experienced Level IV work may be unprepared to deal with patients for whom meaning, awareness, and spiritual growth are issues. Some family therapists, for example, refuse to acknowledge the importance (perhaps even the existence) of an inner world. For such therapists, referral of Level IV families to an existentially oriented therapist would seem appropriate.

SUMMARY

It is important to recognize the variety of therapeutic approaches currently available and their widely varying uses. In addition, the assets and readiness of the families and individuals that we encounter rule out, and rule in, specific therapeutic thrusts. This chapter has focused on the matching of these two variables. Not discussed were the equally important issues of motivation and will: there are people who may prefer to decorate the livingroom even while the roof is leaking overhead. And there are broadly competent therapists who may agree to such an unlikely contract. This more subjective level of interaction is part of the art of therapy and the chemistry of matchmaking. An awareness of motivation and a sensitive response can help harness the energy that enlivens and empowers the more technical aspects of therapy.

Simplistic as it may be, this schema is an effort to begin a consideration of the complex factors in family and in therapist which determine the success of therapy. Although the precise matchmaking system presented here is quite tentative, the challenge is not. We must increasingly reflect on the need to make conscious, enlightened decisions about what we are offering to each family that seeks our help.[3]

[3]I am especially grateful to my brother-in-law, Ken Holbert, Ph.D., for his generous and deft help in getting this chapter into final form.

Table 3.1
The Family Therapies

	Existential Psychodynamic	Structural	Systems	Communications Strategic

Focus	Feelings
	Family history
	Critical images
		Distance
		Boundaries
		Organization
			Distance
			Boundaries
			Organization
			Historical events
			Patterns from family
			  of origin
				Coping style
				Feedback loops
				Sequences of
				  behaviors

Causality	Historical trauma
	Inner conflict
		Closeness
		Distance
			Residues from past
			Failure to
			  differentiate
				Poor coping style
				Problem-maintaining
				  feedback

Cure	Insight
	Conflict resolution
	Personal growth
		Realignments
		Alternative
		  structures
		Clear boundaries
			Differentiation
			Bridge cutoffs
				Interrupt or alter
				  feedback
				Alter communication
				  pattern

Therapist	Listening Concerned Clarifying Permissive	Active Ringmaster Taskmaster Authoritarian	Active Taskmaster Authoritarian	Active Problem solver Dissembler Authoritarian
Duration of Therapy	Long-term 6 mos.–3 years	Short-term 2–6 months	3 months– 3 years	Short-term 1–12 sessions
Target Families	Stable Insightful Intellectual	Disorganized "Unmotivated" Authoritarian	Insightful Motivated	Resistant Previous Rx failure High authoritarian
Authors	Whitaker Napier Ackerman Kantor	Minuchin Montalvo Aponte Haley	Fogarty Guerin Bowen Kantor	Haley Papp Watzlawick et al. Palazzoli-Selvini et al.

REFERENCES

Ackerman, N. *Family therapy in transition.* Boston: Little, Brown, 1970.

Aponte, H. Underorganization in the poor family. In P. Guerin (Ed.), *Family therapy: Theory and practice.* New York: Gardner Press, 1976.

Alexander, F., et al. *Psychoanalytic therapy.* New York: Ronald Press, 1946.

Bowen, M. *Family therapy in clinical practice.* New York: Jason Aronson, 1978.

Burke, J., White, H., & Havens, L. Which short-term therapy? Matching patient and method.

Archives of General Psychiatry, 1979, **36,** 177–186.

Fogarty, J. On emptiness and closeness. *The Family,* 1976, **3,** 3–12.

Grunebaum, H., & Chasin, R. Thinking like a family therapist: A model for integrating the theories and methods of family therapy. *Journal of Marital and Family Therapy,* 1982, **44,** 403–416.

Guerin, P. *Family therapy: Theory and practice.* New York: Gardner Press, 1976.

Haley, J. *Problem solving therapy.* San Francisco: Jossey-Bass, 1976.

Kantor, D. *Inside the family.* San Francisco: Jossey-Bass, 1975.

Table 3.2
Family Assessment and Intervention

Level	Issue	Intervention Strategy	Intervention Technique
I	—Is executive capacity sufficient to manage all basic nurturant needs? —food, shelter, protection, medical care, minimal nurturance.	—Focus on strengths, not problems. —Survey and mobilize available support to bolster executive capacity.	—Marshal more troops from: A. Nuclear family 1. Parental child 2. Family cabinet B. Extended Family C. Community 1. Friends 2. Agency resources 3. Therapist. —Therapist as convener, advocate, teacher, role model.
II	—Is there sufficient authority to provide minimal structure, limits and safety?	—Focus on strengths. —Develop a coalition of those in charge against those needing control. —Increase clarity of expectation.	—Formation of coalitions. —Use of written contracts. —Charts assigning tasks. —Behavioral reinforcers. —Use of self as authority.
III	—Are there clear and appropriate boundaries? A. Family B. Individual C. Generational	—Focus on problems. —Clarify the "ideal" family structure, in conformity with ethnic or family expectations. —Generational clarity.	—Defend family and individual boundaries. —Balance triangles. —Rebuild alliances. —Develop generational boundaries. —Task assignment. —Paradox.
IV	—Are there problems of inner conflict or problems with intimacy? —Are family members self-actualizing?	—Focus on problems. —Clarification and resolution of legacies and historical trauma. —Insight. —Focus on yearnings.	—Family sculpture. —Critical image work. —Resolution of three-generational issues. —Individual dynamic psychotherapy. —Psychosynthesis.

Mann, J. *Time-limited psychotherapy*. Cambridge: Harvard University Press, 1973.

Minuchin, S. *Families and family therapy*. Cambridge: Harvard University Press, 1974.

Napier, A., & Whitaker, C. *The family crucible*. New York: Harper, 1978.

Palazzoli-Selvini, M., Boscolo, L., Cecchin, G., & Prata, G. *Paradox and counterparadox: A new model in the therapy of the family in schizophrenic transaction*. New York: Jason Aronson, 1978.

Papp, P. *Family therapy: Full length case studies*. New York: Gardner Press, 1978.

Sifneos, P. *Short-term psychotherapy and emotional crisis*. Cambridge: Harvard University Press, 1973.

Watzlawick, P., Weakland, J., & Fisch, R. *Change: Principles of problems formation and problems resolution*. New York: Norton, 1974.

Weakland, J., Fisch, R., Watzlawick, P., et al. Brief therapy: Focused problem resolution. *Family Process*, 1974, **13**, 141–166.

Weltner, J. A structural approach to the single parent family. *Family Process*, 1982, **21**, 203–210.

PART II

Practice and Settings

INTRODUCTION

Systems-oriented therapists have come to recognize that the therapy system cannot be defined as including only the family seeking treatment. Rather, it extends outward to include the therapist, other helping professionals, and the setting within which the therapist works. How these different components of the system interact—the pattern of communication, the clarity of the hierarchy, the flexibility of the boundaries—is the stuff that therapy is made of. How many times have we heard, "I had the greatest treatment plan, but . . . (the school wouldn't fund it, the hospital wouldn't permit it, my supervisor vetoed it)"? Therefore, we need to understand the political, economic, and social structures of the settings in which we operate. Our ability to work within a treatment setting, to understand the possibilities and limitations of that setting, and to intervene effectively within the larger system helps us determine the interventions we choose to make with a family and becomes critical in determining the success of the therapy.

This section focuses on a range of treatment settings and of methods of intervening with families within these settings. Neilans, in Chapter 4, discusses the implementation of a systems model within a Health Maintenance Organization, where treatment is already defined as short-term. Given the requirements of that particular setting, he explores the development and practice of a short-term systemic model for outpatient treatment of adolescents and families. Tavantzis, Tavantzis, Brown, and Rohrbaugh, in Chapter 5, present an intensive home-based structural family program for adolescents at risk for placement. The authors formulate delinquency in family-systems terms, describe their program, and include evaluation data as a way of introducing readers to this unique and effective mode of treatment. Libow, in Chapter 6, focuses on how a consultant can assist both the families of dying or chronically ill adolescents and the staff in a medical setting. She suggests that the tragedy of the dying adolescent may at times lead families and the staff servicing them to behave in a manner that, though well-intentioned and sympathetic, may also support dysfunctional patterns. These negative effects, according to Libow, can be avoided if professionals are aware of the potential systemic issues.

Inpatient psychiatric hospitalization is the topic of Chapter 7, by Mirkin, Ricci, and Cohen. Within this setting, one must look at the interactions among patients, family, therapist, treatment milieu, schools, service agencies, and hospital administration when devising and implementing a treatment program. These authors suggest that a short-term, family-oriented model which attends to the above outlined factors can be an effective treatment modality for disturbed/disturbing adolescents.

DeSisto and Koltz, in Chapter 8, examine a family-oriented approach to residential treatment: a seemingly impossible "marriage" to many family therapists. These authors focus on how the family can be incorporated into a program even when the child is not living at home.

Speck and Speck, the "grandparents" of network therapy, define the therapy system as incorporating a network of friends, relatives, neighbors, employers, and significant others. They explain, in Chapter 9, how such a network can be mobilized to aid problem adolescents, and how to assemble and facilitate such a network.

Paul and Paul, pioneers in the development of Multiple Family Group therapy, describe their own form of network in Chapter 10. Several families meet with the Pauls weekly, and the process of such group meetings is a potent force in facilitating change. Koman, in Chapter 11, examines the Multiple Family Group modality with families of an inpatient population. The "system" here is represented by the therapist(s), five to seven families all at different phases of treatment, and the hospital setting in which the group takes place. Two chapters are devoted to Multiple Family Group because such a modality, the editors believe, is extremely powerful in facilitating change, and because it is implemented differently, depending on its (inpatient or outpatient) setting. In addition, it is helpful to know that the Pauls are the "parents" of multiple family therapy, while Koman is a "second-generation" multiple family group therapist, indicating a generational difference in ideas and strategies.

The school system, which is central in the life of every adolescent, is explored by Green in Chapter 12. Because the adolescent spends, or is *supposed* to spend, more time at school than in any other place, it is the environment where problems are often first noted and interventions first undertaken.

In summary, this section examines the family in its interface with therapist and setting as all three elements come together to define a therapy system.

4

Brief Therapy in a Health Maintenance Organization*

THOMAS H. NEILANS, Ph.D.

*I*n this chapter the development and practice of a systemic model for outpatient treatment of adolescents and families within a Health Maintenance Organization (HMO), are described. The focus is on how the therapy that is conducted pays close attention to the context of the therapist as well as to the family's context.

All too often a particular model, view, or practice of therapy is presented without any consideration for the setting in which the therapy occurs. Typically, this happens because one presenter is focusing on the particular variable(s) that he or she believes is (are) contributing to the outcome of the therapy. A linear or causal perspective is especially susceptible to this approach because one looks for the particular *A* (causal agent) that caused *B* (result). However, to subscribe to a systemic frame of reference and not detail the context of the therapist seems incongruous. If one believes that the behavior of patients can best be understood by assessing their families or the systems in which they interact, then it necessarily follows that the therapy of therapists can best be understood by looking at their contexts or settings. It also seems reasonable to extend this notion and say that models of therapy or programs can best be understood by knowing the contexts in which they exist.

Thus, this chapter is divided into two sections. In the first section, the context or setting for the therapists who do the outpatient adolescent therapy is discussed. This includes a discussion of conducting therapy within an HMO, conducting therapy within a mental-health department within an HMO, conducting therapy within a brief-therapy-oriented program within a mental-health department within an HMO, and being a particular conductor of therapy within all of the above. The second section focuses on the actual therapy for adolescents conducted by these therapists. Several clinical examples are discussed as illustrations of the therapy, as well as the various system influences on the therapy.

---

*At the time this chapter was written, Dr. Neilans was Director of the Family Intervention Program at Kaiser Permanente Health Maintenance Organization in Portland, Oregon.

THERAPISTS' CONTEXTS

Health Maintenance Organization

An HMO is a particular way or plan of offering health care to the public. Subscribers to this type of health plan pay in advance a set monthly payment that enables them to receive comprehensive health care based on need with only minimal additional costs. An HMO does not have the limitations, deductibles, and co-insurances characteristic of other health plans such as Blue Cross–Blue Shield.

The Kaiser-Permanente Health Plan was the prototype of the HMO. It was initiated in the 1930s by Henry J. Kaiser as a benefit for his employees. After World War II, the health plan continuously expanded as it offered the public comprehensive health care at low costs. At present the health plan serves several million subscribers in numerous semiautonomous regions. It is within the Kaiser-Permanente Health Plan of the Northwest that we have initiated a systemic model for working with adolescents. This health plan serves Portland, Oregon, Vancouver, Washington, and Salem, Oregon, as well as surrounding regions. There are mental-health therapists located in six different medical office buildings through the region. Presently, the plan has around 260,000 subscribers. We presently have seven therapists within our program.

An HMO is a closed system; that is, it is intended to offer health care to its subscribers without the need for subscribers to receive care outside of the HMO. Subscribers prepay a certain fee for being a part of the plan and health care is then provided with minimal costs. Because of this process of collecting fees, there exists a considerable incentive within an HMO to reduce the utilization of service or to reduce the number of visits per subscriber. Thus, the system makes more money by keeping the members healthy. Whatever can be done to prevent sickness or keep people functioning well is supported by the system. In the mental-health arena, this means that therapy should be as brief as possible and whatever approaches can be used to keep

people from needing therapy will be supported.

The impetus to keep people healthy is a change of pace from the economic forces that are often present for the mental-health practitioner. The economic variables that usually exist for practitioners in the community suggest that they encourage people to come into therapy and to continue in therapy. Often their livelihood or their continued funding base is dependent on their ability to see a certain number of people for a certain period of time.

Conducting therapy in an HMO also means that the mental-health therapist is working within a health-oriented system—a physician-dominated system. The therapeutic strategies possible are influenced by this fact. Each patient who comes to a therapist has a primary-care physician, that is, a longstanding health/sickness-related relationship with a particular physician within the system. Indeed, most frequently, patients are referred to therapists by physicians. Other times patients come to therapists in spite of physician recommendations. Regardless of the initial reason for contact, the patients' relationships with their primary-care physicians are of the utmost importance. Also, the fact that the therapist typically also has a peer relationship with the physician needs to be taken into consideration when planning interventions.

When a patient is referred by a physician, particular factors come into play. First is the pressure to see subscribers in therapy who are overusing the medical system. Cummings and Follette (1976) found that 60 percent or more of physician visits within a prepaid health plan are made by patients demonstrating some mental rather than organic etiology for their presenting physical symptoms. Given the economic pressures within an HMO to reduce visits, it becomes apparent that effective mental-health work can be economically advantageous. Second, even though physician-referred patients have the endorsement and encouragement of their physicians, the physicians and the patients most often wish to continue their relationship after the mental-health intervention. Thus, it is important to support the physician-patient relationship during the therapy. Active, ongoing communication between physician and therapist about each patient is typically necessary toward this end.

There is another offshoot of the fact that there is a primary caregiver for each patient seen. Therapists have continued access to the patient through the physician. Interventions can be created which use this long-term relationship that does exist within the HMO. Directly related is the fact that there are several professionals involved with each patient: a primary physician, secondary physician specialist, assorted other providers, nurses, secretaries, receptionist, and so on. This situation provides ample opportunity not only for assessment of a patient's relationships and interactions with others, but also for orchestrating some or all of the staff into any intervention.

It is also important to note that the physicians typically do not have a systemic world view. As might be expected, their view of therapy is most frequently based on a medical model. It is the task of the therapist to be able to communicate from a medical-model perspective while being aware of and paying attention to the systemic impact of the communication. This is similar to working with a family that has a different frame of reference. However, due to the continuousness of the task, it can become strenuous.

Mental-Health Department

The next context or setting to consider is the Mental-Health Department. Just as each Kaiser-Permanente Health Plan is semiautonomous to others, so is each department within the Northwest Health Plan also semiautonomous. Presently there are thirty-three departments. Each department has one department or division chief. This person, a physician, reports to one person.

It was within this structure that the Mental-Health Department was created fifteen years ago. The department was located near the only HMO hospital that existed

at that time. The location reflected the intent of the department to provide a specialty service to augment the work of the primary physicians. Over the years several new mental-health workers were hired and the direction of the department shifted. Instead of providing service attuned to the needs of the HMO, the thrust of the department became to set up individualized private practices for the therapists. The department moved to a building that was far removed from any medical offices and the therapists lost touch with the rest of the system. The length of the therapy increased. Therapists gave up consulting to physicians, and entry into mental health became more and more inaccessible. The waiting list for a patient to be seen by a therapist in mental health rose to around 700 with a three- to four-month wait. The mental-health system became isolated from the rest of the system.

It was at this time that our program came into existence. The impetus for the introduction of a brief, system-oriented model came from four sources: (1) the work of Nicholas Cummings and his associates in the San Francisco Kaiser-Permanente Medical Center; (2) information about length of stay collected over a three-month period from the Northwest Kaiser-Permanente office; (3) the pressure currently existing from the rest of the system on the Mental-Health Department; and (4) the fact that at this time, the Mental-Health Department was only minimally serving youth, adolescents, and their families.

Cummings (1977) described the early attempts of Kaiser-Permanente in San Francisco to offer therapy within a prepaid health plan. Initially, the mental-health program there accepted the view that long-term therapy was more effective than short-term therapy. The result was long waiting lists and inaccessible therapists—an overburdened and ineffective system. In a comprehensive study, Follette and Cummings (1967) compared the medical utilization (physician visits, hospitalizations, etc.) before and after psychotherapy of psychotherapy patients who were randomly assigned to three groups (one interview only; brief therapy with a mean of

6.2 interviews; and long-term therapy with a mean of 33.9 interviews). They found the one-session-only group reduced medical utilization by 60 percent over five years and the brief-therapy group reduced utilization by 75 percent. Subsequent investigations (summarized in Cummings, 1977) led them to conclude that psychotherapy could be a cost-efficient part of a prepaid health plan if it were conducted with an emphasis on short-term therapy. Cummings (1977) does state that there is a certain percentage of health plan members who cannot benefit from short-term therapy but that these patients can be managed effectively by seeing them long term and spacing sessions out over intervals of two or three months.

During 1980, data were collected on patients seen by the Mental-Health Department at the Northwest Kaiser. The data on length of stay demonstrated a bimodal distribution with the greatest number of patients seen for three sessions or less and another large number seen for twenty-five sessions or more. This information, however crude, seems to reflect Cummings' work: that most patients could benefit from short-term work, while a certain percentage need longer-term work. Of course, several other interpretations of these data are possible but the impact of these data on the system was consistent with the interpretations presented above.

The pressures impinging on the Mental-Health Department were similar to those found at San Francisco Kaiser when therapists worked under the bias that long-term therapy was better than short-term: long waiting lists and inaccessible therapists. The Mental-Health Department had originally intended to offer service to all subscribers. However, when the emphasis became long-term therapy and therapists found that they could not serve the need, several subscribers were not served adequately. Among this group were youth, adolescents, and families. Faced with the problems of long waiting lists, inaccessible therapists, and incomplete services, Northwest Kaiser, unlike the San Francisco Kaiser, chose not to change the bias of existing therapists. Instead, the decision was to add more staff and have them work within a short-term model.

Family Intervention Program

In May of 1981, the Mental-Health Department of the Kaiser Permanente Health Plan in the Northwest expanded to include a program that served youth, adolescents, and families. A task force had been established in 1980 to come up with a solution to the problem of inadequate psychotherapy services for families. The task force consisted of representatives from several departments within the Health Plan, including representatives from Mental Health. The recommendation of this task force was to hire new staff within the Mental-Health Department to provide service for families which was timely (no more than a three-day wait for service) and responsive to the physician referral (would be available for ongoing contact with physicians in various medical offices).

As a result of these recommendations the Family Intervention Program (FIP) was created. To accomplish the objective of providing accessible service, therapists were hired who would work with patients in three sessions or less. A three-session limit was chosen because the length-of-treatment data showed that the majority of mental-health patients were seen three sessions or less. Also, these therapists were located in the actual medical offices where the health-care providers worked. (The Mental-Health Department at that time was located by itself in a building isolated from the rest of the Health Plan.)

Finally, at the program level, there remained the problem of what to do with youth, adolescents, and families who needed long-term therapy. Any adult seen by a short-term therapist in one of the medical centers who needed longer-term work could be referred to the existing mental-health therapists. Following a similar model, two therapists who would see only youth, adolescents, or families were also located at the isolated Mental-Health Clinic. It became their task to see only patients who might need long-term therapy and were eighteen years of age or younger.

From its inception to now, FIP has undergone several changes that have been the result of its actually existing within the HMO system. These changes have affected the therapy with adolescents in several ways that will be discussed later in this chapter.

EVOLUTION OF DEPARTMENTAL POLICIES

Length of Treatment

From the early stages, one of the most difficult challenges for the brief therapists was being part of a department where the prevailing bias was that long-term therapy is better than short-term therapy. It was easy to feel like a second-class citizen. In response to these attitudes, the short-term therapists pushed for an increase in the number of sessions that they could see a patient. Their rationale was that they could not do effective work in three sessions. Given that the therapists' belief in this was strong, it had to be communicated to patients. After a lengthy struggle, administration changed policy from a three-session limit to a four-session limit. Even though it was definite that patients could not be seen more than four sessions, therapists, given the process, felt good. They could now see patients 33 percent longer than they had seen them before. As the therapists felt more positive about their work, their short-term therapy seemed to become more effective.

Fees

Therapists in FIP had the mandate to be responsive to physician referrals. This mandate was directly at odds with the fee policy of the Mental-Health Department. Contrary to the usual HMO policy, almost all mental-health patients were charged an extra fee for each therapy session. This fee was set at one-half the going fee in the private-practice community.

How did it come about that patients were charged for a service within a prepaid health plan? Administrators believed that if fees were not charged, the department would be deluged with patients. Also, the generated income helped pay for staff sal-aries. Full fees were not charged because there co-existed the belief that some benefit should be given to subscribers. However, as a consequence of charging fees, mental-health service was not available to several members who could not afford it. Also, some physicians were angry that a fee was charged for mental health when it was not charged for health care, and many also felt that the charging of a fee for service was inconsistent with the intent of an HMO.

Faced with the systems conflict of how to be responsive to physician referral and maintain the fee-for-service which existed for mental health, FIP arrived at the following solution: offer consultation to physicians regarding patients without charge. Thus, therapists could see someone for a brief time who could not afford the fee, and consult with the physician regarding the best course of treatment. The patient could then choose between several options, including: no further service; continued contact with the physician (no fee); referral to sliding-fee agencies in the community; participation in a group (less cost); or actually seeing FIP therapists for four sessions or less at the standard fee.

Consultation

The policy of providing no-cost consultation had far-reaching consequences for therapists, physicians, patients, and ultimately the way the entire system operated. Having consultation time in the therapists' schedules meant that the opportunity now existed for the therapists to interact, to communicate with the health-care system of which they were a part. As a result, an avenue or entry point was created through which the therapists could affect the system and the system could affect the therapist.

The consultation time provided an opportunity for the building of the therapist-physician relationship. By building a solid relationship, the therapists were able to be more effective in conducting therapy within the system. This increase in effectiveness occurred in two ways. First, therapist and physician could take different therapeutic positions with various patients in order to facilitate change. For example, the therapist could take a pessimistic view with a patient regarding the likelihood of change, while the physician could be optimistic. This type of positioning might encourage the "reluctant" client to change "to show the therapist." Of course, other types of positioning could also occur.

Second, the enhanced relationship between therapist and physician allowed each to educate the other in various ways. The therapist could educate the physician about ways in which the physician could handle some of the mental-health problems of his or her patients without referring to mental-health personnel. Also, the physician could learn which types of patients were best candidates for mental-health therapy. The therapists, on the other hand, could learn much from the physicians about the effects of physical illnesses on the patients.

In order for the consultation time to be used effectively, the therapist's availability was a key factor. FIP therapists were located in six different medical office locations with the intent of bringing the therapists to the providers rather than isolating psychotherapy from health care. This dispersing of therapists to the different locations facilitated the building of the therapist-physician relationship. Also, since most patients were accustomed to attending a particular clinic, they felt more comfortable coming in to see a therapist in "their" clinic.

An offshoot of the decentralization of therapists to outlying clinics was that each FIP therapist had almost no contact with other therapists. To provide an opportunity for these therapists to share ideas, concerns, and cases with other therapists, a weekly program meeting was established. This forum provided an opportunity to compare and discuss various issues and problems that came up in the various clinics.

Therapists in Clinics

The weekly meetings of FIP therapists prompted identification of particular problems encountered by the therapists in their respective clinics. Some problems were shared by most; others were idiosyncratic to a particular clinic. This section discusses some of the problems that were identified and how they were handled.

A particularly difficult issue facing therapists in the clinics was convincing the providers that they were effective therapists even though they did not offer long-term therapy. Several providers held the bias that the longer the therapy, the better the therapy. The fact that a therapist could be more accessible when using a short-term approach did not affect this bias. Of course, this bias on the part of physicians not only affected the type of patient they would refer, but also resulted in physicians communicating to the patients, at least implicitly, that they would not be seeing the "real" therapist when they saw the short-term therapist.

Each therapist attempted to handle the above bias in different ways. The most successful seemed to be a strategy whereby the therapist assured the referring provider that if the patient did in fact need long-term work, the patient would be referred to a therapist who did long-term work, and moreover, that a referral from a short-term therapist would receive swift action.

Another set of issues that faced outlying clinic therapists emanated from the history of the Mental-Health Department. Because a fee had been charged for many years for mental-health services, many physicians had ruled out using the services in Kaiser. They had referred patients to sliding-fee-scale agencies. Also, because of the inaccessibility of mental health within Kaiser, several physicians had developed an ongoing working relationship with private practitioners in the surrounding community. This legacy from the department was most effectively dealt with via the consultation time with physicians. FIP therapists could distinguish themselves and their program from what had been the case in the Mental-Health Department by being immediately available and stressing this difference from the past.

Of course, the match between therapist styles and interests and physician styles and interests affected the therapist's ability to enter the clinic system. As would be expected, where a therapist could find a common interest or approach with a physician, the better the interaction.

In order to communicate to physicians in the outlying clinics, therapists often needed initially to speak the physician's language. If a therapist began by speaking about circularity and neutrality, the typical provider would most quickly be lost. Whereas, if a therapist could speak of the same issues, using terms such as neuroses and psychoses, rapport and communication would be greatly facilitated.

The issue of whom to refer to long-term therapy, and whom to see in short-term therapy was handled differently by each therapist. The determining factor seemed to be more therapist style rather than type of client seen. Whereas one therapist would refer very few patients, another would refer a particular type of patient. Of course, the context of the therapist's relationship with the referring physician and the referring physician's relationship with the patient affected the referral decision. In general, it seemed that more referrals for long-term therapy occurred when several issues were presented by the patient(s); that is, patients who had a very difficult time focusing on any particular problem or reason for coming to therapy were referred more often than others.

Before moving to a consideration of the therapy, a final point should be made. If one variable could be identified in respect to what made it easiest for a therapist to enter a system, it would be flexibility. The therapist who could approach the therapeutic process with each patient or family without rigid, preestablished guidelines tended to be more effective. Given the complexity of the many contexts surrounding each therapist, it became evident that different ways of proceeding often had to be figured out for the particular interplay that presented itself surrounding each patient.

THERAPY WITH ADOLESCENTS

In the preceding paragraphs a description has been provided of the several settings or contexts in which therapists work. The thrust of this chapter is that a therapist's context distinctly affects the therapy that is conducted. The following clinical examples illustrate the therapy with adolescents conducted by the staff of the Family Intervention Program of the Mental-Health Department of the Kaiser-Permanente HMO. As the therapy is described, the influence of the contexts should be evident.

Initial Contact

Although there are several processes by which an adolescent can come into contact with an FIP therapist, the most frequently used one is through the appointment center. One of the adolescent's parents calls the centralized appointment center, where all mental-health patients are scheduled. The support staff, rather than professional staff, schedule the patients. This is true throughout the organization; it frees up the professional staff to have more time for direct (in-office) contact with patients. When the appointment person receives an intake call and determines the identified patient to be eighteen years of age or younger, she or he is then scheduled with an FIP therapist.

The appointment staff have been instructed to handle the initial appointments for FIP in a certain way. If patients have been referred to a particular therapist, then they are given to that therapist. In cases where there is no specific referral, then patients are scheduled with the therapist in the clinic where they most frequently go for health care. This is done for several reasons: this is the clinic that is generally the closest one for the patients; it is the one they know the most; it sets up an arrangement where the primary-care provider may be used more easily and effectively; and, most importantly, it gives the patients the message that mental-health care is part and parcel of their general health care.

The issue of which members of the family should attend thrapy is dealt with initially in the appointment center. It is also addressed later in therapy by the therapist. Regarding this issue, appointment center personnel are instructed to say that the therapist would like to have all members of the family attend the first session, and that family members and their therapist will decide the course of therapy after that. If the family member who is calling begins to argue or disagree, the appointment center person responds by saying that it is not a hard and fast rule that all family members come. If it is particularly difficult for some family members to come, the therapist will be glad to see whoever is able to attend. By this approach, the appointment center is able to encourage entire family attendance, while not engaging in conflict over this issue. If a conflict is likely, it is better that the therapist deal with it rather than the appointment staff.

The issue of whether the patients are to see a short-term or long-term therapist is not addressed by the appointment center. No mention is made of this unless patients bring it up. If patients do wish to know anything about length of therapy, the appointment personnel tell them. If patients wish long-term instead, they are told that the short-term therapist will refer them if long-term work is deemed necessary. If patients persist, they are put in a long-term therapist's schedule.

At various times, therapists in FIP have been booked solid for up to four weeks in advance. This is not a good state of affairs, as the therapists become less responsive to clinic and patient needs. To handle this situation, no waiting list is created. Rather, patients are still scheduled on a first come, first served basis. Therapists are then responsible for trying to offer the most responsive service possible under less than ideal circumstances. If this state of affairs does continue in a particular clinic for an extended period, more staff is brought into that clinic.

Initial Interview

Each mental-health session is limited to forty-five minutes. Department policy is that each therapist has forty-five minutes for direct patient contact and then fifteen minutes in which to write up a mental-

health note in the patient's chart. Thus, for the initial interview, the therapists have forty-five minutes essentially to do an intake interview and decide the immediate course of treatment, and then fifteen minutes to write up an intake note consisting of problem statement, relevant history, mental status, diagnosis, and treatment plan. Also, it is important to remember that for the short-term therapists, this initial interview is one-fourth of the therapeutic time that they will be able to give each of their patients.

At the beginning of the first session, the therapist usually broaches the issues of how many members of the family are there and the four-session limit. The attendance issue is usually brought up with a question that asks if all the members of the family were able to attend. This question is usually asked to the person in the family who set up the appointment. From the answer to this question, the therapist is able to obtain several valuable pieces of information about the views of the family and their particular patterning. If the answer suggests that only the adolescent is here because it is his or her problem, then the therapist further attempts to clarify whether the adolescent believed it was his or her problem or was it the parents that believed such. In cases where it is the adolescent who believes it is his or her problem, then it is usually systemically best to see that person alone. If one or more family members believe it is the adolescent's problem, then they need to be included in the therapy, most often framed as helpers to the problem person. If the family is saying that it is a family problem, then of course the entire family is seen. It is interesting to note that more and more families seem to be coming to therapy stating that it is a family problem. Most likely this is an offshoot of the proliferation of the family therapy movement. The world views of families are being influenced by the changing world views of therapists.

It is probably becoming clear from the preceding points that the therapist does not try to conduct battle with the patients. Battles are generally time-consuming. They involve attempting to alter the patient's view of one situation to match that of the therapist. This is generally a symmetrical interaction that can last for a great number of sessions and accomplish nothing. In order to be effective in four sessions, a symmetrical interaction should not be entered into. More will be said about this later.

The issue of the four-session limit is also brought up very early in the first session. Typically, the therapist tells the family members present that the therapist operates within a four-session limit and that he or she does this in order to provide helpful, effective service to the greatest number of patients. Of course, if there is a need for further therapy, referral to longer-term work can always be made. Most patients readily accept a four-session limit when it is presented in this way. Most want therapy to be as short and as inexpensive as possible. Generally, there are two types of cases where someone reacts against this message of a four-session limit during the first session. One case is the adolescent and/or family that feels firmly that the only way he or she can possibly be helped is by long-term therapeutic contact with a therapist. The other situation is where a family unit is present that feels their problems are so numerous that it will take more than four sessions just to tell of them. When the short-term therapists face either of the above types of family contexts, they generally refer the family to a long-term therapist after the first session.

Sometimes, during the initial session, an adolescent and/or family will assume a "doubtful" position regarding the potential helpfulness of four-session therapy. When this occurs, therapists generally take a "try it and see" approach. Therapists tell the patients that after all, they are only running the risk of gaining some help quickly. If at the end of four sessions it seems as if more therapy is needed, then of course referral can be made to someone who can see them for a longer period. Also, therapists can tell the family that they can come back to see them (the same therapist) if they feel after a period of time (a few months) that their present problem was not solved or that another problem had come up. The last part of this message, probably the most

important part, will be discussed further in the section addressing the four-session therapy.

Another set of questions asked during the initial interview concerns how the family came into therapy. The primary purpose here is to find out if a physician is involved in the entry into therapy. Of course, the referring person is a critical piece of information over and above whether or not it happens to be a physician within the HMO. However, given the time available for conducting therapy, contacting the referring person if he or she is outside the HMO is generally not feasible. If the referring person is a physician, then several other avenues are possible within the four-session model. These will be discussed in the next section.

Often the initial interview takes place during a consultation time. These consultation times are half-hour blocks in the therapist's schedule. There are typically two of these times on any one day. During this half-hour, the therapist has approximately twenty minutes to interview the patient and ten minutes to write an intake note. Most of the same questions mentioned earlier are asked during this time. The difference between this format and the typical intake format (forty-five-minute sessions) is that a physician is involved. Now the physician may have referred this adolescent previously, may be present with the identified patient and/or other family members, or may talk to the therapist without the patient present. Whatever the case, valuable assessment information can be obtained, often in session, about the physician's relationship with the patient. Typically, the therapist wants to know if the physician has had a long-term, active involvement with this adolescent, has been a mother or father figure, or has attempted to give advice or suggest changes. Other questions are what the relationship of the physician is with the parents of the adolescent, whether the physician is feeling "stuck" with this patient, or whether the physician just wants to know if what they are presently doing is right. By finding out the answers to these types of questions, the therapist can direct the therapy most effectively, especially given the context that the primary physician who is referring will probably have contact with the patient for years to come.

Once the therapist has asked the above questions, there is still quite a bit of time left in the first session. At this point the therapist moves into the "therapy." Of course, this is only an arbitrary distinction for the purposes of discussion and does not reflect that what has occurred previous to this should be considered to be "not therapy."

Before we proceed to the next section, it should be noted that very seldom does the therapist spend much time during the first session collecting history. If a family wants to do this or if it will help the therapist collect some specific information, then it does happen. It does not occur as a matter of course.

Four-Session Therapy

As should have become evident in the section on the first interview, the messages given to the patient(s) are extremely important. It is, first of all, necessary for therapists to believe that they can be effective in four sessions or less. It can be very difficult indeed to convince patients to expect therapeutic help in four sessions if the therapists are not themselves convinced that it can be done. Throughout the four sessions therapists find it helpful to remind patients continually that therapy needs to be focused and expedient since little time is available.

Before discussing the typical sequence of the four-session therapy, it should be mentioned that much of the setting immediately surrounding the therapists allows them to be quite directive with their approach. Each therapist's office is in a medical clinic surrounded by physicians. Patients come to this clinic and receive health care from a physician. Since physicians are typically quite directive and quick-moving in their approach, the patients are prepared for a similar style in a therapist who is housed in the same setting.

The four-session therapy begins with the questions discussed in the previous section, questions focused on how the family members came to be in therapy. After these questions have been discussed, therapists most frequently move into problem definition. Therapists work with the family members to have them clearly define a problem and clearly define how they would know when they had been helped with their problem at least a little bit.

Now, as the format or actual process of the therapy is centering on problem definition, the therapist is paying attention to (assessing) the conceptual views of the family and/or identified patient. The therapists are attempting to understand the way the family members talk and communicate, the type of words they use and how they use them. Do they have a very concrete, state-trait view of the way things happen in the world—e.g., once someone in the family has "got something" such as rebelliousness, are they stuck with it forever? Do they want someone to give them advice and would they be glad to change what they are doing? Do they want someone to say "don't worry about the 'problem,' " and would they then stop fussing about the problem? The therapist is actively trying to obtain enough sense of the language and communication within the system to be able to offer an intervention that will have impact.

While assessing the conceptual views of the patient and/or family members, the therapist is also assessing the interactional patterns that are present. Is the thrust of the parents' actions to keep adolescents from growing up or to encourage them to leave the nest? How do adolescents respond to messages from mother and father? Do the adolescents go to see their peers after an altercation at home or do they go to their room and smoke dope? Is an adolescent taking steps toward individuation or is he or she retreating from it, or is he or she moving forward and retreating intermittently? Are the parents moving toward finding an activity or an involvement to replace childrearing? What position does the adolescent assume in the peer group?

It is important to note that therapists are

assessing patterning not on the basis of the content of what is said, but on the process of the session as well as on the information collected about the various interactions occurring outside the office. Thus, it can be seen that the actual content the family brings up is not critical. This actual content is valuable in determining what therapists will focus on when they intervene, but it will not determine the thrust or primary intent of the intervention. This will be determined by the assessment the therapists have obtained of the patterning present in a particular family.

It is often the case that the therapists will have enough information to attempt a minor intervention at the end of the first session. If the therapists feel that they have some sense of what the family is defining the problem as, of what the conceptual views or "language" of the family is, and of what the patterning for the family is, they will go ahead and come up with some type of verbal prescription. The intervention is very frequently a verbal prescription as opposed to a raised question or a reflective statement, because patients for the most part expect and will respond well to a prescription from "an expert in a medical building."

For example, consider a family where the identified fourteen-year-old female patient has attempted suicide. The reason presented for the attempt was conflict regarding whether or not the girl should live with her mother or father. The therapist's assessment of one pattern was that this girl did not like the restrictions her mother had placed on her and wanted to avoid these by going to live with her father. Further, the mother and father were able to communicate about the daughter with each other, but the mother did not feel the father could provide the care their daughter needed. Also, the therapist assessed that both parents would listen to what he said and follow through on it. The therapist's intervention after the first session was to say that the best mothering the mother could do would be to let her daughter live with her father. Of course, the father would need guidance and the best resource would be for the two parents to consult as

parents over the phone regarding rules for their daughter. Also, it would be important for the father to take breaks from this new responsibility and have his daughter spend at least every other weekend with her mother. It would be the responsibility of both parents to work out over the phone without the daughter the rules for these weekends. The family came back once more after one week and then once more after two months. The initial intervention was not changed and the last two sessions were primarily follow-up.

Of course, the preceding was an intervention that worked. Some do not. When this occurs, at least more information is provided. The therapist now knows what doesn't work—an extremely valuable piece of information. In cases where a first-session intervention does not work, the therapist still has three more sessions and the impetus that comes from a four-session limit to proceed with an alternative strategy.

If the therapist does not have a good sense of where to go after the first session, an assessment/intervention is still possible. Typically, the frame for the intervention would be the therapist saying that more information is needed and this can be provided by the adolescent and/or family doing certain prescribed activities.

For example, therapeutic effectiveness for a family that describes their teenaged son as rebellious often can be enhanced by asking them at the end of the first session to track this rebelliousness over the next week or two to see how often it occurs and under what circumstances. Of course, the family is not to try to initiate this rebelliousness because, if they did, the therapist would not be able to obtain as clear a picture of the extent of their son's self-generated rebelliousness.

By attempting to move quickly and prescribe activities, therapists are giving the family the message that it is possible to solve problems by doing something. The family is bombarded by several messages (four-session limit, quick problem-definition, prescriptive setting, etc.) that they can solve their problem by acting. If the therapist at any point in the course of the four-session therapy finds the pattern developing in which a prescription by the therapist is inevitably undermined or "resisted" by the patient(s), then, of course, a different strategy is in order. Typically the therapist would say that it has become quite clear to him or her that this family is not able to change at this point and that this is an okay state of affairs, because it means that however painful the problem may be, the family does need to have it. The therapist would therefore suggest that the family come back after a longer period of time (usually one to six months) and try again, and that they as a family or the adolescent as an individual may have reached a point by then at which they are able to move past their problem.

The therapy that occurs during the remainder of the sessions is similar in process to the examples already mentioned. The therapist is seeking a prescription or message that will provide the adolescent or family with enough impetus to make some small change. This small change may then reverberate throughout the system and be sufficient for the family to go on about their lives. At least it almost always will have the effect of helping the patient/family past the particular difficulty that has brought them to therapy so that they are able to avoid a prolonged association with this problem. And if they were to need specific help with a specific problem in the future, they could always return for more of the four-session therapy.

Several examples of actual prescriptions could be included. This is not the intent of this chapter. Seekers of actual prescriptions are referred to the works of Haley, Selvini, Watzlawick, Minuchin and other writers who ascribe to systems-oriented approaches.

While the therapists are conducting the four sessions, they are careful to avoid symmetrical interactions. Whenever therapists sense they are involved in a symmetrical exchange with the patient, the therapists know they need to proceed differently. This is not to say that the therapists feel confrontive work is never effective. They have generally found that within the context that therapists work within their clinics, it is generally not possible. Con-

frontation that arises out of the therapist's attempt to change the family context to match what that therapist believes it should be takes too long. Confrontations that are used strategically to move the patient(s) in a different direction are typically not helpful because the patient(s) can leave the field. They can return and complain to another provider, complain to Membership Services (consumer complaint department) or go to a different therapist. In any of these cases, the therapy has not been systemically helpful to the patient's and/or the therapist's systems.

If a physician has referred the patient and/or if a physician is or has been actively involved with the patient or patient's family, the therapists typically involve the physician in the therapy in some manner. By doing this, the therapists obtain more information, have increased the number of possible therapeutic strategies, and can use the physician's relationship with the patient in a maintenance prescription.

A typical example of the use of a physician is as an expert back-up in the area of physical symptoms. Thus, the physician can be very helpful with presenting problems such as anorexia, bulimia, nocturnal enuresis, chronic stomach pain, and the like. For example, a thirteen-year-old female is referred to a therapist with the presenting problem of anorexia. The physician collaborates in the therapy as the one to determine if the girl reaches a certain weight where she will need to be hospitalized. This frees the therapist from needing to be the one to focus on weight and allows the therapist to deal with patterns for the girl and the family which have resulted in the present problem.

Before moving to the next section, a few points need to be made about the fourth or last session. As mentioned before, the most frequently used message during this session has to do with telling the patient(s) that they should see how things go for a while and then come back in a few months if another problem arises or if the presently identified problem persists or returns. This message is effective for the majority of patients. Some patients, however, do feel they definitely need more therapy now. If this is the case, argument does not ensue.

The therapists state that they will help the patient be transferred to a long-term therapist.

Long-Term Therapy

The long-term therapy with adolescents may or may not be dissimilar to what has been described for the short-term therapist. The primary and distinct difference is in the pace. At the point that a patient and/or family are referred to a long-term therapist, for one reason or another the set or expectation has been firmly established that long-term therapy is indicated. Thus, there typically does need to be a certain number of sessions, more than four. Very few adolescents and/or families, however, have been seen for more than fifteen sessions.

The long-term therapists have additional extremely valuable assessment information that the short-term therapists did not have. They are familiar with the process that occurred between the short-term therapist and the family. This information is very helpful in figuring out which strategy or strategies did not previously work in therapy.

Typical long-term therapy cases involve adolescents who cannot figure out what they should do with their lives. The adolescent and family feel greatly stressed by this state of affairs and also feel that figuring this out is a very difficult and long-term process. The usual course of therapy is to allow a certain number of sessions for listening to the dilemmas and then attempting to move with the adolescent and family in some specific directions.

Ending therapy, as might be expected, is much more difficult in long-term work than it is in short-term work. If ending has become difficult, the best strategy is not to end but simply to keep increasing the intervals between sessions until they are up to six months apart.

CONCLUSION

The fact that "usual" and "typical" processes have been described should not be misconstrued to mean that all therapists proceed in the same way in the same circumstances. Indeed, the commonality that exists among therapists is that they strive to be aware of the systems with which they are interacting and then proceed in what seems to them to be systemically "best." Each of the therapists has the utmost respect for trying to offer the most helpful and effective service for the greatest number of individuals.

We are in the process of collecting data. We of FIP have been conducting therapy at Northwest Kaiser for three years now. Measuring success is difficult. We have found that upwards of 85 percent of the patients seen by short-term therapists have not needed further therapy and that only a very small percentage have complained that they did not receive the help they desired.

Will the approach described in this chapter work in other settings? The answer, of course, is that it depends on the setting. Each therapist and/or program director should assess his or her context before deciding on what therapy to offer. We feel that much of what we do can be used in other settings. However, the most important message is that the therapist must work with the setting actively in mind when conducting therapy.

REFERENCES

Cummings, N. A. The anatomy of psychotherapy under national health insurance. *American Psychologist*, 1977, **32**, 711–718.

Cummings, N. A., & Follette, W. T. Brief psychotherapy and medical utilization: An eight-year follow-up. In H. Dörken & Associates, *The professional psychologist today: New developments in law, health insurance and health practice.* San Francisco: Jossey-Bass, 1976.

Follette, W. T., & Cummings, N. A. Psychiatric services and medical utilization in a prepaid health plan setting. *Journal of Medical Care*, 1967, **5**, 25–35.

5

Home-Based Structural Family Therapy for Delinquents at Risk of Placement*

THOMAS N. TAVANTZIS, Ed.D.,
MARTHA TAVANTZIS, M.S.W.,
LARRY G. BROWN, M.S.W.,
and MICHAEL ROHRBAUGH, Ph.D.

A merican society has a long tradition of solving family problems by placing people in out-of-home care. In this way, elderly, retarded, delinquent and disturbed people have been segregated and cared for along with other exiled family members who have similar problems. In families where parents are abusive or neglectful, or where youth are chronically troubled or troublesome, a common response has been to rescue a good child from bad parents, or vice versa, by placing the child in foster care.[1] In the 1970s, mounting concern about the costly and ineffective use of fos-

ter care as a band-aid solution to family problems led to legislative reforms aimed at keeping families together. The landmark Adoption Assistance and Child Welfare Act of 1980 (Public Law 96-272) began to reverse a longstanding social policy that had in effect subsidized foster care at the expense of efforts to prevent it.

*We would like to thank the Schenectady County Departments of Social Services and Probation, the Schenectady Junior League, the board members of the Northeast Parent and Child Society, and the New York State Office of Mental Health for the financial support and encouragement that made the placement prevention program, *Families Work*, possible. We are also greatly indebted to the *Families Work* Staff.

[1] "Foster care" refers to any out-of-home placement in an institution, group home, foster home, or temporary shelter.

Now, with changing federal and state reimbursement incentives, effective methods of preventing unnecessary placement and reunifying separated families are of growing interest and concern. Some of the most promising developments in the area of foster-care prevention involved home-based family-centered services. Evaluation data from model projects indicate that counselors working intensively with families, in the home, can help most families avoid placing their children, at costs well below those of foster care (Maybanks & Bryce, 1979; Bryce & Lloyd, 1980).

While home-based prevention projects treat the family as a unit of service, they have had surprisingly little cross-fertilization from developments in the field of family therapy. In our view, the structural, strategic, and systemic models of family therapy (Minuchin & Fishman, 1981; Haley, 1980; Madanes, 1981; Hoffman, 1981) offer a useful framework for understanding problems that lead to placement and practical approaches to resolving them. This chapter describes a placement prevention program dealing primarily with delinquent and unmanageable adolescents—*Families Work*—which combines the principles of home-based service and structural family therapy. After reviewing the legislative context of foster-care reform and the growing field of home-based prevention, we will describe the program in detail, highlighting principles, procedures, and some preliminary evaluation data collected in the program's first two years.

FOSTER-CARE REFORM

Two curiously contradictory American traditions must be considered in relation to foster-care reform. On the one hand, as De Toqueville noted over 150 years ago, we rely heavily on institutions such as asylums and reformatories to manage social problems. On the other, we place a high value on family life and abhor the thought of children growing up without it (Bryce, 1979).

In this century, the institutional tradition

has gained ground. Since 1910, institutional placements increased at twice the rate of population growth, and from 1961 to 1977, the number of children in foster care tripled while the total number of U.S. children declined (Dodson, 1983). As more children entered the vast and disorganized system, fewer came out. Eventually, the enormous human waste and staggering public cost set the stage for reform.

After amassing overwhelming documentation on deficiencies in the foster-care bureaucracy, Congress passed the Adoption Assistance and Child Welfare Act of 1980, and in so doing created unprecedented financial incentives for "pre-placement prevention" and "reunification" programs to help children remain with their families. Concurrently, several states had developed similar legislative initiatives on their own. In New York, a task force commissioned to study the state's child welfare system found it:

essentially a foster care system, despondently biased toward the long-term placement of children whose family environment had been disrupted. The reasons why the thrust of the system was directed toward foster care were many, but one, in particular, stood out. The primary reimbursement system for child welfare agencies, both public and private, was based on each child's stay in foster care at a more or less fixed per diem rate. This reimbursement formula all but dictated the traditional nearly complete reliance on foster care. (Pisani, 1982, p. 2)

In 1979, New York passed the Child Welfare Reform Act and became the first state to mandate that preventive services be provided whenever (a) a child would be placed or continued in foster care without such services, or (b) providing the services would allow the child to remain or return home. The intention was to gain control over spiraling costs of foster care while improving prevention services to families.

California, Washington, and Ohio attempted similar legislative remedies, while other states such as Iowa and Oregon encouraged innovative prevention within existing frameworks. Today, some states have barely begun to address the problem, and larger states, like New York, are experiencing predictable resistance from entrenched child welfare and juvenile justice bureaucracies. Despite problems of implementation, there are encouraging signs: officials in some states that have addressed the problem of a growing foster-care population are optimistic about success (*Prevention Report*, 1982, 1982–1983); parent and child advocates are establishing legal arguments for asserting a family's right to services as an alternative to disruption (Dodson, 1983); and most important, home-based family intervention programs are showing that foster placement can indeed be prevented.

HOME-BASED PREVENTION

Home-based intervention programs have been both a stimulus and a response to legislative reform. In the early and mid-1970s, projects such as Homebuilders in Tacoma, Washington, Families of West Branch, Iowa, the Home and Community Treatment Program in Madison, Wisconsin, and the Lower East Side Family Union in New York City began to demonstrate that foster placement can be prevented by working intensively with families in their homes, usually for a limited period of time. The fact that something could be done helped to promote foster-care reforms, which in turn stimulated broader application of home-based services.

Another important development in the emergence of home-based services was the Department of Health, Education, and Welfare's funding of the "National Clearinghouse on Home-Based Services for Children," headquartered at the University of Iowa School of Social Work. Under the direction of Marvin Bryce, the Clearinghouse organized a landmark national symposium in 1978 (Maybanks & Bryce, 1979) and published a number of manuals and monographs on home-based care. Now, with a different name and different funding arrangements, the National Resource Center on Family-Based Services continues to advocate for home-based prevention and publishes a quarterly newsletter called *Prevention Report*.

In general, home-based prevention programs report excellent results. According to Bryce and Lloyd (1980), program evaluation data consistently indicate that between 70 and 90 percent of the families who receive these services are able to stay together. Some programs, such as Homebuilders, claim even higher success rates, ranging from 84 percent for delinquents to 98 percent for abuse-neglect cases (*Prevention Report*, 1982–1983). There are several reasons, however, why statistics like these should be interpreted cautiously.

First, figures on avoiding placement usually pertain only to the period during which services were provided. Whether families continue to do as well after home-based services have been withdrawn, and traditional (office-based) services resumed, cannot always be determined. The available data suggest that success rates do shrink somewhat over time, but that effects are usually enduring. Families of West Branch, for example, recently reported that 91 percent of their cases had avoided placement when services were terminated, whereas 70 percent were still together a year later (*Prevention Report*, 1982–1983).

A second limitation is that outcome studies have usually not included randomly selected control families with comparable problems and motivation, for whom services were not provided. Yet, most families who receive these services have been defined by state agencies as needing them, which usually means that placement has already been approved or is imminent. An evaluation study conducted several years ago by the State of Oregon did find that each of nineteen control families experienced placement during the time when over 90 percent of 128 families receiving intensive family services avoided placement (*Prevention Report*, 1982–1983).

Finally, it must be remembered that statistics on home-based services are provided almost exclusively by program advocates and administrators who rely on the results to justify budgets and insure program survival. Even if we make allowance for this bias, however, the results are impressive and highlight a modality that has probably not received the attention it deserves.

The potential savings are as impressive as the placement outcomes. The National Resource Center estimated in 1980 that providing intensive home-based service to one family usually costs less than an average foster-home placement and one-half to one-tenth as much as residential or psychiatric care for one person (Lloyd & Bryce, 1980). These estimates, however, are based on a single child entering placement. In reality, home-based family service benefits other family members as well, including other children who avoid placement. Indeed, home-based services are an efficient and coordinated way to serve the entire family.

Given that home-based services work, what are their defining characteristics? The most fundamental is that they address the family, not just the child, as the unit of service. In addition to this family focus, Bryce (1979) lists the following as characteristics of home-based programs that have been developed in the past decade:

1. Home-based care is provided primarily in the home.
2. The parents remain in charge and are counted on to participate.
3. The family system and natural habitat are utilized and the family is related to as a unit.
4. The program will help, or arrange for help, with any problem area presented by the family or observed to be a problem by the service providers.
5. Extensive use is made of the natural resources of extended family, neighborhood, and the community. (p. 20)

Beyond these characteristics, specific methods and models vary widely. One of the best-known programs is Homebuilders of Tacoma, Washington, where staff contract with a family to be available twenty-four hours a day for a four- to eight-week period, spending as much time in the clients' home as is necessary to resolve a given crisis. While Homebuilders disavows any particular theoretical orientation, its philosophy has been strongly influenced by humanistic/experiential approaches such as Roger's Client-Centered Therapy and Gordon's Parent Effectiveness Training (Kinney, 1978; Haapala & Kinney, 1979). The Home and Community Treatment Program of the Mendota Mental Health Institute uses a behavior modification approach based on social-learning theory. Parents are first taught child-management techniques in a group setting, then helped to apply them at home, with intensive intervention lasting four to six months (Cautley, 1980a, 1980b). The Lower East Side Family Union in New York City emphasizes community outreach and in-home care by workers who are themselves residents of the neighborhood they serve. Finally, in the state of Oregon, good results have been obtained with Multiple Impact Therapy, where a team of therapists conducts marathon sessions in the home, attempting to produce major changes in how a family functions in a short period of time (*Prevention Report*, 1982–1983).

In all of these projects, the family group is considered to be the unit of service. Yet, with a few exceptions (Stephens, 1979), intervention is based mainly on individually oriented theories of problem formation and change. Most techniques of behavior modification, values clarification, or assertiveness training, for example, are based on the idea that families change when their *individual* members learn better living skills or get in touch with their feelings. What seems to be missing is a theoretical framework linked specifically to the organization of the family as a group, and ultimately to the broader ecology of which it is part.

A SYSTEMS FRAMEWORK

An eco-systemic view of problems that lead to placement is that they do not occur in a vacuum: there are nearly always other people involved, the most important being members of the child's immediate family (Stanton, 1979). The premise is not that delinquency is caused by prior unfortunate experiences in the family (e.g., broken marriage, inconsistent discipline, abuse, neglect), although such a linear view could probably be supported by research. Rather, it is assumed that how problems are maintained is more important than how they originated—that present causes are more relevant than past causes. The emphasis, therefore, is on how problems persist as an aspect of current, ongoing disturbances of family life (Weakland, Fisch, Watzlawick, & Bodin, 1974; Minuchin, 1974; Hoffman, 1981; Rohrbaugh & Eron, 1982).

In a hypothetical and oversimplified example, two parents may get into an argument, following which their teenage son misbehaves by breaking a window next door, overdosing on drugs, or being truant from school. The parents stop fighting and focus their attention on the child. The father, who is usually preoccupied with his work, joins the mother in taking charge of the teenager, who then begins to behave normally again. Eventually the father disengages from teenager and spouse, and the parents have little to do with each other for some time. They reengage later, another argument ensues, and the pattern repeats itself. In this situation and in many like it, assigning blame or determining what causes what depends on where one punctuates an essentially circular sequence of interaction. It is also evident that the functioning of each family member is intertwined with the entire context of family life, which includes the system of relationships among all family members (Stanton, 1979).

Whereas psychodynamic and behavioral approaches localize problems in individuals, the problem unit from an eco-systemic perspective invariably involves several people. The important issue is not how many people the therapist sees in an interview, but how many people are involved in the therapist's way of thinking about the problem (Madanes & Haley, 1977). A therapist thinking in terms of a problem unit of one may concentrate on helping a delinquent youth express his feelings more appropriately, or learn better social skills or impulse control. She or he may view the parents as contributing to the problem because they provide inconsistent discipline and affection, or are overly crit-ical and rejecting. The therapist may even try to help them change, but will usually prefer to work with the child directly to provide corrective therapeutic experiences and counteract the parents' toxic influence.

By contrast, a therapist who assumes that the problem unit involves several people will attempt to understand how delinquent behavior supports and is supported by the current family organization. This therapist will assume that the young person's problems are inextricably interwoven with the context in which they occur, and that the problem will not change unless the context changes also. Rather than protecting or removing the child, she or he will want to work through the parents, not against them, and will be reluctant to work with the youth alone, since the therapeutic goal is to support a workable family structure.

Two useful models for understanding adolescent problems and introducing change are the structural family therapies developed by Salvador Minuchin and colleagues at the Philadelphia Child Guidance Clinic (Minuchin, 1974; Minuchin & Fishman, 1981), and by Jay Haley (1976, 1980) and Cloé Madanes (1981). Structural approaches assume that problems reflect a dysfunctional organization of relationships, both within the family and often between the family and the community. A key concept in Minuchin's approach concerns the boundaries between individuals or groups of individuals—the unspoken rules that govern "who participates and how" (Minuchin, 1974). The most important boundaries are between generations of the same family (grandparents, parents, children) and between the family unit and the outside community. Problems arise when boundaries are either too permeable or too rigid, when people are too involved with each other (enmeshed) or not involved enough (disengaged). Some of the most difficult situations are those in which cross-generational groupings have stronger boundaries than subsystems within generations, as when a parent is more involved with a child than with his or her spouse (Stanton, 1979).

For Haley and Madanes, confusions of

organizational hierarchy are the basis of most clinical problems. Thus, in families with troublesome adolescents, there are usually sequences in which "the parents tell the youth what to do but he does not do it or the parents do not tell the youth what to do but complain about what he does or the youth tells the parents what to do and the parents do it" (Madanes, 1981, p. 190). But the most problematic situations, again, are those in which covert coalitions cross hierarchial lines. When members of generations *A* and *B* align against another member of generation *A*, or members of *A* and *C* align against *B*, the organizational requirements for what Haley (1976) called a "pathological system" are met. This pattern is not limited to families; systems involving outside helpers can also be pathological.

While issues of hierarchical confusion and control are paramount in families with delinquent or pre-delinquent adolescents at risk of placement, the structural context of the presenting problem varies considerably from case to case. In one way or another, youth in these families are experienced as "out of control." In some families, overinvolved parents monitor their child's (mis)behavior very closely, attempting to control it in ways that only provoke further acting out, which in turn provokes more strenuous efforts to control. In other families a key parent may be disengaged, seeming to abdicate authority by providing too little supervision and granting more autonomy than the youth can handle. At this stage in the family life cycle, when the generations face the difficult task of disengaging from each other, either too much or too little control can easily abort the transition. Negotiating adolescence successfully requires a family organization that is complex enough to allow a young person to be independent and dependent at the same time.

Structural family therapy attempts to alter interaction patterns in ways that support a workable family structure (Minuchin, 1974; Minuchin & Fishman, 1981). In practice, this might involve challenging patterns of overinvolvement or disengagement, helping estranged spouses unite as parents to take charge of a child, or arranging that

a grandparent move to an appropriate supporting role. Key structural techniques include: *joining* (accommodating to the family); *enactment* (eliciting and changing problematic interactions in the therapy session); *restructuring* (rearranging enmeshed or disengaged relationships, clarifying hierarchies); *reframing* (redefining the meaning of events and behavior to create a more workable reality); and *creating intensity* (pushing a family or subsystem past its threshold of comfort with the present pattern of relationships).

A final implication of an eco-systemic view deserves special comment. When families with children at risk of placement are involved with a number of different helping agencies or therapists at the same time—as most are—the effective problem unit often extends beyond the family. Just as youth problems can be understood in the context of family interaction, so are they also shaped by the family's interaction with school officials, probation officers, child welfare workers, and other representatives of the community. To ignore the possibility that well-intentioned helpers (including oneself) can be part of a problem-maintaining process is to err in the manner of an individually oriented therapist who ignores the family system (Auerswald, 1968; Aponte, 1980; Haley, 1980; Coppersmith, 1983).

There are at least two ways in which outside helpers can inadvertently make things worse. Both involve incongruous hierarchies in which helpers participate, and both, in form, resemble structural confusions that occur within the natural family groups. One pattern arises when multiple helpers or agencies work on the same case. Even though all want to help, their specific goals, service philosophies, and methods of treatment may vary widely. In this climate, unrecognized or unacknowledged conflict may develop between helpers, as it does between parents in the families they are trying to help (Coppersmith, 1983). As several helpers struggle with the same case in an uncoordinated and conflictual way, clients are easily drawn into coalitions with one helper against another, creating a "pathological system" in which covert coalitions cross hierarchical lines. The more helpers involved with a case, and the more disagreement there is between them, the greater will be the opportunity for hierarchical confusion. The remedy, of course, is for helpers to clarify the hierarchy by organizing themselves before taking on the task of organizing families.

A second iatrogenic pattern occurs when services are child-centered rather than family-centered, regardless of how many helpers are involved. Whenever outside helpers attempt to change a child directly—or to offer the limits, consistency, affection, or understanding that parents have not provided—they risk undermining the parents' position in the family hierarchy. In this manner, well-intentioned probation officers, child-care workers, foster parents, big brothers and sisters, and psychotherapists can find themselves supplanting parents rather than supporting them. If parent and child are attached at all, the helper who does not empower the parents by working *through* them is effectively working against them. In many such situations, an implicit struggle develops over who is in charge of the youth (i.e., who is the "best" parent), leaving the youth in an impossible position: if he shapes up at the request of outsiders, he is being disloyal to his parents; if he does not, the struggle only intensifies. The tragedy is that competitive relationships between parents and helpers not only undermine the integrity of the family group, but usually aggravate the problems everyone is trying to solve.

FAMILIES WORK

Families Work, a prevention program for adolescents at risk of placement, combines the principles of structural/systemic family therapy and home-based care. The program was developed three years ago at the Parkhurst Parent and Child Center,[2] a private, nonprofit voluntary agency serving youth and families in Schenectady County,

[2]Parkhurst Parent and Child Center has since merged with the Children's Home of Schenectady to form the Northeast Parent and Child Society.

New York. In February 1979, a needs-assessment survey conducted by the County Department of Social Services identified 506 children at high risk of placement and cited a major need for expanding foster-care prevention efforts. Prompted by the survey results and the 1979 Child Welfare Reform Act (Pisani, 1982), Parkhurst undertook a pilot project in 1980 aimed at preventing placement through in-home family therapy. The early results were encouraging enough that an expanded program organized along similar lines was funded in April 1981. At that time, we knew of no similar attempts to apply home-based structural family therapy in a systematic way.

While *Families Work* was inspired by developments in home-based prevention and structural family therapy, two other influences should be mentioned as well. First, the literature on brief, family-oriented crisis intervention indicates that crisis provides an opportunity for constructive change (Flomenhaft, Kaplan, & Langsley, 1972; Pittman et al., 1981). Parents who come to *Families Work* are typically very ambivalent about placement. On one hand, placement offers problem relief and respite from a seemingly impossible situation; it is usually viewed by the parents as their only viable alternative. On the other hand, the pain, guilt, and sense of failure associated with the anticipated separation are difficult for most families to bear. Participating in the program offers another option—one designed to address the family's need for guidance and support at this time of crisis.

Another influence was research on family intervention with juvenile delinquents. Gendreau and Ross (1980), in reviewing delinquency outcome studies, conclude that the most successful programs have been the most intensive in terms of actual time spent by the treatment staff with family members. This suggested that the density of home-based contact would be an important factor in the success of *Families Work*. In an important series of studies in Utah, Alexander and his colleagues (Alexander & Parsons, 1973; Barton & Alexander, 1981) found that families with delinquent adolescents are more defensive (nonsupportive) in their verbal communication than families of nondelinquents. In addition, they demonstrated that a "system/behavioral" intervention program aimed at modifying these dysfunctional patterns had a greater impact on later recidivism than other, more traditional forms of therapy. This research provides the clearest evidence to date that delinquency and family interaction are interrelated, and that changing the family system is an effective approach to treatment.

The Population

The primary target population for *Families Work* was, and continues to be, families with youth between the ages of ten to sixteen who come to the attention of Family Court or the County's Probation or Child Welfare agencies. To be referred, a family must have at least one adolescent who, in the judgment of the referring agency, is "at imminent risk" of being removed from the home within sixty days. According to New York law, prevention services are mandated for any family meeting this criterion and can be reimbursed by state and federal funds.

As of April 1983, forty-four families with fifty-seven youth at risk of placement had completed the program. These youth ranged in age from ten to sixteen, with a median age of 14.4 years. Approximately half (52 percent) were female, and all but one of the families were white. Nearly half of the families had a youth designated as a Person In Need of Supervision (PINS) and an additional 25 percent had an adjudicated Juvenile Delinquent. The most common presenting problems were stealing, truancy, assaultive behavior, running away, and physical abuse by a parent. Half of the youth had been suspended from school at least once in the year prior to admission, and 56 percent were achieving below grade level. Thirty percent of the families had a youth in placement when they entered the program, and over half had experienced placement previously.

In terms of composition, roughly 30 percent of the families were intact, with both natural parents living in the same household. Forty-five percent were single-parent families and 25 percent were remarried families. The average household had 4.7 members. In 30 percent of the families a custodial parent had received some form of public financial assistance in the past year; in 35 percent, a parent had had at least some college or technical training beyond high school.

Sixty-two percent of the families were referred to *Families Work* by the County Probation Department, and in many cases a Family Court Judge had ordered the family to receive counseling. The remaining referrals were from the Department of Social Services, primarily the Child Protective Unit. Over three-fourths of our cases had been in counseling previously, without success.

Procedures

INTAKE/EVALUATION

Evaluation begins with the first phone call from the referring agent, when the *Families Work* supervisor solicits information about the presenting problem in its family context. The supervisor calls the family within twenty-four hours of referral to schedule an assessment interview, so that intervention can begin as near to the time of crisis as possible. The interview is scheduled at a time convenient to the family—usually in the evening—in order to accommodate members who could not otherwise participate. All members of the household and significant others who may be outside the household are strongly advised to attend. As a rule, the interview is postponed if a key adult is unable or unwilling to participate.

The initial assessment is conducted in the home by the supervisor and another family therapist.[3] One therapist usually takes the lead, allowing the other to observe the interaction between therapist and family. The interview may last from 1 to 2½ hours, depending on the level of crisis

---

[3]All *Families Work* therapists have Master's degrees in social work or counseling.

presented by the family. Additional meetings can be scheduled if this is not enough time or if other significant people need to be included.

In addition to gathering information about the family and its problems, the interviewers' goals in the initial assessment interview are (a) to join with and accommodate to the family; (b) to probe members' motivation to stay together; (c) to offer a slightly different definition of the problem, which implies hope for change; (d) to frame the problem as something everyone in the family must work on together to solve; and (e) to leave the family with the task of deciding together if they want to participate in the *Families Work* program.

Near the end of the initial interview, the family is told how the program operates and what will be expected of them in terms of attending scheduled sessions and being observed by other team members at the agency. In addition, family members are asked to agree to take a vacation from other counseling or therapy activities while they are involved in the program. They are also told that the team will be meeting to decide whether or not to accept the family in the program.

At the agency, usually the next day, the staff reviews the case. In general, families are accepted if: (a) a custodial parent lives in the county; (b) at least one parent wants to keep the family together; and (c) there is minimal risk that a therapist working in the home will be in physical danger. If the decision is favorable, a primary therapist is assigned and there is a preliminary discussion of treatment strategy. After the team meeting, the supervisor calls a parent as prearranged in the assessment interview. If family *and* team have agreed to participate, treatment is ready to begin. To date, over 95 percent of the families referred have entered the program.

TREATMENT

The first therapy session is always in the home. At this session the therapist presents a standard (written) contract for all family members to sign. The contract specifies that all parties agree to participate in therapy for a period of six weeks. It also clarifies client and agency responsibilities regarding confidentiality, sharing of information with other agencies, one-way mirror sessions, twenty-four-hour availability of a therapist, and use of the home as the primary treatment site. The therapist then helps the family identify three problem areas which family members will work on in the first six-week cycle. Specific goals for each problem area are defined at this time. Since family members choose them, goals can be both child-focused (e.g., Johnny will go to school) and family-focused (e.g., Johnny and Dad will talk without yelling). Both the therapist and family members then rate their discomfort with each problem and expectations for change. At the end of the first meeting the therapist gives the parent(s) the twenty-four-hour phone number and encourages them to call in case of any emergency.

In subsequent meetings, the therapist concentrates on joining the family and implementing a treatment plan developed in ongoing consultation with the supervisor and team. A strong emphasis is placed on the therapist's establishing a solid relationship with the family, especially with the parents, and being accepted by them on their own terms. The therapist starts where the family sees the problem, by addressing the goals established in the first session. In the meantime, the team helps the therapist formulate *structural objectives* related to organizational characteristics of the family (and its relationship to outside helpers) that will need to be changed in order for the family to achieve its goals. Structural objectives usually involve strengthening or modifying boundaries between parents and children in a way that allows more distance or puts parents more clearly in charge.

In the second or third week, the therapist meets with the family at the agency so that the supervisor and other team members can observe from behind a one-way mirror. These mirror sessions provide consultation and supervision for the therapist, training for other team members, and an opportunity to implement specially planned interventions. The supervisor usually interrupts the interview at least once to give the therapist suggestions, and sometimes enters the room to support a particular line of intervention or reverse directions if things are going badly. Other team members also see the family at first hand and are better prepared to deal with crisis calls that may come later in therapy.

Mirror sessions may be repeated later in therapy depending on how the case is progressing. In the middle stages of treatment they have been especially useful when a case seems to be stuck. At these times, the consultation format helps in building intensity, creating crises, and delivering authoritative messages from the team. In later stages, mirror sessions may be used to help the therapist disengage and prepare the family for termination.

At the end of each six-week contract period, the progress of therapy is reviewed by everyone concerned. Therapist and family members independently rate the progress made toward attaining each of the goals defined at the beginning of treatment and jointly discuss whether to recontract for another six-week cycle or to begin planning for termination. The *Families Work* supervisor also consults with the referring agency at these times, requiring that all three parties (family, team, and referring agent) agree with a recommendation for recontracting in order to proceed. To date, families that have completed the program have contracted for an average of 2½ six-week cycles.

As the family crisis stabilizes, the team begins to plan for discharge. This requires decreasing the intensity of contact with the family[4] (and successfully disengaging our own therapist) while, in most cases, increasing the family involvement with other

---

[4]Program statistics confirm the decreasing intensity of program involvement. During the first six-week cycle, direct service time ranged up to 66 hours with a median of 26.5 hours. By the third cycle, the median dropped to 10 hours, though the range of hours remained constant. The number of emergency (beeper) calls showed a similar trend. Families in the first cycle made a median of 1.3 calls (range: 0–6) while emergency calls in the third cycle were rare (median = 0.3; range: 0–2).

supportive services in the community. After-school programs, boys clubs, parent support groups, and marriage counseling are among the after-care services that have been recommended. Most families, of course, continue to have a relationship with the agency(s) which referred them.

Follow-up

Included in the discharge plan is a standard follow-up procedure for the therapist and family. Follow-up meetings are planned at six weeks, three months, six months, and one year after discharge from the program. At these times, the therapist and family review the family's continuing progress and the therapist makes an assessment of their current functioning. The therapist attempts to reinforce gains and structural changes that have occurred, while being alert to signs of increasing stress and impending crisis. Family members are invited to discuss their concerns about the youth who had been at risk of placement, as well as any other problems family members may be having. In this way, follow-up sessions become prevention sessions in which therapist and family anticipate problems and discuss ways to deal with them.

Principles of Intervention

Cutting across the operational aspects of *Families Work* are principles of structural family therapy that have been consistently helpful in working with adolescents at risk of placement. Several of the principles are especially well suited to the home-based treatment format; others are useful because they orient us to isomorphic structural patterns within and between the family, community agencies, and our own team.

Join Before Restructuring

In structural family therapy, identifying and restructuring dysfunctional interaction patterns requires that the therapist first join the family and become part of the system she or he wants to change. This "inside position" gives the therapist an opportunity to experience and understand what the family structure is, and the leverage and credibility necessary to begin to change it. In supervision, we now refer to effective joining as "enmeshing" to underscore the idea that a high level of therapist-client involvement—even *over-*involvement—in the early stages of treatment is a key part of the process. Being so enmeshing, however, requires the outside support of the team. With this safety line, therapists were able to become part of family patterns in order to change them.

There are several ways in which the home-based format facilitates joining. Since over 90 percent of our treatment occurs in the home, the therapist has rapid access to the family atmosphere and to relationships that may need special attention in the joining process. In one family, for example, a grandmother living upstairs had a large easychair reserved for her in her single-parent son's apartment. By acknowledging the grandmother's importance in the family and including her in several sessions early on, the therapist was able to gain her valuable support in empowering the father. Other factors in joining are frequency and availability of contact. During the first six weeks, therapists have spent an average of five hours per week in direct contact with the family, with nearly half of the sessions scheduled in the evenings or on weekends. Therapist accessibility is assured by the twenty-four-hour on-call system which clients are encouraged to use when the need arises.

The principle of joining before restructuring also applies in working with other agencies and in the internal operation of the *Families Work* team. It is assumed that working effectively with a family will depend on gaining the support and cooperation of others involved with the case, and on how those helpers (who will continue to be involved after we disengage) view the family and its capacity for change. Consequently, careful attention is given to nurturing a collaborative relationship in the course of receiving each referral, and to consulting with the referring agents and keeping them informed as therapy progresses. A similar process occurs within

the team. The meeting prior to each mirror session, for example, is essential in allowing the supervisor to "join" the therapist explicitly before attempting to restructure the relationship between therapist and clients during the family interview.

ORGANIZE HELPERS BEFORE FAMILIES

Since helpers can so easily become part of the problem, we work towards organizational congruence not only within the family, but in the broader system of helpers with whom the family interacts. It is imperative that structural considerations such as clear boundaries and congruous hierarchies include therapists as well as clients. Within the *Families Work* team, for example, decisions are coordinated by the supervisor. This individual is the clinical and administrative authority within the team, just as parents are the authorities within the family. It is important for the supervisor to support the therapist's relationship with the parents just as it is important for therapists and other helpers to support (and not undermine) the parents' relationship with their own children.

Just as parents should not struggle with each other through their children, the efforts of multiple helpers working with the same case should be reasonably coordinated—or at least not in conflict. Some dexterity is required to coordinate these efforts. Fortunately, we have generally been successful in arranging for the *Families Work* team to be in charge of a case during the time a family is in the program. As noted above, family members agree to take a vacation from other therapies as part of the treatment contract. In the meantime, the supervisor contacts the key helpers to explain the program and ask their cooperation, and the therapist continues to keep them informed on a weekly basis as therapy progresses. At the end of each six-week cycle, the team consults with the referral agent about whether to renew the treatment contract.

Where children are at risk of placement, it is especially important to organize helpers to support rather than supplant the parents. In one family, two teenagers whose natural father was in jail ran away from home repeatedly and complained that they were being beaten by their stepfather, to whom the mother deferred in all matters of discipline. The children were placed in a temporary shelter pending investigation of the alleged abuse. Although the abuse charge turned out to be unfounded, the multiple problems of this isolated, blended family came to the attention of the DSS Child Protective Unit, which referred them to *Families Work*. Once in the program with the children at home, the mother and stepfather began to work on their problems, but it soon became apparent that well-intentioned helpers in the community were making the task more difficult. The two children, it seems, were being protected from the parents by school, police, and social-service representatives, as well as by members of their own extended family. Policemen brought them pizza when they ran to the police station, aunts and uncles took them in without informing the mother, and two teachers reportedly told the children they wished they could live with them. At the same time, the Child Protective Unit worker kept her distance from the mother and stepfather, preferring to see only the teenagers and view the situation mostly through their eyes. In effect, all of the helpers in this situation were aligning with the children against their parent(s), giving the message, "Your parents are incompetent and cannot care for you properly."

Intervention in this case focused on the internal structure of the stepfamily, but more significantly on the relationship between the family and the helpers. A series of meetings with those concerned helped to reframe the "bad parents whose children needed protection" as "good people who need all the help they can get to keep their family together." As the helpers began to communicate directly with the mother and her husband about the youths' activities—working *with* the parents rather than against them—the running-away behavior decreased dramatically.

SET LIMITED AND SPECIFIC GOALS

In the face of overwhelming problems, taking things one step at a time can help clients regain a sense of mastery in their lives. The rituals of contracting, setting goals, and reviewing progress in each six-week cycle are designed to engage family members in a clearly defined task in which they are likely to have some success. Few clients have experienced this degree of concreteness in previous dealings with helpers.

Contracting for only six weeks also communicates the expectation that change can occur in a reasonably short period of time. Progress is easier to see when goals are as limited and specific as "Johnny keeping his curfew" or "Mother being able to say 'no' without getting angry or upset." Furthermore, by empowering the parents to decide what the goals will be, the therapist helps them take charge of the situation in a way that supports the structural objective of a workable family hierarchy.

The overall goal of intervention is not to help families self-actualize or communicate openly and honestly, but simply to help them resolve whatever problems they are facing in order to get on with life. Structural changes are never permanent, especially in multiproblem families where dysfunctional configurations can arise repeatedly as adaptations to transitions inside and outside the family. Sometimes problems recur after an apparently successful course of therapy. In one case, for example, the team was able to accomplish the structural objective of helping a disengaged, single-parent mother take charge of her 13-year-old son Larry, who had a habit of stealing. As mother became more effective in parenting, the presenting problem disappeared—but four months after discharge the boy was in trouble again, and the exasperated mother was requesting placement.

In studying this "failure," we learned that Larry's behavior was not all that had changed in the family since discharge. Grandmother had moved next door, mother had begun working an 11 to 7 nightshift, and Larry's biological father, who had returned to the area, was again seeking mother's affection. The single-parent family we had successfully restructured earlier was no longer the family unit. Cases such as this led to a policy that allows families to reapply to the program if they have special problems after discharge. Thus, several "treatment failures" (including Larry's family) may yet experience a more enduring success.

CONSTRUCT WORKABLE REALITIES

Much of therapy consists of reframing the meaning of events and behavior in ways that make change possible (Minuchin & Fishman, 1981; Watzlawick et al., 1974). If a parent paints a picture of an adolescent as impossible since birth, the therapist must somehow redefine the situation as amenable to constructive intervention. For example, when parents view a child as totally out of control, the therapist may accentuate the youth's "immaturity" and the importance of their pulling together to help him or her grow up. It can also be useful to ascribe noble intentions to even the most destructive behavior (Stanton, Todd et al., 1982). Thus, a father may strike his children because he is "frustrated by not being a better parent." Or a youth who destroys property in the community might be "trying to protect his family in some way . . . although [the therapist tells the parents] you don't seem to be the type who need protection."

While reframing may resemble interpretation, its goal is to provoke change rather than provide insight. Reframing messages are used throughout therapy, and can be especially effective during mirror sessions, when reinforced by the supervisor and team.

The principle of constructing workable realities applies equally to helpers. For example, when our own therapists become so enmeshed with a family that the family's reality becomes their own, the supervisor or team is often able to reframe the situation in a way that helps therapist (and family) get unstuck.

USE CRISIS TO PROMOTE CHANGE

The positive side of a family crisis is that it provides an opportunity for reorganization and change. *Families Work* is set up to intervene as close to the time of crisis as

possible, and during therapy, additional smaller-scale crises may be induced deliberately as part of the strategy for helping the family change. The therapist does this by having family members enact a particular problem pattern in the session, then raising the intensity of interaction and "pushing" the pattern to a new resolution.

As a general rule, the first intensity-oriented interventions with a family are implemented during a mirror session, when the team is available for support. In one such session, the identified client was John, a 14-year-old with two juvenile delinquency adjudications for burglary and several PINS petitions. John's mother was aware of his criminal activity, but had taken few steps to set limits for him, despite requests by the judge, the probation officer, and her own husband (John's stepfather) that she do so. The therapist observed that the mother was protecting her son by ignoring stolen goods in the home, hiring an expensive attorney, and on several occasions lying for him. She told outsiders that everything at home was fine, but twice, when tensions were mounting, the mother reported John to the probation officer and requested that the authorities deal with him, putting herself in a position to protect John by fighting for him in court. A similar pattern occurred in the home. When John misbehaved, mother appealed to her husband to provide discipline, which she later felt was too severe. Once again, she was in a position to intercede on John's behalf.

The plan for the mirror session was to challenge mother to disengage from John and set limits on his behavior, with the husband-stepfather in an appropriate supporting role. As the therapist began to do this, the team noticed that the mother closed her eyes each time she told John to do something. Seizing the metaphor, the therapist and supervisor pressed the issue of mother "closing her eyes to John's misbehavior." For most of an hour, they challenged the mother to control her son, and prevented stepfather from coming to her rescue. As intensity rose, mother became angry with John and mentioned some concrete steps she could take to restrict him at home. At this point, the therapists allowed mother to turn to her husband for support, and for the first time, mother and stepfather began to work together on finding ways to supervise John at home.

ENACT CHANGE IN THE SESSION
BEFORE REQUESTING IT AT HOME

The case of John's family illustrates another principle: that change should be planned and rehearsed in the session before the family is asked to try it on their own. Near the end of the same mirror interview, the mother and stepfather decided they should monitor John's behavior very closely until his court appearance three weeks later. The mother came up with the idea of establishing a "detention center at home," which she and the stepfather would supervise together.

The next day therapist and parents rehearsed the details of the arrangement in a session at home, where the plan was to be implemented. When the parents actually began the new regimen, the therapist visited them on a daily basis to monitor progress and support the new family organization. Interestingly, the task channeled mother's closeness to John into constructive limit setting, while the marital dyad evolved a much closer working relationship. Over the next month, signs of John's criminal activity decreased and he was able to stay at home, where he remains one and a half years later.

PROGRAM EVALUATION

We collect data on families before, during, and after their participation in *Families Work*. One reason for careful program evaluation is to demonstrate to board members, funding sources, referring agencies, and the community at large that *Families Work* prevents placements and saves money. The data have also been used to identify characteristics of successful and unsuccessful cases, examine key clinical issues, and test basic assumptions of the clinical model in order to improve the program.

Effectiveness

In the forty-four families discharged as of April 1983, forty-nine of fifty-seven at-risk youths were living at home at the time of discharge and one was with a family friend. Thus, 89 percent had avoided placement. Follow-up data collected during the year after discharge indicated that 90 percent of these youths were not in placement at three months ($N = 49$), 88 percent were not placed at six months ($N = 43$), and 87 percent were not placed at twelve months ($N = 23$).

In terms of the main criteria of avoiding placement, these figures are well within the 70 to 90 percent range claimed by other home-based prevention programs (Lloyd & Bryce, 1980). However, there are several factors that should be considered in interpreting our data. First, the unit of analysis was youth at risk rather than family at risk. Since some families had more than one child at risk, both "success" and "failure" could have occurred in the same family. Second, since our 80–90 percent success rate is based on living arrangements at the time of follow-up, it is also possible that temporary placements may have occurred during the interval between discharge and follow-up. Taking these factors into account gives a more conservative view of outcome, but one which is still quite favorable. If success is recomputed on the basis of whether a family group experiences any placement at any time since discharge, the 90 percent figure for three months shrinks to 81 percent and the six-month figure to 72 percent.

An even more conservative view of outcome might take into account whether the presenting problem recurred, or whether the family had other problems that required community intervention after discharge. If the criterion of negative outcome is expanded to include any recurrence of any presenting problem by any family member (e.g., stealing, truancy, abuse), the success rate drops to 69 percent at three months and to approximately 50 percent at six months. This measure, however, does not account for severity of problem recurrence, only that it did occur. Unfortunately, since there is no untreated control group of families equally at risk and equally motivated to stay together, it is not clear what proportion of our families would have avoided placement or problem recurrence had they not been in the program.

Cost

Cost-effectiveness is best illustrated by comparing the cost of the program to the cost of its alternative—placing children in a foster home, group home, or institution. Referring agencies estimated that of thirty-two at-risk youth seen in the first eight months of the program, thirteen would have been placed in foster homes, twelve in group homes, and seven in institutions. Had all of these anticipated placements happened, the total potential cost would have been $253,082 (per year). The actual cost of *Families Work* during that time was $35,290, with an additional $30,818 spent on youth who actually went into placement after the program. This assumes, of course, that each of the 32 mandated children would have been placed for the entire period, which might not have been the case. But if only three institutional placements had been made, the cost would still have exceeded the cost of *Families Work* for the same time period.[5]

It is also important to note that per diem rates for foster care apply to each child, whereas *Families Work* charges one rate no matter how many children in the family are "at risk." Furthermore, since entire families are seen in their homes, everyone in the family receives services. Of the twenty-three families served during the first eight months, thirty-seven parents, thirty-two mandated "at-risk" youth, and thirty-six nonmandated siblings (a total of 105 people) received family therapy services.

[5]These calculations do not include the cost of after-care services, if any, during the months following discharge from *Families Work*.

Correlates of Outcome

Characteristics of successful and unsuccessful cases have also been studied. Information on the families seen and the treatment they received was entered into a computer data base and correlated with measures of outcome. *Family/case variables* included characteristics of the referral process; prior out-of-home placements; the nature and duration of presenting problems; family composition and living arrangements at the time of intake; and the parents' education, employment status, and problem history. *Treatment variables* included the density of treatment (hours per week); unscheduled contacts and beeper calls; therapists' and family members' expectations of success at the beginning of therapy; their later ratings of goal attainment; the family's cooperation with treatment; and therapist ratings of youth and family-group functioning at the beginning, middle, and end of therapy.

The research strategy centered on determining which of the family, case, and treatment variables predicted placement and problem recurrence after discharge. The two outcome criteria were: (a) whether or not a family experienced placement at any time between discharge and the three-month follow-up interview (19 percent had), and (b) whether or not *any* presenting problem had recurred during the same period (in 31 percent of the cases, one had). Ratings of goal attainment at discharge by therapists and parents were also analyzed as outcome measures, but these did not correlate highly with the criteria of placement and problem recurrence. Statistical analyses were based on thirty-four families for whom complete three-month follow-up data were available.

The following were the main correlates of outcome:

REFERRAL SOURCE

Families referred by the County Probation Department were at greater risk of negative outcome than those referred by the Department of Social Services. The problems presented by probation cases were also more numerous and more severe (e.g., complicated by drug or alcohol abuse), yet of shorter duration, with at-risk youth coming into contact with community agencies at a later age.

PROBLEM PROFILE

Placement and problem recurrence were less likely if the main problem was physical abuse or neglect by a parent (25 percent of the cases) rather than acting-out behavior by a child. On the other hand, better results were obtained when the youth at risk was an adjudicated juvenile delinquent, while PINS cases appear to have been more difficult. In terms of specific presenting problems, alcohol abuse and truancy by the child at risk were most clearly associated with poor outcome, although parents of alcohol-abusing, truant, and runaway youth gave *higher* ratings of improvement at the end of therapy.[6]

FAMILY COMPOSITION

The most favorable outcomes occurred in intact families where the biological parents were married and living together. The worst outcomes, by contrast, were in blended or remarried families, where the probability of placement in three months was over 40 percent, compared to under 10 percent for other types of families. Single-parent families, comprising the largest subgroup, were intermediate. Interestingly, single parents and their therapists gave the lowest rating of goal attainment in the first six weeks of therapy, suggesting that these families may have been the most difficult to engage.

Our failures with blended families have been instructive. In most of these cases the mother and at-risk child(ren) were living with a stepfather who was in conflict with the mother over discipline. A common pat-

tern was one in which the stepfather attempted to exert too much control over the children and the natural mother too little, with (uncontrolled) adolescent behavior and parental conflict escalating to a point where placement seemed necessary to save the marriage. Looking back on our work with these families, we might have given more attention to the unique structural characteristics of stepfamilies. Specifically, the home-based approach focused mainly —and perhaps too narrowly—on members of one household, overlooking the fact that children in blended families usually have significant (if unacknowledged) loyalties to adults living elsewhere. In the past six months, since the program evaluation data have become available, stronger efforts have been made to include absent parents in treatment plans—if only by gaining their permission to work with members of the youth's current household (Montalvo, 1982).

PARENT PROBLEMS

A surprising finding was that youth whose parents had been most overtly dysfunctional in the past were *less* likely to be placed or to relapse after discharge from the program. A parental dysfunction index based on the number of different problem areas the custodial parent(s) had experienced (e.g., drug, alcohol, psychiatric, medical, and legal problems) correlated with both positive outcome at follow-up and goal-attainment ratings at discharge. The specific problem area showing the strongest association with positive outcome was past parental alcohol abuse. (Recall that alcohol abuse by the youth in these families predicted *negative* outcome.) Positive outcome was also more likely if a parent had been placed as a child.

These relationships are difficult to interpret. It is not clear, for example, whether parents who had experienced (and overcome?) problems of their own were able to make better use of the program, whether their willingness to disclose these problems was simply an indication of cooperation with therapy, or whether engaging dysfunctional parents in therapy somehow took the pressure off the youthful symp-

[6]While there were few sex differences generally, drinking problems were more common among girls than boys (50 percent versus 15 percent), whereas boys more often had alcoholic parents (50 percent versus 15 percent).

tom bearer, so that further acting out was no longer as "necessary" to the system.

TREATMENT DENSITY

The density of both treatment (hours per week) and unscheduled contact (beeper calls per week) predicted whether or not placement occurred after discharge. Although all families received intensive services (see footnote 4 above), those receiving the *most* intensive services had the worst outcomes. Of course, these may have just been the most difficult families. Indeed, correlations between treatment density and negative outcome were reduced appreciably (though not reversed) when characteristics of the presenting problem were statistically controlled in a partial correlation analysis.

Interestingly, the density measures did correlate with positive ratings by family members of goal attainment during the first weeks of therapy—although by discharge there was no relationship. The fact that families having more contact with program staff early on felt they were making more progress supports the idea that treatment density and off-hours availability may have facilitated the joining process. On the other hand, these same (well-joined) families were also more likely to require unscheduled crisis intervention and have face-to-face contact with *Families Work* staff after discharge from the program, suggesting that effective joining in the early stages of therapy may make later disengagement more difficult. Other authors note that dependency sometimes develops among clients in intensive home-based programs (Bryce & Lloyd, 1980), and that therapists may have difficulty "letting go" (Haapala & Kinney, 1979). In any case, we now give more attention to termination/disengagement issues in the *Families Work* supervision process, and are exploring ways that the team approach can be used to (re)connect families with supporting resources in the community.

COOPERATION WITH TREATMENT

While seeing families in their homes seems to have enhanced cooperation with treatment, roughly 70 percent of the families did cancel at least one scheduled session, and in half of the cases a family member refused to attend at least one meeting. The frequency of cancelled sessions and refusals to participate correlated modestly with problem recurrence after discharge; however, there was no relationship between outcome and whether or not the family followed through on referral recommendations for other community services after discharge.

CHANGES IN FAMILY FUNCTIONING DURING THERAPY

An important assumption of family therapy is that changes in patterns of family interaction correlate with changes in the presenting problem and outcome. To check this, ratings of family functioning made by therapists at the beginning, middle, and end of treatment were examined in relation to outcome status at follow-up. The family functioning ratings were based on an instrument developed by Bryce (1980), which gives an index of overall family functioning.[7]

In general, changes in family functioning during therapy correlated with outcome in the manner that had been predicted. The families who improved least in their functioning from admission to discharge were more likely to experience placement and problem recurrence later on. Conversely, positive improvement scores were associ-

---

[7]Bryce's scale includes 13 bipolar dimensions such as Trusting Relationships (low versus high), Boundaries (unclear, protected versus clear, safe), Roles (Dysfunctional versus appropriate), and Place in Community (isolated, cut-off versus belonging, involved). Since these dimensions were highly intercorrelated (with one factor accounting for over 60 percent of the common variance), they were summed to give a single index of family functioning.

Correlations between independent ratings of each family made by the therapist and program supervisor following the assessment session(s), and between repeated ratings of the same family made by the therapist, indicate that interrater and test-retest reliabilities for the Bryce instrument, as we used it, were approximately .60.

ated with positive outcome.[8] The relationship between family change and positive outcome is all the more striking because changes from admission to discharge in ratings of the at-risk adolescents' level of functioning were not correlated with outcome.[9] Our results, then, support the idea that changing the functioning of the entire family group is an important ingredient in successful outcome. In fact, changes in family interaction may be even more relevant to avoiding placement than observed changes in the behavior of the at-risk youth.

Also of interest were several variables that did *not* correlate with outcome. First, the duration or chronicity of the presenting problem was unrelated to placement and problem recurrence, although therapists tended to see more improvement when problems were longstanding. Second, outcome had little to do with whether a youth was in placement when therapy began or whether the family had experienced placement previously. Third, therapists' and family members' expectations of improvement, measured at the time of initial goal setting, seemed to have little bearing on what later happened. Fourth, placement and problem recurrence were unrelated to the educational or (un)employment status of the parent(s), although more highly educated parents *and* their therapists gave higher goal-attainment ratings. Finally, success was not correlated with the number of children at risk in a family, which suggests that the program prevented several placements as effectively as one.

Perceptions of Referring Agencies

Another perspective on the program was obtained by surveying the Social Service and Probation Department workers who referred the cases. In May 1982, a program evaluator interviewed by telephone the referral sources for the families who had been seen up until that time. The interview focused on whether the referring caseworkers knew how the program worked, what they saw as it strengths and weaknesses, and how they perceived "outcome" for each of the at-risk youths they had referred. For only four of forty-seven youth (8.5 percent) did the referring worker say there had been "no change" in the presenting problem. For twenty-one youth (44.7 percent), the presenting problem was considered "successfully treated," and for an additional twenty-two (46.8 percent) it was "significantly improved."

At least 80 percent of the ten caseworkers interviewed had a good knowledge of the program. For example, they knew about the six-week contracts, the mirror sessions, the twenty-four-hour beeper service, and that intervention was based on "structural family therapy." While a variety of program strengths were cited, the main criticisms concerned the limited number of cases that could be served by the program at any given time.

[8]This was confirmed through direct comparisons of admission-to-discharge change scores for successful and less successful cases, and through analysis of covariance performed on discharge scores with admission ratings as the covariate. However, since several youths were placed *at* discharge, ratings of family functioning made around the same time may have been influenced by the therapist knowing that placement had occurred. When statistical analyses were repeated with discharge-placement cases excluded, correlations between changes in family functioning and outcome were still significant.

[9]These ratings were based on the Global Assessment Scale (Endicott, Spitzer, Fleiss, & Cohen, 1976), a psychiatric instrument adapted for use with children and adolescents. The GAS yields a single score from 1 to 100 representing an individual's level of functioning. Its interrater and test-retest reliabilities in our project were .62 and .68, respectively.

COMMENT

The experience of *Families Work* indicates that home-based structural family therapy can be an effective modality for adolescent delinquents at risk of out-of-home placement. While other home-based modalities may be equally effective, the advantage of the structural approach is that the family comes sharply into focus as the appropriate unit of assessment and intervention.

Consistent with an eco-systemic orientation, we have given progressively more attention to contextual influences beyond the at-risk household as the program has developed. With stepfamilies, for example, there is now a much stronger emphasis on including absent parents in the treatment plan. And when several therapists or agencies are involved with a case, we are finding that "organizing helpers before families" is the key to successful intervention.

As *Families Work* matures, however, we are also becoming more aware of its limitations. It is clear that the program cannot solve all of a family's problems. To date, about half of the families completing the program have required continuing supportive services after discharge. Yet most of these families have stayed together, and the problems that brought them to the brink of placement, if not eliminated, are at least being managed in the community.

Despite encouraging results, the future of projects such as *Families Work* is uncertain. In New York, where the 1979 Child Welfare Reform Act made possible unprecedented funding of placement-prevention services, increased expenditures have not appreciably reduced the foster-care population. Consequently, cuts in prevention funds are probably inevitable. Part of the problem with mandated prevention is that more youths are being defined as "at risk of placement" so that they will be eligible for services. Yet few of the services provided are either home-based or family-centered. Since the children most clearly "at risk" are those who actually go into placement, a fertile (and fundable) testing ground for family-centered intervention in the future may be reuniting families that are already separated. It will also be necessary to compare approaches that are truly family-centered and/or home-based with those that are not. Only with rigorously controlled outcome studies can the effectiveness of this promising modality be evaluated with any degree of certainty.

REFERENCES

Alexander, J. F., & Parsons, B. W. Short-term behavioral intervention with delinquent families: Impact on family process and recidivism. *Journal of Abnormal Psychology*, 1973, **31**, 219–225.

Aponte, H. Family therapy and the community. In M. Gibbs, J. R. Lachenmeyer, & J. Sigel (Eds.), *Community psychology: Theoretical and empirical approaches*. New York: Gardner Press, 1980.

Auerswald, E. H. Interdisciplinary vs. ecological approaches. *Family Process*, 1968, **7**, 202–215.

Barton, C., & Alexander, J. F. Functional family therapy. In A. S. Gurman, & D. P. Kniskern (Eds.), *Handbook of family therapy*. New York:Brunner/Mazel, 1981.

Bryce, M. E. Home-based care: Development and rationale. In S. Maybanks & M. Bryce (Eds.), *Home-based services for children and families*. Springfield, IL: Charles C. Thomas, 1979.

Bryce, M. *Placement prevention and family unification: Planning and supervising the home-based family centered program*. Oakdale, IA: National Clearinghouse for Home-Based Services to Children (University of Iowa, School of Social Work), 1980.

Bryce, M. E., & Lloyd, J. C. (Eds.) *Treating families in the home: An alternative to placement*. Springfield, IL: Charles C. Thomas, 1980.

Cautley, P. W. Family stress and the effectiveness of in-home intervention. *Family Relations*, 1980, **29**, 575–583. (a)

Cautley, P. W. Treating dysfunctional families at home. *Social Work*, 1980, **29**, 380–386. (b)

Coppersmith, E. I. The family and public service systems: An assessment method. In B. P. Keeney (Ed.), *Assessment in family therapy*. Rockville, MD.: Aspen, 1983.

Dodson, D. Preventive and reunification services. *Legal Response: Child Advocacy and Protection* (Washington: American Bar Association), 1983, **3** (2); 3–5, 16.

Endicott, J., Spitzer, R., Fleiss, J., & Cohen, J. The Global Assessment Scale. *Archives of General Psychiatry*, 1976, **33**, 766–771.

Flomenhaft, K., Kaplan, D.M., & Langsley, D. G. Avoiding psychiatric hospitalization. In G.O. Ericksson & T. P. Hogan (Eds.), *Family therapy: An introduction to theory and technique*. Monterey, CA: Brooks/Cole, 1972.

Gendreau, P., & Ross, R. P. Effective correctional treatment & bibliotherapy for cynics. In R. R. Ross & P. Gendreau (Eds.), *Effective Correctional Treatment*. Toronto: Butterworth, 1980.

Haapala, D., & Kinney, J. Homebuilders' approach to the training of in-home therapists. In S. Maybanks & M. Bryce (Eds.), *Home-based services for children and families*. Springfield, IL: Charles C. Thomas, 1979.

Haley, J. *Leaving home: The therapy of disturbed young people*. New York: McGraw-Hill, 1980.

Haley, J. *Problem solving therapy*. San Francisco: Jossey-Bass, 1976.

Hoffman, L. *Foundations of family therapy*. New York: Basic Books, 1981.

Kinney, J. Homebuilders: An in-home crisis intervention program. *Children Today*, January–February 1978, **35**, 15–17.

Kinney, J., Madsen, B., Fleming, J., & Haapala, D. Homebuilders: Keeping families together. *Journal of Consulting and Clinical Psychology*, 1977, **45**, 667–673.

Lloyd, J. C., & Bryce, M. E. *Home-based family centered services*. Oakdale, IA: National Clearinghouse for Home-Based Services to Children and Their Families, 1980.

Madanes, C. *Strategic family therapy*. San Francisco: Jossey-Bass, 1981.

Madanes, C., & Haley, J. Dimensions of family therapy. *Journal of Nervous and Mental Disease*, 1977, **165**, 889–894.

Maybanks, S., & Bryce, M. *Home-based services for children and families*. Springfield, IL: Charles C. Thomas, 1979.

Minuchin, S. *Families and family therapy*. Cambridge: Harvard University Press, 1974.

Minuchin, S., & Fishman, H. C. *Family therapy techniques*. Cambridge: Harvard University Press, 1981.

Montalvo, B. Interpersonal arrangements in disrupted families. In F. Walsh (Ed.), *Normal family processes*. New York: Guilford, 1982.

Pisani, J. R. *The temporary state commission on child welfare: Final report of the chairman*. Albany: New York State Senate report, March 1982.

Pittman, F. S., DeYoung, C., Flomenhaft, K., Kaplan, D. M., & Langsley, D. G. Crisis family therapy. In R. J. Green & J. L. Framo (Eds.), *Family therapy*. New York: International Universities Press, 1981.

Prevention Report. Oakdale, IA: National Resource Center on Family-Based Services (University of Iowa), Spring 1982.

Prevention Report. Oakdale, IA: National Resource Center on Family-Based Services (University of Iowa), Winter 1982–1983.

Rohrbaugh, M., & Eron, J. The strategic systems therapies. In L. E. Abt, & I. R. Stuart (Eds.), *The newer therapies: A source book*. New York: Von Nostrand–Reinhold, 1982.

Stanton, M. D. Family therapy: Systems approaches. In G. P. Sholevar, R. M. Benson, & B. J. Binder (Eds.), *Treatment of emotional disorders in children and adolescents*. New York: Spectrum, 1979.

Stanton, M. D., Todd, T., et al. *The family therapy of drug addiction*. New York: Guilford, 1982.

Stephens, D. In-home family support services. In S. Maybanks & M. Bryce (Eds.), *Home-based services for children and families*. Springfield, IL: Charles C. Thomas, 1979.

Watzlawick, P., Weakland, J. H., & Fisch, R. *Change: Principles of problem formation and problem resolution*. New York: Norton, 1974.

Weakland, J. H., Fisch, R., Watzlawick, P., & Bodin, A. Brief therapy: Focused problem resolution. *Family process*, 1974, **13**, 141–168.

6

The Care of Critically and Chronically Ill Adolescents in a Medical Setting

JUDITH A. LIBOW, Ph.D.

As psychosocial factors continue to gain recognition as important aspects of the health and illness process, mental-health professionals are becoming increasingly active members of the health-care team. Recent literature indicates that the numbers and visibility of psychologists and related clinicians and researchers have expanded dramatically in such settings as public and private general hospitals, health maintenance organizations, medical schools and pediatric hospitals (Mickel, 1982; Stapp & Fulcher, 1981; Tuma, 1982). This entry into the realm of care traditionally restricted to medical practitioners has allowed for a more comprehensive and effective approach to treatment of a wide range of conditions and types of patients. Mental-health professionals have been able to make significant contributions in such areas as preventive health education, stress reduction, psychosomatic illness, and chronic pain control. But one of the most unique and valuable contributions brought by the mental-health professional to the

health-care setting is that of a broader, systems-wide perspective of the patient both in the family system and in interaction with the larger hospital system. By virtue of training and his or her role as consultant, the mental-health professional can help the patient and medical staff better understand the psychosocial context of the patient's physical symptoms, behavioral problems in the hospital, and the particular difficulties these medical and social behaviors generate for hospital staff.

As in so many other human-service settings, adolescents experience in themselves and stimulate in those around them a number of intense and difficult although predictable issues because of their rapid growth in this transitional period. Adolescents experiencing a sudden critical accident or a chronic and serious illness, as well as the treatment and confinement that follow, are likely to have an even more difficult adjustment than the average adolescent. Serious repercussions for their families, their health-care providers, and the institutions that serve them are virtually unavoidable.

This chapter explores the impact of a critical illness on family development and life-cycle issues, the structural impact on the family, and the effect of hospital subsystem problems on the institutional care of adolescents. Given these very important influences on the adolescent's health care, the goal of this chapter is to define the emerging role of the mental-health consultant in the hospital setting and the value of a systems perspective in this very complex task.

ADOLESCENCE IN THE HEALTH-CARE LITERATURE

A substantial medical, psychiatric, and nursing literature exists elaborating the unique developmental issues of this age group and possible adaptations of medical treatment to meet these needs. In particular, the impact of illness in threatening the adolescent's newly emerging needs for separation and autonomy, intensifying concerns about body image, appearance, and sexuality, and disrupting peer acceptance are among the most prominent themes cited in the literature (Blake & Paulsen, 1981; Brunquell & Hall, 1982; Hughes, 1982; Kaufman, 1972; Ravenscroft, 1982; Schowalter, 1977). While most of the literature is descriptive or anecdotal, some empirical studies have been undertaken. Zeltzer et al. (1980) compared a group of over 300 healthy adolescents with over 100 adolescents with various chronic illnesses. They found that freedom and popularity were most often reported as disrupted for the ill adolescents. Illness seemed to have more of an impact on female patients in terms of feelings about their appearance, and diseases with more uncertain prognoses seemed to provoke the most anxiety and have the greatest overall impact for both sexes. But interestingly, they found that even minor illnesses for the "healthy" control group were experienced as major disruptions with high self-reported impact.

Koocher (1981) studied the more long-range impact of a very serious illness on young adult lives. He studied 117 child-hood cancer survivors who were interviewed an average of 12.44 years after their initial diagnosis. Koocher's group found that the degree of the patient's physical impairment was not related to his or her long-term psychological adjustment. However, cancer survivors often experienced later employment and insurance discrimination which led to increased anxiety and lowered self-esteem. Married patients' spouses often had concerns about their survivor partners' sexual functioning and potential health of progeny.

As in the overall mental-health literature of the past fifty years, the focus of almost all the literature on adolescent illness has been the individual "identified patient" rather than the family system as a larger unit, with the notable exception of the structural family therapists and their work on psychosomatic illnesses (Minuchin, Rosman, & Baker, 1978). In most of the other pediatric/adolescent literature, reference is often made to the significant impact of a child's illness on his or her parents, sibling(s), or family, and there have been some excellent reviews (for example, McKeever's [1983] work on the psychosocial effects on siblings of chronically ill children). But the elaboration of these issues on a family systems level, discussion of systems approaches to treatment during the course of pediatric/adolescent illness and the application of family therapy concepts to the young person in the hospital setting have yet to be explored in any depth. A somewhat better beginning has been made in the discussion of the hospital as a system and the impact of its institutional rigidity, interstaff competition, interdisciplinary conflict, and hospital cultural procedures and rituals on young patients and their families (Hofmann, Becker, & Gabriel, 1976; Johnston, 1981; Marten & Mauer, 1982).

It is interesting to note that the most prevalent family systems–oriented literature that does exist focuses on the family's reaction to the death of a child. Several authors have directly addressed the impact of the death of a member on the family system as a whole, both experimentally (Videka-Sherman, 1982; Williams, Lee, & Polak, 1976) and by case study (Herz, 1980;

Hare-Mustin, 1979; Tietz, McSherry, & Britt, 1977). A number of articles have also addressed the effect on children of the death of their sibling (Cain, Fast, & Erickson, 1964; Feinberg, 1970; Krell & Rabkin, 1979). A more extensive literature is available on the family impact of a child's death rather than on a child's chronic or critical illness for a number of reasons, including the fact that it is only relatively recently that young people with very serious illnesses such as cystic fibrosis or cancer had the opportunity of long survival. The study of Spinetta and Deasy-Spinetta (1981) detailing the impact of childhood cancer on over 250 children and family members is a good start in the direction of studying the psychological and family adjustment of seriously ill patients while they are still living and actively interacting with the health-care system.

This chapter will explore in more depth the reciprocal effects of hospitalization, the crisis of illness, and the adolescent patient's family system in order to look more closely at issues the hospital practitioner will face when consulting in health-care settings. Effective and meaningful approaches can only be designed when the adolescent patient's crisis is understood in its broader contexts.

ILLNESS AS A FAMILY DEVELOPMENTAL CRISIS

The concept of a "Family Life Cycle" (Duvall, 1977; Carter & McGoldrick, 1980) is a useful developmental approach to the predictable change processes and growth experienced by most families over the course of their years together as a living unit. This cycle, no matter which labeling system is used to compartmentalize it into sequences of normative tasks and "crises" for the family, follows the development of the family unit from a couple's courtship through their parenting years and into retirement. Concepts of the family life cycle are based on the changing ages and developmental needs of both children and adults, as well as changing demands by external forces and crises as the family matures.

Among the many predictable phases of the family that require particular strength and flexibility within the system is the adolescent period. This is often one of the most tempestuous and difficult periods for the family unit to weather. It can well be termed a "crisis," due both to the extremes of pressure it exerts on the adolescent and his or her parents in terms of new behaviors demanded, and to the special issues of autonomy, separation, and sexuality that are intensely highlighted for all members of the family. As the adolescent pushes the limits, imports ideas and language from the outside world, forces adjustments in family rules, and brings sensitive issues to the surface, the rest of the family is equally challenged. Parents are forced to redefine their own marital relationship to adjust to more separation from their teenager. The family positions of younger siblings are shifted as the balance of power and the adolescent's family role changes. More attention to issues of appearance and sexuality affect other members of the family.

Serious illness in a child or adolescent is a significant and unusual stress on the family that in itself constitutes a major crisis at any time in the life cycle. When it is superimposed upon the adolescent phase of the family life cycle, it can interact with the simultaneously emerging issues of autonomy and sexuality to unbalance or seriously threaten even the most competent, intact family. Both long-term, chronic illness in the adolescent and sudden, serious illness or accidents can have a devastating impact on the developmental unfolding of adolescence and the family's ability to respond appropriately.

Barnhill and Longo (1978) have conceptualized that the family system as a unit can become fixated at a life-cycle stage or even regressed to an earlier, inappropriate level of functioning when a crisis or special stress obstructs the family in its transition between life-cycle stages. Surely the intense emotional stress, uncertainty, disruptive hospitalizations, dashed hopes of future potential, and changing swings of patient needs such as separation-closeness and independence-dependence have the potential for severe disruption of the family's progression along its life-cycle development. Although some realistic alterations of the usual adolescent adjustments will have to be made, it is very important for the family to progress into the adolescent life-cycle phase, for the sake of both the patient and all members of the system. Regression to latency-age phase functioning may be called for at some points in the patient's hospitalization, but it cannot help but impede the healthy functioning of the other siblings as well as the adolescent patient him or herself as the patient's needs inevitably change over time.

Chronic Illness

In the case of chronic illnesses often diagnosed at younger ages such as cystic fibrosis, juvenile rheumatoid arthritis, sickle cell anemia, and cancer, the youngster learns to cope with an unpredictable world of a vulnerable body, frequent hospitalizations, episodic pain, and in some conditions, the spectre of possible death. The necessary dependence on medical personnel and medication, restrictions on activity and mobility, and the almost unavoidable protectiveness of family members not only make dependence-autonomy a constant issue for the chronically ill child and parents, but also often inhibit the adolescent's ability to develop a network of healthy peers. At the same time, these issues seriously complicate his or her ability or motivation to think about self in terms of future parenthood or careers. If one considers how difficult the patient role and physical dependence on nursing staff can be—even to many healthy adults (presumably secure in their autonomous functioning) enduring a brief hospitalization—its meaning can assume epic proportions to a seriously, chronically ill fourteen-year-old. A youngster at this age is beginning to grow very sensitive and modest about his body, wants some sense of control and ability to "do for himself," and worse yet, sees no end in sight for his perpetual patienthood.

Given that this chronically ill adolescent has limited access to the tools and activities used by his peer culture to challenge and differentiate from adults, it is no wonder that he often finds ways to act out his frustration and anger within the hospital system. Among the few options available to the seriously ill, bedridden adolescent are noncompliance with medical procedures/treatments (e.g., refusing physical examinations, pulling out intravenous lines) and depressed or provocative verbal behavior. Both these expressions of frustrated autonomy needs often have the unfortunate paradoxical effect of increasing the surveillance and intrusions on the adolescent, thus escalating the crisis. As the teenager begins to refuse his medication while home, for example, his dependent contacts with parent and medical center are actually increased; as the adolescent on the ward starts verbally attacking nursing staff or refusing to be examined, there are often increased efforts to coerce the young adult into dependent interactions with staff. If the more basic autonomy and generativity issues of the adolescent are not recognized and directly addressed in some way, there will be destructive battles ahead.

Acute Illness

The adolescent who is stricken suddenly with a serious accident, such as a near-drowning or auto-pedestrian accident, or serious illness, such as Reyes syndrome or herpes encephalitis, must contend with a somewhat different type of crisis. For chronically ill adolescents, their autonomy and sexuality issues emerged gradually as they and their chronic condition slowly passed through earlier developmental stages on the path to adolescence. Patients and their families had some time to test out various ways of adapting the demands of the treatment and the family's interactional style to the growth needs of the adolescent. In the best of circumstances, perhaps over time, they found ways of allowing the adolescent some modified increases in autonomous functioning within the limitations of their condition. The acutely stricken adolescent and his or her family, on the other hand, are hurtled into the frightening, unfamiliar world of the intensive care unit or hospital floor without warning or preparation. Often the first several weeks after hospitalization offer greater uncertainty than for the chronic patient accustomed to the usual treatment, as the acutely stricken family awaits news of whether their six-teen-year-old will come out of coma, their twelve-year-old will regain movement in his legs, or their fifteen-year-old daughter is ever likely to breathe independently of the respirator. The degree and extent of permanent impairment is often the pri-mary concern for all family members. The threat to the adolescent's body image and sexual identity are also often major con-cerns of the family.

Loss of limbs or body function can result in a serious regression to more infantile and dependent behavior by the teenager; the sudden short-circuiting of the young-ster's expected developmental progression (either through death or serious perma-nent loss) can provoke a severe shock to the family. Even in cases of only temporary loss of function (e.g., temporary inability to eat or open eyes due to severe facial burns, brief confinement to a wheelchair due to a neurological insult), the threat to the adolescent's sense of her- or himself as a physically intact and competent person can be so severe that even a brief disability can be experienced as a permanent and ter-rifying loss that is mourned as intensely as any permanent disability.

As the acute phase resolves itself and the adolescent patient enters the rehabilitative stage, many of the issues of the chronically ill adolescent (protracted dependence, un-certainty as to future hopes, etc.) are also visited upon the acute patient, with its see-saw life-style of periodic improvement and deterioration resulting in frequent returns to the hospital or to the family physician's office.

STRUCTURAL IMPACT OF ILLNESS ON THE FAMILY SYSTEM

The serious illness of a child can have significant impact on the structure of the family system itself, in addition to the in-dividual meaning and developmental im-pact of the illness on separate family members and the family life cycle. In struc-tural family systems terms, the illness pro-cess can precipitate dramatic disruptions in family *boundaries* and family *coalitions*.

As defined by Salvador Minuchin (1974), "boundaries" refer to the rules defining how different family members and sub-systems participate in family interactions. The function of boundaries is to protect the differentiation of the system (or subsys-tem) and its freedom from interference by other subsystems. The external boundaries of the family system can be thought of as invisible but implicit rules defining the family's interaction with the world outside the nuclear unit, including in-laws, neigh-bors, school, work, and governmental sys-tems. These external boundaries serve the purpose of helping the family to function as a differentiated, somewhat autonomous unit which serves as a "refuge from the multiple demands of life" (Minuchin, 1974, p. 57).

"Coalitions," in structural family ther-apy terms, refer to alliances between in-dividual family members, generally across subsystem boundaries, which often serve to undermine the effectiveness of subsys-tem functioning. Because these dimen-sions of family functioning are rarely labeled, discussed, or even openly recognized by families, structural disruptions can be the most elusive and destructive to the overall functioning of the sick adolescent's family.

External Boundaries

Both chronically and seriously acutely ill adolescents spend a great deal of time in the hospital and in medical settings. While the former tend to have a greater number of hospitalizations spaced sporadically over long periods of time and the latter tend to have fewer in-patient stays but possibly of longer duration and intensity, the hospi-talization experience in either case inher-ently forces certain changes that threaten the integrity of a family's external bound-aries. The seriously ill child is forced into an intense and intimate relationship with the new extended family system of the hos-pital world. Both chronically ill and intensive-care-level acute patients tend to have greater continuity of nursing and medical staff than the routine medical/surgical patients. In a relatively short period of time they become absorbed into what can be thought of as a new family, complete with new "parents" (primary nurse and/or physician), "siblings" (fellow patients), and "aunts and uncles" (additional nurses and ancillary staff). Not only do these new "family members" relate to the adolescent patient in parentified caretaking and protective roles, but the relationships of the health-care team are also clearly structured in a system with identifiable boundaries, subsystems, coalitions, and interactional rules of their own, which the adolescent patient, although seriously ill, still quickly manages to comprehend.

Thus, the adolescent patient's acute or chronic entry into the hospital "family system" is bound to have repercussions for the family system at home. The family's external boundary is forced to accommodate the intrusion of hospital staff's frequent directives, communications, and investigations of routines and behaviors practiced at home. The authority of medical staff to dictate to the family new procedures, equipment, schedules, and ways of interacting with their patient in the hospital and home clearly blurs the family's external boundary system. It may be analogous to the meddling grandmother or father-in-law who maintains frequent contact with the family and generously volunteers advice on childrearing that is often unsolicited and difficult for the parental subsystem to challenge. The parents' sense of competence and authority, not to mention their ability to protect their child adequately from pain and deterioration, can also be seriously undermined by the parents' dependence on medical staff. The parents must not only rely on the staff to treat their teenager competently as the physicians make their decisions on a rapid-fire basis, but they are also dependent on the most fundamental level for interpretation of the frightening symptoms, medication reactions, and hospital procedures unfolding before their eyes as they helplessly stand at their teenager's bedside.

Thus, parents are virtually forced to loosen their control of their family unit's external boundary with the outside world as they find themselves increasingly dependent on the hospital system as an extended family.

In other concrete ways, the family's integrity and protective space can also be threatened by the physical intrusion into the home of symbols of their child's attachment to the medical system. Portable equipment, such as intravenous lines and suctioning equipment, and visiting nursing staff were no doubt designed to enhance parents' control of their child's illness by shortening the hospital stay and allowing more care by family members in their own home. Yet it is paradoxical that the entry of these innovations into the home also represents the ultimate violation of the physical boundaries of the family as a safe haven that is independent of the hospital system.

Finally, the family's external boundary is also threatened by the inevitably public nature of their adolescent's status as patient. Suddenly there are other parents and families in the hospital and neighborhood inquiring about their child, as well as overtures from innumerable social-service agencies and parent support groups. In cases of tragic accidents or terminal illness, the nuclear family is often the focus of neighborhood fund-raising efforts, news stories in the press, and/or renewed involvement with previously distant extended family. Many of these social supports can be welcome and highly useful adjuncts to the family's coping resources; yet it must also be recognized that in conjunction with the impact of the family's entry into the medical-care system, these factors add up to a massive assault on the family's integrity as a contained, differentiated "refuge" with parental subsystem firmly and confidently at the helm.

Internal Boundaries

The boundaries between subsystems of the family unit itself are also subject to severe strain when the adolescent is critically or chronically ill. In structural family therapy terms, a well-functioning family system requires a well-bounded parental subsystem that is separate from, yet accessible to, the well-bounded subsystem of siblings. Yet the practical demands of the sick child's entanglement in the health-care system can severely test the limits of these subsystem strengths and their within-family boundaries.

In the case of the chronically ill adolescent, the prolonged vulnerable and threatened status of the child (particularly when the chronic illness, such as cystic fibrosis or sickle cell disease, can be terminal) cannot help but intensify the bond of this child with the most involved parent. This caretaker, generally the mother, is most intimately involved in the daily care of the sick teenager, the daily details of the hospitalization, and the intense emotional experience of this vulnerable child. This may be particularly true of the adolescent patient whose chronic illness was identified in early childhood when mother (or most involved parent figure) was most likely to spend weeks and months at the bedside of the seriously ill child. It is not simply a matter of an "overprotective" maternal style that can develop, but an intensely enmeshed mother-child relationship in which child and parent become emotionally overreactive and poorly differentiated as individuals. Given the exhausting demands for parental vigilance regarding the child's symptoms and needs for care, the greater degree of time spent together, and the extremes of suffering shared by parent and child, it is little wonder that so many chronically ill children and their parents find themselves in highly enmeshed relationships as adolescence approaches. Yet as issues of autonomy and sexuality begin to emerge, the adolescent patient finds himself or herself at the developmental stage where a previously rather comfortable enmeshment with mother becomes quite conflictual. It will require a sensitive, adaptive parent as well as a great deal of support for the adolescent patient for the youngster to find a comfortable resolution of his adolescent autonomy needs with his illness-related dependency needs.

Despite the physical weakness and emotional neediness of the ill adolescent, it is ironic that these youngsters often find themselves drawn into a protective, caretaking role with mother (or closest caretaker) as they become increasingly enmeshed with this person. These adolescents can derive a great deal of support from mother and sense of potency and importance in their emotional caretaker role, but it can be heartbreaking to witness a sick and suffering child placing the needs of parent(s) before his or her own. For example, a sensitive and enmeshed child may well comprehend that mother is not yet ready to let go of her own denial and openly deal with the fact of her child's hopeless situation. Thus, a sixteen-year-old terminally ill, rapidly deteriorating patient may find herself struggling to contain her own anger and fear because she is unwilling, for her mother's sake, to acknowledge the fact of her own impending death.

The reverberations of the mother-child coalition that can be cemented by serious illness extend to the rest of the family. Father, lover, grandmother, or mother's most "significant other" may feel excluded from an appropriate degree of time and physical and/or emotional closeness with mother as they find her continually at the hospital. They realize that she seems more attached and intimate with her teenager. Many couples with other resources, flexibility, and sufficient awareness of the dangers will manage to weather these stresses on the parental subsystem, particularly when these shifting alliances are episodic and coincide with medical crises. In other families, the exclusion of father/boyfriend or other adult from appropriate attachment to mother can result in severe splits in the family, including eventual marital dissolution or formation of inappropriate coalitions such as an alliance of the father with a remaining well sibling.

The intense involvement of mother with hospitalized child may not necessarily erode the marital relationship if mother is a single parent or father prefers a disengaged parental subsystem. However, what may result is the long-term destructive disengagement of one or both parents from well siblings at home. Particularly in the case of younger siblings, either the chronic or suddenly intense loss of parent(s) to their critically ill adolescent sibling can be experienced as frightening and depriving. It can also be fraught with guilt as they perhaps find themselves wishing the sick sibling dead or otherwise long for mother's emotional return. In some cases, siblings may begin exhibiting their own behavioral or physical symptomatology in a bid for their fair share of parental interest and energies, which may only backfire in further parental rejection and exhaustion. Research has also indicated that siblings of seriously ill patients may suffer less visible but equally damaging effects such as lowered self-esteem, cognitive impairment, and emotional distancing from parents (Spinetta & Deasy-Spinetta, 1981).

In more adaptive situations, the well sibling may be able to strengthen the sibling subsystem and find creative ways of meeting each others' needs through the crisis. There are cases in which parents make efforts to incorporate the well sibling(s) into hospital life in order to preserve the integrity of the sibling bond. For example, in one family, the seventeen-year-old brother of a fourteen-year-old who had suffered a spinal-cord injury in an automobile accident was given the role of brother's daily homework tutor. As long as these task assignments do not put an excessive caretaking burden on siblings, they can be useful ways of preventing the breakdown of the sibling subsystem and the destructive, exclusive coalitions of patient and parent which take their toll on all family members.

Cases of terminal illness may be particularly unbalancing to the family system because the situation forces at least two major disruptive periods. Not only is the family subject to the stresses on family boundaries and changes in coalitions during the often long period of the terminal child's physical decline, but the period after the child's death once again destabilizes the family structure that had evolved in response to the illness. The removal of the sick adolescent is one additional and massive shift for the family system to endure.

INTERACTIONS WITHIN THE HOSPITAL SYSTEM

Because of its extensive network of interdependent members, roles, work functions, communication pathways, and lines of authority, the accomplishment of high-quality patient care is dependent on the healthy and effective functioning of the huge metasystem known as the hospital. As in the nuclear family unit, the hospital system's effectiveness and viability can be analyzed along structural lines in terms of the functioning of its subsystems, boundaries, and interactional patterns. When a seriously ill child enters this hospital system for an extended period of time, the patient and family unit cannot help but become another component that has to accommodate to the numerous other subsystems within this structure, including nursing staff, medical staff, social work staff, administration, other patient families, and specialists. Like any extended family, the hospital's subsystems can serve as helpful resources to the nuclear family, or can function to complicate and undermine the family subsystem.

The degree to which the hospital system itself maintains clear and functional boundaries between its subsystems, finds mechanisms to limit destructive coalitions, and adapts to changing developmental needs of its members will largely determine its effectiveness and value to its patient families as well as its professional staff.

Staff-Patient Coalitions

One of the potentially destructive types of coalitions that can develop when an adolescent patient enters the hospital system is that of an alliance between a health-care provider and patient which emotionally excludes the parent. The adolescent developmental stage is typically a stormy and conflictual one for many people, and can have repercussions long into early adulthood. There seems to be a particular vulnerability for the young nurse, medical resident, or other health-care provider to become overidentified with certain types of adolescent patients. Terminal illnesses and conditions affecting appearance, adolescent body image, and sexuality are particularly immediate and anxiety-provoking issues for the young health-care provider. The adolescent patient's struggles with accepting his illness and coping with his own grief, anger, and helplessness may at times, with the collusion of a staff member, become inappropriately channeled into a struggle for autonomy from the patient's parent or an unconscious coalition to defeat the "bad parent." Parents who are particularly vulnerable to the "bad parent" label are those who visit their child in the hospital less frequently than the norm, criticize or discipline their child in what is perceived as an overly harsh or infantilizing manner, or appear excessively anxious, controlling, or disinterested to staff. While these staff observations are often quite accurate and meaningful to overall patient care, overworked and stressed health-care providers generally do not have the time or the skills to explore the meaning of these behaviors or their possible cultural and psychological determinants. Thus, there is always the risk that disapproving observations of and attitudes toward parents will be acted out destructively rather than utilized in the overall context of the family's treatment.

In more benign cases, negative attitudes about the child's parent may be shared among hospital staff but controlled through open discussion and monitoring by alert and sensitive supervisors. Nursing supervisors in particular seem to be well trained and experienced in handling the milder forms of parent scapegoating that can inhibit optimal parent-nurse collaboration.

If the nurse (generally the provider who is most intimately and emotionally involved with the patient) is less conscious of his or her attitudes toward the parent, the coalition with the adolescent may take more overt forms, such as allowing adolescent behaviors and routines (e.g., using profanity, eating forbidden foods, or keeping late bedtime hours) that are specifically disapproved by the parent. The parent may be excluded through the selective release of information, when a provider chooses to share critical information first with the adolescent or with the less involved parent before it reaches the more involved parent. There are also ways in which decision-making power can be used to include or exclude a parent, as when information about whether or not to proceed with experimental medication or try a risky surgical procedure is manipulated in such a way that the "bad" parent is given no real choice to make.

Finally, even seemingly innocuous acts of kindness or attachment toward the patient need to be explored carefully for their impact on the parent–child bond. Even with the most benign motivation, the possibility exists that these gestures may be experienced by the sensitive parent as a violation of parental prerogative. Expensive gifts given by nursing or medical staff to seriously ill adolescents such as video games and tape recorders or specially arranged trips to amusement parks or visits to the homes of staff members can be very threatening to a parent. This is particularly true when the parent is not included in these decisions or has a low income and is acutely aware of being unable to provide these gifts him- or herself. A further complication arises when a parent is already involved in some emotional parent-child struggle with a teenager, and experiences these unexpected gifts as poorly timed rewards that undermine the parents' position.

In the case of Anna, a critically ill, long hospitalized daughter, nursing staff went to great lengths to provide a lively, well-attended seventeenth birthday party for the patient—probably the last birthday she would experience. Anna's father, who worked long hours at a considerable distance from the hospital, was invited to the party but had been given a very peripheral role to play in its planning. The father's feelings of alienation and resentment resulted in Anna being forced to return most of the birthday gifts on his insistence that they were too expensive and inappropriate. The nursing staff and the disappointed patient were left regretting the whole incident.

Thus, it is critically important for the nursing and medical subsystems to be appropriately allied with the parental subsystem, in order to spare the adolescent from unwitting entrapment in a coalition against a parent. Despite the relevance of autonomy issues for the adolescent patient, the seriously and/or terminally ill teenager is in desperate need of emotional support from parent(s) and cannot afford to drive them away.

Parent-Child Coalitions

There are also cases in which the adolescent and his or her parent may join in a coalition that threatens the family's cooperative working relationship with one or more hospital workers. This is more likely to occur when parents have preexisting emotional problems. These parents may find it useful to control their anger and helplessness regarding the disease process and perhaps a host of other personal issues by depositing their anger, guilt, or feelings of worthlessness on a particular doctor, nurse, or other provider. While a parent may actually distrust or experience anger toward physicians in general, the unavoidable dependence of the parent of a critically ill child on the medical system makes it much more functional to focus negative feelings on a limited number of "bad" service providers. Given the extensive array of medical specialists called upon to treat a seriously ill patient and the numerous shifts of nurses and daily ward personnel coming in contact with the adolescent patient, it is not surprising that some staff members will be experienced as less caring or competent or will be associated in the parent's or child's mind with the patient's deteriorating condition. When the parent handles his or her doubts and negative feelings by sharing them with the young patient, or accepts the youngster's emotional reactions at face value and readily joins in the condemnation of a particular health-care provider, a potential exists for destructive acting-out by the adolescent with the overt or covert approval of the parent. For example, the sudden or gradually emerging noncompliant behavior of a previously cooperative adolescent patient must not automatically be handled as denial of the medical condition or misguided efforts at greater independence from the hospital system. A possibility to be considered is that the youngster may be acting out the despair of a parent or expressing the parent's fading confidence in a particular treatment and the hope for a cure or remission.

For example, Steven was a sixteen-year-old boy with a serious and chronic renal condition, being maintained as an outpatient on a regimen of fifty pills a day to prevent future renal failure. It became clear that this young man was extremely inconsistent in, and resistant to complying with his medication. His single father expressed bafflement and despair about gaining his son's cooperation despite the fact that this chronic noncompliance was becoming life threatening. A number of individual approaches to this patient, including an attempt at individual therapy, were unsuccessful until Steven's father was brought in for family sessions. Father revealed for the first time that his own wife had died several years earlier from an overdose of prescription medications mixed with alcohol. Although he "trusted" his son's doctor and encouraged the boy to take his pills, he secretly feared that the doctors again might be "making a mistake." It was not until these feelings and the son's respectful cooperation with his father's fears were brought to the surface and challenged that Steven became free to take better care of his own medical needs.

Another form of inappropriate parent-child coalition may emerge as a joining strategy by parent and child to diffuse their own struggle over such issues as autonomy or to compensate for a parent's feelings of helplessness and guilt at not being able to take adequate care of his or her own child.

Samuel was a hospitalized eighteen-year-old patient with chronic respiratory disease who had a very vocal and controlling mother. He rather suddenly began having daily conflicts with the regular day nurse with whom he had previously worked well for three years. He began complaining about her intrusiveness, laziness, and tendency to "baby" him. Samuel's mother, in a rare show of solidarity with her son, joined in his insistence on the assignment of a different nurse. The rejected nurse, who had prided herself on her sensitive relationship with this patient, was hurt and humiliated by this turn of events. The psychological consultant realized that this joint maneuver by mother and son was a technique the family had discovered to distract themselves from their own conflicts over autonomy by projecting onto this nurse issues that seemed too threatening for them to confront head on. The nurse was temporarily able to remove herself from the case, hopeful that the mother-son issues would gradually be addressed as the pair seemed able to tolerate it, with the help of mental-health intervention.

Triangulated Patients and Families

Another destructive indication of dysfunction within the hospital system is the phenomenon of warring professional subsystems. With the complexity of individuals with overlapping job functions who must continually work cooperatively to offer the best, most efficient care to a large caseload of stressed and stressful patients, it is no wonder that treatment disagreements and interpersonal conflicts within the hospital staff occur daily. These problems can be dealt with through a number of channels, including interdisciplinary staff meetings, psychological consultation, the use of supervisory mediation, and, as a last resort, reluctant compliance with traditional lines of authority.

However, as in a marriage between two strong-willed partners, the inevitable conflicts between the "parents" (in our case, two professionals or groups involved in a child's care), if left unresolved and unbounded, have the potential of spilling over into the care of the child/patient and trapping him between these two parties. This is analogous to the triangulation process described by Bowen (1978) in which two persons in a relationship who are subjected to increased internal stresses from within or outside their relationship have a tendency to emotionally involve a third, vulnerable party. The involvement of this third party tends to dilute the anxiety and help stabilize the twosome. The hospitalized child and his/her family are quite vulnerable to involvement in the conflicts between caregivers, particularly when the

patient's care is the ostensible or actual focus of the conflict. This process can be quite subtle, and can find reflection in behavioral problems exhibited by the patient. The danger is that attention may be focused on the family as the identified problem rather than on the actual subsystem conflict.

In the case of Sarah, a twelve-year-old patient who was terminally ill with cancer, a mental-health referral was made by the ward staff who expressed concern that this child was eating poorly and grandmother (Sarah's primary parent) was observed to be screaming at the child and engaging in coercive struggles to make her eat. This child was on one of her many courses of radiation for her advancing tumors. She was vomiting frequently and was seriously endangered by her marginal body weight in combination with her vulnerable overall condition. While the child-grandmother eating battle certainly was disturbing to all parties and was not helping this child gain weight, an interdisciplinary meeting involving members of nursing, nutrition, and housestaff revealed a number of intense conflicts underlying Sarah's treatment. The youngster's private pediatrician felt that the nutritional problem was sufficiently serious to warrant moving from oral feeding to intravenous hyperalimentation. Several of the residents, with the support of the attending physician, were working to avoid hyperalimentation at all costs until it was an absolute last resort, and felt that vigorous enforcement of eating by mouth was psychologically preferable. Many of the nursing staff not only felt that oral feedings were never going to provide sufficient calories but were also angry that Sarah was being subjected to yet another course of radiation, given its very poor probability of success. Finally, two of the three nurses most intimately involved in the daily care of this child (and grandmother) admitted that they were having personal difficulty setting firm limits on Sarah's oral intake. They hated to engage in further battles with this young girl when she was already suffering so much from her illness and constant nausea. Meanwhile, the one primary nurse firmly supporting the eating-limits program was feeling undermined because Sarah informed her that the day and night shift nurses were not being as "mean" to her about forcing her to eat.

In the context of this highly conflicted field, it is small wonder that child and grandmother were receiving contradictory messages and became drawn into the center of this storm. As a consequence of their "triangulation," the family subsystem began acting out their own drama involving food and were only able to stop fighting about eating issues when the staff sorted through their own conflicts and emerged with a consistent treatment strategy. It also became obvious that for child, grandmother, and all staff involved, the focus on the eating problem had become a convenient but unacknowledged symbol of frustration and despair about this child's survival.

It is clear even from this one example that the treatment of any seriously ill patient requires frequent alterations in treatment strategy that must be individualized to the rapidly changing needs of each patient. There is often room for significant difference of opinion among medical and nursing staff as to choice of treatment and timing of certain decisions, especially when the consequences of these decisions can be life-threatening or can engender increased pain and suffering. When these decisions involve critically ill patients, particularly young patients with whom many staff have developed long-term "parental" relationships, there is likely to be an element of emotional investment, active disagreement, and anxiety about these decisions. Families become highly sensitive to the communications they receive from their caregivers and will quickly respond to any indication of uncertainly, disapproval, or noncooperation among significant health-care team members. When staff members cannot find the time or the means to contain their own anxieties and conflicts, the emergence of behavior problems in the adolescent or family unit often signals a serious dysfunction in the larger system.

THE ROLE OF THE MENTAL-HEALTH PROFESSIONAL

As can be seen from the previous discussion of developmental, structural, and systemic implications of an adolescent's illness and hospitalization, the hospital-based mental-health professional has an impor-

tant role to play as a member of the total health-care team. As a service provider trained in working with systems such as the family and larger institutions, and with the rather unique role of "floater" among several units and specialty services within the hospital, the mental-health professional can bring a more neutral and integrated perspective to other members of the health-care team. By their very training and job function, medically trained members of the health-care team tend to be more specialized in treating circumscribed aspects of the patient.

Clarification of the Consultation Request

Regardless of the actual nature of a consultation request for mental-health involvement, there are two major decision points essential to the design of an effective intervention. The initial and most critical step in the mental-health professional's approach to a consultation request is the clarification of the nature and focus of the "problem." Just as family therapists very quickly learned that they could not take at face value the labeled "identified patient" child as the source of the family problem, clinicians working in medical settings have found that "identified patient" consultation requests must be explored thoroughly before a treatment approach is designed. The first step, of course, is a thorough discussion with the referring physician, nurse, parent, social worker, or interested party to clarify the nature, history, duration, specific precipitants, and context of the behavioral problems they are encountering with the adolescent patient and/or family. Sometimes rather simple suggestions and reassurance to staff about normal developmental responses to illness and hospitalization are more effective and efficient interventions than the automatic commencement of direct patient-oriented therapeutic intervention.

For example, a group of nurses originally requested psychotherapy for Raymond, a fifteen-year-old patient with third-degree burns on his trunk who was creating a great deal of stress and anger in the nursing staff by his demanding, angry, and verbally abusive behavior. A discussion with the nurses revealed that this young man was in a great deal of pain, was angry about the circumstances of his accident, and required frequent treatments from his nurses which were extremely painful for him to receive and emotionally draining for the nurses to administer. The staff was reassured that Raymond's screams and anger were quite appropriate to his situation rather than signs of maladjustment or psychopathology. They were also encouraged to set consistent guidelines for verbal behaviors they would tolerate (screaming, expressions of pain and anger) and those they would *not* accept (swearing directly at nurses, intolerant demands). The staff was highly relieved to have some forum for discussing their feelings about this stressful case and for sorting out the limits of appropriate and inappropriate patient behaviors. This allowed the reframing of this problem, from "Raymond's mental illness" to a staff tolerance and limit-setting issue.

Beyond the clarification of the referral request, it is important to seek out information and feelings about the identified patient from a number of other sources, including staff with similar job functions as the referral source and other professionals involved in the case. This helps to clarify whether the problem is situation-specific, unique to a certain kind of caregiver, or perhaps a more personal issue of the referral source. The mental-health professional might question whether the night shift is observing the same depressed and withdrawn behavior as the day shift. He or she might try to determine whether a child's refusal to be examined by certain physicians might be related to their manner of obtaining cooperation from the child, or whether the refusal might stem from the child's reactions to such provider characteristics as sex or ethnic group. Again, in some cases, surprisingly simple changes of procedure or personnel can avert more major crises.

Often a very useful intervention in working within a complex system is the use of emergency interdisciplinary meetings on a target patient as a forum for re-defining a "problem," avoiding rumors, confronting differences of approach, and develop-

ing a consistent plan for a particular behavioral problem. These plans should be cleared with the most critical caregivers if they cannot be in attendance at the meeting and clearly written up in the nursing notes as well as posted in the child's room (if a behavioral contract with the child is developed) to ensure awareness and cooperation from all relevant parties.

Another approach involves the mental-health professional calling and attending special meetings to mediate problems between a parent and a particular staff member, or between two professionals who are having interpersonal difficulties involving treatment of a particular child. In other cases, making simple recommendations for structural changes (such as requesting a change of physical therapist, having only one nurse give the daily injections, or rearranging the hours of a child's treatment schedule) can directly address a problematic situation and prevent it from escalating.

Finally, mental-health professionals have an educational role to play, particularly when they encounter similar issues in several cases. Regularly scheduled talks and case conferences illustrating common psychological issues in the hospital setting as well as brief, informal discussions on an ad hoc basis are important contributions offered by the mental-health consultant.

Choice of Direct Intervention

If the mental-health professional has received a consultation request, clarified and defined the problem, and determined that the situation requires more than consultation with staff, a careful examination of the adolescent individually and in the family context is necessary. It is at this point that the adolescent is assessed as to his or her level of emotional and cognitive development, achievement of appropriate adolescent milestones, and the impact of the chronic disease process or acute medical crisis on this youngster's physical and social development. The mental-health professional can coach other involved providers (such as the physician) or can him- or herself address common adolescent developmental issues concerning illness with the patient in supportive and therapeutic ways. Helping the child and caregivers devise creative ways of allowing for progressive increases in autonomy (for example, through allowing the teenager increasing responsibility for home procedures and medications) can help counterbalance the unavoidable limitations of a particular illness.

The structural impact of the child's medical crisis or hospitalization on the family as a whole can be assessed through observations by staff closest to the family and the routine exploration of relevant issues with family members. These would include questions about which family member is most closely involved in the care of the sick teenager, who is now watching the younger children at home, how much time the parents spend alone together, who in the family may be showing symptomatic behavior, and how routines at home have changed since the accident or onset of illness. Brief family therapy can be useful in helping the family weather some of these unavoidable changes and/or strengthen their subsystems to prevent more serious and permanent damage to the fabric of the family.

For example, fourteen-year-old Shawn was referred for mental-health services because she was observed to be very depressed and wracked by guilt over the condition of her three-year-old sister, a patient in the intensive care unit. The three-year-old, under the care of her older sister at the time, had fallen into a neighbor's swimming pool and was a near-drowning victim, not expected to survive. While the parents were not openly blaming Shawn, the potential existed for serious emotional problems and family dysfunction. Shawn was openly resistant to individual therapy and found it too painful to discuss the drowning or her feelings in family sessions. Shawn's parents were unable to acknowledge any possibility of underlying anger or resentment toward their daughter. However, the therapist actively engaged this adolescent in family sessions under the guise of having Shawn serve as "play therapist" to the only other sibling, a seven-year-old brother. Encouraged in the belief that she was the only person capable

of helping her younger brother adjust to the loss of his baby sister (who died within three days of the accident), Shawn was slowly able to discuss the accident with him and work through her grief and loss through expressive play. At the same time, this process allowed Shawn's reintegration into the family as an important and worthwhile member still capable of being entrusted with the care of a younger sibling.

The brief family therapy model seems to be particularly welcomed by families undergoing severe emotional stress and disorganization in the midst of a medical crisis. Fairly directive strategies including assignment of tasks in the session itself and homework assignments for individual family members can not only effect useful structural changes, but also provide a sense of control and nurturance to a family feeling powerless and endangered. Therapeutic interventions designed to join the therapist's authority with the parents and empower the parents in their caretaking role are particularly important because the parent of a critically ill child is already struggling to maintain some semblance of control and usefulness within the disempowering context of the hospital culture.

The brief family therapy model is also especially useful with families of critically ill patients because the medical crisis is more likely to be time-limited than in cases of chronic illness. Once a child has recovered or been transferred to another institution, parents are often eager to terminate their connection with the hospital rapidly and completely (including the connection with their mental-health professional) to facilitate their entry into their next phase of adjustment. In the case of more tragic outcomes, families are often motivated by a desire to escape the painful memories associated with their hospital experience. While this hasty escape is not always therapeutically indicated, patients or families who are anxious to "move on" and separate from their hospital-based therapists are more likely to complete a therapeutic contract within a time-limited model than when therapy has been conceptualized as an open-ended, long-term process.

CHALLENGES OF WORK IN THE HEALTH-CARE SETTING

The number of mental-health professionals working in health-care settings has been steadily increasing, yet clarification of their role and their mastery of some of the obstacles to entering the hospital system fully has evolved somewhat more slowly. Carving out a job definition and a meaningful role within the complex system of services previously limited almost exclusively to the physical care of the pediatric patient is a challenge to each mental-health professional who attempts this entry. There are some familiar but formidable obstacles generally encountered in the struggle to gain acceptance within this setting which, if overcome, can ultimately lead to a very rich and satisfying professional role.

Obstacles

One of the most immediate difficulties for the mental-health professional is that of coming to grips with the authoritarian structure, model of service, and assumptions embedded in the traditional medical model. Maintaining one's own psychological and social-systems conceptualizations while translating one's clinical input into a terminology and service model acceptable to medical staff requires a high degree of flexibility and cultural adaptability. Finding acceptance by physicians and nursing staff as an autonomous professional who can function in a collaborative but nonsubservient relationship requires persistence and the ability to demonstrate one's competence over time. It also requires that the mental-health consultant redefine the expectations of the medical staff who may at first expect the same rapid, quantitative, one-shot assessment of the passive patient which they have come to expect of the consulting neurologist, dermatologist, or allergist.

Redefining one's role to include broader systems interventions such as interdisciplinary conferences and consultations directed at staff process, rather than being limited to a direct-service model, may at first produce confusion and resistance. The mental-health professional must take a fairly active, assertive stance in order to gain entrance into the numerous family and institutional systems and must learn ways of joining with stressed and overwhelmed families and staff without alienating them with overintrusiveness. Few of the luxuries of the quiet, private therapy office, with its motivated clientele or its protective time and spatial boundaries, are available to the professional who must constantly devise means of working around the daily treatment schedules, crises, hospital routines, and personnel changes of the bustling hospital floor. Developing a therapeutic relationship with patients or staff who may not perceive themselves as needing these services is also a continual challenge.

As in any complex institution, issues of defining and protecting one's "turf" can also cause problems for the newly emerging mental-health consultant in the hospital. As their role and skills become more clearly defined, mental-health professionals may encounter resistance if not overt hostility from social workers, nursing supervisors, occupational therapists, or other team members whose own professional boundaries or self-defined roles may overlap with or be threatened by those of the new consultant. It is essential for the mental-health professional to understand the roles and interrelationships of the existing members of the system before actively defining a role for him- or herself and intervening. Few, if any, medical teams are adequately staffed to meet the overwhelming psychological needs of their patients and staff. Few can afford to reject the services of a mental-health consultant provided the entry is made in a sensitive manner with due credit given the preexisting structure, style, and needs of the system.

In the course of defining the limits of the consultant's role and abilities, one potential trap that can be as destructive as being excluded from the hospital system is that of being overenthusiastically swallowed up by an institution. If adequate education is not provided to fellow team members about the limitations of the therapy process and the definition of appropriate referrals, an overburdened health-care team may start flooding a consultant with therapy referrals for their most tragic and difficult cases, or for those that cause the greatest anguish and helplessness to staff. For example, the consultant/therapist who finds herself getting a number of referrals which expect her miraculously to "cure" the appropriate and unavoidable depression of a dying adolescent is likely to very quickly feel helpless and defeated. Thus, the mental-health professional must not only prove the value of his or her skills and unique role to gain acceptance by the health-care team, but must also clearly indicate the limits of these abilities so that his or her role is not stretched beyond its capabilities. When unrealistic expectations concerning direct-service referrals become apparent, it is generally a sign that it is time to consult directly with health-care staff about handling their own feelings of sadness, helplessness, and failure in their more difficult cases where a certain degree of human suffering is unavoidable.

Benefits of Working within the Hospital

The role of consultant in a hospital setting has a great many rewards for the mental-health professional who succeeds in defining a viable, realistic role within this system. The broad range of children and families who are seen in a large hospital offers a fascinating diversity of socioeconomic, ethnic, and cultural groups to work with and the opportunity to provide preventive as well as crisis services to many families who would not ordinarily seek out mental-health services. Immersion in the culture and daily workings of the hospital system plunges the mental-health consultant into dramatic issues of life and death decision making, complex social interactions, and interesting ethical and treatment problems. In this setting, the contributions of a thoughtful, systems-wise but nonmedically trained professional can be quite useful to a system that is dominated by scientific specialists and technicians.

As for the benefits to the mental-health consultant as an individual, work in the hospital system allows a much greater degree of daily social interaction, public visibility of one's work, opportunity for teamwork, and critical feedback than is normally encountered in the private office or clinic. The continually changing field of medical problems, health-care providers, and interactional issues provides a very rich context for creative thinking and individualized approaches. Adequate time and energy are the only real obstacles to the unbounded possibilities that exist for creative therapeutic interventions, staff training, and research opportunities available in almost any health-care institution.

Finally, the mental-health professional in the hospital setting has the opportunity to observe, study, and work with "normal," functional patient families as well as the disorganized and dysfunctional families generally seen in more traditional mental-health settings. Although these families are encountered in periods of great stress and turmoil, access to functional families allows the mental-health consultant to maintain a more balanced perspective on the mechanisms of the "healthy" functioning of family systems. The courage and strength of these adolescents and their families serve as a powerful inspiration and counterbalance to the otherwise tragic and sometimes overwhelming crises encountered in the hospital setting. The ability of many families to provide nurturance and support and make dramatic and even heroic adaptations to the needs of their critically or terminally ill children provides great encouragement to those of us in the mental-health field who see the family system as a powerful and essential resource in our work with young people.

REFERENCES

Barnhill, L. R., & Longo, D. Fixation and regression in the family life cycle. *Family Process*, 1978, **17**, 469–478.

Blake, S., & Paulsen, K. Therapeutic intervention with terminally ill children: A review. *Professional Psychology*, 1981, **12**(5), 655–663.

Bowen, M. *Family therapy in clinical practice*. New York: Jason Aronson, 1978.

Brunnquell, D., & Hall, M. D. Issues in the psychological care of pediatric oncology patients. *American Journal of Orthopsychiatry*, 1982, **52**(1), 32–44.

Cain, A. C., Fast, I., & Erickson, M. E. Children's disturbed reactions to the death of a sibling. *American Journal of Orthopsychiatry*, 1964, **34**, 741–752.

Carter, E. A., & McGoldrick, M. (Eds.) *The family life cycle: A framework*. New York: Gardner Press, 1980.

Duvall, E. M. *Marriage and family development* (5th ed.). New York: Lippincott, 1977.

Feinberg, D. Preventive therapy with siblings of a dying child. *Journal of the American Academy of Child Psychiatry*, 1970, **9**(4), 644–668.

Hare-Mustin, R. Family therapy following the death of a child. *Journal of Marital & Family Therapy*, 1979, **8**, 51–59.

Herz, F. The impact of death and serious illness on the family life cycle. In E. A. Carter & M. McGoldrick (Eds.), *The family life cycle: A framework*. New York: Gardner Press, 1980.

Hofmann, A. D., Becker, R. D., & Gabriel, H. P. *The hospitalized adolescent: A guide to managing the ill and injured youth*. New York: Macmillan, 1976.

Hughes, M. C. Chronically ill children in groups: Recurrent issues and adaptations. *American Journal of Orthopsychiatry*, 1982, **52**, 704–711.

Johnston, M. Rituals of the hospital culture. In P. Azarnoff & C. Hardgrove (Eds.), *The family in child health care*. New York: Wiley, 1981.

Kaufman, R. Body image changes in physically ill teenagers. *Journal of the American Academy of Child Psychiatry*, 1972, **11**, 157–170.

Koocher, G. P. Surviving childhood cancer: Issues in living. In J. J. Spinetta & P. Deasy-Spinetta (Eds.), *Living with childhood cancer*. St. Louis, MO: Mosby, 1981.

Krell, R., & Rabkin, L. The effects of sibling death on the surviving child: A family perspective. *Family Process*, 1979, **18**, 471–477.

Marten, G. W., & Mauer, A. M. Interaction of health-care professionals with critically ill children and their parents. *Clinical Pediatrics*, 1982, **21**(9), 540–544.

McKeever, P. Siblings of chronically ill children: A literature review with implications for research and practice. *American Journal of Orthopsychiatry*, 1983, **53**(2), 209–218.

Mickel, C. Innovative projects earning psychologists spots on hospital health care teams. *American Psychologist*, 1982, **37**(12), 1350–1354.

Minuchin, S. *Families and family therapy*. Cambridge: Harvard University Press, 1974.

Minuchin, S., Rosman, B., & Baker, L. *Psychosomatic families: Anorexia nervosa in context*. Cambridge: Harvard University Press, 1978.

Ravenscroft, K. Psychiatric consultation to the child with acute physical trauma. *American Journal of Orthopsychiatry*, 1982, **52**, 298–307.

Schowalter, J. Psychological reactions to physical illness and hospitalization in adolescence. *Journal of the American Academy of Child Psychiatry*, 1977, **16**, 500–516.

Spinetta, J. J., & Deasy-Spinetta, P. (Eds.) *Living with childhood cancer*. St. Louis, MO: Mosby, 1981.

Stapp, J., & Fulcher, R. The employment of APA members. *American Psychologist*, 1981, **36**(11), 1263–1314.

Tietz, W., McSherry, L., & Britt, B. Family sequelae after a child's death due to cancer. *American Journal of Psychotherapy*, 1977, **31**, 417–425.

Tuma, J. *Handbook for the practice of pediatric psychology*. New York: Wiley, 1982.

Videka-Sherman, L. Coping with the death of a child: A study over time. *American Journal of Orthopsychiatry*, 1982, **52**, 688–698.

Williams, W. V., Lee, J., & Polak, P. R. Crisis intervention: Effects of crisis intervention on family survivors of sudden infant death situations. *Community Mental Health Journal*, 1976, **12**, 128–136.

Zeltzer, L., Kellerman, J., Ellenberg, L., Dash, J., & Rigler, D. Psychological effects of illness in adolescence: II. Impact of illness in adolescents—Crucial issues and coping styles. *Journal of Pediatrics*, 1980, **97**(1), 132–138.

7

A Family and Community Systems Approach to the Brief Psychiatric Hospitalization of Adolescents

MARSHA PRAVDER MIRKIN, Ph.D.,
RUSSELL J. RICCI, M.D.,
and MARC D. COHEN, M.S.W.

*T*he past two decades have seen an explosion in the rate of adolescent admissions to inpatient psychiatric facilities (Gibson, 1974). Statistics indicate a frightening rate of suicide, crime, and drug use among adolescents. One response to such destructive behavior is hospitalization.

Once the decision is made to hospitalize an adolescent, one can choose from a variety of different treatment models that may differ in many respects. Three differentiating factors will be mentioned here. The first factor is length of stay. Programs vary from brief treatment (Abend, 1968; Madanes, 1982) to long-term hospitalization (Holmes, 1964). The second factor is family involvement. Traditionally, psychiatric units believed that it was best for the adolescent not to speak to, or be visited by, his family at the start of treatment. At the other end of that continuum are programs which require that the family in its entirety be hospitalized (Abroms, Fullner, & Whitaker, 1971). The third factor is the physical set-up of the inpatient unit. Some programs combine adolescents and adults on the same unit (Falstein, Feinstein, & Cohen, 1960), while others advocate for separate units and programs for each population (Glasser, Hartmann, & Avery, 1967; Parmelee, 1983). It is beyond the scope of this chapter to address the variety of program models mentioned above. Instead, we will focus on the theoretical and applied components of what we consider to be a very powerful treatment setting: a short-term, family-oriented adolescent program in a psychiatric hospital.

RATIONALE FOR SHORT-TERM FAMILY ORIENTATION

The authors of this chapter advocate short-term, family-oriented hospitalization for several reasons. First, removal of the child from the home and community for long periods of time increases the adolescent's isolation, thereby making reintegration more difficult. Second, family resources, when reorganized, provide the most effective means of immediate intervention and long-term, follow-up care.

Regarding the first issue, a hospitalization which separates an adolescent from his or her family, school, and community and fails to return him/her to roots in the real world with the skills to grow and develop can leave the adolescent more at risk than prior to hospitalization. An adolescent who has at least some ties to family, even destructive ones, has relationships and roots. If hospitalization severs those lingering attachments and fails to replace them with a more healthy alternative, then the child is truly alone. An intense relationship with an individual therapist is no substitute for an extensive community network.

A major problem in long-term hospitalization is the adolescent's loss of involvement in peer group and school activities. Many of these youngsters are already experiencing school problems. Removal from the academic setting may further alienate the adolescent from the peer group to which he/she is returning, and place him/her even further behind academically. Short-term hospitalization minimizes, although it does not eliminate, these risks. In addition, if one uses a short-term, community-oriented model, one can choose to return the child to school during hospitalization and as part of the treatment plan. The adolescent can then discuss school issues with the hospital staff and therapist after returning to the grounds each day. In this way, those stigmatization and educational risks are further minimized.

The second issue emphasizes that separation of an adolescent from the family fails to recognize the importance of the family in both maintaining and ultimately ameliorating the problem. Symptomatic adolescent behavior is often a red flag for family dysfunction. If one looks at the meaning of the symptom which led to hospitalization, the futility of long-term separation from the family becomes more evident. For example, we have found that troubled adolescents are often members of family systems where growing up (separating) is a threat to the family's sense of well-being and is experienced by the family as disloyal (Minuchin, 1974; Mirkin, 1983). The symptom allows the adolescent to remain a child by requiring that parents continue to monitor him/her.

Thus, the difficulty the family has in making the transition into and out of the adolescent phase of the life cycle (Carter & McGoldrick, 1980) is played out through the teenager's dangerous symptom. Long-term separation from the family during hospitalization, as in a traditional psychiatric model, does not allow work on these dysfunctional patterns. In fact, it creates the conditions which promote the family's sense of intrusion and danger. As a result, it is likely that both adolescent and parents will undermine treatment since the family perceives the hospital as putting a wedge between them and since they view separation as the ultimate act of disloyalty.

Intensive family involvement is the cornerstone of the program model we are recommending. Such a program can help the family negotiate the adolescent phase of the life cycle and establish the hierarchy and boundaries necessary for more positive adolescent functioning.

Structural and strategic family therapists (cf. Haley, 1980) argue that in order for the problematic behavior to change, parents must regain control of the disturbed/disturbing adolescent. Removal of the child from home and the failure to involve the parents as central therapeutic agents will disempower them further and make it less likely that they will regain their position of authority within the family. Traditional hospitalization tends to inadvertently support the dysfunctional hierarchy since staff replaces parents rather than empowers them. In such a situation, it is staff, not parents, that responds to both the limit-setting and the nurturance needs of the adolescent. The staff become authority figures and parents take a back seat.

An effective hospital program also helps the family with boundary problems—issues of distance and closeness, of who's in and who's out in any given context (cf. Minuchin, 1974). A long-term unit without a family focus may continue to support dysfunctional boundaries. The boundary created around the child in a hospital prevents family access and decreases the family's chances of developing more flexible boundaries among its members, as well as between its members and outside helpers. Indeed, a typical family response to outside intrusion is to tighten its boundaries, thus undermining the treatment goal of increasing flexibility.

A positive hospital experience will help families navigate the waters of life-cycle changes. Haley (1980) sees adolescent problems as a failure to disengage from parents. In this regard, adolescent incapacitation continues the teenager's reliance on parents. Therefore, continuing to hospitalize the adolescent without working on fundamental disengagement issues will maintain the problem. The adolescent will continue to exhibit difficulties, parents will continue to treat him as ill and to care for him, and hospitals will reinforce the idea that the child needs care-taking and is incapable of living independently. Thus, the cycle continues unless therapy is guided by the expectation that the problem person will become normal and will function in society. Haley specifies treatment strategies that promote the family's "launching" of its offspring.

The research in this area confirms our clinical impression that programs emphasizing family involvement are effective over time both in terms of clinical improvement and cost effectiveness. While outcome research *is* limited and methodology leads one to interpret results cautiously, Rosenstock and Vincent (1979) concluded that if parents refused involvement, the adolescent's treatment failed almost 100 percent of the time versus a 64 percent success rate with parental involvement. Success was defined as the absence of presenting symptoms at the eight-month-to-one-year, post-treatment follow-up. After the treatment of adolescents in a short-term, family-oriented hospital, parents *and* adolescents believed that the hospital had produced improvement by the time of discharge and up to six months afterwards, especially in conduct-disordered adolescents (Fineberg, et al., 1982).

AUTONOMOUS ADOLESCENT UNITS

While the authors believe that short-term, family-oriented programs can be implemented on either an all-adolescent unit or on a combined adolescent/adult unit, there are reasons to believe that the former is more effective (Orvin, 1974). Glasser, et al. (1967) indicated increased hostility among staff, adult patients, and adolescent patients when adults and adolescents were mixed on the same unit—alarming news for those concerned with milieu safety.

The case for autonomous adolescent units is also supported by our therapeutic focus on hierarchy, boundaries, and family involvement. A systems perspective (cf. Haley, 1980) may predict that the placement of adolescents on a unit with dysfunctional adults and unspecialized staff recapitulates the family's ineffectual hierarchy and results in continued symptomatic behavior. Simply put, when no one clearly knows how to be in charge of an adolescent, negative behavior escalates.

Mixed adolescent and adult units are also ripe for serious boundary problems. When the same program is applied to two different populations without differentiating the developmental needs of each, the result is often chaos. For example, we found that adolescents were very disruptive during the slow-paced, insight-oriented meetings they shared with adults, but were helpful and supportive during the shorter meetings that focused on problem-solving and that were more in line with their stage of development.

On an adolescent unit with its own philosophy and program, the staff is trained in adolescent development, behavior management, and family issues. As will be seen in the following literature review and program description, such a unit can provide a powerful treatment setting.

REVIEW OF FAMILY-ORIENTED TREATMENT PROGRAMS

Many authors have described family-oriented treatment programs. Most dramatically, some programs have chosen to admit other family members along with the identified patient (Abroms, et al., 1971). Bhatti, et al. (1980) describe a hospital program in India in which a patient is hospitalized with the one or two family members identified as important in the pathological interaction. They write that recovery is faster, discharge earlier, and relapse minimized since the family learns how to deal with the identified patient as well as how to modify their own behavior. Combrinck-Graham, et al. (1982) describe a program at the Philadelphia Child Guidance Center in which a family with a child identified-patient is hospitalized on a short-term basis. The goal of treatment is to disengage a usually over-involved family system, develop individual competencies and, seemingly most important, reengage a parent who formerly had no network with persons and activities outside the family grouping.

Other inpatient programs describe the family-oriented treatment of adolescents when only the identified patient, and not the family, is hospitalized. The treatment ranges from parent participation in their own therapy (cf. Rosenstock & Vincent, 1979) to intensive family involvement in many aspects of the treatment program (cf. Harbin, 1979; Ricci, et al. 1980; Suchotliff, 1978). In the latter type of program, parental involvement is seen as critical at every stage of treatment. Byng-Hall and Bruggen (1974) involve parents from the first moment by requiring them to decide together whether to admit their child. They explain that, from the beginning, this creates a more viable family authority structure in a situation where, prior to admissions, parents felt helpless in dealing with their child. Second, requiring parents to work together may thus repair an out-of-joint hierarchy.

Orvin (1974), Suchotliff (1978), Stern, et al. (1981), Mirkin (1983), and Parmelee (1983) describe other family-oriented adolescent programs. Suchotliff suggests that

if the goal is to return a child home, then the unit must approximate the home situation and involve the parents. When a child initially acts out on the unit, the family and the staff will together determine disciplinary procedures, which the staff will then implement. As treatment progresses, parents should continue to decide on a response to inappropriate adolescent behavior, and the staff, to implement the parental decision. Finally, parents take over both limit-setting and limit-enforcement during home visits. In this way, parents are able to define their contribution to the positive change in the adolescent's behavior and to see their role as critical. Suchotliff hypothesizes that if parents do not see themselves in that role, (a) they feel inadequate and skeptical about maintaining the change, and (b) the child may attribute any changes to being away from home and thus tend to downgrade the effectiveness of the parents. Orvin warns that the unit should not duplicate those dysfunctional elements that characterize the home from which the patient has come and that family therapy and (multiple) family group therapy are integral to the treatment of the adolescent. Along the same lines, Stern, et al., combine the concepts of psychodynamic-developmental therapy with those of family therapy in suggesting that the hospital staff function as "good-enough parents" for the entire family and thus model the parenting responses that facilitate separation-individuation. Mirkin describes the interaction of the therapist, therapeutic milieu, family, and outside agencies in the treatment of a hospitalized anorectic adolescent. The focus is on working with the family, empowering the parents, and returning the adolescent as soon as possible to her home and her community school.

Other writers focus on the family-therapy aspect of family-oriented treatment. Madanes (1980, 1982) discusses the stages of therapy during a brief hospitalization. First, the therapist outlines the agenda (the prevention of rehospitalization and the return of the adolescent to work or school), and requests the parents to take charge of making decisions for the adolescent. During the second stage, parents avoid taking the power, and the therapist must countermove in order to help parents take charge. In the third stage, there is a crisis and escalation. The therapist supports the family through the crisis, which may take place during the actual hospitalization or after discharge. In the fourth and final stage, the youth returns to normal activities, and is shortly thereafter disengaged from therapy. Madanes, like Haley (1980), believes that a youth's problems result from incongruities in the family hierarchy, which can be repaired in the above process.

Other writers underline the importance of family therapy aftercare. Leavitt (1975) reports that families did not view the patient as ready to be discharged when discharge approached. Recognizing that treatment should not end abruptly with discharge, Ricci, et al. (1980) specify that aftercare is part of the treatment plan, which is provided by the inpatient therapist unless another therapist is already seeing the family. Norton, et al. (1963) suggest that one goal of inpatient hospitalization is to provide the motivation and opportunity for subsequent outpatient therapy.

In summary, the growing literature on a family-therapy orientation to adolescent inpatient treatment suggests that this outlook may not only be viable but essential to the successful treatment and reintegration into society of troubled/troubling adolescents.

THE FAMILY-ORIENTED PROGRAM AT CHARLES RIVER HOSPITAL[1]

Charles River Hospital is a 58-bed, private psychiatric hospital in Wellesley, Massachusetts. The ideas for this adolescent program were conceived primarily by the

[1]We would like to thank the administration and staff of Charles River Hospital for their support in developing and implementing this program. The first & third authors would like to extend gratitude to the second author, Russell Ricci, M.D., on whose ideas the program is based and who advocated for this model when everyone else seemed skeptical.

second author, Russell Ricci, M.D., at a time when only a handful of adolescents were treated at Charles River. The first author would like to acknowledge that through Dr. Ricci's foresight, dedication and administrative support, an integrated program was developed and expanded within a five-year period. Charles River now treats twenty-six adolescents, 12 to 19 years old, on two units. This part of the chapter will discuss the admissions criteria, underlying assumptions, and application of the program. Much in the following treatment is based on papers and/or chapters by Ricci, et al. (1980), Parmelee (1983), and Mirkin (1983); and on the *Charles River Hospital Parent Guide* (1983).

Admissions Criteria

An adolescent is admitted to Charles River Hospital when:

1. he/she is in life-threatening danger, either from a direct threat, such as a suicide attempt, or from an indirect threat, such as drug or alcohol abuse.
2. outpatient agency and/or family feel that outpatient intervention has not been successful. In situations involving rebellious adolescent behavior at home and in school—such as truancy, fighting, difficulty with police, and running away—outpatient intervention is generally the treatment of choice. However, when good outpatient treatment has been tried, and the full battery of interventions exhausted, then the authors recommend inpatient hospitalization.
3. the adolescent is out of touch with reality and thus needs observation in a more contained environment.
4. increasing demands are placed on the social service and legal systems for guidance in dealing with a given dangerous adolescent. Frequently a court will turn to a psychiatric hospital for recommendations for treatment planning. In such situations the support and clout of the court can be critical in containing an adolescent, and, within such a clear set of judicial expectations, realistic treatment interventions and recommendations can be made.

Assumptions

In order to design and implement a family-oriented program, we have made four assumptions about families and intervention goals.

The first assumption is that families are caring and that they attempt to solve their problems in the best way they know how. Their intentions are noble and loving. Unfortunately, their solutions often maintain the problem patterns (Walzlawick, et al., 1974), but intervening in those patterns can lead to more successful functioning. Therefore, we assume that we can intervene in a given pattern and that the child in question will return home.

The second assumption of this model is that the problems exhibited by a hospitalized adolescent reflect dysfunctional family patterns. According to this model, problems are not conceptualized linearly, by cause and effect, but rather circularly, whereby the behavior of any family member instigates, is a response to, and interacts with, the behavior of other family members. It is not just that an adolescent has problems separating, but rather that each member contributes to and responds to the difficulties surrounding separation.

The third assumption is that if the intervention can begin to restructure the family, far-reaching changes can be obtained within a relatively short period of time and can be enduring if supported by a useful aftercare program. However, the longer an adolescent is hospitalized, the harder it can be for him/her to successfully reintegrate into family, school and community life. Therefore, hospitalizations are relatively short, typically four to eight weeks.

The fourth assumption is that important therapeutic work also occurs outside the therapist's office and outside the hospital. From the start of hospitalization, adolescents are expected to go home every Saturday and Sunday with their parents. Families are often assigned tasks to complete at home.

Program Description

All aspects of the treatment program are planned to dovetail with the systems-oriented clinical philosophy.

ADMISSIONS

The family first comes into contact with the hospital during the admissions process. It is here that the first intervention is undertaken: Parents must agree to have their child hospitalized and agree to participate in the program. This is the first step toward repairing a toppled hierarchy (Byng-Hall & Bruggen, 1974). Families in which the parents are controlled by the child and often by other agencies who say the child needs hospitalization are reengaged immediately. We have found that at times public agencies unwittingly undermine the parents' authority in the process of hospitalizing an adolescent by not involving the parents in the decision-making. When the hospital refuses admission to adolescents whose parents have been left out (or have left themselves out), it reminds both the parent and the agency of the parents' importance. The admissions staff reviews the program with the parents verbally and gives each parent a booklet explaining the program. Parents are then requested to sign a contract in which they agree to: (1) participate in family therapy during their work hours (usually 9-5); (2) participate in multiple-family group one evening a week; (3) take their child on pass for the weekend; (4) cooperate in any suspension or discharge of their child from the hospital.

This excerpt from the *Charles River Hospital Parent Guide* (1983) explains our philosophy in language readily understandable to most parents:

> Why all this emphasis on families? The reason is that we believe you know your child better than anybody else, and can help us help your teenager. We will only know your child for a 4-8 week period. It is your insights and approaches that can guide us in formulating a treatment plan. We ask you to take your child home for the weekend so that he/she can practice what has been worked on during the week. (p. 1)

We also explain to parents our expectations for their child's behavior in the hospital. This intervention is intended as a means of joining (with) the parents through agreement on a code of "normal" behavior for the child as well as preparing parents for subsequent interventions which will occur when their child inevitably breaks the rules (see Disciplinary Procedures). In essence, we are expecting that their teenagers behave like respectful, civilized human beings. However, we also expect that a process of testing and response is necessary for changes in behavior patterns to occur. High expectations are critical since we also expect them to return home and reintegrate into school and family life within a short period of time. By establishing a code of behavior as our mutual goal, parents and hospital forge a therapeutic alliance which aims to block old family habits, restore parental confidence, and promote satisfaction and pride within each family member.

Comprehensive Therapy

Central to the treatment philosophy of our family-oriented program is the notion of the comprehensive therapist—the social worker, psychologist, or psychiatrist who coordinates the course of hospitalization. This professional provides the individual and family therapy, coordinates and intervenes with outside agencies, and interfaces with the milieu in which the adolescent resides. Together with the family and milieu team, the comprehensive therapist decides on weekend passes, discharge date, and aftercare plans.

The initial staff reaction to the concept of a comprehensive therapist was skepticism: which treatment philosophy dictated that one person wear so many hats? However, we believe that this unified model of treatment is the single most important aspect of our program. Such a model—which supports the family and decreases the adolescent's propensity to cause polarization in the treatment team, school, and family—requires a degree of organization best maintained by fewer "cooks." In addition, a short-term hospital should not be a parental substitute; rather, to be most effective, it should reunite the child with the parents in a more functional manner.

The comprehensive therapist must develop equally effective alliances with all family members. One of the major problems of traditional hospital programs has been the unbalanced investment in the child by the hospital staff and therapist which blocked parents' attempts to regain control of their child. Therefore, much of individual therapy focuses on how a youngster will bring up critical issues to his/her parents and siblings. The therapist at family meetings can focus on clarifying boundaries, intervening in maladaptive patterns, and helping parents to assume the hierarchical responsibilities of limits and nurturance while dealing with some very critical issues.

This point is clarified by the following example:[2]

Joan is a sixteen-year-old girl who entered the hospital feeling depressed and decided she needed a group home placement upon discharge. Prior to hospitalization, Joan had an individual therapist plus an individual school counselor. She and her parents also met occasionally with a third counselor. During the course of hospitalization, Joan informed us that she had been sexually molested by her uncle. Her individual counselors knew of this but honored Joan's request to keep it confidential and told Joan that when she was ready, they would support her when she told her parents. Since the abuse had stopped when the uncle moved to California, there was no immediate danger involved in the waiting. However, the counselors had inadvertently reinforced Joan's insecurity: She had to make the adult decision (to inform on her uncle) rather than having authority figures do so for her. Since at Charles River Hospital the individual and family therapist are the same person, Joan was told that her choice was whether she or her therapist would bring the issue up to her parents. The message was clear that such secrets would not be hidden—that the therapist would not collude in that dysfunctional process. Joan was assured by her therapist that she and her parents would be given all the help available to cope with this problem. The message was that Joan could entrust her therapist to

[2]We would like to acknowledge Pamela Slater, Ph.D., for discussing this case and the treatment rationale with us.

protect not only Joan, but her family, who Joan was afraid would disintegrate upon hearing the news. Joan told her parents at the family therapy session, and the therapist helped her parents take a protective, nurturant stance toward Joan. Joan no longer wanted to leave home following discharge.

The comprehensive therapist did not assume that she could help Joan completely work through the turmoil of incest. Instead, she assumed that the very fact that this was kept secret indicated a dysfunction on the parenting level (i.e., Joan was afraid they would fall apart with this information). The therapeutic task was to help the parents accept their role and support Joan. With the hierarchy thus repaired, Joan could feel safe returning home.

When we look at the therapy system, we include not only the family, but also the therapist, the hospital system, and community agencies. If the therapist's role were limited to providing individual and family therapy, the treatment, we hypothesize, would be undermined and progress slow. Interventions at all levels, then, become critical, as in the following example:

Cathy was hospitalized for anorexia nervosa. Individual and family treatment indicated that the symptom was being maintained by Cathy's difficulty in separating and her belief that mother needed her to remain a "little girl." Mother, who had insufficient support from father, was panicked at the upcoming empty nest. In response to the need for an aftercare school plan, Cathy's school offered to provide her with home tutoring. However, the comprehensive therapist was not in favor of this plan because it failed to take into account the critical family dynamic. If the comprehensive therapist did not intervene with the school system, then the dynamic of Cathy being mom's "little girl at home" would have been reinforced and replayed. A plan was needed to interrupt this pattern while also respecting Cathy's need for individualized school attention to catch up on her work. An in-school tutorial program resulted. (Mirkin, 1983)

At times the comprehensive therapist must deal with outside agencies that have a treatment philosophy different from the hospital's:

Betsy was hospitalized after attempting suicide and then placed for two months in a foster home. After that time the foster program was adamant that Betsy had not yet attached to the foster mother and needed a long-term placement to be able to do so. Betsy's parents were adamant that she return home. It was important to make a decision that would not alienate any member of the system. Yet, our evaluation indicated a return home, with continued family therapy on an outpatient basis. This was explained to the foster agency as follows:

"What a great job you did with Betsy! Two months ago, she was too suicidal to return home and now she has been safe at your program for two months and asking to go home. I can see your point that her work is far from completed. However, by keeping her now, you'll have both parents and the kid working to undermine your good work. Why not send her home and let parents know that when they can no longer handle Betsy, they should call you? In that way, when they call, they will be appreciative and not resistant."

The agency, in their frustration, understood and, feeling that the family could call upon them in the future, agreed to the disposition plan. The family also felt that their wishes were respected, and the parents were reempowered after feeling helpless and peripheral.

The comprehensive therapist must also attend to issues that arise in the hospital system itself. Administrative support is critical for the functioning of any program. While the clinical director is responsible for establishing that working relationship, individual cases sometimes bring out a potentially dangerous split between hospital administration and the therapist/milieu team or even between the therapist and the milieu team:

Fifteen-year-old Carole was brought to the hospital after a sensational newspaper article described her last months of being sent from agency to agency, all of which were labeled inadequate to meet her needs. The therapist was told by the hospital administrator that this was clearly a political case followed closely by the newspapers. Within twenty-four hours, Carole had run away. Upset about the negative publicity and concerned about the well-being of the youngster, the administrator spoke to the therapist. The therapist explained that Carole's running away was evidence that this was indeed the type of program Carole needed: When she had run away in the past, her parents would get into an argument with the service provider. Carole would thus not have to answer for her behavior and often would be transferred to a "more appropriate" facility. This time the therapist had already predicted to the parents her running away and framed it as her test to see whether parents could hold her accountable for her behavior. Together, therapist and parents planned how to deal with Carole when she returned. Parents did not feel excluded, nor that the hospital was taking over their role—both of which they had felt in the past. If anything, they had more faith in the hospital for being able to predict their daughter's behavior so accurately. And in responding to their daughter they also felt, for the first time, part of a team. Carole came back, the plan was enacted, and eventually she returned home, no longer suicidal. The administrator, expecting to meet with angry parents, instead found they supported the hospital.

The comprehensive therapist also interfaces with the treatment milieu. Its critical role in inpatient treatment will be elaborated upon in the next section.

MILIEU TREATMENT

The milieu is where the adolescent lives—his/her "home away from home." At Charles River the adolescent lives on one of two units with twelve other teenagers and three shifts of staff; the staff comprises ten to eleven members per unit.

The purpose of milieu treatment is to assess and intervene in the family dynamics as evidenced by the adolescent reenactment of those dynamics; to help parents gain control of their child so that the child can more successfully reintegrate outside of the hospital; to coordinate the treatment plan with the comprehensive therapist; and to promote appropriate, non-regressive behavior in the adolescent. Parmelee (1983) states:

To be maximally effective, treatment must grow out of a philosophy which will promote a young person's acceptance of fuller re-

sponsibility of all of his actions, thoughts, and feelings, and which will assist his parents in moving away from infantilizing struggles and attitudes. (p. 272)

He goes on to specify the guidelines for a therapeutic milieu. They are, primarily, that expectations for behavior should parallel those in society. Adolescents are not allowed to exhibit behaviors that would be condemned in society just because they "are in the hospital." Threats, acts of violence, and drug use are forbidden. When such a behavior occurs, it must be addressed quickly with everybody on the milieu as well as with the youngster's parents.

The adolescent has infinite possibilities for recreating family dynamics on the unit. The staff must constantly be cognizant of the possibility and intervene to provide the adolescent with a different experience. For example, an adolescent typically will make a request of one staff member. When denied, s/he will ask another. The staff must be unified in order to avoid recreating the jumbled family hierarchy that the milieu and therapist are attempting to repair.

Not only can the adolescent replay family dynamics on the milieu, but staff can also fall prey to the tendency to replace the child's parents in providing him/her with a "corrective parenting experience." The problem with that strategy is that within six weeks the child is back home. If s/he starts seeing staff as "good parents" and his/her own as "bad parents," then changes are unlikely to maintain. In addition, if s/he senses a competition between staff and parents for the "better parent" role, the child is placed in a loyalty bind: If s/he gets better, then s/he is disloyal to parents by allowing staff to help; if s/he stays the same, the hospitalization is a waste of time. Children in this predicament can often be recognized by an escalation in their negative behaviors, which decrease only when staff and parents are back on the same team.

At times, staff falls into the trap of trying to supply a corrective parenting experience because they feel that the child is the victim of bad parents. This belief system is often in conflict with other staff members who believe that the child is victimizing his hapless parents. Simplified, this means that some staff members see the youngster as the "good guy" being destroyed by "bad" parents, while others see the adolescent as the "troublemaker" destroying his bullied parents. Given family-systems reasoning, it is likely that both are correct—that each member, in turn, plays the roles of victim and victimizer. The staff's understanding of such family dynamics prevents them from falling prey to the polarization. With this knowledge, they, in turn, help parents with the same issue. For example:

> Ben was a twelve-year-old, waif-like youngster who immediately appealed to the staff with his puppy-dog expression and ragged clothing. Some staff members were angry at his mother, whom they overheard yelling at Ben, saying that she hated him. Within a few weeks other staff members became angry at Ben for slyly breaking rules and innocently denying knowledge of those rules. The angrier the staff was at Ben, the more rules he seemed to "innocently" break. At one staff meeting a member stated, "I can't stand the kid. He's always breaking rules and coming up with good excuses, so it seems as if I'm persecuting him." We were then able to examine the self-perpetuating cycle between Ben and his mother: a cycle that could be started by either actor, with either actor being the respondent. Ben's rule-breaking *led to* a destructive verbal response from his mother, as well as *resulted from* such a response. The challenge was to intervene in and break the pattern.

Often, staff polarization serves as a "red flag" marking a central feature of the family problem. In the above example, some viewed Ben as the victim, while others viewed him as the bully. A systems approach of viewing him and his mother in both roles helped the unit to stop reenacting the dynamic and to intervene in the pattern. As with the comprehensive therapist, if the milieu counselor worked only with the adolescent, therapeutic success would be limited. Rather he/she also works closely with the parents and comprehensive therapist for optimum effect.

When a child behaves well in therapy but acts out on the unit, or vice versa, it is a strong indication that there is a problem in treatment, and that somehow the adults aren't unified in their approach to the adolescent. Just as parents and teacher, and/or mother and father, need to work together consistently, so do therapists and unit counselors. Goals for therapy and the milieu must be clear and mutually reinforced by therapist and milieu staff. This is equally true for discipline. Limits for behavior must be agreed upon and enforced by both parties. Treatment cannot succeed if there is a therapist/unit split. If a child breaks a major rule and is suspended, the unit staff and therapist must carry it out in a consistent, mutually agreed-upon manner in order for the parents and adolescent to get the message that discipline is an important aspect of the treatment program. When parents are angry at the hospital for a child's suspension, it often means that they have not gotten a consistent message—that the whole treatment team feels that the suspension is the best possible intervention for their child.

Milieu staff also works closely with parents. This relationship usually begins by working together on plans for weekend passes. Before they leave on their passes, the goals to be derived from treatment are negotiated among unit staff, adolescents, and parents. During this interaction, staff is able to model appropriate parenting responses by intervening if it appears that in the hierarchy a parent is giving up power to the adolescent or blurring the boundaries between parental and adolescent functions. Staff, parents, and teenagers also review the passes when they are completed, and parents decide on what privileges the child should receive in the milieu following a day out with parents. Staff and parents thus form a team: The adolescent's behavior on Friday, in part, determines home privileges on the weekend; while weekend behavior determines unit privileges on Monday.

DISCIPLINARY PROCEDURES[3]

Disciplinary procedures at Charles River have been developed to promote systemic change, as well as to help the adolescent develop more of a sense of responsibility and behavioral control. Different types and degrees of behavioral interventions are employed in accordance with treatment goals. Milieu staff and the comprehensive therapist are intimately involved in formulating and carrying out these plans.

On a daily basis, adolescents are on individualized point systems. Expected behavior (e.g., attending therapy) is specified on a daily list, and adolescents earn points for fulfilling their responsibilities and behaving in accordance with these expectations. Privileges are based on total point accrual. This system assists the adolescent in taking responsibility for his/her own behavior and minimizes power struggles between adults and adolescents.

A high-risk time for adolescent acting-out is on a weekend pass, when families are together and away from hospital supervision. To minimize the risk, teenagers and parents set goals (such as agreeing to separate into different rooms when angry and discussing the problem once the adolescent "cools down"), contract to abide by certain rules, call milieu staff at prearranged times, and implement point systems at home. However, either in the initial phase of treatment—before parental authority is reestablished—or prior to discharge—when the adolescent tests out the newly established hierarchy—weekend be-

havior can be unacceptable. If a youngster is out of control on pass, parents are invited to bring the adolescent back to the milieu. At that point, the adolescent is sent to his/her room, and the parent spends the rest of the pass on the unit, conferring with staff and working out plans with both staff and child.

A multiple-level suspension policy is also sometimes implemented at Charles River and serves both to respond to an adolescent's misbehavior and to intervene systemically. Suspensions at Charles River are in actuality intensifications and rearrangements of the routine disciplinary program and are implemented when the routine program fails to shape family attitudes and behavior. We often notice that an adolescent's negative behavior escalates if the parent does not seem committed to the treatment program and deescalates when the parent is reengaged. There are many possible reasons for parental disengagement. For example, parents may pull back when they feel powerless over their child's behavior, and/or when they feel staff has usurped their role. If the primary treatment goal is to reestablish parents as authority figures, their continued involvement is fundamental. Therefore, the goal of the suspension policy is to reinvolve parents with their adolescent in a more positive, empowered manner.

The first-level suspension is in-house. Parents are invited onto the unit to support the staff's enforcement of behavioral consequences and to demonstrate that the adults are unified in their approach to the adolescent. When parents feel that only staff can deal with the child, they are invited to the unit in order to take on more responsibility and gain more confidence in their parenting. If they seem to be disengaging, their presence at the in-house suspension allows them to participate more fully and thereby reduces their feeling that the parental role is being usurped by staff. When parents and staff join together, the parents often demonstrate a renewed commitment to treatment, and the adolescent often settles down. During the in-house

[3]We would like to acknowledge our colleague, Stuart Koman, Ph.D., for conceptualizing and implementing creative ways of using suspensions and readmissions. Given that most insurance policies have limited hospital days, it is critical to maximize the hospital stay. Through these alternative treatment possibilities, many adolescents can receive highly effective treatment, with the interruptions in their hospitalization used therapeutically, and within the constraints stipulated by the insurance carriers. In addition, Marsha Mirkin, Ph.D., developed and implemented the concept of milieu-wide point systems at Charles River Hospital.

suspension, families attend special meetings as well as all therapy sessions.

Off-grounds suspension is the "bottom line" of this graded series of responses to continuing problem behavior. Off-grounds suspension, usually for two days, highlights the seriousness of the misbehavior, while being accepted back gives adolescents the message that we still want to work with them. Continued adolescent acting-out is often a red flag for some covert conflict between parents, parents and staff, or staff and therapist. During the suspension, both parents and staff must work together in a unified way in order for the suspension to be successful. This is often the first time that the teenagers have seen adults so unified, and they often then feel secure enough to settle down. The pre-suspension "split" among the adults can be highlighted by the actual suspension, since parents may openly argue about whether the child should return to this particular hospital. This suggests that their prior overt commitment to hospitalization was covertly rather tentative. Disagreements among unit staff or among staff and therapists can also become evident in the process of deciding a suspension plan. Some want to discharge the adolescent totally while others want him/her to return following the suspension. Once these issues are made overt, a step has been taken toward their resolution. Emergency meetings are held among family and staff during suspension.

A variation of the off-grounds suspension is a brief transfer to a more secure unit at the same or another hospital. This decision is made if home suspension is unsafe and the milieu needs time to "cool off" from the influence of an adolescent who breaks unit rules or provokes others to do so. Generally, the rationale for this type of suspension is the same as that detailed above. However, brief transfers to other hospitals can also be used when a youngster does not take responsibility for his/her own behavior, and parents block the consequences for misbehavior. For example, John destroyed hospital property. Parents insisted that they pay for the damage, but did not support a plan for John to repay them. This was a repeat of past behavior:

When John destroyed neighbors' property, parents either paid the neighbors directly or paid the fines if John was arrested. The transfer to a different facility as a consequence for this behavior placed the parents in the new position of not being able to protect John from the consequences of his behavior. It also pushed John to decide whether to take responsibility for his actions at our hospital, or to have somebody else in a more secure facility do so for him.

Most adolescents who are suspended from Charles River do return to complete a more successful hospitalization, because the suspension causes a crisis, and crisis is a time ripe for change.

In summary, the milieu is an active, learning environment, which provides clear limits, nurturance, and permission for individuation; in it self-control and self-responsibility are expected. In its best form, the unit reflects the hierarchy, boundaries, and alignments which promote adolescent autonomy, and helps families stuck in the individuation-separation phase of the family life cycle to become "unstuck."

GROUP THERAPY AND MULTIPLE-FAMILY GROUP THERAPY

Each weekday, five to seven adolescents meet with a group therapist.[4] One evening a week, parents and siblings also attend the group meeting, forming a multiple-family group (see Chapter 11). In forming these groups, a family-oriented, systems approach was again taken. Many parents feel isolated and alone in their problems. Isolation often counteracts their ability to allow children to separate. As Combrinck-Graham, et al. (1982) write, one of the purposes of hospitalizing a family is to find an alternative support group for the parents so that the child is not placed in that supporting role. While we do not hospitalize a whole family, multiple-family group therapy does serve the function of decreasing isolation and providing support. In addition, as a family gets habituated in its patterns, it often loses sight of alternative

[4]The authors are indebted to H. Rollin Ives, Ed.D., for inspiring us to pursue an adolescent group therapy program.

ways to interact. But the group offers opportunities to demonstrate many different ways of interacting, and a family's strengths and healthy patterns gradually become clear. For a family considered deviant for such a long time, its ability to help other families and to be recognized for its strengths is an important confirmation of its changing self-perception.

Families also show their similarities in multiple-family group. Most families with troubled adolescents are having difficulty navigating the waters of individuation-separation. While the adolescent's symptoms might vary, the families' concerns are often the same: uncertainty of how to separate in a healthy way. Families, therefore, either launch adolescents too soon, resulting in youngsters feeling vulnerable and unprotected, or they cling too long, resulting in adolescents who must break away dramatically and yet feel incapable of leaving. Discussion often centers around the "pull" of adolescents and parents to stay in the childhood phase and the counteracting "push" toward adulthood. The adolescent's role in diverting parents from their own problems is also highlighted in group. Sometimes it is easier for parents to take advice from peers in similar predicaments than from professionals:

Mrs. L. reported being angry that Beth did not do her laundry on pass even though they had agreed on it. Mrs. L. was then stuck doing it. Other parents and teenagers asked Mrs. L. why she just didn't leave it. Mrs. L. responded that, if she did so, Beth would have no clean clothes. What emerged were her feelings of responsibility for Beth, which would have been more appropriate with a younger child, and the blurry boundaries in which somehow Beth's messy appearance would be a reflection on the mother. Mrs. L. agreed not to do Beth's laundry. The next weekend Beth left it again, and with group support and much agony Mrs. L. controlled her impulse to do the laundry for her. After two days of wearing dirty clothing Beth did her laundry at the hospital. During the following multiple-family group sessions, she told the group that she was angry at her mother for treating her like a baby and that she got even by leaving her laundry, thus acting like a baby. The cycle then continued.

We will never know which came first: Beth's behavior, which resembled that of a

younger child, or mother's propensity to treat her like a younger child. Important was breaking that cycle, so that both could move onto a more stage-appropriate relationship. From this simple beginning, Beth and her mother were able to grapple with more difficult autonomy issues. The parents' own issues then became more visible, and the group began to address those issues.

Much of the time, adolescent group therapy is utilized to prepare for, or review, multiple-family group. Adolescents often get feedback from other patients which reframes their parents' behavior in a more positive way:

Twelve-year-old Stacy said that her father didn't show up at family group because he was angry that she had run away from the hospital for several hours the day before. She also complained that he was always mean, while her mother was very sweet. During multiple-family group, an adolescent asked Mr. G. about his absence from the prior day's meeting. He said that he was extremely worried about Stacy, spent most of the night looking for her, and was too tired, worried, and angry to show up the next day. While his manner of showing his concern would later be confronted, at this point the group focused on the caring which was reflected in the father's gruffness and behavior of the previous night. Stacy was more able to hear this from the adolescents than from the adults. It also served as an important family intervention since thereafter Stacy no longer viewed her father entirely as the "bad guy," nor her mother, therefore, as a "good guy." The family structure was thus unbalanced, and a new structure fell into place.

Often milieu staff are asked to join the adolescent group or the multiple-family group in order to make the program even more consistent and unified. This promotes continued discussion of the adolescent and family issues on the units.

PSYCHOPHARMACOLOGY VS. MEDICAL CONSULTATION

Haley (1980) writes:

The disease theory held that the patient was responding inappropriately . . . because he suffered from an internal defect. The family view held that the strange behavior was adaptive . . . to the person's social situation. Attempting to combine these views led to a therapy of mystification and confusion, not only for the therapist, but for the clientele. While taught that psychotics had an underlying biological defect which was incurable, the therapist was also taught that he should do therapy to cure them. (p. 11) . . . The more the emphasis on medication, the more the family cannot be put in charge of the problem. (p. 73)

At Charles River Hospital we find both psychopharmacology and medical consultation to be critical components of treatment for certain adolescents. Just because certain problems are viewed by hospital and parents as illnesses does not mean that family therapy is useless or undermined. If a child lost the use of his legs, a wheelchair would not be withheld for fear that the parents would not be in charge of the problem. Instead, both parents and child would be helped to learn the usefulness and limitations of the wheelchair and what the child can/cannot do as a result of both the illness and the tool to deal with the illness. If the child, getting stuck while navigating in the wheelchair, expressed his frustration by throwing and breaking vases, and if parents allowed him to do so, the issue would be how to help the youngster tolerate, and improve his/her use of, the wheelchair as well as put an end to the unacceptable behaviors. If the child used the wheelchair as an excuse not to attend school, parents would have to deal with that, too. In short, the child is still expected to be a useful member of society. The same can be said for the psychotic and depressed person. Medication can relieve suffering and even help to remove the focus from the illness so that the family can be approached on the other issues that inhibit the adolescent's development (e.g., refusing to go to work or to school).

Medicating youngsters is a critical concern not only because of what it symbolizes but also because of how it is administered. Control of medication upon discharge is tied to the goals of family treatment. At that point, who dispenses medication is a structural issue for the family. If an adolescent is acting irresponsibly and parents are demonstrating their control over the youngster, then parents could be placed in charge of dispensing the medication. For example, a distancing father might dispense medication so that he is more involved in the day-to-day care of his child. Alternatively, giving the father that role could signal the message that only illness can draw father in, in which case perhaps a cooperative effort between parents is indicated. On the other hand, parental involvement in the child's domain may be a central concern. In that case, medication could be left to the adolescent, unless the adolescent is deemed too potentially suicidal for the plan to be viable. Perhaps a therapy goal is to help a single parent find a support group. In that situation, enlisting a friend or relative of the parent to refill the prescription or to dispense it while the parent is away is a potential intervention. What is critical is recognizing that how medication is dispensed is an intervention in itself, which should be based on the assessment of family structure and dynamics.

The presentation of the medication issue to the family is also critical. We do not want to reinforce the idea that the child is ill—translated to mean not responsible for his/her behavior. We want medication to be viewed as an adjunct to therapy, a tool, but not a replacement for work on other issues. One psychiatrist on our team presents the necessity of medication as similar to brakes in a car. Brakes alone cannot make a car drive. Yet a car functioning without proper brakes is life-threatening. Similarly, medication alone will not help the adolescent move through this developmental phase and into the next. But without the medication component the adolescent is not safe.

Since we maintain a child-focus while doing family therapy, the fact that medication underlines the concept of the adolescent as the identified patient does not interfere with treatment. The challenge for the family therapist in a hospital setting is how to utilize the child-centered definition of the presenting problem to implement changes throughout the family system.

EDUCATIONAL AND ACTIVITIES PROGRAMS

Adolescents at Charles River Hospital are required to attend tutoring sessions four days a week as well as three activities a day.[5] Activities include didactic seminars on substance abuse and sex education; art and home economics projects; and off-grounds athletics. In preparation for outside responsibilities, adolescents are expected to follow the hospital regimen as they would the regimen of a school day. The only excuse for not going to activities is serious illness, and in that case, the adolescent is required to stay in bed all day. This eliminates the power struggle. We accept the adolescent's evaluation of his/her health and employ a consequence that makes sense only if the child is truly sick. If not, the adolescent is so bored that s/he rarely attempts that excuse again. In addition, this places the adult, rather than the adolescent, in charge of the situation.

The hospital's educational coordinator and the comprehensive therapist work together and with the school system to plan a rapid reentry into an appropriate school program. When family-therapy and educational goals seem to be different, careful coordination is needed to avoid replaying the family chaos within the helper system:

Jane, thirteen, refused to go to school and threatened her single-parent mother. Mother was afraid to make Jane go to school because she did not want to escalate her daughter's volatile behavior, did not feel that she (mother) had the support needed to enforce her limits, and was concerned that the school program was inappropriate to meet Jane's needs. In addition, the mother had recently lost her own father, it was the tenth anniversary of her husband's departure, and she was lonely and fragile. It was hypothesized that Jane did not go to school because (a) she was concerned about her mother's ability to manage without her at home, and (b) she was testing her mother's strength and authority.

After two weeks as an inpatient, Jane was told by her mother and therapist that she was

to return to school from the hospital within the next two days. Mother would drive her to school and pick her up after school. If Jane refused, mother would order bed-rest at the hospital. If Jane complied, mother would take her out after school for a brief pass. However, psychoeducational testing concurrently revealed that Jane could not do seventh-grade academic work and needed an alternative program. Specifically, the educational specialist informed the treatment team that returning Jane to her former class would set her up for failure and that she should await an opening in a new program which more adequately met her educational needs. The two plans obviously conflicted, and a meeting was immediately called, at which it became clear that two separate issues were involved, one relating to content and the other to process. Jane could not handle the academic program. However, if we waited until she was admitted to an alternative program, the momentum of the family work would have been lost: The "process" required immediate reentry, for mother was now ripe to enforce her daughter's school attendance.

The solution accommodated both treatment goals. Jane was required to go to her old school until a new program was in place. However, she attended only the classes in which she would not experience failure due to her specific auditory processing problem. For example, while she did not attend her Spanish class, she did attend gym and fine arts. In that way, both her need for an appropriate hierarchy (mother enforcing the rule that Jane attend school) and her need to avoid the inevitable failure of certain classes were addressed.

PREPARING FOR DISCHARGE

Throughout this section, we have indirectly been discussing methods of preparing an adolescent for discharge from the hospital. In a short-term program where adolescents are expected to go home, discharge planning must begin the day of admission. Usually a community support system must be organized during hospitalization in order for the adolescent to succeed. For example, the educational specialist works with the school system so that an appropriate academic or vocational program is in place or in the making by the time of discharge.

Often we prepare for discharge by hav-

[5]We are grateful to Edith LaBran, M.Ed., and Ann Cunningham, M.Ed., for initiating the educational and activities programs, respectively.

ing the adolescent return to school while still at the hospital. At times, it is astounding to see the issues that arise when such a plan is implemented! For example, sometimes a parent does not show up to take the child to school. The parent's role in maintaining the problem behavior then becomes evident, and interventions are planned. The school system also feels supported by this procedure, since school officials know that the child is returning to the hospital and not being "dumped" back at school, after discharge, without preparation. Sometimes, the distance between home and hospital is too great to have a parent pick the adolescent up in the morning and return him/her the same day. Since hospital insurance will not often cover overnight passes, we may arrange for short (2- to 5-day) discharges, during which time the adolescent is expected to abide by a school contract, and families to continue with therapy and to call the hospital when advice is needed. The adolescent is then readmitted to deal with the problems that surface during the interlude.

An aftercare therapy plan is also critical. If the adolescent already has a therapist, that person is involved throughout the hospitalization, whether by phone with the comprehensive therapist or by seeing and talking to the patient face-to-face. As a transitional step, adolescent and parents are encouraged to see the outpatient therapist in the outpatient office before discharge. If no outpatient therapist is involved, the comprehensive therapist will offer treatment or help the family devise a more economical or geographically feasible plan. The hospital also offers transition groups, to which the patients can return for two post-hospitalization sessions; and one free-of-charge, follow-up, multiple-family group session and/or long-term, aftercare, multiple-family group therapy.

If the adolescent has dropped out of or completed high school, s/he is encouraged to job hunt while at the hospital. Extra passes are available for job interviews, and hospital staff help with finding prospective jobs and by teaching the adolescent interview skills.

In order to prepare parents for their ad-

olescent's discharge, we encourage them to form their own support groups. In that way, the intergenerational boundaries are clearer, parents are less dependent on the adolescent for support, and the adolescent may pursue his/her developmentally appropriate tasks. For example, some mothers expand their support system by getting jobs, some parents find friends within the inpatient multiple-family groups, and other parents are reconnected with extended families.

While preparing a patient for discharge, we will, at times, plan a rehospitalization.[6] Sometimes it is clear that while it is safe enough for a formerly suicidal adolescent to go home for the time being, further hospitalization might be needed. Generally, this is because the problem-maintaining solutions reappear since there has not been enough time for the new structures and patterns to settle and solidify. Rather than waiting for a crisis, we intervene during the hospitalization by predicting the crisis and normalizing it. Predicting a crisis and a setback is also used with disordered adolescents. Recently, we began a new and very effective plan for some suicidal cases, which we label "planned readmissions." Prior to discharge, a date is set for readmission. Depending on the severity of the safety risk, this could be one to six weeks from the date of discharge. The adolescent is required to be readmitted for a set period of time, generally for seven to ten days, on a repeated basis. Therefore, before the family becomes desperate, before the adolescent feels that the situation is hopeless and makes a suicide attempt, s/he has the alternative of hospitalization.

Multiple admissions may also be planned for several other clinical purposes in addition to preventing a desperate family from precipitating a self-destructive move. First, this plan can be used if an adolescent has organic problems and the family needs a respite or reevaluation to assess the prog-

[6]Stuart Koman, Ph.D., and the first author (Marsha Mirkin, Ph.D.) were responsible for developing the concept of planned readmission. Dr. Koman also assisted in formulating ideas for this section of the chapter.

ress of treatment. Second, some adolescents grow so attached to the hospital that they may fail at home in order to return to the hospital. In these cases, readmission is contingent on fulfilling a contract over a certain number of days or weeks:

> Donna had a history of refusing to go to school. She claimed that she was not ready to leave the hospital on her discharge date, and might not "have the strength" to go to school. A week's readmission was made contingent upon her attending school for five consecutive days. At that point, Donna and her family could decide not to return to the hospital, since she was coping with school, or to return for the week's stay.

Third, some families take a "flight into health" and seem to be better in a miraculously short time. It is predictable that these families may once again have problems, and planned readmission can provide them with help while allowing them to save face (they don't have to call the hospital to tell us that they really weren't doing as well as they tried to appear). For example, thirteen-year-old Michele came to the hospital with dizzy spells which could not medically be explained. Her dizzy spells disappeared on the first day after admission, and she and her parents agreed that since everything else in her life was going well, there was no need for her to stay in the hospital. The therapist predicted that the dizzy spells would most likely return if they were based on some problem that Michele was not yet ready to explore, and if that were the case, they would most likely return within eight weeks. Therefore, a readmission was planned for that time, and the family could certainly opt to refuse the admission offer if Michele continued to be symptom-free. Michele returned in eight weeks, ready to work on the issues underlying her dizzy spells.

Finally, planned readmissions are a way of avoiding hospital failure. For example, research coordinated by our colleague, Pamela Slater, Ph.D., indicates that certain youths are at high risk to be discharged from the hospital due to severe misbehavior. After a certain number of weeks, the adolescents begin to break very serious rules. Therefore, upon admission, a plan is made for them to earn a "vacation" from the hospital after a brief period of successful treatment, and then to be readmitted. This pacing of their treatment plan keeps them from reaching that critical time when they are at risk for a disciplinary discharge and thus averts another round in their failure cycle.

Initially, a plan for rehospitalization helps families to feel secure and makes their crisis predictable. At some future time, as the new family structure solidifies, the family no longer wants and, in fact, resents the hospital intrusion. If the entire family decides that repeated hospitalization is unnecessary, and argues convincingly against the treatment plan, then the therapist tells them that s/he will go along with the family decision since they know their own needs best. This helps to wean them from the therapist, develops confidence in their own decision-making ability, and avoids dependence on the hospital. This strategy is taken, in part, from the Palo Alto use of restraining techniques (Walzlawick, Weakland, & Fisch, 1974).

Discharge is not merely a date, it is a process. It is the process of preparing the family and the community for the adolescent's reentry, of setting up support groups, of assessing educational needs and planning accordingly, of encouraging more off-grounds responsibilities, and of developing confidence in the family's ability to meet and handle crisis without dependency on the hospital.

ADMINISTRATIVE SUPPORT

The best program cannot be developed and maintained without administrative support within the hospital.[7] Thus, the establishment of institutional support for a

---

[7] We were very fortunate to have the support of our administrators—Frederick Thacher, President; Robert Cserr, M.D.; Ethan S. Rofman, M.D.; Peter Morris, M.B.A.; Claudine Swidler, M.S.; and Gerald Stechler, Ph.D.—as we developed, implemented, and revised the adolescent program.

separate adolescent program with a unified clinical philosophy is a necessary prerequisite to this and similar programs. Adolescents make noise, are physically active, and appear intimidating. Professional staff can be equally resistant to the development or implementation of the program. If administration officers do not support the clinical philosophy and treatment program, then chronic difficulties will occur. These problems often manifest themselves around budget review or space allocation and reflect underlying institutional resistance to treatment of this age group or to the philosophy behind the treatment. Therefore, a clinical director with a total systems perspective—family, community, hospital—is critical. This person must understand the effects of upper administration on the functioning of the program and be able to intervene accordingly.

SUMMARY

In this chapter we discussed the conceptualization and implementation of a short-term, family-oriented, inpatient adolescent program. Our major perspective is a systems approach, taken not only with the family in the therapist's office, but also in the entire development and implementation of the program. The adolescent, family, therapist, milieu staff, hospital staff and administration, school system, and community agencies are all defined as parts of the system that must be organized to allow for far-reaching change and rapid reintegration of the adolescent into his/her home and community school.

REFERENCES

Abend, S. B., Kachalsky, H. & Greenberg, H. R. Reactions of adolescents to short hospitalization. *American Journal of Psychiatry*, 1968, **124**, 949.

Abroms, G., Fullner, C. & Whitaker, C. The family enters the hospital. *American Journal of Psychiatry*, 1971, **127**, 1363–1370.

Bhatti, R. S., Janakiramaiah, N., & Channabasavanna, S. M. Family psychiatry ward treatment in India. *Family Process*, 1980, **19**, 193–200.

Byng-Hall, J., & Bruggen, P. Family admission decisions as a therapeutic tool. *Family Process*, 1974, **13**, 443–459.

Carter, E., & McGoldrick, M. *The family life cycle.* NY: Gardner Press, 1980.

Charles River Hospital. *Charles River Hospital parent guide.* Wellesley, MA, 1983.

Combrinck-Graham, L., Gursky, E. J., & Brendler, J. Hospitalization of single-parent families of disturbed children. *Family Process*, 1982, **21**, 141–152.

Falstein, E. I., Feinstein, S. L., & Cohen, W. P. An integrated adolescent care program in a general psychiatric hospital. *American Journal of Orthopsychiatry*, 1960, **30**, 276–291.

Fineberg, B., Kettlewell, P., & Sowards, S. An evaluation of adolescent inpatient services. *Journal of Orthopsychiatry*, 1982, **52**(2), 337–345.

Gibson, R. The intensive psychotherapy of hospitalized adolescents. *Journal of the American Academy of Psychoanalysis*, 1974, **2**(3), 187–200.

Glasser, B. A., Hartmann, E. L., & Avery, N. Attitudes toward adolescents on adult wards of a mental hospital. *American Journal of Psychiatry*, 1967, **124**(3), 317–322.

Haley, J. *Leaving home.* NY: McGraw-Hill, 1980.

Harbin, H. A family oriented psychiatric inpatient unit. *Family Process*, 1979, **18**, 281–290.

Holmes, D. *The adolescent in psychotherapy.* Boston: Little, Brown, 1964.

Leavitt, M. The discharge crisis: The experience of families of psychiatric patients. *Nursing Outreach*, 1975, **24**(1), 33–40.

Madanes, C. Strategic family therapy in the prevention of hospitalization. In H. Harbin, (Ed.), *The psychiatric hospital and the family.* Jamaica, NY: Spectrum Publications, 1982.

Madanes, C. The prevention of rehospitalization of adolescents and young adults. *Family Process*, 1980, **19**(2), 179–192.

Minuchin, S. *Families and Family Therapy*, Cambridge: Harvard University Press, 1974.

Mirkin, M. P. The Peter Pan syndrome: Systematic approaches to short-term inpatient treatment of anorexia nervosa. *International Journal of Family Therapy*, 1983, **5**(3), 289–295.

Norton, N., Detre, T., & Jarecki, H. Psychiatric services in general hospitals: A family oriented redefinition. *Journal of Nervous and Mental Disease*, 1963, **136**, 475–484.

Orvin, G. H. Intensive treatment of the adolescent and his family. *Archives of General Psychiatry*, 1974, **31**, 801–806.

Parmelee, D. X. The adolescent and the young adult. In L. I. Sederer (Ed.). *Inpatient psychiatric disorders and treatment.* Baltimore: Williams & Williams, 1983.

Ricci, R. J., Pravder, M. D., Parmelee, D. X.,

& LaBran, E. A comprehensive short-term inpatient treatment program for adolescents. Symposium presented at the 88th annual meeting of the American Psychological Association, Montreal, 1980.

Rosenstock, H., & Vincent, K. Parental involvement as a requisite for successful adolescent therapy. *Journal of Clinical Psychiatry*, 1979, **40**, 132–134.

Schiedeck, R. A. A treatment program for adolescent on an adult ward. *Bulletin of the Menninger Clinic*, 1961, **25**(5), 241–248.

Schween, P. & Gralnick, A. Factors affecting family therapy in the hospital setting. *Comprehensive Psychiatry*, 1966, **7**(5), 424–431.

Stern, S., Whitaker, C., Hagemann, N., Anderson, R. & Bargman, G. Anorexia nervosa: The hospital's role in family treatment. *Family Process*, 1981, **20**, 395–408.

Suchotliff, L. Crisis induction and parental involvement: A prerequisite of successful treatment in an inpatient setting. *Adolescence*, 1978, **13**(52), 697–702.

Walzlawick, P., Weakland, J. H. & Fisch, R. *Change: Principles of problem formulation and problem resolution*. New York: Norton, 1974.

8

The Role of the Family in Residential Treatment

*A. MICHAEL DeSISTO
and NEWTON KOLTZ*

P arents with a seriously acting-out child have available to them a number of choices. One of these is residential treatment, even though this involves a temporary or long term physical separation of the child from the family home. For a number of reasons, some of which we will discuss later, many families and therapists find this an appalling choice. To "break up" the family temporarily seems as unacceptable as breaking it up permanently. Whatever reasons or fears give rise to this thinking, our experience is otherwise. Residential treatment of troubled children in close association with a program that intimately involves the rest of the family often allows these families to grow more deeply and richly connected—more passionately alive as a family—than most "normal" families.

Residential treatment is often seen as the last resort for families in which the youngsters seem so out of control that their parents can't in any way handle them and take care of them. This is not the way we see our kind of residential treatment. Rather, the choice to send a child to a school such as DeSisto is a choice that any family might want to make, based on its own perception of its needs, objectives, and resources.[1]

In this chapter we will be looking at the program that operates at the two DeSisto schools (in West Stockbridge, Massachusetts, and in Howey-in-the-Hills, Florida). It's the program we know best. But also, and more important, there is a wide diversity in the mixture of the children here, ranging from "normal, well-functioning kids," whose families have been impressed by the program and have felt it offered themselves and their children opportunities they couldn't find elsewhere, to fairly seriously emotionally disturbed children; and ranging in background from upper-middle-class children, to children who are publically funded and referred to us by the courts or other public bodies.

[1]Several parents whose children do not act out in any major way have sent their children to DeSisto because they believe the family will benefit from the program. This will not be the case with most other residential facilities, where the focus will usually be somewhat narrower.

Academically, the DeSisto schools offer a college preparatory program. Consequently, each child has to be bright enough to handle that program. The only other criterion for admission is that the child must not be organically dysfunctional. But most important, at least for the purposes of this chapter, the treatment program at DeSisto involves the entire family; the parents' participation is essential. If they don't take part, the entire family is expelled from the school until the parents commit themselves to taking part.

First, we'll discuss, generally, the choice of residential treatment. Then we'll focus entirely on the DeSisto schools: their philosophy; program structure; family participation; and the actual process children and parents go through.

THE CHOICE OF RESIDENTIAL TREATMENT

The choice of residential treatment is not a single, simple choice. There are at least four significant and complex questions to be answered: (1) Should the child be separated from its parents? (2) What are the conditions that indicate residential treatment for this child? (3) What facility is best for the child? (4) When should the child reenter its family?

Should the Child Be Separated from Its Parents?

The answer to this question often has little to do with the actual behavior of the child or with the parents' ability to cope with that behavior, but with the predisposition of the family or therapist to keep the family physically together at all costs, or not.

Just as one segment of the population would never, never think of their children growing up without boarding school, and another segment thinks that sending their children to boarding school and depriving them of home and family is one of the cruelest acts parents can commit, so there are

many parents and therapists who believe there is nothing better for the children than the right residential treatment; and other parents and therapists who would *never* consider that option. For the latter, the conviction that the family must be kept physically intact amounts to a powerful, unconditional imperative.

We have no argument here with those—especially therapists—who are thus predisposed, though it should be obvious that we will be delighted if our chapter changes some of their minds. Many, indeed, turn away horrified at the prospect. "I mean, my God!" they say to themselves. "It's like *my* child is in jail or reform school!" To many parents it feels like the ultimate failure to give one's own child up into others' hands. For many there is a feeling of powerlessness even greater than the feeling of impotence brought about by their own inability to handle the outrages of their children. Parents say to themselves, "If my love is not great enough, and if I am not strong enough to take care of my own flesh-and-blood's problems, how can some absolute stranger—who probably doesn't give a damn for my child, much less care for her or love her—do what I couldn't do?" For these parents—and there are many of them—the risk of residential treatment apparently means risking just about everything that matters deeply—heart and soul, flesh and blood—on a process that is much less controllable than a throw of the dice.

A mother of a boy who is now at DeSisto recently told us how she came to bring her son to the school. She is a strikingly elegant, direct-speaking woman. One would never think, on meeting her, that she was a woman who had ever felt in any way powerless or out of control. But she told us how out of control things had gotten:

My son was acting out to the point where my husband and I could absolutely not cope with it. We were sending him to therapy; and he would take his bicycle (we were living on the West Side of Manhattan then), go into Central Park, get stoned, and never show up at his therapists on the East Side. This went on for a long time, yet his therapist, a woman, did not believe in sending him away . . . and she was effecting nothing, absolutely nothing. I was also in therapy at the time, and I was at such a point where I was really ready to jump out of a window, when my therapist said, "Have you considered sending your son to a residential treatment center—or at least getting him to somewhere out of the house? Obviously, as a family, you can't live with him anymore." He started to build up enough confidence in me and to take away enough guilt so that in time I was able to go forward. But if he hadn't encouraged me or allowed me the space to do it myself, I don't know whether I would have had the energy to go through with it. I would have just suffered and my son would have gone down the tubes.

This mother's story, in our experience, is not unusual. The child acts out in order to call attention to whatever he or she needs to call attention to. The parents, for whatever reason, are unable to handle the acting out, much less satisfy the need (doubtless a very powerful one they are unable to satisfy in themselves) which the acting-out is crying out to satisfy. The child panics—just as infants burst into tantrums—and, as it were, raises the volume of acting out until he or she feels totally panicked and out of control, and the parents totally helpless. The child has taken over control of the family, which for the parents is an experience rather like having their home hijacked by a mad, raging terrorist whom—because it is their child—they love passionately and dearly. Tragically, everyone in the family feels impotent to do anything. And the kid is calling the shots. Now the point has been reached when such options as residential treatment should be seriously considered.

Nearly twenty years of experience watching hundreds of families undergo a process very like the one above leads us to the conclusion that the real choice of residential treatment is much of the time made by the *child*! The child and not the parents, in these cases, "knows" how bad things are, "knows" that s/he will find what is missing only outside the family, and acts out (the usual form of communication in such cases) until parents take the necessary action. Parents, in other words, can't or don't see or acknowledge what is going on in their families, so the children, by acting out, convince them that there are problems.

It is, of course, hard to say at what level of awareness the child "knows" what he or she needs to do. The child certainly will not come up to parents and say in measured, rational tones, "Uh, say, Mom, Dad, I have a serious problem you may or may not be aware of and which I certainly believe requires immediate attention. I've considered all the options and concluded that residential treatment is the best course of action for me." A kid who would make that speech to parents is probably truly insane or an emotional prodigy and beyond the need for treatment. The child's acting out is the real message—the true language—spoken to the parents.

It is not the particular vehicle, the particular kind of acting-out behavior, in our experience, that counts; it is whatever finally gets a child noticed—gets parents' attention enough for them to take action. Some children, for instance, whose parents are heavy drug users, will become heavy alcohol users. Those kids would never *think* of taking drugs, since their parents would not notice. Others get punk haircuts or have their heads shaved; and that will be enough. Others go further:

> A girl, Rebecca, lived in Westchester County. Her parents had been Jewish, but became the Waspiest of Wasps, the highest of high church. They belonged to a fox-hunting club in Connecticut, and there they spent their Sabbath. So, given this, Rebecca tried every trick in the book: she smoked dope, cut school, acted out sexually—the works. But there was no real response to all this, no significant action taken, so finally the girl bought a used black gabardine overcoat and had her hair almost completely shaven. Rebecca became the most Orthodox of Jewish Orthodox. And *that* got attention. Soon after she was at DeSisto.

Similarly, children will let you know by acting out that they need to stay in residential treatment. They want to make sure that their parents are aware that it's not yet time for them to return home for good.

> Connie is a fifteen-year old going on forty. She is stunningly beautiful and *very* mature.

She had to grow up early because her parents didn't take care of her. Connie went home from school for eleven days of an eighteen-day vacation, and she was perfect for the entire eleven days—until the final night. Her parents—she knew—wanted her to stay home for good. And Connie thought she agreed with them. So she returned to school and met with her therapist. "I'm so *upset* with myself!" Connie told the therapist. "Why did I have to be so bad the last day? I had my parents all convinced that I should stay home. And then this one last night I went out and had sex and drank and took dope, and didn't come home until early in the morning. So they sent me back to school; and now they won't keep me home." The therapist replied, "And suppose you were home for thirteen days. What night do you think you'd do it?"

Connie "knew" that her parents didn't parent her properly and that school was the best place for her. So she went home and had a lovely vacation, then acted out the night before she was supposed to come back in order to send a message to her parents that she really needed to be at school.

What Are the Conditions That Indicate Residential Treatment for This Child?

Again, the answer to this question often has little to do with the actual behavior of the child, but with whether or not the parents have resources left with which to handle the behavior of the child. Though they may not acknowledge this consciously, at bottom the parents may feel that they are no longer able to be parents. They no longer feel capable, on their own, of taking care of their child, or of providing the nurturing and the role modeling the child needs. And they feel helpless in setting up and enforcing limits on the child.

Clearly, such parents have *not* failed, any more than any of us is a failure when our car breaks down and we can't fix it. In some areas or departments, these parents simply don't know how to parent (probably because their own parents didn't know how to parent in these areas and could not pass these abilities on).

It's not a surprise that many parents are unable to face the intense feelings of fear, guilt, loss, and failure that such thoughts inevitably bring up. These parents will thus often refuse to admit to themselves that they have exhausted their own resources in dealing with their child and that action must be taken beyond what they can do on their own—or with the help of therapists or other support facilities available to them. So these parents will often let things go along, let things run their course, let time sort things out, until the child (as we have just seen) takes matters out of the parents' control and gets the action that he or she "knows" is needed.

Finally, for those who—with *justification*—would like to see clear and explicit guidelines for choosing a residential school, we have few to give. Like the decisions about where to live, to work, to vacation, to go to school, to get therapy, the decision about residential treatment needs to flow out of the family's awareness of its needs, resources, and objectives. Generally, as we have earlier pointed out, families, by a process of elimination, make their choice to send their child away to a school like DeSisto. The other courses of action they have tried have not worked to their satisfaction, so they come to us.

What Facility Is Best for the Child?

It's important that those involved in making the choice for or against residential treatment understand that they are not choosing for or against some monolithic entity, Residential Treatment, any more than a family choosing to add a religious dimension to its life is thereby choosing a monolithic entity, Religion. They don't choose Religion; they choose a church, a synagogue, a temple, or maybe even a quiet upland meadow. The range of residential programs is simply enormous. This means, of course, that parents looking for a program for their child, or therapists looking to recommend a program for a family, have a load of rather disagreeable labor to go through before they find the program that best seems to fit the child's needs.

There are not even directories to help them. They are pretty much completely on their own. On the other hand, paradoxically, the variety of programs available should offer considerable comfort to parents and therapists, since *somewhere* there's a place that can offer the best hope that this child's needs and problems will be taken care of.

Thus residential treatment ranges from "normal" boarding schools where there are one or two psychologists hidden away, as it were, in back rooms (often parents with children in such institutions don't want to know if their children have "problems," or else the children don't want their parents to know, or else the institutions don't want the parents to know), all the way up to institutions—usually for extremely disturbed children—that are nearly pure therapeutic communities that offer little or no academic training.

There are also wide differences in these institutions. Some take only children with a particular kind of problem, for instance, very seriously emotionally disturbed children, or children with severe learning disabilities. Others deal with a particular problem for a time, and then when they see an improvement they ask the child to leave. Others, such as DeSisto's, encourage a very heterogeneous grouping, ranging from disturbed youngsters all the way up to youngsters who are well functioning. We expect our students to complete their high school at DeSisto; and indeed, some of them take college courses we've made available in association with a local college.

In some institutions the family is part of the child's treatment program—or rather, and more properly, the entire family is treated. In other institutions the family is not. And there are gradations. The families who send their children away to prep school, for example, are often families where problems such as acting out or depression simply do not exist—by definition, by fiat, and/or by tradition. Then there are the parents and families who are so hopeless that there would be no gain in involving them in a residential treatment program. Similarly, if the child is severely abused, it may be impractical to involve the

parents. And finally there are times when, through death or desertion, one or two parents are simply not available.

One remedy for the scarcity of information about the variety of residential treatment choices available is for each therapist entering family therapy—as part of the training or at least as a point of personal responsibility—to try to visit and experience at first hand as many different kinds of residential settings as possible. Personal experience is much more valuable than directories, which are quickly outdated anyway.

When Should the Child Re-enter Its Family?

As residential programs differ, so the ways the child reenters the family differ. Some programs will recommend a halfway house or some other half-way program between the very tight residential, institutional model and the home. Other programs will recommend that the child enter a regular residential school after leaving the program. Other programs will bring the child to the point where he or she can reenter the home; here the reentry and transition are themselves part of the program of the facility.

Even when a program is working successfully and a child is beginning to function well, that does not mean that he or she will yet—or maybe ever—be able to tolerate even a short stay with the family. Likewise, the parents may not be able as yet—or ever—to tolerate or handle the child. Parents, children, school, and therapists have to be able to deal with the possibility of that impasse. A lot of the answer to the question about reentry of the child into the family often depends on how well the child and the parents feel they can tolerate the dynamics that go on between them; it depends on their own sense of their own readiness to make the move: When they're ready to do it, they do it (with the help and advice, we hope, of the school and the therapists). How soon and under what conditions does the family feel "ready"? That depends on its own personal goals and objectives. Parents who are not comfortable with more than a short-term physical separation of their child from their home will often choose a program that will quickly modify the child's behavior enough to accomplish that goal. There are a number of programs that do this quite successfully.

At the other end of the spectrum are programs such as DeSisto's where the objective is to try to discover the causes that underly the family's crisis and pain and to start both parents and children on the way to permanent change and growth.[2] Such change usually takes a long time to achieve; and the child might stay with us for several years, though the family is vitally present and active in the child's life even though it may be, much of the time, several hundred—or a thousand—miles away. A number of other programs exist whose objectives lie somewhere between those that offer short-term crisis intervention and those such as ours that seek to attain more permanent results.

Finally, though this is not true in every case, we have observed that many parents who remove their children from our program before completing it do that because they (the parents) are not ready to let themselves grow. They have learned enough to be able to deal with and handle the acting out and craziness of their child or their children, but they haven't yet learned to acknowledge what is missing in their own personalities. So, as often happens in such cases, even though the child may not be significantly "healthier" than when he or she came to DeSisto, the parents will take the child home. The child will then act out in all the old ways, but there is now a slightly newer dynamic: The parents can now handle it. The child's behavior no longer causes them to feel impotent, helpless, and out of control. But in a deeper

[2]A discussion of how we try to do this comes in later sections. It's probably useful to say here that we don't believe that the DeSisto program is in every case the best way for a family to achieve this goal. Some families try DeSisto and find it doesn't work for them. So they go on to something else.

sense, the old dynamics remain. The parents need to have to spend their lives dealing with their acting-out kids in order *not* to have to face their own problems. The acting-out kids are the parents' addiction. We have found that when the children from such families go on to college (*if* they go on to college), they very often fall apart after they get there. As long as the kids remain at DeSisto, however, the possibility exists that that dynamic will change, and if they, with their families, complete our program, they usually go on to college and do well.

THE DeSISTO PROGRAM

Philosophy

Writing about the philosophy of the DeSisto program, in the sense of its theoretical framework and sources, makes us a bit uncomfortable. On the one hand, we like to hope that we are too eclectic (defined as: the theft of any method that will help us) to be pinned down with a philosophy; and, on the other hand, we like to think that what we do that works is experiential, coming out of the shared experiences, over many years, of hundreds of families, staff members, dorm parents, teachers, and therapists.

The program starts, the process starts—and one might say this is the starting point of our philosophy—when messed-up families come and acknowledge to themselves that they are messed up and commit to doing something about it. Having said this, we can describe a few working principles we have inferred from our trials and errors, mistakes and successes. These have to do with the nature of parenting and growth, of love, and of therapy.

PARENTING

In its most primitive form, the relationship between parent and child is the relationship between the "taker of care" and the "needer of care." The parent, the "taker of care," knows both how to take care of him/herself and how to take care of the child. And the child, at least in the beginning of its life, is absolutely needy. The child grows to be a parent (or adult; the terms are interchangeable in this context) by learning—especially from its parents—how to take care of itself. In this less-than-best of worlds those of us who are parents find ourselves all too often not knowing how to satisfy any number of important emotional and other needs for ourselves and for our children (often because our own parents also didn't know how). Sometimes children figure out for themselves how to get for themselves what they are missing from their parents. These times the children are parenting themselves and growing. Other times the children don't figure out how to get what they need. Then they seek other satisfactions, often non-nurturing ones like drugs or promiscuity, in order to replace, make up for, or anaesthetize the loss. Or they bury the need—"act in." "Acting in" is our term for a process roughly equivalent to displacement or repression. There is a strong parallel between "acting out" and "acting in." The lonely, depressed girl who buries herself all the time in books "acts in," while the lonely, depressed girl who is promiscuous "acts out." The book reader is usually seen as a "good" girl. The promiscuous girl is seen as a "bad" girl, and her promiscuity as a "crisis." Actually, the issue for each of them is the same.

None of these last ideas, we imagine, will much astonish anyone likely to be reading them. But it seemed necessary to us to state them here anyway, since what follows from them is so crucial to our understanding of what we are doing: The school—the DeSisto school—has to *be*, for the children who go there and for their parents, whatever is missing in their families. It has to parent the children in those ways their parents do not know how to parent. And it has to provide for the parents—to the extent that they are themselves children and needy—ways to learn for themselves how to parent themselves. Doing this is, of course, good for the parents, but it is also good for the children, who need to see their parents doing it, role-modelling it, and growing from it. Sometimes, wonderfully, children grow faster than their parents, and the parents learn from the children. It often happens, for instance, that parents who do not express tenderness or anger very well, learn how to do that from their kids.

Since we see the school as an extension of the family and not a replacement for it, we expect the parents to take an active part in those areas of the program, especially the parent groups, that pertain to them (see Parent Groups). If parents find ways of avoiding taking part, then, as night follows day, their children will probably also find ways of avoiding taking part. But more important, we see the family's commitment to participate as more than just a commitment to the school; it's a commitment to itself. Reneging on that commitment is reneging on the family, which may well be one of the main reasons the child came to DeSisto in the first place. Thus, if a parent regularly misses attending his or her parent group, the entire family is expelled from the school until the parent commits to take part. (See also Expulsion, below.)

LOVE

Humankind has a large, unused capacity for joy and, beyond that, a large, unused capacity for ecstasy. Many of us fear joy. We're frightened of pleasure. We go to enormous pains in order to keep ourselves from having as much fun as we are capable of. And we are terrified of more and greater intimacy than we now enjoy. We keep our relationships stable—unmoving. Or hardly moving. We take comfort in what comfort we have. Like tires spinning on ice, we stay in the same place, apparently going forward but really going nowhere.

Thus in many, many families in crisis, there is enormous love. But all too often the love does not come out. It does not show. It is not felt. It does not pass from parent to parent, from parent to child, or from child to parent. It is as though no one is speaking the same emotional language, or else, to alter the metaphor, it is as though from fear and disuse the emotional "umbilical" joining each person has atrophied. Without love, most of us turn rigid and icy, or else we panic, flail around, and act crazy, as though a plastic bag covered our head and kept us from breathing.

It's often said of families in crisis that they are suffering from the absence of love. In our experience, this is hardly ever the case. The love is there and in abundance. The problem, rather, is that it doesn't pass through the "umbilical" (we also call this the "atrophied intake valve"), and then the crisis is the acting out of the resultant feelings of deprivation.

One piece of the program at DeSisto, consequently, is that we attempt to reconstruct the emotional "umbilical." We assign parents and children exercises that are personal and timely—much like some of the exercises Gestalt therapists use—exercises in taking in and sharing love.

Therapy

Therapy, with or without the help of a "therapist," happens whenever either or both of the following events happen: (1) a person does something (usually but not always emotionally) he or she was not able to do previously; and/or (2) a person comes to be closer to another than s/he was previously. Therapy is, in other words, learning to take care of yourself in ways you couldn't before, and learning to love in ways you couldn't before.[3]

Though therapy, most of the time, focuses, of necessity, on serious emotional difficulties, it would be well for therapists to recall from time to time that infinite growth is possible. The end of therapy is not just getting somebody's personality enough together so that he or she does not collapse in catastrophic disarray. Sadly, sometimes this is the best anyone can expect. Still, it would be nice if *everyone* could be in therapy. It's hard to imagine anyone who would not like to find new levels of closeness to loved ones, or who would not

like to find new feelings, or ways of feeling, or ways of expressing feelings.

Just about everyone at the DeSisto schools is in therapy—all the students and all the faculty and staff who have direct contact with the students. The children are in therapy for all the obvious reasons, as well as to learn to parent themselves and to love. The faculty and staff are in therapy for the same reasons, and also because these kids we are trying to parent are among the world's most skilled and successful manipulators, saboteurs, and messers-up of other people, and especially of those who try to parent them. Anyone who takes them on needs all the help s/he can get.

Though the DeSisto schools are not "Gestalt" schools, the therapists are Gestalt-trained, since we have found that that mode of therapy tends to work well with the segment of the population we deal with.

In most residential facilities, either the therapeutic role is seen as functionally superior to the academic role; or the academic role is seen as superior to the therapeutic one. There are usually powerful, concrete reasons why each facility chooses its system. At DeSisto, however, we have tried to merge academics and therapy into a system that allows each to be equal and separate, operationally and legally. There are two corporations, an academic corporation and a therapeutic one; and each has its own responsibility towards the entire school community.

The therapist's job is to be the child's advocate in the community, to keep the youngster in school, to fight for the kid, to be his or her ombudsperson, to deal with the kid in the best possible way, and to adjust the community to the child. The academic's job—which includes dorm parents, faculty, and administration—is to look out for the entire community and to adjust the child to the community. Each of these separate but equal components operates from its own special vantage point. Nothing can be done until they both agree—and they often disagree about how a particular child should be handled. From this tension comes the treatment plan for the particular child. All concerned have to

[3]What we mean by "therapy" and what we mean by "growth" are virtually identical. The difference is that in "therapy" there is usually but not always a "helper" who facilitates the growth.

get together and put together a plan they can all agree to implement.

Every kid comes to school with specific needs, and he will put specific stresses on the community. The therapist's job, then, is to elucidate that: What is *this* kid's need to do what she does? How can the community handle and take care of *her* specific needs? Some kids will fight, for example. One kid fights as a defense against cooperating and out of a fear of being taken over and controlled. Another kid fights in reaction to his parents' leaving the country for three months. The therapist advocates for the process that each youngster needs.

The therapist will also keep in touch with the parents. Confidentiality will be maintained, but parents will be kept up to date about how the child is doing and how they can help.

As we have said earlier in other ways, we are not just seeking behavior change. It's not our aim simply to turn the "criminal"—after a few weeks or months in confinement—into a "guard." By the same token, most kids, in time, will get smart. They'll learn how to go along and pretend they are better. We don't want kids to figure out how to beat the system so they can get "parole." What we are after therapeutically is change in depth. We want the child to be able to build in his or her own personality the strength to tolerate his or her experience and the pains and vicissitudes of life without having to act out or use other ways of escape.

In order to do this we try to make the therapist the catalyst in a close alliance between school, parents, and teenager. It happens, of course, that parents and teenagers resist the alliance in various ways. They stonewall us. They try to sabotage the alliance. They fight us. They run away. And so on. But these resistances are to be expected. They are part of the therapeutic process.

Practice

Over the years certain systems, structures, and methods have evolved at De-Sisto. Some of these we've discovered as a result of working through our own problems and difficulties. Some we've taken from elsewhere. We'll describe briefly those few that we believe will provide a sense of the personality of the program.

COMMUNICATION

Parents need to know what their children are up to; and children need to know that their parents are there for them. Since both of these pieces are often missing in the families that come to us, we work especially hard to ensure that they are not missing at DeSisto.

Consequently, everyone dealing with the kids—from director to dorm parents to therapists to faculty—has to be accessible to them as close to "all the time" as is practical and possible. All the faculty and most of the staff live on or near the campus in apartments provided by the school. The dorm parents live in the dorm. But therapists, however, because they have a different function in the community from these others live off-campus. Still, they are expected to be present and "on tap" for a few days a week (it's wonderful to have a therapist handy to help sort out a crisis while the crisis is actually occurring).

Students are free to attend and to participate in all meetings except those where confidentiality is necessary. And there are no private offices with secretarial barricades for the administration and senior staff. Senior staff, administrators, and secretaries are all together in one large room. It's noisy, and there is more traffic than most people like, but the openness and accessibility created outweigh those discomforts.

Even as we try to make ourselves available to the kids and be there for them, we also *have* to be aware of what each of them is up to. We can't as "parents" take care of them and help them to grow (or to put this more formally, we can't develop and implement a treatment plan for them) unless we are tuned in to how each of them acts in the daily situations that really matter. In practice, this means that we—those dealing with the students—have to be all the time sensitive and aware of what's going on around us. And then we have to be able to share these perceptions as soon as possible after they happen. Thus, throughout the day there are *many* meetings, formal and informal, faculty meetings, therapists' meetings, dorm parents' meetings, dorm meetings, and so on, where staff *and* students can all share their feelings and perceptions.

A lot of group therapy goes on in these meetings, and this is no accident.

THE DORM

A youngster's immediate family at DeSisto is his or her dorm. Each dorm has fifteen or so kids of the same sex but mixed in age and in level of development. This mixture is very important, since the Level Three and Level Four kids (see below) help and act as role models for kids at lower levels. Each dorm has a "mother" and "father" (dorm parents).

The dorm is not just *like* a family (it's not a metaphorical family); it's the place the children play and replay, more than anywhere else, all the old games and ways of acting out that they played at home. It's here that they most tellingly recapitulate their old family dynamics. So good dorm parents, the ones who are *there* when all this happens, are crucial to the success of the program. We have found that no academic, professional, or even age qualifications determine who is going to be suitable for this role (we've had very fine dorm parents who have scarcely been older than the kids themselves). What we require are personal characteristics: Dorm parents have to be warm. They have to be eager to be emotionally involved with the kids and to share their own growth processes with them. This means that they don't just show the kids how to do things right. Much more than that, it means that they have to be willing to let the kids see them when they screw up, fail, and do the wrong thing—and then see them recover from that. Most of these children have had much success at failure. They do that all the time, and they do it very well. But they have had little experience with recovery from failure. They don't know how to han-

dle that. This is one of the major lessons dorm parents have to teach them. Dorm parents also must be firm and flexible. They need to be strong enough to enforce the limits that are set. And finally, they must be willing to be in therapy.[4]

CONSENSUS

The groups that make up the total program—dorms, faculty, therapists, parent groups, and so forth—each govern their own affairs. And this is done by consensus. That is, each member can vote "for" an action, "against" an action, or "I'll go along with" an action. The group cannot proceed as long as there is a *no* vote outstanding. Each negative has to be worked through and resolved until a proposed action can be defined in such a way that all the voting members will work for it—or at least won't work against it. In a system where the majority governs, the minority ends up either disappointed or angry; and some of the minority may actively try to sabotage, undermine, or destroy the majority's programs. But once a consensus is reached and everyone agrees to go along with it, then the entire energy of the group is directed toward completing the action they've agreed to take. Often it takes a while—*quite a while!*—to achieve a consensus. But that means less time wasted over all.

Reaching consensus has another benefit for us: Once consensus is reached, everyone in the group shares equal responsibility for the group's actions. Many of the families that come to DeSisto—children and parents—have very successfully evaded taking responsibility for their actions. Group consensus is one of the ways we use to urge them to begin to take responsibility.

LIMITS

You very rarely hear the word "discipline" at DeSisto. You are very likely to hear from the kids that we are very strict, and from their angle they probably have

[4]In addition to their academic function, teachers must also spend some time every week in a dorm working with dorm parents.

a point; but "discipline" is not what we believe we are up to.

Discipline, as we see it, is some kind of authority's way of imposing external order. Its aim is to keep those who are disciplined in line. It shapes them up, but it lasts only so long as the external authority is around to impose it. Sailors on ships are—more or less—disciplined. Sailors on shore-leave are not. For an acting-out adolescent, discipline becomes just one more system to try to beat. "How can I break discipline and not get punished for it?" So we try to avoid the "discipline-punishment" system.

At the same time, every community (from families on up) needs to set certain limits and conditions under which it has to operate. If some of these limits and conditions aren't met, then certain consequences follow. If enough of these are not met, the community ceases to function and breaks apart. And if one or more members of the community seriously and habitually break the community's limits to the point where the community feels severely disrupted or threatened, then the community needs to expel those members until those members can convince the community that they are ready to return and to handle the community's limits.

A made bed and an unmade bed doubtless stand pretty equal in the sight of God, but for most people living in a community, made beds are nicer. And dishes need to be clean. And screaming is noisy; it hurts the ears.

Thus, at DeSisto, there are firm and secure limits. Kids are expected to attend all classes and meals and to be there on time. They're expected to keep their rooms clean and neat and to make their beds. They're expected to have their homework done on time. There is no sex; no drugs; no alcohol. None of these limits or any of the others in effect are in any way unusual. In fact, most of those that directly concern the life of the kids are devised by the kids themselves through such forums as the dorm meetings, which occur regularly and frequently.

All of these rules or limits are broken, whichever ones the kids broke at home.

We know that they will break the rules. And we expect them to keep doing that until they have found ways of replacing the need to break them with behavior that's more enjoyable and nurturing. So we also expect them to be committed to—or at least working towards commitment to—trying to work on and replace their need to get high on drugs or alcohol, or their need for indiscriminate, promiscuous sex, or their need to escape and run away, or their need to lie, or, at bottom, their need for whatever bond that keeps them destructively locked into their families even when their families are miles away.

The consequences of breaching limits vary: If you don't make your bed or clean your room, some other kid, as a result, has to do that for you. So your failure costs you a portion of your weekly allowance, which portion is given over to the one who does the job. If you act up with such hostility and violence that your presence becomes intolerable to others, then your dorm may, by consensus, vote you out; and you have to find someone else on campus who will take you in (which usually happens), until you've demonstrated to your dorm that you are capable of living there again. And if you run away with your boyfriend to a hotel room and stay stoned for a week with him, you'll likely be expelled from school. You won't be allowed on campus until you have demonstrated your willingness to deal with all that. You can get back into school and into your dorm by asking the school and your dorm for a consensus on whether or not to let you back in. Someone who is expelled from a community, of course, has no vote in that community. He or she has lost their "citizenship" in the community until the community takes them back in.

TURN-INS

A lot of times in a conventional family a parent will find the cookies gone or a joint smoked, go to the kid, grab her, and demand that she own up to what she did.

"But I didn't eat the cookies," the kid says.

"You *did*! You had to."

"I didn't."

"You did."

And it goes on and on, back and forth, until at last the kid decides to be honest and admit that she did it. Whap! She gets hit in the head. She's punished at the moment when her dishonesty turns to honesty, demonstrating the sometime futility of honesty. If there are enough scenes like this one, she'll probably learn how to sneak.

We have tried something different at DeSisto, called "turn-ins." A kid who turns herself in for breaking any limit has instant amnesty. And if a kid turns anyone else in for breaking any limit, the limit-breaker too has instant amnesty. The kids can make turn-ins any time they want, and they can make them to whomever they feel comfortable with—therapist, dorm parent, director, teacher, and so on.

Making turn-ins does not give the youngster license to go back and continue doing what he turned himself in for, since a turn-in implies a commitment to change. Turn-ins are about practicing honesty. A turn-in without a commitment to change is dishonest.

LEVELS

One of the things that has most amazed us as we have observed the families who have passed through our schools is how predictable the changes are that each child and family will go through. Of course, each person and each family grows in its own individual way and at its own special rate. Yet almost all who come to our schools pass through similar phases. We've come to call these phases "levels." Parents and children go through the following levels:

As soon as families bring their child to school, they feel wonderful. They have looked incredibly hard to find the *right* place. And then they have heard so many nice things about DeSisto School. "And now *here we are*! We're just so lucky! And we're so thrilled!" . . . That euphoria lasts maybe a week or two. After that everyone starts to ask questions (Level 1a). What they see going on doesn't seem to make sense. And they are right. It does not make

sense. It's not like anything the parents and child have ever experienced before. It scarcely relates to any experience they have ever had. Which is as it should be, because all that they've done did not work. Later, when the answers to their questions still don't seem to be forthcoming (there *are* answers, but they don't appear to be there), questioning turns into a kind of negative tolerance (Level 1b): "I don't like what you are doing at this school. I don't understand what you are doing. And I don't believe in what you are doing. But we're here, so we might as well stay." Sometimes at this stage parents will pull their child out. Their fear and bafflement are just too overwhelming. These first phases (Level 1a and Level 1b) are on a continuum.

When fear, confusion, and hostility change to *positive* tolerance, the children or the parents move on to Level 2. The parents will say, "Well, okay, we'll suffer through this. We'll go through the year and do what they want us to do. We've got nothing to lose. And the kid does seem to be acting sort of together. He's never done that before." The kid will be less articulate. For him, it's: "Okay, I'm stuck here. So I might as well let it go on a while and see what happens."

Later still, the program starts to become really important to them: To the parents, it starts meaning something *for them*, not just for their child. For the child, it's, "Jesus, I really think I'm getting somewhere. And I like what I'm doing!" At this point they are at Level 3.

At Level 4 they are all deeply involved in the program and see what it means and does for them. Now they begin to reach out and start to take care of other people.

Children, faculty, parents, and dorm parents all pass through similar phases—though often not at the same rates. This can be very disturbing and threatening. A child often grows faster than the parents, and the parents will try to pull him or her back. They often need the child *not* to grow. They need to keep the family dynamics unchanged. They need to keep the family system working in the same old way. Without these, the parents themselves might have to start to acknowledge their own problems and begin to change and grow. Often too, a youngster who has grown faster than the parents will want them to catch up, and might urge them to try therapy or some other positive kind of behavior.

We have found these phases of development so universally applicable to those who go through our program that we have made the levels into a formal system. For the students, their levels of emotional growth are to their emotional and personal development what grade levels are to their academic development. Thus, in order to graduate one must not only be a senior who has passed all the required courses; one must also be a senior who has reached Level 4. For faculty, dorm parents, and staff, there is also a level system that closely resembles the one outlined above and that determines, among other things, their pay.

A person moves from one level to the next when he knows he is ready to make the move. And then the person will let people know that the time has come to move up. If the person is mistaken or dishonest, and other people perceive that, then the issue will be thrashed out in the appropriate meetings until a consensus is reached. There are times when a person has reached a new level but is afraid to see it or admit it. Then it's up to the others to let him know, and that issue is thrashed out until consensus is reached.

FAMILY INVOLVEMENT

Families are involved in the treatment program at DeSisto in the following ways:

1) The parents work with other parents, primarily within their parent groups. There are DeSisto parent groups throughout the country.

2) At school, the children deal mostly with that community, but since each of them will inevitably try to recreate his or her own family and the family dynamics he or she is used to, each is, in reality, going to be dealing on many occasions with his or her own "mother" and "father," in spite of their physical absence.

3) The children visit home, and inevitably old dynamics turn up. But also, they might try new dynamics and find them more satisfying.

4) The parents visit school—and, again, old dynamics turn up, though at school there are therapists and other "school parents" available to help sort out what is really going on.

5) And finally, throughout the year there are a number of "Parent-Child Groups" scheduled at the schools and throughout the United States. These are either weeklong or weekend, intensive, multi-family group therapy sessions.

Each of these will be discussed elsewhere in the chapter.

Entry of Families into the Program

REFERRAL.

Families usually hear about the DeSisto schools in the following ways: (1) word of mouth; (2) referrals by therapists and other professionals; (3) referrals by courts and other public bodies; (4) referrals by school guidance counsellors and the like; and (5) media appearances by Michael DeSisto.

Except for the last of these, residential treatment facilities generally find their patients—or students—in pretty much the same way—by networking—which argues for a broader and better information network.

Interestingly, this is confirmed in another way when I, Michael DeSisto, appear on radio or television. Frequently I have brought a student, or a student and his or her family, to appear on a talk show; and we have discussed—sometimes movingly and in great depth—some of the family dynamics. And we discover, wonderfully and astonishingly, that many in the audience begin to recognize themselves, for afterwards we usually receive many letters telling us this.

What is important in these appearances is not just the personal gratification, which is fleeting, or even the opportunity to advertise and promote our schools, but being able to show people that they are not alone, that others are not a lot different from them, and that help is available. Judging from the responses to our media appearances, armies of family therapists and thousands of residential treatment facilities would be required to handle all the families and all the children who need what we can provide but haven't yet availed themselves of it.

ADMISSION

Admission to our program is neither complicated nor formal. There are the usual transcripts and other academic information. And there will usually be psychological reports on the child and/or family, psychological test results, and the like. And sometimes there will be consultation with the child's or family's therapist(s). It's important for us to know this information, partly because there may be insights into key factors in the child's personality, but more importantly for negative reasons: We find out what has *not* worked previously. (If it had worked, the child would probably not be at DeSisto.) If the child or family has been to one therapist or six different therapists; if the one therapist tried six different approaches, and none worked; or the six different therapists tried six different approaches or the same approach, and none worked—then we know from all this how not to make our diagnosis and therapeutic plan. We know we have to create a plan that takes us up a completely new and maybe untraveled road.

Sometime during the course of the admission procedures, the family will come to the school for an interview. They have to look us over and see how comfortable they feel with us; and we need to know if this is a family or a child we simply can't deal with. We also want to begin to make the parents supportive and trusting of the program. (The child usually won't be ready for this yet.) Because the parents are nervous and frightened, and the child is nervous and frightened—and probably diffident and hostile—the initial interview accomplishes little else of importance. Rarely will parents and children remember afterwards what went on, and what they do remember they rarely believe.

ENTRY

This likewise is uncomplicated and informal. The parents bring the child to school, and there is a new-parent meeting, where the rules are explained. The kids are buddied, and the buddy stays until the child knows the rules and is comfortable in the situation.

Our hope is that during this period trust between school, parents, and children will grow a little. Our expectation is—and experience shows—that this hardly ever happens so early, because of the dynamics of each family.

FAMILY CHANGE IN THE DeSISTO PROGRAM

Parent Groups

Our program, with its emphasis on the involvement of the entire family—parents and children—in the life of the school, did not spring up instantly and in full flower. Neither did our system of compulsory parent groups spring up instantly and in full flower.

There are two reasons why the parent groups evolved into what they are now: First, the children needed to learn to grow by learning how their parents grow, and we realized that this was not happening because the parents themselves did not know how to grow. Second, we realized that positive peer culture is every bit as important for parents as it is for children. The children did not know how to place themselves in a peer culture that was good for them because they had never learned how from their parents—who probably did not know how to place themselves in a peer culture. The vehicle that has proven best for us in satisfying both of these needs is the parent groups.

ORGANIZATION

Parent groups are for DeSisto parents what dorms are for children. That is, parent groups are "families" for the parents (see "Philosophy," above), where they can find emotional nurture and help, learn to parent themselves, and find role models for more effective and satisfying parenting. Attendance has been mandatory for the last three years.

Each group has a parent chairperson, chosen by the group. Supervising all the chairpersons and acting as liaisons between the groups and the school are three former parents employed by the school. The school pays the liaisons a salary commensurate with this responsibility. The liaisons represent the groups to the school and the school to the groups. They do not "run" the groups, however; the groups run the groups.

Each group elects its own parent chairperson, who acts as the "mother" or "father" of the group. Each group *must* have a parent chairperson, which is the last order of business for the group at the end of every school year in preparation for the next school year (the liaison acts as chairperson for a newly forming group until they reach consensus about a chairperson). If a group, for some reason, fails to reach a consensus about who is to be chairperson, then the group ceases to exist, and all the families in the group are expelled from the school until the parents reach a consensus on their chairperson.[5] Once a group was very nearly disbanded because they couldn't arrive at a consensus on a chairperson. So their liaison decided to appoint someone who would be suitable. The school refused to accept this, fearing it would create a bad precedent. The group "mommy" or "daddy," the "parent" to whom they must answer, *has* to come out of the group. He or she can't be imposed from outside. Faced with the threat that their kids would be sent home, the group

[5]There are normally several steps—letters, phone calls, or personal contact—before expulsion. No family is expelled before we have attempted to explain the issues involved. And too, the expulsion is never permanent unless the family decides to make it permanent. There is always a way back in. The child's or the parents' therapists—if the parents have chosen therapy—can often be extremely helpful at these moments.

quickly found a chairperson—whom it fought with the rest of the year. However, if the school had appointed the chairperson, things would have been much worse.

COMMITMENT

The commitment each parent in the group has to make is to begin to confront him- or herself, other individual parents, and the group as a whole on a real basis, and whatever issues then arise. In doing this each parent is going to be confronting issues that they have doubtlessly never dealt with before; and in this way they, and ultimately their children, grow.

One father we have in our Chicago group is an appeaser. He appeases *everyone*. He lets everything go by him. He goes along with anything. His daughter acted out and made such outrageous trouble for him that at last he had to take action and make a stand—which in his case was still a kind of evasion. Rather than face the discomfort his daughter caused, he put her out of sight and entered her in a boarding school. But now, in the parent group, this father can't appease the others. They won't let him *not* take a stand. In doing this, in forcing this father to stand on his own, the others are role modeling how the father needs to learn how to parent. They are also reinforcing behavior that most of them need to reinforce in themselves.

Beyond that, the parents have to learn to respond emotionally in ways they have never before in their lives responded. There is a very lovely lady, who is one of our parent liaisons. Her job as liaison brings her from time to time to parent meetings in Michigan and in other parts of the country. This woman is a person who is not usually disliked; neither is she used to having other people tell her that they hate her. In her own family (she has two boys, one of whom is a DeSisto graduate), though both her boys may at times make trouble for her, both love her and will always rein-in their troublemaking when it gets near the point where their mother might be emotionally destroyed.

Once, on a visit to the Michigan group, she was almost forced beyond that point:

In that group there are a pair of parents who are absolutely outrageous, acting-out "adolescents." Though now divorced, the two have continued their old relationship at group meetings. Their "love" for one another runs the emotional gamut from cold, nasty hostility to physical violence. On good days they gnaw emotionally at one another and the group like rats. On bad days they throw chairs. So in the recent meeting that the liaison attended, these two, as usual, started to act up; and the liaison responded to them very emotionally and very powerfully. Like a good parent, she confronted them, and shouted at them that their behavior was crazy and intolerable. Then she showed them how they might try to confront one another without destroying each other. And they said to her, "We don't fuckin' care about your fuckin' feelings. We don't give a shit. This is our time and our meeting. And we don't fuckin' care how you feel." So here is this very nice lady who has never in her life been so powerfully enraged and who has never shared anything like that before. And these two tell her they don't give a damn about her rage, that they don't give a damn about her, that she's nothing to them, so why does she even try to make her presence felt? These two have pushed the woman closer to the lip of the abyss and the vertigo than she has ever been. And she finds that she can live through it, that she can handle it—as painful and agonizing as it is. So even though the two acting-out "adolescent" parents do not grow as a result of this encounter, she does (and many of the others do, too). Now the woman can handle the pain and conflict that she would have run away from (somehow) before. So now she is a stronger person who'll role model her new strength for the other parents and for her own kids, too.

Thus for the group and for the woman, positive results came about, but only as a result of the group. Without the group, these would not have happened.

Breaking Commitment

The school makes various commitments to child and parents regarding what it is going to do for them. The child makes various commitments, too, regarding what he or she expects, or is expected, to do. And parents, too, have commitments to the child and to the school. Inevitably, some of these commitments will be broken. And

whoever is concerned will have to deal with that.

For instance, parents make a commitment not to let their kids drink at home on vacation. If the kid does drink, then his parents are expelled by the parent group (see Expulsion, above). They lose their vote in the group and their "citizenship." They then have a month to undo the breaking of their commitment and to convince the others that they understand what they did and are now trying to change that. If the group still does not feel convinced by the expelled parents, then their child is taken out of school until the family elects to do something about their negative attitude.

One parent, a physician, has a son, Aaron, at school. Aaron is a nice boy who wants to be liked and who wants you to think he knows exactly what is going on. He likes you to think he knows all the tricks, but in reality he is not present. He's a body whose soul is somewhere else. He has no genuine commitment to *be there* or to grow and change. Aaron's father is exactly the same. His identity is his profession. He *is* "Doctor." The Doctor never came to parent meetings, though his ex-wife, Aaron's mother, did. So the Doctor had absolutely no idea what we were trying to do at the school. He had absolutely no commitment to be involved with the school. And in the end he had no commitment to parent his child. During the summer Aaron ran away from school for a very long time. The Doctor called the school and ferociously harangued us. "You're not doing your job. You've let Aaron get away. Why do I send him to your school if you can't keep him there?" We suggested that there was a connection between Aaron's running away from school and his father's running away from parent meetings. But the Doctor did not see that. Later, Aaron wanted back in, and the school agreed, so long as the Doctor attended parent group regularly. He said he would. He didn't. Not once. Next there were notices, form letters, personal letters, telephone calls urging the Doctor to attend meetings. Excuses. More excuses. The father, like the son, is, in the depths of his personality, a runaway. Finally, there was a special meeting where the group had to deal with several parents like the Doctor. He came to this one—late. The stakes were explained to him. "Sure. Sure. Sure," he answered. He still wasn't *there*. And he didn't show up for the next meeting. So the school sent Aaron home until the Doctor decided to make a real commitment to regularly attend meetings. There was another special meeting, and the Doctor, now contrite, promised to try to change. This convinced the group enough to let Aaron come back to school. Which is where the matter now stands.

At first when we announced three years ago that attendance at parent groups would be compulsory, chairpersons and liaisons were shocked: "But why punish the children for parents' failures?" Later, as the groups grew stronger, and the chairpersons and liaisons grew stronger, and as they began to put more and more pressure on the ones who didn't show up, they began to see how really important attendance was. And they began to see with greater clarity how crucial parent growth is to the growth of children. When the Doctor starts to *be there* for others *as himself* and not as he masks himself as respected and honored healer, then Aaron will also probably begin to be really present at school. Of course, it's possible that Aaron will learn to change and grow on his own, but that will not be easy.

So children are not "punished" for parents' failures, just as parents are not "punished" for children's failures. Blame, punishment, or judgment is not the issue. What is important is that the entire family work together and *with* the school, rather than in opposition to each other and to the school.

Parental Visits to School

There are regular times for parental visits. At these times, long-standing family dynamics often come to light. These can be discussed and dealt with by the family with the help of therapists and staff. Sometimes too, the families will try new behavior that they haven't been able to try before.

There are also times when a child is in a great deal of trouble—he or she has run away, say, and wants to come back to school—and may need to be with parents. We will then ask the parents to come and

stay with the child for a few days at school. The parents take care of, parent, and nurture the child, have conferences with appropriate staff members, and take therapy. They will also attend staff meetings and other staff activities. At such times the parents become rather like deputized staff members.

Visits Home

Visits home by the child are often very "heavy" undertakings for both parents and child. Parents want to spend time with their child, and the child wants to be with parents. Yet often coexisting with the desire to be near and close is its opposite: "We don't want to be together, do we really? Can we stand one another? Have we all changed enough to handle being together? And for how long?"

Child, parents, dorm, therapist, and administration are all involved in the decision about vacations at home. Almost all decisions at DeSisto are made pretty much the same way: Whoever has a stake in a decision takes part in the decision-making process. (Many parents don't want to do that; they would rather others do it for them.)

Sometime near vacation time (vacations are usually eighteen days), each dorm will meet to decide whether each kid will go home and for how long. At times a youngster can handle no more than a day or two. Sometimes he or she can handle perhaps a week. Sometimes a child can take the entire eighteen days. But sometimes there are kids who can't tolerate going home at all.

The measure of the length of a child's vacation is how well he or she handles him- or herself in the dorm meeting. For instance, the kid may have been in lots of trouble—thrown out of the dorm three times, been on drugs or alcohol—and yet he says to the dorm parent, "Look, I know I've done all these things, but I really know, man, that I can handle the full eighteen days." So the dorm parent might say, "I don't believe you. And I don't think *you* believe you." And the kid blusters, postures, and puffs up; and the dorm parent continues. "That's what I mean. You don't believe you. I'm glad you acknowledge you've been in lots of trouble. But you don't really think you can handle the full eighteen days, or else you wouldn't be putting on such a phoney act and throwing so much bullshit at us. Let's go back and start at the beginning. How long do you really think you can do?" Or a kid who has been in similar trouble might say, "Look, I've done pretty well. I mean I'm really ready to go home for eighteen days. I'm right for that." But the dorm parent or another kid says, "Jesus Christ, that's crazy. You haven't been out of trouble in three months, and now you're telling me you can go home and make nice and stay straight for eighteen days? If you last a weekend without getting stoned out of your head, I'll be astonished." And there are kids who are honest, who might say something like, "Shit, I don't know, last vacation I tried a week and I went buggy on the sixth day and got stoned. Maybe I should try only five days this time." And the dorm parent might agree; but then the others in the dorm might say, "We're not sure you're right. You've gotten yourself a lot more together since then. Why don't you try a week?" And so forth.

Thus the child's interactions with the other kids in the dorm and with dorm parents give everyone a sense of how long that child can deal with his parents at home, where, if anything, the dynamics apparent to the dorm will be even more pronounced. This does not mean that a youngster can act nice, eager, pleasant, and open, and then get handed to him what he thinks he wants and deserves. Many of these children are terrific actors. Acting nice and pleasant is desirable; but acting nice and pleasant can be a lie, too. The dorm has to handle that as well. Naturally, mistakes are made, but these will probably be caught at other stages of the decision-making process.

So each dorm reaches a consensus about each child's vacation and about the commitments the child will make for vacation. This plan is written down and sent to the administration for approval. The administration accepts or rejects the entire plan without giving reasons (with this exception: sometimes the administration will feel that there are special reasons why a particular child needs to go home, in which case, a note is added to the plan). If the plan is rejected, the dorm has to figure out why—on its own. Consequently, they are forced to think as adults and try to put themselves in the administration's place, so that they can try to understand why the administration made the choice it made. (The goal is for the members of the dorms, dorm parents included, to try to parent themselves and figure out for themselves what they need and not to have administration be a "good" daddy and hand that over to them.)

Therapists are also involved, as are parents (usually by phone), and they add their input. There are times, for instance, when parents will want to have the child for a longer vacation than he or she is scheduled for. So we'll deal with that. And at times parents will want the child for a shorter vacation. And that will be dealt with.

When the child goes home, he or she has agreed and committed to keep within certain limits structured by the school. These limits will often be broken; and child, parents, and school will have to handle that. Usually, in time, child and parents will learn to handle contracts and commitments better. They learn to see that commitments are not necessarily burdensome behavior imposed by an external force, but the necessary condition for making genuine human connections that grow and increase in intimacy.

Parent-Child Communication Groups

The kind of therapy I, the first author (Michael DeSisto), have always found most effective and congenial is multi-family therapy, groups of families in which as many members as possible can be present. These are brought together to live in a comfortable but somewhat isolated space for periods of up to a week. I've come to call these sessions "Parent-Child Communication Groups."

Since both children and parents often

experience significant change and growth as a result of their attendance at a Parent-Child Group, and since, consequently, Parent-Child Groups have become a major element in the school program, their structure needs to be described in some detail.

My first concern is to make the environment that the families experience at the Parent-Child Group as homelike and natural as possible. Limits are set by the therapist that are firm and fair, so everyone is allowed to feel secure enough that no one has to worry about any externals—only self. I try to take great care, therefore, over material comforts: food, temperature, sleeping facilities, places for people to be intimate and alone together, as well as places to congregate and relate.

The intention is to give each family time and space to work together and with other families so that they can share with each other, share with other family members, work off one another, and just see that their inmost fears and secrets are the very same fears and secrets that many others feel.

Family therapy, as I see it, is not like a surgical procedure, not a time that anesthetizes and blots out the normal flow of life. It is as much a part of the normal flow as eating a cheese sandwich, taking a shower, touching your spouse on the neck, or yelling at your child. So when I practice therapy, I try to create a setting as close as possible to the normal settings in which people live. This allows the families and me to see more clearly and easily the dynamics that prevent them from actually enjoying themselves in their own normal living settings.

To rephrase it, family therapy is any experience in which family members participate, the end of which brings about a closeness and intimacy that were not there previously. The aim of family therapy is to facilitate the growth of intimacy, to help families see the barriers that stand in the way of intimacy, and then to help them try and reinforce new kinds of behavior.

I've found, after trying various approaches over the years, that the best and most effective length of time for Parent-Child Group is a week, but since that amount of time is not always available, the more usual time span is a weekend.

Since weeklong sessions are more useful than weekend ones, I'll confine my discussion to weeklong Parent-Child Groups. In the course of that time I can take a family and give it a chance to look at and talk about the old dynamics. Then family members can begin to flush them out.

The first order of business for the family in a Parent-Child Group is to rerun all the old movies they've acted in, all the old *Casablanca*'s ("Play it again, Sam,") all the old passionate connections that clutter up their perceptions of one another: the times the socks weren't washed, the times Daddy got drunk and violent, the times Keith came home stoned, the times "you" didn't get my car back in time, the times Jessica stole from her grandmother, the times Bryan embarrassed us in front of our friends, the time my ex-wife (Leah's mother) gave Leah dope, the time Karen had an abortion, the times Scott got thrown out of school.

The families will present as many of these stories as they can to the therapist and the group; and it's very important that they do this, even though by so doing they are using the past to avoid the present. They need to do this for two reasons: First, in order to prove to the therapist and to one another that their care, concern, and love for one another are real. Second, to flush out and exhaust the rot and decay so that they can begin to look at the intimacy and closeness that really exist. Reliving the passions of the past is a necessary stage in the growth of the family, but it must be only a stage, because real growth begins when the family runs out of old issues and begins to look at themselves as they are now.

When that happens, when they are left with only today, then they can begin to look at and work on today's dynamics and begin to try a little bit of new behavior and practice it. In so doing, they learn to trust one another more. In the meantime, they develop relationships with the therapist and other people in the group, which allow them to be honest and to bring up the issues, feelings, and thoughts that really matter to them.

After the old dynamics are flushed out,

I like to send everyone out to do with their families some nice, normal, ordinary things together—anything that appeals to them: go out for a pizza or ice cream or dinner, ride horses, go to a museum or a movie, go sailing or shopping—anything pleasant. Two results come of this: they will usually not enjoy themselves and one another as much as they had hoped, so that when they come back to the sessions, they can look at the ways they keep themselves from having fun with one another. But more important than that: in going out they can begin to try new behavior in small doses; and if they find that it works, they can try the new behavior in larger doses. Consequently, the families can begin to work on their dynamics not just by sitting in a room and talking, but by going out together and doing real-life activities.

PARTICIPATION

Though it's best to have in the group as many family member as are willing to come, I make no demands that everyone be there.[6] Sometimes I've started with only the child, without his or her parents; or the parents without the child. And if, later on, another family member decides to join the group, the door is not closed.

Therapists should not try to measure and judge what *they* see. (Therapists have their own need to put value judgments on what people are doing and what they themselves are accomplishing.) Rather, some of the finest, most exciting growth I've seen happened in people who never said a word in a session. And I only discovered what was really going on years later. Some of the finest work, also, that I've seen done in those groups happened at the "break-

fast" table, over cheese and coffee. Beautiful, incredible sharing has gone on there. Secrets were spoken. Openings were made.

LIMITS

There have to be some rules made for Parent-Child Groups, schedules that have to be met, behavior that is not permitted, and so forth. I try to make these limits few and reasonable. I am not a rules fan, though I do believe that some rules are necessary. People need to feel firm and secure and that they are being taken care of. They also need to feel that the therapist—the rule-giver—is a good, warm, careful, and attentive parent.

Often people—children or parents—will try to break the system, just as at home, kids will watch TV when they shouldn't, or parents will smoke in bed when they shouldn't. And the rulebreaker will attack the rulemaker for the silly and absurd rules, or for not stating the rules clearly,—just as at home.

And so, I try to state those rules very clearly and in a friendly way. And then I try to stick to them. Of course if something is wrong, and if a rule needs altering or changing, then I do that. But I don't do that often; families need to know how important I believe what I'm doing is, by seeing how willing I am *not* to give up what I believe in. They can see how much I value what I say by how much energy I put into sticking to it.

And then, when parents or children attack me about the rules, they can see me living through the attack while I stick to my rules. And parents can perhaps learn from that and start to do it at home—if they haven't already. And children too learn from that.

---

[6]Attendance is voluntary and not compulsory at Parent-Child Groups because families—parents *and* children—have to be able on their own to feel they are *ready* to go through the pain and terror of looking at themselves *together*. Though the reality of Parent-Child Groups is not nearly as frightful as families sometimes expect them to be, families still have to feel they're strong enough to handle their pain and terror. Most of the families do, in time, take part in Parent-Child Groups.

COMFORTS

In the Parent-Child Groups, we pay careful attention to the comfort of the families.

In the old days, religious orders used to try to make sure that their monks and nuns were not comfortable, the better to enable them to set their attentions on the pleasures of the spirit instead of the pleasures of the world and the flesh. Our idea is rather the reverse. We want our families to be comfortable, so that they are better able to look at themselves and their own discomforts—the ones *they* are responsible for—not the external discomforts that could distract them from their own. We try to take away all their excuses for not being comfortable.

External discomfort is often an addiction that allows people not to look at the pain and discomfort inside. Similarly, acting-out children are some families' addictions. By making families comfortable, we remove their addictions to discomfort, and so their excuses.

The End-of-the-Week High

Very often at the end of a Parent-Child Group, family members will experience new joy and exhilaration. The therapy will have left them with a high. And this is good. Unhappily, the exhilaration they feel on Sunday afternoon will have drained away by Wednesday. So I try to get them to realize that the permanent benefits they are taking away with them don't include permanent joy. The real benefit is the realization that they can interact differently—and that there is hope they can now trust.

CONCLUSION

A lot of the time you hear words like the following from people who don't have the experience of residential facilities that work: "Oh yeah, I remember the Harmons. They've got a kid at *X* School. It's a dumping ground for burn-outs and other toxic wastes." Or: "You know the Wallaces. Well they're *such* failures as parents that

they had to send their kid to *Y* School. She's such a mess they just couldn't handle her." Or: "I think the Diamonds must really *hate* Sandra. I mean, they threw her *out*, cast her *out*, *ejected* her from their home and sent her away to some godforsaken school in Central Florida, of all places." Or: I just can't understand what got into Mike and Sue O'Donahue. They've sent three of their children to some damned school where all the kids are arsonists and perverts. But Jesus, those three kids are so *good*! They never once in their lives acted up!"

The actuality is different. Sure, a child at a school like DeSisto is physically out of his parents' home. And yes, very often those parents feel that they have failed terribly as parents and that they are no good. And yes, their children may well have done terrible, destructive things. But the point we want to repeat about programs like DeSisto's is that for us physical separation does not mean break-up. We aren't in business to provide after-care for families where children are divorced from parents. We aren't there to handle fall-out from a family that has gone into fission. Our parents don't "expel" their children into DeSisto. Not just the children are at DeSisto; the *families* are at DeSisto. The physical space between the children and their homes gives everyone the emotional space to begin to change and grow—to become more intimate and close.

The end of the program is not necessarily reached when the family can permanently reunite under one roof (though if that happens, fine). The end of the program is reached after parents and child have been allowed to grow through the four "levels" described earlier and the child is ready to graduate. Most of the students who come to DeSisto stay and graduate. And ninety percent of the students who graduate go on to college and do well there.

9

Social Network Intervention With Adolescents

JOAN L. SPECK,
and ROSS V. SPECK, M.D.

*A*dolescents are in a particularly vulnerable position as they experiment with the process of individuating from the family of origin. The natural and usual way to proceed through this process is to begin to identify more strongly with the peer group—a subculture of young people in similar circumstances. This network frequently has—often to the dismay of the parents—its own set of heroes, its own music, fashion, even its own *patois*. In Western culture this is frequently enhanced and exploited as a commercial bonanza by industry. The teenagers are a large and profitable market of consumers.

In dysfunctional families the individuation process becomes a much more difficult growth period than just "growing pains." Letting go is probably one of the most difficult tasks of parenting. For a fused, symbiotically enmeshed family, it can be nearly impossible. Conversely, the isolated, disengaged family is unable to model the use of support systems as a means of transition.

We have found that in extreme cases of dysfunction (symbiosis and threatened suicide are particular examples) a network assembly can provide support systems for all family members, and in doing so can shift the balance and alliances within the index family into more favorable, functional units.

INTRODUCTION

Mobilizing Networks in the Treatment of Adolescents

Network therapy is now almost twenty years old. Although we prefer to call this process social network intervention, the term network therapy so originally suggested by Jay Haley has persisted. We would like to emphasize, however, that the network is the therapist. The professional team merely assists in getting the index family to convene the network, and then to catalyze the process through its various phases until the network is skilled enough to run its own course with its own goals. We still see ourselves as intervenors in a social network intervention. The team's goal is to train and activate the friends, relatives, neighbors, service people, and whoever else assembles to provide whatever assistance the index family needs in solving difficult human problems.

HISTORY

In the late 1950s and early 1960s, one of us (RVS) was involved in an NIMH-supported research project under the direction of Alfred Friedman, Ph.D., at the Philadelphia Psychiatric Center. The project was titled "Family Therapy of Schizophrenia in the Home." Young schizophrenic persons under the age of thirty, often hospital failures, were seen on a once or twice weekly basis along with all family members living in their home. The therapists worked in co-therapy teams, usually a psychiatrist and a social worker or psychologist. Co-therapy was just becoming popular in working with groups or with schizophrenics, following the work of Whitaker, Malone, Warkentin, and the Peachtree Clinic group in Atlanta.

Although family therapy is a major modality today, at the time of this research project there was much professional distrust and dissension regarding working in the homes and with the whole family. However, the work was exciting, and the concept of a socially shared psychopathology allowed radical departures in conceptualizing the cause, course, and even cure of the schizophrenic person. Drugs and hospitalization were avoided and in about 75 percent of cases (our teams saw upwards of 100 families), some shifts occurred in the families allowing improvement in the labeled schizophrenic.

We began to pay attention to our treatment failures. We observed that in eight out of ten of these families, a member, usually a manifestly healthy member, would absent himself from the treatment sessions either intermittently or permanently. The families did not miss the absent member and would frequently make excuses for him. In our view, the absent member rep-

resented a maneuver utilized by the entire family as a defense against anxiety generated when fixed and stereotyped relationship patterns are threatened. When we could get the absent member to attend family therapy sessions on a regular basis, we could frequently make changes in the family system which appeared to ameliorate the schizophrenic symptoms.

In several families there was an extended family member who absented himself from the family, but who played a secretive, powerful role in the family and in the family therapy. This absent extended family member could frequently bring about strong resistance to, or even termination of, family therapy. For instance, after three months of family therapy following discharge from hospital of both a 50-year-old mother and her 19-year-old son (the father had previously been hospitalized at the same psychiatric facility), the mother revealed that her brother-in-law was paying for the treatment. He contracted with them that they visit him after each session and hold a debriefing in which he instructed them as to what to accept or not from the therapy. Frequent attempts to contact him failed, and when he finally suggested (via the mother) that the therapist accompany him on a plane trip when he would have time to discuss the family, he cancelled the day before the proposed flight. A month later he advised the family that they did not need more family therapy and had them terminate.

What these experiences taught us was that families are subject to multiple influences, both internal and external. Working in the homes during the evening, we found that at times friends, neighbors, or relatives would drop by. We began to invite them to stay and help in the family therapy and enlarge the family circle.

In 1964, in a conversation with Erving Goffman about societal factors in the etiology of schizophrenia, he referred to the work of Elizabeth Bott, a British anthropologist who had published a book, *Family and Social Network*, in 1957 (1971), on her research with the social networks of twenty "ordinary" families from East London. This book gave us the concept of an invisible group of friends, neighbors, and relatives surrounding the family and in many ways mediating between it and the larger society. We began to plan the assembly of such a family network and to try to use its power and influence to solve such difficult human dilemmas as schizophrenia, suicide, symbiosis, social isolation—dilemmas that had been failures in other modes of treatment intervention.

The first network therapy assembly occurred in 1964 with the goal of resolving the symbiosis between a widowed mother and her only child, a late adolescent boy. This network intervention is discussed in some detail later in the chapter.

HISTORICAL CROSS-CULTURAL ROOTS OF SOCIAL NETWORK INTERVENTION

While we were working with the first network assembly much more frequently and for a much longer time than we do now (weekly for almost a year), it became obvious that assembly of the network was like assembling the tribe in time of crisis. This first modern network assembly (for therapeutic purposes) labeled themselves a "family of families" and sometimes spoke of themselves as a tribe or clan. In the past the tribe was assembled for ritually important occasions, such as weddings, funerals, rites of passage, and sometimes family crises, either physical or emotional.

Many cultures assembled the network to expedite healing processes. The Hawaiians used the Ho-Ho-Pani-Pa, a ritual in which an intervenor went around to all the friends and relatives of a family in crisis asking them to forgive past hurts and grievances. After several months a large feast was planned, and the network assembled with solutions for the family's dilemma in mind. Some American Indian groups use the peyote healing ritual. In this ritual, a family selects an intervenor who will assemble the network. An all-night session in the teepee will be accompanied by drum beats, use of peyote, speaking out by participants—and eventually a plan for solution of the family problem. Meanwhile, some of the women are outside preparing a huge meal for the next day when the network's healing plans will be implemented.

The !Kung bushmen of the Kalahari desert have an ongoing healing ceremony that assembles the total tribe on a once-weekly basis. In midlife, the bushmen go through a ritual called "passing to the other side"—a change of consciousness to a state of bliss called "Kia." Reaching this state is very painful since the person becomes consumed with a fiery energy called "n'um," which is characterized by severe abdominal and chest pain. When this stage is reached, the initiate can deal in two worlds or levels of consciousness. Chants call upon the dead relatives to help the living. Living friends and relatives and the ancestors on the "other side" are mobilized to help the sick person.

NETWORK DESCRIPTION

A network is the total relational field of a person or family and may be represented horizontally by space or vertically by time. Although networks are relatively invisible, they have high degrees of information exchange. Our definition of a network is that group of persons who have the potential of giving significant help in time of distress. A shorter definition is one's important social relations. A network has few formal rules, or boundaries, no real hierarchy, and each person in it is fundamentally equal. It consists of relationships between people, some of whom are known to many others in the network, while others merely form a linkage, which is often unknown to the two persons linked by the third. *A* may know *B*, and *B* may know *C*, but *B*'s relationship to *A* and *C* may be unknown to both. An individual's network is the totality of human relationships that have a lasting significance in his or her life. The importance of "loose-knit" or "weak" ties between people in networks has been repeatedly observed since these "casual" relationships give potential entree for jobs or other information into many other networks that would otherwise not be available. We all have many networks. Thus, the "weak" ties allow entrance to networks of networks. Social networks are larger than therapeutic groups; the usual range is from twenty to two hundred persons. We prefer to work with networks of forty to fifty persons. This is empirical, based on our techniques and experience. Other network intervenors prefer smaller network assemblies, comprised of ten to twenty-five people.

As adolescence is frequently a time of crisis, most cultures have invented a rite of passage, a sort of passing through a boundary between childhood and the beginning of adult responsibility. The Hopi Indians have a particularly poignant one: children are repeatedly told by their elders that a terrible devil, *Chaumoogra*, will get them and eat them up if they are bad. At puberty, in a ceremony, they are told the secret of *Chaumoogra*, which is known only to adults. The secret is that there is no *Chaumoogra*.

Normally the clan or network in Western culture only assembles at weddings, births, funerals, holidays, or family reunions. The total network assembly of nuclear and extended family, friends, neighbors, and significant others in times of adolescent rebellion, suicidal preoccupation, or serious emotional disturbance can be an overwhelming experience of help, support, reassurance, and relief to the adolescent and his whole family.

We asked each family member of the index adolescent person to telephone their support network—all of the people who would be willing to help with the difficult situation they face. In the week before network assembly, 400 to 800 telephone calls are made within the network. The process, thus, begins even before the network assembles.

Our technique of large network assembly is used only when simpler methods such as individual, group, or family therapy have failed. It is a very powerful technique that uses the energies of many people in the network as well as the network intervention team.

A network assembly can be very helpful to break up symbiosis. We know of no other method that mobilizes such strong support systems for both persons involved in the symbiosis. Cases of adolescent suicidal crisis, antisocial behavior, and psychosis have been most frequently treated by social network intervention.

Network meetings are usually held in the evenings. Experience has shown that 7:30 P.M. is a suitable time when people have rested, eaten, and can assemble after work. Some sessions have been held during the day on weekends. An exhausting variant is a weekend marathon. We only recommend this to younger network therapists. Most regular network assemblies last for about 2½ hours, after which the intervention team departs. However, we make sure that at the end of the session when the hosts serve refreshments everyone in the network is subgrouped. This ensures that discussion, planning, working through, and even blaming goes on for another one to three hours after the team departs.

In our present format, we do one to three network sessions with the adolescent, his family, and their network. The single-session approach is used when people assemble from long distances such as California, South America, or Europe. It is not uncommon for significant persons such as grandparents, uncles and aunts, or others to want to attend a tribal assembly for therapeutic purposes. The team may get telephone calls or letters from persons who heard about the network assembly. Information in a network is passed with electronic speed. American Indians even tell a story about when an American president died suddenly in El Paso, Texas, and the "moccasin network" relayed the news to Washington before the telegraph message got there.

There is always extra energy, power, and excitement in a network when long-gone relatives appear from great distances. A magical expectation occurs and is frequently fulfilled. It is also a sign of a high degree of problem-solving motivation.

We have held large network assemblies in many locales; among them have been a bank boardroom, motels, hotels, churches, a YMCA, hospitals, and private offices. None of these, however, is as suitable as the home of the index family or other network member. We even held one network assembly on a farm with part of the session in the farmhouse, part outdoors, and part in the barn. An ordinary Philadelphia row house (two stories with three bedrooms and one bath) will, with a little crowding, accommodate forty-five to fifty people for a network meeting.

We prefer to work with a network of forty to fifty persons. We have found that, using our large assembly technique, we can count on six or so "indigenous leaders" turning up during the network sessions. We call them "activists," because they mobilize the network's energies and do the most to clarify the presenting problems and propose workable solutions. We have done networks with twenty-five people, as well as with nearly two hundred. The latter group is too large and practically requires microphones.

Since we have been working with networks for nearly twenty years, families are referred to us for "network therapy" by other therapists. Some families refer themselves after reading *Family Networks* (Speck & Attneave, 1973). We prefer to go to the family home for a family session before deciding on network. By doing this we can meet the cast of characters, assess motivation, and evaluate the physical surroundings. In a large network we might ask to have the meeting held in a relative's home, which might be larger. We also would exclude cases with insufficient crisis or those where we believe other family therapeutic modalities might suffice: you don't do major surgery where a bandaid or a dressing will suffice.

THERAPISTS' ROLES

In the first large network assembly, I (RVS) worked alone and met with the network weekly for several months. It was only later that I realized I was using a large-group therapy model and was slowing the progress of the network by accepting a leadership role. Also, with so many people present, the network intervenor needs a team who will function as additional eyes and ears, and will bring other perceptions such as group and subgroup affects to the intervenor's attention. We now function with a team of three to five persons. The team leader is called the intervenor. The others feed information to him or her. Another team member gives the leader a break or is called in to soften resistances by using brief-encounter techniques. The other team members are called consultants. They move about the network collecting information that may be conscious or preconscious in the network. They huddle and give their hunches and opinions to the leader. It is important to know what phase the network is in and where to focus next in order to allow the network to solve its problems. However, the team serve only as conveners and catalysts. The network itself is the "therapist." In large or exceptionally difficult networks we have had as many as ten professionals on the network team.

In our experience, a network has to be composed of at least forty people to achieve an optimal therapeutic thrust. Each member of the family must be able to have a mobilized support system. Further, the support system must be large enough to comprise a group with a built-in system of checks and balances. Checks are needed to curb extreme strategies; balances, to support activists in sometimes daring a strategy that might seem unconventional or too innovative.

In each network assemblage, a group process becomes evident and must be choreographed by the network convenor and his or her team. We have identified the following six phases in the network process:

1. *Retribalization*: an assembly of the network with a specific sense of being there to help or heal the index family.
2. *Polarization*: occurs when the various issues are delineated and "sides" are drawn (e.g., youth versus age, male versus female).
3. *Mobilization*: activist-members of the network state various alternative behaviors and options; support systems develop for each index family member.

4. *Resistance-Depression*: the inevitable sense of failure and frustration when it hasn't happened yesterday.

5. *Breakthrough*: strategies and the means to implement them are clearly defined and achievable goals are determined.

6. *Exhaustion-Elation-Termination*: the end phase of the process where the participants have a shared sense of hard work that will lead to change and healing.

Each of these phases will occur in the course of a successful network meeting, though not necessarily in such a neat and consecutive fashion. Frequently, in order to break through the resistance-depression phase, it will be necessary to return to retribalization exercises, or if polarization is getting out of hand, it may be necessary arbitrarily to mobilize certain segments of the network; for example, in the latter case, one part of the polarized group might be sent to another room to work on strategies.

The job of the team headed by the network convener starts with the decision to use network intervention rather than other therapeutic modalities. Usually, by the time network intervention is decided on, most of the more conventional systems have been tried and observed to have little impact on the chronic crisis of the family. One team member serves as a conductor and moderator, but together the team evaluates the degree of stress and its manifestations, the depth of pathology, and also, importantly, its capability to explore its latent potential. In addition to evaluating historical, cultural, clinical, and socioeconomic factors, the team must also plan strategies for intervention and ways of sharing cognitive and affective data perceived by the various team members. The sharing of information with the leader and other team members cannot be overemphasized for it is only through this sharing that the team can keep a finger on the network's pulse. It is this pulse that differentiates between chaos and ordered disorder.

In all uses of network, the team must have a time to debrief, both to preserve their own sanity and to validate their experience of their experience. It is also ab-solutely essential if further meetings are planned with that particular network to evaluate past and current strategies and to plan strategies for the future. A caveat is in order here: the team must have an easy flexibility with the sure knowledge that the network is the therapist and the function of the team is to facilitate and choreograph the network under the conductor's direction.

In the confusion of the assembly of forty to seventy people unknown to the team, it is useful to create a network map for identifying the network members and the potential dynamics of the group (see Figure 9.1).

CASE STUDIES

The illustration in Figure 9.1 shows one form of network mapping. It clearly depicts the clusters and alliances. In addition, it defines the paucity of kinship available as a support system for the Smiths. There are five defined clusters and a sixth potential cluster. In this kind of map the inner and outer circles can be used to depict emotional closeness and/or distance, or alternately, to demonstrate geographical space. The circle can also be divided in two halves—one side showing kinship, the other side friends and neighbors. The Smith family clusters are grouped as follows:

1. Mother's employers.
2. Mother's sister and her husband (children under six are usually not at the network session; the two-year-old is included because issues about him were actively discussed).
3. Father's co-workers.
4. Index patient John's group of friends (who, as described by the parents and sister, Betty, appeared to be a group of "hippies").
5. Daughter Betty's friends, all of whom turn out to be "girlfriends."
6. The final cluster is the unknown potential; it consists of participating friends, neighbors, and service people (e.g., the mailman, hairdresser, etc.).

A Clinical Example

In the Smith family, the presenting problem was 19-year-old John who had dropped out of school and did not have a job. Both he and his 23-year-old sister lived with their family of origin (see Figure 9.2). John was actively hallucinating. He was convinced that his sister, Betty, a spot announcer on a radio station, was broadcasting his thoughts. The whole family was frequently kept up at night because of John's agitation. They were often forced to trace the wiring of the house in efforts to allay John's anxiety. On numerous occasions the family ended up in the local hospital's emergency room at 3 A.M. The

Smiths were never able to bring themselves to sign John in for observation. The family was at a point of total exhaustion when they were finally referred to us. This was only after a series of psychiatric interventions had been tried.

The initial interview elicited the following impressions and information: Mr. Smith was an unassuming, rather passive man with a veneer of cockiness which, somewhat quickly, cracked. He was an insurance collector, a debit man who collected a dollar here and a dollar there from his low-income clientele. Aside from her visible exhaustion, Mrs. Smith had a job as a business manager for three young businessmen who owned an automotive parts store. It was at once ob-

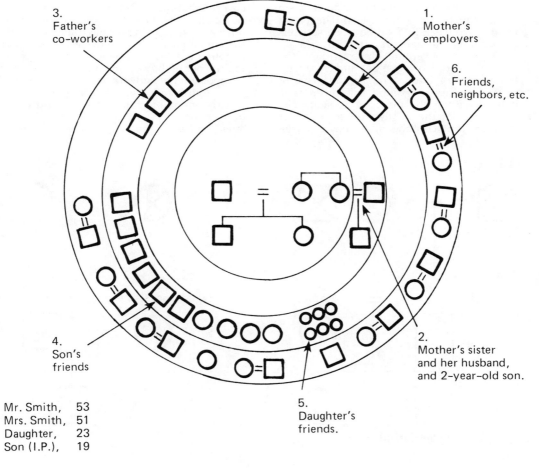

3.
Father's
co-workers

1.
Mother's
employers

6.
Friends,
neighbors, etc.

4.
Son's
friends

2.
Mother's sister
and her husband,
and 2-year-old son.

5.
Daughter's
friends.

Mr. Smith,   53
Mrs. Smith,   51
Daughter,   23
Son (I.P.),   19

Figure 9.1
A network map of the Smith family.

vious that she enjoyed her job and was highly regarded by her employers; further, that they valued her services and were concerned about her and the toll that was being exacted on her. Mr. and Mrs. Smith sat as far from each other as was possible in the office. John fidgeted constantly as he sat apart, occasionally interjecting inappropriate remarks. He also looked drawn and somewhat emaciated. Betty sat near her mother and kept glancing anxiously at her; her manner and dress were mousey. She had little to say. As we discussed with the Smiths who should be asked to attend the network session, we drew the network map that quickly showed the clusters of potential support systems and also of potential polarizations available in the network (see Figure 9.1, as well as the list of clusters above).

In the planning session a contract was made for three network sessions to be held at two-week intervals, the first to be held two weeks from the planning session. The reason for the two-week interval between sessions is to permit the network effect to operate. Unlike most conventional interventions, the network can be in process day and night with face-to-face or phone contacts available at any time. Certain ground rules were also defined during the planning session. The first was that the family themselves must make the contacts either in person or by tele-

phone to mobilize the network. This is a vital step as it keeps the responsibility with the individuals of the network and, equally importantly, begins the network process. A poll of this particular network showed a tally of 600 phone calls made concerning the network.

The second rule was that any contact with the team must also include contact with the convenor, in this case, Ross. It was promptly broken by Mr. Smith who tried, unsuccessfully, to terminate network meetings after the first session by contacting another team member instead of Ross. Termination was averted by the support system's insistence on further network sessions.

A third rule was that the usual patient-doctor confidentiality be suspended. Not only is it impossible to keep confidentiality in a group, but also not keeping it assists in shifting bases of power. Thus, when it was discovered that one of Mr. Smith's co-workers was a volunteer narcotics agent (though unofficial), a serious threat that John's support system could be disrupted was averted by negotiating with this co-worker who agreed to drop out of the network and promised not to report on the network to narcotics agents.

The fourth rule, though seemingly trivial, was that no food or drink be served during the session. It is felt that such hospitality must wait until the official session is over

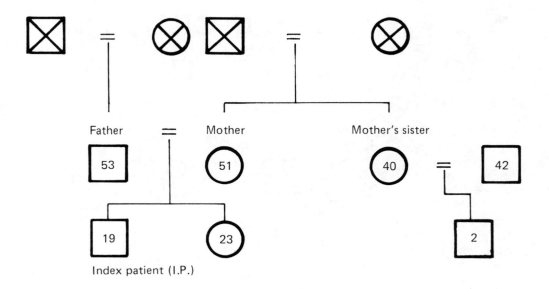

Figure 9.2
The Smith family genogram.

and the network team has left. This is to stress the fact that the network meeting is a *work* session at which there is a job to be done. The party must wait.

A typical network session is scheduled from 7:30 P.M. to 10:30 or 11:00. It may also be held on weekends when the labor force is available. The Smiths' network convened on Thursday evenings. At the end of each session the team makes sure that any unlinked individuals are linked to a subgroup, and then the team departs. The network usually continues informally for several more hours. Again, we are making sure that the responsibility for getting the job done is left to the network.

The focus of the sessions, here condensed, was to replace the symbiotic enmeshment of the family with an autonomous and functional set of behaviors and interactions, as well as to try to achieve replacement of the ambivalent dysfunctional paralysis with achievable, and therefore positive-enforcement, goals. We felt that secondary goals would follow in the natural couse of events; they included relieving Betty's feelings of guilt and responsibility for her mother's unhappiness and permitting her to move away from her family of origin to young selfhood, which in turn would force the parents to look at their own marriage and needs.

The tasks that emerged in the first session's polarization were:
1. How to get John away from his family and living somewhere else.
2. To get John off speed.
3. For John to find a job.
Primarily, the first meeting's emphasis was on retribalization and polarization with support groups forming from the unknown clusters (e.g., John's friends for John).

In the second session, depression-resistance was very evident; there had been no miraculous changes. Mr. Smith voiced his resistance to change by trying to cancel the meeting. However, in this session, network news that Mrs. Smith had discovered a spoon, syringe, needle, and some "powder" in John's room mobilized the group. At first chaotic anger threatened to immobilize the group back into depression but the strategy of dividing the "hippie" peers from an angry parental group permitted fresh energy from an intermediate group, aged 25 to 35, to start functioning and offer more realistic options. Breakthrough occurred as John's hippie friends started both to challenge and to support the parental group after they were themselves supported by the more realistic intermediate group. A committee to support John was formed.

In the final session the network news was discouraging, although John's committee had come up with five job offers and three separate living arrangements. John was not cooperating with them. There was more than a strong suspicion that he was being reinforced in this by other members of the family. By shifting the emphasis from John to the rest of the family, the energies of John's committee were renewed. At the same time, it forced mobilization of committees for the parents and the sister.

Breakthrough came with termination. A job was found for John. He went to live with his aunt. Free of family and peer drug pressure, he no longer used drugs.

Follow-up over the last twelve years has produced some encouraging information. John has maintained jobs, remained drug-free, and continued to live on his own. Two weeks after the last meeting the parents took a trip to California, their first vacation together in the history of their marriage. The sister, by latest report, has her own apartment and lives quite independently of the family.

Since the time when we did that network of young adolescent drug-abusers, we have done many more. Frequently we can achieve network intervention and change in one network session. This is particularly true in the case of inner and outer networks. An exhausted inner network is relieved by an outer one that has fresh perspectives and resources. Geographic change can bring about the infusion of new energies in a similar way.

Another Clinical Example[1]

Mrs. Jones contacted the network intervention team because of family problems which mainly involved her inability to manage or control the behavior of her fourteen-year-old daughter, Carla. She had taken Carla to a number of psychiatrists but Carla was uncooperative, blamed the psychiatrists for her difficulties, and refused the numerous medications that had been offered. Finally,

[1]This clinical case is to be published as part of a chapter in *Macrosystemic Approaches to Family Therapy*, edited by John Schwartzman (New York: Guilford Press, in press).

the whole family had been put on megavitamin therapy by the last psychiatrist seen, who had made a diagnosis of schizophrenia and hypoglycemia. He also advised a diet for Carla. As my wife (an anthropologist and psychotherapist) and I see all families conjointly, we started by seeing the entire Jones family, who resided together. This consisted of Mrs. Jones, a fortyish woman who looked much younger and seemed more like one of the children; Jane, 17; Bill, 15; Carla, 14; Jerry, 12; and Dorothy, 9. Mr. and Mrs. Jones had recently divorced, and Mr. Jones lived in a different city with the woman he was about to marry. A striking feature of the family unit was the hopelessness and exhaustion of all family members. Carla had dropped out of school some months previously. She refused to bathe, did not eat with the family, stayed up all night and then insisted on quiet during the day so that she could sleep, left rotting food hidden around the house, and constantly littered and dumped garbage about the house. At times, she attacked her mother or her sister Dorothy. In the family therapy sessions Carla would sit mumbling or complaining about the family, her hair completely concealing her face except when she rubbed her eyes with a mixture of water and spittle which she kept in a jar in her purse. Jane and Bill gave a lot of history and behaved in a parentified way. Both said that they couldn't take the tension and the disruption in the home. Both wanted to move out. Jerry wanted to move in with his father. Dorothy was frightened of Carla but wanted to stay with her mother.

About six family therapy sessions were held. Mr. Jones attended one of these meetings. He tended to blame Mrs. Jones for not understanding Carla, for having been absent in the past, and for being a slovenly housekeeper. He was glib, used a good deal of denial, and could not be convinced that Carla showed any symptoms of psychotic disorder. He too seemed like one of the children.

Because of the amount of family disorganization and total exhaustion, social network intervention was suggested to help build up support systems for each family member. An additional factor was the three-hour drive, dangerous to all because of Carla's aggressive impulsivity, that the family had to undergo to visit us.

A single four-hour social network intervention was planned in their home. Mrs. Jones and the rest of the family were asked to compile a list of all the people they knew who might be willing to meet in their home and help to change their predicament. Mr. Jones was also seen with his new wife. They agreed to attend and Mr. Jones' sister was invited from a distant state. Mrs. Jones invited her parents and several of her siblings from out of state. Mrs. Jones and Jane and Bill invited their friends. By the time of the meeting, ten days later, they had invited over sixty persons.

The intervention team consisted of six persons with myself (RVS) as team leader, Dr. Uri Rueveni as encounter specialist, Joan L. Speck and Mira Rueveni as group process consultants, a young psychologist as trainee and process consultant, and an audiovisual expert who video-taped the network intervention.

The team arrived at the home at 7 P.M., about half an hour before the meeting was to start. Already a few of the invited network members had begun to arrive. We made a tour of the house and selected the living room and archways spilling into the hall and into the dining room as the space to be used for the main session. We met with Carla who refused to attend and was hiding in the garage. She said she might listen to the meeting from the basement where there was an "escape" door. A team member was assigned to get written permission from everyone for video-taping. Only one couple refused "because they were in politics." After consultation with Mrs. Jones, they were encouraged to leave, as it was doubtful that they would be of help anyway.

By 7:45 P.M., sixty people had arrived and we decided to begin. We pointed out to the network that there are six recognizable stages in social network intervention: retribalization, polarization, mobilization, resistance-depression, breakthrough, and exhaustion-elation-termination. I pointed out that the Jones family was exhausted; that their friends, neighbors, and relatives should begin to think of ways to help the various family members; that support committees for each member would have to be set up; and that the group could help in making Mr. and Mrs. Jones' divorce more effective. (Mr. Jones had been appearing unannounced for dinner and criticizing Mrs. Jones' housekeeping, and had taken pictures of the interior that he threatened to take to the public health department.)

Each network member was asked to introduce himself and tell his relationship to the network. Then the Jones family was asked to sit in the center of the group and tell the group what the trouble in the family was and what they hoped to achieve from the network intervention.

Carla remained in the garage, and later, went to the basement. The team decided not to force a frightened and hostile 14-year-old to sit through the long session. She would undoubtedly have tried to escape and the resulting disruption would fragment the network rather than unite it as a functioning social system.

Jerry said that he could not stand being called "dirt" at school and that he wished he could have a chance to live with his father, "to see if he liked it there." Jane said that it was impossible to live in the same house with Carla and that she wanted to move out, either to California or to go to college. Bill said he was sick of Carla drinking out of milk and juice bottles and of her smelling up the house. He too would like to move. Dorothy said the house would be all right if Carla weren't there. Mrs. Jones said she could no longer put up with Carla and wanted help in getting her into a school. Mr. Jones said the problem with Carla was exaggerated and that Mrs. Jones, with her untidy housekeeping, was the real problem.

The polarization phase had now begun. Dr. Rueveni began to confront Mr. Jones about inconsistent statements he had made. The polarization continued—about whether Carla was sick, about blaming Mr. Jones for the family problems—and then focused on the unresolved divorce between the Joneses. At this point, the larger network was called upon for their reactions to what had happened so far in the meeting. The majority of the network was very supportive of Mrs. Jones and there was some hostility to Mr. Jones. His new wife became very angry, took his side, and attempted to align Jerry with herself and Mr. Jones. She invited Jerry to come live with them.

A few network members began to make suggestions about school or new living arrangements for Carla. This began the mobilization phase of the meeting. At this point, the intervention team asked each of the assembled network members to pick one of the seven Jones family members (including Carla), and to form a small group to discuss in greater detail what assistance might be needed. The small groups met in different rooms of the house for the next hour, with the intervention team members sitting in or "floating" from group to group. Each group chose a representative to report back later the results, in summary form, of the small-group meetings to the entire assembled network.

After several hours of group work, there commonly is a feeling of depression-resistance which appears when the work of polarization and mobilization is met with a sense of frustration and difficulty in solving the tasks. When the groups reported back, there were numerous suggestions about different alternatives to help individual family members. The groups volunteered to act as committees to whom family members could turn to over the next several weeks for advice and help. An aunt offered to take Carla into her home with her own children. A lawyer present suggested that Mrs. Jones needed legal help to stop Mr. Jones from barging into the house whenever he felt like it. A teacher offered to help Carla prepare for the eighth-grade exams. An artist offered her art lessons. Many offers were made to other individual family members. It was pointed out that the unresolved divorce between the Joneses threatened Mr. Jones' new marriage, and marital counseling was recommended.

As the meeting ended, Carla appeared (after having met with her small group) and offered to go with several people to get pizzas. The team left at this point, but the network stayed together discussing until nearly 2 A.M. what had happened.

A follow-up three months later indicated that Carla went to live with her aunt, but after about ten weeks arrangements were being made for residential care because she was causing too much trouble and was uncooperative. The other Jones family members were much relieved. Jane was starting college and the others were back in school. Mr. Jones seemed much happier and his new marriage seemed to be intact.

Social network intervention is a viable and promising therapeutic approach to suicidal, disturbed, or antisocial adolescents. Rueveni's *Networking Families in Crisis* (1979) supplies some of the techniques available. Trimble (1981) and Kliman are beginning to publish some of their results with networks and adolescents. The network team headed by Paul Schoenfeld at the Mount Tom Institute in Holyoke, Massachusetts, does several network interventions weekly. Several studies have shown that the network approach is more economical than conventional methods.

REFERENCES

Bott, E. *Family and social network: Roles, norms and external relationships in ordinary urban families.* London: Tavistock Publications, 1957; New York: Free Press, 1971.

Rueveni, U. *Networking families in crisis.* New York: Human Sciences Press, 1979.

Speck, R. V., & Attneave, C. L. *Family networks.* New York: Pantheon, 1973.

Speck, R. V., & Rueveni, U. Network therapy—A developing concept. *Family Process,* 1969, **8**, 182–191.

Trimble, D. W. Social network intervention with antisocial adolescents. *International Journal of Family Therapy,* Winter 1981, 268–274.

10

Outpatient Multiple Family Group

BETTY BYFIELD PAUL, L.I.C.S.W.,
and NORMAN L. PAUL, M.D.

*I*n 1963 the second author, Norman Paul accidentally booked three couples into his office at the same time. Following an educated hunch, he met with them together. The couples astonishingly discovered that they had much in common; they could learn from each other as well as from the therapist. They also learned, to their relief, that they were not "sick," nor as "unique" as they thought they were. They were able to reframe their difficulties and see them not necessarily as signs of mental illness, but as human difficulties. Later on in treatment, Norman Paul included children, siblings, and parents. Everyone was pleased with the results. There began to generate in the therapist's mind the notion that perhaps there is basically one human family and that what we see day in and day out in our offices are simply variants of that family.

The Multiple Family Group (MFG) has now been in progress for over twenty years. (The first author, Betty Paul, started to work as co-leader in 1970.) On Thursday night each week, four to eight families converge in the library/studio to learn from each other, to teach each other, and to teach us, the leaders. Approximately one thousand men, women, and children have come and gone. We get to know them; they get to know us. We watch them grow; they watch us grow. And we miss them when they leave.

What causes our increasing sense of excitement as the participants arrive? It is pleasing—even exhilarating—to see that the group has survived the week and come back. Possibly it is the model of work that brings satisfaction. Here human beings meet simultaneously in a combination of natural, extended families and multiple-family-group networks. (*Family* is defined here as any group of people—not necessarily living together—related by blood, marriage, or adoption. It can include ex-spouses and their parents.) Working together and challenging each other, group members discover who they are as individuals, how they interact as families, and how their most intimate experiences and relationships affect both their daily living and their work experience in the larger community. They are challenged by the leaders also, who serve mainly as enablers to the changing process, as each person struggles to evolve a new sense of self and self-esteem. As John M., age fifty, says, "This group is like taking a course in human relationships alongside my parents, my wife, and my sons. I'm going to stay here until I feel I've completed the course."

Although each person seems to get more attention in a small group, the larger, more clan-like group provides more challenge for us and more opportunity for peer support, peer insight, and the exchange of energies and life experiences. It propels individuals, couples, and families to reflect, self-observe, and then find new solutions to old dilemmas. As McClendon and Kadis (1983) have noted, "Families and individuals in trouble are like a record with a scratch completely across it. If you move the needle only a little bit, it always travels back to the place where it gets stuck." The MFG allows families to pull together to get "unstuck."

THE GROUP

Structure

The group at any one time varies, depending on family availability and their immediate need for input from other families to neutralize maladaptive, obsession-circular family patterns. The leaders choose family members who are most "stuck" and dysfunctional in their relationships within the family and in their work settings. Clients suffering from acute psychotic episodes or organic brain syndromes are usually *not* included. Candidates are also screened for potential interest in taking the risk of joining such a group. Prospective participants are informed that generally it will be either "anxiety-evoking" or "frightening" to start this venture as new experiences often are. And, yet, they can expect that in a brief period of time (two or three weeks) they will begin to feel acclimated and discover that they have much in common. People generally need to be reminded that any type of new experience

is associated with some level of anticipatory anxiety. Perhaps this relates to the culturally reinforced, magical belief that one should be anxiety-free as one goes through life in some preprogrammed, machine-like mode.

The group meets once a week from 7:30 until 10:00 p.m. Three weeks out of four, the heads of the families, whether a single or a couple, meet and bring along available adult family members over eighteen years old from their nuclear or extended families. This means adult children, brothers, sisters and/or parents, aunts, uncles, etc. In a typical session, one might see, among others, a forty-year-old man and his 45-year-old brother visiting from out of state with whom he "always" has had a marginal, "minimal" relationship; a woman, aged 35, with her 91-year-old grandmother; and a woman with her older sister and niece.

On the fourth evening (once a month), children, eighteen and under, are invited and/or strongly urged to attend. At those times when parents are told that this "children's" night is mandatory, almost all children attend. (New members do not join on children's night.)

Setting

The large room where the group convenes can accommodate up to thirty people arrayed in a circle along the room's periphery. The co-leaders sit on opposite sides of the room facing one another. Two microphones hang visibly from the ceiling and record onto a reel-to-reel audio tape recorder the proceedings of each meeting. Sometimes families borrow the tape to review what has transpired. Other times the co-leaders will replay a session or part of it during an MFG. Fruit and candy are available for all.

This setting is in the heart of an upper-middle-class neighborhood. Permission from the Town had to be obtained, which is renewed on a five-year basis. The setting illustrates our willingness to convey that we regard the proceedings as normal and educative, even though many in the surrounding community continue to generate anxiety about "mental health" clients coming into their neighborhood. In this setting the group comes to resemble a small tribe bonded together in their collective intention to transcend their generally restricted individual family environments. The ultimate goal is the more open expression of the anxieties, fears, and secret terrors that tend to stifle life for all of us.

Method

When a new couple enters the group, they share identifying information, such as name, age, presenting problem, and tell what they expect from the group; it is part of the incoming ritual. Usually two new couples join at the same time. This is designed to allow each person to feel more comfortable and not to be the only "new person" joining the group. Occasionally, it is necessary to introduce only one new couple if it happens to be facing an "emergency," such as an imminent court decision determining custody of their children. Facing and welcoming the new family will be six or seven other families who have been in the group for a while. These "old families," in turn, will usually comprise two groups: those who have been coming for more than a year and those who have been coming for under a year. Those coming for more than a year are generally knowledgeable about their own patterns of behavior and from where in time and place these derive. They also have learned a broad new repertoire for effective problem-solving and act as co-facilitators with the leaders to orient the new families.

There are only two binding rituals adhered to in this group process: "entering" and "leaving." The entering ritual has been mentioned above. The leaving ritual includes: (1) letting the group and leaders know at least three weeks in advance that an individual and usually the entire family are ready to leave; (2) asking leaders and group whether they agree they are ready to make this move; (3) reviewing what has been accomplished by each person in the family and by the family-as-a-whole during their time in the group; and (4) showing,

with permission, an early videotape of an individual family therapy session at the multiple family group session.

The video playback is used by the co-leaders to focus both on behavioral and relational change. All members are asked: "What has changed?" "What thoughts do you have now about the people you see on the videotape?" "Although you know the date that tape was made, how long ago does it feel?" This level of inquiry is used to enable members to develop observational skills, as well as to illustrate the difference between a client's intention or desire for change versus video evidence of such change.

Somewhat routinized for the monthly Children's Night is the Family Sculpture activity. Family Sculpture is a three-dimensional tableau created by a family member (e.g., Family A) using MFG members (not necessarily from their own family) to depict a scene from Family A's past, present or future. Adolescents often vie for the opportunity to sculpt their families, step-families, and dream families. Often different members from one family are asked to re-create a given family scene as they have experienced it. It can come as an enormous surprise, even shock, for parents to become aware of how the family is seen by an adolescent son or daughter. Family sculpting (Duhl, Kantor, & Duhl, 1973) is a means for experiencing the emotional sense of what family members have lived through and provides a type of experiential feedback to other MFG members.

On Children's Night emotions are identified and each person's life experiences can be shared. Emphasis is on empowering and reinforcing individuality in each person present, both adults and children. Empathic listening is emphasized as a critical and desirable skill. Images from the past are sorted out, often with members of the original family in the room. Children are present while patterns of behavior from their parents' original families are examined and then compared with their own present behavior. Participants learn to separate behaviors they wish to keep from the past and what they would like to discard. Strengths are emphasized; "weaknesses" are tolerated and normalized. Members are encouraged to become aware of the bonds of loyalty to past generations that inadvertently maintain the integrity of incapacitating types of behavior.

There is no restriction on members comingling or meeting socially outside the group. About thirteen years ago two young people in their early twenties got sexually involved and such acting-out became a concern. At the present time we deal with sexual acting-out among group members as part of a problem to be handled within the group process. Group discussion is used as one technique to promote resolution. When individuals are expected to behave responsibly and act in more adult ways, they generally will do so, especially in what they come to view as a safe space.

Theory: MFG as Forum

A crisis of middle age is the departure of adolescent children from home and the parents' resultant search for meaning, as individuals and as spouses, in the second halves of their lives. The crisis of adolescence is leaving home to discover an identity and purpose in the first half of life. In adolescence a change in status between parents and children occurs. This challenge to accept new realities is paced principally by the parents. Children are entering adulthood, and they want their new role acknowledged, but often parents have forgotten the struggles of their own adolescence.

The ambivalence of this adolescent/middle age era is such that both generations basically wish to learn how to acknowledge the emotional bonding while simultaneously determining different identities for themselves. The task for the adolescent is to leave home while modifying the emotional bond with parents. The task of parents is twofold: (1) to learn how to allow and encourage their adolescents to leave home with some measure of grace and self-respect; and (2) to become aware that their couple-related problems stem in large part from oscillating, reciprocated (from partner to partner) ambivalence about their own

aging process and their unresolved relationships with their own families of origin. These inevitable transitional phases are natural and normal parts of the living process. The MFG, then, is a place for adolescents, their parents, and even their grandparents to become aware of and to tolerate their own ego-alien and ego-syntonic behaviors as these important life crises are met.

TRANSCRIPTION: AN ACTUAL MFG INTERCHANGE

What follows is a transcription of an actual group process from a recent MFG meeting that focused on two adolescent girls and their families. (Only the names and professions are fictitious to protect identities.) The kind of interchange here is a reflection of the middle-class suburban families of which these groups are composed. The dialog is typical of those that take place when a majority of the group have been working together for a year. (A "year" equals ten months of weekly work.)

The "Characters"

Those people highlighted in this particular segment are the *H* and the *L* families, plus other members of the group. At this session the *H* family is represented by the couple JOHN and BONNIE and their nineteen-year-old daughter DORIS, the oldest of three children. DORIS is a student at an out-of-town college. At the time of this interchange JOHN and BONNIE are separated on a trial basis. JOHN, the youngest of three boys, had been in a family business that failed. The great ambivalence he had toward his own father and older brothers was reactivated when he and BONNIE had children. He had ten years of psychoanalysis and an eighteen-month period of hospitalization for alcoholism ten years before he and his wife were referred by a family physician to family-focused therapy. BONNIE, also a youngest child with four older sisters, chronically deferred to JOHN and thereby nullified her own sense of self. The temporary separation had been encouraged to assist both her and her husband to focus more on self—without the distraction of a spouse's presence.

The *L* family represented here include another oldest daughter, ANNE, aged eighteen, and her mother, MARTHA. MARTHA has been attending group recently with HORACE, her new boyfriend, with whom she has been living while awaiting completion of a divorce from ANNE's father, who had formerly attended the group. MARTHA's problem in her marriage had been complicated by increased amounts of guilt: (1) She has a non-identical twin sister, whose son drowned eight years previously; and (2) the sister's marriage dissolved, influencing MARTHA's marriage adversely. MARTHA's ex-husband MELVIN replaced a stillbirth in his family of origin by about two years to the death date, and his identity had suffered chronically from an unconscious demand from his recurrently distressed parents—as he experienced it—to be both his dead sister and himself. HORACE, the new boyfriend, is a somewhat confused, yet articulate lawyer, who has been married and divorced twice and is presently courting MARTHA. HORACE's father, who died of a heart attack when HORACE was eight, left no life insurance. His mother placed HORACE off and on in an orphanage. Over the years he has had recurrent anxieties about dying, especially since fathering a son. He left his first marriage when his son was eight years old.

Note that both DORIS and ANNE are teenage girls who are oldest daughters caught between partners—in the *H* family, the actual parents; and, in the *L* family, a mother and her lover (a potential stepfather to ANNE). (HORACE and MARTHA eventually do marry.)

The Scene

The scene is an MFG session attended by eight couples and some of their adult children. The bulk of the conversation in

the following segment takes place among the *H* family and *L* family members delineated above; Stephan, a member of the group and a father, who generally contributes a lot of questions; and various Group Members, who ask questions and/or contribute briefly to the segment. Our comments, on some of the interchange are interspersed to clarify our philosophy and method of leadership. Non-verbal behavior ("stage directions") appears in italics and parentheses.

JOHN. My feeling about this is that I don't want Doris to get really fucked up again like she was getting back in the middle again. At the same time, I don't want her to get back in the middle and help, uh, screw up our problems. We've all got to relate, to communicate, but somehow—

This statement is made in the context of when John himself was an adolescent and had found himself "in the middle" between his own parents.

BONNIE.—I know it. This became apparent after she was home for a couple of days.

BETTY PAUL. Do you think that her being at home affects what goes on between the two of you?

The therapist is providing the couple with a meta-view (a broader perspective) of Doris' being at home, giving them a chance to look at themselves as though they were in a play.

JOHN. It could. We had a discussion—is it possible to be at home and not be depressed and not feel that you're losing your individuality? If so, maybe it's workable. Maybe it isn't workable, and if so, maybe she shouldn't be at home.

Depression was John's problem at home with Bonnie. That was his problem as a child in his original family. (The only thing that passes is time. Of course, changes in "inherited" behavior patterns can occur, with work and with appropriate interventions, in therapy settings and outside.)

BONNIE. In all fairness to Doris, my feelings have been—

JOHN. (*Interrupting.*) I'm not at home. I'm in an apartment downtown.

BETTY PAUL. Well, who's at home?

GROUP MEMBERS. (*Everyone talks at once.*)

JOHN. Doris is back from school for the summer, and she is living at home.

GROUP MEMBER. I know that, but when I heard you talk, I was wondering whether you were talking about yourself—your own depression, your own loss of individuality.

John ignores this statement. It is too painful for him to address. The therapists also choose to let it go by.

JOHN. One of the issues we've discussed about living at home is: Doris wanted to get a job and try to make some money. Living at home she could save some money. If she goes to the Cape, it all goes for rent. That's one of the practical issues of living at home.

Anne interrupts suddenly.

ANNE. There's a feeling I've gotten, because of my relationship with my mother, and let me start by saying that it's hard for me to talk about it, and it makes me feel uncomfortable, but I've been getting the feeling that since I moved back to my mother's house . . . from school, I've been feeling a lot like Horace resents my presence and in some ways I'm, I don't know, some kind of interference, some kind of a block with his relationship to my mother. I don't know, I feel that way, and I feel that I should talk about it tonight. I saw Dr. Paul today and he suggested that I do, tonight.

GROUP MEMBER A. Are there any parallels between the father/daughter relationships we were talking about before?

ANNE. No, it's different.

It seems different to Anne. Yet hearing the previous conversation gave her the confidence to talk about her own feelings about being "inbetween." Next, Martha attempts to divert the flow from Anne by answering another group member's question about the younger two boys.

MARTHA. Are the boys living at home now? My son is in the intense social season right now, and every now and then he calls and lets me know that he might need some clean clothes. He lives at home, but he's very, very busy.

Group members briefly draw out Horace about his scene. And Horace, though uncomfortable about Anne's directness, refocuses the attention of the group on the issues Anne raised about him and her mother.

HORACE. Would it help if I responded? (*He and others laugh.*) I didn't want to jump in. (*Sighs.*) I think that your perception is accurate.

This is an example of cross-generational support.

HORACE. I think that there is some resentment, and I think that my feeling has been that your presence in the house has been a block and obstacle to the relationship between your mother and me. I think that I can probably define it, though, in a way that you would accept as reasonable. Your presence in the house means if I'm there and sleeping with your mother—with my particular feelings about sex, my sexual behavior—I see you in two different ways at two different times. At times you are your mother's daughter, and I feel that our sex life is something that should be done, engaged in, without your knowing it, but I know that that's stupid—(*Laughter.*)

The above is a typical dilemma that exists in reconstituted marriages if there are adolescents involved.

HORACE. —since you are pretty well aware of what it's all about. Anyway, I'm conscious of your presence when I go to bed with your mother, and that makes me self-conscious, as I am now, and I resent whatever the source of that self-consciousness is—I don't want to be self-conscious, and you're it—and it isn't your fault, and

I don't dislike you, but I'm resentful, okay? (*Sighs.*) And then, too, your friend Janet sleeps in the house . . .
MARTHA. (*Laughs.*) She's a boarder.
HORACE. No, no, I'm telling you how I feel.
MARTHA. I was totally uninvolved in that decision . . .

The important words there are: "I don't dislike you, but I'm resentful."

HORACE. I know, but she's one of your best friends, she's your age and has your general attitude about things, and she's in a sense a child; somebody else is her mother, but her mother is not here. (*Laughter in the group.*) Wait a minute. Wait a minute . . . I'm struggling with this. So, anyway, she comes and sleeps upstairs and you sleep downstairs in the television room. And I can't watch the goddamned television 'cause all your stuff is all over the place. (*Laughter from the group.*) So, now I have two reasons. But, actually, deeper than all that and much more meaningful than all that, when we think about it and your mother and I talk about it: It's more important to me to know that you and she are together than those other things are. So, I'll still sleep with her when you are there, and I'll get over it. And . . . what else can I say? . . . I think of you as older than any daughter of mine could ever be, even though my number-one son is older than you, but somehow I met you when you were older, and grown up and sexy, and . . . you know, it's impossible that I could be old enough to be your father, but I'm older than your mother, so, of course it's possible. I think of you as a person that has two roles: One is your mother's daughter, but also, on the same level, maturity-wise, there's a little bit of competitiveness there, and I can't be as friendly to you as I am to her, because I'm going to marry her and all those romantic things (*Laughter from the group.*) And I . . . I'd like to know what you think about that, how you feel about that.

Horace's attraction to Anne also confronts him with his own aging process. Paradoxi-

cally, his attraction to Anne can be looked at as a denial of his aging process. On one level he would like to think that he could be a lover to both women. He remains loyal to Martha "because I'm going to marry her and all those romantic things."

ANNE. Well, it's reassuring that my perceptions are not totally unfounded, and my imagination—I'm always afraid I'm perceiving things that aren't really there. It also, just, you know, it makes me feel bad . . . I can understand all this. . . .

Anne is not necessarily rattled by Horace's sexual fantasies about her or his relationship with her mother. She is quite relieved that her perceptions of how he felt about her were realistic and that she is not "crazy."

HORACE. Can you understand that it's my problem, it's my hang-up?
ANNE. Yes.
HORACE. Can you understand that if I were really totally healthy that it wouldn't be a problem at all and that you wouldn't be resented?

Is there such a thing as being "totally healthy"?

ANNE. Yes, it would definitely be different. Nobody's totally healthy.
HORACE. It's true, probably not.
BETTY PAUL. Why do you say that? What does this have to do with health?

The therapist is questioning the use of such labels as "healthy" and "unhealthy."

HORACE. Well, if I were . . . the fact of . . . the business about the resentment. I just think that there is a psychological problem in me about sex that hasn't been totally worked out yet. Intellectually, cerebrally, I know that's my problem. I want Anne to know that my problems are not her fault.

Only now does she know. That's what she's learning in the safety of the MFG.

GROUP MEMBER B. I'm not sure I understand about her being a child and her being a sexy adult at the same time.

HORACE. Okay. I know how I feel about my seventeen-year-old son who has always been my child, so I assume that's the way Martha feels about her daughter, that no matter how big and old she gets, she will be a daughter, and she will be protected and all.

GROUP MEMBER B. From an awareness of sex?

HORACE. Oh, no.

GROUP MEMBER B. Do you mean that you feel attracted to Anne? Maybe I misunderstood.

HORACE. I think you misunderstood. I don't recognize that.

GROUP MEMBER B. Yes, but you called her sexy, you know.

HORACE. Yes, she's attractive, and she's . . . this comes back to the other one. I can see my own daughter growing up to be seventeen, eighteen, nineteen—and attractive. Anne is very attractive, but somehow, something has stopped me, or some power; it really isn't supernatural, because I know it's right there. I have no great sexual, no sexual urges toward Anne, for myself, but I have thought of all kinds of men that I know that are single and looking for women and considered introducing them as a favor to them, and I think what has prevented me is—

MARTHA. Old men, with my daughter! (*Laughs.*)

HORACE. Not old. (*Group laughs.*) I have confidence that Anne will at least go to her mother with these things that she won't go to me [with] yet. She'll go to her mother, because they are close, and I would like to feel that my daughter can talk the same way with her parents, so that if my daughter grows to be as attractive as Anne—and I hope that my daughter can tell me, and I certainly will tell her, that she's sexually attractive, and I'm your father, but boy, you really turn me on—I really expect to be able to say that to her.

. . .

GROUP MEMBER. But there's a conflict in that. It's a confusing thing. It's confusing for you; it's confusing for the child.

HORACE. It's confusing if you come in on it at eighteen or nineteen.

GROUP MEMBER (female). That would have made me feel panicky if my father had said that to me.

GROUP MEMBER (female). My father said that to me, and I felt pretty panicky.

GROUP MEMBER (female). I get upset when my husband starts putting his hands all over my daughter's fanny. I can't even imagine if he said something like that. I just think it would be terrible.

DORIS. I think if my father said something like that I would be able to—I mean, if that's the way my father felt about me at certain times, I think I would probably be able to sense it. If not, if nothing was brought out, I think it would make me uncomfortable. I mean, I told my father how I felt that time in the apartment. I wasn't just telling him that I, myself, was having these feelings about this man who was my father. How did you react?

That time Doris had felt her father was coming on to her as though she were his "date" after he and his wife were separated. Critical in the family of an adolescent child is for parents to learn the value of generational boundaries, how to work out more accommodating, affectionate relations between them rather than unconsciously seducing a child's interest and attention to themselves as was probably done to them when they were adolescents (and unfortunately presently forgotten).

JOHN. I'm kind of in the middle here, because I've spent many sessions with Dr. Paul trying to fantasize sleeping with my mother.

(*Group laughs.*)

BONNIE. There's also the element of homosexual fantasy that we tried to recreate.

BETTY PAUL. That's what I'd like to talk about, because we all have so much difficulty with the fact that we all have sexual fantasies, about anybody, which doesn't mean that we have to act on them.

GROUP MEMBER. Do you have to tell them?

BETTY PAUL. No, I don't know if you have to tell them, but I think a lot of these uncomfortable feelings—I mean Anne felt better when she shared these feelings. I think that if we tell ourselves that we have a fantasy, we can also learn to tell ourselves that we don't have to act on it.

NORMAN PAUL. And that they are not abnormal. They are all normal.

GROUP MEMBER (male). Sometimes it's hard to believe that they're normal. To acknowledge them makes them so much easier. You don't have to say, gee, I want to go to bed with you, but to know that there is a feeling there and to acknowledge it, and not to work on the basis that it's going to take place, but just that it's there. With any strange feeling, sexual or not . . .

GROUP MEMBER (male). I just wonder about saying that to a girl who wasn't having similar feelings, what the effect would be.

HORACE. That's when you can say, I feel strange.

This is part of the "magic": beginning to be able to share images.

HORACE. I get a certain sense in my mind that there is a great deal of danger in having certain thoughts, sexual thoughts, about your children. I've successfully blocked it out with my daughters; they are growing up, and I've blocked it out. I never fantasize.

Is this one of the reasons a husband/father leaves home—when he begins to notice "dangerous" sexual fantasies about his children? It might seem better to him to leave home and find a new woman rather than deal with these so-called lethal thoughts. The quandary for the father of an attractive adolescent girl is how to deal with the increasingly uncomfortable sexual fantasies in a society that has generally been unable to assist the normal adult to know that such fantasies are normal and that the parents should be able to share them with each other. As an addendum, sex education should be made available in a comfortable and supportive manner for parents and then should be available for their adolescent children. Things are often done in a backwards way. Parents are generally hurting with the pretense, for they often know very little about basic sexual matters.

GROUP MEMBER (female). Would you

have been able, when your daughter started maturing—you've been hugging your little girl since she was this high, then suddenly she's fourteen, and you give her a hug, with this different context, and I can remember him going like this. He didn't know what to do with his hands, because he wasn't sure, in our old inhibited way, that it was proper. I don't know what went through your head. What did go through your head?

GROUP MEMBER (male). Well, generally when a male puts his arm around a female, and he feels her contours, and he feels her breasts, and it's different—now it's your children.

GROUP MEMBER (female). Okay. So do you say, "I felt strange when I put my arms around you this time"?

HORACE. I didn't say I was afraid of what I felt, but that I was afraid of what I might feel.

GROUP MEMBER. Okay, but did you say this when it was going on? I think it's unrealistic to say that you can.

(*Everyone talks at once.*)

GROUP MEMBER. No, no, I'm just setting up a situation. Say, she is only fourteen.

GROUP MEMBER (female). Well, I think at that point in time I would have—I wouldn't have expected him to say that. I think maybe if you've ever had a relationship—father/daughter, mother/daughter —of talking about your innermost feelings that maybe at that point it wouldn't sound so strange. I think that maybe at that point I didn't really know what I was thinking at that point. I don't think it would have been constructive for myself.

What group members are learning here is that sharing is a process that demands a sensitive appreciation of the other person's readiness for learning certain things. Timing is always important.

HORACE: Well, I don't really think it's impossible or unrealistic, and I think that the development of breasts in a female can be just as much a part of that father as of the mother, and I think that a bra can be purchased by the father with the daughter on a Saturday, just as well as by the mother, and I think that you don't have to get erotic to be appreciative of the developing body with fathers and sons. My God, my son has this modesty thing of going to the bathroom and closing the door before he gets undressed. I can see it with either sex, but the whole thing to me seems to be an honest relationship where there's no fear of being exposed. That was my whole thing.

JOHN. You are just saying, and I agree with you, but I also feel that erotic feelings can arise, and the questions that come up are should or when or what should be expressed between a father and daughter?

GROUP MEMBER.—Even if you are uncomfortable with them?

GROUP MEMBER. Expressed in what sense? Expressed that you have them?

HORACE. Sure, that you have them. I think so, I really think so.

GROUP MEMBER. You [Horace] brought this up.

GROUP MEMBER (male). I never had an erotic feeling for my mother.

STEPHAN. No, but you [Horace] are assuming that she would be comfortable with you coming to buy a bra with her. You are making that assumption, too. That she would be comfortable? I'm saying that if things are communicated—And that's not erotic, excuse me, I'm separating that.

HORACE. No, that's not erotic.

STEPHAN. And that implies that you expect a particular response, some kind of response, and also acceptance of what you said.

HORACE. It's a hell of a lot of conjecture on my part. My daughter is only eight. All I can say is that I would like it to be that way.

STEPHAN. And you'd like her to be able to respond how? Because she would respond to you.

BETTY PAUL. So, if you can think of yourself as a child, perhaps you can begin to think how a child might feel.

HORACE. Well, I do believe that I did have erotic feelings. I just don't remember them. I can't speak for anybody else, but I would dare to believe that my daughter has already had some kind of subliminal erotic feelings of sexual attraction for me, as I have for her. But they are not intercourse, nor desires for intercourse.

BETTY PAUL. Yes, but why is it so easy for you to talk about your daughter, and so hard for you to talk about your mother?

HORACE. I guess because I love my daughter, and I don't love my mother, probably.

"I don't love my mother"—What he really means is that he's so scared to become aware that somewhere inside he loves his mother.

GROUP MEMBER. Is your mother still alive?

HORACE. Yes. I didn't intend to say that I don't love my mother. I didn't plan it.

NORMAN PAUL. Maybe you should ask your mother if she remembers when you had erotic feelings toward her.

HORACE. She would say, "What do you mean by erotic?"

NORMAN PAUL. Then you spell it out, E-R-O-T-I-C.

HORACE. What has that kind of thing to do with it?

NORMAN PAUL. I was thinking ahead—to take the heat off your daughter.

BETTY PAUL. That's what I was thinking. You're so gung ho when you talk about your daughter.

HORACE. I think there's an exaggeration taking place. You remember, don't you, that I don't even have custody of my daughter. Chances are that—I would like to make a statement to the group—I've decided to leave law. When I leave law, I'll be leaving my daughter behind, so I don't imagine we'll ever bring this off the way I'd like to bring it off, so I'm engaging in wishful thinking. We won't be together much.

It sounds like Horace is going to desert his daughter just as his mother deserted him when she sent him to an orphanage.

GROUP MEMBER (female). You can't just take her for a bra on Saturday if you meet her once a month. [But] I know what you are saying.

GROUP MEMBER (female). But you can still—I mean, I grew up without my father's presence until I was about four, and I wanted to have a relationship with him. I wanted to have a communication, even though I didn't see him more than twice in my teen years. The quality of that, I mean if the quality of interaction has been there, the infrequency wouldn't have mattered much. I could have picked it up when I saw him again when I got married and moved to that area. I don't think it's going to matter much that you see her less frequently if you have good quality dealings with her.

The group goes on to discuss the quality of a relationship versus the frequency of interaction.

DISCUSSION AND CONCLUSION

As shown so clearly in the above transcription, the main power of the Multiple Family Group is the fact that families help each other. It is a safe spot to share fantasies and dialog within and among families. This is usually not possible in any other setting. The MFG creates an automatic de-stigmatizing atmosphere. This type of interchange can also occur in individual or family therapy. But in the MFG the atmosphere is different and more conducive to learning. "Self-help" and "normalcy" are emphasized here.

When we have presented this interchange at workshops and have had it "role-played" by workshop members, they have often expressed anxiety about our low-keyed style. But we, the therapists, take a deliberate laid-back position, so that each client can function as a co-therapist—can learn how to observe behavior and to share such observations.

We want the group members to do the "intervening," which they do well here. When clients learn to take the initiative in MFG, they usually can begin to take the initiative for themselves in the outside world. In the main, we redirect only when the group becomes obviously "stuck" or where there is an opportunity to promote cross-sharing between two families or between two generations. Then, one of us might say: "What does A's comments re-

mind you of?" Or, "what thoughts do B's comments bring up for you?"

One of the main tasks of adolescence is to leave home and establish autonomy, but part of the process, reflected above, should include dialog between generations. It makes separation much less painful for both parents and children. For example, the perceptions of the adolescents here are validated by the adults in the MFG. The adolescents do not have to feel that they are going "crazy." The existence of such sexual fantasies are also validated among the various families. This is an important experience for both parents and children. The atmosphere gives all concerned an opportunity to differentiate and relate at the same time. The dialogue creates "parental readiness" to separate emotionally from the adolescent, and begin to generate in the adolescent readiness to leave home—figuratively, if not literally. "Parental readiness" for letting the adolescent go is related to a "marital readiness," wherein each parent can renew an earlier love and both can grow together by dialoging. The marital relationship (including a sexual relationship) has to become mutually fulfilling as well as reinforce a sense of selfhood. The challenge is important for each marital partner and for the whole family unit.

All families and adult members, and some of the adolescents in the group have individual sessions with the therapists. Individual therapy for adolescents and their parents offers certain benefits. While these individuals are growing apart emotionally, the MFG offers them a strong forum for negotiating the separation.

One of the strong points of this MFG is the fact that it is led by a male and a female therapist, trained in related professions (medicine and social work) and also married. As Albert Schweitzer said, "Example is not the main thing in influencing others; it is the only thing." The group members use us—individually and as a couple working in partnership—as role models, sounding boards, and people handy to rebel against or relate to.

Though we have focused above on two adolescent girls, much of what occurs with adolescent boys is similar. Both boys and girls attempt during their adolescence to evolve and integrate their present emerging senses of identity with visions of future lives as adults.

Generally, boys are more shy and reticent in participating in the Multiple Family Group setting. They require more support and assistance to realize it is okay for them to be aware of their experiences and to share them, including those that make them feel disquietingly vulnerable. To do this, they first require the endorsing sanction of experiencing either their fathers, older brothers, or grandfathers engaging openly in the Multiple Family Group.

The Multiple Family Group setting is a safe context to have such experiences happen. Parental participation with their children can help neutralize the negative consequences of parents' natural tendencies to dictate, without dialoging, arbitrary wishes and behaviors (e.g. dress codes) to their children, which generates rebelliousness. Usually one finds that one or both parents in adolescence had some similar humiliating experience with his/her parents. These earlier scenes are natural setups for replication in the next generation twenty to twenty-five years later. The normal adolescent of today behaves unconsciously like his parent did, and usually this parent has forgotten his own earlier adolescent behavior.

In the introduction to *Normal Adolescence*, the Committee on Adolescence (1968) states:

> It is of interest to note, also, that the adult experience of having been an adolescent usually is of little or no value in aiding him to understand those who are now the adolescents. It is today's adolescents who tomorrow, from their position as the new adult generation, will express the same kinds of concerns about adolescents as were only recently expressed about them. This, too, seems to be an inevitable and therefore presumably normal condition in human relationships. (p. 7)

Thus, parents, irrespective of their desire and wishes to the contrary, are often unable to become important, valuable, and enduring resources for their children's emotional growth during adolescence. The Multiple Family Group represents a vehicle to counteract such limitations. By offering the opportunity to dialog, it introduces empathic connections between the generations.

REFERENCES

Benningfield, A. D. Multiple family therapy systems. *Journal of Marriage and Family Counseling*, 1978, **9**:25–34.

Bowen, M. Principle and techniques of multiple family therapy. *Family Therapy in Clinical Practice*. New York: Jason Aronson, 1978.

Bowen, M. Family therapy and family group therapy. In H. Kaplan, & B. Sadock (Eds.), *Comprehensive group psychotherapy*. Baltimore: Williams & Wilkins, 1971.

Committee on Adolescence, Group for the Advancement of Psychiatry. *Normal adolescence: Its dynamics and impact*, 1968, **6**:751–858.

Duhl, F., Kantor, D., & Duhl, B. Learning, space, and action in family therapy: A primer of sculpture. In D. A. Bloch (Ed.), *Techniques of family psychotherapy: A primer*. New York: Grune & Stratton, 1973.

Framo, J. L. Marriage therapy in a couples group. In D. A. Bloch (Ed.), *Techniques of family psychotherapy: A primer*. New York: Grune & Stratton, 1973.

Guldner, Claude A. Multiple family psychodramatic therapy. *Journal of Group Psychotherapy, Psychodrama and Sociometry*, 1982, **35**:47–56.

Laquer, H. P. Multiple family therapy. In A. Ferber, M. Mendelsohn, & A. Napier (Eds.), *The book of family therapy*. New York: Jason Aronson, 1972, 618–636.

Leichter, E., & Schulman, G. L. Emerging phenomena in multi-family group treatment. *International Journal of Group Psychotherapy*, 1968, **18**:58–69.

McClendon, Ruth, & Kadis, Leslie. *Chocolate pudding and other approaches to intensive multiple family therapy*. Palo Alto, CA: Science & Behavior Books, 1983.

Minuchin, S. *Families and Family Therapy*. Cambridge: Harvard University Press, 1974.

Paul, Norman L., Bloom, Joseph D., and Paul, Betty B. Outpatient multiple family group therapy: Why not?. In: L. Wolberg & M. Aronson (Eds.), *Group and Family Therapy*. New York: Brunner/Mazel, 1981.

Satir, V. *Peoplemaking*. Palo Alto, CA: Science & Behavior Books, 1972.

11

Conducting Short-Term Inpatient Multiple Family Groups

STUART L. KOMAN, Ph.D.

*T*he complex system that is created when five to seven families are joined in a group presents a host of dilemmas for beginning Multiple Family Group (MFG) therapists: "What do I pay attention to? How do I organize this? What is the purpose?" Before answering these questions, however, it is necessary to survey the scene and develop an overview of the MFG experience.

MFG is unlike any other "real-world" situation. The only time that entire families come together *en masse* is for special occasions—family reunions, birthdays, weddings, funerals, holidays—and at those times the purpose is quite different and well defined by the occasion. In contrast, MFG brings together families who are unknown to each other for what are initially vague purposes. There are no natural situations from which new MFG members can generalize and prepare. This "facing the unknown" is obviously an anxiety-producing situation. It can be similarly or even exceedingly anxiety producing for the group leader if there is no way to conceptualize and make plans for the group.

There is, however, a metaphorical approximation which I have found useful—the symphony orchestra. Taking each member of the group as an instrument, and each family or subgroup (children, adults, males, females, etc.) as a section, the orchestra develops its potential by learning to blend and contrast all of its sounds. Through the building of themes that are played and replayed in seemingly unending variations, each instrument establishes its own unique place and the orchestra expands its repertoire. With this in mind, the jobs of the leader/conductor become clear. These are: (1) to help choose the pieces that will challenge the orchestra to evolve beyond its present ability; (2) to control and structure the orchestra so that all of the instruments can be heard; (3) to provide guidance, nuance, feeling, and interpretation so that the resulting product has meaning beyond the notes played; and (4) to model tolerance and respect for each sound and family of sound.

The MFG is far more like the orchestra in rehearsal than the orchestra in performance. Imperfection, the constant reworking of themes, and striving for improvement are the main fare. Drama, elegance, excitement, and resolution are extremely powerful, but less often seen. The leader/conductor has some control over the group, but the metaphorical crutch fails to describe adequately the mutual development and participation of the group and the leader in writing the "symphony" as the group evolves. Unlike the real orchestra, the MFG has no finished piece to play. Rather, the group works on each other's problems, aided by the leader's expertise in promoting a context for resolution.

In creating a context for problem resolution, the leader/conductor must be in contact with the group at both the content level, *what* the orchestra is playing, and the process level, *how* the orchestra is playing (the word "process" is shorthand for "process of interaction"). This monitoring of the group at two levels provides a means of checking the group's progress: the orchestra may sound beautiful, but if only some of the instruments are playing all the time, there may be little change in the overall development. Interventions are based on discrepancies between what is occurring at the content and at the process levels of the group. For this reason, a strong co-therapy relationship is the most effective way of leading an MFG. One leader can be "in," conducting the group, while the other is "out," monitoring the group process.

A major responsibility of the leader/conductor is to achieve an effective balance between comfort and tension for the member families, individuals, and the group as a whole. This dynamic tension is fueled by the very reasons (i.e., family problems) that brought participants to the group in the first place, and can be dampened or stoked by the leader in many different ways. Some specifics will be discussed later, but the primary means of both increasing and decreasing tension come from

focusing on or focusing away from particular problem areas. Given the overwhelming number of problems, issues, and themes which a group of thirty people can present, there is ample opportunity to change subject. However, changing subject (i.e., content) does not necessarily mean changing focus (i.e., process). For example, two husband-wife pairs can be discussing seemingly different problems but the focus on the power and control issues in the marriages is quite similar.

A major problem in MFG leadership, sensory overload, is implied in the preceding analysis. The leader of an MFG is responsible for providing some order to the chaos that is initially presented so that the group is not merely a continual restatement of problems, but a means of promoting change. Differentiating process themes from content themes and finding different ways to focus on interaction are the key to effective MFG leadership. This is especially true of a short-term group. Returning to the orchestra metaphor, the conductor attempts to amplify the sound or group of sounds that offers the orchestra the greatest opportunity to develop itself interactionally. This is a complex task, requiring knowledge of the sounds available, some idea of what sound is desired, and the flexibility and skill necessary to influence (cajole, bully, paradox, beg) the orchestra to develop its repertoire.

DEVELOPING A MULTIPLE FAMILY GROUP IN AN INPATIENT SETTING

The practice of seeing several families in a single therapeutic group originated in the treatment of hospitalized schizophrenics and their families (Bowen, 1971; Laqueur, 1972). Few current inpatient programs, however, have pursued the development of MFG. This section describes one program that has developed multiple family group as a central component of an inpatient adolescent experience.

The adolescent program at Charles River

Hospital in Wellesley, Massachusetts, is a short-term (six- to eight-week), family-centered treatment program for families in which an adolescent member has exhibited enduring symptoms that have prevented his or her continued residence in the home. Virtually 100 percent of the families admitted to the program have been previously involved in outpatient therapy, social agency intervention, or both. Upon admission, families commit themselves to:

1. Participation in family therapy during regular work/school hours;
2. Participation in a weekend pass (adolescents leave the hospital for both weekend days); and
3. Participation in a multiple family group.

These requirements support the basic philosophy of the program—that the vast majority of adolescent symptoms can be relieved enough through planned systems intervention to allow the continued inclusion of the adolescent in his or her family. The admission requirements were established to insure family participation. Although the demands of the program can at times be inconvenient for the family, we believe that the intensity of the program is necessary for the kinds of problems we deal with, and further, that the imposition of hospitalization serves as an incentive to end the inpatient phase of treatment.

Multiple Family Group (MFG) evolved as a natural expression of the adolescent program as it moved from a more traditional, individually oriented perspective to a fully developed systems perspective. It developed through several formats before arriving at the present one, each step representing an advance in understanding of systems intervention in a hospital setting. It is likely that further changes and additions in the format will develop as we become more sophisticated in our thinking.

MFG in its embryonic form was not actually a family group but a parent group (Ricci et al., 1980). Prior to the initiation of parent groups, there was no group therapy for family members except for adolescent group therapy which the hospitalized adolescents participated in during the day.

Aside from family therapy on the average of once per week, family contact with the hospital was mostly limited to informal meetings between parents and milieu staff. This contact often focused on the adolescent's progress and behavior (i.e., lack of progress and misbehavior), vain attempts by parents to express their sense of inadequacy and frustration, and uncoordinated attempts by staff to teach parents alternative methods of handling their children. Given the lack of planned coordination between parents and staff, parents often felt threatened by staff suggestions and staff often felt that parents "caused" the adolescents' problems. The usual results of these meetings were increased hostility and distance between the hospital and parents—easily recognized in systems logic as a breeding ground for further symptomatology.

Parent group was an initial attempt by the adolescent program to enhance individual family therapy and reduce the parents' sense of isolation and guilt. It was correctly assumed that parents would be far more understanding of each other's frustration and that this understanding would provide much needed support. Through the medium of the group, parents provided each other with several types of support, including both general social acceptance and specific suggestions relating to behavior management. Informal gatherings of parents after group in which parents continued to give and seek advice or make weekend plans with each other developed spontaneously. Often, when the parents met outside of the group, their children would be present. Thus, the first multiple family groups probably met without staff or a formal group structure. Another major surprise was the quality of advice given by group members. Initially, staff believe that parent group would be an ideal place to teach parents the basic techniques of behavior management in a time-effective manner. It was soon observed that many parents already knew a "few tricks of their own" and that other parents were more open to suggestions from "their own kind." With the encouragement and wise counsel of the group behind them, individual parents quickly improved in their ability to set limits with their troubled and troublesome children. In addition, parents openly acknowledged the group contribution. Thus, it was not uncommon to hear one hospitalized adolescent tell another, "Get your father to shut up. He's ruining my weekend with his stupid ideas."

It soon became clear, however, that staff involvement in parent group was important. Although the reasons behind this were different than anticipated, in retrospect, they seem completely obvious. The group provided a forum where parents could express their feelings about themselves and their children as well as the staff and the hospital. Parents often felt that staff "blamed" them for their children's difficulties and expended great effort to understand the children but not the parents. In short, parents expressed the feeling that they were being short-changed in the treatment. From a system's perspective, this was in fact true. With an improved understanding of the parents' position and new respect for the parents' strengths and abilities, the milieu staff became more adept at supporting parents and fostering independent family functioning.

Over the course of the program, parent group became the place where parents bonded together to reaffirm their shaken self-respect and to confront representatives of the hospital about problems which they perceived in the hospitalization. In short, parents acted more competently with the help of the group. However, a disturbing phenomenon was observed: the group discussion invariably centered on the hospitalized adolescent, thereby reinforcing the identification of the adolescent as *the* problem. Despite leader attempts to focus on family and/or couples issues, the group resolution was mostly, "What's the matter with kids today? When I was growing up . . ." Thus, while parent group succeeded in supporting parent competence, improving the relationship between the parents and hospital, and improving the communication of different ways to interact with their troubling children, the group inadvertently presented a context in which

the absent identified patients were continually triangulated. MFG was an experiment to see if including the entire family in a group would reinforce the idea that hospitalization and adolescent symptomatology were family problems and would promote broader systems change.

In retrospect, however, it is clear that the "old way" of looking at problems was still alive. Family therapy was one thing (i.e., you can do it in the privacy of your office) but MFG was "really strange." There was a general belief that no one would talk about the "real" problems or even *should* talk about family problems in a group. The old adage, "You don't wash your dirty linen in public" was as much ingrained in the staff as it was in the participating families. (Privacy issues are discussed later in this chapter.) There was also concern that parents would lose their special place in the treatment that parent group provided. In order to quell the rising skepticism, it was decided that parents in the MFG would continue to attend the parent group and that only the highest functioning families (i.e., families who already identified their problem as a family problem and would be better able to tolerate the group) would be referred. Milieu staff, in particular, thought the idea of putting four to six acting-out or depressed adolescents and their families together in a group that would be comprised of a total of twenty to thirty people, laughable and uncontrollable. MFG was soon dubbed "family fight night" and regarded as "one of those ideas that looks great on paper but never actually works." Respect for the leader's bravery was coupled with questions about his or her sanity.

The immediate success of MFG was both surprising and revealing; surprising because a virtually untrained MFG therapist could make the group successful, and revealing because the families needed so little instruction on what to do. The instructions were, in fact, minimal:

MFG is a place where families use their own expertise in various areas to help find solutions to each other's problems. It is not a place where a professional tells you what to do. No one will be forced to reveal anything or do anything that they would feel uncomfortable about.

Faced with the mutual dilemma of their severe problems and given each other as their primary resource, the MFG families quickly developed an attitude of concern and helpfulness. This attitude enabled the group members to accept the probings and suggestions of other group members regardless of their ages as potential paths away from their family quagmires. This is not to say that there were no problems in launching the first MFGs; the first meetings were awkward.

Natural resistance to change and the potential for embarrassment in a public forum strongly supported a maintenance of the status quo. This was reflected in the group in several ways. Some families insisted that they had nothing in common with the others. Some families persisted in viewing the problem as belonging to their child alone. And some demonstrated their general distrust through verbal hostility toward the hospital and the group leader. However, an initial intervention designed to structure the group toward problem definition and problem solving supplied enough of a boundary to allow the natural forces within MFG to develop. More will be said about specific techniques later in this section, but it is important to acknowledge and recognize the role of resistance in MFG; failure to do so will likely result in a "stuck" group and a frustrated leader. Once the group structure has provided for the protection of the family by reducing the risk of sudden exposure, extrafamilial alliances developed to explore similarities between individual members, confront one-sided problem definitions (e.g., the view that the adolescent is the problem), and pursue alternative methods of communicating.

Within a short period of time, accounts of the MFG experience were publicized by the members themselves and by staff witnessing changes in the families and adolescents whom they treated. The spontaneous development of a "community" expanded with the total family membership of MFG. MFG families began to question the need for a separate parent group and other families, hearing about the experience of the MFG members, began to inquire about and request the group.

The present format of the MFG program represents another step in the general acceptance of a systems philosophy in the adolescent program. As the demand for MFG increased, it became more difficult to decide which families should be included and which to exclude. Systems logic assumes that all families are competent when provided with a context that supports higher functioning.

With the ending of parent group, many parents were initially concerned about losing their special "time"; however, the "trade-off" was obvious and many parents were quick to notice the unique contribution of the hospitalized adolescents and their siblings to the group. Nevertheless, parents were reluctant to discuss certain problems, particularly those relating to marital and sexual issues, in a group with nonadults of varying ages. At the same time, the parents had gained much from watching the adolescents function more responsibly. Outside consultation with Norman and Betty Paul suggested that the group could be flexible in its membership—meeting at times with the entire group and at other times in subgroups. With this in mind, it was decided to tie the daily adolescent group program together with the MFG program such that the membership in both groups was constant.[1] The yoked design combines group therapy for the hospitalized adolescent five times per week with MFG for the same adolescents and their families once a week. This provides an effective bridge between group and family treatment which promotes a continued focus on important issues across treatment contexts. This "crossover effect" is maximized by preparing the patients and families in their individual, group, and/or family sessions for their participation in the MFG. In this way, the therapy system

---

[1] This plan was formulated by Marsha P. Mirkin, Ph.D., and the author.

serves as a model of open communication and joint problem solving for the family system.

The inclusion of MFG as one of the three program admission requirements underscores the importance now accorded it, but it is the general change in attitude on the part of the families and milieu staff that accurately reflects its coming of age. MFG, once regarded as a doomed, quirky idea, is now recognized as a major part of the therapy which plays an all-important role in integrating the various aspects of the program. Much time and effort is spent in adolescent group and family therapy to prepare for participation in MFG and MFG leaders report back to the family's therapists and milieu staff following each MFG session.

Families and milieu staff have demonstrated their enthusiasm for MFG in different ways. The recent development of mini-MFGs by staff for time-efficient processing of weekend passes is proof of its acceptance in the milieu. Families have indicated their approval by returning for an additional nonmandatory, postdischarge MFG and by opting for aftercare MFGs as part of their continuing treatment following hospitalization.

THE UNIQUE CONTRIBUTION OF ADOLESCENTS TO MULTIPLE FAMILY GROUP

The processes of change in MFG have been reviewed comprehensively elsewhere (Laquer, 1972; Paul, Bloom, & Paul, 1981). In the following section, some of the effects of these particular groups are described, focusing specifically on the unique contribution of the adolescents to the group and the important lessons that adolescents and their parents learn as group members. The groups are composed of a varying number of families (usually five to seven), who are at different stages of hospitalization. It is common to have around two families starting in a group, around three families midway through treatment, and around two families in the final phase of inpatient treat-

ment. The entire cycle rarely lasts more than six to seven weeks. However, despite limited time and changing membership, these groups progress rapidly to provide effective intervention in family systems, largely spurred by the contribution of the hospitalized adolescents to the group.

Adolescents in MFG: Catalysts of Change

The role of adolescents as catalysts of change has been documented in other MFG's. Leichter and Schulman (1968) noted:

> We had not anticipated the children's ability to relate, sometimes quite deeply, to underlying feelings of adults and to perceive total family problems as astutely as they did. Because the children were so genuine and sometimes profoundly perceptive, the adults felt less threatened by them and could, therefore, often respond with less defensiveness. [p. 60]

Perhaps because of their central position in the family turmoil and their intensive training as hospital inpatients, the hospitalized adolescents in our groups tend to be the group members who provide the initial push toward meaningful interaction, either through comment on another family's problems or through an enactment of their own family's problem. It is assumed that the adolescents and families are at the hospital in order to change and there is great pressure exerted on them to do so. This is often done by one adolescent confronting another in relation to some irresponsible or self-destructive behavior.

> Floyd, a seventeen-year-old hospitalized for his increasing use of drugs and alcohol, refusal to go to school, and disregard of the rules at home, stated that he had had a "perfect weekend" pass and should now be discharged from the hospital because he "had kicked the habit forever." His father, a nice but ineffective limit setter, agreed that things had gone "much smoother in general" and that he had only been concerned a couple of times when Floyd "disappeared without permission," but that "probably didn't mean anything." Don C., another adolescent in the

group with a similar problem, broke in abruptly, "Don't be so naive, Mr. P., Floyd told me that he got high three times this weekend and that he could get away with it as long as he kept it short or did it while running errands for you. He still doesn't take you or this treatment seriously."

In this one act, several group norms are established. These include a redefinition of "loyalty" as the group member's obligation to respond honestly to the subject at hand, not an obligation to support each other's problem-maintaining construction of reality or problem behavior. The establishment of this norm is of utmost importance to families in which "loyalty" has led to the protection of family myths and secrets, thereby preventing the development of the natural process of separation. The pressure to change exerted on the adolescents by each other is thus transferred to the MFG through their modeling of responsible behavior.

Another way in which the hospitalized adolescent promotes the group development is through providing an enactment of the specific symptom and the underlying family problem. This can take numerous forms, such as an emotional outburst, refusal to participate, a statement about family structure or organization (e.g., underlying marital conflict, sibling rivalry, or disclosures of other family problems). These episodes can be interpreted as challenges to the status quo and serve to define the group's work, as in the example that follows.

Marilyn G., an "experienced" fourteen-year-old hospitalized for her increasingly dangerous suicide gestures and violent threats to her parents, opened a session of MFG by leaping out of her chair and shouting, "If my father isn't going to come to this group, neither am I." Her mother, a suspected alcoholic who regularly advised other group members on how to handle their children, angrily responded, "Who are you to demand anything from your father? I COME FIRST AND IF THERE IS ANYTHING LEFT, THEN YOU MAY HAVE IT. If you walk out of this group, you will be severely punished by your father when you come home this weekend." Sensing a standoff, several group members attempted to intervene, but the sequence had

already gone too far. Marilyn taunted her mother, "Tough words and besides, he's never home anyhow." Marilyn departed with a theatrical flair.

The group then went to work on the problem of Marilyn's disobedience and, later, when the father was present, on the lack of support and consistency between the parents. As the group is pushed to find solutions for the dilemmas proposed by the adolescents' symptoms and views, a spirit of seriousness, commonality, and competency emerges. Though individual families may be quite stuck in their dysfunctional patterns, and isolated by them as well, the group is capable of summoning vast resources of experience, caring, and instrumental action with which to address the needs of the individual members and families flexibly and effectively. The group's effectiveness in problem solving and its support for its members create an atmosphere in which individual responsibility and vulnerability are temporarily relieved and the potential for new learning and change is maximized. Under these "protective" conditions, individuals are more likely to accept their roles in the family pattern, try out new behaviors, express themselves more openly, confront difficult issues, and reorganize themselves. This is not to suggest that changes in interactions between family members "magically" occur in one, or even seven or eight, sessions just by virtue of being in an MFG. Rather, the process of change seems to take place through a variety of different processes operating at several levels over a period of time that extends beyond the actual MFG contact.

The Effect of Being Valued

One of the important processes operating in group which directly affects the adolescents' functioning in and out of the group is the acceptance of the adolescent as a valued member. According to Leichter and Schulman (1968), this acceptance emanates from two sources: (1) the inclusion of the adolescent and his or her siblings in a group with adults, a very rare occurrence in everyday social interaction, and (2) the MFG leaders' acceptance and communication supporting the adolescent. This quickly gives way, however, to the more powerful valuation which the MFG adults communicate as they respond to the adolescents' contribution to the group. Yet, it is important to avoid confusing equality between adolescents and adults with the valuation and acceptance of adolescents. Maintaining generational boundaries is often a rather difficult task, especially when the adolescent is functioning in a more responsible manner. Nevertheless, support for the family hierarchy is essential to the families' ability to function independently. This support for the adults in the group as the family leadership is communicated structurally. While all group members may have an equal opportunity to express themselves, all final group decisions that involve adults, such as membership, agenda, rules, and the like, are made by adults.

It is usually the case that praise of a particular adolescent in the group comes first from another parent but the effect is not lost on either the adolescent or his or her parent. Adolescents and parents from different families model successful ways of interacting while other family members observe their previously hostile, withdrawn, or depressed relatives acting differently. Once demonstrated, these new ways of interacting become expected or at least possible in the family of origin, thereby redefining the family system. Unsuccessful behavior (hostility, withdrawal, blaming, passivity, denial, etc.) is no longer a symptom but a choice that can be addressed by other members. This behavior is no longer "out of control" but deliberate and confrontable. Similarly, the praise of an adolescent by a parent or of a parent by another adolescent is a powerful intervention in the family's previously held beliefs about their personal anad collective failures. The adolescents' and parents' peers provide a new view of some behavior which an observing parent or child can

then appreciate, as in the following example:

> Commenting on his son's lack of family involvement, Mr. T. suggested that maybe his son just did not have similar interests and was bored when he was with the family. The son, Sal, answered coldly: "No that's not it, I just don't want to be with you. You're always bugging me to do something." Another adolescent, Paul, remarked matter of factly, "Isn't it funny how one person's problem is just what another person is looking for," and with that he told the group how his father had left the family when he was five and how jealous he gets when he sees other fathers and sons doing things together. Sal looked at Paul and said, "I never thought about it that way."

The valued participation of the adolescent in the MFG also serves as a model for a similar involvement and acceptance in one's own family. Through participation in the group, the adolescent can develop a new, more mature role that is supported by other group members who have no vested interest in maintaining the problem behavior. Various members of the group—again usually not members of the same family—come forward to supply "objective parenting"—parental advice which is unbiased in the sense that it is not influenced by the particular family history and patterns. An analogous process occurs in the other direction. Adolescents of other families supply "objective childrening," an unbiased view of what they would feel or be like in a particular family and advice on what needs to be changed to include, protect, and promote the adolescent's growth and how to make the changes. A newcomer to MFG is often surprised at the suggestions made by adolescents to parents regarding discipline. Their advice is almost always in favor of stricter enforcement of house rules and they are extremely accurate in supplying the most effective consequences for undesired behaviors. They are also quick to point out instances in which parents have been manipulated or "conned" by their children and to question parents when they do not follow through on their stated plans.

MFG as a Laboratory for Separation/Differentiation Phenomena

The previous section described the powerful group influence on changing the hospitalized adolescent's role in the family. Where the adolescent had previously been viewed as the problem in the family, he or she can now be seen as contributing positively to the group and the family. The adolescents in MFG can more freely demonstrate their skills in relating to peers and other adults and can express themselves in a forum that recognizes their right to be heard, appreciates their contributions and holds them individually responsible for their actions. Similarly, parents who have previously been blamed for their children's problems and isolated by the stigma of family failure can resume their positions as competent helpers and receive support for the life issues that challenge all human beings and affect each family's ability to function. Under these conditions, the processes of separation and differentiation, the major tasks of the adolescent phase of the family life cycle, can proceed.

Separation is a dual process involving a redirection or refocus of both the adolescent and the family away from each other. From the adolescent viewpoint, effective separation occurs when the parents are convinced of the adolescent's ability to function in the community, such that their primary focus on parenting is no longer necessary. MFG provides a unique opportunity to work on problems in separating partly because it is one of the few places where all group affiliations—family, peer, community—exist simultaneously. This makes it possible for families to observe their members in their peer group, for peers to observe each other in the context of their respective families, and for all members to participate in the community. This unique arrangement introduces new information to each distinct group, which provides an "organic reframing" or changed perception of the family members' views of each other which is mainly supplied by the fact of the larger group composition.

This "organic reframing" can take many different forms. One example, which I have already discussed, is the effect the larger group perspective can have on the adolescents' acceptance and inclusion in their own families. The larger group provides a more objective view of the adolescent's behavior and a wider range of helpful responses, which allows the adolescent to express and modify him or herself. This, in turn, enables the group to accept and value the adolescents' participation and serves as a model of inclusion and interaction for the adolescent and his or her family. Individual families learn the art of negotiation and compromise from viewing the group process and are encouraged by the participation of their previously unyielding children.

Another important process involves the observation of family members in their peer groups. It is easy to appreciate the relief that a parent experiences when observing his or her child responsibly confront the destructive behavior of another adolescent, or similarly, the adolescent's pride when observing a parent competently advising another parent. Separation is enhanced when this occurs because adolescent and parent are reassured that each can get along independently—that the adolescent does not need as much supervision and that the parents do not need protection. This process also aids in the development of social skills that will allow each group member to meet his or her needs through peer interaction rather than solely through the family.

A third viewpoint that promotes adolescent autonomy is direct observation and interaction with the family of the hospitalized adolescent by the adolescent's peers. Previously held attitudes of the peer group about another member's family which were based mostly on the report of that member are challenged by the new "data," as in the following example.

The B. family, an intact upper-middle-class family with three children, placed a high value on achievement. The parents communicated this to their children in several different ways. Carol B., the middle child, hospitalized because of running away and fighting with her younger sister, had complained bitterly to her inpatient adolescent group for several weeks about the way her parents compared her to her siblings and never gave her credit for her efforts. During one MFG session, Mr. B. responded to another parent who was expressing his concern that what had hospitalized one of his children might affect his other children as well, by saying, "Well, I'm sure that won't happen in our family. My son [Carol's older brother] will be going to Harvard in the fall and my daughter [Carol's younger sister] was just elected president of her class and captain of the soccer team and I know they won't let me down. They never have any problems." Hearing this, one of the other hospitalized adolescents spoke to Carol, "You were right about the lack of support but your brother and sister have it worse than you. After all, at least your parents compare you to human beings, they compare your brother and sister to Superman."

In the Charles River arrangement, the new information from MFG often resurfaces in the daily adolescent group and enables the group to effectively hold each member responsible for him- or herself. Prior to MFG, the individual was able to "cop out" by blaming his or her parents or by distorting the actual situation. Separation is enhanced through the adolescent's confrontation with a different perspective supported by peers, which then forces the adolescent to change and adapt. This serves as a preparation for entrance into the "real" world where previously held beliefs and behavior would not be tolerated.

MFG aids separation in another major way. By providing a series of dilemmas which the group is responsible for solving, MFG forces its members to consider a great number of alternative methods and styles of problem solving, thereby increasing the flexibility of the participants. Modeling, trial and error, and group evaluation are central to the acquisition of these new skills. This increased flexibility paves the way for the family to reorganize itself so that it can permit its members, particularly the adolescent, to change the form and intensity of his or her involvement while at the same time continuing to provide for the

individual needs of the other family members. For parents, this may mean a return to a primary emphasis on the marital relationship as opposed to the parenting tasks, to greater attention to other children, the development of a wider social network, or the development of a new interest. For the adolescent, the change may involve more participation in household chores, less attention or a different kind of attention from parents, and more involvement with siblings. Separation of the adolescent is effectively achieved, however, only when there is a complementary reorganization in the family system as a whole.

Short-term, inpatient MFGs demand that the families participate in continual restructuring since the membership is continually changing. During its cycle through the group, each family experiences several different positions. New families are often timid observers who identify themselves as a single, undifferentiated entity, whereas veterans of MFG are identified both as members of a family and as individuals who have established roles in the group (e.g., leader, villain, peacemaker). Seating arrangements often reflect the group structure: members of new families tend to sit together and act as a unit; members of veteran families intersperse themselves according to their group alliances and respond from their various family and group positions. In our groups, these relative positions change swiftly to accommodate the continued entrances and exits of the member families. This provides a certain "practice effect" for families learning to adapt to change. Over the course of their involvement in MFG, each family is put in the position of "welcoming" and "saying goodbye" to many others, as well as joining and leaving themselves. This has obvious benefits for families learning to separate. The accumulated experience of MFG is apparent in the sage advice which the group "grandparents" give in their last MFG sessions. Their respected position in the group reaffirms their experience of themselves as competent people/parents and their reflections on the MFG experience provide an orientation and motivation for new MFG families.

While the emphasis in this section has been on the process of separation, the process of differentiation is taking place simultaneously and providing an incentive to further family evolution. In much the same way as separation is enhanced in MFG, differentiation, the clarifying and accepting of differences in individual family members, is also supported. As this process evolves, the undifferentiated family who previously responded to problems with each other and the outside world in a predictable, one-dimensional manner, begins to appreciate the acceptance of differences as a positive thing that results in more effective functioning for the individual and the family. Each member is seen as a unique contributor to the family "bank" whose reserves can then be used for the good of all members. When fully appreciated inside the family, each person's uniqueness becomes the basis for the development of a more equal and adult relationship between two family members as well as the catalyst to further personal development for all family members.

The Siblings of Hospitalized Adolescents

This section would not be complete without a word about the siblings of the hospitalized adolescents in these groups. The degree and type of participation of siblings, especially when they are close in age, stand out in stark contrast to the participation of their hospitalized brother or sister. In fact, our observation is that these siblings are extremely resistant to attending the group and, frequently, the last family member to participate actively once there.

To understand why they are so resistant and to explain this radically different involvement, several viewpoints should be considered. From the viewpoint of the hospitalized adolescent, a sibling's negative attitude is a continuation of their former relationship in which perceived rejection, quarreling, and overt hostility are the basic rules. The reluctance of parents to demand participation of siblings is seen by the hospitalized adolescent as favoritism, weak-

ness, or a lack of commitment to the therapy. From the viewpoint of the sibling himself, his involvement in MFG is seen as nonessential—it's not his problem, he's been behaving, so why should he attend the group? From the parents' viewpoint, their nonhospitalized child's reluctance is viewed as a stand against the tyrannical control that their hospitalized child has exercised over the entire family. In obvious and subtle ways, parents support the resistance of the siblings because it expresses their own feelings. However, a systemic viewpoint would suggest a different explanation. The degree of participation of a sibling is a barometer of change for the family. In this conception, hospitalized adolescents and their siblings work as a team to provide protection and support to the family as a whole. The change that has occurred is really an "exchange" or trading of family roles between the hospitalized adolescent and a sibling.

The protective envelope provided by the hospital and the MFG removes this responsibility from the hospitalized adolescent. Symptomatic behavior no longer serves the function of family protection and therefore decreases. Instead, the hospitalized adolescent is directed into a new role that involves putting into action the communication skills he or she has learned and helping the family to address directly the difficult problems that brought them to the hospital. Siblings, however, are part of another reality as well. The family changes that are apparent during therapy meetings may not be quite so clear at home. Protection away from the hospital environment may still be needed or at least perceived to be needed. With the change in the hospitalized adolescent's role, the protection that was so badly needed before is no longer present and the other siblings may be pulled, wittingly or unwittingly, into a resistant stance toward therapy. Nonparticipation prevents the family from moving "too fast," keeping certain information out of the group or by keeping the focus of the group away from certain areas. Nonparticipation also communicates to the group the message that the significant family issues have not been fully addressed and they should not be fooled by the family's "health veneer." This is illustrated in the following case example.

> The F. family had experienced continual turmoil since the suicide death of the father eight years earlier. This turmoil finally culminated in the hospitalization of the youngest of two children, a daughter, who was refusing to go to school, abusing drugs and alcohol, and running away. Mother and daughter attended MFG and although they participated little, they both stated that their relationship had improved to the point that they could talk about their sadness together and not react by becoming overly dependent [mother] or independent [daughter]. When questioned about the absence of the older brother, Mrs. F. insisted that he had been inconvenienced too much by the hospitalization already and besides, he was quite stable. At each session, the group persisted in its interest in the brother and Mrs. F. grew angry in her response. Finally, toward the end of the hospitalization, the brother appeared at MFG. The group indicated that they were pleased to have the entire family present and inquired about his opinion of the family's progress. His response was sad but emphatic, "The whole family is not here. My mother and sister are putting on a big act. And I sometimes wonder if my father had the right answer."

In this example, the nonparticipation of a sibling served the dual purpose of temporarily protecting the family against the overwhelming effect of the father's suicide while keeping the group concerned about the brother's absence. When he finally came to the group, he supplied the necessary information that allowed the group to address the continuing problem of unresolved grief and anger in relation to the father.

TECHNICAL ASPECTS OF LEADING SHORT-TERM MULTIPLE FAMILY GROUPS

The discussion of therapeutic technique in leading MFGs in this section is meant as a reference for understanding the preceding sections and as a springboard for practitioners to acquire skills. It is not a prescription to be followed point by point, nor is it an exhaustive description of even one method of leadership. Furthermore, it must be recognized that this discussion is limited in scope: the techniques described were developed with a specific population (hospitalized adolescents and their families) and a specific program (from six to nine ninety-minute sessions) in mind. The reader *cum* therapist is urged to take a curious and playful approach to the material. The benefit that one might derive will then be a combination of what is suggested directly and what is made of it.

Beginning the Group: The Problems of Anxiety

Beginning MFG therapists faced with the prospect of "doing something therapeutic" with twenty to thirty-five people will invariably attempt to allay their own anxiety by moving immediately to structure the group. This is not a bad instinct, especially in short-term groups, as the group membership is usually more anxious about the beginning than the therapist, and structure—telling the group members what to do or what to talk about—will decrease their anxiety. It should be realized from the start that MFG is an awkward experience with, as previously noted, no known correlates in the real world. Thus, the leader must realize that new members will not know what to expect and are likely to be uncomfortable, and even veteran members take a short time to get comfortable at the beginning of each session. Jumping immediately to a new task, however, often has an undesired effect: it communicates the leader's anxiety, thereby confirming the group's anxiety and increasing feelings of awkwardness by not allowing for necessary social and informational exchange. Rather, the beginning of the session is the time to define the group purpose and attend to the job of group building through reflecting on the mutual experiences of group members during previous sessions and sharing information about the family in an introductory manner.

In our groups, each session begins with a short description of the group's purpose by either one of the leaders or veteran group members. The main points communicated here are: (1) that family members have come together to help solve family problems, and (2) the expectation that, despite whatever problems each family is experiencing, there is a great deal of expertise within the group to help each other. This orientation serves as an initial intervention, promoting the two major goals of the group: the family shares responsibility for the functioning of all of its members and the members experience themselves as competent individuals. The leader also reassures the group that no one will be forced to divulge any information or to do anything about which they feel extremely uncomfortable. A colleague of mine refers to this as the "pass rule" and instructs the members to indicate their own discomfort by simply saying "pass" when necessary.[2] This is one way in which anxiety is alleviated. In groups where leadership has developed from the membership, these opening tasks are performed by the members themselves.

A short period of information may follow the opening statements. Members of each family are asked to introduce themselves and may briefly review the period between group sessions or inform the group of important events. New families often participate by giving a short account of their reasons for coming to the group (e.g., why their adolescent has been hospitalized, what problems exist in the family as a whole) and the leader helps the family to define the problem or series of problems on which the group may focus in future sessions. This portion of the group is intended as an "ice breaker," a time for some member of each family to talk to the group in a nonthreatening situation. Equally important is the information the leader gains about the specific membership for a given session and the pressing issues of the group. This then allows the leader to mod-

ify the treatment plan to better "fit" the group. This is not to suggest that one should not plan for the session, only that the plans be adjusted to the group rather than the group to the plans. It is not essential to focus on every family at every session of MFG. Participation often occurs in relation to another family with similar problems and/or dynamic issues.

Problem-Solving—The Main Focus

The second and longest portion of the group (forty-five minutes to an hour) is devoted to problem solving. In this conception, "problem solving" is used interchangeably with "problems in interacting" between family members. Families can volunteer, be coaxed, or at times thrust into the spotlight by the leader or other group members to work on the reasons why they have joined the group. The "pass rule" is still in effect so that no one is forced to comply, but the family issues, combined with the group's support, are often compelling. MFG is not intended as the panacea to all the family's ills. As part of an intensive therapeutic program, it has a more restrained focus. The themes most often examined are those shared by families with hospitalized adolescents—namely, authority versus autonomy, freedom versus responsibility, and closeness versus distance—and the patterns of interaction that manifest these themes. As previously stated, the group attempts to promote the two major goals: helping families share responsibility for family problems, and increasing members' competency in problem solving.

Usually the leader will select a theme or group of problems to address in this portion of the session. If the group is strongly motivated toward a certain topic, however, it is wise to follow their lead. The format varies between open discussion and experiential exercises and between working as a group and working as subgroups, families, or individuals. The possibilities are infinitely varied; the only limitation is the imagination of the group and its leaders. Major interventions such as choosing top-

---

[2] The "pass rule" was developed by Pamela Slater, Ph.D.

ics or exercises, defining interactional problems, and structuring the group are made at this point. The leader attempts to strike a therapeutic balance in directing the group. Too little direction often results in an increasingly anxious and ultimately frustrating experience for group members, while too much direction undermines the leader's assertions of the group purpose in using its own expertise to change. Interventions that help to define the group direction without specifying in detail how the group should work promote movement without stifling creativity. These organizing interventions are made as early as possible to allow the group ample time to function on its own. The leader may then assume a "consultant" role with the group, responding to questions and suggestions by the group when invited.

Special Problems

REFUSAL TO PARTICIPATE: NONATTENDANCE BY FAMILY MEMBERS

This is a major problem which occurs frequently. It can take the form of either active or passive resistance and may be the product of overt or covert collusion between family members. It is obviously a major obstacle in promoting shared responsibility among family members because inactive members are either relieved of consideration ("They're not a part of the problem so why should they come?") or held fully responsible for the family's problems ("How can we do anything with that attitude?").

Intervening in this problem may require a multidirectional strategy involving both family and group dynamics. I generally start by positively reframing the behavior as self-protective ("Any family member who has tried often but failed or been rejected would be crazy to come to this group—they might end up being rejected again"), or protective of the family ("By not participating, that member prevents the family from putting forth their best effort and thereby protects them from the

pain of possible failure"). This often focuses the family on their feelings of helplessness, inadequacy, hurt, and anger, which have developed as a result of their previous attempts to address the problem. The group will respond to this, as well, by sharing similar feelings and suggesting possible solutions. The shared experiences among families promote a sense of being understood ("These people know what I'm talking about; they've been there"), which serves as a basis for trust and hope in resistant families. Once this is established, the need for protection is diminished and permission for participation by all members is given.

Another strategy for intervening in this problem takes a paradoxical approach, encouraging the resistance and exploring the value of it. The leaders structure the group to concentrate or "brainstorm" about the possible advantages of non-participation, thereby highlighting the reasons for the family's ambivalence toward the treatment. To resist this strategy, a family must supply the disadvantages of non-participation (i.e., the advantages of participation), leading them to comply with the initial request of the group—involvement by all members.

Other strategies concentrate on group dynamics. These are particularly useful when a larger portion of the group is not participating. In our groups, it is often the siblings of the hospitalized adolescents or the adolescents themselves. This type of "silent rebellion" may indicate a general group issue such as a lack of trust among members or the existence of a group norm suggesting that discussion of certain issues constitutes disloyalty. Less frequent but still possible is the situation where a subgroup of the adult membership is not participating or is openly resisting. This reflects a problem between that subgroup and the group leaders, usually a perception that the parents are being blamed for their child's problems or that the leader is usurping their authority. When these problems occur, the most effective strategies are those that alter the group structure or return the problems to the group. Examples include temporarily relinquishing the leadership of the group, dividing the group into subgroups with varying agendas (e.g., competition among subgroups often increases participation; cooperation and dependency among subgroups increase subgroup cohesion), and openly discussing the fact that both the group and the leader are "stuck." Regarding this latter idea, the leader must accept his or her ultimate dependency on the group and be able to admit to failure and oversights when they exist. Once his or her humanity is restored, the group will accept the burden of responsibility for its treatment and trust the leader's direction.

ALL TALK—NO ACTION

This is a particularly dangerous problem with a multitude of variations. It is dangerous because the leader and the group can be easily fooled by apparent change in a family or individual member and then devastated by eventual failure. It can take the form of a "flight into health" by entire families such that everyone in the family agrees that all the problems have been solved and the therapy has been incredibly successful in a very short time, when in fact a "deal" has been made between factions to prevent outside intervention (e.g., family agrees to forget about an alcohol problem if parents ease rules and adolescent agrees to go to school). It can, also, take the form of an emotional catharsis where family members make frequent, solemn vows to change their behavior or interactions during a session, but appear unchanged during subsequent sessions or between sessions. In instances where this type of scenario occurs, the group often becomes enmeshed in the family's emotional rollercoaster, experiencing joy and satisfaction initially, but anger and failure at the end.

Intervention strategies to address the problem of "all talk, no action" should, like those strategies suggested for nonattendance, take into account both individual family and group dynamics. This is especially true in relation to open confrontation by the leaders of the "cured" family. The rest of the group, hoping for major changes

in their own situations, will be rather intoxicated and protective of the "cured" family. Confrontation of their superficial change will evoke a strong protective reaction from the rest of the group which may result in various forms of resistance and a perception that it is the leader and not the cured family who is demeaning the group effort. Yet the leader will not want to become part of the problem by pretending to be in agreement either. Several options are available to deal with the situation with finesse. The best possible situation exists when another group member voices some doubt about the family's changes. In this instance, the leader is not required to voice an opinion, only to amplify the doubting member's concerns. Another effective strategy that can be used when no dissenting opinion is present in the group is a prediction by the leader. It is wise to make the prediction in the manner of a friendly warning, based on "other families *I* have seen in similar situations who found out too late that they fooled themselves and everyone else around them." The predictions should not be made definite but more along the lines of "I could be wrong but . . ." so that the group reaction will be muted. Also, the leader does not want to be in the position of saying "I told you so" when the expected turnaround occurs, because this would detract from the major goal of increasing the group's sense of competency.

Another type of intervention involves the use of psychodrama techniques such as role playing and doubling (Moreno, 1946). These techniques require that group members actually enact a specific situation or interaction rather than report on it. Thus, the group can observe directly whether or not the reported changes have occurred. Families who claim to be "cured" are asked to participate as "good examples," "teacher," or "coaches" for the rest of the group.

In role-playing, the family may be asked to enact a specific problem in their family (e.g., arguments at the dinner table) or to coach another family through a problem. Different practitioners use variations of the procedure. In our MFG, a family will enact the situation twice: the first time to represent the current situation, the second time to alter the situation so that the problem is relieved. The group participates as observers and coaches, reflecting on their own situations and suggesting alternatives and solutions. All psychodrama exercises take place in the middle of the room with the rest of the group circled around.

Psychodrama techniques, developed by Moreno (1946), are especially effective in MFG because they require the participants to involve themselves totally—cognitively, emotionally and behaviorally—and they have strong affective impact on observers. For this reason, it is necessary to prepare for the exercises and to review the experience after its completion. When used properly, psychodrama techniques tend to have an energizing and concentrating effect on the group, which is reflected in references to the exercises in later sessions. When used improperly, particularly when the group is not developed enough to tolerate the affect that is released, the techniques can have a detrimental effect. The "pass rule" should always be observed when employing these techniques. Also, these techniques have a wide range of application beyond the usage directly indicated here.

Another psychodrama technique known as "doubling" occurs in a similar arrangement with two members facing each other and two "doubles" sitting slightly to the side and in back of the two working members. The two working members are assigned the task of solving a problem in their relationship. The two "doubles" are responsible for voicing the "unspoken thoughts and feelings" that are present in the interaction. Each person speaks in turn: one working member, then his or her double, the other working member, then his or her double. Either the leaders may serve as doubles or the working members may choose their doubles from the group. The remainder of the group participates or observes and reflects on their own experiences (what the exercise evoked in them about their own situations) but does not make interpretations about the interaction.

DIFFICULTY WITH SEPARATION

Difficulty with separation is reflected in individual families and in the group dynamics in a multitude of ways. It can be seen simply in the behavior of a parent who continually talks for his or her child or in the habitual pattern of rule breaking, which results in an adolescent's being "grounded" for long periods of time. In the group dynamic, difficulty with separation is implied in an overreaction to the entrance or exit of members.

In truth, MFG is a difficult test for these families. The short-term format combined with the intensive emotional involvement of the group and the hospital program create a constant tension between taking care of oneself and becoming overinvolved in the problems of others. Families with poor internal boundaries will evidence overinvolvement, or as a reaction, underinvolvement, in their individual interactions as well as in their interactions with the group.

Separation in families is enhanced when boundaries are clarified and protection of members is not perceived to be necessary. Operationally, this is accomplished when individuals are successful at "doing things"—interacting with others, progressing at work or school, etc.—and family's relinquish the responsibility over time for caretaking. Families with underfunctioning members or in which the responsibility for family problems is not shared may be having difficulty with separation. In MFG, this is reflected in family members' blaming an adolescent for all of the family's problems or in the "guilty parent syndrome," a situation in which a parent accepts total responsibility for the existing problems.

Several types of intervention are possible in this situation. Veteran MFG members are usually effective at confronting these issues without the leader's intervention, but it is often necessary to draw attention to the underlying separation issue. Again, a positive reframing of the behavior can accomplish the dual purpose of confronting the behavior and drawing attention to the underlying issue. Once this occurs, the group can work together with the family to explore their feelings and fears and suggest solutions. Some examples of positive reframing are: "The family is working hard to toughen up its offspring for the outside world"; "The disruptive adolescent has unified the family in preparation for the pain of his departure"; "The parent has accepted responsibility for all the child's problems because he/she expects that the adolescent would be overwhelmed by them."

When this type of intervention is not effective, the family structure may be problematic (e.g., an adolescent involved in a marital triangle, a distant parent, or a disowned sibling). I have on occasion brought a family into the center of the group for a session of structural family therapy (Minuchin, 1974) and used the group as observers or co-therapists. The group is responsible for reflecting back to me and the family various observations about similarities between the current experience and the situation in their own families and for suggesting solutions.

Another intervention that has the advantage of creating group involvement without verbal exchange is family sculpting. This technique, developed by Satir (1972), asks a family member to place his or her entire family in a spatial arrangement (e.g., a photograph or sculpture) that best reflects their association with one another. Group members may be asked to become absent family members for the exercise and also take part in asking the sculpted family questions about the experience, such as, "Are you comfortable? Why not? How could you be more comfortable?" The exercise can then be repeated so that all the family members are more comfortable with the structure.

Psychodrama techniques can also be useful in aiding the separation process. In this context, the use of ritual relating to "rites of passage" and mourning are particularly applicable themes for dramatization. Specific examples include graduation ceremonies for older adolescents moving into adulthood, mourning of a deceased family member or a troubled childhood, fantasized reunion of an adoptive child with the biological parents, and others. These techniques require imagination and are best carried off when there is substantial planning by the group. Roles, props, and scripts help create an atmosphere of plausiblity and seriousness during the experience. The use of humor is effective in promoting discussion afterward, especially by helping members to laugh at themselves.

Another strategy that aids the process of group separation phenomena is a technique called "inside-outside." The group is arranged in two concentric circles. Group members are asked to select the group in which each belongs—the inside group initially composed of those members (i.e., families) who are veterans and soon to be departing, the outside group composed of new members and those who have yet to belong fully. The leaders can either make the choice themselves or have the group choose where the members belong. Generally, the leader sits with the inside group but variations of structure and theme are possible. The division of the group in this manner serves to underscore the connection of the members with the proper reference group and to assign the joining-leaving tasks to the appropriate people. The inside group is presented with two problems. The first problem is to assign a role to the outside group. The second problem is to evaluate the progress of the group and its individual members and make realistic plans for the remainder of their time together. The two groups then exchange seats and repeat the process. Often, the newer group will ask for advice from the veteran members to help define the group goals. Joining and leaving are enhanced by the identification of the proper reference group, the development of realistic group goals, and the clarification of group tasks.

POSTSCRIPT

The preceding pages have concentrated on providing the reader with a rationale, explanation, and "game plan" for the initiation of a short-term inpatient multiple family group. A short-term group with changing membership creates a structure that demands action. As a leader, I am constantly thinking about ways to structure the group such that a slightly different reality or changed perception can be experienced. The hope is that this "ripple in the pond" will serve as a nodal event which, amplified over time, will provide the impetus for a new way of being. This is no small order for a short-term group. When one considers, also, the fact that the group is composed of families in which the problems have become so severe as to warrant hospitalization of children and, moreover, that major decisions about the integrity of the family are forthcoming, a sense of urgency that can deteriorate into panic is all but assured.

This must be considered further. Obviously, very little will be accomplished if the leader and therefore the group are in a panic. However, there are two related factors that relieve the leader's burden of responsibility somewhat and decrease the likelihood of panic. The first is structural; the second rather spiritual.

Regarding the first point, the MFG leader can decrease his or her own anxiety by simply remembering that MFG is part of a total systems approach to family problems. Although it has a unique place in the treatment, it is not expected that all therapeutic requirements will be obtained from MFG. What, then, is the minimal contribution that MFG must provide? In our view, MFG has been successful if families: (1) accept responsibility as a whole for solving their problems, (2) experience themselves as competent problem solvers, and (3) develop new ways of interacting with each other. But there is another level at which the group as a whole impacts the family—the more personal level of acceptance and belonging.

To really understand how the group works and, by induction, how to avoid working oneself into a panic, an MFG leader must understand the relieving and healing power of human contact. Less has been said in this chapter about the human contact that occurs there, although it is hoped that some of this can be appreciated in the case examples and from reading between the lines. It is, I think, impossible to know precisely how this healing contact is working at all the various levels of experience when considering a group of twenty to thirty people. For some, it is simply knowing that another person shares or appreciates your dilemma. For others, it can take the form of a gentle reprimand, an objective analysis, a flattering comment. It is present in the informal gatherings in the parking lot which seem, at times, to last for hours after the group is over. I know that I cannot describe it adequately, although I have seen silent evidence of its work in other places as well. One place where I have seen it is in my own surprise, often shared by other group members, when families who seemingly could not have cared less about the group come to a follow-up session with an air of comfort, belonging, and matter-of-factness unlike anything previously seen in their behavior. They are invariably surprised when I or other group members show surprise. Why are they there? A second shred of evidence comes from my personal experience as an MFG leader. At those times when I am "stuck" and about to hit the panic button, all I have to do is inform the group about my dilemma in leading the group and the group members are there to "take me off the hook." It is at that moment that I feel the strongest connection to the group and experience its healing power.[3]

REFERENCES

Bowen, M. Principle and techniques of multiple family therapy. In M. Bowen (Ed.), *Family therapy in clinical practice*. New York: Jason Aronson, 1978.

Bowen, M. Family therapy and family group therapy. In M. Kaplan, & B. Sadock (Eds.), *Comprehensive group psychotherapy*. Baltimore: Williams & Wilkins, 1971.

[3] The author would like to acknowledge the special contributor of Denise Moretti, R.N., for her efforts in the development of MFG and this chapter.

Framo, J. L. Marriage therapy in a couples group. In D. A. Bloch (Ed.), *Techniques of family psychotherapy: A primer*. New York: Grune & Stratton, 1973.

Laqueur, H. P. Multiple family therapy. In A. Ferber, M. Mendelsohn, & A. Napier (Eds.), *The book of family therapy*. New York: Jason Aronson, 1972.

Leichter, E., & Schulman, G. L. Emerging phenomena in multi-family group treatment. *International Journal of Group Psychotherapy*, 1968, **18**: 58–69.

Minuchin, S. *Families and family therapy*. Cambridge: Harvard University Press, 1974.

Moreno, S. L. (Ed.) *Psychodrama and group psychotherapy*, Monograph no. 18. New York: Beacon House, 1946.

Paul, N. L., Bloom, J. D., & Paul, B. B. Outpatient multiple family group therapy—Why not? In L. R. Wolberg, & M. L. Aronson (Eds.), *Group and family therapy*. New York: Brunner/Mazel, 1981.

Ricci, R. J., Pravder, M. D., Parmelee, D. X., & LaBran, E. *A comprehensive short-term inpatient treatment program for adolescents*. Symposium presented at the meeting of the American Psychological Association, Montreal, 1980.

Satir, V. *Peoplemaking*. Palo Alto, CA: Science & Behavior Books, 1972.

12

Systems Intervention in the Schools

BARBARA J. GREEN, Ph.D.

*U*pon entering junior and senior high school, adolescent and family find themselves facing an influx of new people, new ideas, new situations, and new challenges. The adolescent period is a time which impacts not just on the individual adolescent, but on the entire family. During this period the adolescent's world becomes an interacting combination of two key systems: family and school. These systems generally function as separate entities with their own distinct qualities, characteristics, and agendas. This poses a particular challenge, as both school and family must help promote the adolescent's continuing growth along cognitive, social, emotional, and physical dimensions while simultaneously confronting the push/pull of the adolescent's struggle for independence. The family must develop more elastic boundaries in order to accommodate the increased spectrum of the adolescent's environment, while still providing structure, guidance, and limits. The transitional developmental period of adolescence is eased when there is some collaboration between school and family. All too often, this is not the case. Frequently with adolescents who

are in trouble or distress, one or both systems are operating in a dysfunctional manner. Problems may first be spotted in the school; these might include school refusal, school phobia, poor academic performance, change in academic performance, or blatant disregard for rules. Or the problems may arise within the home; these might include running away, verbal disrespect for parents, or lack of respect for discipline and limits. Regardless of where the difficulty is first spotted, there is a need for school and family to function as two systems but in an integrated manner. When a difficulty occurs in one system, it has an effect on the other. Likewise, intervention in one system will have an effect or impact on the other.

Traditionally, there has not been strategic integration of the two systems, family and school, during the adolescent years. There are significant reasons for this. The adolescent is in a normal developmental phase requiring increasing movement and time away from the family and its influence. The school becomes a very important site for them to extend their independence from home and family, to increase social

193

contact and reliance on peers, to further clarify their individual self-identity and perspective on the world, to develop appropriate ways for relating with adults, and to begin to develop some direction for the future (Gallatin, 1975; Guardo, 1975). For parents to integrate effectively with the school system requires some entry into the adolescent world of junior/senior high school. While this may in itself be difficult for the adolescent, it can become a bewildering task for the parents. Schools at this level often have a closed-system quaity to them. In actuality, they may appear more monolithic than they actually are. Parents may also relive or revive old memories when confronting problems in schools. Nevertheless, there is typically much less parent involvement and contact than with elementary schools. Junior and senior high schools tend to have very structured hierarchies, standard rules of conduct, standard procedures for discipline, and an implicit agenda for focusing primarily on academic issues and needs.

Navigating the transition of adolescent and family through the adolescent years can be greatly facilitated and enhanced by joining the two key systems of family and school. Notably little has been written concerning strategic integration of these two fundamental systems. This chapter will present a discussion of what has been the traditional form of consultation intervention with schools, and gives examples of more optimal ones—of strategic, planned systems intervention in the schools. Examples will be drawn from cases highlighting specific instances of the interplay between the family and school with relevant interventions and maneuvers. Issues pertinent to effective systems consultation with schools and families will be discussed.

TRADITIONAL MENTAL HEALTH CONSULTATION

Consultation as a process came into vogue in the early 1960s as community mental health services shifted toward primary prevention of emotional and mental problems (Caplan, 1970). There had been increasing concern about the efficacy of treating emotional problems through traditional psychotherapy. Attention to the social and emotional milieu, as well as to early identification of problems, was seen as a welcome target for the mental health consultant. The schools became an important focus of the mental health consultation movement.

The goal of the mental health consultation process was to help consultees gain more insight into normal and abnormal emotional development and personality dynamics. The supposition was that through this increased understanding of the affective domain of children, teachers would experience better emotional health and therefore be able to create a healthier climate for children in the schools. Consultation generally focused on difficulty in dealing affectively with children, a lack of objectivity, or personal emotional interference in dealing with children. The consultant would help consultees become more sensitive to, and increase their understanding of, their feelings and the child's feelings. Through this client-centered, psychodynamic focus, the consultant would aim to establish a non-threatening atmosphere, which could then promote free, open emotional expression to enhance the analysis and understanding of their own feelings and those of the children. The basic tool for traditional consultation was the relationship itself as it developed through communication and sharing. As the relationship between consultant and consultee formed and strengthened, the consultant aimed to influence and guide the consultee toward a fuller understanding and coping with his/her own feelings and concerns. Thereafter, the consultant would then help the consultee apply positive psychotherapeutic principles and concepts to the feelings and concerns of the client.

This traditional form of consultation generally involved a mental health consultant and consultee, usually a teacher or schol-involved professional. It did not normally include the child nor the child's parents. A frequently stated weakness to this type of consultation is that it did take an exclusionary approach toward involvement of non-professionals, meaning the clients themselves. In addition, there were questions as to whether increased understanding of feelings and personality dynamics would actually result in behavioral changes and more positive situations. In light of this, traditional mental health consultation was often regarded as an insufficient model for approaching school-related difficulties with adolescents (Reschly, 1976).

BEHAVIORAL CONSULTATION

Behavioral consultation, in contrast to the traditional consultation, is based on the social-learning-theory approach to human behavior, with an individual's behavior being viewed as the direct result of the interaction of the behavior and its controlling environment. Schools are generally very concerned about students' problem behavior and tend to frequently utilize behavioral consultation to deal with it. The goal of behavioral consultation is to reduce or eliminate the client's presenting problematic behavior and to initiate and maintain the consultee behaviors which are necessary to implement the behavior-change program (Russell, 1978).

Behavioral consultation is usually conducted by a trained professional, such as a school psychologist, counselor, or mental health professional, and may involve teachers, parents, or nurse. It generally consists of a five-step process: observation, functional analysis, objective setting, behavioral intervention, withdrawal of the intervention and assessment. Although behavioral consultation relies on social learning theory to develop behavioral change programs, the consultant is not limited to intervention based on this theory. The aim of the behavioral consultant is to find the intervention which changes the behavior and can be empirically validated. The behavioral data is used to determine the effectiveness of the intervention and whether the consultation goal has been reached.

The advantage of behavioral consultation lies with the specificity with which problems are addressed and resolved within the school. (Dinkmeyer & Carlson, 1973; Keat, 1974) The behavioral consultant enters the school system and designs an intervention program linked directly to the presenting problem in coordination with the available skills of the school personnel. The consultant may utilize a variety of behavioral techniques toward this end, including behavior modification programs with positive reinforcement, modeling, contracting, and stimulus control.

The gap in this approach lies with the fact that it ignores the role of the adolescent's problem behavior within the larger context of his/her life. Behavioral consultation generally does not view the symptomatic or problematic behavior in terms of its role in the family and the interaction of the family system and the school system. In this regard, behavioral consultation does not extend the perceptual field and context of the problem to include how it impacts the family as a whole system.

SYSTEMS ORIENTATION TO SCHOOL CONSULTATION

Hobbs (1966), as President of the American Psychological Association, spoke to the 74th annual convention in a keynote address describing his work with emotionally disturbed children. In his address he stressed the imperative need for the various parts of children's lives to begin working together as a collaborative system of inseparable parts. The child or adolescent exists in a family, goes to school in a neighborhood, sees a physician, and may have clergy or social service agency involvement—and therefore shuttles between assorted aspects of one large ecological unit. The adolescent's parents must be collaborators with all the segments of the whole and are largely responsible for making the youngster's environment work harmoniously. The goal should not be to provide perfect, flawless living, but to establish a way in which the systems function effectively as one whole ecological unit.

Hoffman and Long (1969) and Auerswald (1968) further elucidated the dilemma facing social service systems as these systems attempt to provide services and meet their stated delivery goals. They coined the term "ecological system theory" to describe the functional aspects of the transactions between individual, family, and social/educational/community systems. They discussed the need to equilibrate the power between the systems in order to promote positive growth and direction. If one system, or part of a system, becomes too powerful, it can easily induce the demise of the entire unit. With this in mind, it becomes clear how easy it is for the different parts of the ecological system to inadvertently combine in such a way that frustrates the whole system's activities and actually inhibits the growth of the family. In order to avoid the sabotage of efforts by parts of the ecological system, Hoffman and Long, as well as Auerswald, advocated for communication and coordination between the parts of the whole system, including school, therapist, physician, social service agency, grandparents, and the family itself.

Therapists whose consultation adheres to the viewpoint of working with the entire ecological system view the problem from the perspective that he/she may be performing a significant function within the system. In order to deal effectively with the presenting problem, or the metaphor it represents, consultation must involve the parts of the system in an orderly manner.

As early as 1958, Ackerman (1958) proposed that children with school-related difficulties may be performing an important function for the family system. He suggested that an adolescent's school symptom, such as retarded reading development, provides an issue on which the child's parents can collaborate and is supported by the collusion of other members of the family. Grunebaum, et al. (1962) and Staver (1953) also discussed the role of children's learning difficulties as having fundamental links to parental difficulties, be they mother's or father's. Miller and Westman (1964) investigated one specific learning difficulty, retarded reading development

in boys, and concluded that in each of the eighteen families they studied, the families resisted change with regard to the reading difficulty, as this provided a bond around which the parents could organize. The reading disability thus served as a "glue," contributing to the family structure and survival. They found that the symptom acted to keep the parents together; it tended to help put a cap on marital discord and therefore helped maintain a homeostatic quality within the family.

Aponte (1976) described an adolescent's problem as being systems-interrelated in an ecological context, where there is a common issue that serves as a linkage. The challenge, as he stated it, was to develop methods for intervening effectively in all parts of the system, where the systems come together. From this perspective the adolescent having trouble in school is not having trouble alone. There are interactional patterns that promote the problem and often inhibit the solution. The consultant must take the lead in directing the involvement of the key people in an adolescent's life by including the family system and the school system as partners. In both the family system and the school system there are issues of hierarchy, rules, boundaries, power, structure, and communication that must be evaluated by the consultant and included in the treatment planned. The consultant must be active in the assessment of how the boundaries of the systems are relevant to the problem, of whether alignments are cooperative or oppositional, and whether the distribution of power serves to exacerbate the problem and, if so, how to redistribute the power in order to permit successful change.

Smith (1978) and Solomon (1973) discussed the role the adolescent's problem plays in acting as a wedge in the marital relationship and serving to maintain the system between the parents. The adolescent is faced with a growth dilemma as he or she gets caught in serving as a stabilizing force in the family. Thus, he or she is not free to further develop independent functioning but is stuck in a dependent, nongrowth mode. It is important for the family therapist/consultant to examine the developmental stage of the family in order to assess whether the family has been able to successfully complete one stage and resolution of tasks before moving on to the next stage (Solomon, 1973). The life events of the family are pertinent to the consultant's task of determining the developmental stage of the family and what function the adolescent's problem behavior is playing for the family. Again, these problems are often first noticed in school but serve a vital function in maintaining the homeostatic quality of the family. Smith (1978) recommends looking for the ways in which the family system inhibits learning in school for the symptom-bearing adolescent, or looking to see whether the symptom is a signal of marital discord. Families often get stuck or detoured during the transition phase into adolescence if the parental/marital role gets submerged in favor of focusing on the adolescent. Then it becomes increasingly difficult for the adolescent to freely move through the individuation process and prepare for departure from the family. Systems consultation involving the school and the family help free the adolescent from his/her mired position in the family.

Ehrlich (1983) has described five transactional patterns that have been identified as supporting the presence of a school disturbance with the problem child. The school becomes a natural environment for the displaced and transferred symptoms of the family's struggles. Friedman (1969) characterized one of the five patterns that Ehrlich labeled, citing that erratic classroom behavior may be promoted by inconsistent and contradictory procedures by the mother and father. The adolescent has learned that his/her parents will counteract each other in the application of family rules and carries this over to his/her lack of adherence to school rules. One or more of the family dynamics and interaction patterns of enmeshment, overprotectiveness, rigidity, lack of conflict resolution, and the adolescent's intrusion in the marital conflict are frequently found to be supporting a difficulty at school. Viewing family and school difficulties in an interactional pattern assists the family therapist/consultant to simultaneously treat the two systems. In doing so, Ehrlich recommends strengthening the marital dyad, improving communication in order to increase the family's ability to resolve difficulties, and removing the adolescent from the role of protecting the family. The school disorder is an integral component of the family functioning and must be treated as such.

The school psychology literature has begun to present a systems-orientation approach to understanding problems (Green & Fine, 1980; Fine & Holt, 1983). The latter underscore the concepts of the adolescent being a key member of two systems, family and school, and that the systems are interconnected through the adolescent. They warn that family problems are often couched in the school difficulties frequently observed with adolescents. The overlap between the two systems becomes fundamental in helping the adolescent either grow or stagnate. With the exception of true learning disabilities or learning problems, the adolescent's problem does not necessarily reside with the adolescent, the family, or the school. The goal of the systems approach should be to assist the interactive systems of school and family to learn to emotionally disengage so they can collaborate on behalf of the adolescent. Working with the interactive systems of family and school, the family therapist/consultant needs to be alert to the possibility of becoming a part of the triangle of consultant/family/school (Carl & Jurkovic, 1983; Fine & Holt, 1983; Minard, 1976; Tucker & Dyson, 1976). It is very easy for families to relegate their fighting to the school and the therapist and thus escape confronting and resolving their own difficulties. The school, family, and therapist cannot operate as separate worlds without adversely affecting the child, yet it can be difficult for the therapist/consultant to steer the course without becoming caught in an adversarial relationship with one or the other. School personnel tend to take on the characteristics of a family, and can pull an outside consultant into the triangle of the systems. It is important to maintain the lens on the adolescent as a member of the family unit, and for the therapist/consultant to serve as a director and catalyst for change within the two systems. In so doing, the therapist/consultant should help school and family focus on problems and resources. Promoting a collaborative, communicative, supportive relationship between school and parents removes the adolescent as communicator and shifts the blame from the adolescent. It is critically important for the adolescent to observe the systems, learning to function in a cooperative manner that does not cultivate blame and scapegoating.

There are helpful procedures for developing effective systems consultation between school and family. Aponte (1976) and Fine and Holt (1983) recommend direct observation and involvement of the adolescent, the family, and the appropriate school personnel together. The formulation of hypotheses in a circular fashion and the development of rationales for the interventions should flow from this meeting. The therapist/consultant should then implement interventions based on the hypotheses and rationales. These may include structural moves to put the parents and school personnel in charge of the adolescent in a collaborative fashion, meetings to define boundaries and roles, behavioral programs to elucidate the rules and limits and clarify communication, the involvement of heretofore absent family members or school personnel who play a significant and influential role, paradoxical interventions to assist breaking resistances, precision diagnostic testing to provide clear data and information, reframing, homework assignments, giving directives, and so forth.

The therapist/consultant serves as a joiner of the two systems. He/she becomes an insider within the systems and must be alert always to the possibility of becoming triangled in. He/she needs to maintain leverage and a clear perspective on the role of the symptoms and the function of the systems. The therapist/consultant should demystify the adolescent's behavior in relation to events and, through positive reframing, help the family and school focus on present interactions. It is important to be alert to the specific details of each meeting, such as who calls it, who attends, where it is held, who sits where, and who conducts

it. The systems therapist/consultant must be creative in formulating interventions and alert to coalitions, collusions, triangles, boundaries, destructive alliances, false assumptions, and unclear power distribution.

Consultation and intervention with the school and family—utilizing this strategic, systems-oriented format—can be a very potent aid to treatment. Success requires a planned approach to working with the two key systems in an adolescent's life. In this regard, the therapist/consultant becomes a catalyst for directing the interaction patterns of the systems and helping them combine in a more fruitful, productive manner, thereby freeing the adolescent to pursue positive growth.

CASE EXAMPLES AND INTERVENTIONS

The following cases presented to highlight the systems issues as they appeared with these adolescents and their families, and the process of intervening with school and family. They are drawn from an outpatient private practice, in a suburban, middle- to upper-middle-class community, from a junior and senior high school population.

Bobby: The School and Family Scapegoat

Bobby was referred to therapy by his junior high school counselor at his teacher's request three months into his eighth-grade year. He was the oldest of four children and lived with his mother and father. Both of his parents worked at blue-collar jobs. All the siblings had a history of minor learning disabilities. Bobby had a long history of mediocre school performance through elementary school, which worsened when he reached junior high school. He was referred because of his teachers' concern for his extreme lethargy, total lack of attention to and effort in his school work, complete social isolation, and total lack of responsiveness to teachers' verbal initiatives. His teachers and his parents had become very angry and frustrated with his lack of response and improvement, despite efforts to engage and challenge him. At the time of the referral, school and parents had become involved in a blaming, accusatory interaction pattern, with Bobby as the scapegoat. His behavior in school had worsened to the point that he would fall out of his chair if he was not resting his head on the desk. Bobby was caught in the crossfire between parents and school and getting worse rather than better.

After an initial office visit the following hypotheses were developed and an initial intervention strategy was planned. Bobby's behavior was instrumental in halting his adolescent development, as well as the family's movement into the adolescent stage of the family life cycle. The parents were not functioning as a team; mother was taking an overly involved, but ineffectual position, leaving father to burst forth in unpredictable fits of anger and despair. This behavior was being mirrored at school by Bobby's team of teachers and his counselor. Until the systems could align in a collaborative effort and maintain order in a firm and precise manner, I predicted Bobby's behavior would remain the same or worsen.

The first intervention was to request a meeting at the school involving the team administrator, the team teachers, the counselor, the parents, and Bobby. I requested the meeting with the goal of joining the two systems, school and family, in a non-hierarchical manner so the scapegoating could stop. As a result of the meeting the school was placed in charge of school-related matters (e.g., diagnostic testing, teaching, and correcting). The parents were placed in charge of supervising school readiness, motivating Bobby, and providing incentive. Bobby's behavior was reframed, a process that gave his behavior a different meaning and perspective. In so doing, his lack of output at school was termed "laziness," and "teenage behavior with no energy for school work." Reframing his behavior as laziness placed it on a much less toxic level for Bobby and his family and made it more approachable for them. The adults were all told that they were working too hard and that they too were expending too much energy. The intent was to slow down everyone's efforts at rescuing Bobby so that the pattern could adjust in an appropriately collaborative, hierarchical frame. Slowing the pace was important for the school, his parents, and Bobby to give them time to consolidate the new behavioral patterns, and to give the patterns a chance to

become more natural and familiar and thus become an integrated aspect of everyone's normal approach.

Initially Bobby turned around his behavior and started looking more alive in school and becoming more involved in his schoolwork. His parents and teachers were buoyed with the changes and his new vigor and interest. The changes did not last long, however. He had been referred for full educational diagnostic testing, which had been delayed, due to a backlog of referrals. When Bobby encountered work that was too difficult, he shut down once again. The school finally agreed to provide a tutoring program in reading and a buddy in his academic classes to help him. The buddy was a social youngster with whom Bobby was able to start breaking out of his social isolation. He had begun looking more teenage-appropriate after the initial reframing of his behavior and no longer stood out quite so much. Parents and school had implemented weekly progress reports marking his efforts in class and the completion of homework assignments. Teachers agreed not to ride herd over him and to take a joking stand on his expert laziness. The counselor suggested that she support the teachers in their efforts but not see Bobby individually; individual sessions had inadvertently served the purpose of hand-holding for Bobby and wrongly permitted him extra attention for his laziness. But she joined forces with the teachers and served as a progress-reports monitor and conduit of on-going information between the parents and teachers.

The parents had a great deal of work to do at home to set up a synchronized system to support the progress reports and the laziness training. Mother and father started to collaborate as partners when it was suggested to father that his lack of on-going, predictable involvement was cheating his son out of a role model. Mother was so exhausted that it was not difficult for her to permit her husband to join her. They set up household guidelines for study time, TV use, chores, curfew, and allowance. They agreed to foster his steps toward teenage socialization by linking Saturday afternoon movies with acceptable progress reports. In addition, they started to alternate nights serving as supervisors to briefly check over his homework.

It should be noted that several setbacks did occur that served to test the partnership of the two systems, but, through on-going contact with each other, parents and school were able to continue working together. Bobby even started to give his brothers and sister advice not to do what he had done.

Sally: A Case of School Refusal

Sally was referred for therapy at the beginning of seventh grade by her junior high school counselor and the assistant principal due to her refusal to attend school. She was living with her mother and older brother, who was in the high school. Her mother was unemployed and had a history of periodic unemployment. Sally's father and stepmother lived within walking distance. Despite the close geographic location, Sally and her brother had very minimal, sporadic contact with their father. He was a local businessman with a steady history of employment. Sally's parents had divorced when she was four years old. Her father had been remarried for two years, while her mother had never remarried.

Sally had been in and out of therapy for approximately six years with at least five therapists, for a variety of referral reasons including physical aggression toward mother, and school refusal. Her mother reported that Sally had always been an immature child and had a long history of physical illnesses and complaints. Sally's older brother had always been the responsible child and was currently functioning adequately socially and academically, although engaged in intensively rivalrous interactions with Sally.

At the time of the referral both Sally's mother and the school had been unable to get Sally to attend school regularly or willingly. Neither the school nor mother had contacted father about the current difficulty nor difficulties in the past. The school and mother appeared locked in an enmeshed pattern, which mirrored the enmeshed pattern of Sally and her mother. The pattern of enmeshment had been clearly present for a number of years. Sally's history of school refusal and her mother's unemployment always had occurred simultaneously. Sally and her mother still shared a bed; daughter still sat in mother's lap at meetings. Both school and mother seemed frazzled and helpless in dealing with the girl.

After an initial meeting with Sally, her mother, and her brother and a telephone consultation with her school counselor, it was hypothesized that Sally's school refusal protected mother from seeking and maintaining gainful employment and that it served to keep the family locked in the developmental stage of Sally being a young child, which she was at the time of the divorce. It also served to provide mother with sufficient material on which to focus her anger and resentment at her husband for leaving her

and inhibited full emotional resolution concerning the divorce. In addition, it prevented mother and father from joining together in a collaborative parenting relationship. The hierarchy was inappropriate as Sally was clearly in charge, and the boundaries between mother and daughter and school and home were entirely too fuzzy, as mother would always turn to the school assistant principal for help, an action which excluded father. Not surprisingly, the communication between mother and school and mother and daughter was so mystifying that it was difficult to determine what anyone really wanted to happen.

The plan was to involve Sally's father in an appropriate way with both systems in an effort to mediate the enmeshment pattern present in both systems. In so doing, I hoped to establish a hierarchy with the adults in charge of Sally in a collaborative, non-sabotaging manner. An anticipated by-product would be clearer boundaries between school and home so that Sally's educational issues could be addressed by the school and her family issues could be addressed by the parents.

After I met with father and his current wife, father called both the school and his ex-wife to offer his help and involvement to try to get Sally to attend school. Then a meeting involving both parents, Sally, Sally's brother, Sally's counselor, the assistant principal, and Sally's two teachers, was held at school. The meeting produced a plan for the parents to work as partners getting Sally out of bed and into the car if she refused to go to school. School officials agreed to meet them at the driveway and assist the parents if they needed it. The possibility of mother sabotaging the plan was indirectly addressed through a paradoxical intervention. Mother had said she wanted desperately to go back to work, if only Sally would go to school. It was suggested that this would probably not be possible, that she would likely need to prepare herself for many more years of battling with Sally to go to school. The school cooperated in this paradox by telling Sally's mother that the high school was not prepared to help her the way they had and that at that stage, she would be left on her own to deal with Sally. The parents and school personnel agreed on justifiable reasons for Sally to stay home (i.e., temperature) and presented them to Sally. The combination of pulling in Sally's underinvolved father and assigning him the job to help strategically "manage" his daughter by joining with his ex-wife as his partner; the paradox with mother which the school supported; and the school taking an appropriate assistant role to the parents—was sufficient to get Sally attending school regularly within two weeks' time.

Once Sally was attending school, further interventions were planned. The school routinely contacted both mother and father regarding all school matters. Sally started doing homework at her father's house after school. In a follow-up school meeting, parents requested a core diagnostic educational evaluation, which revealed significant learning deficits. This enabled the school to utilize the Federal legislative act (Public Law 94–142) resources and to provide academic support by tutoring one hour a day and sending weekly reports home in duplicate so parents could successfully monitor Sally's progress during the rest of the school year.

Carol: Over- and Underinvolvement

Carol, a high school senior, had just completed a four-week psychiatric hospitalization following an alcoholic binge and was referred for therapy by her in-patient therapist. As a youngster, Carol had been abused by her father and neglected by her mother. Her parents had been divorced for five years, during which time she lived with her alcoholic, now terminally ill mother and had very infrequent contact with her father. Carol cared for her mother for almost two years. A few months prior to Carol's hospitalization her mother died. After her death Carol lived on her own at home, with visits from her father. She had very close connections with several adults at high school, including her guidance counselor, her assistant principal, and her physical education teacher, but none with peers. During Carol's hospitalization she and her father did work on the issues around his abuse of her and her anger toward him, which helped them begin a more meaningful, mutually supportive relationship. School personnel had played a very important role in Carol's life for several years, essentially serving as parental-role figures. During her hospitalization they had visited frequently, brought gifts, and taken her out to dinner. Discharge plans called for Carol to live in a foster home, continue her senior year, and participate in individual therapy for herself and family therapy with her father.

After several visits with father and Carol, it became clear that school personnel and foster parents played a significant role in this family system. For Carol, they were her surrogate parents. She turned to them for help and emotional support. For her father, they held a double-edged position. He found their "quasi-parenting" work helpful as it permitted him to have to do less parenting, but he felt very angry and resentful toward them because he knew they had an extremely negative opinion of him. It became clear that the interactions between the school, the foster parents, Carol, and her father were very potent, and not producing beneficial outcomes for everyone in their present structure.

Based on the hypothesis that Carol had done the caretaking of her mother and had missed being a teenager, even by her own description, it was hypothesized that she needed to enjoy a respite from her role of taking care of herself and to see that she could receive help and caretaking from adults, including father, foster parents, and school. In this respect, it was postulated that father, foster parents, and school personnel needed clarification of their roles as caretakers so they could, in fact, be helpful and supportive to Carol without canceling each other's efforts.

The plan was to place school personnel in charge of educational endeavors while continuing to serve as personal supporters. Through a meeting with Carol's counselor, assistant principal, and teachers a program was established based on an additional half-year of school during the following year to make up for missing credits and to plan Carol's future. During this extra school time she would have an individually taught English class with the assistant principal, check in daily with her guidance counselor, and take an extra typing class to better her vocational skills. The rest of her credits would accrue through a work-study position, giving her additional work experience. It was suggested that she could participate in the upcoming graduation ceremony if she wished, but the school agreed to a private ceremony for her with invited guests following the successful completion of her credits. This ceremony was intended to underscore the school's commitment to Carol and extend to her her right to a personalized ritual marking her graduation from high school. In addition, it was decided that information concerning school should be conveyed to her father as well as to her foster parents.

After the development of this plan, it was presented to Carol's father by the therapist in a session in the office rather than the school. It was decided that an immediate meeting at the school would be moving too quickly and that the adults needed some time in their new roles prior to face-to-face contact. This turned out to be a judicious move as school personnel were inclined to remain overly involved and had not yet forgiven Carol's father. Thus, they were unable to fully support him in his renewed role as father, despite his efforts. A combination of two interventions helped school, foster parents, and Carol's father to solidify their roles with Carol in an appropriate way, and to an appropriate degree. Carol had a crisis, which did not involve school issues or concerns. A paradoxical intervention was designed to hold back the school personnel and to give Carol's father a chance to step in and help her with the crisis. It was suggested that school personnel take full financial, medical, and legal responsibility for Carol, as clearly this crisis indicated that they should do. The proposition alarmed them and delayed an immediate response and reaction. During this brief interlude Carol's father saw that they were not going to react or shut him out. He became very concerned about what was going on and went to the school unannounced. He met with school personnel for over two hours and then went on to the foster parents' for a visit. School personnel witnessed his action of fathering and proceeded to use the time to clear the air and give the proposed amended roles for everyone a chance to work. Through indirect suggestions both school and father maintained the changed roles long enough for everyone, including Carol, to become more familiar with them and to sustain them.

Anne: Rediscovering Lost Relationships

Anne, a ninth-grade student, was referred for therapy by her mother after a meeting with Anne's school counselor. Her mother had become very alarmed at Anne's drastic decline in academic performance, her increased lethargy, and the onset of frequent lying episodes. Anne's parents had been divorced for a year and a half. Prior to the divorce Anne had always been very social, very trustworthy, and a very good student. It was close to the end of the school year, and her teachers and mother were pushing her very hard to pass ninth grade, precisely because she had been a good student.

After an initial meeting with Anne and her mother, it was decided to see Anne alone. She had been very reticent during the first meeting, allowing her mother to do most of the talking. Anne's mother was a very successful, intelligent career woman who seemed

very interested in not having anything else go wrong. She related that the divorce had been amicable but devastating and that she didn't want Anne to experience any more emotional events, such as failing school. Anne's mother said her ex-husband had never been a good student and was not interested in education or in Anne's schooling, therefore leaving all of the responsibility to her. During the individual session Anne related that she missed her father terribly, that she had enjoyed a very close relationship with him and his extended family prior to the divorce, but that she rarely saw him anymore. She felt this was because he was angry with her, despite the fact that she had kept the secret about his girlfriend. As far as she was concerned, her life was at a standstill.

It was hypothesized that Anne's decline at school and lying episodes were designed to halt her momentum. To continue with her previous behavior would have permitted father to be out of her life and to permit her overly competent and rigid mother to fully control the shape of her future. She needed to reunite with her father, and her parents needed to reconcile the divorce and learn how to co-parent. It became clear that Carol might fail the school year and need to repeat it.

A plan was developed, which included reframing both Anne's school failure and her lying as intended to draw attention to her need to reduce the pressure and demands on her to perform at school; involving father with the school program; and restraining mother and the school from pushing Anne. It was decided to hold off on having a normal meeting at the school until after Anne and her parents had done some work on reconciliation and joining. The school was given father's address and phone number and asked by the therapist to continue to send, in duplicate, notices and progress reports to Anne's mother and father. (The progress reports had previously been ineffectual in changing Anne's behavior, despite her mother's efforts and her teacher's pushing and attention.) It was also requested that Anne be allowed to drop out of the divorce group led by the school psychologist.

After a series of sessions involving Anne with her mother, Anne with her father, and her parents alone, a school meeting was held. This meeting included teachers, counselor, the psychologist, Anne, an parents. Anne's continued poor performance in school was reframed to suggest that everyone had been working too hard to help Anne get through ninth grade and move on and that she was trying to slow down the rate of change and responsibility in her life. It was suggested that the adults were working too hard and that Anne would probably not be able to make it in the tenth grade without their continued level of help and involvement. It was a difficult task to convince a school system that it might be in the best interest of the student to repeat a year of high school. Parents and school agreed to use the progress reports in a modified approach, with the intention of monitoring her successfully through the ninth grade but putting the responsibility on Anne. Her parents told her that they were fully prepared that she might need an additional year in the ninth grade and that they could benefit from an additional year of doing what they had learned to do. This effectively placed Anne in charge of engineering the pace. They did agree to withdraw the option of attending summer school should she not pass her courses.

Anne started to improve her academics, but not enough to pass the year. She stopped lying and was clearly more energized, and related that she felt another year of ninth grade would be good for her, in that she felt she had missed too much and wanted a chance to catch it a second time around. Her relationship with her father continued to flourish and her parents continued working on successful co-parenting.

These case examples illustrate various approaches to working with adolescents, their families, and school systems. The therapist in these cases was strategic in planning and implementing interventions, including reframing, use of rituals and meetings, and behavioral strategies such as progress reports, diagnostic testing, and paradoxical interventions. The interventions were designed to join the family and school in a beneficial, productive interaction and utilized to correct mystifying communication, inappropriate hierarchies and boundaries, unbalanced power distribution, and destructive family collusions and coalitions.

ISSUES IN SCHOOL/FAMILY INTERVENTIONS

Strategic consultation has the goal of drawing on community resources to promote positive mental health (Alpert, 1976; Conoley & Conoley, 1981). Success depends on attention to a number of relevant issues. Among these are points of entry, timing of entry, dealing with resistance, being a guest in the system, establishing a follow-through framework, guarding confidentiality and privacy, understanding the distinctive styles of individual schools, appreciating the differences between junior high school and senior high school, knowing when to withdraw from the system, and effectively utilizing resources within the school system, including P.L. 94-142.

The point of entry in the system and the timing of entry into the system are two critical issues. It must be remembered that the therapist/consultant is a guest and outsider to both school and family systems. In this respect, he/she faces a difficult task of joining with the school system while still maintaining a connection with the family system. This requires sustaining relationships with two systems and not becoming a part of a triangle. In making the entry into the system, it is important to determine the formal and informal power strata, as systems consultation does not occur in a power vacuum. One must pay attention to who in the system might be helpful for the tasks of introduction into the system, insuring the implementation and effectiveness of the interventions, and providing ongoing support and contact with the system. These tasks may be accomplished through different people. Administrators are generally integral to the formal power structure, with popular school counselors or teachers representing the informal power structure. It is important not to neglect the formal power structure of the administration, despite the fact that they may not be involved after the initial contact, as administration support can be a very potent tool for achieving modification of rules and specialization of programs. The informal power strata is often the part of the system where the bulk of the contact occurs and therefore the work toward creating change. The timing of the entry into the system depends on the goals and needs for joining the systems and when these might best be undertaken.

As a guest in the two systems, the therapist/consultant must be alert to the possibility of resistance and the inherent difficulty of producing change in systems when resistance is present. This requires an alert perspective and the flexibility to move with or around the resistance as needed. Effectively handling resistance to change can often make the desired change possible. This may be done through reframing, redirecting attention, or open discussion. This can be a critical area of concern toward meeting the goals of the consultation, the needs of the two systems, and their respective capacities for initial change and sustaining change. Deciding when to withdraw from the systems dovetails with the follow-up plan and established framework. This may vary from case to case. Premature withdrawal may mean relapse of a sort, but it can also be illustrative of the degree of permanence of the change. The therapist/consultant may reenter the systems from time to time thereafter, until they demonstrate effective self-monitoring and functioning.

The therapist/consultant has the task of guarding the family's privacy and confidentiality. Aponte (1976) and Friedman (1969) have described a school-based family interview. Many of the interventions described in this chapter are based on the premise of joining family and school. It is important to briefly prepare both the family and the school personnel for the joint interview and for the therapist/consultant to remain in a directing role. This can help circumvent the unnecessary spilling of information, which could lead to resistance and apprehension regarding further contact. Many communities are closely knit environments where school personnel are influential, well-connected, important people. The concern for privacy and confidentiality should not be minimized nor overlooked.

It is also important for the therapist/consultant to understand that schools have distinctive styles and personality characteristics, and that there are significant differences between the junior high and senior high school settings. Being alert to the individual qualities of the school and the personnel involved can be useful in planning goals and interventions. In addition, it is common to find junior high school personnel more flexible and involved than senior high school personnel, for the junior high school serves as a bridge between the close structure of elementary school and the increasing degrees of freedom of senior high school. Despite the increased freedom, the therapist/ consultant has a responsibility for dealing with the senior high school system, if the need exists for joining the two systems in a positive interaction and structure for the adolescent. It often necessitates that the therapist/consultant be more ingenious in utilizing the resources and joining the systems.

Being familiar with resources within the school system, such as resource rooms, tutoring, diagnostic services, alternative programs, etc., is a critical aspect of being an effective systems therapist/consultant with the schools. In addition, one should be familiar with P.L. 94–142, a federal mandate signed into legislation by President Ford in 1975. It guarantees a youngster's right to full and free educational services in the least restrictive setting possible. It is often viewed as the handicapped children's educational act, but it should be recognized that "handicap" does not only apply to physical problems. P.L. 94–142, which was modelled from Chapter 766 legislation in Massachusetts, provides for special learning services for all students who need them, be they educationally or physically related. This law has changed, in some fundamental ways, the manner in which schools deliver special services. Parents' and children's educational rights are protected by this law; parents are required to sign educational plans, have the right to due process, and are assured of regular follow-up evaluation. This mandated structure of parent involvement has opened up a whole new arena for school and family. It is imperative that the systems therapist/consultant be familiar with the particulars of this legislation. In addition, there are a multitude of other resources that can be effectively and strategically utilized in the school setting, and these should not be overlooked.

CONCLUSION

While there has been increasing attention recently to the task of working with the complete ecological system for the adolescent, involving family and school, it has generally not received as much formal recognition as other aspects of the therapeutic process. The systems therapist/consultant faces the task of joining the two key systems of school and family together in a sensible, positive manner. This may require changes in the structure, the hierarchy, the power disbursement, the boundaries, the coalitions and collusions, the communication style, etc. There are a variety of interventions that can be useful in achieving these changes, such as reframing, behavioral strategies, meetings, paradoxical interventions, homework and role assignments, structural moves, and utilizing available resources. The therapist/consultant needs to be alert to the issues regarding point of entry into the system, establishing follow-through procedures, guarding confidentiality and privacy, knowing when to withdraw, being familiar with the idiosyncratic nature of schools, and being knowledgeable about P.L. 94–142 and school resources. Strategic systems consultation with the school and family can be a very potent source of change.

REFERENCES

Ackerman, N. W. *The psychodynamics of family life*. New York: Basic Books, 1958.

Alpert, J. C. Conceptual bases of mental health consultation in the schools. *Professional Psychology*, 1976, **7**, 619–626.

Aponte, H. J. The family-school interview: An ecostructural approach. *Family Process*, 1976, **15**, 303–312.

Auerswald, E. H. Interdisciplinary versus ecological approach. *Family Process*, 1968, **7**, 202–215.

Bowman, P., & Goldberg, M. Reframing: A tool for the school psychologist. *Psychology in the Schools*, 1983, **20**, 210–214.

Caplan, G. *The theory and practice of mental health consultation*. New York: Basic Books, 1970.

Carl, D., & Jurkovic, G. J. Agency triangles: Problems in agency-family relationships. *Family Process*, 1983, **22**, 441–452.

Conoley, C. W., & Conoley, J. C. Strategic consultation: Community care givers in the schools. In J. C. Conoley (Ed.), *Consultation in Schools*. New York: Academic Press, 1981.

Dinkmeyer, D., & Carlson, J. *Consulting: Facilitating human potential and change processes*. Columbus, OH: Charles E. Merrill, 1973.

Ehrlich, M. F. Psychofamilial correlates of school disorders. *The Journal of School Psychology*, 1983, 191–199.

Fine, M. J., & Holt, P. Intervening with school problems: A family systems perspective. *Psychology in the Schools*, 1983, **20**, 59–66.

Friedman, R. A. A structured family interview in the assessment of school learning disorders. *Psychology in the Schools*, 1969, **6**, 162–171.

Gallatin, J. E. Adolescents and individuality: A conceptual approach to adolescent psychology. New York: Harper, 1975.

Guardo, C. J. The adolescent as individual: Issues and insights. New York: Harper, 1975.

Green, K., & Fine, M. J. Family therapy: A case for training for school psychologists. *Psychology in the Schools*, 1980, **17**, 241–248.

Grunebaum, M. G., Hurwitz, I., Prentice, N. M., & Sperry, B. M. Fathers of sons with primary neurotic learning inhibitions. *American Journal of Orthopsychiatry*, 1962, **32**, 462–472.

Hobbs, N. Helping disturbed children; Psychological and ecological strategies. *American Psychologist*, 1966, **21**, 1105–1115.

Hoffmann, L., & Long, L. A systems dilemma. *Family Process*, 1969, **8**, 211–234.

Keat, D. B. *Fundamentals of child counseling*. Boston: Houghton Mifflin, 1974.

Miller, D. R., & Westman, J. C. Reading disability as a condition of family stability. *Family Process*, 1964, **3**, 66–76.

Minard, S. Family systems model in organizational consultation: Vignettes of consultation to a day-care center. *Family Process*, 1976, **15**, 313–320.

Reschly, D. J. School psychology consultation: Frenzied, faddish or fundamental. *Journal of School Psychology*, 1976, **14**, 105–113.

Russell, M. L. Behavioral consultation: Theory and process. *Personnel and Guidance Journal*, 1978, **56**, 346–350.

Smith, A. H. Encountering the family system

in school-related behavior problems. *Psychology in the Schools*, 1978, **15**, 379–386.

Solomon, M. A. A developmental, conceptual premise for family therapy. *Family Process*, 1973, **12**, 179–188.

Staver, N. The child's learning difficulty as related to the emotional problem of the mother. *American Journal of Orthopsychiatry*, 1953, **23**, 131–140.

Tucker, B. Z., & Dyson, E. The family and the school: Utilizing human resources to promote learning. *Family Process*, 1976, **15**, 125–141.

PART III

Issues in Treatment

INTRODUCTION

This section is designed for the practitioner looking for concrete treatment suggestions following a grounding in systems theory.

Why include a section on special topics in the treatment of adolescents in a book devoted to a systemic approach? Why even assume that adolescents have their own "special issues?" From a systemic viewpoint, there are three reasons. First, the adolescent him- or herself is a system: a biological and intrapersonal system, which, in the throes of time, is undergoing rapid, critical change. Such times of change, though ripe for growth, are also ripe for problems in making the transition. Second, the adolescent is a member of a family system that is going through the adolescent stage of the family life cycle, the stage of individuation and separation. In a family that becomes "stuck" at this transitional point and unable to successfully negotiate this new phase of life, the adolescent may become symptomatic. The symptoms of the adolescent, explored in this section, often reflect the difficulty of his/her family in transition. Third, the adolescent is part of a still larger community system, and, legally, certain problems are defined as offenses only in childhood and adolescence (e.g., running away) or as crimes only when committed against a child or adolescent (e.g., adult sexual involvement with a child).

In Chapter 13, "The Prevention of Rehospitalization of Adolescents and Young Adults," which originally appeared in *Family Process*, Madanes presents a family-oriented therapy approach for the prevention of rehospitalization of adolescents and young adults with diverse diagnoses. The dilemma of the family is presented in terms of the incongruities evident in the organizational hierarchy of these families. The main premise is that if the hierarchy is corrected so that the parents are jointly in charge of the youth and the extended kin cooperate, rehospitalization can be prevented. A therapeutic strategy is presented with the emphasis on overcoming the family's attempt to avoid a hierarchy in which the parents are in charge of the family. Todd, in Chapter 14, explores the problems of anorexia nervosa and bulimia, both of which have reached epidemic proportions in the female adolescent population. Todd discusses the family dynamics surrounding eating disorders and possible interventions, with the family as well as with the medical and nursing communities involved with the eating-disordered adolescent. Substance abuse, another widespread problem among adolescents and their families, is explored by Kaufman in Chapter 15. Kaufman fuses structural-strategic and psychodynamic methods to intervene with substance-abusing families. He recommends that the therapist be knowledgeable about substance use and abuse and a dynamic, active participant in the therapy. He explores how each family member contributes to either the maintenance of, or change in, the substance abuse pattern, and also explores the pseudo-individuation of the addicted teenager as one of the functions of substance abuse.

Crumbley, in Chapter 16, examines the physical and sexual abuse of adolescents in an overall generational context where boundary problems are evident in families with young children, as well as in families having adult children with aging parents. How the clinician "does" family therapy in a charged situation where safety is at risk and the problematic dynamic is longstanding creates many challenges for the family therapist.

Keshet and Mirkin, in Chapter 17, describe a model for defining and intervening in divorced and remarried families with troubled adolescents and highlight the teenager's special role in these family structures. They describe the stages of forming a step-family, which include acceptance, authority, and affection; and the dynamics of reunion, diversion, and replacement, which may occur in families where the divorce process goes awry. In Chapter 18, Morris takes a multidimensional view of the psychotic adolescent. He notes that integrating biological, individual, and family-treatment approaches within the framework of a family systems conceptualization is helpful in treating adolescent psychosis. He suggests that there be a sequential approach to therapy, using elements of strategic, structural, and contextual therapies. He rec-

ommends the merger of treatments previously considered conflicting: medication suggesting a biological difficulty, and family
therapy reflecting a systemic difficulty. Landau-Stanton and Stanton, in Chapter 19, explore the family with a suicidal adolescent.
On the basis of their track record—no suicidal adolescent with
whom they or their colleagues have worked has died—the authors
propose a family oriented model of intervention. They suggest
that unresolved loss must be dealt with by the family, and that
parents must take on the executive role of vigilantly monitoring
a suicidal adolescent until the young person once again assumes
a safer and more effective way of living.

In Chapter 20, Mitchell and Rizzo deal with the complexity of
defining ''adolescent'' as they explore the problems and promise
of teenagers with special needs. They suggest that while a special-
needs adolescent may be chronologically an adolescent, one must
assess whether he/she is socially, physically, and/or cognitively
functioning at similar levels. The authors suggest that families
with a special-needs member have additional responsibilities and
more psychic stress than other families. Therapists must be sensitive to the family and understand that the time of the onset of
the disabling condition is a critical factor.

Lappin and Covelman, in Chapter 21, discuss runaways, a problem area exclusive to childhood and adolescence, since only in
this age group is running away a status offense. They review the
limited previous literature on this topic and propose an approach
from a structural/developmental perspective—based on the issues
of generational hierarchy, conflict avoidance, and the triangulation of the runaway by the parental dyad.

In the final chapter Landau-Stanton looks beyond the family
system to the changing contexts of families making the difficult
transition between cultures. She suggests that knowledge of culture, tradition, and ethnicity is critical in understanding these
families, and that the key to treatment is recognition that their
problems arise because different family subsystems adapt at different rates.

In conclusion, this section is devoted to issues that specifically
concern the treatment of adolescents in a systems context.

13

The Prevention of Rehospitalization of Adolescents and Young Adults*

CLOÉ MADANES, Lic.

A current problem in psychiatry is planning for the discharge and post-hospitalization adjustment of patients leaving a mental hospital. With the trend toward releasing patients back into the community as soon as possible, there is a need to ensure that the progress achieved in the hospital will be continued and rehospitalization prevented. This chapter presents a method of therapy designed to prevent the rehospitalization of adolescents and young adults with severe problem behaviors involving aggressive or self-destructive acts, abuse of drugs or alcohol, bizarre communication, extreme apathy, or depression. These behaviors often become so extreme or upsetting to the family that the youth is admitted to a psychiatric hospital. When the young person and the family eventually calm down, the youth is discharged. After some time he begins to cause trouble again and, if rehospitalized, the chances are that he has begun a career as a mental patient.

The difficulties of the young person, the trouble he causes, and his failure in life often become the main theme in the parents' lives. A parent may have problems with his own parents or trouble at work, he may be depressed or ill, or his spouse may be threatening separation, but all these problems become less important in contrast to the tragedy of the youth's life. The focus on the youth, and the need to be available to him, provide the parents with a primary goal. They must overcome their own deficiencies and hold themselves together in order to help him. In this sense, the young person's disruptive behavior has a positive influence on the parents, even though it tyrannizes, threatens, and incapacitates them. The youth may passively threaten that, if stressed, he will go crazy or take drugs or harm himself in

*Originally published in *Family Process* (**19**, June 1980) and reprinted with permission. Many of the ideas in this chapter were worked out in collaboration with Jay Haley, but the sole responsibility for the presentation lies with the author.

some way, or he may actively do physical violence against the parents. The parents become unable to attempt to change the young person's behavior because they are afraid of causing him harm or afraid that he will harm them.

Two incongruous hierarchies are simultaneously being defined in the family: one, in which the youth is incompetent, defective, and dependent on the parents for protection, food, shelter, and money, with the parents in a superior position providing and taking care of him; the other, in which the parents are dominated by the youth because of his helplessness or threats or dangerous behavior. If the parents are to be competent parents, they must demand from the youth the behavior that is appropriate for his age, but doing so may trigger extreme and dangerous behavior from him. If the youth behaves normally, he loses the power that the threats of extreme behavior gave him over his parents.

It is possible to hypothesize that this power of the youth over the parents has the function of protecting them or of holding them together.[1] In many families a child dominates benevolently by having a symptom and being helpless. But when an adolescent, for example, sprinkles gasoline around the foundation of the house and then plays with matches, when he beats up on the parents and extorts money from them with threats, there is little question of who has the power in the family, and it is difficult to see this power as benevolent. It is possible, instead, to assume that the only function of the disturbing behavior of the youth is the exploitative power derived from it. It may be that originally the disruptive behavior had a protective function, but when the incongruous hierarchy stabilizes and the system of interaction becomes chronic, the disturbed behavior persists as a function of the system and independently of what set it off. It may be that at a certain point in time,

there is no longer a hierarchical incongruity but simply a hierarchical reversal with the youth in a superior position of power over the parents and with few or no situations in which the reverse is true. (This is often the case in violence, delinquency, and addiction, but it is also sometimes the case in psychoses.)

As the youth gains power over the parents, they try to restore their position in the hierarchy by resorting to agents of social control (the police or the mental hospital). The youth is institutionalized and consequently behaves more helplessly and with less control. This gives him more power over the parents because they must focus more and more on him in their attempts to help him. Yet this helpfulness of the parents defines the youth as even more helpless (or out of control) and contributes to the power that can be derived from such helplessness. In this way, a system of interaction can be established that perpetuates itself over time, particularly if there is a certain stigma attached to the situation of the youth and if society (through social agencies) contributes to maintaining it. Whether the youth's behavior originally had a protective function, whether it was meant to prevent a separation between the parents, or whether it was only related to a bid for power is quite irrelevant. (In any case, power always has its benevolent aspects. The most tyrannical dictator is also a benevolent benefactor.) The issue is that to solve the problem the hierarchy must be restored to one in which the youth does not dominate the parents through helplessness and/or abuse.

In these cases, there often is a similarity between the youth's behavior and that of one of the parents. The youth might be apathetic and do nothing, and a parent might be similarly depressed; the young person might be addicted to drugs and a parent to alcohol; the youth might hear voices, and a parent might talk to himself; the young person might be violent, and the father might physically abuse the mother. This similarity indicates that the disturbed behavior of the youth is metaphorical of the disturbing behavior of a parent. Along with other problems, the therapist can

---

[1]For a formulation that proposes that the youth's disruptive behavior has the function of preventing a separation between the parents, as well as for a detailed exposition of the stages of this therapy, see Haley (1980).

work on the symbolic communication of the family, changing metaphors, and analogies (Madanes, 1980). Here, with severely disturbed young people, a different, simple, straightforward approach is recommended. The therapist focuses on resolving the incongruity in the family hierarchy so that the parents will consistently be in a superior position to the youth. As the parents become more powerful, they are able to deal with their own problems more successfully, and the youth no longer needs to express their difficulties metaphorically. In this approach, the therapist focuses only on the literal meaning of the messages exchanged. When pathology is severe, it is easy for a therapist to get lost in a morass of metaphorical meanings. A simple way to avoid getting caught in conflicting levels of messages by family members is to become very literal and concrete and to deal only with the most basic, mundane issues. In this approach, the therapist takes the position that a youth should go to work or to school, do his chores, avoid drugs and violence, and have one or two friends. The content of the therapy is to organize the family so that this takes place, and metaphors and analogies are largely ignored, in the sense that, although the therapist might understand the analogy in the family's interaction, the therapeutic strategy will not be to attempt to change the analogy but only to deal with literal issues.

The double-bind theory (1) describes conflicting levels of messages in families of schizophrenics. The communication therapists, influenced by this theory, attempted for years to get family members to communicate clearly and congruently. There was no realization that incongruent messages are consistent with incongruous positions in a hierarchy—that for parents to talk consistently as parents they have to be consistently in that position. The double-bind theory refers to a framework of communication. The concept of hierarchical incongruity refers to a wider framework of organizations in which communication takes place. If a parent is simultaneously defined as a person in charge of a family *and* as tyrannized and exploited by his own child, the family members involved in this situation will communicate in incongruent ways that reflect their incongruent positions in the hierarchy.

The approach to therapy presented here is based on the idea that the therapist must respond to only one of these definitions, the one in which the parents are in charge of the youth, and must discourage and block the other incongruous definition of the family hierarchy, that is, the one in which the youth is in charge. The therapist must elicit from the parents messages that define them as competent, responsible adults and discourage communications that imply they are weak, incompetent, or helpless. With respect to the young person, the messages that he is in charge of the parents must be discouraged, and he must be encouraged in defining his position as a member of a younger, more inexperienced generation. In this approach, only certain messages from certain family members are encouraged and allowed, in contrast to a communication approach that encourages the clear expression of all kinds of messages. The focus is not on the congruence of messages per se but on the congruence of relationships. When the reversal in the communicational and hierarchical organization of the family is resolved, the young person will behave normally.

The view that there are hierarchical reversals[2] in these families might not be the only relevant factor to etiology and to the reconstruction of the past. It is relevant,

[2]For research data that support the hypothesis of hierarchical reversals in these families, see Madanes et al. (1980). There are also therapy outcome data that support the approach. In training programs with live supervision by me and by Jay Haley at the Department of Psychiatry, University of Maryland, and at the Family Therapy Institute of Washington, D.C., out of twenty-eight cases (age range: late teens to twenties) that had been hospitalized prior to the therapy, and were followed, six were rehospitalized after therapy—a failure rate of twenty-one per cent. The time between when therapy terminated and an inquiry was conducted ranged from six months to 2.5 years, the mean being 1.5 years. The cases included several different diagnoses, but in all cases there had been at least one hospitalization before the therapy started.

however, to the most powerful factors operating in the present. It is a perspective that developed from the need to select, from the multiplicity of data presented by disturbed youths and their families, the events that form a pattern that is intelligible and useful to the therapist for the purpose of changing the young person and his situation. More complex theories of etiology can make it more difficult to derive operations that will produce change.

It is possible to view the youth's behavior as protective of the parents in that it holds them together, preventing a separation and divorce (see Haley, 1980). It is also possible to view the function of the youth's disruption as preventing an agreement and an alliance between the parents. In my opinion, when the case involves a first break, a first criminal offense, or a few drug episodes, the therapist should give careful consideration to the possibility that these behaviors may have a protective function in the family. The therapist should think about whether the youth is expressing metaphorically a parent's problem and wonder if his acts are self-sacrificing. In the more chronic cases, where there have been rehospitalizations or several encounters with law-enforcing agencies, it is best for the therapist to think mainly in terms of the hierarchical reversal—the power that the youth has over the parents—and to focus on understanding the problem from the point of view of how the youth's disturbing acts contribute to maintaining that power. The emphasis of this presentation is on the hierarchical incongruities in the family organization and on the communicational maneuvers that parents use to disqualify themselves from a position of authority in the family hierarchy. This emphasis developed from my research on the communication of parents of schizophrenics, heroin addicts, and delinquents (Madanes et al., 1980; Sojit, 1969 & 1971).

THE THERAPY

In order for the therapist to achieve the goal of the therapy, he must restore the family to a single hierarchical organization with the parents in a superior position to the child. The therapist needs first to define a situation in which the parents are in charge of the youth, in which they tell him what to do as if he were younger than his actual age, and in which the youth obeys them. For this purpose, the therapist must encourage all communication from the parents that defines them in a superior position in the hierarchy and discourage all messages by which they are disqualified from this position. The therapist needs also to block all attempts from the youth to put himself in a superior position.

The First Stage

As a first step in correcting the hierarchy, the therapist should begin treatment by meeting with the parents and the young person to plan his discharge from the mental hospital. The parents need to make decisions in this interview about where and how the youth will live once he is discharged. In these cases, it is best, in the first interview, not to start by asking what the problem is. It is important to orient the youth as soon as possible toward a normal life out of the hospital. Inquiring about the problem will focus the family on past difficulties and failures in a way that may not be consonant with this goal. The therapist should begin the interview by stating that his goal is to avoid further hospitalizations and have the young person lead a normal life involved in work or in school.

Before the first interview with the family, the therapist should have arranged with his colleagues that he be in charge of the case so that he can say that to the family. In difficult cases, where there are serious problems and disagreements among family members, there are bound to be disagreements among the staff that will interfere with the therapy unless it is clear that there is only one therapist in charge.

If the therapy is started before the youth is released from the hospital, the therapist can make the discharge contingent upon the plans that the parents make for the young person. This gives power to the therapist in relation to the family since he will not discharge the young person if the family does not collaborate and agree on a feasible plan. This is also a strategy that gives power to the parents since it makes the youth's release from the hospital dependent on them.

During the first interview the therapist should ask the parents what their expectations are for the youth (who is also present) when he comes out of the hospital, in terms of where he will be living and what he will be doing. It is best to encourage the youth to come home to his parents rather than go to a halfway house or to some other living arrangement. If the young person is not living at home, it is difficult to reorganize the hierarchy so that he will ultimately be able to leave the parents successfully. The family should be told that at this time, when he is just coming home from the hospital, the youth needs the parents' guidance and that when he has established himself in a normal way of life, then he will be able to leave. The parents must be asked to express what they expect the young person to be doing. Do the parents expect him to go to school or to look for a job? How is he expected to behave at home? At what time must he get up in the morning? At what time should he be home at night?

As the parents begin to discuss their expectations, the therapist should request that they talk to each other and agree so that it is clear to all present, particularly to the youth, that the parents are in agreement. Reaching agreement is not an easy task and often requires a great deal of effort and ingenuity on the part of the therapist.

As the parents begin to agree on expectations, the therapist should begin to require that these expectations be phrased as rules for the young person. These rules should be as specific and practical as possible. For example, a rule could be that the youth must get up at seven every morning and look at the employment columns in the newspaper or that he must be out of the house for x hours a day looking for a job. The therapist should not let the parents proceed to the next rule until there is agreement between them. This is impor-

tant because the therapist wants to have both parents in a superior position in the hierarchy, which occurs if they both set the rules.

After the parents have agreed on a few rules, the therapist should ask them to agree on what the consequences will be if these rules are not followed. The parents often need some examples from the therapist of what is meant by consequences. For example, for not coming home on time the consequence could be no use of the car; for not getting up to look for a job, no allowance, etc. Depending upon the severity of the problem, the consequences should vary from mild to extreme. Coming home late may entail the loss of telephone privileges, but the use of drugs may necessitate a more severe consequence such as confiscation of funds or house arrest. While the parents discuss rules and consequences, the young person should only listen. Interventions from him should be discouraged. He will have a chance to speak later when the parents' decisions are communicated to him. Once the parents have made some rules, they must explain them to the youth, even though he has been present during the discussion, and they must obtain some commitment from him that he will obey the rules. It can be expected that the youth will object to the parents' rules and to the consequences and will demand more independence. The therapist's position should be that the young person's irresponsible behavior has landed him in the mental hospital and that the parents have to give the guidance that he needs until he shows that he behaves like a responsible person.

In cases in which the young person is apathetic, the parents should be encouraged to mobilize the youth by setting rules ensuring that he will be minimally active and prescribing consequences if this activity does not take place. A useful technique is to set a deadline, a date after which if the young person does not have a job or is not looking for one or going to school, they will, for instance, put him out of the house for a certain number of hours each day. It is best for the therapist to take the position that it is not possible to wait until the youth is motivated to do something and that only after he has begun to be active will he abandon his apathy.

As the parents deal with the issues around daily living with their child, the behaviors that initially precipitated the hospitalization are sometimes brought up by the parents. These behaviors are usually related to violence, bizarre behavior, drugs, or alcohol. If the family does not bring up these issues, the therapist should do so in order to anticipate and plan for future difficulties. That is, the steps are for the therapist first to plan the youth's life with the parents in terms of the normal activities that will be expected of him. Then, after there is such a plan, to bring up the issue of the behaviors that precipitated the hospitalization, not with the purpose of focusing on the past or of attributing blame, but in order to prevent a repetition of these behaviors. The therapist should reformulate the behaviors that precipitated the hospitalization in such a way that it is possible for the parents to make rules to control and discourage their occurrence. The therapist's reformulations should put these acts in the context of misbehavior and not of mental illness so that they are in the realm of expertise of parents and not of professionals. The parents must agree on a plan to handle the next episode of extreme behavior if it occurs. It is best to encourage the parents to use their own resources to control the youth even if this involves restraining him physically and requesting the help of relatives or neighbors. The therapist should make clear to the parents that hospitalization should not be part of their plan. Severe consequences should be planned ahead of time to discourage the youth from behaving in extreme ways.

Ideally, the young person should be discharged from the mental hospital only when the therapist is satisfied that he is going home to a situation in which there are clear rules about how he is to behave and consequences if he does not abide by these rules, and in which there is a plan for what he is to do that involves school or work. It is important to make these plans with the family before the youth is discharged from the hospital, because usually both the parents and the young person want the discharge and are therefore more cooperative with the therapist.

The Second Stage

Most of the work in the therapy of these families consists of arranging a hierarchy in which the parents are in a superior position to their offspring. Each week the therapist must review with the parents whether the rules they have set for the youth have been followed. If they have not been followed, the therapist needs to know whether the consequences were applied. As the parents begin to demand more adequate behavior from the young person, new rules and consequences must be set up. Sometimes it is necessary to establish a hierarchy of consequences, so that if the youth has broken a rule and also refused to comply with the consequences for breaking it, there is then another consequence of a more serious nature. The young person can be expected to put the parents to the test, and the therapist must struggle to maintain them in a superior position.

As the therapist struggles for a definition of the hierarchy in which the parents together are in charge of the young person, he strives for communication sequences between family members that will define the situation in this way. That is, the therapist wants mother and father to talk about the young person and to agree on what the latter should do, and he wants the youth to listen to the parents and obey their rules. Instead, the parents typically use a series of communication maneuvers to avoid a definition of the hierarchy as one in which they have power over their offspring. They do so because they are losing or have already lost their superior position in the hierarchy, because the youth is more powerful than they, because society has intervened to take power away from them, because they are afraid to do the wrong thing and harm the youth, because they are afraid they are to blame and wish to do no more harm, or because they are afraid to lose their child. A parent avoids a definition of the hierarchy as one in which he has power over the youth by communicating (a) that he is not qualified to participate in the therapy because he cannot occupy an executive position in the hierarchy; (b) that the other parent is not qualified; or (c) that the therapist is not qualified to be in charge of the therapy. It is these maneuvers that the therapist must counteract so that the proper hierarchy can be defined.

Parent Disqualifies Self

At the beginning of the therapy, parents will often disqualify themselves from a position of authority by invoking the authority of others, by giving authority to the problem youth, or by defining themselves as inadequate.

GIVING AUTHORITY TO EXPERTS

Parents might invoke the authority of experts by saying, for example, that the therapist or the chief of the ward should make the decisions concerning the disturbed young person. The therapist must decline giving power to the professional experts, including himself, and give it to the parents. To transfer power to the parents, the therapist must relabel the young person's problem so that it is in the area of the expertise of the parents rather than of medical or psychiatric experts. As the therapist describes the youth as misbehaving, confused, childish, rebellious, in need of guidance, etc. (instead of using words like mental illness, schizophrenia, emotional problems, psychological conflicts, etc.), the parents, if reluctant to take charge, will protest that this is not the way the youth has been described by other experts who have talked about years of intensive therapy, the need to avoid any stressful situation, etc. The therapist must use all his authority and the backing of the institution to counteract such statements, whether or not they were truly made by other experts, or it will be impossible to achieve the goals of the therapy.

A tactic that the therapist can use is to project the parents into the future and predict that if there is no change, the young person will come out of the hospital (or jail) and eventually cause trouble again. He will be hospitalized once more, but after a period of time he will be discharged and returned to his parents, and so on, so that the parents understand that the youth will always be returned to them, that society will not take him over, and that he is their problem, which they must solve.

Each inappropriate behavior of the youth must be carefully reformulated so that it is not a psychiatric symptom but a behavior that the parents can change. It is important for the therapist to relabel even the most bizarre behavior as discourteous communication, in that others cannot understand it or it upsets others. Then the parents can be asked to require that the youth communicate more clearly and politely. If the problem is apathetic behavior, it can be reformulated as laziness so the parents can be moved to demand regular activities. If the case involves drug addiction, the therapist can emphasize that it is not a physiological dependence that cannot be overcome. The parents must be convinced that the young person's problem is one that they can handle by establishing clear rules and prescribing severe consequences if these rules are not followed. If the youth is on medication, the therapist must state that he will reduce the medication and discontinue it altogether as soon as possible. As long as the young person is on medication, he is a mental patient under the care of psychiatrists instead of a misbehaving son whose behavior must be changed by the parents. A similar issue often comes up with the question of whether the youth should be on disability benefits. If the therapist accepts this idea, he is defining the youth as a mental patient incapable of making a living like a normal person.

Parents often disqualify themselves from the tasks of the therapy by communicating their ignorance about what expectations and rules to set for the young person or what consequences to levy if the rules are disobeyed. Typical examples are statements such as, "It depends on so many things"; "I couldn't make rules that would contemplate all the possible eventualities";

"How could I know what is good for him?"; etc. One of the ways to counteract this maneuver is for the therapist to repeat a request and give a rationale that the parents will have difficulty arguing against. For example, if the parents express ignorance about what rules to set for the son, the therapist can say, "I know it is difficult to set rules for him but your son was hospitalized because he was confused. For him to be clear in his own mind, you, his parents, have to be very clear with him about the rules for his behavior in your house when he comes home from the hospital." It would be a mistake for the therapist to believe that the parents are actually ignorant. Their expressions of ignorance serve the purpose of arranging for others to take charge, i.e., the therapist, other doctors, or the youth himself, so that the parents will not have to come together in agreement as joint leaders of the family.

The therapist should avoid the temptation of taking over the parents' task and himself setting the rules and consequences for their child. Since the therapist wants a hierarchy with the parents in a superior position, he cannot put them down in front of the offspring by taking over a parental position. Only if the therapist feels strongly that the parents' decisions about the young person are seriously wrong should he undermine their authority by suggesting an alternative, and then this should be done with the parents alone, not in the presence of the youth.

GIVING AUTHORITY TO THE PROBLEM YOUTH

Sometimes the parents will offer the authority to the disturbed youth. For example, when asked to make a decision about him, the parents might turn to the youth for advice. The therapist should emphasize that the young person needs parental guidance, and only when he is behaving properly will he be in charge of himself. If the youth objects, the therapist can explain to him what there is in this approach for him. It can be emphasized that the youth will live in a predictable world, knowing exactly what his obligations and privileges

are, and will therefore not find himself in situations in which he will be punished or mistreated arbitrarily or without warning.

When the parents begin to talk to each other and there is the possibility of an alliance between them that will give them power over their offspring, the youth will behave in bizarre and disruptive ways. The threat of a parental alliance will end as the parents focus on the youth. It is important for the therapist to know that at the beginning of therapy chances are that every time the parents begin to talk to each other, the young person will intervene and call their attention to himself. The therapist must quiet the young person or ask the parents to do so.

DEFINING THEMSELVES AS INADEQUATE

Sometimes a parent will present himself as inadequate by behaving in disruptive ways. He or she might scream and cry in a session so that nobody else can talk. When a parent behaves in disruptive ways, it is better to deal with this behavior without the offspring in the room. The therapist should emphasize that he or she has been a good, dedicated parent and ask litle of the parent—e.g., one more week of patience until there is a plan for what the young person will do with his life.

Parent Disqualifies Other Parent

Sometimes one parent will define the other parent as incompetent or defective. If one parent is incapacitated and disqualified from taking charge of the offspring, the two parents cannot reach agreement and an alliance to be jointly in charge of the youth. There are a series of tactics the therapist can use to counteract this maneuver by one of the parents. He can say that one of the parents may or may not have been too harsh or too weak, withdrawn or depressed, in the past, but whether or not that was so is not the issue; this is a new situation in which they will be working with the therapist, who will help them to get together, agree, and take charge jointly of their offspring. Whatever happened in the past is irrelevant. The therapist can reformulate the disqualification of one parent by the other parent so that weakness becomes sensitivity, harshness or brutality becomes desperate attempts to provide clear guidance to a disoriented youth, depression and emotional instability become dedicated concern. Once the incompetence has been reformulated, it can be discarded.

Disqualifications of one parent by the other parent can sometimes be avoided or corrected by reformulating the behavior of the disqualifier. This reformulating may be inaccurate and closer to what the therapist wishes the parent did than to what he or she actually does. For example, if a critical parent is defined by the therapist as supportive, he or she will behave more supportively.

Sometimes a parent will suggest that there are secret, unsavory facts about the other parent, with the purpose of arousing the therapist's curiosity so that he will become interested in these facts and will focus on the parent's difficulties. The therapist should be prepared to avoid being distracted from his goal by other issues. It is a good idea for the therapist to say that he will be interested in the parent's difficulties and willing to discuss them, if this is the parents' wish, only after the disturbed youth is leading a normal life. The first priority now is the young person who needs the parents to take charge and guide him. This message implies that no matter what secret or unsavory facts there are about a parent, he or she must take charge of the youth and provide the necessary guidance. Also, in this way, the therapist is only postponing, without rejecting, the parent's bid for attention.

Parents Disqualify Therapist

The parents can ignore the therapist's requests that they be in charge of their offspring by disqualifying the therapist from being in charge of the therapy. If the parents put the therapist down, it is difficult for him to help the parents be in a superior position in their family. They need not follow the directives of a therapist they do not respect.

The parents might disqualify the therapist by suggesting that he is incompetent and does not know what he is doing. They can object to the therapist's age, sex, or professional degree. They might quote the opinion of other professionals whose position differs, or they might state that the therapist will fail as other therapists have failed in the past. In order to counteract these maneuvers effectively, the therapist must realize that often the parents would rather discuss the therapist's competence than face the difficulty of taking charge of their family. The parents, however, have the right to information on the therapist's qualifications, and even though they might bring up these issues in order to avoid dealing with other matters, this should not be pointed out to them but answered briefly.

When the issue of conflicting opinions from other professionals is brought up, the therapist must state that he is aware that there are different positions in the field and does not agree with some of them. To the prediction that the therapist will fail as other therapists have failed in the past, the answer can be that this approach to therapy is different and the family should give him a chance to do his job. The therapist can suggest that the parents try this approach for a limited period of time, for example, for three months. In this way they will understand the modality of therapy, and after the three months they can decide whether to continue or not. Also, after three months the young person might be on his feet and the therapy might no longer be necessary.

Sometimes the parents refuse to comply with the therapist's requests as a way of disqualifying the therapist from being in charge of the therapy. The therapist needs to use certain tactics to ensure that his directives are followed. He must state and restate the goal of the therapy, which is to prevent rehospitalization. He can explain the cycle of rehospitalization, discharge, and rehospitalization that can occur if the issues are not dealt with immediately.

nied on the basis that the requested behavior took place many times before. The
therapist should reply that this is a new
situation, since he, the therapist, is now
involved with the family. The therapist
should repeat his requests time and time
again until he succeeds. A great part of the
therapist's tactics within this approach involve repetitiousness and tenacity.

The Third Stage

Changes in other relationships in the
family inevitably follow changes in the hierarchical relationship between parents
and child. Sometimes a sibling will make
an alliance with the disturbed youth to support him against the parents and to rein-
state an organization in which the parents
are not in a superior position. Often a
grandparent or other relative will ally with
the youth, and there will be the danger
that two incongruous hierarchies will again
be defined in the family. In fact, the more
disturbed the young person is at the beginning of the therapy, the greater the possibility that as soon as the hierarchical
organization of the nuclear family begins
to become congruent, the therapist will
discover involvements with extended kin
that define a hierarchy that is incongruent
with one in which the parents are in a superior position. The therapist must block
these coalitions and shift the relatives from
allying with the disturbed youth to supporting the parents in their efforts to guide
him. In order to do this, it is often necessary to have the relatives present at one or
more sessions.

As relationships change, the difficulties
of the parents can become exacerbated.
Demanding more of their child, the parents
may also begin to demand more of each
other, which may result in a threat of separation. In struggling to provide guidance
to the youth, a parent might become more
aware of his own deficiencies and failures
and, consequently, become upset or depressed. Sometimes the upset is related to
a struggle with his own parents as he tries
to keep them from allying with the youth
across generation lines.

Sometimes what the therapist asks is de-

When a threat of separation occurs, it is
sometimes useful to exaggerate the power
of the youth by his extreme and incompetent behavior to bring the parents together in order to take care of him. If this
power is presented benevolently, emphasizing the young person's concern and self-
sacrifice in preventing a divorce, the family
will not be antagonized, since no one will
be accused of bad intentions. They will respond, however, by reorganizing in more
appropriate ways. This intervention is similar to those described by Selvini Palazzoli
et al. (1978). The fact is that the youth's
extreme behavior does bring the parents
together to take care of him and that the
kind of power that the young person holds
over the parents requires extreme involvement with them at the cost of other attachments. The youth's behavior, however,
although preventing the parents from separating, causes so much disruption and
pain in the family that it also prevents the
parents from coming together in joy and
good feeling.

When the youth's behavior is extremely
bizarre, hospitalization is often considered.
To hospitalize would be an error because
it disqualifies all the therapist's efforts to
put the parents in charge of the problem.
If the parents threaten to put the youth
back in the mental hospital, the therapist
must state that this is no longer an option
because parents and therapist have agreed
that the goal of the therapy is to keep the
young person out of the hospital. The therapist can help the parents by suggesting
alternative consequences if the young person misbehaves, such as no money, no
food, or confining him to his room. If there
is violence or the threat of violence, the
therapist might suggest that the parents
call the police. If there have been previous
hospitalizations the police will probably
take the youth to the hospital. This is better, however, than if the parents resort to
hospitalization directly. Sometimes the
young person demands to be taken to the
mental hospital. The therapist should anticipate this possibility with the parents
and suggest that they refuse to do this. If
the youth wants to go to the hospital, he

must get there himself. If hospitalization occurs, the therapy must start all over again following the same steps that were carried out previously.

Sometimes, when the youth is very disruptive, the parents do not threaten him with hospitalization but with expulsion from the family home as the only consequence for the youth's misbehavior that is available to them. This threat must also be blocked. The therapist must emphasize that ultimately the young person will leave home but that this separation from the parents must happen when the youth is behaving competently and when the parents know and approve of where and how he is going to live. Depending upon the nature of the problem and the age of the young person, however, expulsion from the home might be accepted as the ultimate consequence if the rules as well as the consequences for disobeying the rules are not respected. It is better, however, to avoid expulsion—first, because it is a threat that is rarely carried out and, second, because the chances are that as soon as the parents are in difficulty the youth will involve them again in his troubles and the cycle will be repeated.

Avoiding rehospitalization is more difficult if the young person threatens suicide. In this case, there are two possibilities for the therapist: (a) to hospitalize the youth, which means that the therapy will have to start all over again when the young person is discharged; or (b) to put the parents in charge of the youth and help them organize to prevent the suicide. This is a difficult decision to make and should depend on the seriousness of the suicide threat, on whether there have been previous attempts, on an evaluation of the parents' investment in keeping their offspring alive, and on their ability to work together to prevent the suicide. If the therapist decides against hospitalization, he should carefully help the parents organize to prevent the suicide. They should institute a 24-hour watch and take turns watching him so that the youth is never alone. This usually tests the limits of the parents' patience and helps them to take a more firm position in demanding normal behavior from the youth.

The Fourth Stage

As the youth becomes oriented toward a normal way of life centered around work or school, the therapist begins to meet with him separately to plan tasks related to work, school, and social relations with peers. There are also meetings with the youth and the parents to plan how the young person will eventually leave home, where and how he will live, how he will support himself. As various goals are accomplished, the sessions become more spaced in time (usually once a month) until the therapy is discontinued.

The Single Parent

In cases in which there is a single parent, it is best to obtain the cooperation of a relative in the treatment—for example, a grandmother, aunt, mother's boyfriend, etc. This relative should be the most significant parental surrogate in the young person's life. The therapy will then proceed in the same way, except that instead of two parents there will be one parent and one parental surrogate. If there is no relative to involve in the therapy, the stages and the treatment plan are still the same. The only difference is that instead of having two parents talking to each other and making decisions jointly, the therapist will have to use himself more in the discussion with the single parent. That is, the therapist needs to become more involved with the single parent in encouraging her or him to make the decisions that are necessary during the course of therapy.

Organicity

The question of whether certain types of pathology that typically occur in young people, such as schizophrenia and manic depression, have an organic basis, is quite irrelevant to this therapy. Even if these pathologies have an organic or genetic basis, the medications in use today must be used sparingly and with caution, and the goal for the therapist must still be to organize a life for the young person that is as normal as possible, keeping him out of the mental hospital. In fact, the same approach has been used with mentally retarded youths, patients with tardive dyskinesia, young people with irreversible neurological damage from Phencyclidine (PCP)—angel dust—use, and epileptics.

Summary of the Therapeutic Strategy

When a severely disturbed youth is discharged from a mental hospital, the therapist is typically presented with a situation in which there is an incongruity in the family hierarchy. The young person has superior power over the parents and threatens them with his behavior. The therapist's goal is to get the parents to take away from the youth this power that is based on disturbed behavior.

Hierarchy in a family is defined by repetitive sequences of who tells whom what to do. Normally, sequences in which the parents tell the children what to do and the children do it, occur in families more frequently than the opposite kinds of sequences. In families of severely disturbed young people, the therapist faces a situation in which the youth is still economically and emotionally dependent on the parents; yet the most frequently recurring sequences are ones in which the parents tell the youth what to do but he does not do it, or the parents do not tell the youth what to do but complain about what he does, or the youth tells the parents what to do and the parents do it.

The therapist must intervene to change these sequences to ones in which the parents tell the youth what to do and the youth obeys. Through the repeated occurrence of these sequences a hierarchy will be defined in which the parents will be in a superior position to the young person.

The content of the communicational sequences between parents and youth must be one in which the parents set expectations and rules for the youth and establish consequences if these are not followed. Since at the beginning of treatment the parents are at a power disadvantage, the therapist must influence them to establish rules and consequences that are stringent enough to build up their power vis-à-vis the youth. When the young person loses his power over the parents, he will behave normally, become independent from them, and eventually leave home.

The strategy used in this therapeutic approach is based on the manipulation of power, with the therapist redistributing power among family members. The process for carrying out this strategy consists of eliciting from family members the communicational sequences that define an appropriate hierarchy and counteracting the communication maneuvers that disqualify that hierarchy.

REFERENCES

Bateson, G., Jackson, D. D., Haley, J., & Weakland, J. Toward a theory of schizophrenia. *Behavioral Science*, 1956, **1**, 251–264.

Haley, J. *Leaving home.* New York: McGraw-Hill, 1980.

Madanes, C. Protection, paradox and pretending. *Family Process*, 1980, **19**, 73–85.

Madanes, C. Dukes, J., & Harbin, H. Family ties of heroin addicts. *Archives of General Psychiatry*, August 1980, **37**, 889–894.

Selvini Palazzoli, M. D., Ceccin, G., Prata, G., & Boscolo, L. *Paradox and Counterparadox.* New York: Jason Aronson, 1978.

Sojit, C. Madanes. Dyadic interaction in a double bind situation. *Family Process*, 1969, **8**, 235–259.

Sojit, C. Madanes. The double bind hypothesis and the parents of schizophrenics. *Family Process*, 1971, **10**, 53–74.

14

Anorexia Nervosa and Bulimia: Expanding the Structural Model

THOMAS C. TODD, Ph.D.

*T*he past decade has seen considerable evolution in the conceptualization and treatment of anorexia nervosa and other eating disorders, particularly with regard to the role of the family. This chapter will discuss in some detail one model, Structural Family Therapy, which has proven to be successful in the treatment of anorexia and other psychosomatic disorders of childhood and adolescence. In addition, the chapter will examine the work of others who have attempted to include the family in their theories and treatment approaches for eating disorders.

Recently, there have been efforts to address and move beyond the limitations of the structural model and the more general limitations of a purely family-therapy approach. These efforts will comprise the backdrop for the model offered in this chapter. This model emphasizes working simultaneously at several levels of system, attempting to strike an appropriate balance between an emphasis on the homeostatic tendencies that keep the system stable and the developmental processes that tend toward change. While this model may lack theoretical elegance, it is hoped that it will provide clinically useful principles for effective treatment.

Bulimia is included along with anorexia nervosa, since bulimia is also quite common, frequently overlaps with anorexia, and generally shares many clinical features with anorexia. However the major focus of the chapter is anorexia, since most of the early family-oriented work, particularly from the Philadelphia Child Guidance Clinic, dealt primarily with anorexia, a bias that is gradually being overcome. Where appropriate, comments on similarities and differences between the two syndromes are offered, including contrasting case examples and differential treatment implications. Obesity will not be included in this chapter, although some writers such as Bruch (1973) have argued that the dynamics of obesity are similar to anorexia and bulimia. It is the author's impression, however, that while there may be similarities in the clinical picture, the treatment is quite different.

At this point, it seems appropriate to offer a brief sketch of my background, in order to shed some light on the evolution of my approach to the treatment of psychosomatic disorders and to clarify the relationship between treatment context and overall treatment plan. From 1970 to 1975, I was on the staff of the Philadelphia Child Guidance Clinic (PCGC), where I was one of the original members of the psychosomatic research project which later culminated in *Psychosomatic Families* (Minuchin, Rosman, & Baker, 1978). Since 1975, I have worked in New York and Connecticut, directing a comprehensive community mental health clinic and treating in private practice a large number of cases involving eating disorders. It is probably also important to note that strategic and paradoxical influences have been increasingly important in my work (Todd, 1981) and that M. D. Stanton and I have made several attempts to integrate structural and strategic therapy. (Stanton, 1981a, 1981b; Stanton & Todd, 1982; Todd, 1983)

EVOLUTION OF FAMILY-THERAPY APPROACHES TO EATING DISORDERS

The Early Efforts of Bruch and Selvini Palazzoli

Bruch (1973) and the early writings of Selvini Palazzoli and colleagues (Selvini Palazzoli, 1974) clearly acknowledged the importance of the family in anorexia, but stopped short of a truly systemic model. Instead, the family was seen as an etiological factor in the early development of the disorder or a current stressor affecting the disorder.

Bruch has shown a long-standing interest in the role of the family in the etiology of eating disorders. In one of her early papers, "The Family Frame of Obese Children" (Bruch & Touraine, 1940), she explored consistent interactional patterns and other characteristics of families with obese children. In her 1973 book she applied a similar "family frame" to fifty-one cases of primary anorexia:

> The parents emphasized the normality of their family life, with repeated statements that "nothing was wrong," sometimes with frantic stress on "happiness," directly denying the desperate illness of one member. Often they emphasized the superiority of the now-sick child over his siblings. The mothers had often been women of achievement, or career women frustrated in their aspirations, who had been conscientious in their motherhood. They were subservient to their husbands in many details, and yet did not truly respect them. The fathers, despite social and financial success which was often considerable, felt in some sense "second best." They were enormously preoccupied with outer appearances in the physical sense of the word, admiring fitness and beauty, and expecting proper behavior and measurable achievements from their children. (Bruch, 1973, p. 82)

On a more general level, Bruch contends that obese and anorectic individuals lack awareness of the internal cues of hunger. She has examined distortions in the early mother-child interaction that would lead to such a lack of awareness, as well as a more general lack of awareness in living one's own life. She found evidence that the mother would feed the child according to her own perception of the child's needs and would often ignore feedback from the child which conflicted with her ideas. Similarly, these mothers would make many decisions for their children, again based on "mind-reading" rather than the stated preferences of the child.

Selvini Palazzoli subtitled *Self-Starvation*, (her 1974 book): *From Individual to Family Therapy in the Treatment of Anorexia Nervosa*. This is obviously a transitional work in evolution toward her later, more systemic thinking. Nevertheless, these early writings contain many valuable observations, collected in her efforts to describe a "model system" for the family of the anorexic patient. Although the patterns of communication and interaction in these families were not as skewed and distinctive as those of the families of schizophrenics, she noted many characteristic patterns.

Selvini Palazzoli found, in agreement with Minuchin and Barcai (1969), that the parents typically refuse to assume personal leadership of the family. Rather than make decisions, the parents will ask other family members to decide, even very small children. Even when decisions are made or actions taken, the parents will rarely acknowledge any link to their own desires, and usually the children learn quickly the dangers of taking responsibility. "So the actions of each member are never attributed to personal preferences but to the needs of another member; all decisions are for the good of someone else." (Selvini Palazzoli, 1974, p. 209) In a sense, the anorectic can be said to "lead" the family, but only through her symptoms, which are not attributed to her.

She also found the same prohibition against exclusive dyads seen in Minuchin's concept of enmeshment:

> Clearly the members of the family behave as if an alliance between any two is a betrayal of the third. They seem to have great difficulty in entering into a two-person relationship; the exclusion of the third strikes them as a grave threat to their pseudo-solidarity —only in the absence of all open alliances can this threat apparently be averted. (Selvini Palazzoli, 1974, pp. 210–211)

Within this overall pattern, the anorectic typically plays a pivotal role, in which both parents invite her[1] to ally with them. Since the parents maintain a facade of normality, these alliances can never be openly acknowledged.

According to Selvini Palazzoli, the fathers and mothers of anorectics display predictable characteristics, with the anorectic daughter playing a stereotyped but ambiguous role. The mothers see themselves as "Ladies Bountiful," who are completely dedicated to the welfare of others. The

---

[1]At times throughout this chapter, the anorectic or bulimic patient will be described in the female gender, since roughly 90 per cent of such patients are female.

fathers see themselves as essentially good and decent men, who are conscientiously trying to do their best. The two partners are engaged in a struggle that must remain hidden, since they present themselves as a model couple to the outside world.

In summary, both Bruch and Selvini Palazzoli offered observations of the family systems of anorectics which remain accurate to this day. These are important works, even though neither represents a complete transition to a family systems view. Even now, Bruch does not acknowledge the primary importance of the family, although she regards family therapy as a useful adjunct to treatment. Selvini Palazzoli's work made it clear that she was grappling with the inclusion of the family into her view of anorexia and other symptoms, yet in her early work she was unable to move beyond her psychoanalytic training and find ways to include the family in treatment.

Structural Family Therapy

The work of Minuchin and his colleagues at the Philadelphia Child Guidance Clinic represented a major step forward in developing a systems perspective on eating disorders and other psychosomatic problems. The Minuchin group pointed out in an early paper (Minuchin, Baker, Rosman, Liebman, Milman, & Todd, 1975), that while writers such as Bruch and Selvini Palazzoli acknowledged the importance of the family, such a view still represents a *linear model* in which the family is simply added to the list of causal factors. By contrast, the Minuchin group proposed a *circular model* in which the family is part of a mutual feedback process. In this view, the psychosomatic symptoms are influenced by family interaction and simultaneously influence family interaction. According to this conceptual model, there is a constellation of family characteristics which are practically universal in families exhibiting psychosomatic problems. The structural family therapy treatment model, described more fully in *Psychosomatic Families* (Minuchin, et al., 1978), is explicitly designed to deal with these family factors.

THE STRUCTURAL CONCEPTUAL MODEL

Four factors have been identified in this conceptual model which are thought to be typical of "psychosomatic families." (While the use of this term probably perpetuates a tendency to blur the characteristics of the family and those of the identified patient (IP), it does provide a convenient shorthand for a group of families with extremely predictable features.) These four factors are:

(1) *Enmeshment*, a characteristic pattern of overinvolvement and blurring of boundaries at the individual, subsystem, and family levels;

(2) *Overprotectiveness*, a high degree of concern on the part of family members for the welfare of other family members, which is not limited to the welfare of the IP;

(3) *Rigidity*, the tendency to maintain the status quo, even in situations calling for flexibility, change, and growth;

(4) *Lack of conflict resolution*. Most psychosomatic families have an extremely low tolerance for the expression of conflict, particularly between the parents. Occasionally, this takes the form of overt conflict which is never resolved. More typically, however, there is little or no expression of conflict, so that resolution is impossible.

The above factors are general characteristics of psychosomatic families; by themselves they say little about the unique role played by the child with psychosomatic problems. In this conceptual model, the symptoms of the IP are seen as having particular interactional significance as a regulator in the family system. The symptomatic child is typically involved in parental conflict in one of several distinctive ways:

(1) *Triangulation*. The spouse dyad is openly split at times of conflict, and extreme pressure is brought to bear on the symptomatic child to take sides. (This pattern is highly stressful and is usually seen only briefly in transition to other patterns.)

(2) *Stable Coalition*. The symptomatic child is involved in a relatively stable coalition with one parent against the other, again with spouse conflict openly expressed. (As mentioned above, open conflict is somewhat unusual in psychosomatic families.)

(3) *Detouring*. Open conflict between the parents is avoided or quickly submerged by having the parents unite with respect to a child. In psychosomatic families, this detouring usually has a protective quality, unlike families who unite by scapegoating a child in a negative fashion.

TREATMENT PRINCIPLES

Minuchin et al. (1978) have also developed a treatment model for the anorectic family which is tailored to this conceptual model. (To employ these treatment principles effectively, the reader should already be familiar with the basic structural family-therapy techniques outlined in Minuchin (1974), and Minuchin and Fishman (1981).) The structural family therapy treatment model for anorexia provides for the following:

(1) *Identifying Short- and Long-Range Goals*. In this model, the initial aim of therapy must be to deal with the life-threatening behavior. This is typically achieved through a combination of behavioral intervention and family therapy. (See the discussion of Liebman's work below.) Only after some initial symptomatic improvement has been achieved can the therapist turn to the equally important goal of altering long-standing patterns of family interaction.

(2) *Forming the Therapeutic System*. The therapist must join with the family to form a therapeutic system. To do this, the therapist must accommodate to the family, yet maintain a position of flexible leadership.

(3) *Challenging Realities*. Early in therapy it is necessary to challenge the family's portrayal of their child as "sick" and the parents as helpless bystanders. The term "challenge" may be misleading, since it implies more direct confrontation than is typically used in the structural approach to psychosomatic families. A gentle example of challenging realities occurs in the film, "Anorexia Is a Greek Word" (Minuchin, 1982). When the parents attempt to use the exotic disease of "anorexia" as an excuse for deferring to the medical expert, Miuchin counters by claiming that he does not understand Greek, and that the patient's disease is "being special." At times, more direct confrontation is needed, such as the induction of a therapeutically generated crisis (Minuchin & Barcai, 1969).

(4) *Challenging Enmeshment.* Enmeshment is challenged in three ways—supporting the individual's life space, supporting subsystem boundaries, and supporting the hierarchical organization of the family.

(5) *Challenging Overprotection.* Similar to challenging enmeshment, the therapist must challenge overprotection when it occurs, whether it is protective of the IP or of other family members.

(6) *Challenging Conflict Avoidance.* Successful conflict resolution can be promoted by blocking the intrusion of other family members when a dyad is discussing a conflictual issue. In addition, it is usually important to help the dyad to transcend their usual tolerance for conflict, by prolonging the conflict or even by allying with one of the participants.

(7) *Challenging Rigidity.* While anorectic families are typically overtly compliant, their patterns of interaction are remarkably impervious to change. To confront this, the therapist must make repeated use of the interventions of intensifying conflict and boundary-making. Enactment and the assignment of tasks can also be used to effect lasting change.

(8) *Challenging Conflict Detouring.* The anorectic child typically plays a unique role in detouring parental conflict. To counteract this, the therapist must strengthen parent-child boundaries, doing so with a combination of confrontation and support.

THE FAMILY LUNCH SESSION

No discussion of the work of the Minuchin group would be complete without highlighting the role of the family lunch session, one of the most important single ingredients in the structural family-therapy treatment of anorexia. Because of the family characteristics noted above, it can be extremely difficult to gather the observations about family transactions that are necessary for the therapist to challenge old patterns of interaction. Descriptions of the family's behavior around the patient's eating problems are typically bland and uninformative, and the family's commitment to conflict avoidance and protectiveness makes it difficult to intensify the conflict. The family lunch session was devised as a means of "crisis induction" (Minuchin & Barcai, 1969), which enables the therapist to observe and challenge the family's characteristic patterns. The family is brought together around the lunch table, and the parents are confronted with the task of making something different happen around the patient's refusal to eat. Naturally they cannot do this unaided by the therapist. Seeing the patterns firsthand, the therapist can use the techniques outlined above to move the family beyond their usual threshold of conflict avoidance to produce positive change.

EVIDENCE OF EFFECTIVENESS

The structural family therapy model developed by the Minuchin group is relatively unique, because it has research data to confirm both the presence of the hypothesized family characteristics and the effectiveness of the family therapy model. Several sources of data were used to confirm the presence of the family characteristics hypothesized in the conceptual model. Videotapes of Wiltwyck Family Tasks (Minuchin, Montalvo, Guerney, Rosman, & Schumer, 1967) were used to study family interaction. In these tasks, the family is asked to perform standardized tasks, such as planning a menu together, without therapeutic intervention. Observation of these tasks, particularly with the opportunity to review them carefully on videotape, allows the assessment of stable patterns of enmeshment, overprotectiveness, conflict avoidance, and rigidity.

A second method was used to highlight the unique role played by the symptomatic child. A structured Family Diagnostic Interview (Minuchin et al., 1978) was used to arouse parental conflict through experimental manipulation and then to study the patterns of involvement of the child in response to this conflict. (The psychosomatic families are generally so successful at avoiding conflict in relatively neutral situations that it is necessary to utilize such conflict-inducing procedures to activate their patterns of conflict-avoidance.) These patterns were observed and recorded on videotape. In addition, the project monitored the physiological response of the child to observing parental conflict and to becoming more directly involved in this conflict.

Extensive outcome data were collected for fifty-three anorectic patients in order to evaluate treatment effectiveness. The results of this treatment were impressive—for the fifty patients that remained in therapy longer than two sessions, eighty-six per cent recovered from both the physical symptoms of anorexia and its psychosocial components. (See Minuchin et al., 1978, pp. 126–133 for details.) These results have been maintained over a follow-up period of two years or more and contrast dramatically with treatment results reported by other investigators.

An interesting related finding is the effectiveness of the lunch sessions mentioned above. Weight-gain data were examined for eight individual anorectics by comparing daily weight gain (or loss) prior to the lunch session and following it. Dramatic reversals were reported for these patients, most of whom were declining in weight prior to the lunch session. The authors are quick to point out, however, that the lunch session should not be regarded as a "quick cure," and that the results of the lunch session are unlikely to hold up without further treatment. (See Minuchin et al., 1978, pp. 122–125 for further details.)

ADDRESSING THE LIMITATIONS OF THE STRUCTURAL MODEL

Limitations of the Structural Model

The structural school has come under increasing ciriticism in recent years, particularly by those of a more strategic or systemic persuasion. (Benjamin, 1982; DeShazer, 1982; Hoffman, 1981, 1983; Selvini Palazzoli, et al., 1978) These critics see structural therapists as overemphasizing homeostatic "stuckness" and resistance, while underestimating the system's tendency toward change and morphogenesis. Structural therapy is also seen as over-using powerful techniques such as crisis induction to push a family toward goals set by the therapist, rather than letting new patterns of family interaction evolve more

naturally and with less intervention by the therapist. Finally, critics find that the structural model overemphasizes the nuclear family and underemphasizes other system levels, including the extended family and the larger peer and community networks.

An example of this trend, as applied to eating disorders, is the work of Harkaway (1983a, 1983b) on obesity. She describes a shift from her early work, conducted within a structural/strategic framework, to Milan-style systemic therapy. She finds structural work too "aggressive," and values the neutrality of the systemic approach. (The issue of neutrality will be discussed at greater length in the next section.)

Systemic Therapy

In many family therapy circles, the label "systemic therapy" has become virtually synonymous with the influential work of the Milan group (Selvini Palazzoli, Cecchin, et al., 1978). Despite the importance of Selvini Palazzoli's 1974 book on anorexia, it is interesting to note that little of the later, more systemic writing of this group has been specifically addressed to anorexia and other eating disorders. Other systemic therapists, however, have begun to demonstrate the utility of the systemic model for eating disorders (Caillé, et al., 1977).

The systemic model typically makes use of a team that includes observers behind a one-way mirror. During the session itself, the therapists in the room strive to remain neutral. Through the use of "circular questioning" (Selvini Palazzoli, Boscolo, Cecchin, & Prata, 1980), the team attempts to develop and test hypotheses about the case. At the end of the session, considerable time may be devoted to developing a final intervention for the family. In this final intervention, the behavior of the family members, particularly symptomatic behavior, is reframed in a more positive way. Prescriptions and rituals are assigned, in an effort to remove the family members from their paradoxical bind. For example, the anorectic might be given credit for remaining loyal to her family while still expressing her independence indirectly. The whole family might be instructed to perform a ritual together, which might involve food or some other significant issue.

While it is admittedly difficult for me to be objective in this area, it does seem that the systemic model offers some advantages while creating new difficulties. The work of the Milan group has definitely provided a useful antidote to the sometimes heavy-handed application of structural techniques. It is particularly important for therapists to avoid imposing their goals when it is unnecessary; in this respect, the Milan team's emphasis on having the system find its own new stability is commendable. On the other hand, there seem to be inherent problems in applying this model in its pure form to typical cases of eating disorders. This is particularly true of extreme weight loss. It is generally conceded by therapists of most persuasions that the dangerously low weight must be dealt with before utilizing verbal forms of therapy that require considerable time for effectiveness (Stern, et al., 1981).

Such considerations have led me to be selective in the use of paradoxical techniques with eating disorders. The techniques of positive connotation (Selvini Palazzoli, Cecchin, et al., 1978, pp. 55–66) and other forms of reframing are used almost routinely, since there is so much polarization of issues as Good and Bad, Strong and Weak, etc., with so much underlying ambivalence. Full-blown paradoxical treatment, in which the symptom is prescribed, is generally reserved for cases in which the symptomatic behavior is not life-threatening and where the family system is ultra-stable (Todd, 1981).

The author employed paradoxical treatment in the case of a young woman whose family had known about her vomiting for fourteen years but had never managed to get her into treatment. She agreed to come for one session with the family, on the condition that her vomiting not be discussed. In view of these impossible conditions for treatment, there seemed to be little alternative to a paradoxical approach. Her behavior was reframed as extremely loyal to the family, especially to her dead father, whom she allegedly hated. The vomiting behavior was not mentioned, but was dealt with by anal-ogy through an elaborate ritual of wastefully throwing things away. The family was given specific instructions to get together at prescribed times, with the patient given the role of leading a discussion of throwing away items that had belonged to her dead father. This ritual thus addressed the central role of the IP, her loyalty to her father, the significance of her "wasteful" eating practices, etc.

As promised, the patient failed to attend any further sessions, although her mother and sisters came for several additional sessions. The strategic team continued to respect the reluctance of the family to address conflictual issues directly. To do this, additional rituals were devised to deal with issues such as independence, intrusiveness, and mother's role conflict.

Combining Structural Therapy and Behavior Modification

Another way to expand the structural model is to utilize to a greater extent the opportunities provided by inpatient treatment. Liebman, a member of the Minuchin project, was one of the early advocates of an inpatient program that combined family therapy and behavior modification (Liebman, et al., 1974a, 1974b). Much of his work has been incorporated in the standard approach at the Philadelphia Child Guidance Clinic (PCGC) with hospitalized cases (Minuchin, et al., 1978, pp. 113–118). Behavior modification approaches such as the approach of Blinder, et al. (1970) are now widely used in inpatient programs and have been reported as achieving remarkable gains in the hospital. Unfortunately, if behavior modification is used exclusively, these gains are often short-lived, vanishing quickly when the patient leaves the hospital (Bruch, 1974; Pertshuk, 1977).

It is important to understand the general application of the behavioral program, although details can vary. All contingencies are based upon weight gain and weight loss, rather than food intake. This avoids having nursing staff engage in the detective work and power struggles around eating that have typically preoccupied the family so unproductively. Instead, the range of privileges and possible restriction to bed rest are made dependent on weight

criteria. (This usually requires careful spec-
ification of when and how the weighing
will occur, to prevent the issue from dom-
inating all interaction with the patient.)
The rationale offered to the patient must
be a nonpunitive one, typically that the
nursing staff must prevent unnecessary
expenditure of energy so long as the patient's weight remains at a dangerous level.
Nursing staff are specifically instructed to
avoid engaging in discussions of how
much or what to eat. Weight gain is portrayed as the patient's major task in the
hospital, a task she needs to approach in
a businesslike manner, even if she is not
hungry at first. Power struggles can still be
expected, but will hopefully focus on issues of obeying the rules, rather than on
life-threatening issues of eating.

The approach at PCGC was designed to
incorporate many of the desirable features
of the behavioral program into a family
therapy program. Combining behavior
modification and family therapy is particularly important in maintaining progress
achieved during hospitalization. The behavioral program is used to facilitate weight
gain in the hospital, while work with the
family insures that the parents follow up
effectively when the patient is discharged.

As noted above, hospitalization at PCGC
is typically very brief. The behavioral program is only used to begin a pattern of
weight gain and to get the patient out of
danger, rather than to achieve a desirable
final weight. Achieving an ideal final weight
in the hospital takes too long and leaves
the family too uninvolved in the process.
Initial weight gain typically begins five to
seven days after initiating the program. As
soon as this pattern is established and a
safe target weight has been reached, responsibility is quickly transferred to the
family on an outpatient basis. Often they
are encouraged to use a similar behavioral
program in the early stages after discharge.

The Work of Garfinkel and Garner

An impressive comprehensive model of
anorexia nervosa has been developed by
Garfinkel and Garner (1982). Their work

has attempted to incorporate multiple
etiological or predisposing factors: physiological, psychopathological, perceptual and
cognitive, family, and sociocultural. Garfinkel and Garner view anorexia as a syndrome that is the product of the interplay
of a number of such factors, although the
exact mechanism of etiology is not known
(Garfinkel & Garner, 1982, p. 188).

Given a predisposition to anorexia, a
number of initiating factors are seen as important: separation and losses, disruptions
of family homeostatis, new environmental
demands, direct threat of loss of self-esteem, and personal illness. Finally, there
are a variety of factors that may sustain the
illness, once it has begun: the starvation
syndrome, vomiting, gastrointestinal
physiology, distorted body perceptions,
cognitive factors, personality features, secondary gain, cultural emphasis on slim-
ness, and iatrogenic factors.

Not surprisingly, the treatment approach recommended by Garfinkel and
Garner is multimodal and somewhat eclectic. Hospital management can include
such diverse elements as behavior modification, medication, tube-feeing (hyperalimentation), and even ECT.
Psychotherapy is also advocated, which
can include psychodynamic issues, reality-
oriented feedback, cognitive behavior therapy, and family therapy.

The work of Garfinkel and Garner is
praiseworthy for its dispassionate and scientific examination of existing evidence
concerning etiology and treatment, avoiding the dogmatic and simplistic advocacy
of a single approach. To some extent, it is
obviously important to consider each case
separately, as they suggest, and to indi-
vidualize the treatment approach. What is
disappointing is their failure to furnish an
overall organizing principle that would
help to integrate the treatment approach.
While their observation is undoubtedly
valid that combining methods at times
creates a "synergistic effect" (Garfinkel &
Garner, 1982, p. 260), they offer little guidance concerning what combinations may
be particularly efficacious and under what
circumstances.

All of the treatment models discussed in

this section either explicitly or implicitly address some of the limitations of the structural approach, especially its overemphasis on the nuclear family and its comparative neglect of other system levels (peers, community, etc.) and a similar underemphasis on treatment modalities other than family therapy. Still missing is a comprehensive framework that can include work at several levels of systems, which would integrate hospitalization and medical management, individual therapy, family therapy, and larger systems issues.

THE EXPANDED FAMILY SYSTEMS MODEL

The Crucial Features: An Overview

Major features of the expanded family systems model are presented below in cursory form on a more abstract, theoretical level. Specific clinical guidelines and case examples will be provided in later sections.

First, the model emphasizes working simultaneously at many levels. (This book provides numerous examples of current efforts in the family therapy field to move beyond a narrow focus on the family.) Increasingly, the family therapy field is acknowledging that the family is only one level of system, and that it is simplistic to ignore other levels. General systems theory provides a clear framework for conceptualizing the family as one of many levels of system, which include the individual, the family, the family's immediate context (including the extended family), and the larger community. These levels can be thought of as nested within each other, similar to a set of Chinese boxes, but with each level influencing and being influenced by other levels. Emphasizing multiple system levels is not important on purely theoretical grounds. Later in the chapter there will be examples of the practical consequences of expanding the focus of therapy to include other levels of the system.

Second, the model highlights the importance of developmental processes. Along

with the need to recognize multiple levels of system, it is also important to consider the developmental processes operating at each level. On the individual level, each family member can be seen as having individual needs shaped in part by that individual's stage of physical and psychological development. Similarly, the nuclear family and the extended family can be viewed as progressing through a family life cycle (Carter & McGoldrick, 1980; Haley, 1973), with each stage having distinctive developmental tasks.

Third, this model attempts to place equal emphasis on "stuckness" and the developmental impetus to change. At each level there are change-inhibiting and change-encouraging factors at work; both tendencies need to be considered by the therapist. In many cases of eating disorders, both the individual patient and the family typically appear to be arrested at a particular stage of development, such as leaving home (Haley, 1980). This is only a partial view, however, because there are a whole host of developmental processes, at the physiological, psychological, family, and larger system-levels that tend to promote change.

Setting the Stage for Treatment

USE OF THE SYSTEMIC MODEL AS ORGANIZING FRAMEWORK

The overall treatment plan includes a varied mixture of therapeutic modalities in the treatment of eating disorders. These can include individual psychotherapy, behavior therapy, inpatient hospitalization, and family therapy. While the precise ingredients vary with the case, the treatment setting and therapist preferences, it is the systemic model that provides the overall organizing framework. This model guides many treatment decisions, especially decisions regarding the ground-rules for treatment.

ENSURING FAMILY SUPPORT FOR TREATMENT PLAN

It is critically important that the family (particularly the parents) support all aspects of the treatment plan. This includes the necessity of psychotherapeutic treatment, the ground rules for inpatient hospitalization, issues of privacy and confidentiality, and a strong commitment to family therapy. A variety of techniques are useful in achieving this. The therapist can join with the parents in recognizing their concern for the child. S/he can predict, however, that they may have second thoughts about whether treatment is really necessary and whether all possible medical causes have been ruled out. If they still express any ambivalence on this issue, they should be encouraged to pursue any such concerns and come back when they are ready to make a whole-hearted commitment to therapy. (Usually, at this time, they do not choose to pursue alternatives, but the family may need to be reminded of the therapist's warning when the predicted period of ambivalence arises.) Similarly, the parents should be prepared in advance for the inevitable efforts of the IP to sign out of the hospital against medical advice, to persuade the parents that the ward staff are unreasonable, etc.

Hospital/Medical Issues

It is equally crucial (especially for a nonmedical therapist) to have a clear contract with those hospital/medical staff who will play important roles with the patient, especially during hospitalization. One of the major virtues of an inpatient behavior modification program is that it provides unambiguous rules for treatment. This provides consistency across staff members and minimizes the tendency for them—in a "boom and bust" cycle—to become overhelpful and then disappointed and angry. It also allows ward staff to combat the inevitable attempts at manipulation on the part of the anorectic.

While the behavior modification plan is extremely helpful, usually it does not cover all the issues that may arise in inpatient treatment. The therapist should anticipate having to provide explicit guidance for staff concerning the handling of power and control issues. For example, ward staff are in-

structed to avoid any discussion of eating, no matter how hard the anorectic tries to engage them on that topic. It is also helpful to explain the overall goals of the program to staff, and to inform them, for example, that it is healthy for the patient to show assertiveness in the form of challenges to other parts of the treatment plan (such as confinement to bed and obeying other rules.)

In most cases of eating disorders, conflict will develop between the parents and the inpatient staff. The exact form of this conflict is unpredictable and depends on the stage of hospitalization. The IP may initially attempt to enlist the parents in a power struggle with staff; hopefully this has been ancitipated in preliminary discussions with both inpatient staff and parents. As the hospital stay progresses, it becomes more likely that one or more staff members may begin to sympathize with the IP as the "victim" (Mirkin, 1983) and blame one or both parents. (See Haley, 1976, 1980, for typical examples.) Since the tendency for such polarization in staff attitude increases over time, the simplest way to minimize this trend is to keep the hospitalization brief. Such conflict can also be reduced if it is anticipated and viewed by the therapist as inevitable (rather than "bad.")

Even when the treatment team attempts to remain consistently systemic in its approach, the IP sometimes succeeds in persuading a team member to depart from the treatment plan and become overinvolved and overly helpful. At times, discussion among team members will be sufficient to restore a systemic focus, but at other times this helpfulness may persist despite such efforts. At such times it is usually preferable to attempt to redirect the helpfulness, rather than opposing it directly.

The author encountered such a problem when working with a twelve-year-old anorectic boy. His parents were in constant conflict on a covert level, leading both of them to ignore the boy. Partly in response to this apparent neglect, the chief pediatric nurse became overinvolved with him to the extent of coming into the hospital to see him while she was on vacation. Rather than opposing her directly, I attempted to channel her helpfulness and encourage it to the point of overload. Her zealousness was preempted and neutralized by assigning her readings (at her request), having her organize a staff conference, getting her to make elaborate notes, etc.

While some clinicians might view my actions as somewhat manipulative, the response of the nurse made it clear that this had been a respectful intervention. She felt that her helpfulness had been validated, while being brought within reasonable bounds. Above all, this was accomplished without confrontation or power struggle. There is a variety of situations in which redirection is preferable to direct opposition. To be effective, however, it is best to see the behavior of the over-involved team member as a manifestation of the system of patient/ family/ treatment team, rather than some "character defect" of the team member. No one, including the family therapist, is truly outside the system, and no one has a corner on truth.

The case of Lisa, a seventeen-year-old anorectic, offers many examples of potential pitfalls in establishing a workable treatment contract among parents, physicians, therapists, and inpatient staff. During the first two outpatient family therapy sessions with her and her parents, there was little agreement among the participants concerning the existence of a significant problem or what should be done about it. The parents, who were divorced, took polarized positions on every issue. Mother, a militant feminist, favored nontraditional approaches, such as homeopathic therapy. Father, an extremely conservative lawyer, rejected such unconventional treatment and clearly had misgivings even about the value of psychotherapy.

During the following week I was attending a conference out of state. The mother learned this when calling my office. Rather than stating that there was any urgency in contacting me, she contacted a local psychiatrist to hospitalize her daughter. (One of the few things that she and father were able to agree upon was that I had been derelict in my duty by failing to warn the parents of my absence.)

When I returned and made a routine phone call to the family, I was quite shocked to learn that Lisa had been hospitalized in a local general hospital without their consulting me. Fortunately, there were two factors working strongly in my favor—First, the case was clearly going to be difficult, so that the psychiatrist had no interest in continuing with the girl and her family in therapy. Second, the hospital was eager to have the girl transferred to a different hospital which had a psychiatric unit; and arranging this transfer was proving, for the psychiatrist, to be an extremely difficult and time-consuming task.

The situation clearly had the potential for developing into a major power struggle between the psychiatrist and me, with me at a distinct disadvantage in several respects: (1) The parents were still angry at me. (2) The patient felt abandoned by me and that the hospitalization was my fault. (3) She was now the psychiatrist's patient in a general hospital where I had no staff privileges. Clearly it was pointless to oppose the current plan in an open confrontation; more strategic methods therefore seemed necessary.

I apologized profusely all around and expressed my gratitude that the psychiatrist had been available to pick up the pieces. I repeatedly emphasized how much time and effort the psychiatrist had already invested and how much more would be required; I labeled this as particularly praiseworthy, since the psychiatrist would not be keeping the case in treatment. To the patient and her parents, I exposed the prospect of lengthy and expensive inpatient treatment, as well as their having to start all over with yet another therapist. I voiced no opposition to this plan, but began gently to suggest that I might be able to arrange her transfer to a hospital where I was a consultant. Not only was this preferable from the standpoint of continuity of care, but it also relieved the psychiatrist of a considerable amount of unrewarding legwork. The plan met with everyone's approval, and I was transformed from scapegoat to "hero."

While the hospitalization was easily arranged, the problems were, by no means, over. It was unusual at the hospital for an outside psychologist to be allowed to remain directly involved in an inpatient case as the primary therapist and decision-maker. It was possible in this case because of my reputation and my status as faculty member and consultant at the hospital—a situation that possibly brought with it unrealistic expectations! Also, the author's decision to include a staff member as co-therapist[2] added the probability of resentment for her involvement, because she had direct access to the outside

---

[2]The co-therapist, Sandra Rigazio-DiGilio, was very helpful in preparing this case example.

consultant (me) not typically available to the inpatient staff. It was likely not only that the unrealistic expectations would be disappointed, but also that the resentment would surface and lead to problems with the team psychiatrist, medical specialists, and nursing staff.

Deliberate efforts were made to scale down the expectations regarding hospitalization by having the female co-therapist (the most accessible of the co-therapy team) take a deliberate one-down stance. This stance was also utilized with Lisa to keep her from taking advantage of her relationship with the female therapist (who saw her individually), and from manipulating the direct-care staff on the unit. Some of the specific strategies employed will be discussed in later sections of the chapter.

Integrating Individual Therapy with Family Therapy

Although many family therapists write as though individual psychotherapy and family therapy are irreconcilable, this has not been the author's experience. Combining these two modalities is not only possible but often quite desirable, although the combination can definitely create major problems in case coordination. Combining the two is probably more common than has been usually acknowledged; for example, in my cases in *Psychosomatic Families* (Minuchin et al., 1978), individual sessions with the IP were quite common. This practice is not uncommon with other structurally oriented family therapists, who often use individual sessions to achieve purposes such as boundary-making.

The inclusion of individual sessions (or parts of sessions) with the IP has multiple advantages. Usually parents and other family members (as well as other professionals) expect such a focus. I have noted (Todd, 1981), it is unlikely that an individual's symptom as severe as anorexia can easily be dismissed and relabeled solely a "family problem." Including individual sessions can reduce the tendency for power struggles with the parents over the issue, and can have similar effects with the IP, who is more likely to feel, after individual contacts, that the therapist is sympathetic.

Seeing the IP individually can also be an important move toward individuation. The author's typical practice is to agree to see her individually, not because she is the "patient," but because she is becoming an independent young adult who will undoubtedly have things she will want to discuss alone. Often the content of the individual sessions is less important than the structure. In one family, for example, it was clear that I was the first male whom the parents had allowed to have any private time with the patient. (She had become anorectic when she began to be interested in dating.) While the therapist was clearly regarded as "safe" by the parents, the sexual overtones were not lost on any of the participants. A particularly blatant example was a crisis call by the patient to me at home; the "crisis" concerned trying on a new bikini!

The classic use, in anorexia cases, of individual sessions is to remove the issue of weight from the family arena. Such individual sessions are useful: (1) after significant weight gain has been achieved in a family context; and (2) when the treatment has reached a point where the therapist fears progress may be eroded if the girl reengages her parents in nagging and fighting with her about eating. At such a point, it is appropriate for therapist and patient to make an individual contract to exclude the parents from these issues. Typically, it seems that parents allow the contract because they are reassured to have someone take charge of, and put limits on, their daughter. This step of developing an individual contract with the patient is premature if it's done before there has been a breakthrough in the usual pattern of family interaction; establishing such a contract too early can set the therapist up for taking over the role of the parents and inheriting all the power struggles that belong more appropriately to them.

The significance of individual sessions for boundary-making should not be underestimated. As noted above, the families of anorectics prohibit any stable relationship between two family members; instead, some other family member can be counted upon to intrude and interrupt. Enmeshment is such a pervasive characteristic in these families that the therapist should not count on the teenager being aware of such intrusions and lack of privacy; if necessary, the therapist must be prepared to take the lead in making an issue of privacy.

Maria, age nine, became anorectic shortly after her oldest sister Nancy entered puberty and became increasingly attractive sexually, altering Nancy's intense relationship with her father. At a middle stage in treatment, the therapist raised the issue of what changes there had been in the family as Nancy had started to become a teenager. Discussion revealed many of the classic examples of intrusion throughout the family, with Maria a prime offender. Maria spied on Nancy in the shower, listened in on her telephone conversations, read her diary, etc. Nor was the therapist surprised to learn that the doorknob on Nancy's door had been removed and somehow never been replaced, leaving a large peephole and preventing her from closing out family members. Neither Nancy nor her parents expressed any concern over this pattern; Nancy began to protest only after the therapist made an issue of the lack of privacy and gave her considerable support. Following this, the parents began to keep Maria from intruding on Nancy; mysteriously, it suddenly became possible to replace her doorknob, as well.

Combining Cognitive Behavior Therapy and Family Therapy

Individual treatment can far transcend its use for individuation and boundary-making. A particularly promising combination seems to be that of family therapy and cognitive behavior therapy. A few years ago, I began incorporating elements of cognitive behavior therapy (Beck, 1976) into an overall treatment plan for eating disorders. A similar development seems to have been occurring simultaneously at several other centers, the best published example being the work of Garner and Bemis (1982). This development should not be surprising, since distorted body image and other thought distortions have long been recognized—by Bruch (1973, 1977, 1978) and by Crisp and associates (Ben-Tovim, Hunter, & Crisp, 1977; Crisp & Fransella,

1972)—as important components in the clinical picture of anorexia and other eating problems.

Garner and Bemis (1982) have used the categories of cognitive distortion originally proposed by Beck (1976) to identify patterns characteristic of patients with eating disorders, especially concerning topics such as eating and weight:

(1) *Selective abstraction*. A conclusion is based on isolated details without considering contradictory evidence, as in: "The only way I can be in control is through eating."

(2) *Overgeneralization*. A rule is developed based on a single event and then assumed to be applicable to other—not necessarily similar—situations, which are for example: "I used to be of normal weight, and I wasn't happy. So I *know* gaining weight isn't going to make me feel better."

(3) *Magnification*. The prediction of undesirable consequences is overestimated, such as: "Gaining five pounds would push me over the limit."

(4) *All-or-none reasoning*. The categories of thinking are black and white—extreme and absolute, for example: "If I'm not in complete control, I lose all control. If I can't master this area of my life, I'll lose everything."

(5) *Personalization*. Events are given an exaggerated interpretation of self-reference, such as: "Two people laughed and whispered something to each other when I walked by. They were probably saying that I looked unattractive. I *have* gained three pounds."

(6) *Superstitious thinking*. Cause-and-effect relationships are attributed to non-contingent events, such as: "If I eat a sweet, it will be converted instantly into stomach fat."

These principles have been used by the author with clinical success, particularly in the treatment of bulimia. With anorectics, it is a mistake to attempt to apply them in individual therapy until later in treatment, after the first stage of massive denial (of the weight problem) has been overcome. With all patients, it is important to avoid lecturing or proselytizing. The goal of the therapist is to bring thoughts about eating, weight, etc., and underlying assumptions into conscious awareness so that the patient can evaluate their accuracy. With most patients, but especially with anorectics and bulimics, it is usually ineffective

(Beck, 1976) to argue strongly about the distorted quality of thinking; such efforts will probably meet with strong resistance.

It may not be intuitively obvious that cognitive behavior therapy can or should be combined with family therapy. Additional case material regarding Lisa provides a graphic illustration of the inevitable link between the two.

> After Lisa was discharged from the hospital, I began working with her individually to overcome her black-and-white thinking. During this time she was staying with an aunt, who described to the therapist the kinds of pressures the patient was receiving from her parents to make choices they framed as extreme, all-or-nothing alternatives. In reference to her niece's tendency to think in polarities, the aunt noted, "After all, she comes by it [this thinking style] honestly." In treatment, the cognitive therapy for Lisa was combined with direct efforts to reduce the all-or-nothing pressure from the parents.

It might seem self-defeating, or at least unnecessarily self-limiting, for the therapist to work exclusively on a cognitive level when the interpersonal (family) context repeatedly reinforces such distortions. On the other hand, it often seems that cognitive distortions tend to persist even after interpersonal patterns have been altered, so that cognitive therapy can be an extremely useful adjunct to family treatment.

Just as the anorectic's polarized thinking reflects her family's, so does her belief system. White (1983) describes the anorectic family as having a system of rigid and implicit beliefs, transmitted from one generation to the next and restricting the choices available to family members. These include both general beliefs, and specific expectations about the role of women. Loyalty is highly valued and maintained through the "currency of guilt." There is also a belief in "insightfulness," which is akin to the mind-reading noted by the Minuchin group (Minuchin, et al., 1978), in which family members believe they can see into each other and know the true motivations and intentions.

White attempts to expose these beliefs, without arousing unnecessary resistance, by employing a strategic approach. He describes to the family how mechanisms such as the "currency of guilt" operate, continuing across generations, but he does not do this in an interpretive manner. Instead, he validates the compelling nature of these transactions and predicts that the family members will have extreme difficulty in breaking out of these patterns, even questioning whether it is wise to do so.

Elements of cognitive therapy can also be used effectively by members of the inpatient ward staff. It was noted earlier that formal cognitive therapy for the anorexic is premature in the early stages of treatment when it is so difficult to establish a working relationship in individual therapy. During these early stages, the inpatient staff can be extremely useful in overcoming cognitive distortions and breaking through denial. Inpatient staff should be systematically coached in providing reality-oriented feedback to the anorectic. If she looks awful, she can be told so in a matter-of-fact manner. Her emaciated appearance, straggly hair, etc., should not be ignored, since ignoring it would fit into the existing pattern of denial; neither should it be harped on in a nagging fashion, which would allow the patient to resist and thus escape responsibility.

ALTERNATIVE MODELS OF DIVIDING CASE RESPONSIBILITY

Combining individual and family therapy creates several possible ways to divide up case responsibility. These models, each of which has its advocates, include the solo therapist model, where one therapist conducts all of the treatment; the split treatment model, in which responsibility for individual therapy and family therapy rests with different therapists; and the strategic team model. Each has its advantages and pitfalls and may be most appropriate for a particular context.

In the solo therapist model, the model I most frequently employ in my outpatient practice, the same therapist treats the family, the IP, and any other subsystems (such as the parental couple). Often a session will be split, with part devoted to individual work with the IP or to some sub-system. Working solo makes it easy to vary the mixture of individual and family sessions strategically; the same is true of the time allotted each modality. For example, early in treatment with an anorectic, it is unlikely that individual sessions will be very productive. They can therefore be kept quite brief and serve an almost purely symbolic purpose. At later points in therapy, the situation may be reversed, with a brief part of the session to "check in" with parents, and most of the work done individually.

When there is more than one therapist, there are several possible ways in which responsibility can be shared and divided. For example, Whitaker and his colleagues (Stern et al., 1981) conduct as much of the clinical work as possible as a team. However, there is one model of inpatient collaboration that I have found particularly consistent with my overall treatment approach. One therapist, who typically comes from the inpatient team, works individually with the patient. A second therapist (the outpatient therapist, where relevant) has primary responsibility for the family sessions. During inpatient hospitalization, both therapists are present at family sessions. Their mutual presence allows both family therapist and parents to be "outsiders" with respect to inpatient treatment but offsets the "inside" knowledge of the individual therapist and his/her tendency to side with the IP.

When the two models are compared, the most immediate source of appeal of the solo treatment model is its simplicity and efficiency. Treatment can be conducted with a minimum of need for continuous coordination with other colleagues. Working solo is particularly consistent with a structural approach, as Haley (1976, p. 16) has noted. The solo therapist can also allocate his/her time flexibly, as noted above, spending more time in family sessions early in treatment and gradually devoting an increasing amount of time to individual work. And, when done skillfully, the solo therapist can provide a useful model of combining support with firmness and balancing a concern for the needs of the family with those of the individual.

There are also potentially significant disadvantages. The attempts at evenhandedness on the part of the therapist may leave both family and IP, particularly the IP, feeling inadequately supported. Many therapists feel the burden of responsibility is too much for a single therapist to bear alone, particularly if the symptoms are extremely life-threatening. This potential for over-responsibility is probably the biggest single trap in the solo model.

Working with more than one therapist offers the clear advantage of the greater objectivity afforded by multiple perspectives. Responsibility is clearly shared, which can help prevent the therapists from being overwhelmed. A male-female team can model the successful handling of gender-related issues, which tend to be paramount in these families. For example, the team can model shared decision-making instead of male dominance and female passivity.

Often the inpatient treatment program requires too much work for any single therapist, especially if that therapist works primarily in an outpatient context. Splitting responsibility can allow the outpatient therapist to continue with the case even during the inpatient phase. Under the solo therapist model, this is usually possible only if hospitalization is brief.

One of the biggest dangers of using two therapists is that the team will be split by the skillful manipulation of the IP. Even if the conflictual issues do not reach a "toxic" level, there is still the possibility that the team will become polarized into relatively rigid and stereotyped roles—for example, one therapist typically siding with the anorectic and the other therapist siding with the parents.

The case of Lisa offers an intriguing example of the creative use of a two-therapist team to defuse the issue of weight and eating. Individual therapy was designated as the place where the issue of eating would be handled. As mentioned earlier, this has the inherent danger of taking power away from the parents and deemphasizing the importance of family sessions. The individual therapist deliberately emphasized her one-down stance by eating constantly in the individual sessions and whenever the patient saw her on the unit. This made it impossible for Lisa to view the therapist as a powerful expert, particularly in the area of eating. The culmination of this strategy was a session in which the therapist brought in three of Lisa's favorite binge foods and chided Lisa for introducing her to such attractive new foods. Halfway through the session, Lisa exclaimed, "Will you stop eating!" The therapist (apparently) tried to control herself, but kept sneaking bites during the session. Eventually she had to excuse herself and returned with her package of Lorna Doones empty. Lisa seemed to recognize this interchange on some level as playful, but she could not be sure.

The one-down strategy was extremely successful on several levels: (1) Lisa was prevented from manipulating the individual therapist. (2) Similarly, since the individual therapist was "powerless," Lisa did not try to use her to manipulate the inpatient staff. (3) In family sessions, the individual therapist functioned as a naughty and powerless sibling, frequently whispering with Lisa. In this way, it was possible to support Lisa without the parents being overpowered.

The final model of collaboration is the strategic team. This model has been used successfully by many therapists, including myself, for cases involving eating disorders (Bartholomew, 1984; Caillé, et al., 1977; Harkaway, 1983b; Moley, 1983). As typically employed, in this model one or two therapists in the room conduct the family session, while other team members watch through a one-way mirror and send in messages during the session. The model has many variations, from the neutral style of the Milan team (Selvini Palazzoli, Boscolo, et al., 1980) to the consistent use of paradox (Todd, 1981), with most practitioners falling between the two extremes (Papp, 1980). A common feature of most applications is the use of a final intervention devised by the whole team and delivered at the end of the session.

As noted previously, it is the author's contention that this model, especially in its most paradoxical variations, should be used only under carefully selected conditions. Strategic therapy can be useful when the system is ultra-stable and the symptoms, not life-threatening. Under such circumstances the paradoxical prescription of

the behavior of the IP and the family can be extremely effective in destabilizing the system. When the patient is in danger and may require hospitalization, however, it is dangerous and inappropriate to maintain an attitude of neutrality and nonintervention, as the Milan model advocates. Such situations require a model that allows direct intervention, which may include crisis-induction methods or the use of hospitalization.

During inpatient treatment it is also difficult to maintain a stance of neutrality and nonintervention, especially if the team members are affiliated with the hospital. It is difficult to utilize techniques such as warning of the dangers of change, and positively relabeling and prescribing the symptom, if the strategic team also has responsibility for decisions such as inpatient privileges, medication, and discharge. For example, a strategic team might caution a bulimic not to give up vomiting too quickly or might question whether she should assert herself. It is obviously difficult for those same therapists to assign the patient to an educational program on the medical consequences of vomiting or to an assertiveness group. For such reasons, strategic techniques are more effective when the strategic team can be insulated from other components of the inpatient treatment.

Strategic therapists who utilize elaborate final-interventions believe that such interventions work best with a relatively long interval between sessions (Selvini Palazzoli, 1980; Todd, 1981), and when the family is forced to deal with such interventions without making contact with other helpers between sessions. None of these conditions are easily achieved in inpatient programs, which emphasize short time-frames, and the intensive involvement of many therapists.

There are advantages to the strategic team model, however, even for inpatient cases. The primary attraction is the use of the one-way mirror, which allows some team members to remain comparatively insulated from the pressures inside the therapy room. This position gives the observers greater objectivity, allows them to offer interventions that would be difficult to suggest from inside, and enables them to avoid power struggles with the family. The clearest disadvantage is that of cost, since the strategic team often uses four to six person-hours per session.

The Relationship Between the Family and Other Systems

On both a family level and an individual level, it is almost invariably true that psychosomatic families and the patients themselves are extremely isolated in their connections outside the family. It is important to stress that the primary issue is the *quality* of relationships, not the quantity. From a quantitative standpoint, the family contacts of anorectic families may be misleading, since both parents and anorectics often have a multitude of outside relationships and activities. On closer examination, however, these relationships are typically performance-oriented and invariably experienced as rather empty. The parents are usually extremely child-focused, with most activities being community and church-related and revolving around their children. Other activities may be charitable in nature. What is rare is for an activity to be purely pleasurable and self-centered.

RELATIONSHIP TO THE FAMILY LIFE CYCLE

In view of the difficulties in allowing outside relationships, it is not surprising that psychosomatic families have particular difficulty with the life-cycle stages of adolescent autonomy and leaving home. Anorexia nervosa typically emerges during the stage of beginning independence, as these girls begin to move outside the family, particularly to form heterosexual relationships. While the stage of adolescent autonomy is difficult for these families, the stage of leaving home is actually the "acid test" of releasing the child from a constraining role. Steps toward autonomy, such as holding a job and having a boyfriend, are important, but these are nowhere near as stressful as the actual act of leaving home. I have

made it routine practice to consider therapy incomplete until the IP goes off to college or leaves home. While it is not always possible to continue formal therapy until this point, my expectation is conveyed to the family, and some contact is maintained with them until it is clear that the patient is "home free."

In order to negotiate this stage successfully, both IP and parents must begin to establish outside relationships that are qualitatively different from previous ones. The IP need to begin to establish relationships and engage in activities less governed by "shoulds." She will also feel much freer to do this as she sees her parents receiving more satisfaction from outside relationships and depending less on indirect satisfaction through her. Often a key ingredient appears to be the decision of the mother to resume or initiate a career or job outside the home, instead of submerging her needs in favor of the roles of mother, wife and daughter.

> Sally, age eighteen, appeared to be a highly successful and popular student upon graduation from high school. In her first semester of college, she revealed to her parents that she had been vomiting secretly for several years. She dropped out of college, returned home, and discontinued all her outside activities, which she had previously pursued in a driven fashion. She felt that these steps were necessary in order for her to understand clearly which activities she genuinely enjoyed and pursued voluntarily, and which she felt obliged to continue. Her parents were instrumental in giving her permission to do this and in showing her that they had other satisfactions besides her accomplishments. As she regained her confidence and began to make concrete steps toward independence, they endorsed these changes as healthy. Eventually she was able to feel that she chose activities voluntarily and derived much more satisfaction from them.

THE ISSUE OF SKILLS

It is important for the therapist to evaluate the degree to which the IP actually possesses the requisite social skills needed to form satisfactory outside relationships. In the most dysfunctional cases of eating disorders, the IP may totally lack these skills; this is particularly likely to be true in cases with an extensive history of psychosomatic illness, school avoidance, etc. In other cases, the skills are definitely present and merely need to be unblocked. In such cases, the girl needs to receive parental permission to proceed; in addition, she may need to "go backward," as in the case mentioned above, in order to experience outside activities as voluntary.

Cases in which the IP lacks the necessary social skills require the most painstaking therapeutic effort. When these deficits are extreme, the patients may be good candidates for day treatment programs or other intensive socially oriented programs. In cases with such deficits, it will usually be necessary for the therapist to take an active role in devising a gradual series of learning experiences for the patient. The family—parents and more socially adept siblings—can play an important educational and supportive role in this endeavor. This has the twin advantages of removing pressure from the therapist to devise and monitor these activities, and also of ensuring that the family is consistently giving the IP permission to move in this direction.

INVOLVING THE PARENTS IN SYSTEMS BEYOND THE FAMILY

As mentioned before, the success in getting the parents to engage in meaningful relationships outside the family is a critical factor in the successful resolution of eating disorders. This can be particularly problematic with mothers, who have often immersed themselves in a care-taking role, while living vicariously through their daughters. Real independence for the daughter is difficult to achieve unless these two factors are diminished. Unfortunately the therapist is asking the mother to do the one thing that she consistently finds most difficult, namely to put her own needs first.

For this reason, it is often useful as a first step to make strategic use of the child-focused nature of these families. For example, it is often possible to persuade the mother to do something to help her daughter, even though it may be difficult to mo-

tivate the mother to do something for herself. For instance, if her daughter has difficulty making friends or finding outside activities, the mother may be asked to do some of the preliminary research on possibilities. This assignment will require her to make outside contacts, which can ultimately be used as bridges to forming relationships on her own behalf.

Similarly, the therapist may strategically "blackmail" parents into finding activities they can enjoy as a couple. S/he can join with them in their stated belief that they have a healthy marriage. Whether or not the IP expresses doubts about the healthy marriage, the therapist can portray the IP as needing concrete reassurance by observing parents as they enjoy activities together (Mirkin, 1983). It is probably not important whether they actually enjoy these activities, so much as it is important that they both give the daughter the *message* that they are enjoying them. In this respect, the technique is similar to the "ritualized prescription" being used by Selvini-Palazzoli and Prata, in which parents are given the secret instruction to disappear together mysteriously; what they do is not as important as maintaining the shared secret from the children.

DEALING WITH THE EXTENDED FAMILY

At times the above material may seem to imply that all eating problems begin with the parents. If so, this is an unfortunate result of oversimplification. While it is true that therapy conducted according to the principles outlined above can often succeed with little or no involvement of the extended family, this should not be taken to imply that the parents are the cause of the difficulties. It is doubly important for the therapist to avoid such an implication, since the parents often already feel that they are to blame, even though the guilt is originally masked by denial.

There are usually strong parallels between what is occurring in the nuclear family and the patterns in both families of origin. Whether or not it will be necessary or useful to deal with such parallel issues depends on the particulars of the case (and, of course, on the biases of the therapist.) When there is extreme evidence of intrusiveness from the extended family, it is generally necessary to deal with extended-family issues, usually by getting the parents to set boundaries more effectively. Even when extended-family issues could be avoided, addressing these issues may speed up therapy and reduce the scapegoating of the IP. White (1983) offers a case example in which mother is led to deal with an issue strikingly similar to one of the primary difficulties of the IP. She attempts an "experiment" to free herself from the sense of obligation and guilt experienced when dealing with her own mother. Her success appears to be a helpful example to her daughter of being less governed by obligation and guilt.

THE PROBLEM OF OTHER HELPERS

Often a family therapist inherits an eating-disorders case in which patient and family are entangled in a web of well-meaning helping agencies. As is true with many psychosomatic disorders, these patients have often missed considerable amounts of school and managed to elicit the sympathy of an impressive array of school personnel, truant officers, social workers, etc. The inertia of these helping efforts can become a severe problem when a patient who has recovered in dramatic fashion is still faced with helpers who view her as sick or disabled. Getting such helpers to "back off" can be a difficult task for the therapist, yet an important one. It is often also helpful to anticipate that many people the girl encounters will treat her as sick or fragile, and to rehearse with her and her family how to deal with such encounters.

PROSPECTS FOR THE FUTURE

As mentioned at the outset, this chapter should in no way be regarded as a finished product. While the systemic framework seems to provide a powerful means of organizing the treatment of adolescents with eating disorders, so far the potential of this model has not been fully realized. That it has not been realized is probably inevitable at the present time, because the field of family therapy, like the field of psychotherapy itself, is only beginning to emerge from a period of myopia in which each therapeutic method is touted as a panacea. New and promising techniques for the treatment of eating disorders are developing rapidly in diverse fields, including family therapy, behavior therapy, psychodynamic psychotherapy, chemotherapy, and inpatient treatment. Unfortunately, because the field is so politicized and because so few practitioners even read the publications of the other "camps," efforts at integration are rare. I can only acknowledge my own limited vision and hope that this chapter may stimulate others to develop a still more inclusive model of treatment.

REFERENCES

Bartholomew, K. L. I would eat for her if I could. *Journal of Strategic and Systemic Therapies*, 1984, **3**(1), 57–65.

Beck, A. T. *Cognitive therapy and the emotional disorders*. New York: International Universities Press, 1976.

Benjamin, M. General systems theory, family systems theories, and family therapy: Toward an integrated model of family process. In A. Bross (Ed.), *Family therapy: Principles of strategic practice*. New York: Guilford, 1982.

Ben-Tovim, D. I., Hunter, M., & Crisp, A. H. Discrimination and evaluation of shape and size in anorexia nervosa: An exploratory study. *Research Communications in Psychology, Psychiatry and Behavior*, 1977, **2**, 241–257.

Blinder, B. J., Freeman, D. M., & Stunkard, A. J. Behavior therapy of anorexia nervosa: Effectiveness of activity as a reinforcer of weight gain. *American Journal of Psychiatry*, 1970, **126**, 1093–1098.

Bruch, H. *Eating Disorders: Obesity, anorexia, and the person within*. New York: Basic Books, 1973.

Bruch, H. Perils of behavior modification in treatment of anorexia nervosa. *Journal of the American Medical Association*, 1974, **230**(10), 1419–1422.

Bruch, H. Psychological antecedents of anorexia

nervosa. In R. A. Vigersky (Ed.), *Anorexia nervosa*. New York: Raven, 1977.

Bruch, H. *The golden cage*. Cambridge: Harvard University Press, 1978.

Bruch, H., & Touraine, G. Obesity in childhood, Part 5: The family frame of obese children. *Psychosomatic Medicine*, 1940, **2**, 141–206.

Caillé, P., Abrahamson, P., Girolami, C., & Sørbye, B. A systems theory approach to a case of anorexia nervosa. *Family Process*, 1977, **16**, 455–465.

Carter, E. A., & McGoldrick, M. *The family life cycle: A framework for family therapy*. New York: Gardner Press, 1980.

Crisp, A. H., & Fransella, K. Conceptual changes during recovery from anorexia nervosa. *British Journal of Medical Psychology*, 1972, **45**, 395–405.

De Shazer, S. *Patterns of brief therapy: An ecosystemic approach*. New York: Guilford, 1982.

Garfinkel, P. E., & Garner, D. M. *Anorexia nervosa: A multidimensional perspective*. New York: Brunner/Mazel, 1982.

Garner, D. M., & Bemis, K. M. A cognitive-behavioral approach to anorexia nervosa. *Cognitive Therapy and Research*, 1982, **6**, 1–27.

Haley, J. *Uncommon therapy: The psychiatric techniques of Milton H. Erickson, M.D.* New York: Norton, 1973.

Haley, J. *Problem-solving therapy*. San Francisco: Jossey-Bass, 1976.

Haley, J. *Leaving home: Therapy with disturbed young people*. New York: McGraw-Hill, 1980.

Harkaway, J. E. Obesity: A family systems perspective. Workshop presented at the Annual Conference of the American Association for Marriage & Family Therapy, Washington, DC, 1983a.

Harkaway, J. E. Obesity: Reducing the larger system. *Journal of Strategic and Systemic Therapy*, 1983b, **2**(3), 2–14.

Hoffman, L. *Foundations of family therapy: A conceptual framework for systems change*. New York: Basic Books, 1981.

Hoffman, L. A co-evolutionary framework for systemic family therapy. In B. P. Keeney (Ed.), *Diagnosis and assessment in family therapy*. Rockville, MD: Aspen Systems Corporation, 1983.

Liebman, R., Minuchin, S., & Baker, L. An integrated treatment program for anorexia nervosa. *American Journal of Psychiatry*, 1974a, **131**(4), 432–436.

Liebman, R., Minuchin, S., & Baker, L. The role of the family in the treatment of anorexia nervosa. *Journal of the American Academy of Child Psychiatry*, 1974b, **13**(2), 264–274.

Minuchin, S. *Families and family therapy*. Cambridge: Harvard University Press, 1974.

Minuchin, S. *Anorexia is a Greek word*. Boston: Boston Family Institute, 1982.

Minuchin, S., Baker, L., Rosman, B., Liebman, R., Milman, L., & Todd, T. A conceptual model of psychosomatic illness in children: Family organization and family therapy. *Archives of General Psychiatry*, 1975, **32**, 1031–1038.

Minuchin, S., & Barcai, A. Therapeutically induced family crisis. In *Science and psychoanalysis* (Vol. 14). New York: Grune & Stratton, 1969.

Minuchin, S., & Fishman, H. C. *Family therapy techniques*. Cambridge: Harvard University Press, 1981.

Minuchin, S., Montalvo, B., Guerney, B. G., Rosman, B. L., & Schumer, F. *Families of the slums: An exploration of their structure and treatment*. New York: Basic Books, 1967.

Minuchin, S., Rosman, B., & Baker, L. *Psychosomatic families*. Cambridge: Harvard University Press, 1978.

Mirkin, M. P. The Peter Pan syndrome. *International Journal of Family Therapy*, 1983, **5**(3), 289–295.

Moley, V. Interactional treatment of eating disorders. *Journal of Strategic and Systemic Therapies*, 1983, **2**(4), 10–28.

Papp, D. The Greek chorus and other techniques of family therapy. *Family Process*, 1980, **19**, 45–57.

Pertshuk, M. J. Behavior therapy: Extended follow-up. In R. A. Vigersky (Ed.), *Anorexia nervosa*. New York: Raven, 1977.

Rosman, B., Minuchin, S., & Baker, L. Family lunch session: An introduction to family therapy in anorexia nervosa. *American Journal of Orthopsychiatry*, 1975, **45**(5), 846–853.

Selvini Palazzoli, M. *Self-starvation: From individual to family therapy in the treatment of anorexia nervosa*. New York: Jason Aronson, 1974.

Selvini Palazzoli, M. Why a long interval between sessions? The therapeutic control of the family-therapist supra-system. In M. Andolfi, & I. Zwerling (Eds.), *Dimensions of family therapy*. New York: Guilford, 1980.

Selvini Palazzoli, M., & Prata, G. Snares in family therapy. *Journal of Marital and Family Therapy*, 1982, **8**, 443–450.

Selvini Palazzoli, M., Boscolo, L., Cecchin, G., & Prata, G. A ritualized prescription in family therapy: Odd days and even days. *Journal of Marriage and Family Counseling*, 1978, **4**(3), 3–9.

Selvini Palazzoli, M., Boscolo, L., Cecchin, G., & Prata, G. Hypothesizing—circularity—neutrality: Three guidelines for the conductor of the session. *Family Process*, 1980, **19**, 3–12.

Selvini Palazzoli, M., Cecchin, G., Prata, G., & Boscolo, L. *Paradox and counterparadox: A new model of the family in schizophrenic transaction*. New York: Jason Aronson, 1978.

Stanton, M. D. An integrated structural/strategic approach to family therapy. *Journal of Marital and Family Therapy*, 1981a, **7**, 427–439.

Stanton, M. D. Marital therapy from a structural/strategic viewpoint. In G. P. Sholevar (Ed.), *The handbook of marriage and marital therapy*. New York: SP Medical & Scientific Books, 1981b.

Stanton, M. D., & Todd, T. C. Integrating structural and strategic therapy. Workshop presented at the Philadelphia Child Guidance Clinic, 1982.

Stern, S., Whitaker, C., Hagemann, N., Anderson, R., & Bargman, G. Anorexia nervosa: The hospital's role in family treatment. *Family Process*, 1981, **20**, 395–408.

Todd, T. C. Paradoxical prescriptions: Applications of consistent paradox using a strategic team. *Journal of Strategic and Systemic Therapy*, 1981, **1**, 28–44.

Todd, T. C. Structural and strategic therapy: The case for integration. Paper presented at the national meeting of the American Association for Marriage and Family Therapy, Washington, D.C., 1983.

Tomm, K. One perspective on the Milan systemic approach: Pt. 1. Overview of development, theory and practice. *Journal of Marital and Family Therapy*, 1984, **2**, 113–125.

White, M. Anorexia nervosa: A transgenerational system perspective. *Family Process*, 1983, **22**, 255–273.

15

Adolescent Substance Abusers and Family Therapy

EDWARD KAUFMAN, M.D.

Adolescent substance abuse has reached every geographical area and social class in our country. It is therefore essential that this phenomenon be understood and that an approach be developed to cope with the problem (Kaufman, 1976).

Not only is adolescent substance abuse spreading, but it is occurring earlier and earlier, with onset in the latency period as well as in early adolescence. In every situation in which there is an adolescent drug abuser, there is a profound effect on the family. The majority of past investigations into the relationship of adolescent substance abuse to family function have focused on parental dysfunction and how it leads to substance abuse in children. Recently, however, we have begun to look at the reciprocal patterns in families. We have found that the most appropriate focus is on how substance abuse affects the entire family and how the entire family affects substance abuse. Adolescent substance abuse serves an important function in every family in which it occurs. These functions, which will be discussed in detail, range from keeping parents together to distancing them to a point of separation

and divorce. When substance abuse occurs, the family develops new relationships and role assignments which constitute a new homeostasis that tends to perpetuate itself and to resist change. This reciprocal involvement of the family in the adolescent's substance abuse makes it essential that family therapy become an integral part of intervention with these problems.

EARLY FAMILY SYSTEM REACTIONS TO ADOLESCENT SUBSTANCE ABUSE

Substance abuse and related behavioral problems frequently begin upon entry into junior high school when the child first becomes seriously vulnerable to substance abuse. Drug-abusing adolescents generally refuse to follow parental rules for behavior at home (Hendin et al., 1981). They associate with individuals whom their parents consider bad influences and bring them into the house. They come home just sufficiently later than curfews and without calling in a way that infuriates their parents

245

(Hendin et al., 1981). They drive the family car without permission and frequently get traffic citations which they can't afford to pay and which require parental court appearances. They are constantly in trouble at school, particularly through tardiness, absence, not paying attention, and unruly behavior, yet they develop a multiplicity of ways for intercepting messages from school to parents. Shoplifting as well as theft from and damage to friends' homes are also common and the adolescents may either conceal or flaunt these activities. Parents are lied to about needs for funds that are diverted to drugs and when these lies are discovered, parents are coerced into continuing to provide funds by threats of violence from debtors or of commission of crimes, and through promises of protection from incarceration. They continue to drink and to use drugs at home after they've been prohibited from doing so even with legal reinforcement. They lie about their substance abuse and destructive behavior and the lies themselves frequently become a major concern to parents. They also engage parents in frequent power struggles about whether they are high or have used drugs.

This type of defiance leads many parents to feel they have totally lost control of their children. Some parents respond by attempting to abnegate responsibility altogether but find it impossible to maintain a detached state because the adolescent still manages to draw them into their problematic behavior even after they have moved out of the parents' house. Other parents respond by becoming extremely controlling and limiting (Hendin et al., 1981), at times to a point where the child is totally grounded and has lost all privileges. The child then still manages to act out and the parents feel powerless because they feel they have no means left to enforce structure and control. At such times parents may resort to physical brutality and violence, which only serves to escalate defiance, adolescent substance abuse, and other self-destructive behaviors. In these cases, parents frequently become totally preoccupied with the adolescent's behavior and their own inability to contain it,

causing a great deal of parental anguish and suffering. Their concern for their adolescent child may create distances between the spouses, which may function as a needed buffer or may create painful sexual and emotional withdrawal. Many of these patterns are seen in families with defiant or antisocial adolescents, even when there is no substance abuse. However, these patterns of family interaction are rare without some drug or alcohol abuse, as this abuse is consistently a part of teenage defiance and causes cycles of increasing antisocial behavior.

In some families there may be an extended period of years in which the adolescent's drug use and other problems are consistently denied, even in the face of overwhelming evidence. Even these families may shift to overinvolvement when the drug abuse is discovered. In later stages families may attempt to totally abandon the adolescent emotionally; the abandonment, however, is only partial and enmeshment will be reactivated by extreme crisis.

FAMILY REACTIONS TO SEVERE AND PROLONGED ADOLESCENT SUBSTANCE ABUSE

The family system frequently revolves around the drug abuser as a scapegoat upon whom all intrafamilial problems are focused. Often, the family's basic interactional pattern is dull and lifeless and only becomes alive when it is mobilized to deal with the crisis of drug abuse (Reilly, 1976). At times the adolescent's difficulties keep conflictual parents together or are an attempt to reunite separated parents. Guilt is a frequent currency of manipulation and may be induced by the drug abuser to coerce the family into continued financial and emotional support of drug use, or by parents to curb individuation (Kaufman & Kaufmann, 1979). Many mothers have severe depression, anxiety, or psychosomatic symptoms that are blamed on the Identified Patient (IP), thereby reinforcing the pattern of guilt and mutual manipulation. Mother's drug and alcohol abuse and suicide attempts are also blamed on the adolescent substance abuser (Kaufman & Kaufmann, 1979).

Physical expressions of love and affection are either absent or used to deny and obliterate individuation or conflict. Anger about interpersonal conflicts is not expressed directly unless it erupts in explosive violence. Anger about drug use and denial of it is expressed quite frequently and is almost always counterproductive. All joy has disappeared in these families, as lives are totally taken up with the sufferings and entanglements of having a substance-abusing child. In many cases, however, the joylessness preceded the addiction. As Reilly (1976) noted, communication is most frequently negative and there is no appropriate praise for good behavior. There is a lack of consistent limit setting by parents in which deviance may be punished or rewarded at different times (Fort, 1954).

Adolescent substance abuse is frequently an expression of defiance which actually leads to infantilization and continuing intense family ties, albeit conflictual ones. These families frequently undergo pseudoindividuations through institutionalizations, runaways with crises which result in brief reunions, and scrapes with authorities which result in incarcerations or parental bail-out. Thus, although the drug-abusing adolescent may be hundreds of miles from home, his or her behavior continues to affect and be affected deeply by parental ties.

The role of siblings of drug abusers has been consistently overlooked. In my own studies (Kaufman, 1977), siblings tend to fall equally into two basic categories: the very good and the very bad. The "bad" group is composed of fellow drug abusers whose drug use is inextricably fused with that of the IP. The "good" group includes children with parental family roles who assume an authoritarian role when the father is disengaged and/or are themselves highly successful. Some of these successful siblings had individuated from the family, but many were still enmeshed.

Another small group of "good" siblings were quite passive and not involved with substance abuse. Some of these develop "anger in" disorders, such as depression and headaches. Enmeshed drug-abusing siblings provide drugs for each other, inject drugs into one another, set the other up to be arrested, or even pimp for one another. At times, a large family may show sibling relationships of all the above types. Many successful older siblings were quite prominent in their fields and in these cases, the patient sibling withdrew from any vocational achievement rather than compete in a seemingly no-win situation. In a few cases, drug abusers are themselves parental children who had no way of asking for relief of responsibility other than through drugs. More commonly, they are the youngest child and their drug abuse maintains their role as the baby. They are frequently the child who gets the most attention and whose drug abuse keeps them from ever abandoning the parental nest, serving an important function for parents who need to have children around to be concerned with and/or prevent them from experiencing strong feelings of boredom in their spousal relationship.

Hendin et al. (1981) also noted that drug-free siblings are frequently the "good ones" even before drug use begins and that this dichotomy contributes to the difficulties of the I.P.

Cleveland (1981) noted that the good children in these families obey family rules and work hard in school, attempting to meet their parents' high expectations. They bear the burden of their bad sibling (the IP) and of their incompetent parents. They feel that if they can only be good enough they will erase the effect of the bad IP and make their parents look good. Good children are rigid, lonely, and suffer guilt and remorse for the rest of their lives.

As adolescent substance abuse becomes more progressive, many mothers suffer an agitated depression whenever their son or daughter "acts out" in destructive ways. Mothers who took prescription tranquilizers or abused alcohol frequently increased their intake whenever the drug abuser "acted out." These mothers will do anything for their addict sons except leave them alone (Fort, 1964). In a comparison of mothers of drug addicts, schizophrenics, and normal adolescents, the mother's symbiotic need for the child was highest in the mothers of drug abusers (Attardo, 1965).

In addition to family systems issues, there are other family factors that are known to predispose heavily to the abuse of drugs and alcohol by adolescents. The most common finding in the families of adolescent substance abusers is parents who are themselves substance abusers, specifically alcoholic fathers and prescription-drug-abusing mothers. Parental abuse of drugs and alcohol is a much more important determinant of adolescent abuse than parental attitude towards the child's drug and alcohol use (Kandel et al., 1978). Even parents who use minor tranquilizers in prescribed doses have a greater incidence of drug- and alcohol-abusing adolescents (Kandel et al., 1978). Parental as well as adolescent smoking also predisposes adolescents to drug and alcohol abuse. Alcohol- and drug-abusing siblings also statistically predispose other siblings to substance abuse although it may at times spare them through the family dynamics described above. Parental mental illness, divorce, separation, and frequent moves (Gibbs, 1982) also predispose to adolescent substance abuse. Another predisposing factor is birth trauma (Gibbs, 1982), perhaps because it leads to diminished coping skills and the need for drugs as compensation.

In general, a traditional family structure insulates the adolescent from drug abuse (Blum et al., 1972). Thus, in a family where there are greater degrees of parental control, a high premium on achieving, high expectations and structured, shared parent/child activities, there is a lower likelihood of substance abuse (Brook et al., 1978). However, if any of these attitudes are overdone and excessive, then the converse may be true, and these overconcerned attitudes may lead to or perpetuate substance abuse. The key to determining if these traditional values are overdone is the adolescent's response. If the child vigorously and repeatedly defies parental controls, is overwhelmed by expectations, and

avoids activities, then the parents' escalating but ineffective demands may lead to drug abuse or secondarily be associated with it (Brook et al., 1978).

FAMILY FACTORS THAT PREVENT ADOLESCENT SUBSTANCE ABUSE

A healthy family system will prevent adolescent substance abuse even in the face of heavy peer pressure to use and abuse drugs. As warm and mutual family ties diminish, the adolescent becomes more vulnerable to peer pressure. The key to healthy family functioning is the family's ability to adapt flexibly to different stresses with different but effective coping mechanisms. Thus, extreme closeness is necessary when children are small, but as they enter adolescence, the family must permit them to become autonomous without imposing excessive control and guilt. The healthy family requires a balance in the following processes: assertiveness, control, discipline, negotiation, roles, rules, and system feedback (Olson, Sprenkle, & Russell, 1979). A family should be able to adapt not only to expected stresses in the life cycle, but to unanticipated stresses such as physical illness, accidents, job loss, relocations, deaths of family members, divorce, inclusion of new members (including stepfamilies), and external catastrophes.

GENERAL PRINCIPLES IN THE FAMILY THERAPY OF ADOLESCENT SUBSTANCE ABUSERS

Many of the techniques used in the family therapy of adolescent substance abusers are identical with those used in other adolescent disorders. My personal approach is a synthesis of six basic approaches to family therapy: psychodynamic, systems, structural, communications, experiential, and behavioral. The six approaches have borrowed greatly from one another to a point of substantial integration; however, there are discrete differences that have at times led to conflict between approaches. My major approach is a structural one which incorporates the other techniques. It is my impression that many different styles or systems of family therapy can be successful with adolescent substance abusers if the therapist understands substance abuse, can recognize typical patterns (described previously) and is cognizant of several basic "rules of thumb" in regard to the treatment of this group.

Basic Rules of Thumb in Treatment

Confused families of adolescent substance abusers need structure and guidance. Too many alternatives only confuse them. Simple, direct courses of action are most helpful.

A critical general principle deals with establishing a system for enabling the substance abuser to become free of abuse chemicals to a point where family therapy can take place effectively. The specific methods employed to achieve this vary according to the types of chemicals used and the extent of use, abuse, and dependence.

If a drug is interfering with family functioning but there are no signs of dependence, I will suggest abstinence as the goal that will best restore family functioning and facilitate individual rehabilitation.

My approach is to contract for abstinence, utilizing the "one day at a time" approach of Alcoholics Anonymous. If the IP is or has been physically dependent, then I will inform the family that therapy is generally quite successful when members work toward abstinence, but it almost never works (with me as the therapist) if controlled drinking or substance use is their goal. One problem with the approach of controlled drinking or substance use is that the individual cannot take advantage of AA or NA (Narcotics Anonymous) as a support group while they are using any abusable substances. Many adolescents are notable exceptions to this rule, which has

been developed with more long-term substance abusers. Some adolescents may use substances in a peer-appropriate way without any impairment of function. In these families, the major problem may be the parents' overreaction or scapegoating. Here, the therapists' approach may need to go in quite the opposite direction from that described above; e.g., to normalize this level of substance use and join with the family sufficiently to focus on other problems. Thus, the therapeutic contract made in the beginning of treatment should focus on how the family will deal with substance abuse. Often, mild to moderate drug and alcohol abuse can be controlled if both parents can agree on clear limits and expectations and how to enforce them. However, if the substance abuser's intake is so severe that he or she is unable to attend sessions without being under the influence, if functioning is severely impaired, if there is substance-related violence, and/or if there is physical dependence on alcohol, narcotics, or sedatives, then the first priority in treatment is to stop substance abuse immediately. My first goal therefore is to persuade the family to pull together to initiate detoxification or at least some measure to achieve temporary abstinence. Generally, this is best done in a hospital and, if the abuse pattern is severe, I will require this in the first session or very early in the therapy.

If the substance abuse is only moderately severe or intermittent, and without physical dependence, such as binge alcoholism or weekend cocaine abuse, then the family is offered alternative measures to initiate this temporary substance-free state. I insist, however, that the family adopt some system that will enable them to continue to stay free of abuse substances such as teen-oriented AA groups and Al-anon for the rest of the family. Some moderate substance abusers who are resistant to self-help groups may find a system that helps them stay off of drugs through involvement in religion or dedication to a sports program. Even adolescent substance abusers who are not drug or alcohol dependent may benefit from hospitalization in a specialized drug-dependency program. Such programs may cool down high-conflict-level family systems, immerse the IP and family in educational programs as well as multiple therapeutic modalities, and permit establishment of a therapeutic alliance with the IP. For some severely dysfunctional families, long-term residential treatment such as that utilized in Phoenix House in New York City, Pride House in Los Angeles, or a specialized long-term hospital unit may be necessary. Most families will not accept this until other methods have failed. In order to accomplish this, a therapist must maintain long-term ties with the family, even through multiple treatment failures. On the other hand, it may be more helpful to terminate treatment if the substance abuser continues to abuse chemicals rather than continue treatment, which allows the family the pretense that they are changing when actually they are not. This excludes temporary "slips" into substance abuse, which are an expected part of treatment. Treatment should not be terminated for these slips but may best be ended if the family does not adopt any workable system for enforcing abstinence.

When I have properly joined with such families and they truly believe that I am terminating in their best interest, they invariably return to treatment a few months or a few years later, ready and willing to commit abstinence.

With a commitment and a system to achieve abstinence, the family therapy of formerly dependent substance abusers can take place. If the substance abuse is not so severe, then the family approach is very similar to that used with other acting-out adolescents. Thus, my method of treatment of adolescent substance abuse is based on a fusion of two approaches: restructuring the maladaptive aspects of the family system and establishing a method for controlling or eliminating substance abuse. This method is described in the following case examples:

A family entered treatment because Milt, age 16, and his brother, Doug, age 17, were arrested together for smoking marijuana in a car and treatment was a part of their probation. I invited the entire family to the first session in order to understand and work with the whole system. Thus, mother, 37, father, 37, sister, Carol, 18, and brother, Jimmy, 5, also attended. The teenagers' pot smoking was symptomatic of overall family and individual dysfunction. Mother had been in psychotherapy for a year for a weight problem and difficulties in relating to others. She was taking amphetamines for weight reduction and had been on them for an extended period of time. Father was a moderately successful small businessman who had difficulty asking for money that was owed to him, leading to frequent family financial crises. Carol was employed as a clerk and was on the verge of moving out of the house. Doug was described as having a personality change that was related to marijuana and admitted to smoking up to twelve joints a week, including smoking during school hours. He had become passive and irritable but generally responded to structure. Milt was much more assertive and had a very lucrative weekend job. He would involve the family in endless debates whenever they attempted to set limits for him. Jimmy had asthma and slept in his parents' bedroom. Doug and Milt had signed a probation contract in which they agreed not to be out after curfew and to abstain totally from alcohol and drugs. Dad generally let Mom take responsibility for every aspect of household and parental decision making. When Mom failed, Dad expressed extreme rage and prescribed rigid prohibitions that he later failed to enforce. One solution that Dad had tried in the past was to have the boys work in his business, but this generally failed because of their defiance and his inconsistency in setting limits. Although mother had most of the power in the family, she felt controlled by father.

I asked the parents to agree in this first session to establish clear limits about marijuana smoking. They came up with the following limits on their own: if they determined the boys were smoking pot (and that judgment was to be strictly up to them), then they were to work for five days without pay and be placed on restriction for one week. If they were caught a second time, the penalty would be doubled, and if a third offense occurred, they would be asked to move out. They were also asked to plan one meal a week where they would all eat together.

The family arrived for their second session with a suitcase full of Jimmy's toys and this helped focus that session on how the family interacts around the youngest child. Jimmy's sleeping in the parents' bedroom was focused on as a way of keeping the parents apart, and the first in a series of tasks to move him into Carol's soon to be vacated room was assigned, e.g., that they begin to talk about his moving out of their bedroom. The family was seen as they generally function when they were asked to deal with getting Jimmy's toys packed with fifteen minutes left in the session. The older siblings all put him down and said he could never do it himself. Mother defended him but father began to put the toys back himself. Dad was asked to support Mom in requiring that Jimmy do it himself and that neither parent do the job for him or leave it up to Mom. Jimmy's getting in between his parents and interfering with their closeness had to be dealt with, as well as how they undermined each other. If they could learn to function together to deal with Jimmy and reestablish their own intimacy, then they could handle their teenagers better. The teenagers were also asked to limit their parenting of Jimmy and to leave these functions to his natural parents.

It required two months of gradual practical steps, such as choosing and hanging wallpaper, to move Jimmy out of the parental bedroom and into his own room. During the exploration of these practical steps, many emotional issues between the parents were also explored, and they began to spend what they termed "quality time" together. Once the parents were able to function as a team sexually, as well as in decision making, the teenagers' marijuana problems abated substantially.

The family functioned well for over a year after the termination of their initial course of therapy, but returned when they learned that Milt was again smoking marijuana and the daughter was asking to come back home. At this point their functioning was at a sufficiently high level for them to agree readily that the daughter was not to come home because "she regresses and pulls the whole family back." They were also able to establish clear guidelines for Milt, who was now 17½, as to their expectations, and to state firmly that if he did not follow them he would be requested to leave the house even if he was in college and functioning well. I supported their position, even though Milt's use of marijuana at this time was apparently not interfering with his functioning. This was because both parents were clearly together on this issue, and because parents have the right to place limits on the drug and alcohol use of children living in their own home even after the age of eighteen.

In this case example, substance abuse was relatively mild and the situation could be resolved by direct structural approaches

including strengthening the spousal bond, removing Jimmy from between his parents and from his overinvolvement with mother, strengthening Dad's confidence, facilitating Carol's moving out and staying out, and some normalizing of the other boys' behavior.

When substance abuse is more severe than in the above case, all early efforts in family intervention are directed towards cessation of substance abuse as a prerequisite for family therapy. A recent case in which the adolescent was addicted to heroin and his mother was directly and indirectly providing the money for his drugs is illustrative of the need for the therapist to take a much "harder line" about substance abuse early in the therapy.

This family consisted of Tom, age nineteen, his wife, Cora, age nineteen, their one-year-old son, John, and Tom's family of origin. The present household included Tom's family and the following members of his family of origin: brother Mel, age seventeen, Mom, a 54-year-old registered nurse, and Dad, a 56-year-old engineer and rodeo afficionado. Julie, a thirty-year-old sister who was living in the Midwest, joined us three weeks later for a pivotal session. Tom and Cora were both on methadone maintenance since the age of eighteen and both had used heroin since fourteen and been addicted for over two years. They had a very lucrative job in which they were given a daily percentage of the money they raised for a charity. Tom had difficulty with the ready, daily access of money and fell behind in the amount of money he was to turn back to the company because he was spending huge sums of cash to inject sufficient heroin to overcome his methadone blockade. Cora would argue with him about his wasting the money unless he shared his heroin with her, which would quiet her protests. Because of the money spent on heroin, Tom and Cora were unable to pay the fees of their private methadone program and were "borrowing" from Tom's Mom to pay their weekly fees. Mom had been holding Tom's money for him but he still managed to withhold enough to buy heroin. He had also stolen goods from everyone in the family and pawned them. Mom would then pay off the pawnbroker and return the goods to the household. Mom's protectiveness of Tom caused constant conflict between her and Dad, and reinforced their distance. Dad repeatedly threatened to kick Tom out but couldn't enforce it because of

Mom's fears that Tom would die if he were outside of the family.

The therapist pointed out to Mom that her overprotectiveness keeps Tom an infant while her constant concern with Tom keeps her apart from her husband. She responded with, "I can't kick him out; what else can I do?" I suggested that a simple answer was to ask her husband for help, but she was not ready to do this yet because they had become so used to being polarized. Mom replied with, "I could send him to Phoenix House." I suggested that we evaluate the situation further and that in order to do that, I would have a session with Tom, Cora, and John, an individual session with Tom (to join with him and work towards his being an ally in his own individuation), and a family session with Julie when she returned home for Christmas. (Christmas week is often a time to hold a family session which includes significant members who have left the household.) I also assigned Mom and Dad the task of going out on a date the next time Tom got high on heroin. In the session with Tom, Cora, and John, Cora tended to manage and deal with John, leaving Tom on the periphery. They revealed one of the typical patterns in co-addicted pairs. Cora would never initiate using heroin on her own but would only use it when Tom provided it. Tom was able to state that he knew his mother would always bail him out if he got into trouble and this was one reason why he felt he could use heroin in safety. They also stated that all of their peer relationships were with fellow heroin addicts and that they felt this contributed to their problems. They were given a task to spend one evening with a drug-free couple and to keep in mind that this would be very frightening to them.

In the individual session with Tom, we explored his fears of success and independence as well as his guilt about manipulating his mother. We explored his feelings about Julie who had been seriously disfigured facially by a gunshot wound when Tom was nine. She had received a great deal of attention around the wounding and ten years of surgery to correct it. His mother felt guilty about the attention she gave Julie and tried to make it up to Tom. Tom denied that he was directly upset about Julie, stating that he did not start to use drugs until three years later, at age twelve.

The session which Julie attended was very poignant because of a powerful presence, despite her facial disfigurement and inability to speak. She communicated in writing. Her notes began with, "I know what you're going through" and "I don't have anyone who can help me by saying I've been there." She wrote to her mother, "You're killing Tom and keeping me alive." She suggested that the family establish a written agreement of ground rules that would permit them all to live together without conflict. When attempts at this failed, she wrote her last note, "I don't think Tom can get out of his habit alone. I think he needs a residential program." The family readily agreed that Tom would enter Phoenix House and Tom agreed to go. I reinforced this by stating that I was pleased they had all agreed to this and that no further therapy was necessary at this time, but that I would appreciate a call about how Tom was doing at Phoenix House and how the family was doing in general.

Four months later Tom called requesting an individual session. He informed me that he did not go to Phoenix House because it was too much like jail. He had quit his job which had solved the problem of having money available for heroin. His mother was now paying for his and Cora's new methadone program. However, he was now devoting himself to golf which was a great pastime of his father's. Thus, they were playing golf together at least three times weekly which was bringing them closer than they'd ever been. Unfortunately, he had pawned his golf clubs a few days before to get money to buy heroin. This permitted us to focus on his self-destructiveness as well as his fear of success.

Since Tom had a "system" for staying off of heroin, i.e., methadone maintenance, and he and his family expressed motivation for change, I agreed to resume outpatient treatment even though he had recently used heroin. I stated to the family that I had gone too fast the last time and that they were not ready to part with Tom because Mom and Dad needed him around to occupy their relationship and keep them apart. They readily agreed with the first part of the paradox, seemingly not hearing the interpretation of the need for the IP to continue his symptomatic behavior. I also suggested that both parents join Al-anon to help them learn to become less involved with Tom, as well as to have an activity that would unite them. Since that time Tom has remained free of heroin for two months and has registered for college. Cora has a job and infuriated the family by stating she wanted to buy an expensive ring before she paid off her debts. She is five months pregnant and a new child will reinforce her and Tom's dependency on the family. Tom got his own golf clubs out of hock with money earned from odd jobs. He began to explore his intense fear of his father and how the fear disappeared when he and his father played golf together.

Tom's stated goal, as well as that of every other family member, is for him and his own nuclear family to leave the household and establish one of their own. In order to achieve this, the tie between Tom and his mother will have to be further loosened. Tom's new relationship with his father is an important step in that direction. However, his mutual tie with Cora will have to be strengthened, as will the ties between his mother and father. Tom and Cora's getting off of methadone is a long-term goal of this therapy but neither expresses any motivation for detoxification at this point.

Although it is unusual for an adolescent to have a drug-abuse history as severe as Tom's, the description of his mother's overinvolvement is not at all atypical, nor is the triangulation between mother and father. Sedative-tranquilizer dependence, severe cocaine abuse, or alcohol dependence can be equally dangerous for the adolescent and devastating for the family. In this case, outpatient treatment was initially terminated to reinforce the family's decision for long-term residential treatment as the only system Tom could utilize to stop using heroin. However, without Julie's continual presence, the family was unable to implement that decision. Four months after that termination, Tom and his family returned to treatment, this time at Tom's urging. With some realignment of the family, particularly Tom's alliance with father, family, individual, and couple therapy had a better chance of being successful this time.

The initial intervention would have been more successful if I had available a multi-family group, which would support maternal letting go. However, unlike during most of my work with the families of substance abusers, such a group was not available to me at the time this family participated in treatment. Without this type of support, I worked paradoxically with the family's need to hold on to Tom. Cora's pregnancy certainly reinforces Tom's need to stay at home for financial and convenience reasons and offers their children more stable parenting through the grandparents.

These case examples illustrate that the actual family therapy of adolescent abusers is not appreciably different from the family therapy of other types of adolescent problems. There are some modifications of specific family therapy techniques that can be very helpful in working with these types of problems. The contract, which is made at the end of the first or second session, should deal with the substance abuse and how the family should react to it. This should include the system used by the IP to detoxify from substances as well as to maintain abstinence. The family's involvement in support groups such as Al-anon or a multifamily group should also be made a part of the contract. The family should also be coached to disengage from their reactivity to substance use or paradoxically to monitor it more closely as part of the contract. Involving all siblings in treatment should also be a part of the contract.

Joining with all family members may be too difficult for one therapist. I have often found it necessary to utilize a co-therapist who treats the adolescent individually and maintains an adolescent-advocate position in the family sessions. This enables me to join better with parents and facilitate their setting limits. In other cases, the adolescent is begging for limits underneath his bravado and a single therapist can easily join with the adolescent as well as the parental system.

Marking boundaries is very important with these families. After I have observed the adolescent's interfering role in parental decision-making during an actualization or enactment, I will work with the parents to restrict the adolescent from such interference while respecting the adolescent's right to his or her privacy. I will often ask the adolescent subsystem to leave the room while parents are agreeing on limits, in order to underline the importance of making such decisions without the adolescent being present or influencing his or her parents. Once decisions have been made, the adolescent can then participate in negotiations as long as an intergenerational coalition or triangle can be avoided. It is also important that all siblings not be treated exactly the same or bumped into categories regardless of whether these are ''actor-outer," "good child," "bad child," "drug abuser," "alcoholic," or the like.

One situation which occurs frequently in these families is parental substance abuse, which may be more extensive than that of the adolescent. However, if the adolescent is clearly labeled "the problem" by the family, then it is very important that the family be given some relief from the adolescent's behavior and/or substance abuse before the drug/alcohol or behavior problems of the parent(s) are addressed. On the other hand, if the adolescent's problems are only a means to get the more seriously disturbed parent into the session and the family clearly labels the parents' problems as major, then primary parental difficulties can be addressed and even made a part of the initial treatment contract. In the former case, once there is some relief for the family from the adolescent's problems, then the parental substance abuse and other problems can be dealt with. When the parents themselves are dependent on drugs or alcohol, it is very difficult for them to acquire appropriate parenting skills; thus, their finding a system for abstaining becomes a very high priority in the treatment.

The therapist must become knowledgeable about the pharmacologic effects of drugs and alcohol, particularly about the dependence process and long- and short-term effects of usage. Frequently, educating the family and identified patient can be extremely helpful if not essential to the family in putting the substance abuse into proper perspective, whether they be exaggerating or minimizing these effects.

These above therapeutic techniques are examples of how structural family therapy can be modified to be implemented with the families of adolescent substance abusers. If the basic principles of working with this group of patients and their families and these modifications are kept in mind, the family therapist can readily adopt his or her own techniques to working successfully with this challenging but workable group of patients.

REFERENCES

Attardo, N. Psychodynamic factors in the mother-child relationship in adolescent drug addiction: A comparison of mothers of schizophrenics and mothers of normal adolescent sons. *Psychotherapy and Psychosomatics*, 1965, **13**, 249–255.

Blum, R. H. *Horatio Alger's Children*. San Francisco: Jossey-Bass, 1972.

Brook, J. S., Lukoff, I. F., & Whiteman, M. Family socialization and adolescent personality and their association with adolescent use of marijuana. *Journal of Genetic Psychology*, 1978, **133**, 261–271.

Cleveland, M. Families and adolescent drug abuse: Structural analysis of children's roles. *Family Process*, 1981, **20**, 295–304.

Fort, J. P. Heroin addiction among young men. *Psychiatry*, 1954, **17**, 251–259.

Gibbs, J. T. Psychosocial factors related to substance abuse among delinquent females. *American Journal of Orthopsychiatry*, 1982, **52**(2), 261–271.

Hendin, H., Pollinger, A., Ulman, R., & Carr, A. C. Adolescent marijuana abusers and their families. *NIDA Research Monograph*, No. 40, September 1981, 17–25.

Kandel, D. B., Kessler, R. C., & Margulies, R. S. Antecedents of adolescents, initiation into stages of drug use: A developmental analysis. *Journal of Youth & Adolescence*, 1978, **7**(1), 13–14.

Kaufman, E. The abuse of multiple drugs: Psychological hypotheses, treatment considerations. *American Journal of Drug and Alcohol Abuse*, 1976, **3**, 293–304.

Kaufman, E. Family structures of narcotic addicts. *International Journal of the Addictions*, 1977, **12**, 106–108.

Kaufman, E., & Kaufmann, P. From a psychodynamic to a structural understanding of drug dependency. In E. Kaufman & P. Kaufmann (Eds.), *The family therapy of drug and alcohol abuse*. New York: Gardner Press, 1979.

Olson, D. H., Sprenkle, D. H., & Russell, C. S. Circumplex model of marital and family systems: 1. Cohesion and adaptability dimensions, family types, and clinical applications. *Family Process*, 1979, **18**, 3–28.

Reilly, D. M. Family factors in the etiology and treatment of youthful drug abuse. *Family Therapy*, 1976, **2**, 149–171.

16

Child and Adolescent Maltreatment: Implications for Family Therapy

JOSEPH CRUMBLEY, D.S.W.

INTRODUCTION

Early research of maltreated children (under eighteen years old) identified children under three and one-half years old as the most vulnerable to abuse and neglect. Later research and statistics identified various developmental and age ranges at which children are at risk of maltreatment.

The adolescent is increasingly being cited as victim in reports and studies of child maltreatment. Studies of sexual abuse are identifying the adolescent as being as vulnerable to maltreatment as children under three and one-half years, if not more vulnerable, because of the adolescent's stage of sexual development.

The purpose of this chapter is twofold: first, to present family characteristics, dynamics and profiles that are generalizable to all maltreating families (regardless of the child's age); second, to identify treatment issues and approaches in family therapy when intervening with the family of an abused adolescent. Many of the issues and approaches discussed in this chapter are also generalizable to all maltreating families.

PROFILES OF THE ABUSIVE AND NEGLECTFUL FAMILY

Sweet (1979) identifies four theoretical approaches for explaining and identifying abusive families and caretakers: psychoanalytical, sociological, social-learning, and psychosocial approaches. Table 16.1 discusses the implications of each approach and the corresponding goals and methods of research and intervention.

From these theories psychodynamic and sociological profiles developed portraying the maltreating family. Descriptors of the *psychodynamic profile* include deprived childhood experiences, social isolation, low self-esteem, parent's misperceptions of

child, "role reversal" in parent/child relationships, and crisis-oriented problem-
solving. The *sociological profile* reflects the
social descriptions of the perpetrator and
victim and their respective socioeconomic
characteristics.

Psychodynamic Profile

PARENTAL IMPRINTING

Parental imprinting is the learned capacity to nurture, care for, and protect a child.
This capacity is acquired through the experience of being loved and cared for during childhood. The maltreating parent has
had childhood imprints and experiences of
being unloved, unprotected, insecure, and
unnurtured. Not cared for or deprived of
consistent nurturance as children, they are
less likely and capable of being nurturant
and protective parents (Kempe & Helfer,
1976, 1972; Polansky, 1972).

Consequently, when their child demonstrates dependent or demanding behaviors, the parent's own anxieties and unmet
needs are recalled. This is further complicated by feelings of parental inadequancy
generated by the child when the parent is
emotionally or empathetically unable to
respond. The need to repress the source
of this discomfort elicits a defensive response from the parent toward the child.
Subsequent withdrawal (i.e., emotional or
physical neglect) or striking out (i.e., emotional or physical abuse)—instead of sympathy, comfort and protection—is the
response to their child's dependency and
helplessness.

LOW SELF-ESTEEM

The parent whose imprinting has been
negative as a child perceives himself or
herself as unworthy, unattractive, inadequate and undeserving. The ultimate result
is low self-esteem. Low self-esteem and
poor self-image are reinforced if the parent
feels he/she elicited or was deserving of
abuse and neglect as a child.

Consequently, abusive and neglectful
parents are described as not having the

"cushions," memories, or reservoirs of reassurance to carry them through periods
of stress, instability, or crisis (Kempe &
Helfer, 1972; Polansky, 1972). Instead, they
are in constant need of reassurance from
external, non-threatening sources, even a
child.

The use of more appropriate support
systems (i.e., spouse, parent, friends) has
been negated by experiences of abuse and
neglect. Deprivation or abuse by significant caretakers (parents, relatives, foster-
parents, etc.) can distort the victim's perceptions and trust of those closest to them.

The parents, who have experienced this
deprivation or abuse, are reported to perceive those closest to them as most likely
to hurt, criticize, reject, or disappoint them.
If generalized to the environment and
other significant relationships, social isolation is the anticipated result (Kempe &
Helfer, 1972; Polansky, 1972).

SOCIAL ISOLATION

Social isolation is demonstrated by the
parent's inability to identify or appropriately use resources when in need of help
or support (Kempe & Helfer, 1972; Polansky, 1972). The ability to turn to others for
support or help is a coping skill which has
been discouraged during the parent's
growth and development. It is the unrewarding risks and punishing experiences
of being unnurtured during moments of
extreme vulnerability and dependency that
reinforces the parent's need to become
withdrawn and socially isolated.

The parent is in a constant search for a
non-threatening, emotionally satisfying,
egocentric relationship. The search for
such a relationship is due to: (1) a need for
external reassurances; (2) the mistrust of
relationships and consequent lack of personal and inter-personal support systems;
and (3) unfulfilled childhood experiences.

The parent's most immediate source of
unconditional loyalty and unquestioned
obedience is the child. The parent's unrealistic perception of the child as a source
of emotional support is based on (1) memories of playing a similar role as a child or

(2) on the perceptions of their personal needs being greater than the child's.

The needs of abusive and neglectful parents, in combination with the perceived role and function of the child, creates "the world of abnormal childrearing" associated with child maltreatment (Kempe & Helfer, 1972). Factors associated with abnormal child-rearing are described in the literature as role-reversal, and adult misperceptions of the child.

Most parents look forward to being nurturant, depended on, and needed by their child(ren). The average parent anticipates an unselfish catering and commitment to the child's needs, with minimal reciprocation or positive reinforcement from the child. What rewards or positive reinforcements there are, may only originate from being a responsible and nurturant parent.

The skills and intrapersonal reassurances necessary for meeting unrewarding episodes of parenting are drawn from memories, models and experiences of being nurtured, cared for, and protected as a child. The literature suggests that abusive and neglectful parents have not had these experiences and are therefore in constant search of methods to satisfy these needs. The ultimate result is a reversal of dependency, nurturing, and protective roles between the parent and the child in abusive and neglectful families.

Role Reversal

The phenomenon of role reversal is defined as a reversal of dependency roles when parents turn to their children for reassurance and protection (Kempe & Helfer, 1972, 1976; Fontana & Besharon, 1979; Polansky, 1972). The results of role reversal are the parent's assignment of unrealistic "adult-like" expectations to the child. When the child fails to meet these expectations, he/she is perceived by the parent as being consciously rebellious and defiant. The lack of personal assurance and of models and experiences of being nurtured as a child causes the parent to respond defensively toward his/her child. The defensiveness can be displayed aggressively (physical or emotional aggression towards the child)

or passively (withdrawal of emotional or material nurturance from the child).

The abusive and neglectful parent is often capable of performing many of the routine functions associated with parenting. However, there is evidence of inconsistency in meeting these functions and in meeting the affective needs of the child.

Adult Misperceptions of the Child

Unrealistic expectations, dependency, and role reversal are influenced by the parent's perceptions of the child. Distortions in these perceptions are due primarily to four factors: (1) a contaminated view of the child; (2) fusion between parent and child; (3) negative experiences associated with the child; and (4) "imagined or real" personality and/or physiological "differences" in the child (Kempe, Helfer, & Ray, 1976, 1972; Kempe & Kempe, 1978; Fontana, 1979; Halpern, 1973).

The average parent usually sees the child as malleable, formative, and extremely impressionable throughout its development (particularly during infancy). The abusive and neglectful parent perceives the child as already having an intact personality, moods, and even feelings about them (the parents) as early as infancy. Consequently, the parent will describe the child's behavior as good or bad. Mood swings and shifts are perceived by the parent as personal attacks and defiance.

Abusive and neglectful parents do not perceive the formative influence, responsibility, and control they possess over the child's personality and behavioral development. This contaminated view of the child renders the parent's perceived influence upon its development as inconsequential. Consequently, the parent perceives his/her role as correctional—if they perceive any influence at all. Or, the parents' role may be passive and apathetic if s/he perceives his/her lack of influence in changing the child's behavior.

The fusion that occurs between parent and child is not unique to abusive and neglectful families. Most parents do perceive their children as extensions of themselves or other family members. In fact, this fusion is frequently a source of satisfaction and personal pride, if perceived as a positive reflection of the parent. However, in abusive families, the parent's projection of his/her own negative attributes onto the child fosters a negative fusion between the child and the parent. Thus, a parent's dislike for himself/herself can lead to a dislike, demeaning, and devaluation of the child (Kempe & Helfer, 1972).

The problem of fusion, and the projection of parent's negative attributes on the child, can result in the attempt to "rescue" the child through constant and inappropriate discipline and punishment, or in ignoring and rejecting the child. When these attempts invariably fail, the parents feel even more justified in their misperceptions to the point of finding themselves "cursed" or "jinxed" again. To make matters worse, there is no escape (except through therapy) since the core of the problem is the parent's own loneliness and feelings of abandonment (Polansky, 1972). Fusion can be demonstrated in the difficulty that abusive and neglectful parents have in separating from their school-age children.

A third source of distortion is negative experiences or situations associated with the child. The child is at risk of maltreatment (passive or aggressive) when he/she is perceived by the parent as a symbol of negative memories. The negative experience could be an unwanted pregnancy, a battering spouse, or even a negative childhood. Due to these distortions, the child is in danger from displaced anger and frustration, which can take the form or abuse and/or neglect. Thus, the parent may relive the anxiety and discomfort of his/her childhood by recreating it for the child. Having been raised in such a fashion becomes the justification for recreating the experience for the child, while simultaneously allowing the parent to identify with and justify the abusive and neglectful actions of his/her own parents (Kempe, Helfer, & Ray, 1976). A lack of individuation of the child from the parent is also apparent in this cyclical process.

A final source of distortion is the parent's perception of the child as "different." The perceived differences may be real or imagined. Throughout the literature there is a constant correlation between the perceived "difference" of the child and child maltreatment. A number of studies reviewed by Friedman (Sweet, 1979) reveal a higher rate of physical and developmental problems among abused and neglected children than in children in control groups.

One interpretation of these results is that the physical and developmental problems are results of the maltreatment (Kempe & Helfer, 1976). However, Wolcott (Sweet, 1979) proposes that the physical health and developmental problems of children and the capacity of parents to provide adequate care are reciprocal—each being the cause and effect of the other.

The literature also suggests high rates of abuse and neglect among premature and low-weight infants. This association is attributed to the unattractiveness of, and difficulty in caring for, the infant, in addition to prolonged hospitalizations that interrupt bonding between parents and child (Elmer & Greg, 1967). Because of the reciprocal relationship of physical and developmental problems with child maltreatment, they require equal attention as independent and dependent variables.

Less tangible but equally significant is the association of incompatible personalities of parent and child with child maltreatment. The incongruencies can be evidenced in (1) energy levels (e.g., hyperactive child matched with passive parents); (2) expressions of affection (e.g., expressive and emotional child matched with intraverted and quiet parents); or (3) degrees of alertness and development (e.g., a slow, socially developing toddler or infant matched with overzealous and socially conscious parents.)

CRISIS-ORIENTATION

A crisis usually precipitates abuse and neglect. The presence of crisis is not unique to maltreating parents. However, the absence of successful experiences and self-assurance to cushion or prevent a crisis is characteristic of the maltreating parent.

To cope with these deficits, the parent

turns to the child for support, assistance, and reassurance. The child's inability to meet these unrealistic expectations exacerbates the parent's stress or anxiety, now symbolized by the child. The child's inability to respond, or its own demands, are interpreted by the parent as deviant, threatening, and the source of their problems. In the name of discipline or protection from further anxiety, the parent strikes out against the child aggressively (abusively) or passively (neglectfully).

Sociological Profile

The sociological profile consists of social descriptions of the perpetrator and victim, and their socioeconomic contexts. Therefore, the age, sex, race, position in family, and socioeconomic status of each become important factors.

Social Context

The American Humane Society (1978) discovered that eighty-one percent of substantiated reports of child abuse and neglect were perpetrated by the child's natural parent (N = 116, 806 substantiated reports). Gil (1979) reports that over seventy percent of the child abuse cases he studied occurred in the home and were perpetrated by a biological parent.

Sex of Perpetrator

The American Humane Society (1978) reports more male (56.7 percent) than female (43.3 percent) perpetrators in studied abuse cases; and forty percent male perpetrators in all reports of maltreatment. Gil reports that fifty-one percent of the children he studied were abused by a female perpetrator (Gil, 1967). In another study (Zalba, 1967), the sex split was fifty-fifty.

Literature on father-to-mother ratios is contradictory and varied. Gil (1979) reports that nearly fourteen percent of the abuse was committed by a stepparent, less than one percent by an adoptive parent; and that fifty percent was committed by mothers in comparison to forty percent by fathers. Steele and Pollack (Sweet, 1979) report that in fifty-seven child abuse cases, the mother was the abuser fifty times.

In Zalba's study (1967), sex splits were equal for maltreating parents (fifty-fifty). Based on 116,806 substantiated reports of child abuse and neglect, the American Humane Society (1978) found that

adoptive fathers and stepfathers were reported at a higher rate (72% and 87%, respectively) than adoptive mothers (78%), stepmothers (13%) and maternal mothers (52%) in abusive cases;
natural mothers were found to be the perpetrator in 52% of substantiated reports, in comparison to 48% indicating the natural father as the perpetrator;
in 70% of the neglected cases, the natural mother was reported as the perpetrator. (Please note, however, that 45% of the neglect cases were single parent female headed households. Gil (1979, p. 183) also noted that 30% of his survey were single parent female headed households. The obvious result is a skewed curve showing less [sic] male perpetrators.) (p. 183)

Age of Perpetrator

Gil (1979) found that serious injuries were committed primarily by a parent under the age of 25. Female perpetrators of serious injuries were generally found to be younger than male perpetrators; fifty-three percent of the women were below the age of 30.

Socioeconomic Status

Out of 34,948 substantiated reports, low income was especially characteristic of families involved in neglect (American Humane Society, 1978). Forty-six percent of neglect cases were from families with incomes under $5,000 (1978 poverty level). Thirty-six percent of all substantiated reports of maltreatment were from families with incomes under $5,000.

Gil (1979) reported that more serious or fatal injuries occurred in families whose annual income was under $3,500. In Strauss's study (Strauss, et al., 1979) there was an inverse relationship between parental income and parental violence. Those families with incomes below the poverty line (less than $6,000 in 1979) had the highest rate of violence toward their children (twenty-two percent), while families with incomes exceeding $20,000 had the lowest rate (eleven percent).

OCCUPATIONAL AND EMPLOYMENT STATUS

Strauss's examination of occupational status found that parental violence was related to the father's occupation. The rate of severe violence by a father who was a blue-collar worker was sixteen percent, while the rate of a white-collar father was only eleven percent.

Gil (1979) noted that the occupational level of parents in his survey was lower than that of the general population. Nearly half the fathers of abused children were unemployed throughout the year, and about twelve percent were unemployed at the time of the abusive act.

Strauss (1979) also found that in families where the husband was employed part-time, the rate of parental violence nearly doubled the rate in families where the husband was employed full-time (twenty-seven percent compared to fourteen percent).

EDUCATION OF PERPETRATOR

Both Gil (1979) and Gladstone (1971) identified and reported maltreating parents as having limited education. The American Humane Society found the educational levels of abusive and neglectful perpetrators lower than levels in the general populace. Sixty-four percent of the general population have graduated high school, and fifteen percent, college; while twenty-eight percent of all perpetrators are high-school graduates, and only two percent college graduates.

FAMILY SIZE AND COMPOSITION

Gil (1979) noted that thirty percent of the abused children lived in female-headed households. The remaining families were predominantly two-parent families (sixty percent). The American Humane Society

(1978), similarly, found that 58.5 percent of all reported families were two-parent in contrast to thirty-seven percent female-headed, while forty-five percent were female-headed households in neglect cases.

Larger families are generally associated with child maltreatment. However, Strauss's results showed that parents with two children have a higher rate of violence than parents with one child. However, the rate did not increase with further increases in family size (Strauss et al., 1979).

STRESS FACTORS

Strauss et al. (1979) found higher levels of stress associated with higher levels of child maltreatment in middle income families than in the very low or very high income families. He did find that for the low socioeconomic families, poverty and unemployment were constant stressors.

The American Humane Society (1978) found broken families, family discord, and the stress of child care associated with substantiated reports of child maltreatment. In Gabarino's (1976) analysis and study of fifty-eight counties in New York, he found that thirty-six percent of the rate variance in child maltreatment was accounted for by the degree to which mothers were subjected to socioeconomic stress.

SEX AND AGE OF CHILD

There was no significant difference between the percentage of female and male victims of child maltreatment, except that for adolescents between thirteen and seventeen (American Humane Society, 1978), more females were abused than males.

Gelles (1979) proposes that the most dangerous period for the "high risk" child is from three months to three years of age. Resnick found that the first six months were the most dangerous for the child (Sweet, 1979). Bennie and Sclare (Sweet, 1979) reported battered children from four months to two years old (Gil, 1979). Kempe and Gladstone also found the battered child to be under the age of three and one-half years (Kempe, 1972; Gladstone, 1971).

Gil found that half the children reported

during 1967 and 1968 were boys. Boys outnumbered girls under age twelve, but girls outnumbered boys among teenage victims (Gil, 1979). Over seventy-five percent of the reported victims were over two years of age, nearly half were over six years, and nearly twenty percent were teenagers (Gil, 1979).

SPECIAL CHARACTERISTICS OF CHILD

In Gil's national survey, approximately twenty-nine percent of the maltreated children revealed deviations from the norm in social interaction and general functioning during the year preceding the abusive incident. Nearly fourteen percent suffered from deviations in physical functioning during the time span of the incident. Among the school-age children, over thirteen percent attended special classes for retarded children or classes below their age level. The above findings are in keeping with the supposition that a higher rate of physical and developmental problems are associated with battered children.

The American Humane Society contradicts this supposition with findings of no significant physical and developmental problems in the children of eighty-seven percent of the substantiated reports (N = 63,424) for 1978.

RACE OF CHILD

In Gelles's study (1980), fourteen percent of the children who were abused were black. David Gil (1979) identified and acknowledged the overrepresentation of nonwhite children in his study.

The nationwide reporting rate of abuse was 6.7 percent per 100,000 white children, and 21.0 percent per 100,000 non-white children. (Note: the higher rate of non-white children reported is attributed to the primary source of reports being public agencies and institutions serving low-income, non-white families). The under- or overrepresentation of non-white children in studies seems in general to be determined by the geographical and racial mixture of the samples, and due primarily to reporting sources, i.e., public agencies or private hospitals and physicians (Sweet, 1979; Gil, 1971).

Summary of Profiles

The *psychodynamic profile* portrays the maltreating parent as the victim of an unprotected, insecure, inconsistent, and unnurturing childhood. The trauma of such a childhood is manifested in the parent-child relationship. The emotional deprivation of the parent is exhibited in the parent's preoccupation in meeting his/her needs over those of the child. In fact, the child is perceived by the parent as a source of nurturance, support and security, particularly during times of stress and crisis.

During extreme stress or crisis, the parent will project anger, anxiety, or aggression onto the child. The child's inability to meet the parent's unrealistic expectations, coupled with the child's own demands, are interpreted by the parent as rebellious acts of defiance, disobedience, or nonsupport. The parent's response may be one of aggression (abuse) or withdrawal and passivity (neglect).

The *sociological profile* of the maltreating parent is based on the social characteristics of the perpetrator and victim, and the social context of the incident. The parent is portrayed as a person of low socioeconomic status (at or below poverty level) plagued with the stress of unemployment and poverty. The limitedly educated maltreating parent usually has a spouse. However, in cases of neglect, the parent has a forty to seventy percent chance of being a single female parent. Neglect is more prevalent in the poorer family.

Child maltreatment occurred within the family in over eighty percent of the reported cases. A biological parent was the perpetrator between seventy and eighty percent of the time. There is usually a fifty-fifty chance of the perpetrator being either male or female. In neglect cases, the female perpetrator is most visible in seventy percent of reported cases. Serious injuries appear to be perpetrated by parents under 30 years of age.

Information about the age of the child is

contradictory; however, the abused child appears to be most vulnerable between three months and three and one-half years old. Literature concerning the sex of the child is equally contradictory. Boys are reported to be most vulnerable or equally vulnerable to girls until adolescence. After twelve years of age, girls seem to become more at risk of injury.

Conclusions about the special characteristics of the child (social, mental, or physical deviations) vary from findings in which the children have no significant characteristics to statistics reporting twenty-nine percent of maltreated children displaying special characteristics.

IMPLICATIONS FOR FAMILY THERAPY

Adolescent abuse is considered symptomatic of family problems and dysfunctional systems. The family problems confronting the therapist include: (1) abnormal childrearing practices and attitudes (e.g., role reversal, misperceptions, and unrealistic expectations of the adolescent); (2) social isolation; (3) inadequate support systems; and (4) socio-economic stresses and crisis.

Addressing these problems will require intervention with various family subsystems including the extended family, the abusive family (abuser's immediate family), and siblings (adolescents of the abusive parents).

Intervention with each subsystem may also require the use of several approaches that include structural and contextual techniques. These approaches are necessary in response to dysfunctions within the family's systems.

Structural issues may include unclear or diffuse boundaries and roles, inappropriate alliances, issues of enmeshment or disengagement. Contextual issues may include unresolved life cycles, issues of entitlement, trust, and loyalty.

The Extended Family

Involvement with the extended family may become necessary because of: (1) the inter-generational nature of adolescent maltreatment; and, (2) the extended family's involvement with the abuser's family or surrogate parents, and grandparents.

Structural issues within the extended family may include: (1) the lack of clear roles, boundaries and hierarchy between the members of the extended and abusive families; (2) the carryover of reversed roles between the abusers and their parents from childhood, adolescence and into adulthood; and, (3) the lack of support systems for the extended family.

The lack of clear roles, boundaries and hierarchy may be directly related to the lack of changes in the relationships between the abusers and their parents from adolescence through adulthood.

The goals of the therapist become helping the abuser's parents to: (1) accept a supplemental role—as opposed to primary caretaker's role—with the abuser and his/her family; (2) accept an advising, rather than a decision-making role in the abusive family; and (3) accept and support the abusive parent's authority and primary commitment to his/her nuclear family.

The carry-over of reversed roles between the abusers and their parents may occur when child maltreatment is intergenerational or cyclical. The abuser may continue to be parentified in the extended family as primary decision-maker, caretaker, nurturer, or mediator between his/her parents. Or, the abuser's parents may need to perceive the abuser as dysfunctional and dependent from childhood through adolescence and into adulthood. The abuser's perceived dysfunction: (1) maintains the extended family's position in the hierarchy of decision-making and primary caretaking; and (2) detours the extended parents from their relationship and their need to develop new goals and purposes, now that their own child is an adult.

Historically, the nuclear family incorporated members of the extended family. As families became more urbanized, the nuclear and extended families appeared to have become more distant and separate in both living arrangements and patterns of interaction. Both extended and nuclear families are functioning more independently and autonomously.

The autonomy is evidenced by the increase in retirement and convalescent communities for the elderly. A financial indicator is the use of retirement funds and allotments as the primary source of financial support to the extended family, rather than support from or by their children.

However, the fixed and/or diminishing availability of financial and social services is creating a crisis for members of the extended family. The results are: (1) lack of support systems for the extended family; (2) an increase in the children's responsibility for elderly extended-family members; and (3) increased stress on the nuclear family members if they are inadequately prepared (financially or emotionally) to incorporate additional family members. The side effects may be elderly and/or parent abuse.

Contextual issues confronting the extended family and their therapist include: (1) middle or late life-cycle stages; (2) issues of entitlement related to being elderly and a member of the extended family; and (3) issues of loyalty between children (now adults) and the extended family.

Middle and late-life stages being experienced by the extended family may include children: existing, becoming adults, getting married and starting their own nuclear families. Adjusting to the loss and to the redefinition of role and function with the exiting adult may leave some gaps and unresolved feelings for the extended family members.

Because of these gaps and losses, the extended family must be helped to develop new purposes and personal goals and roles different from those members had as primary caretakers and as nuclear family for the exiting adult. Now, no longer primary caretakers, the abuser's parents must adjust to being "just" a couple again, rather than parents.

The source of focus and purpose now must originate out of the needs of the couple, rather than the needs of their children.

Finding compatibility and contentment with being together—for each other and not just for the children's sake—may become a task for the extended family.

Changes in entitlement can become a treatment and adjustment issue for the extended family. The exiting adult no longer perceives or accepts the parents' actions and suggestions as being final. Obedience or adherence to the suggestions or recommendations of extended family members is not a given conclusion. The extended family's recognition of their offspring's adulthood and authority for making decisions in his/her own nuclear family may entail a difficult adjustment. Helping the extended family to accept the role of assisting their offspring to become more independent and autonomous as adults and as parents may become a crucial therapeutic task.

Sharing the exiting adult's loyalty with his or her own nuclear family (wife and children) may also be an adjustment for the extended family members. Not addressing the issue of split loyalties may result in: (1) competition for attention between members of both the extended and nuclear family members; (2) resentment between family members; and (3) family members undermining each other's roles and authority.

Delineating clear roles, patterns of interaction, and the importance of each member's role may help the extended family to feel more secure, and less threatened or abandoned by their children's split loyalties.

The Abuser's Nuclear Family

Structural issues for the abuser's families may include: (1) developing clear executive (parental) boundaries; and (2) discontinuing role reversal and the assigning of inappropriate expectations to the adolescent. The lack of awareness and assigning of executive roles by abusive parents is a major problem in maltreating families. The result is a diffusion of boundaries between the parents and the adolescent and the extended family.

Boundary clarification can be facilitated by the therapist if he or she is able to assist the abusive parents through the following tasks: (1) developing uniform rules and consequences for and with the adolescent; (2) developing fair and realistic expectations of the adolescent (e.g. behavior and performance), by understanding adolescent human growth and development; (3) developing uniform techniques in punishing and disciplining the adolescent; and (4) developing supportive roles and shared responsibilities in the discipline, teaching, supervision, physical care, and emotional nurturance of the adolescent.

The lack of clarity in the parent's expressive and instrumental roles frequently results in reversed and diffused roles between the abusive parent and his/her children. Role reversal refers to the reversal of relationships, roles, and functions between parents and their children. Consequently, the roles of problem-solving, nurturance, protection, teaching, etc., may be assigned to the children by their parents. The patterns of role reversal and the parent's assigning of adult-like responsibilities to their children are motivated by the following sources:

   • the unmet needs of the parents, carried over from their missed childhood, adolescence, personal development, or unfulfilling male/female relationships;
   • the parents' repetition of parental behavior from childhood or adolescent memories and exposure to models of parenting;
   • the parents' inability to provide nurturing and supportive relationships for each other.

Attention directed to the parent/adolescent relationship as well as to the parents' relationship as executives is essential. Restructuring and redirecting adult-like responsibilities to the executive system will free the adolescent from unrealistic roles and expectations.

Contextual issues confronting the abusive parents frequently include: (1) separation from the extended family; (2) developing as individuals and as a couple; (3) resolving issues of entitlement and loyalty between each other; (4) balancing the needs and roles of being a couple and of being parents; and (5) beginning to accept and assist the adolescent's growth into adulthood and separation from the family.

Helping the parent to understand and accept the adolescent's growth process into adulthood and separation is critical. The parent's understanding will result in: (1) more appropriate relationships based on adolescent's needs that are different from those of a child; (2) more age-appropriate responsibilities for, and expectations and disciplining of, the adolescent; and (3) more appropriate interpretations of, and responses to, the adolescent's behavior (e.g., limit-testing, peer allegiance, rejection of parents and tradition). Validating the parents' accomplishments and arrival into adulthood through support by the abuser's parents, spouse, significant others, and therapist may increase the parent's self-confidence and self-esteem. Helping the parent through successful experiences as an adult (e.g., decision-making, crisis management, financial and domestic planning, career goals and development) further validates their confidence. This experience can then become a model to be used with their adolescent.

Helping parents to function as a couple requires helping the parents to become successful at anticipating, communicating, understanding, and responding to each other's emotional needs. The couple must then develop communication skills, listening techniques, and an understanding of their partner's developing and emotional needs and stages. With these skills, techniques, and understanding, the couple will be able to develop mutual loyalties that entitle each other to an exchange of trust and shared resources (both emotional and material).

Siblings

The sibling system requires attention because of its independent impact on the entire family system. The child(ren) or adolescent may also initiate, precipitate or elicit abuse.

The provocative or precocious adolescent may elicit a response of physical abuse or neglect. A seductive adolescent may be conditioned to give cues that result in an incestuous relationship. Siblings in a family may scapegoat each other in order to detour attention from each other.

A common practice of abused children, adolescents, or siblings is to create negative situations that comprise attention-seeking behavior. The attention-seeking behavior may not only be meeting the needs of the adolescent, but may also function to detour the parents from their own discord or problems as a couple.

Structural approaches are useful in identifying parentified behavior and attention-seeking behavior, and clarifying limits and boundaries between parents and adolescents. Helping parents not to involve their adolescent in marital/couple conflicts helps eliminate the need for detouring, scapegoating and attention-seeking, behaviors. The parents' development of appropriate support systems and ways of meeting unmet needs decreases their need for role reversal and the unrealistic expectations of their adolescent.

Contextual issues confronting siblings include: (1) transition through childhood, adolescence, and young adulthood; and (2) issues of trust, entitlement and loyalty related to these developmental stages.

Helping siblings and adolescents to understand their own developmental processes, needs, and impulses is essential to their development and transitions. They then become better able to cope with the emotional and physical changes affecting relationships with peers, parents, and the environment.

Siblings and the adolescent will also need to renegotiate personal values related to entitlement, loyalty, and trust. The maltreated adolescent and his siblings have frequently learned values based on: (1) entitlement that is taken forcibly by means of control and power rather than earned through respect and negotiation; (2) loyalty that exists as long as it's to one's advantage rather than being long-term, unconditional, and not manipulative; (3) trust that exists only in oneself and hardly ever with

those closest to them rather than being trustful of others and open to the risks of relationships; and (4) justice that is harsh, prejudiced, and inconsistent rather than humane, objective, and consistent.

This re-clarification of the adolescent's and siblings' values can be done didactically and experientially through their education and interaction with parents and the extended family. However, parents and extended family members must be equipped and involved in reevaluating the family system's values if new values are to be communicated to their children.

The following case study is presented in order to highlight the problems and breakdown within family subsystems and their implications for family therapy.

The therapist was meeting with the family following the placement of a sixteen-year old female who had been sexually abused by her stepfather. Present at the session were mother, stepfather, abused daughter, and older sister (no longer living in the home, but formerly harassed by stepfather). The purpose of the session was to develop a 'map' of the family's lines of loyalty, allegiances and relationships. This involved assessing the kind and quality of the relationships between the spouses; parents and children; siblings; and immediate and extended families.

The therapist began by asking the parents if they wanted their daughter to return home from placement. Stepfather was the first to respond by saying "Yes, of course, she's my daughter." Mother responded by saying "Only if she listens to me and stays in her place." Daughter (the abuse victim) said that she wouldn't want to return home as long as her mother was jealous or threatened by her relationship with Dad. She continued by saying that Mom was jealous of her ability to talk with Dad and always be supportive of Dad. Finally, daughter very proudly stated that she knew Dad "better than Mom" did.

Dad admitted to feeling more loyalty and understanding from his daughter than from his wife, sometimes. Mom also admitted that her daughter had more patience with Dad than she did, and that she did use her daughter as a "sounding board" to complain about Dad and even sometimes used her to calm her husband down when she (Mom) couldn't. However, Mom felt justified in expecting her daughter to "know her place." Mother's feelings were based on her own feelings as an adolescent when she "also had to be a comfort to her parents or help them with their marital problems by breaking up arguments and calming Dad down," but she was still "respectful to her mother" and "stayed in her place" as a child.

The older daughter echoed Mother's sentiments and proudly boasted that she also had the same responsibilities as Mother and her younger sister, but was "able to stay out of the middle and say no to Dad when he went too far."

The abused daughter responded angrily, saying that her sister always sided with Mom against Dad, and that Dad needed someone on his side.

The family dynamics which placed the sixteen-year old daughter at risk of sexual abuse were: (1) the breakdown in the relationship between mother and father (i.e., intellectual, emotional, social, and sexual); (2) the assigning of adult-like characteristics and responsibilities to the daughter (i.e., nurturing, mediating, problem-solving, being a companion); (3) the repetition of childhood and adolescent experiences and roles learned by the parents, now carried into their parenting practices; and (4) the adolescent's sexual activity being perceived by both parent and adolescent as an extension of the adolescent's role as support to the parent.

A structural approach with this family would certainly be useful in helping the family members redirect and define sources for appropriate relationships. Tasks with the parent would include: (1) developing uniform rules and consequences in the home; (2) developing fair and realistic expectations of the adolescent; (3) developing techniques in punishing and disciplining the adolescent; and (4) developing supportive roles and shared responsibilities in the discipline, teaching, supervision, and nurturance of the adolescent. The accomplishment of these tasks would enable the parents to function better as parents and possibly even affect their interpersonal relationship.

Contextual approaches would be useful in helping the family learn how to ask for, establish, and use a relationship. Poor communication and support, and the withholding of nurturance are common interpersonal problems.

Development from individuals to a couple is a long-term goal of the treatment. Tasks with the couple include: (1) helping to develop communication skills; (2) understanding the development of individual members; (3) helping them to develop skills in establishing relationships.

The intergenerational nature of emotional deprivation, poor imprinting, low self-esteem, and isolation reinforces adolescent maltreatment. The mother in the previous case study stated how she was also involved, parentified, and triangulated with her parents in their marriage.

The following case study is indicative of the cyclical nature of family patterns of interaction. It features the same family as in the previous case study.

Present at this family meeting were the parents and maternal grandfather. The parents are discussing a task they were assigned in a previous session. The task was to identify barriers to their spending time together, socially and privately. They gave the typical answers which included the job, domestic responsibilities, the children. These responses were given in joint agreement. Even grandfather was able to commiserate with his daughter and son-in-law. Mother then added "and family responsibilities." Father then stated "not my family." He continued by saying that his wife was "using taking care of the family as a convenient excuse." Mother, in an impulsive outburst, stated, "you mean to say taking care of my father, don't you?" Father said, "Yes! You've always gotten caught up in your parents' problems, like their arguments, their financial problems, physical illnesses, and even problems with your brothers and sisters. You're like his wife and daughter." (Grandmother was deceased.) The therapist reframed the issues by asking grandfather if he knew that his well-being was so important to his daughter and son-in-law that they would even argue over his care. He said he knew they cared, but that he did not need a mother or wife, and that he didn't want to be a barrier between them.

The therapist then asked grandfather to tell his daughter how she and her husband could be helpful to him. Note: The therapist had met with grandfather prior to the session and was able to identify problems grandfather was having. The therapist was able to give grandfather a list of agencies and organizations which were able to assist him. His daughter's role was to provide transportation to these agencies until he could arrange transportation with services for the elderly. Mother could now begin separating from grandfather, becoming less triangulated by redefining her involvement with him.

The structural issues confronting the *extended family* include: (1) the reversal of nurturance, parental, and problem-solving roles carried over by the abuser from childhood, and adolescence to adulthood; (2) the lack of appropriate resources for nurturance and support for the parents of the abuser through later life cycles (i.e., loss of spouse, physiological changes, separation from children); and (3) the lack of clear boundaries and relationships between the extended and immediate family of the abuser.

Contextual issues for the extended family include: (1) the exit and independence of their children; (2) the development of boundaries and new roles with their children (i.e., advisor, rather than decision-maker; supplemental, rather than primary supporter; grandparent to grandchildren, not parent); (3) illness or loss of spouse; being single again; and (4) loss of independence through physical disabilities, which are part of the aging process.

Both contextual and structural approaches will help the extended family learn how to: (1) establish more appropriate relationships; and (2) identify appropriate sources for support and reassurance.

Socioeconomic System

The therapist must anticipate a variety of socioeconomic problems. These problems effect and/or are effected by the family's patterns of interaction. The problems must also be included and considered in therapy since the environment is part of the family's system. Therefore, the therapist must be prepared to help the client connect with networks outside of, but essential to, the family's functioning (e.g., employment, housing, medical care, school). Many of the abused children and adolescents will be in or entering placement. Many families will be involved with

the judicial, law enforcement, or child welfare systems. It is essential that the therapist coordinate services with these agencies and systems. If used properly, agencies can provide the leverage and support necessary for helping a family through a therapeutic process. These agencies can be used for leverage and support when: (1) families are resistant to therapy but must attend because child welfare laws agencies and enforcement agencies mandate therapy; (2) an adolescent who is maltreated, or at risk of being maltreated, needs placement (temporary or permanent); or (3) when families need additional therapeutic or supportive services (e.g., day-care, services to the elderly, parent education, housing). Arranging these types of services can usually be done through local/state child protective services and juvenile aid divisions of local law-enforcement agencies.

Summary of Implications for Family Therapy

In summary, the therapist can anticipate involvement with various subsystems: the extended family, the abusive family, and siblings. Intervention with each of these subsystems may require the use of several approaches, including structural and contextual.

Within the *extended family*, structural and contextual issues are present. Structural issues include: (1) the lack of clear roles, boundaries, and hierarchy between the extended family members of the abusive family; (2) the carryover of reversed roles between parents of the abuser from childhood or adolescence into adulthood; and (3) the lack of appropriate relationships and support systems for the extended family (e.g., spouses, peer groups, and social service agencies).

Contextual issues include: (1) the late or midlife stages of (a) children exiting and becoming adults; (b) separation and the development of new parenting and grandparenting roles as extended family members; and (c) becoming a couple again, following the exit of the children; (2) issues of entitlement related to being elderly and a member of the extended family; and, (3)

Table 16.1

INTERVENTION AND RESEARCH IN CHILD MALTREATMENT: IMPLICATIONS FOR INTERVENTIVE GOALS AND METHODS

Theoretical Explanation and Approach	Implications for Interventive Goals and Methods	Implications for Research Goals and Methods
Psychoanalytical Approach Child abuse/neglect is a result of unresolved personality, behavioral, and emotional disorders (Sweet, 1979)	*Goal* Develop emotional capacity and psychological maturity that will reverse arrested ego and personality development *Method* Restructuring of ego (impulsive controls, self-concept, coping skills). Insight and personality analysis of emotional needs, deprivation, and sources of gratification	*Goal* Identify typologies of abusive/neglectful personalities *Method* Personality tests Tests for psychopathology Test for pathnogenicity
Sociological Approach Child maltreatment is a result of sociocultural and environmental factors that ill-equip parents to meet parental responsibilities (Sweet, 1979)	*Goal* Develop an environmental milieu and child-rearing attitude that supports the family's ability to care for children *Method* Assure family's access to environmental resources necessary for child-rearing (i.e., employment, housing, nutrition) Reeducate community and parent in rights, roles, and perceptions of children	*Goal* (1) Identify sociocultural and environmental factors associated with child maltreatment (2) Identify "high risk" populations and families *Method* Develop sociocultural profiles of maltreating family and battered children, (i.e., stress factors, employment status, housing situation) Develop profile and criteria for targeting potentially abusive/neglectful environments
Social Learning Approach Child maltreatment is a result of behaviors and attitudes learned by the parent from childhood experiences and models of aggression (Sweet, 1979)	*Goal* To develop new attitudes and behaviors that support positive parenting *Method* Behavior modification via parent education, modeling, and positive reinforcement	*Goal* Identify those behaviors and attitudes resulting in maltreated children *Method* Categorizing and contrasting parental attitudes and behaviors associated with maltreating and nonmaltreating families
Psychosocial Approach Child abuse and neglect is a result of the interaction between the individual and environment (Sweet, 1979)	*Goal* To remedy the sociocultural and environmental factors that create the psychopathology and behavior associated with child maltreatment *Method* A combination of the psychoanalytical and sociological methods of intervention	*Goal and Method* A combination of the psychoanalytical and sociological approaches

developmental physical and social issues associated with aging.

Within the *abusive family*, both structural and contextual approaches may be necessary. Structural issues may include: (1) developing clear executive boundaries; (2) identifying shared and delegated parental roles and responsibilities; (3) constructing uniform methods and rules for child-rearing, punishment, and discipline; (4) disengaging parent/adolescent relationships that are inappropriate; and, (5) developing and assigning appropriate expectations to the adolescent (non-parental expectations and responsibilities).

Contextual issues may include: (1) male/female relationships (communication, support, nurturance); (2) transitional experience through early and middle lifecycle phase from individuals to couples to parents; and, (3) entitlements as parents, spouses, and individuals.

Within the *sibling subsystem*, the therapist may use similar approaches. Structural issues include: (1) Disengaging the adolescent from inappropriate relationships with parent(s); (2) reassigning realistic expectations and tasks to the adolescent; (3) reassigning parental roles to executives; and, (4) removing the need for the adolescent to function in parenting and detouring roles.

Contextual issues include: (1) transitions through child and adolescent development; (2) entitlement as children, adolescents, or young adults; and, (3) parent/adolescent relationships and issues related to individual life cycles of the adolescent and those of the family.

Therapists may need to network with other agencies when confronted with the following situations: (1) when families are resistant to therapy but must attend because child welfare laws agencies and enforcement agencies mandate therapy; (2) when the adolescent who is maltreated, or at risk of being maltreated, needs placement (temporary or permanent); or, (3) when families need additional therapeutic or supportive services (e.g., daycare, services to the elderly, parent education, housing).

REFERENCES

Ackoff, Russell L. *A concept of corporate planning.* New York: Wiley, 1970.

American Humane Society. *Incidence reports.* Denver, CO: American Humane Association, 1978, (1970, 1977).

Bandura, A. Institutionally sanctioned violence. *Journal of Clinical Child Psychology*, 1973, **2**, 23–24.

———. *Aggression: A social learning analysis.* Englewood Cliffs, NJ: Prentice-Hall, 1973.

———. *Social learning theory.* Englewood Cliffs, NJ: Prentice-Hall, 1977.

Berdie, J. Violence towards youth. *Children Today*, 1977, **6**, 7–10.

Billingsley, Andrew. *Black families in white America.* Englewood Cliffs, NJ: Prentice-Hall, 1968.

———. *Black families and the struggle for survival: Teaching our children to walk tall.* New York: Friendship Press, 1974.

Biosvert, M. Battered Child Syndrome. *Social Casework*, 1972, **53**, 475–480.

Birmingham, Stephen. *Certain people: America's black elite.* Boston: Little, Brown, 1977.

Blager, F., & Martin, H. Speech and language of abused children. In H. Martin, *The abused child*. Cambridge, MA: Ballinger, 1976.

Blassingame, John W. *The slave community.* New York: Oxford University Press, 1972.

Blau, Zena Smith. Exposure to child rearing experts: A structural interpretation of class-color differences. In Robert Staples (Ed.), *Black family*. Los Angeles, California: Wadsworth, 1971.

Boesel, D. *Violent Schools—Safe Schools.* Washington, DC: National Institute of Education, 1978.

Bolton, F. J., & Laner, R. H. Maternal Maturity and Maltreatment. *Journal of Family Issues*, 1981, **2**(4), 485–509.

Bolton, F. J., Laner, R. H., & Gai, D. S. The study of child maltreatment: When is research, research? *Journal of Family Issues*. 1981, **2**(4), 531–541.

Burgess, R. Family Interaction. Presented at Association for Advanced Behavioral Therapy, 1967.

Bybee, R. Violence Toward Youth. *Journal of Social Issues*, 1979, **35**, 1–14.

Campbell, Donald T., & Stanley, Julian C. *Experimental and quasi-experimental designs for research.* Chicago: Rand McNally, 1966.

Chamberland, T. The method of multiple working hypotheses. *Science*, 1965, **15**, 754–759.

Cooper Joseph. *How to get more in less time.* Garden City, NH: Doubleday, 1962.

Davis, Allison, & Havighurst, Robert J. Social Class and Color Differences in Child Rearing. *American Sociological Review*, June, 1946, **31**, 698–710.

Ehlers, Walter H., Austin, M., Chael, J., & Prothered, Jon C. *Administration for the human services*. New York: Harper & Row, 1976.

Elmer, E. Child abuse and family stress. *The journal of social issues*, 1979, **35**, 60–69.

——. *Children in jeopardy: A study of abused minors*. Pittsburgh: University of Pittsburgh Press, 1967.

Elmer, E., & Greg, G. Developmental Characteristics of Abused Children. *Pediatrics*, 1967, **40**, 596–602.

Embree, R. *Brown America*. New York: Viking, 1931.

Emery, J. Battered Child Syndrome, *British Medical Journal*, 1974, **4**, 43–45.

Endo, Russell, & Strawbridge, William. *Perspective on Black America*. Englewood Cliffs, NJ: Prentice-Hall, 1970.

Erlanger, H. Social class and corporal punishment. *American Sociological Review*, 1974, **33**, 68–85.

Fontana, Vincent J., & Besharon, Douglas J. *Maltreatment syndrome in children*. Cambridge, MA: Harvard University Press, 1979.

Frazier, E. *The Negro family in the United States*. Chicago: University of Chicago Press, 1966.

Garbarino, J. Ecological approach to child maltreatment. *Child Development*, 1976, **47**, 178–185.

Gelles, Richard. *Behind closed doors: Violence in the American family* (2nd ed.). New York: Doubleday, 1980.

——. Child abuse as psychopathology: A sociological critique and formulation. *American Journal of Orthopsychiatry*, 1973, **43**, 611–621.

——. *Sociological critique and formulation*. In D. Gil (Ed.), *Child abuse and violence*. New York: AMS Press, 1979.

——. Violence in the American family. *Journal of Social Issues*, 1979, **35**, 15–39.

Gelles, R. J., & Hargreaves, E. F. Maternal employment and violence towards children. *Journal of Family Issues*, 1981, **2**(4), 509–531.

Gil, David. Violence against children. In David Gil (Ed.), *Child Abuse and Violence*. New York: AMS Press, 1979.

Gil, David. *Violence against children: Physical abuse in the United States*. Cambridge: Harvard University Press, 1973 (1970, 1971).

Gil, David (Ed.). *Child abuse and violence*. New York: AMS Press, 1979.

Giovannoni, J. Parental Mistreatment. *Journal of Marriage and Family*, 1971, **33**, 649–657.

——. Child neglect among poor. *Child Welfare*, 1970, **49**, 196–204.

Gladstone, R. Observations of abused children.

Journal of Child Psychology, 1971, **10**, 336–350.

Gray, J. Prediction and prevention of child maltreatment. *International Journal of Child Abuse*, 1977, **1**, 45–3.

Gutman, Herbert G. *The black family in slavery and freedom, 1750–1925*. New York: Vintage, 1977.

Halpern, Florence. *Survival: Black/white*. New York: Program Press, 1973.

Halpert, Harold P. *An administrator's handbook on the application of operational research to the management of mental health systems*. Washington, D.C.: National Clearinghouse for Mental Health Information, 1970.

Heckscher, B. T. Household structure and achievement orientation in lower class Barbadian families, *Journal of Marriage and Family*, August 1967, **3**, 102.

Herskovitz, Melville. *The myth of the Negro past*. Boston: Beacon, 1958.

Jayarante, S. Child abusers as parents. *Social Work*, 1977, **58**, 5–9.

Jeffers, Camille. *Living poor*. Ann Arbor, MI: Ann Arbor Publishers, 1967.

Jones, James M. *Prejudice and racism*. Boston, MA: Addison-Wesley, 1972.

Kamii, Constance K., & Norman L. Class differences in the socialization practices of Negro mothers. *Journal of Marriage and Family*, 1967, **29**(2), 302–10.

Kempe, Henry C., & Helfer, Ray E. *Child abuse and neglect: The family and community*. Cambridge, MA: Ballinger, 1976.

——. *Helping the battered child and his family*. Philadelphia: Lippincott, 1972.

Kempe, Henry C., & Kempe, Ruth S. *Child abuse: The developing child*. Cambridge, MA: Harvard University Press, 1978.

Kempe, H. C., Silverman, F. H., Steele, B. F., Droegmuller, W., & Silver, H. K. The battered child syndrome. *Journal of American Medical Association*, 1972, **181**, 17–24.

Kent, J. A follow-up study of abused children. *Journal of Pediatric Psychology*, 1976, **1**, 25–31.

Kerlinger, Fred N. *Foundations of behavioral research*. New York: Holt, 1973.

Knowles, Louis L., & Prewitt, Kenneth. *Institutional racism in America*. Englewood Cliffs, NJ: Prentice-Hall, 1969.

Kronus, Sidney. *The black middle class*. Akron, OH: Charles E. Merrill, 1971.

Light, R. Abused and neglected children in America: A study of alternative policies. *Harvard Review*, 1973, **43**, 556–598.

Martin, Elmer P., & Martin, Joanne Mitchell. *The black extended family*. Chicago: University of Chicago Press, 1978.

Martin, H. Prevention and the consequences of child abuse. *Journal of Operational Psychology*, 1974, **6**, 68–77.

——. The development of abused children.

Advances in Pediatrics, 1974, **21**, 25–73.

Martin, Harold, & Kempe, Henry C. *The abused child: Multidisciplinary approach to issues in treatment.* Cambridge, MA: Ballinger, 1976.

Miller, Henry. Social work in the black ghetto: The new colonialism. *Social Work,* July 1969, **3**, 65–76.

Muir, M. Psychological and behavioral characteristics of abused children. *Journal of Pediatric Psychology,* 1976, **1**, 16–19.

Nagi, S. *The structure and performance of child abuse and neglect.* Washington, DC: Office of Child Development, 1975.

Nobles, Wade. *A formulative and empirical study of black families.* San Francisco: Westside Community Mental Health Center, 1976.

Ounsted, D. Aspects of bonding failure. *Developmental Medicine and Child Neurology,* 1974, **16**, 447–456.

Parke, R. An interdisciplinary analysis. In E. Hetherington (Ed.). *Review of Child Development Research.* Chicago: University of Chicago Press, 1975.

———. Socialization in child abuse. In J. Tapp, *Law, justice and the individual in society.* New York: Holt, 1977.

Parker, Seymour, & Kleiner, Robert J. Social and psychological dimensions of the family role performance of the Negro male. *Journal of Marriage and the Family,* March 1969, **31**, 500–506.

Polansky, R. *Child neglect.* New York: Child Welfare League of America, 1972.

Powdermaker, Hortense. *After freedom: A cultural study in the Deep South.* New York: Russell & Russell, 1968 [1938].

Public Law 93-247. *Child Abuse Prevention and Treatment Act.* Washington, DC: U.S. Government Printing Office, 1978 (1973, 1974).

Radbill, S. A history of infanticide. In R. Helfer (Ed.), *The battered child.* Chicago: University of Chicago Press, 1974.

Reid, J. Social interactional approach to the abusive parent. *Journal of Pediatrics.* In press.

Silverman, F. The Roentgen Manifestation of Skeletal Trauma in Infants. *American Journal of Roentgenology,* 1953, **69**, 413–426.

Staples, Robert. The Black American family. In Charles H. Mindel & Robert W. Habenstein (Eds.). *Ethnic families in America: Patterns and variations.* New York: Scientific Publishing Co., 1976.

Steinmetz, S., & Strauss, M. The cradle of violence. *Society,* 1973, **10**, 50–56.

Strauss, M., Gales, R. J., & Steinmetz, S. K. *Behind closed doors: Violence in America.* New York: Doubleday, 1979.

Sweet, J. The maltreatment of children: A review of theories and research. *Journal of Social Issues,* 1979, **35**, 40–60.

Tapp, J. *Law, justice and the individual in society.* New York: Holt, 1977.

Terr, L. Family study of child abuse. *Journal of Psychiatry,* 1970, **127**, 665–671.

Trecker, Harleigh. *Social work administration: Principles and practice.* New York: Association, 1971.

Zalba, S. R. The abused child: A typology for classification and treatment. *Social Work,* 1967, **12**, 70–79.

17

Troubled Adolescents in Divorced and Remarried Families

JAMIE KELEM KESHET, M.S.W.,
and MARSHA PRAVDER MIRKIN, Ph.D.

*D*ivorce and remarriage are major family transitions that become additional stages in the family life cycle (Carter & McGoldrick, 1980). These stages can have a special impact on children who are approaching or are in their adolescent years. Divorce involves adjustment to a different kind of parenting. With a remarriage, new members are introduced and the structure of the relationships among the original family members is changed. The first part of this chapter delineates a developmental model of the changes precipitated by divorce and remarriage; the second part focuses on treatment of these transitional families where the adolescent is the identified patient.

PART I: DEVELOPMENTAL MODEL

For any family, the life-cycle stage of having adolescent children is also a time of change in the structure of family relationships. A child will soon leave the family household and introduce new members as lovers, housemates, or spouses. In Ackerman's (1980) analysis, three major areas of family organization are concurrently being shifted in families with typical adolescents. These are the balance of responsibility in the relationship between the adolescent and each parent, the shifting of intensity in interactions with each parent, and the adolescent's greater involvement with the larger community.

Parental separation, divorce, or remarriage coming at this point in the life cycle may delay the appropriate changes of adolescence or accelerate the process of adolescence to a pace that is not healthy for the parent or the child. The adolescent's troubled behavior may be the result of interaction between stages of family life and the adolescent's developmental stage. When a child in a divorced or remarried family reaches adolescence, all family members have been exposed to a good deal of change, stress, and loss. The family structure that exists at the time of adolescence, even if it has been stable for some time, may become problematic because of unfinished resolution of separation issues and/or the complexity of the relationships, particularly in the stepfamily.

Post-Divorce Family System

A family does not end, "break up," or dissolve with a divorce; it continues in another form. The ideal form is that of the binuclear family (Ahrons, 1980)—two households that share the rearing of the children. However, one parent may be out of the picture permanently or for some time. The varying involvement of biological parents is a critical factor in the adolescent's adjustment following divorce.

Family patterns established during the marriage influence the way in which custody and visitation are determined, the custody arrangements following divorce, and the way in which the children are cared for by each adult (Little, 1982). Some patterns from the nuclear family may be carried directly into the post-divorce situation. For example, a family of four in which each parent has one "special" child is likely to keep these special alliances after the separation. The consequences of divorce for the favorite child of the noncustodial parent are very different from the consequences for the favorite of the remaining parent. Fights among siblings may echo the marital fights.

The divorced family continues to operate as a system after marital separation. The day-to-day caring for the children is done separately by each parent in one of the subsystems created by the divorce. These subsystems include the Former-Spouse Subsystem, composed of the two formerly married people now working together as co-parents in two households; the Custodial Subsystem, consisting of the custodial parent and children (also called the Single-Parent Family); and the Visiting or Noncustodial Subsystem, composed of the noncustodial (visiting) parent and children. In joint custody, there are two Custodial Subsystems rather than one custodial and one noncustodial. When a remarriage takes place, the New-Couple Subsystem is added, consisting of the remarried couple.

Some members of the family are members of more than one subsystem. A parent, for example, may be a member of the Former-Spouse Subsystem, the Noncustodial Subsystem, and the New-Couple Subsystem. A child is a member of the Single-Parent Family and the Visiting Subsystem. The ways in which these subsystems do or do not communicate and cooperate in carrying out family tasks is an important aspect of the system's functioning.

Within each of these subsystems, relationships of affect and power change as the family moves from being a nuclear family to being a divorced family. Behaviors that would be pathological or disturbing in a nuclear family may be appropriate forms of adjustment for the post-divorce family. Recognizing these changes is important for understanding the tasks faced by the stepfamily as it attempts to create a remarried family structure. As the remarried family becomes unified, some of the changes that previously took place in the divorced family subsystems must be reversed or modified.

After Separation

The married couple moves from being a combined marital and parental subsystem of the nuclear family to being a former-spouse and co-parental subsystem of the post-divorce family. This change is characterized by an increase of emotional distance, a limitation in the scope of the relationship, and a greater differentiation between the partners in their parental functioning. This complete transition from married couple to former spouses is often referred to as an "emotional divorce." Although physical distance usually makes conflict less frequent, and the emotional divorce may appear to be complete, many issues often remain unresolved.

Adolescents may experience difficulties when these underlying issues are not resolved and are not addressed openly by the adults; in short, when the emotional divorce is not complete. A lack of resolution is often reflected in the adolescent's attempts to create contact between parents. The adolescent child may carry messages between the two parents, invent situations in which the parents must confront each other, or give the parents reasons to meet together to discuss the child's problems.

One part of the emotional divorce involves mourning for the positive aspects of the former marriage. Any divorced parent, even one who feels that the divorce was necessary and beneficial, has occasional moments of missing the former spouse or being aware of the good parts of the marriage. If the parent cannot express these feelings, a child may nonetheless sense them and attempt to effect a reconciliation between his or her parents.

As the former spouses move away from each other, cooperating as parents becomes a difficult task. This is because many couples have never been able to communicate well or agree on child-rearing issues while married, and it is compounded by feelings of loss and anger from the divorce. In general, the control of divorced parents over their children diminishes during the year following the separation because of their own grieving and loss of self-esteem. When a child is an adolescent at the time of the divorce, the parents may have less individual and combined authority at a time when the teenager needs clear and firm controls exerted upon him or her.

Adolescent Tasks at the Time of Separation

The major task of adolescence is to rearrange family involvement in preparation for greater independence and individuation. An adolescent can ordinarily gain distance from one parent by decreasing his or her involvement with that parent and increasing involvement with the other parent (Ackerman, 1980). Through a series of shifts in intensity between parents, or through one major shift the adolescent moves towards separation and independence.

When one parent moves out of the house, the adolescent has a more difficult time applying this technique, partly because the other parent is not available to help break the intensity. The structure of the post-divorce living arrangements forces the adolescent to have a more intense involvement with the parent who is left at home. This is a shift that occurs, not because the child is trying to redefine his or her family position, but because the marriage is ending. If the parent with custody has not been close to the child, this sudden and forced involvement may be tense and difficult. If the custodial parent is the one with whom the adolescent had a closer relationship, the adolescent may then have a harder time separating or shifting intensity to the visiting parent.

A typical way for adolescents to increase the intensity of an interaction is through anger. However, they may be fearful of expressing angry feelings towards the noncustodial parent because they do not want to be abandoned completely by this parent. If they do use anger to become more involved with the visiting parent, either parent may think the child is taking sides on the issues that led to the divorce. At times, for example, the custodial parent may coopt the adolescent's age-appropriate anger for his or her adult purposes in gaining advantages in the divorce settlement.

Another way in which the adolescent readjusts his or her relationships with the parents is to shift the balance of responsibility, taking more or less initiative than previously. A separation may prevent the child from making this change according to his or her own needs or desires. The adolescent may be pushed into a caretaking role or forced to be more assertive in order to get the simplest needs met. In other cases, the parent may cope with the loss of the mate by investing more energy in the relationship with the child.

Outside activity is also affected by the adolescent's freedom to withdraw energy from the family and become involved with the larger community and peer group. For some teenagers, the moving-out process is blocked or slowed down. The family crisis requires them to do more at home, be more connected with one parent, or play the role between the two parents. The energy a child should be using for his or her growth can be drained by this involvement with adult problems.

These problems are exacerbated when a parent leaves home suddenly at the time that the oldest sibling leaves for college, marriage, or work. In these families, the next oldest adolescent experiences a double loss—that of the sibling and the parent. Moreover, the intensity of the relationship with the remaining parent is increased if the older sibling had acted as a buffer.

Adolescents who adjust best to separation and divorce focus themselves outside the home in what Wallerstein and Kelly (1980) have termed a "strategic withdrawal." By concentrating on school, on peers, and on outside activities in which they have secure identities, these adolescents protect themselves from the tensions and chaos of the home.

Living in the Post-Divorce Family

Even after the initial crisis of the separation has subsided and the family is settling into a new form of parenting within two households, renegotiating involvement with the parents is difficult.

As in the initial separation period, the adolescent is not at liberty to shift the intensity of his or her involvement with each parent. When one parent has left the scene completely, the child may have angry or longing fantasies about the missing parent but is not in a position to act on the desires. A noncustodial parent living at a considerable distance from the child's primary home is also a difficult person with whom to initiate greater contact. Moreover, the child may feel inhibited from expressing his or her anger toward someone with whom the connection is already fragile.

Once the family has become accustomed to one pattern of custody and visitation, a child who wants to initiate a closer relationship with the noncustodial parent can rarely do so in a subtle way. Even a minor change in a visiting arrangement can upset the balance of power between households. Often a teenager must declare a strong desire to "live" with the noncustodial parent in order to decrease the distance. He or she may ask directly or may behave in such an impossible way that the custodial parent chooses to send him or her to the visiting parent. This behavior can overtly alienate the custodial parent while also providing a connection between the former spouses. However, the adolescent's behavior may be doubly determined. The behavior may indicate that the emotional divorce is incomplete, and serve as a means of working out a safe way to move between the two parents. In this way, the adolescent becomes differentiated from both parents.

The Single-Parent Family

The single-parent family is actually a subsystem of the larger divorced family. It often develops as a family unit for several years before a parent remarries, and during this time creates its own style for dealing with the absence of one parent.

The single-parent family develops some of its special characteristics because it is formed at a time of deep pain and grief. Supporting each other through the process of mourning the end of the marriage is often a source of strength for the parent and children. They find a new companionship and intimacy with each other. However, the increased intensity of the parent-child relationship can hinder a child's age-appropriate differentiation from the parent.

The intimacy between single parent and child seems to be strongest when there is an only child or only one child left in the home. If this child is of the opposite sex, there is a temptation to "date" the parent. The love and affection received by the parent from the child compensates, in part, for the divorced spouse's loss of companionship.

The closeness between parent and child can protect them from new relationships. The parent often fears failing in another relationship. Lack of confidence about heterosexual relationships is also a common adolescent response to parental divorce. A mother and daughter may enjoy each other's company and spend time socializing, for example, by going shopping together or going to movies on the weekends and thus, avoiding the world of men. Becoming the parent's companion is a way of growing up within the family rather than growing up by leaving the family. The absence of the other biological parent (who would ordinarily break up this pair) makes it easier for the parent and child to become stuck in dysfunctional intimacy, and symptomatic behavior may result. These dynamics are stronger and more difficult to change when the single parent does not remarry for a considerable time.

The single-parent family may not be a structure that copes well with adolescent anger and rebellion. The single parent, already overloaded with work, financial, and childcare responsibilities, frequently lacks the strength to enforce controls on the adolescent. In a two-parent family the spouse is often helpful in backing up the partner's authority. In some families, one parent acts as a buffer for angry exchanges between the other parent and the adolescent. This other parent can diffuse the charge of these exchanges and keep them from escalating. One teenage girl, complaining about her parents' divorce, said, "It's hard having only one parent home. If I get mad at my mother, I have no one to talk to. I used to talk to my father."

The parent-child hierarchy may also be thrown off by sexual competition between parent and child. An adolescent and parent may both begin dating at the same time. Many divorced adults compare their feelings about meeting new people to the way they felt as adolescents. They may be moody, vulnerable, shy or adventurous. A teenager in this phase of life wants the security of a safe and confident parent to fall back upon when he or she has had enough adventuring. When the parent is going through similar experiences and is clearly as insecure and inept as the teenager, the child may become very resentful and angry. (For example, "How can she borrow my clothes for her dates? She wants to look like a teenager herself. She's disgusting.") The child's sexual activities may be aimed at spiting, outdoing, or encouraging the parent. His or her sexual involvement with peers may also be a form of protection against incestuous feelings or fantasies provoked by the parent's clear interest in finding new sexual partners.

A parent may actually feel jealous of the child's looks, social poise, or attachment to a boyfriend or girlfriend. Sometimes the parent will flirt with the child's friends. The parent may have a hard time limiting the child's freedom or sexual experimentation when he or she is also experimenting. Many parents are baffled when their teenager asks, "If your boyfriend sleeps over, why can't mine?"

The power structure of the single-parent family often differs from the way it was in the nuclear family. The children gain power relative to the parent through participating in the upkeep of the household, providing support and feedback to the parent, being valuable companions, and giving the parent the sense of being a good parent. They perform functions that would ordinarily be the role of the other spouse.

The work necessary to care for children and a home intensifies when one parent moves out. Sometimes an older child takes over many of the parental responsibilities and moves into a position of authority alongside the single parent. Enlisting the aid of the older children and working things out democratically may be an appropriate strategy for the single parent of adolescents. However, the parent must also continue to enforce limits and to determine nonnegotiable standards. The child who becomes stuck in a parentified role to the exclusion of his or her own growth is endangered, just as he or she would be in a nuclear family. The parentified child may be protecting one or both of the parents from the pain of the divorce.

Power is also exerted in a family by setting standards and limits for the children's behavior. In the single-parent family there is an unavoidable loosening of the surveillance of the children. The children become more powerful by increased personal autonomy. The single parent may also

have difficulty when the adolescent with-
draws in anger if this is a replay of the
withdrawal of the other spouse from the
marriage.

In becoming closer to his or her children
as companions, the single parent also consults them about decisions. They are the
most available source of support and feedback. Moreover, some of them become
very good at advising their parents. Some
adolescent children offer unsolicited criti-
cism of their parents' dates, outside activities, or jobs. Sometimes a parent and child
agree to leave each other alone rather than
criticize the other's behavior. The parent
who allows the adolescent to have equal
power in this contract is abdicating his or
her parental role to set and enforce limits
for the child.

When the noncustodial parent is not in
contact with the children, the single-parent
family is relatively well bounded. The children have one home and one set of expectations. They usually share in the chores
and decision making as much as in other
single-parent families. The parent may
have an especially hard time maintaining
control as there is no financial support or
sharing in the child-rearing tasks from the
other parent. The adolescents may have
more difficulty separating from the single
parent. Sometimes the adolescent, unable
to find ways to regulate the distance between him- or herself and the single parent
and without another parent available in the
home to help modulate the intense relationship, leaves home earlier than he or
she would otherwise. One girl chose a college in Colorado although her mother
wanted her to stay nearby on the East
Coast. If the adolescent has reached an appropriate age for leaving home, he or she
may have a more difficult time separating
from a parent whom he or she has supported after a divorce, and may feel guilty
about leaving the single parent and siblings
without his or her services.

The Visiting Subsystem

The Visiting Subsystem (consisting of
the noncustodial parent and his or her chil-

dren) is not well defined or well bounded.
The children and parent live primarily in
different homes. Children may each visit
the parent separately. The minifamily forms
and disbands; it is nonexistent more frequently than it exists. Most visiting parents
try to pack in as much parenting as possible, both by doing things with their children and by teaching their particular views
on life.

Adolescents may object to regularly
scheduled visits with parents. They often
prefer to set the times of their visits and to
spend a fairly short time together. They
can control the intensity better this way.
However, they must frequently commit
themselves to a weekend, a week, or a
month at the other parent's home. This
long period of time away from peer contacts, school, and extracurricular activities
is often very uncomfortable for the teenager. In fact, both parent and child often
wonder what to do with each other. One
teenager, aware that his father "doesn't see
us growing," described how his father
"followed us around" constantly on a
week's visit.

The distribution of power between the
parent and children shifts in a visiting subsystem as it does in the custodial minifamily. The visiting parent usually has less
power than he or she had during the marriage because the custodial parent is defined as the primary decision maker. The
visiting parent often limits his or her power
by a reluctance to discipline the children
on their visits. Adolescents may not be receiving the controls they need from either
parent.

A teenager may be very angry at the visiting parent for having left home. The adolescent, in his or her self-centered fashion,
takes the divorce as a personal affront:
"How dare you move out now when I need
you home so I can move out?" He or she
also feels hurt and rejected by the noncustodial parent. The visiting parent may feel
overwhelmed by these angry feelings as
they emerge, and may interpret the child's
anger as a permanent rejection rather than
a test of the parent's continued love.

Teenage moodiness and unpredictability
are an extra challenge for the visiting par-

ent, who is not as familiar as the custodial parent is with the behavior of the child on a daily basis. A blue mood may look like a major depression. A child's change from withdrawal on Saturday to cheerful playfulness on Sunday may be considered a sign of preference for the visiting parent. The child may resent being taken overly seriously in this way.

The visiting minifamily, if given enough time to develop, can become an important resource for the adolescent. However, a child who is sixteen or seventeen at the time of the divorce may leave home and be out of regular contact with the noncustodial parent before the visiting subsystem finds its own rhythm, style, and identity. The child may feel abandoned by the visiting parent and deprived of his or her care.

Ideal Divorce

The divorced family can foster the adolescent's growth if the change is handled well by the adults. If the system is flexible enough to permit the child to determine the manner and degree of contact with each parent, he or she can learn to differentiate from each one of them while maintaining the safety of the relationship with the other parent. The parents can each be open to the adolescent's expression of angry feelings without blaming the other. Moreover, the young person is exposed to two different life styles, a greater variety of new people and experiences, and two adults who are handling their sexual and social needs responsibly.

Enter the New Person

When a divorced parent begins to build a new intimate relationship, the children are affected by the changes in the parent's behavior. Parents may pull away from the children now that their needs for closeness are met elsewhere. They may make new demands. One mother wanted her children to be neater and have better manners so that they would impress the man she was dating. Adolescents react to these

changes before they have even met the new person.

Children who feel abandoned by their parent will attempt to identify or increase their involvement with the parent who is not yet involved with a new partner. They may prefer to spend time with the, as yet, unattached parent and try to protect and comfort him or her.

Adults in a new relationship are often more open in expressing their affection with each other than long married parents. Adolescents may feel very uncomfortable seeing the parent holding hands or kissing someone new. Their discomfort may lead them to move away from the parent, or to stay nearby as a voyeur or chaperone.

Conflicts develop between the parent-child dyad and the new couple. Both relationships need attention, nurturance, time, and energy. The parent can only give so much and often becomes less available to the adolescent. Resentment and jealousies develop between the child and the new person.

The parent may at times use the parent-child relationship as a safe haven from the new couple. When he or she is feeling less sure of the new person or is threatened by the new closeness, he or she may reinvest in the parent-child relationship. This shift in focus is confusing and disruptive to teenagers. If they have adjusted to their parent's new adult relationship by becoming more independent or forming new relationships with peers, they are likely to resent the parent's desire for renewed closeness. If, on the other hand, an adolescent has responded to the parent's relationship by acting out or by withdrawing from social interactions, the power of his or her negative behavior is reinforced by the parent's reinvestment. It appears as though the parent has "given in" to the child and given up the adult partner. In either case, the child's development is not appropriately facilitated.

Adolescents are especially upset when the new person is someone the parent was having an affair with before the divorce. The parent often tries to introduce the new person before the children are ready. The adolescent is likely to blame the parent and new partner for ending the marriage and hurting the other parent. He or she may form very harsh and rigid moral judgments about the new couple. Remarriages between a divorced parent and the person with whom he or she was having an extramarital affair are not common, but they often create stepfamilies with many problems. The divorced family must cope with divorce and remarriage issues simultaneously, a task that is too demanding for many families to handle.

Unification of the Stepfamily

The stepfamily is formed by joining the new couple and one or two parent-child subsystems. For example, a stepfamily may contain a new couple and a Custodial Parent-child Subsystem, a new couple and a Visiting Parent-child Subsystem, or a new couple, a Custodial Parent-child Subsystem and a Visiting Parent-child Subsystem. An individual is often a member of two subsystems.

These subsystems (also called minifamilies [Keshet, 1985]) retain their distinct identities for some time. Membership in each minifamily is more clear than membership in the overall stepfamily. The boundaries around each minifamily are stronger than the boundary around the stepfamily as a whole. Each parent-child minifamily has its own history, in both the former marriage and the interim period. The strong loyalties to each other and to the parent living outside the stepfamily often exclude the stepparent and stepsiblings. Adolescents have had more time than younger children to develop a sense of history and loyalty from the previous family. They are not eager to join a new family at the time when they are setting their sights on independence.

Combining two sets of children brings special difficulties. Adolescents of the same age may differ greatly in their physical and emotional maturity. One fourteen-year-old may be fearful of staying home alone while another may have a large babysitting practice. Children also lose their special positions in the family; for example, an oldest child may now be in the middle. Stepsiblings can become competitive with each other. Sometimes a teenager is sexually attracted to a stepsibling and feels frightened or overwhelmed.

The difficulties of an ordinary family with adolescent children are multiplied by the complexity of post-divorce parenting. Many extra exits and entrances occur as visiting children arrive and custodial children leave for their visits. Moreover, unresolved problems from the prior marriage or the parent-child minifamily may be carried directly into the stepfamily.

Stepfamily unification, the process of creating one stepfamily out of the existing minifamilies, takes from two to four years (Keshet, in press). It occurs in three major stages: acceptance, authority, and affection. If the family is stuck in one of the first two stages, the unification process cannot continue. The constant level of tension, ambivalence, and frustration in a stuck stepfamily can lead to the termination of the second marriage or the development of symptomatic behavior in one or more family members. Therapy may sometimes be required to help the stepfamily progress through these stages. Education about the process in which they are engaged is helpful in alleviating the stress and isolation experienced by many couples (Brady & Ambler, 1982). A similar educational process for adolescents in stepfamilies might also prove useful.

Acceptance

The members of the stepfamily are the remarried couple and all of their children. The work of the acceptance stage is to recognize one's own membership in this new family and to acknowledge the membership of all the others. Stepfamily members must accept the prior relationships people in the stepfamily have with each other, the history of the various minifamilies, the personality traits of other family members, and the roles that adults and children will play as the family develops. The acceptance process is hindered by unprocessed grief over the ending of the first marriage, extreme loyalty to the previous nuclear family or minifamily, or continuing anger between either adult and the children.

As occurs at the time of separation, changes in the intensity and the quality of the parent-adolescent relationships result from the remarriage. The adolescent may be blocked in his or her moves to shift the intensity of the parental relationships. Moving closer to a parent who is working on a new adult relationship is often impossible. Moving farther away leaves the adolescent with the option of moving closer to the noninvolved parent (or parent who has been remarried previously), or of isolating him- or herself.

The adolescent often sees the stepparent and the stepsiblings as competitors for the parent's affection. He or she may attempt to hold on to the intimate relationship of the parent-child minifamily in the face of such stiff competition. He or she cannot be pushed to accept a stepparent while still intent on winning the contest for the parent's heart. An adolescent who is pressured to accept the stepparent and stepsiblings is likely to withdraw more from the family.

As the stepfamily development proceeds, the children are continuing to grow up. A fourteen-year-old at the time of the divorce may now be seventeen or eighteen. If the children reach the age of leaving home in the acceptance stage, they are likely to function as outsiders to the stepfamily rather than family members. For example, a child calling home will not acknowledge the stepparent but will immediately ask for "Mom." Even teenagers living at home may not be very available physically or emotionally for learning to accept the new family members. Their primary task is to form important relationships with their peers.

The adolescent can delay the process of acceptance not only by rejecting the other stepfamily members but also by causing them to reject him. Teenagers have a dreadful reputation. Even biological parents often find them impenetrable, obnoxious, self-centered, and arrogant. A stepparent has to look beneath the surface behavior of the child in order to accept him

or her as a family member. If a stepparent has younger children, he or she may also be wary of the older child's influence on them.

The acceptance stage is accomplished as the stepfamily members spend time together, get to know each other in a variety of circumstances, and make compromises that respect their different needs. The minifamily boundaries become more permeable and new alliances are formed which cross these boundaries. The stepfamily as a whole develops a boundary and an identity for itself.

The adolescent may also benefit from the parent's involvement in a new relationship. The child can be freed from the role of spousal or parental child. He or she may gain more space and time for personal exploration and age-appropriate activities. A parent who is in a good relationship with another adult can more easily tolerate sudden changes in the adolescent's energy and intensity. He may allow the child to spend more time with his other parent or with friends now that he is not dependent on the adolescent for companionship.

Authority

The second step in the unification process is the establishment of the remarried couple as the highest authority within the stepfamily. The couple then has more power than any of the other minifamilies. Each adult has authority to set and enforce limits for all of the children. The authority stage of the stepfamily's growth is a time of intergenerational conflict which results in a new power hierarchy. The survival of the remarriage frequently depends on passing through this stage successfully. Many couples seek therapy during this stage because they associate conflict with marital instability.

Establishing the adult couple's authority requires a change in the power patterns that had developed after divorce. An adolescent is likely to oppose the reestablishment of a family hierarchy with the two adults at the top regardless of the stepparent's personality. The autonomy and power that the child had in the single-parent family are hard to give up. In addition, he or she does not yet trust that a strong couple can care for him or her. Sometimes several adolescents, siblings, or stepsiblings band together to resist the tightening of parental and stepparental reins.

Working out authority relationships requires that the stepparent and adolescent interact more directly. The stepparent may need coaching in how to discipline. He or she often has unrealistic expectations. Sometimes the stepparent's anger is a sign of difficulties within the marriage. At other times it is a reaction to the frustrations of parenting a teenager.

A common way for the adolescent to get closer to an adult in the family is through anger. The stepparent may find him- or herself the target of angry retorts, rebellious behavior, and insults as the child attempts to build the relationship. If adults cannot recognize these exchanges as a part of a process in which they are being challenged to stand firm and yet show caring, they will often withdraw in anger and frustration.

When a stepparent is willing to discipline the child and demand respect, the parent is often intolerant of the stepparent's anger at his or her child and may collude with the child to undermine the stepparent's authority. It is often the parent who wants the stepparent's help in "straightening out these kids" who becomes threatened when the new partner tries to be authoritative. The parent may fear either the child's rejection of the new stepparent or his or her own exclusion from the new dyad of child and stepparent. This particular couple dynamic is likely to increase the acting-out behavior of the child.

The authority stage is sometimes prolonged because it suits the needs of the adolescent. Although angry and resentful about being displaced by a new adult, the adolescent also has someone new to challenge and reasons that seem justifiable for disliking and therefore rejecting his or her family. The adolescent can challenge the biological parent more freely now that the parent is backed up by another adult and

is less needy. Consequently, the child has a choice of adults to approach at any given time.

The adolescent's oppositional behavior can be a constant challenge to the new couple. Without years of shared childrearing experiences, they are forced to work together in one of the hardest tasks of parenting. They may resent the child's constant demands which interfere with their enjoyment of each other as a couple. The adults may send the child to the other parent or relinquish their responsibility by allowing the teenager excessive freedom and ignoring signs of trouble.

The child's rebellion or withdrawal at this time may indicate deeper problems within the new couple relationship or unresolved problems between the former spouses. Power struggles between either set of adults can be mirrored in struggles with the child. A parent who is avoiding intimacy or commitment to the new partner may be rescued by the child's problems.

The visiting stepfamily (i.e., the visiting parent and his or her remarried family), as in the acceptance stage, is in a weaker position because of the short periods of time spent together. A whole weekend spent in conflict over rules can be exasperating for everyone and can resolve nothing. An adolescent may avoid the visiting couple at a time when they are attempting to be stricter. An adolescent who leaves home permanently at this time may remain stuck for many years, constantly challenging the authority of the stepparent and the primary importance of the remarried couple. Moreover, they have difficulties with others in their own environment who fill in for parents or represent authority.

Successful negotiation of this phase requires a unification of the standards of behavior for the various children in the stepfamily, a sense of security within the family, and a new identity of the family under the clear leadership of the remarried couple. The adults must have clear and enforceable standards. However, a willingness to include the adolescent in certain kinds of decision making is developmentally appropriate. If the adults are too authoritarian, particularly with adolescents who have previously had more power and freedom, their tactics are not as likely to succeed. Adolescents need recognition that they can handle some adult tasks and responsibilities.

Affection

The groundwork for affection is laid by the resolution of the issues of acceptance and authority. Feeling accepted helps both children and adults open up with each other. Getting beyond the authority struggles also brings out positive feelings. New stepparents are more relaxed and responsive when their authority is not constantly being tested. Children who are no longer resisting authority can begin to see stepparents as individuals. The child's security within the stepfamily structure can allow him or her to work on age-appropriate tasks and to use his or her energy more creatively. Children become more appealing to stepparents when they are neither rebelling nor regressing.

Greater flexibility and security characterize the affection stage. The adolescent has a relationship with his or her stepparent which includes respect, familiarity, and frequently, growing affection. As a semi-outsider within the boundary of the family household, the stepparent becomes an available adult with whom the adolescent can try out new behaviors, and someone who can be enlisted as a resource. The stepparent can help the adolescent and parent detach from an overly close relationship. He can use his authority to prevent a child from overpowering the couple subsystem.

The two adults, although not equally attached to the children, may have learned to function as a team and provide a clear family structure. With the adults clearly in charge, the adolescent is released from the role of spousal or parental child. The child can explore and interact with the larger community with the safety of the stepfamily to retreat to. An adolescent moving out of the home at this time takes with him or her a secure place in the family.

The affection stage is not just a bed of roses, however. The new alliances and friendships that form may shift the balance of the relationships in the stepfamily. A mother may want her sons to like her new husband but be jealous when they prefer his company to her own. A child's affection for his stepfather may bring out his biological father's jealousy. A child may feel she is being disloyal when she starts to like the stepparent or a stepsibling.

Moreover, the adolescent's experience of the divorce and remarriage are not eradicated. He or she may fear the anger of the parent or stepparent, which is reminiscent of the anger between the parents before they split up. Moving out into the community may seem dangerous if the child has seen one parent move out and then be excluded from the first family.

Even during the affection stage, old issues between the biological parents may resurface as new questions about curfews, drugs, alcohol, and sex arise and threaten the stability of the stepfamily. A child may be receiving implicit consent from one parent for behavior which the other parent adamantly opposes. As the last child is nearing adulthood, the biological parents may realize that they will have much less contact with each other. Even if one or both are happily remarried, they may have feelings of loss in giving up their post-divorce, co-parenting relationship. A child's behavior may reflect the parents' need to hold onto each other a little longer.

If both parents remarry and have new families or close relationships with stepchildren, the teenager who moves between them may feel that he or she has no real home. The adolescent in a remarried family is in danger of being extruded for many reasons which are thoroughly described by Sager et al. (1983).

The Divorced-Remarried Family System

The divorced spouses, their children, their new spouses, and their children form a larger family system which we call the Divorced-Remarried Family. The stepfamily is a subsystem of this system, as is one former nuclear family. The adults in this family are united by their care of the same children. Unresolved issues of acceptance, power, and jealousy among three or four adults who parent a given child can result in problematic behavior for that child.

For example, first and second spouses of the same sex are in a relationship with each other which they did not choose. They may feel jealous and competitive towards each other. Adolescents are aware of the ways in which these important adults do or do not get along.

Sometimes power issues in the Divorced-Remarried Family are not resolved as long as one of the former spouses is in a new relationship and the other is not. The remarried spouse feels a responsibility to please both the former spouse and the new spouse. A child may remain loyal to the parent who is not in a new relationship since the remarried parent has another ally. The adolescent may refuse to accept or respect the stepparent out of loyalty to the parent who is not remarried. Another adolescent in the same situation may be angry or embarrassed by the "clingy" behavior of the unattached parent.

When both divorced spouses have remarried, the power relationship between the two couples is not clearly defined. Although the custodial couple may consider themselves the major parents, the visiting couple is not willing to accept a lower status merely because they see the children for less time. The two couples may compete with each other to have more control over the children, to be better parents, or to be more popular with the children.

Adolescents respond in various ways to competition among the three or four adults. They may ally with the apparently needier parent or couple. The adolescent who attempts to remain neutral may distance himself from all the adults. Conflict and confusion create an unbearable situation, sometimes resulting in the adolescent's becoming demanding, selfish, and unruly. This behavior may escalate the conflict between the couples, and the adolescent experiences an even greater conflict of loyalty. Facilitating the deescalation of conflict and resolution of differences among the adults of the Divorced-Remarried Family is an important task of family therapy.

Stepfamilies are exposed to changes from many sources. Changes in either household affect the other. A custodial stepfamily may have reached the stage of affection and be much calmer just as the noncustodial parent decides to remarry. A new baby can disrupt the family. There are also three or four extended families that can impact on the adolescent. The death of a stepparent's parent, for example, may move the remarried parent closer to the stepparent and more distant from the adolescent.

Summary

When a family experiences a divorce, several structural changes take place. In the single-parent family and the visiting minifamily, children become more powerful family members and often take the role of companion, protector, or assistant to their parents. Although these changes are frequently adaptive and not necessarily pathological, they may block the normal developmental changes of adolescence for both child and parent. An adolescent may be unable to negotiate the increased distance from the family necessary for maturation or may be pushed into a premature independence.

A remarriage requires another series of changes which take place in three stages: acceptance, authority, and affection. This process of stepfamily unification is often in conflict with the adolescent's need for greater independence and involvement in the community outside the home. A family that becomes stuck in one of these stages is unable to proceed and may be the setting for an adolescent's symptomatic behavior.

PART II: TREATMENT MODEL

The first part of this chapter, as well as much of what has been written in the area (see Visher & Visher, 1979; Sager et al., 1983), concentrates on the problems encountered by divorced and remarried families as they reorganize over time. This section focuses on situations where the quest to reorganize goes awry, and mental-health practitioners are presented with an adolescent identified patient.

In an effort to understand how this reorganization breaks down, as well as how change can be facilitated, we are utilizing a systemic conceptualization of dysfunctional behavior. Such an outlook makes several assumptions. One assumption is that families are caring. While the alliances in divorced and remarried families might be skewed (for instance, stronger between the biological parent and child than between stepparent and child), there are strong bonds and a desire to "make the family work." Families are seen as functioning in the best way they know how, and are often in dysfunctional patterns because they know no other way both to maintain the integrity of the family and to provide flexibility for change.

Second, we assume that symptoms serve a function for the family. Troubled adolescent behavior is often a symptom of a system that is tangled in its efforts to reorganize. The family is uncomfortable with new and often unclear role definitions, boundaries, and hierarchies. The usefulness of a symptom in this context will be discussed further in this chapter.

Although there are differences among divorcing, single-parent, and remarried families, we view them as part of a continuity because they are at different phases in a family's life cycle (see Carter & McGoldrick, 1980). We refer to these families as "reorganizing families."

If role definition, boundaries, and hierarchy are clearly and functionally set during the divorcing stage, it is less likely that an adolescent will exhibit problems during the single-parent or remarried family stages. However, if those issues remain unresolved, if the loss is not dealt with, and if relationships are not defined during the earlier phases, it is quite probable that the adolescent will exhibit disturbed or disturbing behavior during that or a later phase. In addition, a family who has negotiated the divorce may again become "stuck" when the remarriage phase begins. We view the acting-out behavior of an adolescent in a reorganizing family as an extreme of the process which all reorganizing families undergo. There is some disruption and a need for redefinition of roles and relationships in all divorcing and remarrying families. The families discussed here, however, have difficulty negotiating these changes.

It has been our experience that there are three critical systemic dynamics related to the disturbed and disturbing behavior of an adolescent in a reorganizing family. These dynamics, which are not mutually exclusive, will be referred to as reunion, diversion, and replacement. What seems to underlie each of these dynamics is fuzzy boundaries within and between the biological and the step- or divorced family. The emotional divorce in many of these families has not been completed, so there is still an unspoken relationship between biological parents. The adolescent is often triangulated within this relationship, rather than able to form a boundary between himself and each of his parents, as well as to define himself within the context of the new family.

Reunion Function of Symptomatic Behavior

In the reunion mode, the adolescent's behavior serves to reconnect the biological parents. Generally, these adolescents feel that they have caused the divorce, and thus feel responsible for the reunion. Parents in such families have not emotionally separated, and the child receives the message that his biological parents still need each other. The ex-spouse bond does not have to be one of expressed love—ex-spouses may also bond through anger. In many of these situations, ex-spouses fought with each other about their child's behavior prior to the divorce, and continue to blame their child for the marital discord. When the decision to divorce is made, the adolescent assumes that he or she is the catalyst for the divorce.

Often the noncustodial parent in these

families backs off from the parenting role. This can be a way of distancing from the ex-spouse or a way of connecting, since the custodial parent, anxious to be a "good parent," will often pursue the distancing partner. It is not uncommon to be told that a mother will call her ex-husband weekly to ask why he hasn't seen his son. Phone calls thus provide a medium for ex-spouses to connect.

An adolescent in this type of family therefore feels responsible for the divorce and reunion; feels that his or her parents still need each other, even if a stepparent is already in the picture; and fears the loss of one of the biological parents. The disturbing behavior serves to bring the parents together in their efforts to help the troubled adolescent, and fuels the fantasy of reuniting parents in marriage.

This dynamic can be illustrated by the case example of Lisa. Lisa was brought to the inpatient family unit of a psychiatric hospital at age sixteen because of repeated runaway episodes and noncompliance with her mother and stepfather. Lisa's parents divorced when she was twelve and her sister was ten. Her father, Mr. G., with whom she was closely identified, moved back to his family of origin in Arizona. Lisa saw him once that first year, and then visits stopped. When financial burdens became great, Mrs. G. would yell in frustration, "Why did he have to leave us?" Lisa was generally helpful, and often comforted her mother. When Lisa was fourteen, Mrs. G. was remarried to an attractive man, Mr. A., several years her junior. This was Mr. A.'s first marriage. Shortly after the birth of their mutual daughter, Mr. and Mrs. A. began to argue about finances, discipline, and their needs for different degrees of closeness, which had not yet been resolved from the prior marriage. Mrs. A. would often cry about being misunderstood.

At one point, Lisa overheard a conversation in which she heard her mother and stepfather say that if Mr. A.'s stepchildren needed hospitalization, Mrs. A. would have to contact Mr. G. since the children were still covered by his medical insurance. Shortly thereafter, Lisa began to run away and her belligerent noncompliance snowballed. Lisa finally suggested that she be hospitalized to work on her problems. Clearly, the only way that mother could meet that demand was to get in touch with Lisa's biological father,

which she did. Lisa was hospitalized, and Mr. G. came in from Arizona to see her.

By creating a crisis, Lisa's difficulties served as a means of reengaging her father. If her sole purpose was to reconnect with her father, she would have been successful and the crisis would have been over, at least until they again disengaged. However, the unwritten agenda was to reengage her biological parents. Lisa did not trust the new marriage and felt that her mother needed more support than was provided. She also believed that she had been a "bad child" who caused her father to leave. Now, if she could only be a bad adolescent who repented, perhaps he would come back. In addition, mother demonstrated that the emotional divorce from Lisa's father was not complete by insisting that she monitor all interactions between Lisa and her father.*

When intervening with such families, the therapist must understand the complexity of the various roles and interactions, and help the family to reorganize functionally. This requires an acceptance and clarification of the various roles of all the involved adults. The goals of treatment are first to reconnect the child with the disengaged biological parent, as well as to define the child as a member of the new family. The second treatment goal is to define the roles and relationships in the new family. For example, stepfather must be included in treatment as this helps structurally to define him as having a central role. Finally, the therapist assists the biological parents with their emotional separation.

Our suggestion is that therapy remain focused on the child. The first meeting in a family operating with these dynamics is often held with the biological parents and a stepparent and defined as a meeting focused solely on helping the child. It is made clear from the onset that no marital or divorce issues will be touched upon. There are several purposes for structuring the meeting in this way. First, father is reengaged in his parenting role while not

---

*Case examples are from families seen at Charles River Hospital, Wellesley, Massachusetts. Names, ages, and some facts about the cases have been altered to protect confidentiality.

crossing the boundaries into the spouse subsystem. Second, this enhances communication among parents about visitation and financial arrangements for treatment. If we had excluded Lisa's stepfather, we would have fed into the family fantasy that the meeting was for the purpose of reuniting biological parents. If father were excluded, we would have reinforced the previous structure that had not worked. Future meetings with the family in the above case example involved clearly defined subsystems: Lisa and her father; Lisa with her mother and stepfather; Lisa with her siblings; mother and stepfather.

The content of the meetings also must remain child-focused. If a therapist directly tells a parent that he or she has not emotionally separated from an ex-spouse, the parent will either feel blamed for the teenager's behavior or will not connect this statement with the child's behavior. Most likely, the parent will also deny the incompleteness of the separation. An alternative approach, taken with families such as Lisa's, would be to explain as follows: "Lisa is worried that she caused the divorce and is responsible for getting you back together. She's trying very hard to do that. How can we work toward letting her know that you feel stable enough in your new lives that you don't need her in that role?" It was then suggested that Lisa's mother and stepfather go out more with each other to "prove their point" to Lisa. Once they did this, Lisa not only saw the couple working more effectively but also that her mother was indeed getting more attention and affection from her new husband.

The same child focus applies when attempting to reengage the biological parent with the child. The biological parent often feels guilty about abandoning his or her family, and those feelings of guilt and worthlessness often spiral into more distancing. It is therefore usually helpful to ascribe positive connotations to the noncustodial parents' past behavior, for example: "I know that since you love your daughter, you were very concerned that Lisa wouldn't be able to adjust to life after the divorce if you stayed in the picture. But that was two years ago. Lisa does have a

new life now, and she needs you. Are you willing to be part of her life now?" If the biological father agrees, very specific guidelines are set up for visits and calls.

A common reunion dynamic occurs when a custodial parent attacks the other parent for "neglecting" the adolescent, and the child defends the attacked parent. In families where both parents maintain some involvement with the child, the attack-defense dynamic keeps the parent who left present in the household and interferes with the emotional separation between ex-spouses. It is only through enforcing boundaries that respect each parent's relationship with the child, blocking involvement in that subsystem by the other parent, and enforcing the hierarchy such that each parent makes the rules and decisions for the time the child is with him or her, that the cycle is broken and more functional adaptations are made possible.

For example, Jeff is a fourteen-year-old whose parents divorced when he was two. However, the separation remained incomplete and there was much bickering between parents. Jeff's father was often late to pick Jeff up, and at times, never came. Thinking she was comforting Jeff, mother would attack her former spouse on the basis of his unreliability. Jeff would then become furious with his mother and defend his father. Mother in turn felt misunderstood and angry and would tell Jeff to go live with his father. Jeff would leave and return with his father several hours later. The dynamic kept parents involved with each other. Direct interventions asking mother not to discuss father in front of Jeff, and asking father to drop Jeff off and immediately leave when he returned Jeff from a visit did not work. The attack-defense dynamic continued. Finally, Jeff's mother was told that it was very nice of her to sacrifice herself for her ex-husband. Here she was setting it up for Jeff to get angry at her, so he would never have to get angry at his father for being unreliable. She was asked to continue to put down her ex-husband, in order to give Jeff the chance to support his father, see his father more frequently, and develop that relationship.

Father was told that Jeff understood the insecurities that would make him come late or not show. As a result, Jeff would come to him, reaffirming that he had not rejected his father because his father left when he was two. We told him to continue coming late or not showing until he felt secure that Jeff loved him. By telling the family to do "more of the same," but at the same time giving them a new meaning for their behavior, they were placed in a predicament. Should mother continue to talk about father, the message was that she still loved her ex-husband. If father continued to be unreliable in his visits, the message was that he felt insecure. This set the stage for change.

In summary, when presented with a symptom that served to reunite parents in their spouse roles, it is critical to intervene to enforce the parenting role without establishing a spousal role. To detriangulate the adolescent, the parent must no longer send the message that reunion is desired. This is accomplished either by strengthening the boundary around the new marriage, or in the case of single-parent families, by developing an adult support system for the single parent. Finally, the therapist facilitates the reengagement of the distant biological parent while developing a role for the stepparent.

Diversion Function of Symptomatic Behavior

Diversion in a reorganizing family, as well as in a nuclear family, is a protective effort by the child to divert attention away from a parent's marital and personal distress onto the problematic adolescent. In reorganizing families, this dynamic most often occurs when the new marriage is threatened by marital conflict and the child is overly concerned about the parent's unhappiness. The child's behavior allows or forces the parent to mobilize his or her energy to come to the aid of the child, and thus avoid the parent's own issues.

Children in reorganizing families tend to be sensitive to messages received from custodial parents. Divorcing families are ripe for adolescent symptoms because both the structural and the affective foundation of the family are shifting at a time when adolescents would normally be making moves to separate. The adolescents then experience a pull between their need to separate

and their need to remain at home until the home foundation is again settled; between the need to start their own lives, and the need to take care of the parents who often feel depressed and overwhelmed. This is a time for the adolescent to be moving out, but instead, an adult usurped that position and moved out. Instead of the adults being left at home to care for each other, there is the pull for the adolescent to remain at home to care for the remaining parent. The critical determinant for adolescent adaptation is the parent's message that the parent is strong enough to work through the pain and to guide the adolescent toward independence. Diversion is more likely to occur when these messages are not given.

A case example that illustrates this dynamic involves Nancy, a thirteen-year-old girl who was brought to the hospital because of oppositional behavior and suicidal gestures. Her mother, Mrs. D., had married Mr. G. a year earlier. Nancy reportedly got along with Mr. G. until the marriage. This was Mrs. D.'s third marriage, each of the prior marriages lasting less than two years. Mrs. D. refused to change her last name, stating that she had too many medications and couldn't change her name on all the prescriptions. Since the marriage, Mrs. D.'s migraine headaches and functional colitis had worsened. Nancy did change her name, but fought viciously with her stepfather. She defended her mother's reasons for maintaining her last name and threatened to punch anybody who suggested that her mother's physical ailments were psychosomatic.

In this case, Nancy and her mother both had histories that would make it difficult for them to trust that a marriage could last. Mrs. D.'s physical ailments allowed her to keep some distance between herself and Mr. G. Mr. G. never expressed any anger at his wife either for her choice to keep her second husband's name or for her distancing via illness. Rather, the entire family colluded in expressing all their hurt, anger, and fear in regard to Nancy's behavior. The marriage was protected through Nancy's symptoms.

In treating a family where diversion is the purpose of the symptom, we once again focus on boundaries and hierarchy. Intervention seeks to empower the parents and to communicate clearly that they are strong enough to deal with their own issues, and don't need the child to divert them. For example, the therapist in this case suggested that Nancy needed to test her parents, to see if they were really strong enough to deal with her. She was asked to continue to misbehave until she felt sure that her parents could really tackle her behavior. A new meaning is thus given to Nancy's behavior, and the parents are put in the position of working together and developing their parenting style to meet up with Nancy's "test."

In many families such as Nancy's, the stepparent took over a great deal of authority before being accepted as a parent within the family. This is often a reaction to the biological parent's difficulty in maintaining authority during this transition. However, since the stepparent has not yet been accepted, his authority is often defied. An initial strategy in a case of diversion is therefore to place the biological parent solely in charge of the child in order to diffuse the situation described above (see Carter & McGoldrick, 1980). The biological parent can later delegate some caretaking and disciplinary responsibilities to the stepparent. In the above example, Mrs. G. was placed solely in charge of Nancy. In the past, because of mother's illness, stepfather had assumed that role. However, he had assumed it prematurely, in the acceptance stage, rather than the authority stage. When mother felt too sick or "weak" to enforce limits, stepfather was instructed to offer support, empathy, and nurturance to her directly, rather than skipping over mother to the diverting child. In this way, the biological parent was in the role of disciplinarian, while the spouse bond was strengthened by the added support and caretaking given directly by husband to wife. When the marriage was strengthened, the stepfather was encouraged to develop his authority within the family.

In summary, in families where diversion is the function of the symptom, the out-of-control adolescent is often protecting a custodial parent either from his or her own depression and anxiety, or from potential rifts in the new marriage. The remarried couple (initially the bioparent), or single parent (sometimes with assistance from a support group) is again placed in charge of the child. The entire family can thus see that the parent is indeed strong enough to care for the child, in spite of his or her overwhelmed feelings. The overwhelmed parent can get support from other(s) in his or her own generation instead of depending on an adolescent whose task is to begin the separation process.

Replacement Function of Symptomatic Behavior

Replacement occurs when an adolescent attempts to take the place of the parent who left to a degree that is dysfunctional. This dynamic is mostly seen when a child lives with an opposite-sex parent. It is a complex dynamic with three components: first, the adolescent is protective of the custodial parent by making sure that the parent's needs are met. Simultaneously, the parent sends the message that he or she is overwhelmed and incapable of functioning without the adolescent. Second, the adolescent is loyal to the departed parent by not allowing another adult to replace him or her. Finally, the adolescent attempts to gain control of a previously unpredictable life by assuming the role and tasks of an adult. He or she attempts to control the household in collusion with the parent who has lost a mate of his or her own generation.

Some replacement is typical in any reorganizing family. It is labeled problematic only when the generational lines are so blurred that the child can no longer function in his generation (for example, when he stops attending school or shies away from peer relationships), and when family tasks are assumed by the adolescent instead of being delegated to the adolescent by an adult. In order to separate functionally, the adolescent must feel secure enough to leave, and the parent must feel supported enough to let the adolescent go.

The problem of replacement is demonstrated in the following case example:

Jenny, sixteen, lived with her father and nineteen-year-old brother, Michael. Prior to Jenny's having problems with truancy, psychophysiological complaints, and a recent suicide threat, Michael began seriously dating an eighteen-year-old girl. Michael had a very close relationship with his father since the divorce and was rarely home after he began dating. At the same time, father began sporadically seeing a divorced woman, while overtly denying that he wanted a serious relationship. The scenario was played out as follows: father would go to work and wake Jenny on his way out. Jenny would complain of headaches and refuse to go to school. She would spend the day cleaning the house and preparing dinner for her father. When questioned, Jenny responded that her father "couldn't take care of himself" and she was just doing her job. Father did not impose consequences for that behavior.

The primary focus of therapy was to place Jenny back into the adolescent generation so that she could resume age-appropriate tasks. The therapeutic goals were to develop an age-appropriate support group for father so that he was not as dependent on Jenny and to place father in charge of Jenny so that he required her to attend school and to spend time with peers. In addition, father was instructed to delegate household chores to Jenny rather than stepping back and allowing her to take them over.

The adult network is mobilized ostensibly to focus on the child, in this case, to get Jenny to go to school. However, the network also provides support and a peer group for the single parent. The stated goal is for father to develop a source of support when he needs to enforce his authority. In Jenny's case, Michael, Michael's girlfriend, father's girlfriend, and father's colleague at work all offered to drive Jenny to school and father agreed to place Jenny in the car if she refused. This "strong-arm" approach never had to be carried out; it was sufficient for Jenny to see that her father wasn't alone, that he did have support coming from people other than herself, and that he could set limits for her.

In summary, strong bonds with the departed parent in combination with concern over the ability of the remaining parent to function and to support the adolescent's separation may lead an adolescent to fill in for a lost parent. The adolescent may assume the role of the spouse, even if the parent has remarried, and refuses to accept or acknowledge the authority of the step-

parent. A focus on hierarchy, clear limit setting, and development of age-appropriate support groups can be helpful.

Special Issues: Loosened Sexual Boundaries

Sager and his colleagues (1983) refer to the loosened sexual boundaries in remarried families and discuss the dynamics resulting in sexual abuse between a non-biological parent and a child. They hypothesize that remarried families are less likely than biological families to collude in a "conspiracy of silence" and thus are more likely to reveal sexual abuse. It is our experience, however, that this collusion still frequently occurs.

In a biological family, the incest taboo is a powerful injunction, but in remarried families, the taboo is less clear. The stepparent has no history with the child, and history is often what reinforces the sexual taboos when a child reaches puberty. The highest risk for sexual abuse is when the remarriage occurs concurrently with the child reaching puberty or at the time of adolescence. The child is then emerging as a sexual being at the same time that sexuality within the household is heightened owing to the new marriage; the new couple is expected to have sexual relations, and physical affection is more often visible in the household. A healthy atmosphere generally exists in these families. A problem may arise, however, if the remarried adults are afraid of intimacy, especially if the mother is sending messages that she can tolerate neither too much closeness (often for fear of another rejection) nor too much distance. This situation is ripe for triangulation: if mother becomes too distant, she may lose her new spouse; if she allows him to come too close, she becomes frightened. A distance regulator is needed. If the stepfather has poor impulse control and cannot experience his attraction to his stepdaughter (which is common and normal within remarried families) without acting impulsively, he may then initiate sexual relations with the stepdaughter. At times, this abusive relationship can maintain a balance within the family: the daughter enters the role of distance regulator by providing some closeness with father, so that father and mother may have some distance.

Unreported sexual abuse may become more likely if: (1) the child feels guilty about destroying the first marriage and therefore will do anything possible not to break up the new marriage, and/or (2) if the child feels protective over a mother who she believes could not handle either the intimacy of marriage, or the separation that may result from revealing the abuse.

Sager and his colleagues (1983) observed that these families often present themselves as afraid of losing the child to outsiders, deny the importance of the noncustodial parent, and object to the child developing normal social relationships. Indeed, we have found that the biological father is often not involved with the child, and the child may also have concerns about being abandoned by the remarried family should she refuse to participate sexually with her stepfather.

Very often, these sexually abused adolescents do not present with the problem of sexual abuse. They are far more likely to be seen for serious acting out such as self-abuse, lethargy, anorexia, drug and alcohol abuse, and oppositional behavior.

An example is seventeen-year-old Beth who was brought to the hospital for alcohol abuse, staying out all night, and angry verbal and at times physical attacks directed toward her mother. The precipitant was the birth of her mother and stepfather's first mutual child one year earlier. The initial hypothesis was that Beth could not accept the remarriage, and acted out when the birth solidified the reality of the new family. However, her very sexual presentation (tight-fitting clothes, low-cut sheer tops), combined with poor eye contact, a refusal to date, and calling her mother a "slut" when they had arguments made us suspect abuse. We asked Beth about our suspicion directly and nonjudgmentally, an approach that is often effective. Beth told us that the abuse, which involved genital touching without intercourse, began shortly after the marriage. With the birth of the new child, she began to fear that her stepfather would be around for a long time, and the abuse would have no end.

Our typical treatment stance is to inform the child that the therapeutic goal is to protect her, not to destroy the family. The therapist generally brings the issue up to the parents without the child present, which serves as the first clear message that the adults will handle the issue and protect the adolescent. During that session, the critical factor is not whether the stepfather agrees that the abuse occurred, but rather that the mother clearly and unambiguously protects her daughter. The mother's ability to give the stepfather a clear message that he must leave if any further abuse occurs indicates a good chance of reaching a solution. If the mother cannot relate that message and the stepfather cannot contract not to be alone with the stepdaughter, a temporary placement must often be found for the child. The parents are then told that when the family, with support, can provide protection for the child, we will work toward bringing the youngster home. Reporting any suspected abuse is a requirement. We suggest that the family report themselves, which lets the watch dog agency know that the family recognizes the problem, is seeking help, and wants to work cooperatively with the child protective services.

Sager and his colleagues (1983) observed that with incest, there is a bond to father in spite of the abuse, but with stepfather abuse, the adolescent often wants to escape both the assailant and the colluding parent. We have found that although the adolescent wants the assailant to leave and is furious at her mother's lack of protection, she also fears being abandoned by the only biological parent left in her life and is often afraid to express anger at mother. Sager and his colleagues have also suggested that as part of treatment, a genogram be written to emphasize that a noncustodial parent does exist who cannot be replaced by a stepparent.

A second result of loosened sexual boundaries in stepfamilies can be sexual involvement between stepsiblings. When both parties are not consenting, the impact on the victimized adolescent and the family can be devastating. There is no firm set of social rules, however, dictating the relationship between stepsiblings when both are attracted to each other and they meet during adolescence. The devastation is often the result of the youngsters' trying to hide a relationship they sense is socially unacceptable, or it is owing to the response of the family when such a relationship is discovered. Parents must be helped to accept the sexual feelings stirred up both by the remarriage and by having adolescents living in such close proximity, while calmly defining family rules regarding sexual expression.

Special Issues: Suicide of a Biological Parent

When families reorganize after the suicide of a parent, the issues common to reorganizing families are accentuated. In other reorganizing families, an adolescent may feel responsible for the divorce, but in families with a suicide, the adolescent may also feel responsible for not having saved the deceased parent. Adolescents in reorganizing families typically have trouble acknowledging the anger they feel toward the noncustodial parent. When a parent suicides, it is even more difficult and guilt provoking to acknowledge anger toward the departed parent. In divorce, adolescents often feel angry that the custodial parent couldn't maintain the marriage. After a suicide, the adolescent is angry that the remaining parent could not protect, help, and save the parent who suicided. With other separations, the adolescent may feel that he or she must replace the lost parent. In the case of suicide, the adolescent may feel that the remaining parent is so vulnerable that the system requires total commitment by the adolescent to replace the dead parent.

When a parent dies, whether from suicide or any other means, it is almost impossible for a stepparent to be accepted before the grief work is completed. If the death is unresolved, the family may fear the stepparent will also leave them, just as the biological parent did. At times, the family may resist distinguishing the stepparent from the deceased parent and may resent any changes the stepparent imposes upon the family. Alternatively, the adolescent's unresolved anger toward the remaining biological parent may be displaced toward the stepparent: it is just too frightening to become angry directly at the custodial parent for fear that she or he too will die or abandon the child. In addition, the biological parent, also shaken from the suicide, may lose some confidence in his or her own ability to manage a family and thus place too much responsibility, too early, on the shoulders of the stepparent. Since the stepparent has not gained acceptance by the adolescent, a struggle between adolescent and stepparent is set up. Some families form an unwritten rule not to speak about the deceased parent. The adolescent feels a loyalty conflict as she or he is being asked to "forget" the deceased parent and to allow a new parent into her or his life.

An example of this dynamic is Julia, a sixteen-year-old whose mother had committed suicide when Julia was eight. Julia was in the room at the time, but did not recall the details until therapy progressed. Julia was brought to the hospital because fights with her stepmother were escalating and she was not responding to household rules. Sessions revealed that after her funeral, Julia's mother was never discussed. Father told Julia and her two sisters that mother died of a heart attack, even though Julia had seen mother overdose on pills. Prior to her death, mother had been depressed and abusing alcohol. Father, a mental-health professional, felt guilty for not being able to "cure" his wife and provide a better home life for the children. After mother's suicide, he remarried and the family colluded to "begin again," as if their previous life and experiences had never occurred. Father, feeling like a failure, shifted his disciplinary role to the stepmother long before she was accepted by the children.

The treatment plan was: (1) to return the limit-setting function to father so as not to escalate the conflict between stepmother and girls; (2) to discuss mother's suicide openly; (3) to discuss the positive as well as negative memories of mother; (4) to visit mother's grave; (5) to help father and stepmother acknowledge that she could not replace mother; (6) to create an environment in which anger at the denial and collusions could be expressed; and (7) to help father place his responsibility for his daughters above his guilt so that he could be very firm in response to acting-out behaviors.

In conclusion, when a parent suicides, all family members feel a heightened sense of guilt, responsibility, anger, and sadness, as well as a tremendous desire to protect each other from further pain. A stepparent in this arrangement may be set up to replace the parent in a family where a replacement will never be accepted. The family can reorganize in a more positive way once the biological parent resumes a strong and caring parenting role, and the grief work is underway.

SUMMARY

In summary, when families with adolescents reorganize, the results can be positive. The adolescents can see a couple working together, observe physical affection, and be provided with new role models. When the family has not accepted the separation, however, an explosive situation can result. Adolescent acting out may reunite parents in their spousal roles, divert parents from their own difficulties, or replace the parent who left. In addition, therapists must evaluate whether sexual boundaries have been loosened in stepfamilies with severely acting-out adolescents. Finally, unresolved issues following the suicide of a parent can make it more difficult for families to reorganize functionally. Treatment can help families with troubled adolescents by clarifying boundaries, establishing a clear hierarchy, creating functional roles for each family member, acknowledging the multiple family loyalties, and prodding the family onward with the separation process that is so critical to the adolescent phase of the life cycle.

REFERENCES

Ackerman, N. The family with adolescents. In E. Carter & M. McGoldrick (Eds.), *The family life cycle*. New York: Gardner Press, 1980.

Ahrons, C. Redefining the divorced family: A conceptual framework for post-divorce family system reorganization. *Social Work*, Nov., 1980, **25**, 437–441.

Brady, C. A., & Ambler, J. Use of group educational techniques with remarried couples. In L. Messinger (Ed.), *Therapy with remarriage families*. Rockville, MD: Aspen Systems, 1982.

Carter, E., & McGoldrick, M. (Eds.) *The family life cycle*. New York: Gardner Press, 1980.

Goldsmith, J. The post-divorce family system. In F. Walsh (Ed.), *Normal family processes*. New York: Guilford, 1982.

Keshet, J. K. From separation to stepfamily: A subsystem analysis. *Journal of Family Issues*, 1980, **1**(4), 517–532.

Keshet, J. K. *Love and power in the stepfamily*. New York: McGraw-Hill, in press.

Little, M. *Family breakup*. San Francisco: Jossey-Bass, 1982.

Sager, C., Brown, H. S., Crohn, H., Engel, T., Rodstein, E., & Walker, L. *Treating the remarried family*. New York: Brunner/Mazel, 1983.

Visher, E. B., & Visher, J. S. *Stepfamilies: A guide to working with stepparents and stepchildren*. New York: Brunner/Mazel, 1979.

Wallerstein, J., & Kelly, J. *Surviving the breakup: How children and parents cope with divorce*. New York: Basic Books, 1975.

Weiss, R. S. *Growing up a little faster*. Paper presented at the Symposium on Children and Divorce, Wheelock College, Boston, November 3–4, 1978.

Weltner, J. A structural approach to the single parent family. *Family Process*, 1982, **21**(2), 203–210.

18

The Treatment of Adolescent Psychosis: An Integrated Perspective

JESS MORRIS, M.D.

The treatment of young psychotics and their families has been controversial within the helping professions. The psychoanalytic, systemic, and biologic points of view have often been advocated by their proponents in an either/or manner. Theories of etiology have predominated over descriptions of process. The limitation of any single point of view is borne out by the fact that there has been no one successful cure for psychosis. Most clinicians therefore no longer ask what point of view is right; rather, they wonder how to integrate into therapy perspectives that have been presented for so long as mutually exclusive. Recognizing that a multifaceted approach to treatment is useful and compatible with systems interventions, I shall concentrate upon family systems contributions to such an approach. I shall then suggest specifically how systemic modes of thinking—strategic, structural, and contextual—can be used in sequence to help psychotic adolescents and their families.

There is generally uncertainty in diagnosing adolescents. For the purposes of this chapter, I shall refer to psychotic adolescents as a group who become less capable of testing reality for a relatively short period of time, from a few weeks to a month. This chapter does not consider the problems of autistic adolescents and their families, or of those whose psychosis has an easily identifiable organic basis, such as substance abuse. The group considered here does meet DSM III criteria for Schizophreniform psychosis, but does not meet DSM III criteria (American Psychiatric Association, 1980) for schizophrenia, since the perceptual difficulties of the index patient do not persist for six months. However, systemic studies on schizophrenia will be reviewed, both because these studies preceded the revision of the medical nomenclature and because they seem relevant to the group delineated for study here.

Family systems thinking about psychosis began as an outgrowth of psychoanalytic thinking but proceeded to define itself in opposition to that thinking. The term "schizophrenogenic mother" was coined by the analyst Frieda Fromm-Reichmann (1948). The 1950s and 1960s were a period in which increasingly systemic ways of looking at families eclipsed such concepts. Family systems thinking also developed concurrently with the development and widespread use of major tranquilizers. Thus, systems thinking occupied an uncomfortable corner of a triangle including deterministically intrapsychic and biological theories. At times, perhaps in response to the Sputnik-inspired scientific gestalt of the era, nascent cybernetics seemed to be in battle with other theories around the causality of psychosis. This controversy may have lent epistemological confusion to research into family theories of schizophrenia (Dell, 1980), and may have added to the burden of clinicians trying to find ways to be helpful to these families.

DEVELOPMENT OF COMMUNICATIONS MODEL

Reviewing the literature relevant to systemic approaches to understanding and treating the families of psychotic adolescents is like thumbing through an old family album. Here are many original thinkers in the field. Surely the 1956 publication of "Toward a Theory of Schizophrenia" by Bateson, Jackson, Haley, and Weakland marks a critical moment in the history of thinking about families and psychosis. In this seminal work, the authors approach schizophrenia from a base in communication theory which Bertrand Russell (Whitehead & Russell, 1910) called the "Theory of Logical Types." This theory holds that there is a discontinuity between a class and its members. Because a class and its members represent different levels of abstraction, one member cannot be equivalent to the class, nor can the class be a member of itself. Although in real communication, the authors concede that "this discontinuity is continually and inevitably breached. . . . we must expect pathology to occur in the human organism when certain formal pat-

terns of the breaching occur in the communication between mother and child" (Bateson et al., 1956, p. 252).

Contradictions involving two layers of abstraction are one ingredient of what Bateson et al. coin the "double bind." This situation involves a primary negative injunction with a secondary injunction conflicting with the first at a more abstract level and, like the first, "confused by punishments or signals which threaten survival." Three other aspects of double binds are postulated to be essential to the formation of schizophrenia in the offspring. Two or more persons, one of whom is designated the victim, are involved. A negative injunction prohibiting the victim from escaping the field of interaction is said to exist. Finally, there is repeated experience. The latter is significant as the authors disown traumatic etiology for a more repetitive interactional pattern.

Several aspects of the Bateson et al. article mark it as important in family systems thinking about schizophrenia and as pertinent to our thinking about adolescent psychosis. First, the authors espouse a communications mode. Second, they point to the paradoxical mode of communication within these families. Third, they postulate that psychotic symptoms—hallucinations, delusions, and incoherent behavior and verbiage—represent an attempt to step outside of contradicting injunctions into a state of pure metaphor.

Bateson et al. anticipate the use of therapeutic "counterparadox" in their discussion of the therapeutic implications of their hypothesis. They point to an intervention by Fromm-Reichmann, who used a therapeutic double bind in treating a schizophrenic girl whose delusions involved a "God R." Essentially she said, "That world of yours doesn't exist. . . . Go tell God R he must permit you to talk with me." Here there is a contradiction between the concrete ("That world of yours doesn't exist") and the abstract ("Go tell God R . . .") levels of meaning. The therapeutic aim is to elicit a tension in the patient to talk about what have in the past been entirely private delusions.

In subsequent papers, the Palo Alto

Group evolves the communications model further by removing the sense of victimization within the double bind. Jackson (1965) explains, "There is no possible response to a double bind *except* an equally or more paradoxical message, so if neither can escape the relationship, it can be expected to go on and on until it matters little how it all got started" (p. 5). This shift anticipates the radical departure from causal thinking implied in later cybernetic formulations. Like the original double bind theory, however, this reformulation does not address the question of the timing of psychosis, occurring as it so often does at moments of systemic tension—adolescence rather than latency, for instance. In general, such feedback loops were seen without relation to development and with a questionable degree of egalitarian circularity. Such formulations neglect the fact that in the earliest moment of development, the infant is totally dependent upon its parents for survival. Finally, such a viewpoint neglects a corollary, that the psychotic individual invariably has paradoxical power within the family system.

Writing two years later, "Pseudomutuality in the Family Relations of Schizophrenics," Wynne, Ryckoff, Day, and Hirsch (1958) study schizophrenia using the social organization of the family as a model. In this article, Wynne et al. point to the ways in which roles become rigid at times in all families, but with regularity in schizophrenic families. The authors postulate a state of "pseudomutuality" that is characterized by four qualities:

1. Rigid role structure with predominant absorption in fitting together at the expense of differentiation of the identities of the persons in the relationships.
2. An attachment to this form of relating.
3. Concern over any change from this form of relating.
4. Absence of spontaneity, humor, or zest in relationships.

Wynne et al. observe that these families share mechanisms for preserving the pseudomutual status quo. They observe that, "in characteristic schizophrenic relations perceptual and communication capacity is involved in an earlier and more primitive way" (1958, p. 210), than it is in less disturbed families. They point to paired contradictory expectations as facilitating a failure in the selection of meaning. They also postulate a "rubber fence" enclosing such families, stretching "to include that which can be interpreted as complimentary" (p. 211) and contracting to exclude that which is interpreted as noncomplimentary.

Wynne et al. do not see the psychotic family member as a victim, but rather speak of the active investment of the potential schizophrenic in maintaining the family structure. Indeed, anticipating later writers who would connote psychotic symptoms positively, Wynne et al. write:

> In families in which strivings toward a separate personal identity are regarded as a nonintegrated, crazy or chaotic experience, *each* member of the family—not only the patient—experiences frustration of his needs for achieving a sense of identity. The overt psychosis, then, may have a covert function of giving expression to the family's collective although dissociated, desires for individuality. [p. 219]

Singer and Wynne (1965) later show that the test protocols of the parents of schizophrenics reveal communication styles that could be blindly paired with their schizophrenic offspring. The shared nature of the familial "communication deviance" is inferred by these findings.

As Dell (1980) has pointed out, the research of the 1960s, showing mounting evidence of communication impairment in parents of schizophrenics, has been used by family theorists and geneticists as proof of their respective theories of the etiology of schizophrenia. This emphasis on causality has done an injustice to the study of schizophrenia and psychosis in general. It implies that Bateson et al. (1956) and Wynne et al. (1958) have posited an etiological theory, as opposed to a description of process and pattern. Ensuing research, attempting to show that the parents of schizophrenics have thought disorders, has isolated the schizophrenic from his parents. The concept of how the whole family fits together and develops in a co-evolutionary way was lost to concepts of linear causality. The opposition of nature versus nurture did not allow for nature (e.g., multifactorial genetics) *and* process.

Theoretical and qualitative research on communication patterns in schizophrenic families did continue in the 1960s, however. *Pragmatics of Human Communication* (Watzlawick, Beavin, & Jackson, 1967) describes a body of rules by which human communication and behavior may be seen as approaching mathematics. Calling this study "a science in its infancy," the authors expand upon the process and pattern emphasis of the earlier Palo Alto writers. The peculiarities of schizophrenic families in communication receives particular attention.

The communications theorists, in differentiating themselves from the psychoanalysts, geneticists, and biologists, concentrate almost exclusively upon the current relationships within the family. Yet, in eschewing the history-oriented, deterministic approach of other schools of thought, the communications theorists may have overlooked certain aspects of the family that are relevant to treatment. These aspects have to do in particular with the life stage of the family and with vertical communications —that is, communication among generations.

Dialectical Process of Adolescence

Clinically, it is a commonplace to observe the frequency of psychosis in adolescence, yet little of the purely communications literature addresses the phenomenology of this family developmental stage. Helm Stierlin (1981) has conceptualized the family system at adolescence as one that is characterized by a dialectical process. In *Separating Parents and Adolescents*, Stierlin views the ordinary process of separation at adolescence as dynamic rather than fixed. He uses the Hegelian concept of a dialectic, employing it, not with ideas (as Hegel himself), or with economics (as Marx), but to define a characteristic of re-

lationships between separating adolescents and their parents. Stierlin argues that such apparent stances as adolescent disobedience or disloyalty must be viewed in the context of a predictably dialectical process involving its counterpart in parental response and provocation. Thus, apparent disloyalty or disobedience may stand for something far more loyal or loving. Stierlin chooses the biblical story of the prodigal son to exemplify this relationship. In that story, one son leaves home in open rebellion from his father's values. When that son returns home, he is welcomed warmly by his father to the dismay of his brother. In this instance, misbehavior is covertly positive; the paradox of loyalty through rebellion is evident.

Stierlin develops the concept of "transactional modes" to reflect the interplay and relative dominance of forces binding the adolescent to the family ("centripetal forces") and those increasing the distance between adolescent and family ("centrifugal forces"). This interplay is not fixed. It is transitive—in that the adolescent remains captive to parental influences—and reciprocal, as the adolescent molds and influences his parents. The balance of these forces at adolescence varies in different families. A separation drama dominated by the centripetal (inward) force is characteristic of what Stierlin would call the "binding mode." Less relevant to this chapter is the "expelling mode" of families characterized by a predominance of centrifugal (outward) forces at adolescence.

Stierlin argues that binding occurs within the family of a psychotic adolescent with particular intensity both at adolescence and in infancy. This formulation, however, does not see the infant as a passive victim. Rather, Stierlin describes the growing infant as a developing "specialist for symbiotic survival" (1981, p. 128). In adolescence, the binding process is described as a mutual one.

Ego-binding is one form of binding that involves cognitive functions, for instance, reality testing, logical thinking, and consensual validation. Stierlin uses this term for the process of communication deviance described by Bateson, Wynne, Laing, Haley, and others:

Cognitive—or "ego"—binding, thus understood, reveals important features: it implies devious communications which mystify (Laing, 1961, 1965), interfere with the sharing of a common focus of attention (Wynne and Singer, 1963), and disaffirm one's own or the other's messages (Haley, 1959). Such devious communications strain and unsettle the partner in the dialogue and they throw this dialogue off the track. [Stierlin, 1981, p. 42]

Within this setting, the adolescent's newly acquired skills at reasoning and abstract thought become important factors. Rather than use these new faculties in the service of differentiation (helping him to identify and compare his own feelings with those of others within the family, for instance), the adolescent "perverts his ideas into chains which bind him even more closely to his parents" (p. 46). The deflection of cognitive growth into fantasy results in less interaction with the world of peers. In its most extreme form, psychosis, such binding results in a bound family member who appears "sick" and dependent.

Stierlin allows that binding may occur on other levels than simply that of distorted and devious communication ("cognitive" or "ego-binding"). He posits that other categories of binding occur around affect ("id-binding") and loyalty ("superego-binding"). Affect binding involves regressive affectual contact between parent and child. The overgratifying parent receives confirmation of his or her giving by a continuously dependent adolescent. Such affective binding may be stable through the latency of a child because, although no period of development is truly fixed or rigid, the years preceding adolescence most approximate such a time in the family developmental cycle. The nature of the family at adolescence—the stage of shifting dialectical forces as described by Stierlin—is incompatible with such stasis of regressive affect. Loyalty binding, finally, involves a mutual binding via self-sacrifice. Adolescents become "self-sacrificing victim-adjuncts" (p. 49) to their parents whose own overt or covert sacrifice prompts its own return. Separation becomes the "total number one crime." In families characterized by the transactional mode of binding, the developmental task of adolescence,

separation, is too great a challenge. In summary, then, Stierlin's dynamic concept of adolescence lends a family developmental perspective to the timing of adolescent psychosis.

Multigenerational Dimensions

There remains another historical dimension that is relevant to the understanding of adolescent psychosis, that of communication among the generations. Ivan Boszormenyi-Nagy (1973) has developed a theory of family relations which puts current family function into a framework of ethics involving loyalty to generations past. Boszormenyi-Nagy sees legacies as developing naturally in the prior generation. These legacies embody the positive caring and its return (in his term, "positive entitlement") or the interruption of the natural flow of helpfulness (leading to "negative entitlement"). Ultimately, in families in which parents and adolescents are unusually bound, Boszormenyi-Nagy would argue that a legacy was impeding the developmental process in its final goal, the continuation of the generations. This theory may appear superficially to be a return to the theories that posited blame with the parent (such as Fromm-Reichmann's [1948] "schizophrenogenic mother"). Yet, in Boszormenyi-Nagy's theory, caring is seen as reciprocal; he places emphasis on the capacity and wish of the child to care for and give back to its mother. The importance of Boszormenyi-Nagy's theory extends beyond an academic understanding of intergenerational dynamics. It leads to an ethically based mode of therapy, contextual family therapy, which will be discussed at length later.

TREATMENT

Having reviewed some of the systems literature pertinent to adolescent psychosis, we turn to treatment recommendations. A sequential approach to the family therapy of these cases will be outlined. First, however, the field of focus needs to be enlarged, as in my experience, the treatment of adolescent psychosis has involved more than family systems therapy alone.

I am indebted to my friend and family therapist colleague, Beatrice Chorover, M.S.W., for a model that helps to organize analytically and phenomenologically a wider point of view. Three concentric circles (see Figure 18.1) expand outward and interconnect. Innermost is biology—the numerous feedback loops of the individual's central nervous and endocrine systems. Next is the individual psyche, affected and affecting biology and surrounded by the largest circle, that of family and society. These three spheres all need to be considered in our formulation of the psychotic adolescent. Each needs to be placed in the context of time. Time in the biological sphere relates to physiological maturation; in the individual sphere, time pertains to the developmental stages of life; and time in the family relates to a circular time encompassing family development and generational history.

It has been my experience that a treatment model that attempts to intervene in

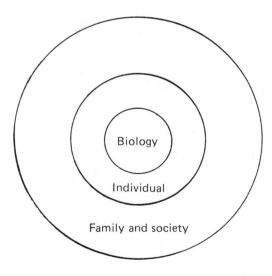

Figure 18.1
Expanding and interconnecting spheres from the field of focus in the treatment of many disturbances of adolescence.

just one of these spheres may prove helpful only temporarily. If these three overlapping spheres can be kept in mind, treatment strategies may be established which aim to integrate consideration of all three spheres. Two areas in particular pose problems for an integrated treatment of adolescent psychosis: possible hospitalization and/or medication of the identified patient.

There are times when hospitalization of a psychotic adolescent is prudent—for instance, when delusions are prompting self-destructive behavior. Bearing in mind our tripartite model, a clear hazard of hospitalization is that the adolescent may be viewed out of context of the larger interactive sphere of the family. In situations when hospitalization is deemed necessary, this inherent problem will have to be met by vigorous activity to involve the family.

Whether or not to medicate an adolescent is also a question often raised early in treatment. There may be reasons to do so. Psychosis is frequently a positively reinforcing state within the individual. For instance, paranoid delusions prompt searching which prompts confirmation of paranoia and further strength of delusions. Whatever can interrupt such a sequence temporarily may be beneficial. Psychotic symptoms per se, such as delusions and hallucinations, are of little benefit in the family work, in my opinion. Finally, the experience of psychosis is often accompanied by panic anxiety, a most dysphoric state of affect which may be ameliorated by medication.

While there seem to be good reasons to medicate in the short term, what are the effects of advocating medication on the individual psyche and the family system? Is the use of medication at all synonymous with the advocacy of "intoxication" as a mode of treatment, as has been suggested by some family systems' thinkers (Haley, 1980)? Does the fact of medication use so bias the family's view of further treatment that it should be avoided at all costs? Both questions imply that there is only one sphere (the family) of helpful involvement or that biological interventions cannot be integrated into a family context.

It seems critical that the therapist present

medication as temporary and only pallia-tive, not curative. There needs to be candor about the benefits as well as potential risks of antipsychotic medication. The fact that medication may well facilitate meeting as a full family sooner and may enable a re-turn to work or school more quickly should be stressed. Finally, one needs to be alert to the tendency of these families to use the recommendation of medicine or hospitali-zation to reify family structure in which the identified patient is seen (and behaves) as a failure and a hopeless dependent.

Although not yet formally defined as such, family therapy begins even at this early stage of intervention in the attitude of the helping professional toward possible hospitalization, medication, and the need for family involvement. The family sphere is not discarded simply because interven-tions in the biological and individual sphere may predominate in the first days of treat-ment. During initial contacts, an effort is made to learn as much about the larger family context as possible. Inquiring about how the family members have tried to help one another in the past and what other problems exist in the family may provide a chance to see the family interact, as well as to gather information. One needs in par-ticular to observe the rules that organize the family and the hierarchy of power within the family at this early moment of therapy.

A Sequential Model

What follows is a proposed sequence for approaching the major portion of the treat-ment of these families, generally after the acute psychotic symptoms have subsided. The model contains three parts, each char-acterized by a particular mode of family therapy. In reality, these stages are not so easily defined, although I am suggesting that the therapist can usefully combine modes of family thinking. The three modes derive from the strategic, structural, and contextual therapy.

Curiously, little has been written by structuralists about the treatment of ado-lescent psychosis. This fact is odd, since numerous systems theorists point to struc-tural components of dysfunction in these families. The "rubber fence" of Lyman Wynne (Wynne et al., 1958) is an early ex-ample of a metaphor denoting a structural abnormality. Stierlin (1981) is describing structure in his comments on binding, al-beit in dialectical and dynamic terms. Nonetheless, approaches to these rigidly bound families which respect family ri-gidity are called "strategic" and paradoxi-cal rather than structural in the systems literature.

Phase 1: Strategic

While the issue of crisis intervention (in-cluding possible medication and hospital-ization) are being addressed, the helping professional will likely be looked upon as a rescuer by the distressed family. As acute psychotic symptoms subside, this attitude may change for two reasons. First, the ther-apist's interest in the family could be felt as a sign of blame. Second, as has been reviewed, these families are used to inter-acting in the binding mode; an agent of change will eventually be felt to be a seri-ous threat. For a therapist to join these change-resistant families is probably im-possible unless entry into the system is change-reluctant. The latter refers to an attitude that concentrates upon what is positive in the status quo. The therapist must ally with the forces of homeostasis, not developmental transformation (change toward greater adolescent individuation, for instance), as Andolfi, Menghi, Nicolo, and Sacco (1980) have described. The more one sees of such truly rigid families, the more sincere such change-reluctance may become. The experience of a family disaster following attempted change is not infre-quent. Thus, what may appear strategic is often based on well-founded prudence.

Another first-stage intervention involves the use of positive connotation, which is defined as finding positive attributes in the behavior of the identified patient as well as in the symptomatic behavior of other members of the family. Credit probably belongs to Palazzoli, Boscolo, Cecchin, and Prata for advocating in *Paradox and Coun-*

terparadox (1978) the use of positive connotation in family therapy with schizophrenics. This is an important concept and one to which the authors devote a full chapter. Palazzoli et al. (1978) justify this therapeutic stance in a number of ways. First, they argue that negative judgment of a family with prevalent homeostatic (over transformational) forces risks losing the possibility of being accepted at all by the family. In intervening critically, they argue that one would be labeling forces of transformation "good," and those of homeostasis "bad." Since both forces are a necessary part of all systems, such a stance would constitute a theoretical error.

There is another compelling reason for positive connotation at this stage of therapy: the dialectical nature of the adolescent-parent relationship. Here the drama of psychosis may well be hiding from the family's view the opposite side of that dialectic—some useful function that psychosis, dependency, or failure provides the system. In terms that Boszormenyi-Nagy (1973) might use, it is the loyalty of the psychotic family member, his or her self-sacrifice, that may be overlooked by the system. Within these families, the task of positive connotation involves finding a way to highlight the silent side of a dialectic that may involve binding, which may take the form of regressive gratification (id binding), linguistic mystification (ego binding), or sacrificial failure (superego binding). For this, the therapist will need other foci than the immediate behavior. For instance, the therapist who knows that an adolescent's dependency through psychosis distracts parents from the self-observation of an empty marriage may find some way of speaking of sacrifice or loyalty on the part of the adolescent.

Early family treatment from a systemic point of view involving change-reluctance and positive connotation exerts a peculiar effect on the therapist's own tendencies to label as pathological, and thereby to disqualify, sequences of interaction. These elements of early treatment require the therapist to address continuously to him- or herself the questions of what possible benefit may be accrued to the system by interactions or behaviors that seem so evidently nonbeneficial. A measure of the success of a therapist's entry at this point will be the degree to which the therapist genuinely feels temporarily reluctant to prompt change and the degree to which the positive connotation is experienced by the family as sincere. At times there may be surprise that an agent of change is urging restraint or validating behavior that has been seen solely as "bad" in the past. In addition to surprise, however, there should be some sense on the part of the family of being—perhaps for the first time—understood.

There are other ways for the therapist to use the structure of therapy itself to respect the family's unwritten rules. When generational boundaries have been crossed in the family and there has been unusually strong parent-child binding, a therapist might initially tacitly support that dyad by meeting with that subsystem. Conversely, if the marital couple seems to have an empty relationship, direct approaches to that subsystem early in treatment should be avoided.

A challenge facing the family therapist early in the treatment of such families will necessarily be to counteract the family's attempt to use the therapist for the purpose of reifying the already rigid structure. Appeals will be made to diagnose as a means of permanently labeling, and thereby fixing the adolescent in time. Conversely, parents may appeal for advice in such a way as to renounce their own authority and make static a view of themselves as inept in the use of parental power. A therapist must be alert to the possible meaning of such requests early in treatment. The therapist must remember that respecting and appreciating structure is not synonymous with reifying it; indeed, the goals are opposite.

Jay Haley has written persuasively about this aspect of the treatment of disturbed adolescents in his book, *Leaving Home* (1980). Haley is sensitive to the unwitting collusion of experts and hospitals in robbing parents of—or complying with parental wishes to divest—authority. The need to encourage the adolescent, who has previously gone to school or worked, to resume those activities as soon as possible is likewise stressed by Haley. Both stances are compatible with family therapy which begins change-reluctant and positively connoting.

In summary, the first stage of the treatment of the family of the psychotic adolescent involves two distinct periods. During the first brief period, the medical treatment of the psychosis and medication-related counseling predominate. Shortly thereafter, a stage of family therapy that is strategically based and involving positive connotation and change-reluctance will be possible. Here the therapist must avoid the reification of structure while attending to the family's fears of change. In addition, by aligning with the forces within the family that favor homeostasis, the therapist paradoxically allows the latent forces for transformation to come to life. Finally, because positive connotation gives voice to the silent side of a dialectic, the therapist sets the stage for the next phase of treatment, in which the family's difficulty mastering this stage of development is more directly confronted.

PHASE 2: STRUCTURAL

The second phase of family therapy may involve techniques that are more directly structural in nature. It is well known that structural family therapy (Minuchin, 1974) aims at changing the organization of the family, encouraging more appropriate hierarchy and alliances. Although Minuchin has not focused on the treatment of families with psychotic members, he does write about the subject in passing in *Families and Family Therapy* (1974). Focusing on the misuse of structural family therapy, Minuchin relates a vignette about the family treatment of a fourteen-year-old psychotic boy who was seen as being enmeshed with his mother. The spouse subsystem was characterized by few and unrewarding interactions. One intervention involved the parents ignoring the boy's psychotic remarks. In addition, the parents were advised to go out one night per week without the boy. On the first night that the parents

went out alone, they returned to find the boy had slashed his clothing with a razor. The therapist then told the parents that this event was a hopeful sign: they were improving, as manifested by an increase in the child's symptoms. The second time the parents went out, the boy broke a window and cut his wrist, then walked into the streets naked. Minuchin describes these interventions as unnecessarily stressful and "possibly dangerous." He cites the case as an example of the pitfall of ignoring some family subsystems. He goes on to suggest that the therapist might have had sessions with father and son in which the mother would be present but not participating. He also advocates sessions with the son alone, as a means of showing concern for him. Minuchin writes: "such an awareness of the child as a suffering individual, instead of as a system member who responds to attempts to restructure with antitherapeutic system-maintaining devices, would have enhanced the total treatment situation without retarding the progress toward the goal" (p. 107).

The use of subsystem meetings that include the identified patient does seem to be a valuable structural tool at this stage of therapy. As Minuchin suggests, one can facilitate an improved bond between the noninvolved parent and the adolescent without initially threatening the overly close bond. Sibling meetings may be useful in this phase of treatment, as such meetings favor the reestablishment of generational boundaries. Sessions with the adolescent, which respect his or her individual pain, may also be beneficial. Ordinarily not beneficial at this time are couples' meetings, other than parenting-focused meetings.

Within sessions the therapist must respect that the overall system will respond with great sensitivity to felt assault. The very process of meeting with siblings, for instance, may be a strong enough structural move for a therapist to make at this stage of treatment. Within such a meeting, direct confrontation among siblings, such as encouraging the expression of envy of or anger toward the identified patient, should be avoided while areas of common interest or interaction should be stressed. There is a trade-off here. The therapist agrees to promote a temporary "pseudo-mutuality" among siblings in return for the potential of greater sibling alliance and interaction in the future. Whatever the format, the instruction that family members should speak of their own thoughts and feelings, rather than speaking for each other, may be helpful and disentangling.

As structural family therapy proceeds, the family rules of organization are slowly made explicit. An ethical question naturally arises in this process: how could it be fair for one family member to play such an important, suffering role as the index patient has played? The therapist does not pose this question directly, but rather engages the parents in wondering about how the family rules originated. The natural assumptions (or legacies) that come into the family from the parental families of origin, become relevant as the family enters the third stage of treatment.

Phase 3: Contextual

Boszormenyi-Nagy's (1973) theory of intergenerational legacy has relevance to the treatment of psychotic adolescents. To reiterate, Boszormenyi-Nagy sees dysfunction as being based upon legacy, the residual of negative entitlements earned in the prior generation. Most generally, contextual family therapy aims to rebalance the relations between the generations with emphasis upon the rejoining of the generations. This goal of rejunction implies the restoration of appropriate give and take among the generations. Such a state is distinct from dysfunctional binding. Bound adolescents have little of value, save their own dependency and failure, to give to their parents. Binding parents may, for instance, replicate another generation's self-sacrifice, but such giving does not meet the genuine needs of offspring (i.e., it does not encourage them to take an active part in the world at large).

The therapeutic process advocated by Boszormenyi-Nagy follows from his view of the intergenerational basis of systemic dysfunction. The structural problems in these families, which Stierlin has described dynamically as binding, embody a living heritage. The final problem for therapy, then, is how to help reverse a process between generations. The balance needs to be shifted in a direction of greater positive entitlement.

There are a number of ways in which a family therapist can encourage such a reversal of legacy. Remembering that all of these family members have been robbed of opportunities both to give and to receive by virtue of a legacy, the therapist may promote new opportunities in the present. To credit (i.e., to acknowledge what has been given) is to earn positive entitlement, for instance. It is of interest that one symptom of binding is the lack of acknowledgment of the help that one member gives to another. In working with an id-bound adolescent in this phase of treatment, therapists may note that the adolescent rarely thanks or acknowledges his or her parents. Since the interior state of the id-bound adolescent is one of deprivation, it is natural that such crediting is new work. Conversely, that a parent in such a bound situation has not asked for a return of thanks is also noteworthy.

The parent whose self-sacrifice replicates the covertly exploitative self-sacrifice of a past generation might be encouraged to include his now aged parents in sessions. The aim would not be insight into the past situation per se—although the wish to understand is a gift given between the generations—but rather the fostering of an opportunity for the earning of positive entitlement. At times the shift in focus in sessions that include grandparents may stir up painful affects. Here, what is essential is the therapist's conviction that blame or the mere abreaction of anger toward grandparents will not reverse legacy. The injustices of past legacy need to be acknowledged, but ultimately grandparents must be offered understanding or helpfulness in order to reverse legacy. Unless this goal is kept in mind, the unresolvable expression of negative affect becomes the new expression of negative entitlement.

The Ordering of Therapeutic Approaches

Contextual therapists may well ask why I have placed this approach third in the sequence described. I do not think that the other approaches advocated are alien to the contextual. Positive connotation might be described contextually as paying close attention to the loyalty demonstrated by otherwise dysfunctional behavior. Boszormenyi-Nagy's (like Stierlin's) dialectical view of relationships at this developmental moment renders a dynamic basis to paradox.

Directly structural approaches precede contextual ones in this schema. Until the dysfunctional structural arrangements within the family have been shifted, contextual work will be premature. The content of the therapy will follow its process. Most contextual therapists probably make structural interventions intuitively as they select who is appropriate to attend a given session. Most importantly in the sequential approach advocated here, the therapy does not end after the structural interventions; some attempt at rebalancing and appropriate rejoining of the generations is viewed as necessary.

To summarize, the stages of family therapy described represent three stances that might be taken sequentially by a family therapist dealing with a family of a psychotic adolescent. In the initial stage, the therapist attends most to the task of voicing the silent part of the dialectic crazy/loyal or helpful. In this phase of treatment, an attitude of change-reluctance is assumed. In the second phase of treatment, the therapist gently urges more appropriate hierarchy and structure, in part by how the therapy itself is organized. Finally, as the living family begins to change structurally, the work of intergenerational rebalancing may take place.

A CASE HISTORY

A case history may help to illustrate these phases of treatment. Fifteen-year-old Carol was referred to treatment because of psychosis and suicidal ideas. She complained that she had recently become convinced that the devil lived in her mother's dresser and that she, Carol, was bad and needed to die. Carol's maternal grandmother had died ten months previously.

Carol lives with her mother, a registered nurse, and three siblings: a fourteen-year-old brother, and two sisters, twelve and eleven. Carol's father died when she was seven. Even before her father's death, Carol had had an unusually close relationship to her mother, who had confided secrets to her (for instance, that she planned to divorce father shortly before his death). Mother and daughter slept in the same bed at night and Carol, who was failing in her schoolwork, frequently stayed home from school to clean the house.

Because of her psychosis and suicidal thoughts, Carol was briefly hospitalized. She was placed on a low dose of a major tranquilizer. Carol's mother asked if Carol would need to take medicine forever to prevent another "breakdown." Carol and her mother were both told that she would be on medication for a short time and that the aim of the medication was primarily to calm some of the panic that Carol was feeling. Our belief that family members could in the long run offer more help than medication was stressed.

Family meetings were instituted in the first hospital week when Carol's delusions were less prominent. In the initial family sessions, Carol's sadness and hopelessness—expressed as suicidal thoughts—were underlined and supported as a valuable statement of family affect around the death of the maternal grandmother. Her upset was supported as loyal in distracting the family from its obvious unhappiness. As the bound nature of the mother-daughter dyad became increasingly apparent, the mutual loyalty of that relationship was supported. Life had been unpredictable owing to the major losses experienced by mother and daughter and their locked embrace was reframed as an island of stability. Carol's current surrender of adolescent individuation was not confronted, but supported as a form of necessary family sacrifice. An attitude of change-reluctance was conveyed to the family.

Each member of this family was suffering in some way. Carol's symptoms were most prominent, but the silent suffering of her siblings bespoke the fact that Carol's position of importance had come at their expense. Each was having difficulty at school and with peers. Carol's mother had become so involved with her oldest daughter's problems that at the time of referral, she had virtually no social life or friends. At this early stage of treatment, these issues were not raised.

During Carol's hospitalization, her individual sessions focused on her own suffering. As her psychosis cleared, Carol emerged as a fearful young woman who frequently expressed concern that people might be watching her. Carol spoke increasingly about her fears of the future—that any step toward autonomy would result in a cut-off from her mother.

Discharge plans included continued individual therapy for Carol, weekly meetings of the full family, and weekly mother-daughter meetings. Positive connotation and change-reluctance were the hallmarks of the therapist's attitude at this stage of the treatment. Individual outpatient meetings with Carol—something that might threaten the mother-daughter dyad—were balanced by meetings involving the two together. The latter were justified to the family on the basis that mother and daughter had been supports to each other for some time and that it was not the intention of the therapist to change that fact. After six months of such meetings, Carol's mother requested individual meetings for herself to obtain parent guidance as she was feeling overwhelmed with the demands of the three younger children. Now, with a separate therapist, mother began to receive parenting help and to deal with her own grief over the loss of her mother the previous year.

At the time that mother's individual sessions began, sibling sessions were suggested. The initiation of these separate therapies marked the beginning of the second, structural, phase of the treatment. Generational boundaries were observed more within the therapy. Carol initially bristled at the suggestion of meeting with her siblings, but later used the meetings as a format in which to chide her two sisters for doing so little housework. Carol's efforts to maintain a parental stance in the sibling meetings were gently confronted. Why did she have to do all the housework before her siblings had returned home from school? Gradually the focus shifted to problems that all four shared: managing without a father and having a working mother who was often tired at the end of the day. For over a year, the therapy gently supported a shift in the boundaries within the family through the use of fewer mother-daughter meetings and more frequent sibling or individual sessions.

In individual sessions, Carol's mother spoke at length about her relationship to her own mother. In the course of this work, she acknowledged anger at her mother for having

pushed her out on her own as an adolescent. She was encouraged to understand more about her mother's own life situation. A session with an aunt was pivotal in helping Carol's mother to understand that her own mother had felt exploited in her family of origin: as the oldest, she had been forced to care for her two younger siblings while their mother drank heavily.

Whether Carol's mother's understanding of her own mother's situation was correct or not is not at issue. She was encouraged to move beyond a position of anger at a felt (and real) injustice to offer understanding to her mother. In this way, she gained positive entitlements. Her attempt to understand was a gift to her mother. Coincidentally, she began to raise concerns with her therapist about Carol's development. Wasn't it time that Carol had more friends outside home?

In the mother-daughter sessions, the question of crediting and appropriate giving was raised. As inappropriately driven to do housework as Carol was, she refused to give her mother what she increasingly needed—privacy with a new male friend. Carol's mother, who had always been enormously sacrificing to Carol, had never given her permission to see her paternal grandfather since her father's death. Encouraged to acknowledge each other and their individual needs, mother and daughter began to shift in their bound state: Carol began to look forward anxiously to graduating from high school; her mother remarried and began to spend more time concerned over the needs of the other children in the family.

This case illustrates the treatment of adolescent psychosis advocated by this chapter. Initial hospitalization and medication are seen as compatible with a family therapy approach, so long as the hazards of these interventions are acknowledged and the direction of therapy toward family intervention is maintained. There are three general stages recommended in this sequential approach to family therapy. In the first stage, an attitude of positive connotation and change-reluctance is seen as facilitating the development of the therapist-family system. A second stage of structural interventions—notably in the structure of the therapy itself—gently moves the treatment in the direction of establishing generational boundaries and hierarchy. In the third stage, a contextual approach attempts to rebalance the relationship between the generations, resulting, in part, in less binding between parents and adolescents.

SUMMARY

In this chapter, some of the history of the family approaches to adolescent psychosis have been reviewed. It has been noted that one legacy of the controversy has been an either/or aura to treatment modalities. The integration of biological, individual, and family treatment approaches within a framework of a family systems conceptualization has been advocated. A sequential approach to the actual family therapy has been suggested. In this approach, elements of strategic, structural, and contextual therapies have been utilized.

Finally, as complex as the problem of adolescent psychosis may be, the progress that has been made over the past years toward helping adolescents and their families has been enormous. In the decades ahead, the current capacities of the helping professions may be augmented as approaches that were formerly seen as conflicting are viewed instead as sharing common ground.

REFERENCES

American Psychiatric Association. *Diagnostic and statistical manual of mental disorders* (3rd ed.). Washington, DC: American Psychiatric Association, 1980.

Andolfi, M., Menghi, P., Nicolo, A., & Sacco, C. Interaction in rigid systems: A model of intervention in families with a schizophrenic member. In M. Adolfi & I. Zwerling (Eds.), *Dimensions of family therapy*. New York: Guilford, 1980.

Bateson, G., Jackson, D., Haley, J., & Weakland, J. Toward a theory of schizophrenia. *Behavioral Science*, 1956, **1**, 251–264.

Boszormenyi-Nagy, I., & Spark, G. *Invisible loyalties*. New York: Harper, 1973.

Dell, P. F. Researching the family theories of schizophrenia: An exercise in epistemological confusion. *Family Process*, 1980, **19**, 321–335.

Fromm-Reichmann, F. Notes on the development of treatment of schizophrenia by psychoanalytic psychotherapy. *Psychiatry*, 1948, **11**, 263–275.

Haley, J. The family of the schizophrenic: A model system. *Journal of Nervous and Mental Disorders*, 1959, **129**, 357–374.

Haley, J. *Leaving home*. New York: McGraw-Hill, 1980.

Jackson, D. The study of the family. *Family Process*, 1965, **4**, 1–20.

Laing, R. D. *The self and others: Further studies in sanity and madness*. London: Tavistock Publications, 1961.

Laing, R. D. Mystification, confusion and conflict. In I. Boszormenyi-Nagy and J. L. Framo (Eds.), *Intensive family therapy*. New York: Harper, 1965.

Minuchin, S. *Families and family therapy*. Cambridge: Harvard University Press, 1974.

Palazzoli, M., Boscolo, L., Cecchin, G., & Prata, G. *Paradox and counterparadox*. New York: Jason Aronson, 1978.

Singer, M., & Wynne, L. Thought disorder and family relations of schizophrenics: IV. Results and implications. *Archives of General Psychiatry*, 1965, **12**, 201–212.

Stierlin, H. *Separating parents and adolescents*. New York: Jason Aronson, 1981.

Watzlawick, P., Beavin, J., & Jackson, D. *Pragmatics of human communication*. New York: Norton, 1967.

Whitehead, A., & Russell, B. *Principia mathematica*. Cambridge: Cambridge University Press, 1910.

Wynne, L., Ryckoff, I., Day, J., & Hirsch, S. Pseudomutuality in the family relations of schizophrenics. *Psychiatry*, 1958, **21**, 205–220.

Wynne, L. C., & Singer, M. T. Thought disorder and family relations of schizophrenics: I. A research strategy. *Archives of General Psychiatry*, 1963 (a), **9**, 191–198.

Wynne, L. C., & Singer, M. T. Thought disorder and family relations of schizophrenics: II. A classification of forms of thinking. *Archives of General Psychiatry*, 1963 (b), **9**, 199–206..

19

Treating Suicidal Adolescents and Their Families

JUDITH LANDAU-STANTON, M.D.
and M. DUNCAN STANTON, Ph.D.

THE POWER OF THE SUICIDAL GESTURE

A suicide attempt by an adolescent is a powerful act. Most people in Western Culture are appalled by the idea of one so young attempting to take his or her life, especially when the young person has a whole future lying ahead. Such an act challenges society's values and shakes the sense of hope and optimism that we all need in order to carry on in life.

Families usually become terrified when an adolescent member attempts suicide. Often they are confused or mystified about the reason(s) behind the attempt and are frightened by its unpredictability. They are unsure as to how to prevent another attempt and subsequently become mistrustful of the adolescent even when he or she is in good spirits—they may feel as if they are walking on eggshells. Suicide is the "ultimate threat," and the family responds accordingly.

Of course, there may be differences in the reactions of different family members. It is not uncommon for some members to downplay, overlook, or ignore the suicidal behavior, to act as if it does not exist. Other members may become angry, seeing the adolescent's behavior as manipulation, misbehavior or disobedience. Still others may be distraught. These differing reactions can often reveal much about the family structure. "Overlookers" tend to be more disengaged, such as in the case of a distant parent, while those who label the suicide as manipulative tend to be siblings who are more attuned to the machinations that occur within the sibling subsystem. Family "reactors," on the other hand, are more likely to be those members most enmeshed with the problem adolescent.

Professional "treaters" and "helpers" involved with a case of attempted adolescent suicide tend to line up with the family reactors, albeit perhaps for somewhat different reasons than the family members. Their role as concerned professionals (who have been called on or invited to rectify the problem) makes it incumbent on them to do something—to take action toward eliminating the problem. They feel a burden of responsibility that does not occur with most of their other clients, since suicide is one of the few life-threatening syndromes in the mental health field. Sometimes they respond by overidentifying with the index patient and moving toward rescuing him or her from the "destructive" family influence. Other treaters may react by practically moving in with the family—by making repeated home visits or being "on call" night and day.

Therapists must contend with additional factors that complicate the situation. If they have treated or seen the patient before, they are faced with the humiliation of a palpable failure when one of their clients subsequently attempts suicide: Whatever they had done before did not work, or did not work well enough to avert the tragedy. In addition, they must attend to the legal complications surrounding the suicidal behavior: Did they act "responsibly" and take the proper precautions? Will they be the object of informal or formal censure by colleagues and regulatory bodies? Is the family likely to sue them if the adolescent successfully completes a suicide?

For all the above reasons, suicidal adolescents tend to mobilize a multitude of helping systems; in fact, they mobilize systems like almost nobody else, and the ensuing activity of family and helpers can be frenetic. The referring person, the therapist, the hospital, and the family all chime in, each perhaps with a different prescription or intervention, and the resulting chaotic skein can be difficult to sort out. Family- and systems-oriented clinicians usually have their work cut out for them when they take on a case of adolescent suicide.

SOME OVERLOOKED ASPECTS OF SUICIDE

Family Involvement

Suicide has traditionally been viewed as an individual phenomenon, stemming perhaps from such factors as severe depression, hopelessness, a need to "send a message" to significant others, or a result of "existential Angst." Less common is a recognition of the involvement of other people, such as family members, in the suicidal behavior of an individual. However, a slow but perceptible shift has begun to occur in the degree to which clinicians attribute importance to the suicidal person's interpersonal relationships (Williams & Lyons, 1976). For example, Meerloo (1959, 1962) has observed that the suicidal individual is often acting out the command of someone with whom he or she identifies, calling this "psychic homicide." Other writers have looked at the specific involvement of family members in a suicide. Cohen-Sandler et al. (1982) note that, compared with depressed children and adolescents who typically withdraw from family and friends, those presenting for suicide usually maintain close family contact. From his research on forty-five adolescents at risk for suicide, Wenz (1978) concludes that, "Regardless of generation, all family members are involved in the process that leads to suicidal acts in one or more of its members. Adolescent suicide attempts may be seen as an extreme form of reaction to family anomie; and the adolescent suicide attempt is merely a symptom of a process that involves the entire family" (p. 47). Rosenbaum and Richman (1972), in a study of forty cases in which suicide was attempted by drug overdose, found that (1) the family often "expected" the suicide, (2) the suicide was frequently an imitation of an earlier, similar act by a parent or older sibling, and (3) other family members participated directly in the suicidal act. Murphy, et al. (1969) found that survivors of suicide by a loved one constitute a high-risk group for committing suicide themselves. Cain and Fast (1972), in a study of children who were survivors of a parental suicide, found that many identified strongly with the deceased parents' impulses, and subsequently maintained a deep conviction that they would die in the same way. Finally, Rudestam (1977), using the "psychological autopsy" method to study responses to suicide in the family, determined that the remaining, post-suicide family relationships may actually have been strengthened. All of this points to the importance of viewing the suicide as perhaps a sacrificial, and certainly a transactional, phenomenon rooted in the family.

Forms of Suicide

At the mention of suicidal behavior, the clinician commonly thinks of overdose and wrist-slashing, and less commonly of gunshot, hanging, or some other direct life-threatening act. There are, however, other, less direct forms of suicidal behavior to which the clinician needs to remain alerted. For instance, there should always be a question as to the "accidental" nature of an adolescent's death from substance abuse, diabetes, asthma, epilepsy, or schizophrenia. When one of these is present, it is all too easy to get caught up in the treatment of the "illness" and overlook the possibly subtle, but frequently self-destructive, aspects of the syndrome. Further, an actual suicidal gesture may be only the end point in an escalating series of self-destructive behaviors, such as substance abuse, sexual promiscuity, conflict with authorities, poor schoolwork, and truancy (Teicher & Jacobs, 1966). Farberow (1980) has regarded such patterns as manifestations of "indirect self-destructive behavior," or ISDB. Several forms of ISDB warrant special mention:

Substance Abuse

Recognition of substance abuse as a suicidal endeavor stems from as far back as 1938 when Menninger likened addiction to "chronic suicide." This view gained support from a study by Pescor and Surgeon (1940) of suicidal behavior among addicts. Frederick (1972), the second author of this chapter (Stanton, 1977), and others have since concluded that the high rate of deaths among addicts "is more than a result of living in dangerous environments and is to a great extent—if not primarily—a suicidal phenomenon" (Stanton & Coleman, 1980, p. 194). Others have also suggested that drugs are an alternative to, or an equivalent of, suicide (Cantor, 1968; Litman, et al., 1972) or that the addict is trying to tell his or her family and society how close they have brought him/her to death (Winick, 1963).

In earlier publications Stanton has made a case for the family basis of a drug abuser's suicidal behavior (Stanton, 1977; Coleman & Stanton, 1979). Such behavior is not just "depression" or despondence over a "worthless" life, but is an active family process wherein the substance abuser acts out a death wish entertained for him or her by all or most of the other family members. The family message is often quite explicit, with members stating openly they would rather see the abuser dead than lost to friends, spouse, or outsiders. The substance abuser "becomes a saviour or martyr who is sacrificed in noble manner through responding to the family's suicidal conspiracy" (Stanton & Coleman, 1980, p. 195).

Schizophrenia

This disorder has many obvious self-destructive manifestations. In addition, Searles (1961) identified fear of death as one of its major adaptive or defensive functions. Ten years later, Welldon (1971) dramatically described the identified schizophrenic patient as symbolizing a deceased family member, a formulation supported by Walsh's (1978) finding that a high proportion of schizophrenics tend to be born in temporal proximity to the death of a grandparent. Further, Paul and Grosser (1965) have noted that families with an emotionally disturbed member have had difficulty in dealing with previous losses, resulting in "resistant," symbiotic family relationships. These reports attest to the frequency of death-related issues in families of schizophrenics and the possibility that these may be dealt with through ISDB and suicide in one or more members.

Physical and Psychosomatic Disorders

The possible relationship between physical and psychosomatic problems and death-related, possibly suicidal, family processes has not been extensively examined in the literature. However, some relevant implications come from the work of Lewis, et al. (1976) on psychological health in family systems. When they looked for longitudinal differences in physical illness, these researchers found a correlation between the family's ability to discuss death in a personal way (as it applied to either the nuclear or extended family) and the number of "well" versus "sick" days among their members. The types of illness studied were largely psychosomatic and included references to ulcerative colitis, duodenal ulcer, asthma, etc. Further, a particularly important family-systems approach to physical disease is Grolnick's (1972) literature review, which suggests that many psychosomatic illnesses are associated with some of the rigid structural components also described in Stanton and Coleman's (1980) discussion of the patterns found in addict families. Thus, it is appropriate to ask, for example, whether exacerbations of cardiac conditions are predictable from knowing a family behavior cycle; or, like many psychosomatic disorders such as anorexia (Minuchin, et al., 1975), whether hyperobesity is predicated on a cyclic, family-based, self-destructive process.

Other forms of physical ISDB merit exploration from an interpersonal and family-systems viewpoint. For instance, does the dying process that hemodialysis patients face compare with the deathlike pattern that some suicidal families engage in? Are traffic accidents partly contingent on unresolved family mourning and covert instructions for a family member to die?

The risk of suicide is also increased when there is obvious self-mutilation, or a history of either child abuse or incest, in addition to a physical symptom. The following case history illustrates a number of these features.

Stephanie, aged eighteen, and the youngest child in her family, was admitted to an adolescent inpatient unit after multiple suicidal attempts by wrist-slashing, overdosing, and the induction of diabetic coma. Early on in therapy it was discovered that she had had an illegitimate baby two years before.[1] Two of her three older brothers were alcoholic, as was her father, and since she had been involved in incestuous relationships with all

[1]The interventions in this case were designed by the first author of this chapter functioning in the capacities of therapy supervisor and unit director for the Adolescent Program of the Fairmount Institute, Philadelphia. The family therapist was Rama Rao Gogenini, M.D.

three alcoholics, there was some question as to the baby's paternity. The family had a lengthy, multigenerational history of substance abuse and of children not completing the "leaving home" stage (Haley, 1980).

During the early stages of inpatient therapy Stephanie had one serious diabetic crisis after another. She held the entire unit at her mercy, remaining very much in charge. She would set herself up as the victim; if somebody else on the unit misbehaved, Stephanie would take responsibility and try to get herself punished. The whole unit—staff and adolescent residents—eventually become impatient with this pattern. The staff were also angry at her because her diabetes would get out of control, leaving them feeling helpless as she went in and out of crisis. Staff members felt intensely guilty because they were not making her physically better. (Nothing affects medical staff more than a diabetic who is not improving and who threatens the staff by hammering repeatedly at death's door.) Further, if the situation began to appear under control, Stephanie would induce an asthmatic attack by hyperventilating. The staff could therefore understand why Stefanie's family felt helpless and incompetent.

In addition to the problems with Stefanie, each time her physical condition improved a little and therapy appeared to be initiating change, a member of the family would either bring her candy or divert the staff into pursuit of a "red herring": Father would ask for help with his alcoholism or depression, mother would ask for couples' therapy, etc. Further, whenever staff members asserted their authority and held Stephanie responsible for her own behavior on the unit, the other (adolescent) residents would threaten riot in an attempt to protect her. These were, of course, well-known ploys to detour change and reestablish family and unit homeostasis.

Eventually the director and the therapist intervened and, in conjunction with the family, appointed a "link" therapist (Landau, 1981; Landau, 1982; see Chapter 22) from the extended family. The link therapist (Stephanie's older, married, non-alcoholic brother) and staff united and informed Stephanie and her family that Stephanie was to be held totally responsible for her own physical well-being, under the supervision of her parents. They were reminded of the privilege system on the unit and the rule that destructive behavior to self or others resulted in loss of privileges. The other adolescents were enraged ("How can you be so cruel?"; "Don't you know she's very ill and has no control?"). However, by strengthening the parents' role and fortifying their involvement, along with establishing clear-cut and firm boundaries and consequences within the unit, the situation was turned around. After several attempts, Stephanie finally realized that her old techniques were no longer effective. Her behavior started to change, and within a week she ceased being a problem on the unit. She gained control of her diabetes and, some eight months later, had continued to exert control over it effectively. In addition, her other symptomatic behavior disappeared, and she remained essentially problem-free during the follow-up period.

Repeating Patterns of Suicide

The success of the suicidal gesture in mobilizing the family system, family friends, and mental health professionals is often so effective as to ensure that the index patient repeats the gesture. One often overhears clinicians in an emergency department sighing, "Oh, not him (or her) again!". This may repeat (similarly to hysterical paralysis, deafness, or mutism) at regular or irregular intervals until the therapeutic system reorganizes and develops a means for preventing the recurring pattern. Until then, it is all too common for the emergency clinician to resort to treating the physical aspects of such "repeaters," while becoming progressively immune to what is transpiring in the family and thereby contributing to the relapse pattern.

In a protypical case, "Mary Jane" becomes a dreadful nuisance. She is always admitted on a weekend when there are other competing acute medical and traumatic emergencies—and always manages to survive. Ultimately, the clinician becomes blasé and almost wishes she would make a successful attempt. Unfortunately, if no systems intervention is considered, she may well do just that. Her death then comes as a "surprise" to everyone, especially the emergency room clinician, who, out of impatience, may have forgotten that repeated attempts are often the precursors of a successful suicide.

Sometimes the clinician reacts to what is perceived as manipulation on Mary Jane's part. Perhaps Mary Jane is viewed as merely trying to get her latest boyfriend back. However, this, too, may be a family-systems problem. Mary Jane's mother and father may be struggling with a stormy relationship, and Mary Jane may be the only child left in the home to provide the necessary detour or focus of attention to protect her parents' marriage. She may be choosing boyfriends who will inevitably leave her, thereby guaranteeing that she will not have to face the prospect of leaving home. She and her parents may claim to be ready, but the choice of boyfriend prevents them having to face the possibility that they are not. The repeated suicidal gestures may be an integral part of a cycle in which: (a) Mary Jane chooses a new boyfriend; (b) her parents start feeling shaky about their relationship and/or begin fighting; (c) Mary Jane's boyfriend leaves; (d) Mary Jane attempts suicide; (e) the parents pay considerable attention to Mary Jane for a while, eventually encouraging her to venture out a little and choose a new boyfriend; (f) Mary Jane gets herself another boyfriend; (g) the mother and father are once again left alone with their relationship; etc. Consequently, the clinician who treats Mary Jane's suicide attempt(s) in isolation may be asking for a lengthy and unsuccessful course of treatment, with the real risk of concluding with a successful suicide.

In contrast to repeated suicidal attempts by one person, some families will demonstrate repeating patterns across several members. The practice might extend down through several generations or might be passed from one sibling to another. The following case illustrates such a pattern:

Ellen, age eighteen, had been hospitalized for attempted suicide on six occasions since age twelve. She was the youngest of four sisters (ages twenty-five, twenty-three, twenty and eighteen), and the family expressed extreme concern about the danger to her life at this latest, serious attempt. (She had made frequent minor attempts and had threatened suicide on numerous other occasions.) Her mother, a bright, attractive woman in her late forties, was terrified of Ellen, who had attacked her physically at times and had, during two such episodes, hurt her badly. She was determined to have Ellen placed out of the home. Ellen's father—a quiet, flabby and almost voiceless figure—had no idea how to handle the situation and refused to take sides with either his wife or his daughter.

During the initial family session with the therapeutic team (led by JLS), it was discovered that each of the daughters, in turn, had given their parents trouble.[2] The oldest had made her first suicide attempt in her late teens after a very disruptive and troublesome adolescence. As soon as she had successfully left home, the second daughter, who had been on drugs for a while, made a hasty marriage at age eighteen to an older man of whom the parents did not approve. The third daughter followed up an adolescence fraught with rebellion, drugs, and suicidal threats with having an illegitimate baby at age eighteen. At that point, she was thrown out of the house. Consequently, Ellen, aged sixteen at the time, made a really serious suicide attempt, which was followed by a nine-month hospitalization.

It was evident to the therapists that Ellen was continuing a long-standing pattern by escalating her symptomatology around the transition of leaving home (Haley, 1980). Her dramatic history was far in excess of that presented by her sisters, as she was the last child to face leaving home; the transitional conflict (Landau, 1981; Landau, in press) was extreme. Consequently, any attempt to continue treating Ellen independently and in isolation from her family had to fail—much as such attempts had in the past. Involvement of the whole family system in therapy was the only logical recourse.

TREATMENT

To Admit or Not

When a suicidal adolescent enters an outpatient or emergency setting, the question immediately arises as to whether to admit (or refer) this person for inpatient treatment. Sometimes an inpatient program can be avoided, for instance, if it is

---

[2]This patient was also treated in the Fairmount Institute Adolescent Program. The family therapist on the team was James Zoto, M.S.W.

the first psychiatric contact for a female adolescent who is trying to mobilize her family after the family has evicted her boyfriend. In such cases, the suicidal gesture is usually of a mild sort, such as token wrist-markings or ingestion of only four or five aspirin. However, if intensity within the family has built to a high point and the pressure needs releasing, another option is to arrange for the adolescent to stay in the hospital overnight. This was the strategy used by the family-crisis team in the landmark project conducted by Langsley and associates (Langsley, et al., 1968). It allows the members to calm down and gain a respite while also interrupting the escalating family process.

If, on the other hand, the patient has made a serious, clearly dangerous, suicide attempt, inpatient (rather than overnight) admission is probably indicated. Of particular note are cases in which a young person makes an attempt more or less secretively, so that he or she is unlikely to be discovered before it is too late. Such incidents are not to be taken lightly, because they indicate a real commitment to suicide rather than simply a plea for help. Other cases that should normally be admitted are those with a family history of successful suicide, and almost any male adolescent who has attempted suicide, since adolescent male suicide attempts are more likely to be in earnest than "manipulative". Furthermore, if family members are panic-stricken that they themselves cannot prevent the adolescent from attempting to kill him- or herself, admission is advised. In the end, if the therapist is in any doubt about the seriousness of the gesture, inpatient admission, often accompanied by medication, is the recommended course of action—the "safe not sorry" rule of thumb.

A third kind of case invoking the question of admission is that of the "manipulative relapse." This can occur during the process of therapy, sometimes as termination is approaching, and is typified by the index patient making a gesture that is clearly of a manipulative sort. Problems of this type will be discussed in a later section.

While some family therapists categorically discourage the use of inpatient services, this may not be a wise position with cases of serious adolescent suicide. The admission relieves the pressure and load on family members without necessarily exonerating them. As will be discussed later, our goal is to restructure the family in order to empower parents and help them manage the problem themselves. If the young person is left in the home in a position of power—to carry on a reign of terror—before the parents are strengthened and empowered (i.e., while they are still immobilized and without the tools to take charge), the parents will remain impotent. Change will therefore be unlikely and probably impossible, leading to escalation and an increase in the frequency and/or intensity of the suicidal behavior. From this viewpoint, inpatient admission is neither a rescuing of the index patient nor a "parentectomy." Rather, it is an early step in bringing about the necessary structural change (Minuchin, 1974). This restructuring starts with elevating the parents by asking them to play a major part in the decision of whether to admit or not. Admission is used, therefore, as a specific, therapeutic, systems-oriented intervention. It becomes one step within the overall course of family treatment, rather than serving as a goal in itself.

Engaging the System While Setting Preliminary Goals

As noted earlier, suicidal adolescents often gather an extensive system of professionals and helpers around themselves. Frequently, this network includes the referring person or agency, an outpatient therapist, and/or the school system. For family treatment to succeed, it must usually include these individuals in some way. This is especially so if the family treatment starts during an inpatient stay and the patient will be discharged to the care of such persons. Therefore, it has been our practice to involve these people in early phone calls and family sessions whenever possible. The primary reason for taking this tack is to prevent the various treaters from working at cross-purposes. By getting everyone who is involved to cooperate toward the

same therapeutic goals, we can gain greater assurance that changes effected during therapy will last.

The system engagement process usually starts at first contact. The therapist gets a sense from the family as to their preliminary goals. He/she should also connect with the other treaters and find out where they are heading. The aim is to include them throughout treatment. Minimally, they should be petitioned to attend at least (a) the first session, so that they can participate in the initial contracting of, and decision-making on, the goals of therapy, and (b) the last session, to help determine whether the goals have been met so that treatment can end. An outside therapist working counter to the direction taken by the family sessions can undo whatever change has come about up to that time, whereas his or her inclusion in the overall process can prevent disaster.

If the other helping professionals will not agree to be involved, the therapist should request that they sign over responsibility to him or her. They must decide to be "in" or "out." Again, this is particularly crucial for inpatient cases. It is less an issue of "too many cooks" as it is of various cooks concurrently trying to prepare different dishes in the same pot. Therapy carried out in this way has very little chance of success and may result in a dead or damaged adolescent.

Some Initial Strategies and Techniques

From the outset of treatment, the therapist needs to be keenly attuned to the life-cycle events a particular family is undergoing. We usually view families with a suicidal member as struggling with both current changes and recent or distant losses, so a certain amount of time is devoted to *transitional mapping*, that is, assessing the family's position along the transitional points in the life cycle (Landau, 1982; Landau, in press; Landau, et al., 1981). Consequently, we always attempt to ascertain who is in the extended family system; which of these people have died and when; what the frequency and nature of contact with the grandparents are, and how the grandparents are faring; whether there have been deaths or losses of children within the family; with which deceased family members the index patient is identified; etc. Such information allows the pinpointing of key family event(s) and structures, and provides the framework for the therapy that follows.

POSITIVE INTERPRETATION[3]

Commonly we "ascribe noble intentions" to the adolescent (Stanton & Todd, 1979; Stanton, et al., 1982). We identify and emphasize the benevolent, sacrificial side of the self-destructive behavior. Some typical tacks, and their accompanying rationale, are:

Grieving. It is quite common for the suicidal behavior to be linked to deaths or losses in the family (Paul & Grosser, 1965). Sometimes the index patient is viewed by the family as a successor to a deceased relative and is imbued with the attributes of that relative. Such losses are often recent, but may also be long-standing and exacerbated by current family-life-cycle events.

Sandra, aged nineteen, had been hospitalized for two weeks for attempting suicide on several occasions. She also claimed to have auditory hallucinations and bulimic symptoms. Her response to antidepressant medication had been minimal. The family, including Sandra's two older sisters (ages twenty-four and twenty-seven), had been involved in one therapy session, and a second session was held with a therapeutic team (Landau & Stanton, 1983) led by Stanton.[4] As the session unfolded, it was found that this family had a history of unresolved grief ex-

periences. Father was almost the sole survivor of a military unit that had been wiped out during World War II. In addition, the mother related, through tears, that the family had lost its only male child at birth. Mother noted later, also while crying, that the son of a next door neighbor had grown violent five years before and killed himself and his mother. These neighbors were like family to Sandra's family, and the deceased mother was Sandra's mother's closest friend. The parents had consequently held on tightly to their daughters, and none of them had successfully traversed the leaving-home stage. The events precipitating the hospitalization were Sandra's completion of a two-year training course and moving out of the house, and the father's loss of his job.

The therapists quickly pointed out that Sandra was giving to her family by serving as the repository of all their grief. They had been racked by a series of unexpected, devastating losses over a long period, and Sandra had volunteered to assume the mourning of these losses for her family. She was performing the services of a loving martyr, allowing all grieving to focus on her so that the other losses could be shelved, thus permitting the other family members to carry on with their normal routines.

Reflecting family distress. While often related to the grieving strategy, this approach may not involve issues stemming from actual deaths so much as problems that are occurring in the family system. For example, a depressed adolescent may be expressing affect for a parent overwhelmed by mounting family responsibilities and changes. Or, the young person may unwittingly be assisting the family in avoiding a painful life-cycle transition, such as that of a member leaving home. In general, the index patient is noted to be performing a service for the family.

Elizabeth, aged seventeen, had been hospitalized twice for suicidal behavior, the latest inpatient admission having extended to ten weeks when the family therapist (Stanton) was called in on the case.[5] In the initial session, it was revealed that the father—who

---

[3]While similar to the Milan group's technique of "positive connotation" (Selvini-Palazzoli, et al., 1978), the more generic term of "positive interpretation," as coined by Soper and L'Abate (1977), is preferred here.

[4]Other members of the team were: Judith Landau-Stanton, M.B., Ch.B., D.P.M. (co-leader), Clifford Jacobson, M.D., Sandra Mitzner, M.D., Gregory Roeder, Ph.D., Carol Zapalowski, and, during the inpatient stage, Ann Marie Rotella, R.N.

[5]Michael Goldstein, M.D., served as co-therapist. During the inpatient stage, the team also included Evelyne Milanese, M.S.W., Deborah Hubbard, R.N., and Terry Lynn Lucko, R.N.

owned a large farm on which the majority of his ten, mostly adult, children worked and lived with their families—had had a heart attack two years before. Since that time the family had been emotionally crippled. They had tried, with only marginal success, to get father to reduce his workload so that he would not suffer another coronary. The family, and especially the mother, lived in constant fear that father would die suddenly. This would present them with a dilemma as to how to maintain the farm after his death, since none of the sons was capable of assuming proper leadership and mother did not care, or have the competence, to carry on. Mother was therefore concerned that, when her husband died, she would be faced with trying to quell a revolt among her sons—a battle over fiefdoms—and she saw no simple solution. On the other hand, the father, who had built his agricultural "empire" from scratch, wanted the farming complex to continue more or less intact after his death—a kind of memorial to his life's work. Consequently, the whole family was terrified of the day he would die and of the resultant dilemma, and was, in part, mourning his departure before it had occurred.

Knowing this, the therapist noted that Elizabeth was expressing for the family the difficulty they were all having in coping with this impending loss (a dynamic that is somewhat different from grieving, and more similar to anticipated loss of a job or a home). She was carrying the load for the other members, so that they could go on with their daily lives. She was also letting them focus on her as an alternative to an anticipated problem that they felt unable to resolve.

Drawing the fire. This intervention involves ascribing to the adolescent a conflict-detouring role that he or she is usually fulfilling. The therapist points out to family members that, while the family may be beset with trying to cope with a problem, or "because Mom and Dad aren't sure they agree on (a given) issue," the adolescent proffers him- or herself as a target for the fire of the other members. He or she draws their energies and allows them to bring focus to an ambiguous, "mysterious" problem.

DEPICTING THE ADOLESCENT AS DISOBEDIENT

The second general reframing strategy is to depict the adolescent as misbehaving, disobedient, thoughtless, or in some way making things more difficult for the family. Usually family members are frustrated and confused by him or her, and the evocation of a chastising stance from them is not difficult because it is so close to the surface. It is important to note, however, that this is not simply a strategic attempt to scapegoat the index patient, but is a clear structural move designed to allow the overinvolved parent to disengage from the index patient through anger, and unite the parents on a common posture. Whether or not this strategy is adopted in the first session depends on a number of factors, such as: (a) How frustrated the family feels with the index patient at that point (in part a function of how many suicidal attempts have occurred to date, and how much energy and time have been devoted to the problem by the family); (b) how defensive the family is toward the therapist and/or the treating institution (they may not tolerate any "blame" by any treaters, no matter who its object); and (c) how manipulatively "pathetic" the index patient presents (the therapist can come across as cruel and heartless if he or she has not subtly tested the family's readiness to join his or her "attack").

With Sandra's family, the team of therapists noted the family members' frustration with her sullen demeanor and her reluctance to share and talk with them. Thus, she was labeled as "uncooperative" by one team member, and her behavior was mocked by another (while other team members upheld the positive aspects of her behavior in line with the "Pick-a-Dali" approach, in which therapists choose points along a conflictual spectrum; Landau & Stanton, 1983). This technique helped the parents and family to (a) verbalize how frustrated they became when they reached out and she rejected them, and (b) mobilize toward taking the necessary steps to get Sandra's behavior under their control.

In the case of Elizabeth, the process was handled somewhat differently. The therapist did not criticize her in the first session, but essentially ignored her, letting her sit in silence in her pouting, noncommunicative stance. By the second session, the parents (toward whom the therapist had exerted much effort in session #1 at positive joining) were feeling strong enough to fight back. When the therapist tried to get Elizabeth to sit on her mother's lap, and, that failing, to hold her mother's hand, she refused adamantly. Mother, who wanted to hold Elizabeth's hand, then burst into tears about how much agony her daughter was causing her, telling her "you have to give in, too." (Father, who also became silently tearful, was moved next to his wife by the therapist, and his hand was put on hers during this interaction—a restructuring that elevated him, helped him support his wife, and united the parents.) Her mother's outburst startled Elizabeth. She softened and eventually apologized, stating that she had not realized how much pain she had been causing her parents. She resolved to try to change her behavior.

COMBINING POSITIVE AND NEGATIVE REFRAMINGS

At times it may be useful to verbally combine the disobedience and positive reframings, in order to relabel the "naughtiness" or "misbehavior" as noble and self-sacrificial, e.g., "Nobody wants to be labeled and treated as bad. Therefore it is lovely of him/her to make the sacrifice of being constantly viewed as bad in order to help the family."

In the case of Ellen, the team chose to describe her behavior of being "as wicked and disruptive as possible," even to the point of risking death, as a self-sacrificial means for detouring her parents from having to deal with the last of their offspring's leaving home. (This situation was particularly difficult due to father's impending retirement, which, with Ellen's departure, would leave the parents alone with their marriage.) Ellen's sacrifice was therefore interpreted as a noble way of drawing the fire and freeing her sisters to leave home successfully, as well as a way of providing her parents with a real distraction from their difficult relationship. This interpretation was then adopted by every member of the inpatient staff. For example, if Ellen made her bed and tidied her room, the housekeeper would chastise her for not making the sacrifice of "badness." As she passed through the hospital grounds, the gardener would ask her, "Ellen, have you kicked a tree today?" If she arrived at the unit classroom on time, the teacher would express surprise and concern at Ellen's apparent lack of consideration for her parents. Within a few days, Ellen became a paragon

of virtue on the ward and a model patient. For this to be achieved, however, it was essential for the *whole treatment team to reinforce the intervention with absolute consistency*. If one team member had deviated from the plan, Ellen and her parents would have immediately joined this staff member and the paradoxical intervention would have foundered. In addition, it was necessary for the team to stick with the intervention well beyond the point that Ellen's behavior improved. It would have been premature, and therefore detrimental, for the team to have backed away from its stance before the parents themselves had begun to challenge the validity of the "badness" paradox. Eventually the parents became ready to take Ellen home, convinced that she was no longer suicidal, homicidal or disobedient—i.e., "bad"—and that she would indeed be a pleasure to have back in the family. At that point, the team shifted its position and validated the parents' new-found perception of their daughter.

It should be emphasized that although the various interpretations and relabelings given thus far have a clear linear flavor to them, they are applied more for their utilitarian value than for their completeness as "truths." Obviously, if an adolescent exerts power in the family or its detours conflict, the other members are colluding in granting him or her these prerogatives. Like the scientist who can become so enamored of his or her research instruments that flexibility to perform new and different experiments is compromised, the therapist should beware of becoming so attached to linear interpretations that he or she overlooks the contributions of all family members to the dysfunctional process.

Principles of Treatment

As may have been obvious thus far, our approach incorporates various components: structural/strategic (Stanton, 1981a; 1981b), transitional (Landau, 1982; Landau, in press; Landau & Griffiths, 1981; Landau, et al., 1981), experiential (Whitaker & Keith, 1981), and contextual (Boszormenyi-Nagy & Ulrich, 1981). It is a brief-therapy model (generally five to fifteen sessions) and rarely exceeds six months. In addition, there are certain specific guidelines that we find essential in treating cases of this sort.

UNITING THE THERAPEUTIC TEAM

Getting *all members of the therapeutic system* to negotiate, agree upon, and reinforce the *goals, direction, means* and an acceptable *point of completion* of treatment is a crucial feature of this therapy. On an inpatient service this entails regular meetings among staff to reaffirm the treatment plan, provide mutual support, avert problematic countertransference, and prevent the treatment team from itself reenacting the family pattern. It is also crucial that one member of the team has primary responsibility for management of the case; management "by committee" increases the risk of suicide, tending to be both sluggish and relatively inconsistent. In their need for stability, adolescents are quick to find gaps in management systems, test them, and possibly exploit them—sometimes with disastrous results.

EMPOWERING PARENTS

Commonly parents or parental figures with a suicidal adolescent feel weakened, due to the incompetence they are experiencing in trying to manage the problem, and perhaps due to their own grieving. They may also feel powerless, and isolated from their cultural and extended family norms (Wenz, 1978). Sometimes this has evolved to the point where a role reversal has occurred, i.e., the parent(s) have allowed the adolescent to parent them—an essentially untenable arrangement for all parties (Anthony, 1970; Kreider & Motto, 1974; Landau, 1982; see Chapter 22; Madanes, 1980).[6]

---

[6]While our reference to "parents" may sound as if we are concerned only with two-parent families, this is not the case. Much of our experience has also been with single-parent cases. However, we agree with Haley (1976) that a problem in an adolescent or child minimally involves three people—the index patient and two adults or adult systems. In a single-parent family, one of the adults may be an estranged spouse, a grandparent, an aunt or uncle, or some other parental surrogate. Consequently, we use the term "parents" here in a more generic sense.

An early and primary goal of treatment is to change the above situation. This is done by exerting considerable, sometimes inordinate, effort in building up parental figures in their roles as both parents and as people. The therapist has to develop a sincere belief in the innate strengths of these adults. While this may sometimes seem like the hardest, it is also one of the most crucial aspects of conducting successful therapy with such cases.

The general procedure in empowering parents is to join with them, empathize effusively with their plight—the difficulties they have been and are facing—underscore their commitment as parents, and emphasize their strengths as individuals. Essentially, we see only "good" in what they do and never blame them: They can do no wrong. We may develop rationales for their behavior—"How could someone in your position do any differently? You want your son to be a whole person, not a whiny baby." By taking this position, we help to free them from guilt so they can feel safe enough to try other options—perhaps they can dare to do something different.

As may be clear from the clinical material presented thus far, empowering parents usually requires neutralizing the patient in some way, by either ignoring him or her, disparaging his or her "thoughtlessness," or some similar means. It is a form of "unbalancing" (Minuchin, 1974). The more one attends to the complaining, verbalized "pain" and distracting behavior of the index patient, the more one is diverted from effecting the necessary building-up of the parents. Inexperienced therapists and those who have been involved in treating the patient individually are most susceptible to making this error. They may feel that the patient should be attended to, that his or her subjective state needs to be explained to the family, and that the therapist is the one best qualified to understand it, coax it out, and clarify it. What such therapists do not realize is that they may unwittingly be encouraging the patient to act out, perhaps even to make another suicidal attempt. By empowering the index patient in this manner, they weaken the parents and perpetuate a family structure that has led to the dysfunctional suicidal pattern in the first place. Such therapist behavior can thus be homeostatic and, as a result, not helpful in bringing about change in either patient or family.

UNITING PARENTS

In line with the work of Haley (1976, 1980) and Madanes (1980), we find it effective to work toward uniting the parents in their behavior toward the patient. While a problem between the spouses may be evident, it is not prudent to deal with this in the early stages of treatment, and certainly not before the desired change in the patient's behavior has been sustained for a month or so. Consequently, it is wisest for the therapist to gloss over disagreements between parental figures and focus instead on getting these people to work together. Only in this way can they present the united front and consistency necessary for them to manage their problem off-spring. If they are already divided, or the patient is allowed to continually divide them, they will be weakened and ineffectual. If the therapist helps them to unite, they will feel more supported by one another and therefore strengthened as a parental subsystem. By cooperating with, and leaning upon each other, they can start to solve problems, to gain mastery over the situation, and to entertain some hope of success. *Parents working together can tame Godzilla.*

EXPOSING SECRETS

Suicidal adolescents often try to seduce therapists and treatment staff by sharing secrets with them that they withhold from the rest of the family. If the adolescent is allowed to succeed at this, therapy can be severely compromised and even neutralized. The therapist who keeps the secret will be rendered impotent when "hot" issues arise, leaving the adolescent in control and the family and treatment team powerless. It is therefore always best for the therapist to avoid confidence pacts and to insist that emotionally laden issues are shared with parents and family.

GENERALIZING INTERVENTIONS ACROSS FAMILY AND INPATIENT CONTEXTS

We have found several procedures to be crucial for conducting effective treatment with adolescents and their families within the context of an inpatient program. One of these is to contract with family members that they will remain intensely involved with the program on a regular basis. This means that they attend both conjoint family and multi-family sessions at least weekly and, where possible, also join the adjunctive activities two to three times per week. (The usual length of stay is two to six weeks.) Admission to the program should be contingent upon their agreeing to such an arrangement.

While it is often easy to convince family members to attend conjoint family therapy sessions, it is equally important that they become regularly involved in the ongoing activities of the unit—as will be described later. This is because, as was demonstrated in the case of Ellen, we *extend interventions that begin in family sessions to every aspect of the inpatient context.* The following case gives additional examples of such generalized interventions:

> Jack, aged thirteen, was admitted to the Fairmount adolescent inpatient unit for suicidal behavior (overdose), drug abuse, beating up his mother, and being expelled from school. This was a single-parent family in which the parents were divorced and Jack had not seen his father for ten years. Jack also had an older brother, aged sixteen, who abused drugs, and a sister, aged fourteen.
>
> The therapeutic team[7] decided upon the following goals: (a) unbalancing Jack and putting mother in charge; (b) engaging father and a maternal aunt to support mother in the parenting endeavor; and (c) reconnecting Jack with his father. After several efforts to get the mother to verbally take charge of Jack, it became necessary to physically assist her in sitting on him until he was ready to defer to her. This was initially undertaken in a family session and was subsequently applied

[7]The team, the adolescent unit and the therapy for this case were supervised by the first author. The family therapist was Jehoshua Kaufman, M.A.

throughout the ward. During the next 7 to 10 days, mother literally sat on Jack eight or ten times—in the recreation room, in the dormitory, during music therapy, in the middle of a baseball game, etc. A large proportion of the unit staff, plus mother's sister, was involved in reinforcing this intervention across a number of ward activities.

Concomitantly, Jack's mother was (a) empowered, by having her teach Jack how to cook, and (b) aided in being nurturant, by helping her to encourage his artistic talents in handicraft class. She was an expert in these areas, so establishing her superiority was not difficult. The activities-therapists involved thus devoted their efforts to coaching and fortifying mother, rather than teaching Jack themselves.

After considerable difficulty, the father, a travelling salesman, was contacted and persuaded to visit Jack. When he appeared, Jack did not recognize him. The father, who placed a premium on education, was only able to relate to Jack from the position of an academic lecturer. Therefore, the classroom context was chosen as the arena for their interaction. During the next month and a half, the father visited Jack almost weekly. They would sit in the classroom and, with the teacher's assistance, design Jack's curriculum, review his studies and plan for his future.

Once Jack realized his father really cared for him, and once his mother was feeling more competent, conjoint therapy sessions involving both parents could begin. Initially these sessions consisted of negotiating the level of father's involvement. This was followed by helping the parents to support each other in parenting tasks and resolve visitation arrangements. By the time of Jack's discharge, his problems had dissipated, and a follow-up seven months later indicated no recurrence.

Not only do we demand parental participation before admission of an adolescent inpatient, we also require that they be *on call* for the inpatient staff whenever needed, day or night. If a problem with their son or daughter arises on the unit, they will be called for guidance, consultation, or advice and may even be asked to come in and settle it. In this way we pay more than lip service to our position that parents know what is best for their kids and that they should be empowered to see that it is done. This is a very different philosophy from

programs which see parents as necessary evils who would best be barred from the unit. If we were *not* to involve parents in this manner, we would be giving them a double message—telling them they are wise in family sessions, while excluding them from key decisions and the settlement of problems pertaining to their son or daughter. Consequently, we routinely call them in if their adolescent has acted out, made a suicide gesture, or engaged in other untoward behavior on the unit. Surprisingly, we have generally found them willing to cooperate, thankful for being asked, and often amazingly insightful as to the best course of action to take.

Specialized Interventions

In addition to the general principles, techniques, and strategies described earlier, we have come to rely on several specialized therapy methods that greatly enhance the effectiveness, and reduce the length, of treatment.

THE FAMILY SAFETY-WATCH

This approach to managing self-destructive and potentially dangerous behavior is a natural extension of our practice of generalizing interventions across family and treatment contexts. The family suicide-watch (Stanton, 1984b) is one type of family safety-watch. We have also applied this safety watch with such problems as child abuse, spouse abuse, self-mutilation, incest, detoxification from narcotics, eating disorders, and alcoholism (Landau & Stanton, 1984).[8]

The family safety-watch is applicable within both inpatient and outpatient settings. Most inpatient units have established procedures for carrying out suicide

[8]This safety-watch method was first used by JLS in 1966 with a suicidal, sixteen-year-old self-mutilating female. Madanes (1980) uses a similar approach. Over the past ten years, JLS has implemented the family safety-watch procedure on a number of inpatient units with considerable success.

checks on an adolescent who is threatening to, or at risk of threatening to, make a gesture. We have altered this procedure so that staff serve only a supervisory or advisory function in the safety watch. Instead, we have the family members conduct the watch. They select the members to be involved from among their nuclear family, extended family, and network of family friends. They establish a shift schedule and determine, in conjunction with the inpatient staff, what the adolescent is to do with his or her time over a twenty-four-hour period, i.e., when he/she is to sleep, eat, attend classes, do homework, play games, view a movie, etc., according to a schedule. They also discuss with staff what problems might be anticipated with the adolescent and what the contingencies (rewards, punishments) and proper courses of action should be. One of the benefits of this overall approach is that if positive shifts occur in the adolescent's behavior, the family, appropriately, gets credit for the change (Stanton, 1981d).

The family safety-watch is not necessarily limited to use in inpatient settings, but can also be extended to more natural contexts. For instance, parents and family can be empowered and coached to manage the suicidal problem at home—the *home safety-watch*. In less severe cases, such a program might be implemented on an outpatient basis at the very beginning of treatment. For inpatient cases it could begin upon discharge—as a logical sequel to the inpatient regimen.

The primary aim is to mobilize the family to take care of their own and feel competent in doing so. The therapist(s) spend(s) time with the family in (a) determining what the family resources and support systems are, (b) figuring out ways for involving these support systems in the effort (e.g., "How much time do you think Uncle Harry can give to watching your son?"), and (c) designing a detailed plan for the safety watch. The latter involves figuring out schedules and shifts so that someone is with the patient twenty-four hours a day. A backup system is established so that the person on watch can get support from others if he or she needs it. A cardinal rule is

that the patient be within view of someone at all times, even while in the bathroom or shopping.

If the patient is a student or is employed, and the family and therapist agree that he or she is well enough to participate in these activities, very clear parameters for supervision must be established. This might entail a family member accompanying the patient at all times, or might be achieved by the family transfering responsibility to specific people in school or at work. If so, airtight provision must be made for coverage of breaks, lavatory visits and transit between rooms.

One might expect the patient to protest a program of this sort—"I want to shop on my own. After *all!*" However, he or she should not be allowed the luxury of being left alone *at any time*, and the family should be informed that the patient may try to thwart the system, such as by slipping away unnoticed. There should be a contractual agreement that if the watch is inadvertently slackened or compromised, and the patient makes a suicide attempt or tries to challenge the program in some other way, the regimen will consequently be tightened up—a therapeutic move that reduces the family's feeling of failure if some slippage occurs during the week. As implied above, it is useful to employ the technique of "strategic prediction" at the beginning of such a procedure: The family is warned that the patient will try tricks to be alone, pretend to be "fine," etc., and that the first month or two will be the hardest.

In conjunction with the tasks surrounding the watch, the family, patient, and treatment team collaborate in determining what the adolescent must do in order to relax, and ultimately terminate, the watch. The behavioral criteria usually revolve around issues such as personal responsibility, age-appropriate behavior, and the handling of family and social relationships. For example, the adolescent might be required to arise in the morning without prompting, complete his or her chores on time, substitute courteous and friendly behavior for grumbling and moping, talk to parents and/or siblings more openly, watch less television, and/or spend more time with friends; the tasks chosen are tailored to the particular problems and priorities of the family. They should be specific, clearly delineated, and observable, so that their occurrence or nonoccurrence can be readily determined and charted.

The decision to terminate the watch is made conjointly by the family and the therapeutic team. It is, of course, contingent upon the absence of suicide-related behavior, as well as upon the achievement of an acceptable level of improvement in the other behavioral tasks assigned to the adolescent. If any member of the therapeutic system feels there is still a risk of a suicide attempt, the watch is continued. In addition, if, after the watch is terminated, the adolescent relapses in any way, a full safety watch is reinstated.

It is surprising how appealing families often find the safety watch. It makes them feel potent and useful and reduces the expense that they may have incurred, for instance, in visiting and maintaining the adolescent in an extended inpatient program. It also reestablishes the intergenerational boundary, opens up communication within the family, reconnects the nuclear and extended families (thus providing support for the nuclear family), and makes the adolescent feel cared for and safe. In addition, it functions as a "compression" move (Stanton, 1981c; Stanton, 1984a), which pushes the patient, parent(s), and family members closer together, holds them there, and awaits the rebound or disengagement that almost inevitably follows. This rebound is often a necessary step in bringing about appropriate distances within enmeshed subsystems and opens the way to attaining a new, more viable family structure—a structure that does not require a member to exhibit suicidal behavior.

RESOLUTION OF FAMILY MOURNING

As noted earlier in this chapter, suicidal behavior is often intimately tied into unresolved mourning and loss within the nuclear and/or extended family of the suicidal person (Paul & Grosser, 1965; Paul & Paul, 1975; Reilly, 1976). However, unless spe-

cifically pursued in therapy sessions, this grieving is rarely shared with a therapist. Family members may not deliberately conceal the losses, but may be completely unaware of how these losses relate to the self-destructive family member(s).

In such cases, we tend to supplement the methods described earlier (e.g., nuclear family restructuring; safety watches) by taking the family directly into the mourning process. In this way we "return" (compress) them to the original, unresolved point of family transitional conflict and escort them through it in a new way, so that they can complete the transitional pathway from the past through the present and into the future. Because the different family subsystems may, perhaps, have been "out of sync" ever since the point(s) of loss, this approach takes them phenomenologically, experientially, and structurally to an earlier point, holds them there briefly, and guides them forward.

Sandra's family, described earlier, had suffered a series of tragic losses extending from World War II. Whereas these losses were discussed in the first team session, sessions two to four focused more on Sandra's discharge and on establishing a home safety-watch. However, the seed of a family-grave visit was planted during session No. 1. The symbolic grave chosen was that of the maternal grandfather, who (a) had died thirteen years earlier, (b) had been the family patriarch, and (c) had been the family member around whom much of the grieving affect seemed to revolve. (In fact, the family reported that his wife, the maternal grandmother, still woke up in the middle of the night, wailing his death and unable to return to sleep.)

Once the home safety-watch was succeeding (i.e., the family had held the line competently, and Sandra was working her way out of this regimen by convincing the family that she was behaving responsibly), we suggested that plans ought to be made for the grave visit. It was recommended that members of the extended family and friends be invited to share the mourning, so that Sandra could be free to be a young girl again. The therapeutic team volunteered to send letters of invitation to these additional family members and friends.

The letter stated that this family had suffered greatly and that Sandra appeared to be bearing the family sadness. It suggested that a ceremony at the graveyard, to mourn grandfather and others lost, would allow family members and close friends to share their grief openly, thus relieving Sandra of her responsibility. The letter stressed that the ceremony would also include a joyful recognition both of the valuable attributes and unique gifts of those who had died, and of the ways in which these have been, and would continue to be, carried into the future by succeeding generations.

After a couple of planning sessions with the family (which included discussion of who should bring what refreshments, music, tape recorders, cameras, etc.), the ceremony took place at grandfather's grave.[9] The grandmother and all her available offspring, sons-in-law, daughters-in-law, and grandchildren attended. The family's minister was also present, along with five team members and two of their spouses. The therapeutic network thus totaled twenty-four people, each of whom, upon arrival, was directed to greet and connect with every other person present.

The ceremony was opened by the minister reading a metaphoric story about dragonflies and their metamorphosis, which he had read to the grandchildren at their grandfather's funeral thirteen years earlier. Members of the family and the therapeutic team then read poems and prose, gave eulogies, and shared experiences of personal loss. Although grandfather was the central figure in most of the family contributions, other losses were also addressed. While there was a fair amount of weeping and hugging, much of the content had an uplifting tone. At times, the group laughed warmly and hilariously while sharing humorous stories about those who had passed on.

Following the formal part of the ceremony, the entire group was directed to embrace each other tightly, with grandmother in the center and the therapeutic team forming the outer layer. This embrace was held for some time, and was followed by the network breaking down into smaller groups, which (a) hugged, talked, cried, and laughed quietly, and (b) dissolved and reformed in different combinations. Throughout this latter

phase, moving music was played. It consisted of the recorded voice of a family member who was unable to attend, but who had sung at most previous family rituals, including grandfather's funeral and the weddings of many of those present.

Afterwards, as had been arranged, the network moved to the family's church. In a room off the vestibule, they shared refreshments, reviewed a collection of family photographs which had been arranged on a table, and chatted freely. The conversations ranged from the father's heroic war experiences and losses, through discussion of other deceased members, to teasing the young adult members about how they had changed from their childhood photographs. Sandra began to bubble about finding herself a boyfriend, and ultimately marrying and having children. (Thus, the transitional pathway was reestablished, stretching from past events to the family's hopes for the future.) Meanwhile, one of the team co-leaders talked with the minister about how he (the minister) could play a crucial role in the family's further resolution of their grieving; essentially, this was a step toward returning the family to its natural support system (Auerswald, 1968).

Eventually, members of the extended family began to feel comfortable in inquiring about Sandra and her problems: A number of them had been kept in the dark as to her situation. When this stage had been reached—approximately one and one-half hours from the beginning of the gravesite ceremony—the team was free to leave. A group photograph was taken, and, as previously arranged, most of the extended family repaired to the home of Sandra's parents.

At the family's request, the final therapy session was held a few days later—the evening before Sandra's birthday. The family was content that the goals of therapy had been achieved. In addition to Sandra's improvement, they felt that they had gained a sense of direction, had accomplished much, and had found the necessary perspective and resources to move on. The team reinforced the family's perception, congratulated them, and, as part of the clinic's evaluation procedure, obtained permission to make "social" follow-up calls in the coming months.

Four months later, Sandra, who had passed the qualifying examinations needed in her occupation, was working steadily, enjoying an active social life, communicating well with her family, and remaining symptom-free.

---

[9]In twelve years of experience with this approach, the first author has found that if an appropriately symbolic grave is not readily accessible, the ceremony can be held in the family home, a place of worship, a garden, or even the therapist's office. Under such circumstances, the family should bring symbolic possessions, photographs and memorabilia to the occasion.

The therapy applied in this case progressed through several stages, many of which overlapped chronologically. These were:

1. Reframing Sandra's behavior.
2. Uniting and empowering the parents in order to establish a functional hierarchy that could take responsibility for keeping Sandra alive.
3. Initiating a retribalization (Speck & Attneave, 1973) and compression around the safety watch.
4. Concomitant with the first three stages, preparing the family for grief work. This was not only important in itself, but was also a crucial aspect of the retribalization—both the nuclear family and the extended family needed to grieve.
5. Gathering the network together and compressing them experientially around the unresolved transitional conflict of the bereavement, eventually resulting, as with the safety watch, in a rebound.
6. Moving them, during the ceremony, both backwards and forwards in "time." By allowing them to ascertain where they had come from and where they were going, they could see a pathway along which they could proceed.
7. Freeing them, eventually, to share information and "secrets" openly, thus loosening up the system and permitting effective utilization of their combined resources in coping with the challenges of the future.

Managing "Manipulative" Relapse

Once therapy is progessing well and appropriate structural shifts begin to emerge in the family, along with improvement of the index patient, it sometimes happens that an apparent relapse occurs. We say "apparent" because the gestures often have a strongly manipulative flavor to them, such as the adolescent's carefully removing a new coat so as not to soil it before superficially cutting a wrist. These ploys can be viewed as testing by the index patient to see if the rules that the parents have been assisted in establishing have any backbone to them. Sometimes it even helps to warn the parents that the adolescent will attempt to stress the system to see if the new family structure (e.g., of parents working together) will hold up. When so forewarned, parents will find it easier to cope with the homeostatic behavior and take proper steps, such as tightening the safety watch, removing privileges, or whatever is fitting.[10]

In some cases, the manipulative relapse is invoked by an outside therapist who continually centralizes the patient, exhorts the patient to share his or her "true inner feelings" with the therapist instead of with the family, or works in some other way toward undermining the parents' competence and responsibilities as parents. Such therapist's actions are rarely helpful to the client or family, even if well-intentioned, and we agree with Duhl and Duhl (1981) that it is much more important that a person talk honestly and revealingly to the members of his or her family than to a therapist. The natural system is the one to be bolstered, not the (artificial) system of identified patient and therapist.

One option the family therapist may have in such instances is to use inpatient readmission as a negative reinforcement. Usually the patient does not really want to return to the hospital. Consequently, therapist and parents can unite in requiring that the adolescent return to the inpatient program (even if, in their own minds, they plan the stay to last no longer than a few days). Or they might threaten to admit the patient to a more restrictive facility, such as a state mental hospital, if he or she does not shape up and stop misbehaving. Indeed, it may require a series of several such brief admissions until the lesson sinks in and/or, if applicable, the outside therapist either (a) begins to understand and to follow the plan, or (b) gives up and turns the case over to the family program and, in essence, the family.

---

[10]This is not meant to imply that we are unaware of the role of parents and other family members in aiding and abetting the relapse. Rather, we find it more efficacious and structurally sound to avoid blaming parents and to maintain a focus on the "responsibility" of the index patient.

THE FAMILY AFTER ADOLESCENT SUICIDE

Adolescent suicide is unfortunately sometimes successful and the family members are left to cope with the aftermath. They ask many questions of themselves, perhaps the most frequent and unanswerable being, "Did he/she mean to do it? Was it something I/we said or did? Could I/we have prevented it?".

The family therapist is rarely asked to see a family with the specific charge of helping them to work through the loss of the dead member, however. Instead, their request for therapy is, in our experience, frequently vague. For instance, the therapist may be asked to see one apparently depressed family member (commonly one of the parents). The presenting index patient may be another adolescent who is acting out or depressed (Rosenthal, 1980), or a parent who is drinking heavily. Information about the dead adolescent is often not volunteered and needs to be elicited:

A family was referred to JLS by the family physician who had known the family for fifteen years. The identified patient was Kent, aged fifteen, who had been threatened with expulsion from school because of poor grades and disruptive behavior. He had recently been caught running away from home.

When the parents completed the intake form, only three children were noted: Greg, aged twenty-one, Millie, aged seventeen, and Kent. During the initial session (to which father came late), it was apparent that the entire family was severely depressed, particularly the mother. Each member sat with head bowed, and all communication was addressed only to the therapist. Kent was vociferously blamed for his behavior, and he in turn blamed father for drinking again after some years of being completely dry. It was only during careful questioning about family-life-cycle events that the question of bereavement was raised. The family burst into tears, sobbing that Jim, aged eighteen, had blown his head off with a shotgun six weeks prior to the session. (It was after this event that the father's difficulties had escalated.) The therapist was able to encourage the family members to hold hands in a circle (closer touch was not possible at that stage) and to begin to share their grief. Jim's name had hardly been mentioned since his death, and the major thrust of therapy was to remove the focus from Kent's misbehavior and father's drinking, and to help the family talk about Jim, thus working through the mourning process.

Parents have great difficulty in overcoming the death of a child and, in the case of suicide, they not only shoulder the guilt of surviving themselves, but also the dread that they were in some way responsible. Secondary preventive work is essential both for the parents and for the siblings.

In the above family, Greg had heard the shot and felt he could and should have prevented it. Kent had given up and felt he ought to follow his brother to the grave. Father, too, had again started down his own self-destructive path. Had the family not been referred for therapy, the systems factors that precipitated Jim's despondence and death would, in all probability, have claimed another life or, at least, perpetuated a disastrous pattern.

The family needed to know that they could take control of their lives and change the script. In this way, they could use Jim's death to improve their future and perhaps make sense of what they had been viewing as a meaningless event. The stages of therapy were somewhat similar to those described earlier in the case of Sandra, and the treatment goals were successfully achieved. A thirty-month follow-up indicated no recurrence of problems with Kent or either of his parents.

From this case and the others presented in this chapter, it should be apparent that the preventive potential of family- and systems-based interventions with suicidal problems is enormous. Therapy that weakens parents can increase the risk of death. Therapy that supports and empowers them can help them save lives.

REFERENCES

Anthony, E. J. The reactions of parents to adolescents and to their behavior. In E. J. Anthony & T. Benedek (Eds.), *Parenthood*. New York: Little, Brown, 1970.

Auerswald, E. H. Interdisciplinary versus ecological approach. *Family Process*, 1968, **7**, 202–215.

Boszormenyi-Nagy, I., & Ulrich, D. N. Contextual family therapy. In A. S. Gurman & D. P. Kniskern (Eds.), *Handbook of family therapy*. New York: Brunner/Mazel, 1981.

Cain, A. C., & Fast, I. Children's reaction to parental suicide: Distortions of guilt, communication and identification. In A. C. Cain (Ed.), *Survivors of suicide*. Springfield, IL: Charles C. Thomas, 1972.

Cantor, J. Alcoholism as a suicidal equivalent. In *Proceedings of the Fourth International Conference for Suicide Prevention*. Los Angeles: Delman, 1968.

Cohen-Sandler, R., Berman, A. L., & King, R. A. A follow-up study of hospitalized suicidal children. *Journal of the American Academy of Child Psychiatry*, 1982, **21**, 398–403.

Coleman, S. B., & Stanton, M. D. The role of death in the addict family. *Journal of Marital and Family Counseling*, 1979, **4**, 79–91.

Duhl, B. S., & Duhl, F. J. Integrative family therapy. In A. S. Gurman & D. P. Kniskern (Eds.), *Handbook of family therapy*. New York: Brunner/Mazel, 1981.

Farberow, N. L. Indirect self-destructive behavior: Classification and characteristics. In N. L. Farberow (Ed.), *The many faces of suicide*. New York: McGraw-Hill, 1980.

Frederick, C. J. Drug abuse as self-destructive behavior. *Drug Therapy*, 1972, **2**, 49–68.

Grolnick, L. A family perspective of psychosomatic factors in illness: A review of the literature. *Family Process*, 1972, **11**, 457–486.

Haley, J. *Problem-solving therapy*. San Francisco: Jossey-Bass, 1976.

Haley, J. *Leaving home*. New York: McGraw-Hill, 1980.

Kreider, D. G., & Motto, J. A. Parent-child role reversal and suicidal states in adolescence. *Adolescence*, 1974, **9**, 365–370.

Landau, J. Link therapy as a family therapy technique for transitional extended families. *Psychotherapeia*, 1981, **7**(4), 382–390.

Landau, J. Therapy with families in cultural transition. In M. McGoldrick, J. K. Pearce, & J. Giordano (Eds.), *Ethnicity and family therapy*. New York: Guilford, 1982.

Landau, J. *The family in transition: Theory and technique*. New York: Guilford, in press.

Landau, J., & Griffiths, J. A. The South African family in transition: Therapeutic and training implications. *Journal of Marital and Family Therapy*, 1981, **7**, 339–344.

Landau, J., Griffiths, J. A., & Mason, J. The extended family in transition: Clinical implications. *Psychotherapeia*, 1981, **7**(4), 370–381. Republished in F. Kaslow (Ed.), *The international book of family therapy*. New York: Brunner/Mazel, 1982.

Landau, J., & Stanton, M. D. Aspects of supervision with the "Pick-a-Dali Circus" model. *Journal of Strategic and Systemic Therapies*, 1983, **2**(2), 31–39.

Landau-Stanton, J., & Stanton, M. D. *The family safety watch: A method for managing abusive and self-destructive behavior*. Manuscript submitted for publication, 1984.

Langsley, D. G., Fairbairn, R. H., & DeYoung, C. D. Adolescence and family crises. *Canadian Psychiatric Association Journal*, 1968, **13**, 125–133.

Lewis, J. M., Beavers, W. R., Gossett, J. T., & Phillips, V. A. *No single thread: Psychological health in family systems*. New York: Brunner/Mazel, 1976.

Litman, R. E., Shaffer, M., & Peck, M. L. Suicidal behavior and methadone treatment. In *Proceedings of the 4th National Conference on Methadone Treatment*. New York: National Association for the Prevention of Addiction to Narcotics (NAPAN), 1972.

Madanes, C. The prevention of rehospitalization of adolescents and young adults. *Family Process*, 1980, **19**, 179–191.

Meerloo, J. A. M. Suicide, menticide, and psychic homicide. *Archives of Neurology and Psychiatry*, 1959, **81**, 360–362.

Meerloo, J. A. M. *Suicide and mass suicide*. New York: Grune & Stratton, 1962.

Menninger, K. *Man against himself*. New York: Harcourt, 1938.

Minuchin, S. *Families and family therapy*. Cambridge: Harvard University Press, 1974.

Minuchin, S., Baker, L., Rosman, B. L., Liebman, R., Milman, L., & Todd, T. C. A conceptual model of psychosomatic illness in children. *Archives of General Psychiatry*, 1975, **32**, 1031–1038.

Murphy, G. E., Wetzel, R. D., Swallow, C. S., & McClure, J. N. Who calls the suicide prevention center? *American Journal of Psychiatry*, 1969, **126**, 314–324.

Paul, N. L., & Grosser, G. H. Operational mourning and its role in conjoint marital therapy. *Community Mental Health Journal*, 1965, **1**, 339–345.

Paul, N. L., & Paul, B. *A marital puzzle*. New York: Norton, 1975.

Pescor, M. J., & Surgeon, P. A. Suicide among hospitalized drug addicts. *Journal of Nervous and Mental Disease*, 1940, **91**, 287–305.

Reilly, D. M. Family factors in the etiology and treatment of youthful drug abuse. *Family therapy*, 1976, **2**, 149–171.

Rosenbaum, M., & Richman, J. Family dynamics and drug overdoses. *Life-Threatening Behavior*, 1972, **2**, 19–25.

Rosenthal, P. A. Short-term family therapy and pathological grief resolution with children and adolescents. *Family Process*, 1980, **19**, 151–159.

Rudestam, K. E. Physical and psychological responses to suicide in the family. *Journal of Consulting and Clinical Psychology*, 1977, **45**, 162–170.

Searles, H. F. Schizophrenia and the inevitability of death. *Psychiatric Quarterly*, 1961, **35**, 631–664.

Selvini Palazzoli, M., Boscolo, L., Cecchin, G., & Prata, G. *Paradox and counterparadox*. New York: Jason Aronson, 1978.

Soper, P. H., & L'Abate, L. Paradox as a therapeutic technique: A review. *International Journal of Family Counseling*, 1977, **5**, 10–21.

Speck, R. V., & Attneave, C. L. *Family networks*. New York: Pantheon, 1973.

Stanton, M. D. The addict as savior: Heroin, death and the family. *Family Process*, 1977, **16**, 191–197.

Stanton, M. D. An integrated structural/strategic approach to family therapy. *Journal of Marital and Family Therapy*, 1981a, **7**, 427–439.

Stanton, M. D. Marital therapy from a structural/strategic viewpoint. In G. P. Sholevar (Ed.), *Handbook of marriage and marital therapy*. Jamaica, NY: SP Medical and Scientific Books, 1981b.

Stanton, M. D. Strategic approaches to family therapy. In A. S. Gurman & D. P. Kniskern (Eds.), *Handbook of family therapy*. New York: Brunner/Mazel, 1981c.

Stanton, M. D. Who should get credit for change that occurs in therapy? In A. S. Gurman (Ed.), *Questions and answers in the practice of family therapy*. New York: Brunner/Mazel, 1981d.

Stanton, M. D. Fusion, compression, diversion and the workings of paradox: A theory of therapeutic/systemic change. *Family Process*, 1984a, **23**, 135–167.

Stanton, M. D. *The suicide watch: An alternative approach to managing self-destructive behavior*. Paper presented at the Departmental Conference, Department of Psychiatry, University of Rochester Medical Center, Rochester, NY, 1984b, May.

Stanton, M. D., & Coleman, S. B. The participatory aspects of indirect self-destructive behavior. In N. L. Farberow (Ed.), *The many faces of suicide*. New York: McGraw-Hill, 1980.

Stanton, M. D., & Todd, T. C. Structural family therapy with drug addicts. In E. Kaufman & P. Kaufmann (Eds.), *The family therapy of drug and alcohol abuse*. New York: Gardner Press, 1979.

Stanton, M. D., Todd, T. C., & Associates. *The family therapy of drug abuse and addiction*. New York: Guilford, 1982.

Teicher, J. D., & Jacobs, J. Adolescents who attempt suicide: Preliminary findings. *American Journal of Psychiatry*, 1966, **122**, 1248–1257.

Walsh, F. W. Concurrent grandparent death and birth of a schizophrenic offspring: An intriguing finding. *Family Process*, 1978, **17**, 457–463.

Welldon, R. M. C. The "shadow of death" and its implications in four families, each with a hospitalized schizophrenic member. *Family Process*, 1971, **10**, 281–302.

Wenz, F. V. Economic status, family anomie, and adolescent suicide potential. *The Journal of Psychology*, 1978, **98**, 45–47.

Whitaker, C. A., & Keith, D. V. Symbolic-experiential family therapy. In A. S. Gurman, & D. P. Kniskern (Eds.), *Handbook of family therapy*. New York: Brunner/Mazel, 1981.

Williams, C., & Lyons, C. M. Family interaction and adolescent suicidal behaviour: A preliminary investigation. *Australian and New Zealand Journal of Psychiatry*, 1976, **10**, 243–252.

Winick, C. Some psychological factors in addiction. In D. Wakefield (Ed.), *The addict*. Greenwich, CT: Fawcett, 1963.

20

The Adolescent With Special Needs

WILLIAM MITCHELL, Ed.D.,
and SALVATORE J. RIZZO, Ph.D.

A family whose child has a handicap is not necessarily a handicapped family. Families have similar needs even though individuals within the families have "special" needs. All families, for instance, must manage transitions. Nonetheless, these transitions are more intense and prolonged for families whose children have handicaps. One reason for this is that a family's psychological adjustment to a disabling condition in any of its members is fundamentally stressful. Even the most well-informed family cannot anticipate the impact this kind of event will have on the entire family. Another reason why transitions may be difficult is that extra work is required to negotiate them. The logistics involved in meeting special needs can become burdensome.

Adolescence is a stage in the individual and family life cycle during which radical shifts in roles occur. As offspring prepare for independence, parents begin to look forward to a renewal of their relationship as a couple. For the family whose adolescent has a handicap, the drama often extends beyond chronological adolescence,

leading parents to believe that they will be trapped in their parental roles. In fact, in the days when fewer educational and community services were available, people with handicaps were often regarded as "perpetual children." Services available today focus on preparation for launching but not on long-term support of autonomous living. This may herald an age in which the family member with a handicap is viewed as a "perpetual adolescent." The question persists: how can the family therapist help these families move beyond this phase of the family life cycle?

Because families with handicapped adolescents are, to paraphrase Harry Stack Sullivan, more simply families than otherwise, family therapy with them is not very different from therapy with any other families. However, understanding the differences that do exist is crucial. A key difference is their usual reason for entering therapy. Rather than psychopathological family processes, we typically find a myriad of logistical difficulties and prolonged transitions that have left family structures rigid and obsolete. Consequently, families with a handicapped member seem to respond most positively to treatment that is oriented towards solving problems and managing resources. Even subtle inferences of family pathology on the part of the therapist can undermine treatment. Short-term work that addresses the pragmatic difficulties directly seems to work most successfully. The goal is to move family members incrementally toward more independent functioning and to promote structural shifts that support the launching of the adolescent with special needs.

The purpose of this chapter is to highlight issues and treatment strategies relevant to families with a handicapped adolescent. In the first section we review the inconclusive literature on families with special-needs youth. In the second section we describe types of disabilities and propose treatment strategies emerging from broad categories. In the third section we offer case vignettes and a model for conceptualizing systemic work. In the fourth section we advocate treatment based on the needs of the family. In the concluding section we discuss those central ideas that may be most useful in family therapy.

Throughout the chapter we subscribe to the notion of handicap as a generic condition, physical and/or cognitive, that substantially limits the individual and makes special demands on the family. We do not attempt to catalogue specific disabling conditions and the corresponding specific treatments. Also, the identification of adolescence by age presents problems for special-needs individuals who may be developmentally delayed. We will therefore define adolescence functionally, rather than chronologically. We regard the adolescent stage as a period of growth and development toward the highest capable level of adult functioning of each family member, a period not necessarily restricted by the parameters of chronological age.

DEBUNKING THE FAMILY DISRUPTION MYTH

Several authors have commented on the extra stresses that a handicapped member imposes on a family (Farber, 1960; Solnit & Stark, 1961; Wolfensberger, 1967; Schild, 1971). It would be naive to believe that a handicapped member has little or no impact on family functioning. Helen Featherstone, parent and educator, writes that, "A disability usually shifts the organization and alignment of a family, as well as the feelings and expectations of parents and children" (1980, p. 141). However, the intensity and direction of these shifts may not take the form that one would intuitively predict.

Early literature associated high levels of family disruption with the presence of a handicapped member. The usual focus was on the parents or siblings and typically on intrapsychic or psychopathological variables. Experimental methodology was unrefined and there was often a tendency to blame the victim. The usefulness of these early studies is limited, but the clinician who is familiar with them can: (1) avoid some of the popular misconceptions about these families; (2) gain a better perspective of systems other than the family; (3) understand historical trends that may have affected these families; and (4) establish credibility with families by demonstrating a thorough knowledge of the field.

Much of the early descriptive and empirical literature written by professionals is surprisingly subjective. The problem lies as much with assumptions as with methodology. The basic assumption seems to be that a handicapped child is a catastrophically negative influence and must result in parental maladjustment (Solnit & Stark, 1961; Olshansky, 1962; Cummings, 1976). Empirical studies have borne out this assumption. For example, in families with a mentally retarded child, marital stress has been estimated to be twice the national average (Love, 1973). The desertion rate of fathers of retarded children has been listed as disproportionately high (Reed & Reed, 1965). In another early study, over half a population of parents of physically handicapped children reported emotional disturbance (McMichael, 1971).

More recent and more sophisticated studies seem to reflect a trend in the direction of less family disruption than was previously reported. Divorce rates of parents of institutionalized mentally retarded young adults and newly diagnosed mentally retarded children did not differ from the norm except that the younger group (who received genetic screening and counseling) showed a lower divorce rate than the general population (Roesel & Lawlis, 1983).

Studies of the effects of a handicapped child on siblings have been contradictory (Wasserman, 1983; Breslau, Weitzman, & Messenger, 1981; Binger, 1973; Graliker, Fishler, & Koch, 1962). Citing Grossman (1972) and Featherstone (1980), Seligman (1983) concludes that there may be differential outcomes among families: "Little impact, a negative impact, or a positive outcome on subsequent adjustment and coping" (p. 529). Wasserman (1983) warns against relying on empirical studies at this point because of the small number of investigations, the contradictions, and the poor controls in the studies done. Although Wasserman focuses on siblings, her caveat applies equally well to the studies of the family as a whole. Earlier studies, then, tended to hold a more pessimistic view, while recent studies have been more positive, but somewhat contradictory.

What sense can one make of such divergent findings? It is possible to find some consistency in all of this. All the studies recognize the extra stress of the handicap on the family. In view of the fewer services that were available in past decades, one could easily imagine that there were less positive outcomes. What is objectionable about the earlier studies is the assumption of pathology. The contradictions of more recent studies may be inherent in the families investigated; that is, they may reflect the differential responses listed by Seligman (1983). The inconsistencies may also result from the complexity of the interacting variables and the inability of current methodologies to tease out those that are most salient. What can be objectionable in recent literature is romanticizing about the resilience of families in crises.

Studies of parents as teachers of and advocates for their children have been positive in tone and useful in practice. Researchers who perform such studies generally do not assume pathology, but instead believe that parents can be competent teachers of their handicapped children. Voluminous evidence over the past two decades has demonstrated that parents indeed are quite effective as teachers (Baker, 1980; Shearer & Shearer, 1977; Tjossem, 1976). Programs that train parents to teach their children have established themselves as an essential part of the network of services offered in clinical settings. For example, Parent Place at the Judge Baker Guidance Center in Boston currently offers training to parents of nonhandicapped as well as handicapped children.

Another very useful body of literature is that written by parents themselves (e.g., Featherstone, 1980). These works tend to be narrative accounts of the emotional reactions, the day-to-day logistics, and the interactions with professionals of these author-parents. They offer an inside view of the special issues in rearing a child with a handicap. All too often, the parents find the understanding of professionals incomplete. Bridging the parent-professional gap are works by parents who are themselves professionals (e.g., Turnbull & Turnbull, 1978). A consistent theme among parent-authors is the need for advocacy for improved services at the community level.

None of these studies deals exclusively or convincingly with the special problems of families with an adolescent with special needs. Taken together, they do suggest that families with a handicapped member are capable of managing pressures without necessarily reacting with disruption or psychopathology. So far, it is not possible to isolate a typical structure or profile of a family with a handicapped member (Rizzo, 1982). Perhaps Minuchin's (1974) description can be applied here: these are "average families in transitional situations, suffering pains of accommodation to new circumstances" (p. 60). Also relevant is Featherstone's notion: "One important conclusion may be that families are too intricately complex to generalize about: it all depends" (p. 165). The systemic clinician must attempt to answer the question: "On *what* does it all depend?" One obvious factor is the type of handicap. The next section delineates three types of disabilities.

CLASSIFICATION OF HANDICAPPING CONDITIONS

A disability, whether developmental or sudden and traumatic, is almost always unintentional and imposed on the family. (An exception would be the adopting of a handicapped child.) Disability is relative, however, and the manner in which the family responds determines in large measure how disabled the young person will actually be. Some children's disabilities are pervasive, but as Gliedman and Roth (1980) point out in their study, *The Unexpected Minority*, only about one-tenth are so limited that the children could not lead normal lives if they were not victimized by prejudice (p. 4). Curiously, much of the confusion and stereotyping that inhibit development and autonomy can exist within the primary unit of socialization—the family. One major factor lies in the lack of a map or model for family members, especially for parents as family executives, to follow which would organize the family to manage the disability most effectively. Unlike other minority groups (e.g., racial minorities), family members are ill-prepared to teach the handicapped adolescent how to contend in the world; family members are simply not members of the same minority group as the handicapped adolescent (Gliedman & Roth, 1980).

There is little empirical data to document the differential impact of various classes of disability within the family unit. Conceptually, clinicians utilize the following three broad categories of disability: (1) developmental disability with prenatal or perinatal onset; (2) disability with traumatic onset; and (3) psychosomatic disability. Because so much has been written about treatment of psychosomatic families (e.g., Minuchin, Rosman, & Baker, 1978), we will focus, except for purposes of comparison, on the first two classes. In these classes, it is clear that there is an unintentional life event precipitating an immediate systemic crisis that has ongoing implications and can complicate the remainder of the family life cycle. Here it is important not to assume pre-event pathology or dysfunction. The disability represents an idiosyncratic stress

that can overload family coping mechanisms, at least temporarily. The major differences between the first two classes lie in timing of onset. Life-cycle demands on the family at the time of birth of a child differ from those occurring later and thus lead to differences in feelings of responsibility for the condition, degree of pre-event attachment, and energy available to manage later transitions.

In the third class, the so-called psychosomatic disability, there is more obvious interaction between physical factors and family organization related to the onset, as well as the course, of the disability. Here the disability seems to emerge from the family organization rather than to be imposed on it. The psychosomatic disability seems to be a stabilizing rather than a destabilizing event in the family system. In such families it is harder to make the assumption of no pre-event dysfunction. In fact, research by Minuchin, Rosman, and Baker (1978) demonstrated structural similarities in families with a psychosomatic child. The family characteristics include enmeshment with the child who is also overinvolved in parental conflicts, overprotectiveness, rigidity, and conflict detouring. A family systems approach to adolescent anorexia is discussed elsewhere in this book (Chapter 13).

Our clinical impression, though as yet unverified, suggests that the greater the time between the onset of the disabling condition and the present, the more similar are the family interactions to those of psychosomatic families. Thus, what appears to be a difference based on the nature of the disability (e.g., an inherent condition, such as Down's syndrome, as opposed to a catastrophic illness or trauma) may in fact be a difference based on the amount of time since onset. This has important implications for treatment modalities. Those families still reeling in the "novelty/shock crisis" (Menolascino, 1968, p. 597; Wolfensberger, 1967) immediately following the diagnosis are in a state of disequilibrium and need supportive treatment. Families entering treatment years later may have become overprotective of the disabled young person and family structures are often inflexible. These families may need treatment that is destabilizing in order to break free from patterns that no longer serve a useful purpose.

For practical purposes, then, we are left with two "types" of families (distinguished primarily by the time since the onset of the disability) with distinctly different needs. These two types can exist at any point after the disabled member's early childhood. During early childhood, families are still destabilized and there has not been sufficient time for family interactions to become rigid. If the disabled member is an adolescent, it is relatively easy to differentiate these types. As a rule of thumb, it takes two to three years for structures to become so rigid that some form of destabilization is necessary. The case vignettes that follow illustrate each type.

CASE VIGNETTES

The Johnson Family

Rosalyn and Jeff, who had been married for less than a year, came in for marital counseling. Jeff complained that Roz was so preoccupied with problems in her family of origin that she had no energy left for him. Roz countered that Jeff simply did not understand that it was impossible for her to walk away from the difficulties in her family since her fourteen-year-old sister's spinal-cord injury shortly before their wedding.

The therapist decided to take the couple's complaint seriously and began to concentrate on concerns related to Roz's family.

Roz, twenty-one years old, was from an intact family and had a fourteen-year-old sister, Joan, who was paralyzed below the waist in a bicycle accident a year earlier. Up to that time Joan had been among the brightest children in her class. Because of her prolonged hospitalization, she fell behind in her school work. When she was ready to resume attendance at school, her family discovered that there were inadequate provisions for wheelchair access in the local junior high school. Rather than make elaborate changes in the existing building, school officials wanted to provide transportation to another nearby junior high school that was already fully

wheelchair accessible. The parents were strongly opposed to this plan because this school had no advanced classes for gifted children such as Joan. Joan was also opposed to the switch because she wanted to attend school with her friends. The school officials argued that Joan could not be among her peers anyway because she had missed too much work. The battle lines were drawn.

Roz's father, whose job as a marketing executive had required extensive travel, had transferred into a less demanding home-based job in order to be more available to his daughter. Neither he nor his family was prepared for his reinvestment of energy into the family system. According to Roz, her parents could not agree on a coherent plan for managing the family under the new circumstances. Her father wished to fight the school system while her mother wanted to negotiate quietly. Roz has been spending several afternoons each week tutoring Joan at her parents' house. Roz felt this was the least she could do to help her sister.

The family's problems were clearly multi-generational and multisystemic. The conflict between Roz and Jeff seemed to mirror the conflict between Roz's and Joan's parents (Ackerman, 1980). Each couple was having difficulty putting their own needs in perspective and was distracted by Joan's needs.

Roz and Jeff were given the task of arranging tutoring for Joan by an educational specialist at the school. In order to insure his active involvement, Jeff was asked to make all the necessary phone calls to the school. Once this task was completed, the therapist held a joint meeting with Jeff, Roz, and her parents to ritualize the transfer of power. In a follow-up session with Roz and Jeff one month later, they reported that their conflicts were manageable. They had resumed jogging together and were looking forward to a weekend trip to the beach.

As a second step, the therapist continued working with Joan's parents. The father's reentry into the family was addressed by assigning tasks. The therapist asked Joan's father to research the problems further by contacting local agencies. In the meantime Joan's mother was asked to build a working relationship with the school officials. In meetings with the therapist, they were soon united in a successful advocacy effort. Follow-up meetings with Joan and her parents at monthly intervals focused on promoting her autonomy within realistic limitations of her disability. This involved supporting the family as they grieved Joan's loss of some physical abilities and adjusted to a new reality.

The Pastor Family

Bob Pastor's parents asked for help in getting Bob to improve his personal hygiene. There were two areas of prime concern: his poor toileting hygiene and his inability to shave. Bob was a nineteen-year-old young man with moderate mental retardation who cognitively and emotionally was barely an adolescent despite his chronological age. His regression in hygiene represented poor execution in toileting and shaving rather than absolute inability. To avoid public embarrassment, his father had been bathing and shaving him daily. Bob was attending his last year of high school where he received vocational training and was on a waiting list for a group residence nearby. In order to move into the group home, he needed to be completely independent in self-help skills. While obtaining a family history, the therapist discovered that after his parents' divorce, six-year-old Bob had been placed in the custody of his alcoholic mother until she abandoned him a year later. His father thereupon assumed custody and remarried when Bob was twelve years old. That same year Bob's maternal grandfather died and Bob attended the funeral with his mother. This proved to be extremely upsetting for Bob. Five years later Bob's stepmother gave birth to a girl. Shortly after her birth, Bob's self-help skills deteriorated.

Bob visits with his alcoholic mother (who lives with her mother several hours' drive away from Bob's home) twice yearly for about one week per visit. He and his mother have great difficulty during these visits and often call Bob's father for help in resolving a crisis.

The therapeutic focus in this case concentrated only on the specific presenting problem of the son's inadequate hygiene. The therapist had to resist becoming distracted by other compelling factors in the family history. Hypothesizing that Bob's father was overinvolved in his son's hygiene, the therapist gave him the paradoxical directive that he was on the right track and that making any immediate changes would probably be disruptive to the family. When asked how often Bob was soiling, and improperly wiping, Mr. Pastor reacted angrily by saying that he was not going to go through dirty laundry to count soiled underwear. The therapist agreed that this was too much of a burden. During the next session the father reported that he had decided to stop bathing and shaving his son. Bob was not doing a perfect job, but was improving. The soiling persisted,

sporadically, for another few months and then disappeared completely. The therapist next began to help advocate for placement in the group home.

Discussion of Both Cases

While the therapist working with the Johnsons needed to widen the focus, the therapist working with the Pastors needed initially to restrict the focus. Therapists must move in steps, concentrating on one problem at a time; they need not have all the answers. In the case of the Pastors, the paradoxical instruction to the father not to change his involvement in his son's hygiene may have helped the father back off a little. The therapist's question about frequency of soiling was not an intentional intervention, but implicitly directed the father to become more involved than he already was. His resultant anger introduced impetus for change. As Bob's father did less for him, Bob was forced to do more for himself or endure the censure of his peers. Thus, independence in bathing and shaving were achieved expeditiously.

The therapist who worked with the Johnsons supported them through a difficult adjustment. The therapist who worked with the Pastors initially used a more powerful technique, that of a paradoxical directive, to shake the family out of a maladaptive structure. In both cases, however, the focus remained on the logistical problems presented by the families.

MULTIPLE SYSTEMS

Family therapists tend to focus exclusively on the family system. The therapists in the above cases were effective because of their willingness to work on several levels. Carter and McGoldrick present a model of stressors on various systems as they move through time (Carter & McGoldrick, 1980, p. 10). We have adapted this model and present it here in a simplified form (Figure 20.1).

The model consists of an individual, represented by the inner circle (with various subsystems operating within it), surrounded by larger systems (nuclear and extended family, community, society), represented by progressively larger concentric circles. The model is described by the following axioms:

1. All systems move through time (develop) and have a history.

2. All systems are open—i.e., they have interaction with, influence, and are influenced by other systems on all levels. Regulation of this commerce with other systems can be viewed as a complex of dynamic equilibria.

3. What appears to be "external" (nondevelopmental) to one system or set of systems is "internal" (developmental) to another. For example, as a community moves through time, it elaborates a history. The chronologically ordered events in this history represent its development as a system and are related

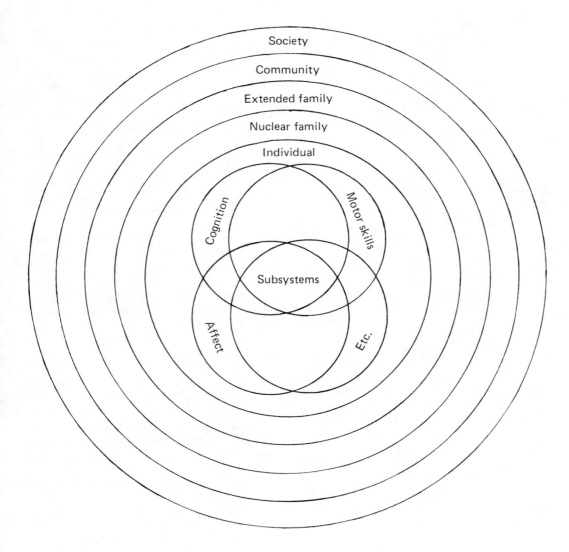

Figure 20.1
Multiple systems model.

to each other systemically. Thus, if the community's school system loses enrollment, adjustments (closing some schools or classroom, laying off teachers, etc.) are made. These are developmental changes from the community perspective. If you are a handicapped student, however, and your neighborhood school is closed, the event is external to you and therefore not developmental.

4. Incongruence with other systems is stressful. For example, the teenager who needs a wheelchair for locomotion is not congruent with the norms of the high school. Arriving at school in a special vehicle, wheeling around back to a ramp, waiting for elevators instead of dashing up stairs, attending adapted physical education, and so forth, the teen in a wheelchair is constantly reminded of his or her "differentness."

5. Working effectively with any systems requires focus on those variables one can influence most directly. One may work at any level but it helps: (a) to be aware of the level at which one is working; (b) to set realistic goals; and (c) to take interplay with other levels into account.

The handicapped adolescent's disability is by definition an incongruence. The individual's subsystems are out of skew. However, the effects of the disability reach far beyond the individual. Stigmatization, for example, is a social rather than intrapsychic process. Often the most devastating implications of a disability are the negative and prejudicial reactions of others. The family may become rejecting (or overprotective) before making accommodations. Likewise, the larger systems of extended family, community, or society at large may reject all those who are seen as contaminated by the stigmatized member. There are, then, many systems that have a profound effect on the well-being of the adolescent with special needs. Therapists working with families of handicapped adolescents must be aware of all these levels/systems and willing to move from one level to another as the need arises. We have deliberately focused here on the nuclear family as the major social system for initial therapeutic consideration.

PREPARING FOR TREATMENT

Adolescent Development

As the therapist gathers information about the family entering treatment, he or she must keep in mind the parameters of normal development as well as the special issues pertinent to the disabling condition. As we have seen in earlier chapters of this book, families with any child in adolescence can expect to have the elasticity of their structures stretched to the limits. The rapid changes taking place "within" (emerging physical and sexual maturity; the acquisition of formal operations in the cognitive domain, etc.) and around (intimate peer relations or "chumship"; sexual exploration, etc.) the adolescent must be accommodated by equally rapid changes in the family. The adolescent typically makes explosive forays into the world outside the family, only to return to the family for refuge. The family may be rejected energetically as the teenager asserts independence, and reembraced as the pressures of the outside world become temporarily overwhelming.

These bursts of independence are the test flights that precede the launching of the young adult. The family—the "ground crew" in this metaphor—may feel somewhat helpless and perplexed at times, but is as important to the successful negotiation of this period as a ground crew is to astronauts during a space flight. The most crucial ingredient of families with adolescents is flexibility. Families that have adjusted to particular routines necessary for earlier childrearing find these routines unsatisfactory during adolescence. A new repertoire of skills and an assortment of interactional patterns are now required and the family must learn to select appropriately.

When there is more than one child, the family is also required to maintain the structures necessary for other children's need attainment. Ironically, it may be easier for parents with younger children to weather the storm of adolescence, because (1) they do not face as rapid transition to the empty nest, and (2) they keep some old patterns of family functioning operative, which gives the adolescent a more secure home base.

Special Needs

In working with families with a handicapped youth, the therapist must be cognizant of the subsystems operating within the identified individual, the systems outside the family domain, and the family itself. Unless the handicap is pervasive, affecting all levels of development or functioning equally, there will be incongruities between areas of strength and weakness. Incongruities, wherever they appear, are stressful. For the individual, the tension between strengths and weaknesses may be difficult to manage. For example, the physically handicapped adolescent whose cognitive development has been within normal limits is likely to become extremely annoyed when the handicap prevents or slows down achievement of a cognitive task. Conversely, the mentally retarded adolescent whose sexual development is progressing like any other teenager's may have difficulty understanding these physical changes. On a more subtle level, the learning-disabled adolescent with an auditory-processing problem may feel "out of it" when forced to rely on this subsystem, and so on.

Most individual subsystem incongruities are experienced as frustrating. We all experience some frustrations of this sort but the handicapped adolescent becomes "stuck," much as a family gets stuck in maladaptive interactive patterns. The adolescent can get caught in a circuitous and self-defeating internal dialogue in which there is a bad, handicapped self and a good, normal self. Adolescence is a time of running from one extreme to another. These shifts can become amplified in the adolescent with special needs. Some teens may deny the existence of a disability and create elaborate fantasies to avoid confronting reality. Others withdraw and become increasingly passive. Most, however, are able to work through the discrepancies between varying skills. The therapist needs

to be aware of such discrepancies and must be prepared to suggest ways in which the special-needs youth and his family can support an integration of subsystems so that the individual may function near the limits of his or her potential.

The mentally retarded adolescent provides an apt example of how incongruities create tension for the individual, as well as for the family and community systems. In mental retardation stages may be "stretched."[1] Lynn Hoffman (1980) has reminded family therapists that discontinuous changes are characteristic of all systems. Individual development illustrates this well. There are plateaus followed by the abrupt emergence of new skills. The plateaus are hardly quiescent and the discontinuity of development is more apparent than real. But the change is experienced as quite sudden. There is one moment in time when the child takes the first step, says the first word, or in the case of the adolescent, shows the first signs of sexual maturity. The mentally retarded adolescent, by definition, has had longer plateaus in cognitive development. Figure 20.2 shows how this occurred in the case of Bob Pastor.

Keeping in mind that we are using adolescence as a functional designation, the illustrated case shows that when Bob reached a chronological age (CA) of nineteen years, his "mental age" (MA) was approximately nine years and his "social age" (SA) was approximately twelve years. Where is the "real" Bob? Adding to the confusion is the fact that while Bob is now about as tall as an average twelve-year-old, he became sexually mature when he was thirteen years old chronologically.

Paradoxically, although most of Bob's developmental stages simply have been delayed or stretched over a longer than normal period of time, this has not made him developmentally simple, but more complex. At nineteen years he now represents a myriad of stages collapsed into one individual. He must contend with the demands of young adulthood, adoles-

[1]We are indebted to Les Rubin, M.D., for this term and the illustration of it.

cence, and late childhood all at once. Bob's solution in the past was to take flight into a fantasy world which was the only place he felt he had any control over his destiny. Bob was stuck, and so was his family.

Family's Fears of Getting "Stuck"

Adolescence is a time of incremental as well as dramatic shifts in a family's structure and sequence. It is a time when both horizontal distance (i.e., between siblings) and vertical organization (hierarchical or generational) need to be sufficiently established to offer guidance and protection, and sufficiently fluid to encourage growth. The primary difficulty that families face in this period of internal transition is becoming "stuck."

The family with a handicapped adolescent is often stuck on the time dimension because of the incongruities of development discussed above. Parents may continue to utilize old strategies based on their perception of the handicapped teenager as an eternal child. A special need usually implies a decrease in independent function-

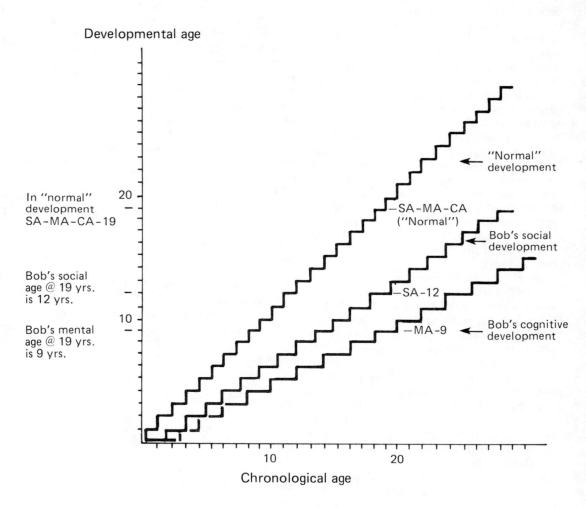

Figure 20.2
Plateaus in development in the case of Bob Pastor, compared with normal development.

ing. For example, a nonambulatory adolescent may require assistance in situations where there are no adaptations (ramps, rails, wide doorways, etc.) in the environment. Well-intentioned and conscientious parents and siblings can become overzealous in their attempts to help. Protectiveness becomes overprotectiveness and the adolescent is trapped. This is an instance where the solution has become the problem (Watzlawick, 1978).

For many families there is a belief of no future beyond the adolescence of the member with a disability. Many believe there can be no launching, only prolonged caretaking by the family. This often translates to a parent or both parents devoting their life to the care of the disabled member and insuring that there will be other resources (perhaps siblings, extended family, or the state) after their own deaths.

Siblings have very powerful effects on the adolescent with special needs and their parents. If the siblings are older, they may become parental children in order to lighten their parents' workload. If the siblings are younger, they can have several effects and may serve in several roles. One effect may be to give the parents the experience of rearing normal children. These children may serve as a reference point and thus restore self-esteem or decrease social isolation for the parents. The younger sibling may also be expected to make up for the incapacities of the older disabled child. The disabled young person (understandably) could be threatened by the competition.

In therapy, siblings may be part of the problem and part of the solution at the same time, as we saw in the case vignettes. We have often found adult siblings to be the key element in helping parents launch a disabled adolescent or young adult.

TREATMENT PLANNING AND IMPLEMENTATION

During adolescence and throughout the life cycle, a family weaves the handicapping condition of the member into the life and organization of the family in ways that become a part of the family culture or ideology. Some of the factors that the clinician needs to consider in working with the adolescent family are presented in Table 20.1. Consideration of these factors for each family provides the therapist with a reasonably comprehensive treatment plan. A table such as this should not be used as a therapeutic cookbook, but as a guide in sorting complex variables. The possible combinations of these and additional variables are too numerous to chart. The most important variable left out here is the therapist's temperament, training, and style. Choices must be made which are compatible with these unknowns.

Families that seem to manage disability best are those with clear and intact generational boundaries, flexibility within and between roles, capacity for direct communication of differences, and strong encouragement of self-differentiation of members. The therapist's task is to move the family in steps toward these capacities.

Therapists sometimes feel overwhelmed by the multiplicity of needs in families with a handicapped child. There is danger in becoming enmeshed and immobilized. Formulating a specific treatment plan and moving in steps toward the goal are crucial to success.

SUMMARY

Neither research nor clinical experience with families with special-needs adolescents suggests that these families are different in significant ways from other families. It is more important to be well grounded as a family therapist than it is to have extensive knowledge about disabling conditions (although, of course, the combination is desirable). What may be different about these families is that they have additional responsibilities and psychic stress. Without prejudice about how a family *must* feel in adverse circumstances and without assumptions about pre-event pathology, the family therapist can gather data in order to inform a rational treatment plan.

Table 20.1
Treatment planning guide

Variable		Approach	Useful Techniques
Onset	Recent	Supportive Educative Stabilizing	Help family learn about disorder; help with resources—parent groups, special equipment or training, etc.
	2 or more years ago	Destabilizing Directive Paradoxical	Paradox often useful; bring in adult siblings.
Family	Parenting:		Since single parent may feel overwhelmed, focus on reducing burdens of special care—e.g., respite care
	Single-parent	Supportive	support groups, financial arrangements such as S.S.I.
	Two-parent	Depends on Onset	Look for style: Do parents alternate in active role? Is one in charge? Is there conflict? Are parents united?
Organization	Extended	Network	Bring in any extended family members who are intimately involved in caring for adolescent with special needs. Beware of cross-generational coalitions that do not work.
	Boundaries: Enmeshment	Directive Stepwise	When parents are overinvolved with the teen, tasks can be assigned which: (1) reinvolve them with one another; (2) integrate teen with peers.
	Distancing	Same as above	Common pattern is 1 over- and 1 underinvolved parent. Assign tasks bringing underinvolved parent closer (e.g., have parents alternate in some crucial task).
	Resources (e.g., education, respite, financial)	*Supportive Educative*	*Therapist can advocate for services by writing letters, attending meetings, making phone calls, visiting facilities with family, etc.*
Treatment	*Presenting problem*	*Clarifying*	*Clarify, but do not try to convince the family that the "real" problem is anything other than what they present.*
	How is family stuck?	*Analysis of patterns*	*What sequences are repetitive and maladaptive?*
	What are therapeutic objectives?	*Team*	*Consult with others. When using educative or directive approach, remain in executive or "T" role. Neutrality is important in paradoxical approach.*
Questions	*What family or social units are to be mobilized?*	*Multisystems*	*Where is leverage? Which units should be dealt with first?*

The time since the onset of the disabling condition stands out as a critical variable. Early on, families tend to be in a crisis and need support and guidance. With time, many families' interactional patterns become repetitive and maladaptive. These latter families may benefit from strategies designed to realign these patterns; a much more intrusive approach usually works better. New concerns may arise after the presenting problem has been solved. The therapist should remain available to the family and encourage periodic follow-up visits.

Although working with the family system will usually result in significant change, additional benefits are derived from considering other systems. The therapist may find it advisable to work with the family on making changes in the larger social network. Conversely, viewing the individual as a system may aid in understanding how an incongruence or inequality of skills may be frustrating that person's growth.

REFERENCES

Ackerman, N. J. The family with adolescents. In E. Carter & M. McGoldrick (Eds.), *The family life cycle*. New York: Gardner Press, 1980.

Baker, B. L. Training parents as teachers of their developmentally disabled children. In S. Salzinger, J. Antrobus, & J. Glick (Eds.), *The ecosystem of the "sick child."* New York: Academic Press, 1980.

Baker, B. L., & Heifetz, L. J. The Read Project: Teaching manuals for parents of retarded children. In T. D. Tjossem (Ed.), *Intervention strategies for high risk infants and young children*. Baltimore: University Park Press, 1976.

Bernard, K., & Powell, M. *Teaching the mentally retarded child: A family care approach*. St. Louis: Mosby, 1972.

Bernstein, N. (Ed.) *Diminished people: Problems and care of the mentally retarded*. Boston: Little, Brown, 1970.

Binger, C. M. Childhood leukemia: Emotional impact of siblings. In E. J. Anthony & C. Kovpenik (Eds.), *The child in his family: The impact of disease and death*. New York: Wiley, 1973.

Breslau, N., Weitzman, M., & Messenger, K. Psychologic functioning of siblings of disabled children. *Pediatrics*, 1981, **67**, 344–353.

Carter, E., & McGoldrick, M. (Eds.) *The family life cycle*. New York: Gardner Press, 1980.

Cleveland, D. W., & Miller, N. Attitudes and life commitments of older siblings of mentally retarded adults. *Mental Retardation*, 1977, **15**, 38–43.

Cummings, S. T. The impact of the child's deficiency on the father: A study of fathers of mentally retarded, and of chronically ill children. *American Journal of Orthopsychiatry*, 1976, **46**, 246–255.

Cummings, S. T., Bayley, H. C., & Rie, H. E. Effects of the child's deficiency on the mother: A study of mothers of mentally retarded, chronically ill and neurotic children. *American Journal of Orthopsychiatry*, 1966, **36**, 595–608.

Dalton, J., & Epstein, H. Counseling parents of mildly retarded children. *Social Casework*, 1963, **41**, 523–530.

Doernberg, N. L. Parents as teachers of their own retarded children. In J. Wortis (Ed.), *Mental retardation: An annual review* (Vol. 4). New York: Grune & Stratton, 1972.

Ehlers, W. *Mothers of retarded children: How they feel, where they find help*. Springfield, IL: Charles C. Thomas, 1966.

Farber, B. Perceptions of crisis and related variables in the impact of a retarded child on the mother. *Journal of Health and Human Behavior*, 1960, **1**, 108–118.

Farber, B. Marital integration as a factor in parent-child relations. *Child Development*, 1962, **33**, 1–14.

Farber, B. *Notes on sociological knowledge about families with mentally retarded children*. Paper presented at the Annual Meeting of the American Association on Mental Deficiency, 1967.

Farber, B., Jenne, W. C., & Toigo, R. Family crisis and the decision to institutionalize the retarded child. *Council of Exceptional Children Research Monograph Series*, 1960, No. 1, 1960.

Featherstone, H. *A difference in the family: Life with a disabled child*. New York: Basic Books, 1980.

Gliedman, J., & Roth, W. *The unexpected minority: Handicapped children in America*. New York: Harcourt, 1980.

Golden, D. A., & Davis, J. G. Counseling parents after the birth of an infant with Down's syndrome. *Children Today*, March–April 1974.

Graliker, B. U., Fishler, K., & Koch, P. Teenage reactions to a mentally retarded sibling. *American Journal of Mental Deficiency*, 1962, **66**, 838–843.

Greer, B. G. On being the parent of a handicapped child. *Exceptional Children*, 1975, **41**, 519.

Grossman, F. K. *Brothers and sisters of retarded children: An exploratory study.* Syracuse, NY: Syracuse University Press, 1972.

Haley, J. *Problem-solving therapy: New strategies for effective family therapy.* San Francisco: Jossey-Bass, 1976.

Hoffman, L. The family life cycle and discontinuous change. In E. Carter & M. McGoldrick (Eds.), *The family life cycle.* New York: Gardner Press, 1980.

Love, H. Characteristics of parents having mentally retarded children as compared with parents not having mentally retarded children. *The Digest of Mentally Retarded,* 1967–1968, **4,** 103–106.

Love, H. *The mentally retarded child and his family.* Springfield, IL: Charles C. Thomas, 1973.

McMichael, J. *Handicap: A study of physically handicapped children and their families.* London: Staples Press, 1971.

Menolascino, F. J. Parents of the mentally retarded. *Journal of the American Academy of Child Psychiatry,* 1968, **7,** 589–602.

Minuchin, S. *Families and family therapy.* Cambridge: Harvard University Press, 1974.

Minuchin, S., Rosman, B. L., & Baker, L. *Psychosomatic families: Anorexia nervosa in context.* Cambridge: Harvard University Press, 1978.

Olshansky, S. Chronic sorrow: A response to having a mentally defective child. *Social Casework,* 1962, **43,** 190–193.

Pueschel, S., & Murphy, A. Counseling parents of infants with Down's syndrome. *Postgraduate Medicine,* 1975, **58,** 90–95.

Reed, W. E., & Reed, S. C. *Mental retardation: A family study.* Philadelphia: Saunders, 1965.

Rizzo, S. J. Working with families through Intentional Family Interviewing. In T. F. Harrington (Ed.), *Handbook of career planning for special needs students.* Rockville, MD: Aspen, 1982.

Roesel, R., & Lawlis, G. F. Divorce in families of genetically handicapped/mentally retarded individuals. *American Journal of Family Therapy,* 1983, **11,** 45–50.

Roos, P. Parent organizations. In J. Wortis (Ed.), *Mental retardation: An annual review* (Vol. 2). New York: Grune & Stratton, 1970.

Ryckman, D. B., & Henderson, R. A. The meaning of a retarded child for his parents: A focus for counselors. *Mental Retardation,* 1965, **3,** 4–7.

Schild, S. Counseling services. In R. Koch & J.

C. Dobson (Eds.), *The mentally retarded child and his family.* New York: Brunner/Mazel, 1971.

Schlesinger, H. S., & Meadow, K. P. *Sound and sign: Childhood deafness and mental health.* Berkeley: University of California Press, 1972.

Seligman, M. Sources of psychological disturbance among siblings of handicapped children. *Personnel and Guidance Journal,* June 1983, **61,** 529–531.

Shearer, D. E., & Shearer, M. S. The Portage Project: A model for early childhood intervention. In T. B. Tjossem (Ed.), *Intervention strategies for high risk infants and young children.* Baltimore: University Park Press, 1976.

Shearer, M. S., & Shearer, D. E. Parent involvement. In J. B. Jordan, et al. (Eds.), *Early childhood education for exceptional children.* Reston, VA: Council for Exceptional Children, 1977.

Solnit, A. J., & Stark, M. H. Mourning and the birth of a defective child. *Psychoanalytical Study of the Child,* 1961, **16,** 523–537.

Tjossem, T. D. Early intervention: Issues and approaches. In T. D. Tjossem (Ed.), *Intervention strategies for high risk infants and young children.* Baltimore: University Park Press, 1976.

Turnbull, A. P., & Turnbull, H. R. (Eds.), *Parents speak out.* Columbus, OH: Charles Merrill, 1978.

Wasserman, R. Identifying the counseling needs of the siblings of mentally retarded children. *Personnel and Guidance Journal,* June 1983, **61,** 622–627.

Watzlawick, P. *The language of change: Elements of therapeutic communication.* New York: Basic Books, 1978.

Weingold, J. T. Recent trends: A parent's view. In J. Wortis (Ed.), *Mental retardation: An annual review* (Bol 4). New York: Grune & Stratton, 1972.

Wolfensberger, W. Counseling the parents of the retarded. In A. A. Baumester (Ed.), *Mental retardation: Appraisal, education and rehabilitation.* Chicago: Aldine, 1967.

Wolfensberger, W. *The principle of normalization in human services.* Toronto: National Institute on Mental Retardation, Leonard Crainford, 1972.

Wortis, H. Parent counseling. In J. Wortis (Ed.), *Mental retardation: An annual review* (Vol. 4). New York: Grune & Stratton, 1972.

21

Adolescent Runaways: A Structural Family Therapy Perspective*

JAY LAPPIN, M.S.W., A.C.S.W.,
and KENNETH W. COVELMAN, Ph.D.

*A*dolescents and running away, in the minds of many, are synonymous. Those who work with runaways and their families are familiar with the party lines: "He's bad"; "The family is no good"; "She's headstrong"; "It's the friends"; "It's the drugs". And so it goes. Yet despite these simple explanations, the problem of running away remains complex. And unidimensional explanations like friends, drugs, "badness," etc., rest on an oversimplified cause-and-effect premise that can narrow a clinician's vision—a vision which can hardly afford myopia when one considers that runaway estimates of between 500,000 and 2,000,000 a year are not uncommon (Brennan, et al., 1978; Sharts-Engel & Lau, 1983). Roughly translated, this means that approximately one out of every seven teens will run away from home (Langdell, 1983).

Because running away is such a prevalent symptom, clinicians must learn how to treat the Huck Finns and the Holden Caulfields of the world.[1] We believe the ability lies, in part, in using a systems perspective, one which encompasses the total ecology of the adolescent. From a systems perspective, running away is viewed as another color in the spectrum of symptoms; it represents the family's difficulty in shifting roles, rules, and structure as they adjust to new life stages. But it must also be seen in the larger context of the helping system. All too often, society has

*The authors wish to thank Braulio Montalvo for his encouragement and conceptual clarity, Marcia Vitiello for her editorial assistance, and Chris Cesarini for typing the innumerable drafts. The chapter is dedicated to CW.

[1]While no exact numbers are available, contact with a Philadelphia-based facility for runaways indicated that less than 10 percent of their cases are eventually placed out of the home. If this is suggestive of the trend at other agencies, then the vast majority of runaway cases will be seen in some form of outpatient treatment.

accepted a definition of runaways that has led to the organization of their treatment in a narrowly prescribed fashion. This means that foster care, group homes, and "independent living" are selected as treatments of choice before thoroughly exploring the family organization. In some cases the child is removed from the home before treatment begins. Helping systems now tend to be organized to accept the runaways' definition of their problems, which are often clouded by their needs to justify their actions. For example, runaways will often tell the clinician that the situation at home is "hopeless," that they "had to leave," or that their parents will beat them if contacted. Geographical distance, false information, reports of incest, or threats to run away again may also seemingly serve to obviate pursuing the family. The helping systems tend also to be organized by the family's response, or lack of it. In short, helpers need to understand that the overt definitions offered by adolescents or parents are, in many instances, a call for attention to a family crisis.

In research, acceptance of the runaway's version of the problem has resulted in sample bias that has cloaked treatment in self-fulfilling prophesies. Runaways have met their own definitions in the mirror, because often the helping systems have bought their image. Unfortunately, this has clouded the issues, hindered objective research, and curtailed systemic treatment. What is needed is a viewpoint that does not share a restricted focus. Clinically, this means that we will need to use our skills to determine if the bonds between adolescent and family are really beyond repair. If, after all our efforts, we have determined that there is no way to knit the family back together in a functional way, then, and only then, should the decision be made to place the child. This is a most delicate decision but, once made, the clinician can continue to employ knowledge of systems to perform this operation in a sensitive and humane fashion.

Removing the child from the family needs to be done responsibly. It must enhance the sense, in all parties, that everything that could have been done was done. This might allow a mother, for example, to be less furious with her child, so that the child could, perhaps, come home to visit once in a while. With responsible placement, a child might get past hating parents who "didn't care." During future times of stress it might be possible for a parent and child to reconnect. We realize that coming home is not always a certainty or, in some cases, even preferable, particularly where physical or psychological abuse is overwhelmingly present. A "responsible" replacement would, however, help determine these contingencies more clearly. Thought and action that can raise those kinds of odds need to be pursued at all levels of the helping system.

Working from a systems perspective would require significant changes in the way treatment is now organized. For example, one might want to permit an adolescent to sit around a shelter or halfway house watching TV beyond the federally mandated 72-hour grace period before attempting to reunite the family, in order to establish a bond of trust with the adolescent.[2] In other instances one might speed the contact process to capitalize on family concern before anger sets in to create warring camps. Flexibility in treatment, however, requires a change at the legal level. Regulations and policies now frequently preclude working creatively. The question remains then: how to treat runaways, given the system we've got.

The first order of business is not to be so organized by the power of the symptom that we forget the systemic lessons we have learned thus far. We must be careful not to accept the family's, runaway's, or society's definitions of the problem. All three of these groups, for their own reasons, need closure around how they see the problem. For example, runaways often portray themselves as psychologically cut-off from their families and for the most part this view has not been challenged. Until

---

[2]The Runaway Youth Act, Title III, Juvenile Justice and Delinquency Prevention Act of 1974, as amended by the Juvenile Justice Act of 1977, Rules and Regulations Section 135/18, suggests contact with family be within 24 hours, and maximally 72 hours, after admission to a federally funded runaway center.

recently this had also been the case with heroin addicts.

Addicts, for years, were thought to have broken ties to their families of origin. They were viewed as street people who were married to their drugs and their deviant lifestyles. Research by Perzel and Lamon (1979) indicated that, across cultures, in contrast to popular belief, close to two-thirds of male hard-drug users under the age of thirty-five live with the people that raised them. A case study demonstrates:

One of the authors was working with a twenty-six-year-old heroin addict. The addict had been in and out of prison and residential treatment centers for most of his adult life. He had hocked his mother's air conditioner from her two-bedroom city row-house in the middle of August to get money for his habit. His mother and father had been separated for over ten years, but the addict lived with mother from time to time, so an attempt was made to involve her in treatment. The son was receiving methadone at the outpatient drug treatment center, and calls were made to mother to recruit her for treatment. Vinnie's mother was adamant. "I ain't got nothin' to do with that little S.O.B.," she raved. "He's no good." And so on. Not so sure about this, the author pressed, "Oh, but you've said that before." The mother was outraged. "No way, I've *really* kicked him out this time. I've even got different locks! Do you know what that kid has stolen from me?" Quite content that Vinnie could now be confronted with the reality of life out on his own, and that Mom meant business, the therapist thanked her and was no longer insistent that she attend sessions. The next day the therapist met with Vinnie. To make a long and painful story short, the therapist asked Vinnie if he was aware of his mother's new resolve and what that would mean for him. Vinnie, nonplussed by the whole thing, said he knew. The therapist was puzzled about this, since Vinnie, according to Mom, was out of the house, living on the street. The therapist wanted to know *how* Vinnie "knew." "Oh, I was sittin' at the table at my Mom's having a bowl of soup when you called yesterday. . . ."

Let the buyer beware.

It has been our experience that adolescent runaways, too, are intimately connected to their families and the families to them. Clinicians need to proceed on this assumption until it's proven otherwise.

Clearly, systems therapists must broaden definitions and come to appreciate the pain and stress associated with change. Adolescents, and their families in particular, are faced with major structural reorganization as they contend with the issues of separation and individuation. Families with transactional coping styles that are either rigidly over-involved, or under-involved, are likely to experience problems in facilitating the adolescent's individuation. Running away is seen as one way in which the adolescent and family deal with the stress that accompanies the structural reorganization brought about by natural development. The symptom may result from the cumulative effect of earlier systemic imbalances, and/or from present arrangements in the family structure which leave the family vulnerable at transition points (Haley, 1973). Families may display these stresses through a variety of symptoms, ranging from an anorectic child or schizophrenic young person, to less dramatic symptoms, such as school failure and behavior problems.

The constraints that life and its exigencies produce requires constant adjustment from the family. Von Glasersfeld, writing on radical constructivism, presents an alternative view to adaptation, evolution, and reality construction that helps to place symptoms in a systemic, non-pejorative context. He says: "In order to remain among the survivors, an organism has to 'get by' the constraints which the environment poses. It has to squeeze between the bars of constraints . . . The environment does not determine *how* that may be achieved." He goes on to say, "Anyone who *by any means* manages to get by the constraints, survives." (Von Glasersfled, 1980, p. 90). Symptoms, in our view then, are one of the ways that families survive.

We feel that given the current level of knowledge in the field, the most pragmatic approach to treating runaways is one that directs therapists to "discover the families' basic problem-solving characteristics"—its universals (Montalvo, 1983). By universals, we mean the following: How does this particular family deal with stress and crisis? Why is there a runaway now? What has shifted in the family structure? What supports are missing? What has changed in the balance between forces in the lives of family members? What are the roles of the family members? What rules govern the family's transactions? How do family members' behaviors complement each other? What is the structure that is presently maintaining the symptom? What is the family's hierarchy arrangement? Has the runaway produced a change in hierarchy? What strengths does this family share with all families? How does it cope with the demands of extrafamilial contexts (i.e., work, school, etc.)? Are the boundaries between individual members and subsystems, and between the family and the outside world, in the process of change? And so on. Rather than being attentive to what is going on *inside* the identified patient, the therapist should be more concerned with what is going on *around* the identified patient. It's a paradigmatic shift from psyche and insight to behavior in context.

Examining these universals places the clinician at the meta-level of pattern rather than in the specifics of the symptom. This is not to say that we are advocating a "damn the specifics—full speed ahead" approach. Certainly knowing as much as one can about the characteristics of runaways and their families is a prerequisite for sound clinical work with this population. And, while statistics may be of small comfort when fielding a two a.m. phone call from a family, they are, in fact, useful in delineating treatment parameters. The task ahead is to put the statistics in a dynamic context. Rather than simply knowing that certain constellations of characteristics appear in 75 percent of all runaways, we need to understand intimately the relationships between these forces. Structural family therapy offers us such a framework.

LITERATURE REVIEW

In reviewing the literature on runaways we have drawn several conclusions. First, while the clinical literature on runaways is voluminous, the family-therapy-based studies are meager. Second, the great majority of the studies are based on anecdotal clinical observations, with well-controlled research studies almost non-existent. Finally, we found no interactional studies of runaways and their families. Thus, there is little reliable family-oriented data available to guide clinicians on treating runaways. The following review covers articles that we felt most directly pertained to adolescent runaways and their families.

Stierlin (1973) offers a transactional, systemic model of runaways and their families based on the family life-cycle. He makes a distinction between successful runaways, i.e., those who "escape their parents and make themselves prematurely independent," and "runaway failures," i.e., those who remain home-bound despite a family life where running away would seem to be justified.

All families must cope with adjusting to adolescent separation. Stierlin describes one dysfunctional strategy that families use to cope with the separation as "centripetal dynamics," which serve to bind family members more closely; autonomy is decreased while proximity to the family orbit is increased. Consequently, adolescents bound to families who operate in a centripetal fashion are most likely to be unsuccessful or abortive in their runaway attempts. Casual or successful runaways, and their families, on the other hand, exhibit the transactional style known as "centrifugal." These expel adolescents from the family orbit and leave them to fend for themselves. Stierlin points out that these patterns are both transitory and reciprocal, i.e., 1) they are life-stage-specific, and 2) parents' and children's behaviors impact and regulate each other in a complementary fashion. Centrifugal and centripetal dynamics operate on both the overt and covert levels and combine in three specific transactional modes: the binding mode; the expelling mode; and the delegating mode.

In examining therapeutic considerations, Stierlin suggests that parents "bind" children to cope with their own developmental crisis, and bind them excessively to compensate for the depression that surrounds the crisis of aging. On the other hand, parents may deal with the sense of depression and emptiness by striking out on new ventures; in these instances, the child is expelled and viewed only as excess baggage—a hindrance. Parents who "delegate," however, neither bind nor expel the children, but "differentially exploit" them; the children are delegated by parents to fulfill their own unmet needs or fantasies. Stierlin points out how the "aging mother who fears life's excitement is passing her by, can delegate her teenage daughter to vicariously supply such excitement" (p. 61).

Stierlin offers three brief guidelines for treatment. For those adolescents stuck in the binding mode, the task is to unbind them and their families. Here, a successful runaway-attempt might even be viewed as a sign of health for both the child and the family. Adolescents running away from a family whose transactional style is characterized by the expelling mode, however, need to experience limits and parental concern and commitment. Lastly, "delegated" runaways need to have the familial missions explored, untangled, and resolved.

Brennan, et al. (1978), drawing on data from two large surveys in one of the few empirical and methodologically sophisticated studies, have attempted to understand runaways from a social-psychological perspective. They emphasize the social environment in which runaway behavior occurs, and maintain that the cause of the problem is not purely in the characteristics of the family or school, nor in the characteristics of the youth, "but in the complex interactions which take place between them" (p. 84).

The Brennan model suggests that one group of runaways shows a critical weakness in both external social bonds and internal personal commitment bonds. As a result of these weak bonds, the runaways are described as having lost their psychological as well as their behavioral connections to both family and school and consequently drift into extremely marginal positions vis-à-vis these two social institutions. They present ample evidence for

what they describe as ineffective, inadequate, and ambivalent socialization processes in the families of runaway children. These processes, they predict, lead to weaker social commitment bonds than for children who have had more effective socialization experiences. They point out that while all runaways do not experience family problems, the family was the dominant social context where most critical stresses and strains were felt by youths who did display runaway behavior. According to this view, inadequate socialization processes within the family are thought to lead to weak bonds between the child and parents. The theory assumes that inadequate parental behavior interacts in complex ways with the child's behavior to produce a situation where there is little or no commitment on the child's part to that context.

Another group of runaways exhibits the attenuation or weakening of already established bonds. It is assumed that family socialization practices have been adequate, but that particular strains or stresses appear at some point in the family's life history. These stresses and strains weaken or attenuate the bond in the family context, heightening the possibility of runaway behavior. Brennan, et al., see these strains as including a wide variety of potentially stressful situations including: frustrations of the youths' needs and aspirations; too little autonomy; undermined competence within the family setting; physical abuse by parents; and parental distancing and withdrawal of love. Even without these circumstances, children who are adequately socialized can find themselves in families in which runaway behavior seems to them to be the only option: The adolescent feels unable to resolve problems at home, with friends, or in school, or feels that their concerns, in general, will not be met.

Stierlin and Brennan offer different views of the map, but not of the dynamic aspects of the territory. While Stierlin's pioneering efforts touch on the reciprocity between systems, there is no sense of the cumulative aspects of this process. Why is it, for example, that a child runs away now and not six months earlier? What were the imbalances in the homeostatic mechanisms that tipped the scale to running away? Here Brennan's work begins to offer useful territorial stakes. He and his colleagues point to the importance of the bonds among peers, school, and family as well as of the internal perspective of the adolescent. They offer data that is able to predict the types of adolescent most likely to run away. They also detail subclasses of runaway types that cross economic and gender lines. While this information is useful, there needs to be an explanation that offers a more complex reality. One knows that a pinch of this and a dash of that will make a great cake. But if one isn't sure about how the pinches and dashes go together, or whether to bake it *before* you mix the ingredients or after, one is not likely to make it like grandma did. One needs chemistry as well as chemicals.

So it is with runaways in their contexts. Future research is needed to investigate the dynamic interplay of forces in the lives of runaways and their families. It could be, for example, that a young person is being maintained at non-runaway status by an interested teacher or counselor (Whitaker, 1976), and that the runaway happened during a particular week, when one area of the young person's life was not able to compensate for a loss of support in another. We may find that there is an "eclipse" effect, where a number of points in the system and the adolescent's subjective experience overlap in just the right sequence or fashion to produce the runaway event. If not restructured, these issues may continue to produce recurrent incidents. Researchers may find that the week when the caring teacher was on vacation, the adolescent's father made a pass at his daughter, and a friend moved to a new school, a runaway event occurred. Or, when father came in drunk, mother wasn't home, supportive sibling was out on a date, father abused adolescent—and "click," events were in synch, the eclipse was complete, the child ran away. These kinds of events indeed produce a "last straw" situation. In understanding them, however, we gain insight into the interrelationship between the act of running away and the life of the run-

away. For example, families with runaway members are typically rigid family systems and have little capacity for developing alternatives to life's demands. The maintenance of the adolescent, in these families is a fragile arrangement, often supported by extra-familial sources. Any subtle shifts in the constellation can throw the system into imbalance and, like a house of cards, it collapses. Awareness of the adolescent's sensitivity to this balance of forces can alert teachers, counselors, and helping professionals to times when a young person may be more at risk.

Mirkin, et al. (1984) outline three ways the female runaway functions in her family: parenting, protecting, and preserving. First, hierarchy is reversed in the family by the way in which the young woman "parents" her parents and siblings. Second, she serves as a protector of the parents' marriage, allowing them to avoid underlying conflict by focusing on her misbehavior; she thus regulates psychological distance between her parents. And third, she preserves the family organization at the pre-adolescent level of development.

In Mirkin's model, runaway behavior by the adolescent is an attempt to straddle the horns of several dilemmas. In such a family the onset of adolescence in the identified patient is seen as provoking a crisis to which the family cannot adaptively accommodate. The family has prescribed parenting behavior for the adolescent and prohibited it for the parents; it needs the adolescent to continue her parenting role. But the adolescent needs to negotiate greater distance and autonomy to accommodate *her* own emerging needs. The family is thus unable to reorganize in a way that allows parents to take over the parenting function and at the same time permit adolescent separation. Running away is seen as one solution to this dilemma. According to Mirkin and her colleagues:

> The runaway overtly abandons her parenting role and adopts a child role in which she forces her parents and/or outside helpers to parent both her and the family by looking for her, seeking help, etc. Covertly, however, she continues to parent by being the one to

bring the family into treatment (Mirkin, et al., 1984, p. 66).

The Mirkin model microscopically examines the dynamic interplay of forces, which Brennan does not address. Specifically, it looks at situations in which there is an attenuation of previously strong bonds in the family. In the above case, it deals with the family's inability to meet the adolescent's needs for separation and autonomy.

In treating these families, Mirkin, et al., have developed a model of intervention which attempts to challenge the inappropriate locus of the protecting, parenting, and preserving functions in the adolescent. Their family treatment makes an immediate attempt to recognize the collapse of the family hierarchy, restore appropriate parental functions to the parents, and disengage the adolescent from her overly powerful and central position. Interventions are geared to return the adolescent to the sibling subsystem and to allow her to deal more adaptively with the developmental tasks of separation and individuation.

In our view, Mirkin, et al., have developed the model most clearly structural and most focused on the current functioning of the family. While they have limited their observations to one subset of adolescent runaways, they provide a useful springboard for further discussion of the structural approach.

A STRUCTURAL PERSPECTIVE

Unlike adolescents with anorexia nervosa—a disorder highly circumscribed in its expression—adolescent runaways are ubiquitous, cutting across ethnic, socioeconomic, and family types. Additionally, the number of male and female runaways is reported to be roughly equal. Faced with this diversity, how can clinicians view adolescent runaways and their families most usefully? What family processes are most intimately involved in maintaining the adolescent's runaway behavior? And where should clinicians focus their interventions?

Using the lens of structural family therapy, we shall briefly explore the issues these questions raise.

Our approach to adolescent runaways is a structural/developmental framework that takes into account the stages of family development, as well as the developmental issues of each family member. The therapist must use a developmental backdrop to observe familial transactions. The structural family therapist assumes, within a very wide range, a certain framework or guideline for normal family functioning (Minuchin, 1974). The key emphasis here is on functioning and not on idealized structural configurations. This enables the clinician to examine a wide spectrum of structural formations and to remain outside the realm of values. Observable events, behavioral bits, and patterns are the materials with which the therapist constructs his or her hypothesis about the structure or "shape" of the family. The clinician is constantly engaged in the process of refining the structural hypothesis based upon events observed with the family. Within this general framework we focus on four characteristics of family functioning that we feel are implicated in the runaway process. The first three aspects of family functioning—dysfunctional generational hierarchy, triangulation of the adolescent runaway, and conflict avoidance—are necessary but not sufficient conditions to produce adolescent runaways. The fourth, parental collusion in the runaway process, is the necessary condition that accounts for this particular symptom choice.

Dysfunctional Generational Hierarchy

A universal aspect of family organization is the generational boundary which prescribes role behavior appropriate to parents and children. The generational hierarchy (Wood & Talmon, 1983) may be thought of as those behaviors which place the parents in charge of the children. In families with runaway adolescents there is often striking evidence that this normative family pattern is reversed. We have observed and others (e.g., Mirkin, et al., 1984) have reported that adolescent runaways frequently function as surrogate parents to their own parents or function as peers with one or both parents. In either case, the generational hierarchy is violated. Cross-generational coalitions between adolescents and parents, along with failure of parents to establish appropriate control of adolescent behavior, are common features of these families. Both of these are examples of a collapsed or reversed generational hierarchy.

In its most extreme form, generational hierarchy violations can lead to sexual abuse and incest between adolescent daughters and their fathers. In milder forms we find daughters being emotional surrogates for their mothers, or sons standing in for their fathers. Often the parents in these families have serious marital problems which go unresolved for many years and in which the children become embroiled. We have observed both male and female adolescents overfunctioning as parents to their parents in both single and two-parent families. These families can have significant problems with all aspects of establishing and maintaining a functional generational hierarchy. Any family can experience difficulty with nurturance, control, and temporary cross-generational coalitions. Families in which these patterns are rigidly embedded, however, will have difficulty meeting the developmental tasks of adolescence that support separation and age-appropriate autonomy. Conversely, a child who feels needed to protect, nurture, or ally with a parent will have difficulty moving into the world of peers. Therefore, one of the first necessary therapeutic operations is to begin to challenge instances of dysfunctional generational hierarchy. The adolescent will need to be blocked from trying to maintain his or her dysfunctional position. Parents need to be helped to rely on each other, and transitionally on the therapist, for support, so that the dual task of nurturing and controlling the children is realized.

Triangulation of the Adolescent Runaway

Families with adolescent runaways frequently present with significant unresolved conflict between the marital couple. These conflicts, however, are usually played out at the parental rather than the spousal level and must be approached therapeutically in this way. In some families the parental conflict is overt, with the adolescent as the clear focus of parental disagreement, while in others the conflict is more covert. In the first instance, the parents may present with complaints about the adolescent's running away, but also about other control issues. Typically in these situations one parent is more closely allied with the child, while the other is more peripheral. Usually the allied parent feels the more distant parent is too harsh or too demanding, or emotionally unresponsive to the adolescent. In another variation the parents present as united in their concern over the acting out of their adolescent, claiming complete agreement. This unity is more apparent than real, serving to mask significant unresolved marital conflicts. In both cases the marital conflict is detoured through the adolescent. The focus on the adolescent's behavior serves to stabilize the couple's marriage and protect them from having to deal directly with their conflicts.

Therapeutically one must deal with the conflicts at the level at which they are presented. Thus, the therapist must initially work with the parents to resolve their differences around the adolescent rather than attempting to deal with underlying marital issues. Even in divorced or separated families the adolescent can continue to be triangulated between feuding parents and serve as a go-between. Again the therapeutic goal becomes to resolve the parental conflict and in the process remove the adolescent from his/her triangulated position.

Conflict Avoidance

Families with adolescent runaways have limited ability to resolve conflict directly.

As previously mentioned, significant conflicts often exist between the partners, both at the spouse and parent levels. Frequently these conflicts have existed for many years without resolution. The families of adolescent runaways, like many other families with a symptomatic child, live in a state of constant tension, with conflicts hidden just below the surface, or manifested in open bickering.

In these families the child's runaway behavior can be seen as part of the conflict-avoidance mechanisms, which serve to support the status quo in the family. Typically the child's running away will occur as part of a sequence in which spouse conflicts are beginning to heat up to a level which the family feels threatens the integrity of the system. This may, in part, explain the "impulsive" nature of most runaways. From the adolescent's and the parent's perspectives the runaway event seems to "just happen." At the family-system level, however, it is part of a larger sequence of conflict avoidance, and forces the parents to re-focus on the child, thus aborting further escalation of the conflict. The parents now unite in their parental concern over the runaway. While this behavior by the adolescent has a protective function, as described by Mirkin, et al. (1984), it also operates to short-circuit any direct resolution of the spouse conflicts and thus maintains the family in a dysfunctional cycle.

Parental Collusion in the Runaway Process

The three dysfunctional family patterns just described, while necessary, usually in and of themselves are not sufficient to produce runaway behavior in adolescents. Hierarchy violations and parental triangulation of the adolescent are dysfunctional processes common to many families with troubled children. In trying to understand the development of the symptom of runaway behavior, as a predominant problem in a family, we have found evidence of some form of parental collusion in the runaway process, and it is this collusion

which determines symptom choice. The parental collusion can take any of several forms:

CROSS-GENERATIONAL COALITION

In this instance a coalition is formed between one parent and the adolescent against the other parent. Here the adolescent often becomes the confidante of the parent, hearing his/her intimate thoughts and fantasies. In a situation where there is significant marital discord, the parent may harbor a fantasy desire to run away or leave the marriage, but feel emotionally unable to leave. Even where this message is not communicated directly, it may be communicated symbolically as, in one case, when a mother withdrew totally to her bedroom for months at a time. The adolescent, aware of the parents' desire to leave and experiencing psychological pressure from the patterns already described, responds with runaway behavior.

ADOLESCENT RUNAWAY ISOMORPHIC TO PARENTAL BEHAVIOR

In some families we have observed a parallel process between adolescent runaway behavior and parental behavior but, as distinguished from the previous situation, no coalition between parents and child. In these families the parent is frequently stressed and emotionally isolated, becoming more and more disengaged from parental responsibilities. The parent may leave the home for hours or days at a time, leaving children or adolescents to fend for themselves without adequate supervision. In a case cited below, a mother took a periodic two-day "vacation" to visit her boyfriend, while checking in with the children by phone. Within a few days of her return, the thirteen-year-old son would run away for more than twenty-four hours before being found.

Structurally these families tend to function more toward the disengaged end of the emotional continuum, and the therapeutic task is one of mobilizing parental concern and engaging parent and child while helping parents find more appropriate ways to meet their adult needs.

PARENTAL SCAPEGOATING OF THE ADOLESCENT RUNAWAY

In this third situation a more direct, open conflict exists between the adolescent runaway and one or both parents. Here the adolescent is blamed for any or all of the family problems and openly told "everything would be fine in the family without you here." Thus, the adolescent's running away is often directly encouraged by either or both parents. We have seen examples of this type in blended (remarried) family situations in which family-formation issues are prevalent. Parents unable to tolerate the anxiety and uncertainty engendered by the difficult process of forming new family systems can easily blame children when their fantasies about the "perfect" new relationship are spoiled by the reality of the blending process. Adults often put tremendous pressure on themselves in these situations and want nothing to go wrong. Such expectations are impossible to meet, but the disappointment is often devastating. The adolescent then becomes a convenient scapegoat, particularly if the adolescent feels caught in a loyalty bind with the non-custodial parent and is slow to accept new family members. In these cases the adolescent may feel personally displaced by the stepparent or protective of the place of the natural parent, who is absent. The therapeutic task here becomes one of helping the adults develop more appropriate expectations relative to family-formation issues, thus interrupting the scapegoating process and helping the adolescent negotiate loyalty issues in more appropriate ways.

CASE EXAMPLES

In the following three case studies we will detail the operations involved in the treatment of adolescent runaways. They are meant to be illustrative, but by no means exhaustive examples of families that

present with a runaway. We hope that they convey the essence of structural thinking and that the reader learns from them as we did.

The Loss of an Ally: An Instance of Exorcism

In this brief excerpt near the end of a one-time consultation with a white, middle-class, fifteen-year-old runaway and her father, certain themes are evident.

THERAPIST: Why do you deny your own power?

FATHER: I don't see how I am, I mean . . .

THERAPIST: Why is she here?

FATHER: Well, because I think she wants help.

THERAPIST: From *you*! She wants help from *you*. That gives you power. That gives you the parental power that your daughter wants you to help her. You insist that she doesn't want anything from you, but she wants your help. Treat her as if you accept her request.[3,4]

The theme for the family is hopelessness, frustration, and distance; the theme for the therapist is restoration of bonds and a call for executive functioning in the areas of nurturance and control.

The degrees to which these themes are played out in therapy is a figure-ground phenomenon that will be determined by the stage of treatment, the setting of the therapist, the point of contact with the family/adolescent, the age of the young person, and the idiosyncratic demands of the situation. In the case cited above, the family had been in treatment at another clinic for

---

[3]The analysis of this case represents the authors' own elaboration and interpretation of Minuchin's discussion of the material and is their responsibility.

[4]The names and some details in this case and those that follow have been altered to protect the anonymity of family members.

several months, around the daughter's inappropriate behaviors including her running away. The therapist, feeling stuck, negotiated a consultation at the Philadelphia Child Guidance Clinic with a senior clinician. The daughter's whereabouts were unknown for over two weeks prior to the session. The mother had committed suicide several years before. The surviving family consisted of the fifteen-year-old identified patient, her two younger brothers, and her father.

The session described below can be viewed as an emotional and structural exorcism. The exorcism that takes place has to do with the interplay of forces operating in the family. In this case, the family is organized as if its present structure included mother. Accommodation to new structural realities has not taken place, and people in the family continue to define their roles vis à vis an outdated context. Father sees himself as he did when mother was alive, tentatively connected to his daughter, unable to understand or control her. His view is supported by the rest of the family system and his efforts at change have become self-fulfilling prophesies of disappointment and distance.

The questions as to why this arrangement continues may be answered by observing the family in action. The therapist needs to ask himself certain questions that would begin to put the runaway behavior in context and complete the picture of mother's role in the family. Why, for example, is father unable to step out of his narrow definition of self and reach out to his daughter? Are there remnants from the old family structure that include a mother-daughter coalition that keeps father distant? Perhaps this could help explain father and daughter's inability to communicate. If so, how is the family currently operating to maintain old roles and boundaries? What systemic reorganization is lacking, specific to the life-stage of the family and its circumstances? Is the family drawn into camps according to sex? What issues need resolution so the family can move on to the next developmental phase? While all of these questions cannot be answered immediately, they do provide the backdrop

with which to understand process and content. In this instance, they will also provide information that will facilitate the reframing of the family's reality and help to exorcise the old structure.

The process of testing the hypothesis and challenging the status quo begins quickly. Approximately ten minutes into the session the therapist catches a glimpse into the family's world when he asks the father and daughter to talk with one another.

FATHER: Amy, why did you take off again?

DAUGHTER: (*Remains silent and looks away.*)

FATHER: I tried to reach you; you wouldn't cooperate. You yessed me on everything I said. You told me you'd clean up your room. You told me you wouldn't be leaving your underwear around. You were going to behave. The next morning I went up and found your menstrual period in your underwear laying on the bathroom floor.

DAUGHTER: (*Crying.*) I don't think that's anybody's business . . .

FATHER: Well, it certainly *is*, Amy. The boys have to see it, and they've been seeing it.

DAUGHTER: They weren't home.

FATHER: Well, I was. It's just your little way of slapping me in the face again.

DAUGHTER: (*Silent, looking down.*)

FATHER: I tried being nice to you since your mother died. I thought it would work, and it sure didn't. You took off three times since your mother's died, and you took off before she died.

THERAPIST: Is that the way that you attempt to contact her? It's clearly not working.

Here we see several things. By creating an enactment, process and structure begin to unfold, and the gap that exists between father and daughter becomes apparent. Within minutes, mother's ghost and the structure it represents is brought to life in the presence of the father-daughter dyad. It is as if there is no permission within the present context for contact between father and daughter without invoking mother's memory. We must also wonder what makes father so angry at his daughter that he violates a very personal boundary? It could be that the distance between father and daughter never permitted a sensitivity to women's issues to develop in him; that distance between father and mother ill-prepared him for his daughter's emergence into adolescence; or that he hears his wife's voice whenever his daughter speaks. To some degree all of these explanations are valid and point to the pre-existence of a mother-daughter coalition against father. The therapist, however, need only be concerned with constructions that will be the most useful in changing their present arrangement. Content becomes the vehicle for process. In the next segment, the therapist, by pushing father to find another way to talk to daughter, begins to provide them both with a new experience of one another.

FATHER: All right then, why don't you tell me what you've been thinking?

DAUGHTER: (Silent, looking away.)

FATHER: What have you been thinking?

DAUGHTER: Wait a minute! I . . . don't believe you . . . about Mom, most of all of it.

FATHER: Completely?

DAUGHTER: Just about.

FATHER: Why?

DAUGHTER: I just do.

FATHER: Well, why—not just because you do—why don't you tell me?

DAUGHTER: Because of all the things that she told me and that I saw . . .

FATHER: Well, go ahead and tell me then.

DAUGHTER: Well—now—then I already told you so many times things she's told me.

FATHER: Tell me again.

DAUGHTER: That you told her that you didn't know if you loved her anymore.

As the session continues, the therapist maintains his call for executive functioning from the father. The family's narrow worldview is challenged by the therapist's joining father in his dilemma of battling his wife through his angry daughter.

In the next sequence, the strains of the cross-generational coalition between mother and daughter are heard more fully. The therapist, noting this, enters as an outsider, challenging long-held beliefs that have bound the family in a dysfunctional structure.

FATHER: I'm asking you when did I tell her? You know when I told her. I told her that the last week that she was alive. When we were at the doctors for her appointment. That's when that was brought up—and I didn't know if I did or not. Now I think I do know.

DAUGHTER: I don't see how you cannot know if you love somebody . . .

FATHER: Amy, I tried so hard with your mother through the whole marriage. I thought it was a great marriage—and it was when we first started as we were raising you—all of you—but she had her problems and she wouldn't go for help until I finally forced her to. Then she finally admitted that it was helping out—but it obviously didn't help in the end.

THERAPIST: May I ask her? You see, I am a stranger so I am listening for the first time. Your mother died two years ago?

DAUGHTER: Yes.

THERAPIST: I didn't hear you.

DAUGHTER: Yes, two years ago.

THERAPIST: O.K., and so, are you not blaming your father because of her death?

DAUGHTER: (Sobbing.) What?

THERAPIST: You are blaming him because she died?

DAUGHTER: Yeah.

THERAPIST: . . . Did he inject her with drugs?

DAUGHTER: No.

THERAPIST: What did he do that he killed her?

DAUGHTER: You know how she died.

THERAPIST: No, I don't know.

FATHER: He only knows she's deceased.

THERAPIST: I met him five minutes ago, and I want to know whatever I need to know from you.

DAUGHTER: She killed herself.

THERAPIST: She killed herself?

DAUGHTER: Yeah . . .

THERAPIST: And do you think she killed herself because your father didn't love her?

DAUGHTER: I don't know why . . .

THERAPIST: But that's what you are telling him.

DAUGHTER: But other reasons too.

THERAPIST: What I hear you telling your father is that he killed your mother and because he killed her you don't want to talk with him. Is that what you are saying to him?

DAUGHTER: That's right.

THERAPIST: Uh-huh.

THERAPIST: (*Turning to the father.*) This means that since she accuses you of killing your wife, you need to defend yourself?

FATHER: I need to explain myself.

THERAPIST: Then she has you really in a corner where you cannot . . . where you do not have too much power.

Later in the session.

THERAPIST: But you are really now in an impossible situation because you are competing with a ghost. You must find a different way of relating to your daughter than as the person who killed her mother. . . . You are her father?

FATHER: (*Nods yes.*)

THERAPIST: You are certain of that?

FATHER: Yes.

THERAPIST: O.K. talk with her as if you are her father, not the guilty husband of her mother.

FATHER: I, uh . . . I don't know how to approach it. I . . .

THERAPIST: But she has been your daughter for fifteen years even though she has also been the daughter of your wife. She is also your daughter and you don't know her—you absolutely don't know her.

FATHER: I agree with that.

THERAPIST: O.K. . . . talk with her, start from point zero. . . .

Slowly, the family begins to bury mother's ghost, father's helplessness, and daughter's anger.

What can be learned about the thinking of the therapist from the preceding segments? One might assume that the young woman and her mother had been very close and that she had not adequately mourned her mother's death; that father needed to be more understanding and give his daughter more space to allow her to mourn. And, indeed, it was learned that the mother had crossed generational boundaries and shared many of her adult, personal concerns with her daughter. The therapist could thus erroneously conclude that running away represented the daughter's need for space and for completion of the mourning process and could intervene accordingly. But the structural family therapist would not be content with this explanation. Throughout the session the therapist is, instead, actively confronting the current organization of the family. The therapist is pushing to reestablish bonds between father and daughter by explicitly supporting the hierarchy of the family, demanding that father and not therapist take responsibility for the structural shift in the family, a shift which is necessary in the wake of mother's death. Nor does the therapist buy father's helpless position. Rather, the alliance is with the executive subsystem in its dual function of both control and nurturance. Father's insensitivity, in this model, is seen as a structural artifact of the family's previous organization, leaving him distant and unaware of the needs of his teenage daughter. Daughter's silence and tears are seen as her response to father's insensitivity, as a validation of the old structure—a monument to mother's memory. Interventions, then, were not to achieve more space, but to responsibly resolve the structural imbalances. In this family, that meant supporting the hierarchy in such a way that nurturance and control could achieve a new, more dynamic equilibrium.

Returning to the end of the session, we reiterate the therapist's supportive response to father's continued helplessness: "[she wants help] from *you*! . . . Treat her as if you accept her request." Then Father can say: "All right—so you are going to come home. We can work out the problems about school and work, but you are going to come home."

This family interchange documents what can happen when boundaries and patterns become crystalized and repeated in a narrow transactional band, limiting options, and replaying an old, familiar song. At one point in the session, the daughter was described as living in a "monastery" formed by the males in the family.[5] Father was comfortable relating to the boys, and they to him. The mother-daughter coalition contributed to this configuration by helping to draw the family into rigid sex camps—thus highlighting the complementarity in the family: For every monastery there has to be a convent.

The goal of the structural family therapist in working with runaways and with all families is to help the family use its own strengths in order to get unstuck and to move on to a new developmental phase showing increased flexibility. To the degree the family has a wider range of roles and can change transactional rules, it has a better chance of success in meeting life's changing demands. The session we have described was a single, mid-therapy consultation and served to exorcise not only mother's ghost, but the structure that supported it as well. The remainder of treatment focused on helping father and daughter to establish connections without an intermediary, and establish a more normative family hierarchy.

In the following cases we will see how conflicting demands have pulled and shaped other families, resulting in the same symptom: running away. While the techniques used in treatment vary, the thinking remains structural.

Creating Motivation for Change: Challenging a Mother's Collusion

In the following case, discussion will center on the task of creating therapeutic motivation in the service of restoring a collapsed generational hierarchy. The issues surrounding hierarchy restoration in families with adolescent runaways are prominent and essential features of successful treatment. Establishing functional levels of protection, control, and nurturance between parent and adolescent is a delicate process. This is particularly true in single-parent families, where mothers or fathers have no other adults available to meet their own emotional needs. In this case, we will see how a mother's attempts to meet her own needs unwittingly fosters the runaway behavior of her youngest son.

Ms. *A.* was a black woman in her early thirties. She had three adolescent offspring: a sixteen-year-old son, a fifteen-year-old daughter, and Peter, thirteen, the identified patient. Ms. *A.* received public assistance and had been separated from the children's father for two years, and divorced for six months. The father had a history of psychiatric illness resulting in several hospitalizations. Since the parents' separation, Mr. *A.* had tried to force his way back into the family using physical intimidation and violent threats against mother. Despite having obtained a bench warrant to protect herself and the children from father's intrusions, mother had been unable to bring herself to use it. In the last year, Ms. *A.* had established a serious relationship with another man, but felt she had to keep this relationship quiet, because

[5]Minuchin is credited with this idea.

of the father's threats.

Peter's running away had begun during the last year. He periodically disappeared from home for one to two days at a time every few weeks. Sometimes the boy would return home voluntarily. Other times family members would search for him, finding him in abandoned buildings in the neighborhood. Occasionally the police would find and bring him home.

In the initial family interviews, which included the mother and her three children, mother presented herself as depressed, overwhelmed, and feeling helpless. Peter came across as a rather passive boy, whose thoughts were somewhat disorganized. The two older children appeared to be coping better with the family situation, and mother frequently looked to them for support. In these initial meetings mother reported feeling hopeless about the father's intrusions into the family and expressed exasperation over not being able to control her children, particularly Peter. She was upset by Peter's running away, but tended to view it as more of a nuisance than anything else. Peter could give no clear reason for it and was labeled selfish by his older siblings. They took the position that, given how difficult things had been over the last two years for the family, Peter should have enough consideration for everyone else and not create further problems. Mother also echoed these feelings.

Diagnostically, it was clear that things were, and had been, emotionally chaotic for this family for several years. Mother and children had been unable to establish an effective boundary between themselves and the rest of the world. They were open to intrusion from without and defection from within. Additionally, mother's parental functions of nurturance, protection, and control had been totally compromised. The parental hierarchy had collapsed under the weight of family stress. From this assessment, it became clear that therapy needed to address two major issues—first, creating a less permeable boundary around the family and, second, establishing a clear, functional generational hierarchy within it.

Initially, the family situation had to be stabilized, and the therapist began working with the mother to help her protect herself and the children from the father's unwarranted intrusions. She was supported and urged to contact the father's family and appeal for help in keeping the father away. When this produced little change, she was encouraged to use the bench warrant she had previously obtained. Gradually mother became more secure in her rights and, with the therapist's support, was able to take a stronger stand with father. Eventually father's family had him involuntarily committed for treatment, and mother and children felt less threatened.

At that point it became possible to focus more on mother's relationship with Peter and the other children. Attention was turned to restoring the generational hierarchy. It was during this phase of treatment in an individual interview that Peter revealed his mother took "vacations" every few weeks for a day or two. During these "vacations" she went to stay with her male friend. The children were not allowed to contact her, but she checked in with them by telephone. Apparently mother initiated this arrangement because she felt she could not risk bringing the new friend home, fearful as she was of her former husband's reaction.

Here we begin to see how mother's finding time for her own emotional needs blinded her from seeing, or at least acknowledging openly, the impact of her behavior on Peter. She had not told the therapist about her "vacations" and acted mystified about the timing of Peter's disappearances, even though they often followed closely on the heels of her own. Thus we can see mother's collusion in the boy's running away; it was her self-protective act, based on her assumption that there was no other way to get legitimate time for herself. The assumption had to be challenged along with her failure to act responsibly towards Peter.

This was a sensitive operation, because mother attempted to detour responsibility and to deny that her behavior had impacted on her son or was related to his runaway episodes. But the therapist confronted mother's denial and increased her motivation for change. We see this in the following sequence:

THERAPIST: I think you underestimate yourself, your importance to Peter. I don't think you realize how much you mean to that kid.

MOTHER: I kind of . . . when I was sick he kind of let me see a little bit. He did.

THERAPIST: I think you totally underestimate your impact on him and how important you are to him and how much you really have an influence over him.

MOTHER: I guess I do because I figure he doesn't listen to me.

THERAPIST: I don't know if you realize that. When he was talking about you in here, you just mean an awful lot to him.

A few moments later in the session, the therapist emphasized the seriousness of the boy's behavior and the mother's need to take charge. As can be seen, mother herself had been worried, but minimized her worries. Only with the therapist's dramatizing the situation could she acknowledge how dangerous it really was.

THERAPIST: I think this thing with Peter is very serious—this thing about 'vacations,' going out in vacant buildings. When you read the newspaper every once in a while you read about what happens to these kids that go into vacant buildings.

MOTHER: The neighborhood that we live in is bad.

THERAPIST: Yeah, I mean it's not a place for a kid to be. I want to bring Peter back in. I want you to be able to tell him that you are going to work hard at being around for him. That you don't want him to take any more 'vacations,' and you are going to work hard at being around for him. I think it is really important that he knows that. This thing is serious that we are talking about here. We are talking about something that could be life or death or something that could have a permanent impact on his life.

MOTHER: I had a nightmare and I woke up screaming and I saw Peter dead in this vacant house.

THERAPIST: It's like your own conscience trying to tell you something. You know it's serious.

MOTHER: Yeah, I know.

THERAPIST: So, I am going to bring him in, and I want you to convince him that you are going to be working at being around more for him, okay?

In the last part of the session mother and son talked together about her worries about him, and she pledged to be more available to him. The session was pivotal in the restoration of the generational hierarchy in the family. Mother gradually began to recover her control, nurturance, and protective functions. This was followed by a subsequent reduction in the boy's runaway episodes. The mother was helped to work out a way to have time for herself. Importantly, she was able to integrate her new boyfriend into the family's life without totally abandoning her job as parent.

We have observed that, with respect to adolescent runaways, generational hier-archy collapse or role reversal in one form or another is a significant clinical phenomenon. Brennan, et al., (1978) and Mirkin, et al. (1984) both emphasize dysfunctional aspects of generational hierarchy as central to their theories about runaways. Brennan focuses on the breakdown of control functions in the family. Mirkin highlights three areas: role reversals in the areas of nurturance and protection; inappropriate cross-generational coalitions; and the premature treatment of teenage girls as spouse substitutes for their mothers. All of these phenomena represent some breach of the generational hierarchy, putting the adolescent in psychological jeopardy. Given their frequency in runaway cases and their centrality in producing family dysfunction, it follows that intervention strategies must be geared to restoring the generational hierarchy to a more normative pattern.

In each of the families thus far presented, hierarchical imbalances occurred. Here, we will cite another clinical example in which the family's hierarchy went awry; however, the more salient clinical phenomenon is that of core structural imbalances.

The Structure Behind the Mask

The following case is presented as a caveat to clinicians. It is also a testimony to the complexity of families.

Debbie, thirteen, the eldest daughter in a family of three girls, was referred for therapy because of poor school performance, running away, and beating up her mother. John, the father, was a recently recovered alcoholic, and June, the mother, a homemaker and full-time college student. The family came to treatment because mother "could not control" Debbie. The picture painted of Debbie over the phone was of a disrespectful, nasty, abusive, self-centered teenager. In person, however, Debbie presented as soft-spoken and shy. Mother appeared to be frustrated, while father, a quiet man, preferred to have his wife do most of the talking. The younger daughters, eleven and nine years, were cute, polite, and age-appropriate. Yet, as the family story unfolded, one wondered if this was the real cast of characters. The shy, little thirteen-year-old had beaten her diminutive mother, causing bruises, no less than three times in as many months. The daughter had run away from home twice, one time walking more than eight miles to a grandparent's house. Debbie, who had been truant, was also disrespectful to the nuns at school, and smoked cigarettes. The family was concerned about Debbie's outbursts and wanted her under control quickly.

The initial interview revealed that the daughter's runaway events coincided with several other dramatic changes in the family's life. Father had successfully detoxified from alcohol approximately nine months before the first family therapy meeting. Mother had entered college just prior to father's abstinence, but then had to drop out because father's hospitalization required much of her time. At the same time, Debbie had entered adolescence. During the previous spring her delinquent behavior had escalated when she had learned she was going to start parochial school in the fall.

Over the year in which these changes were taking place, there were also subtle, but significant, shifts in the composition of the neighborhood. The girls Debbie played with, who were a few years older, had now progressed to the stage of being interested in boys full-time. The only children remaining for her to "hang around" with were a tightly knit group of boys a year older than she. The family lived in a relatively rural area, precluding the possibility of contact with other young people her age. At this stage in her life, her two younger sisters held no interest for a "worldly" adolescent of thirteen. For the family, negotiating all the other changes—father's detoxification, the change in mother's educational plans, and the subsequent reorganization of the family rules and roles—was stressful; for Debbie, it appeared to be intolerable. The parental hierarchy had collapsed under the weight of contextual demands.

So the family, in a short amount of time, was attempting to become "normal." That is, up until now their lives had been organized around father's alcoholism. What they could do, when, and with whom, all had centered around whether or not father was sober. Now that he was sober, their lives were supposed to be problem-free.

Debbie's behavior and running away seemed, though, to continue the family's journey along a troubled path. While, on one level, the family was angry at Debbie for "fouling things up," on another level her behavior served to focus the parents on her and away from each other. It gave the impression that mother and father were together, as indeed they were: Both agreed that the running away and beating up of mother

had to stop.

Unanimity on the parental level, however, masked differences at the marital level. Mother and father still had not resolved what their new roles would be as sober husband, and wife of sober husband. Also, mother still seemed angry at father for all the years he drank and for her own perceived neglect. The running away, the anger, and the abuse of mother all seemed tightly bound to an outdated structure, one that now required reconstruction into a functional hierarchy and appropriate boundaries.

In order to do this, the therapist needed to join with family members in a way that would alleviate the stress they had been under, while at the same time search for a frame that would motivate them to begin the restructuring process. This was done by carefully tracking the chronicle of the family's life. How and when things were handled when father was drinking, and by whom, were carefully noted. During this process an attempt was made to validate each family member's perception of the changes they had experienced; the members slowly began to relax. Then the focus was broadened to how the family had collectively and individually handled the transitions. Debbie's behavior, in a context of many changes, could be redefined from "bad" to being the most sensitive to the family's transitional stress. This frame was expanded when it was learned that when father drank, mother would track him down by phoning bars. Once she located father, mother would go get him and entrust Debbie with watching her younger siblings. At other times, mother would take the children with her, sharing some of her anger at father with Debbie as they drove to recover him from the bar.

Currently, the family was operating with an ersatz hierarchy; i.e., father and mother were in agreement about the severity of Debbie's behavior; one almost felt, however, as if any behavior less severe would not have exerted enough pull to keep mother and father together. With Debbie being so bad, the parents could talk about her and avoid the sensitive issues of talking about each other. At another level it assured father's presence in the system and automatically reintegrated family relationships. He was the only one who could make sure that conflicts between mother and Debbie did not escalate into physical battles. In short, the family needed him. A job had been posted and father took it. Yet on further examination, it appeared that father was not simply policing Debbie. He was attending an Alcoholics Anonymous couples group for recovered alcoholics. He was spending time with the kids. He was working regularly. And he appeared to be available and supportive to mother. Since Debbie's inappropriate behavior was relatively recent and since the family had been through so many changes in such a short time, the therapist felt that the family's dysfunctional arrangement was transitional.

The chosen interventions were designed to do several things. First, the family's experience needed to be normalized. Their transition from an alcoholic system to a dry system had been rapid and emotionally draining. Second, the hierarchy needed restoration, with emphasis on appropriate generational boundaries and functional parenting. Third, Debbie needed to be relieved of her scapegoat position and de-triangulated from marital issues, which in turn would have to wait until a more functional structure was established.

Once the therapist felt he understood the family structure, he planned a session in which he hoped to free Debbie from her position as parental buffer and to begin the task of reuniting parents as a cooperative unit. First he framed the existing arrangement by stating that June had "married" Debbie in order to deal with John's "marriage" to alcohol. Consequently, even though the parents *looked* married, it really wasn't so. The younger siblings were sent out of the room and, unbeknownst to the rest of the family, were given a special job to make something that was kept a "secret." In another part of the therapist's house, in which the therapist has his office, the therapist's wife and son, accustomed to life in the private-practice fast-lane, helped Debbie's younger siblings construct a set of "wedding rings." While this was being done, the therapist had mother and Debbie talk about all the things Debbie had done for the mother. Mother and father were both asked to thank Debbie for all that she had done for them. Then they each, individually, "fired" Debbie from her position as caretaker and mother's confidant. Mother and father agreed that, from this point on, father would handle mother's worries—which meant that Debbie was now free to be a daughter to her mother. The three were then asked if they would be willing to perform a ceremony to "seal the deal." When all agreed, the younger siblings were brought in to act as best man and maid of honor. Debbie performed the marriage ceremony.

As a challenge, the therapist predicted that the family would have a difficult time with the new arrangement and asked Debbie to test it by trying to engage her mother in talk about father. Mother was to respond to Deb-

bie around only appropriate issues. If mother slipped up, it meant that father wasn't doing *his* job. Debbie was returned to the top of the sibling sub-system and could now be both closer to father, knowing that he was taking care of mother, and closer to mother, in a more age-appropriate fashion. It should be noted that the main purposes of the ritual were twofold: (1) to disengage the girl from the marital struggle; and (2) to provide a base for the framing of family issues that was positive and family oriented, rather than negative and individually focused. In these instances it is understood that the ritual may or may not serve to bind a new structure. If it does, so much the better. If it does not, useful information about the system is often gained; and differences and conflicts can be brought out into the open and resolved in a more functional way than by allowing triangulation with the child to continue.

The intervention described above seemed to be working. At the next session, the family reported that they had no incidents of conflict or confidences exchanged between mother and daughter. Debbie had not run away, and was going to school. There had been no battles between mother and daughter, and father and mother had even managed to get a few minutes to themselves. The therapist warned that when things went this well, he got worried. Change had occurred fast—perhaps too fast. Unfortunately, he was right. During the interim between this session and the next, Debbie had taken a handful of aspirins and other assorted over-the-counter pills in a suicide attempt following an argument with mother. Although she was not hospitalized, the attempt was taken seriously, and an emergency session was immediately scheduled.

The anxiety and stress of the suicide attempt proved to be invaluable in clarifying deeper structural issues in the family. It was learned that the daughter had not been wired to the mother in the straightforward way that had been previously described. True, she did share some confidences with her daughter, but on closer examination these were not of an intimate nature. Instead, they were requests such as "Watch the kids. I'm going out to get your father." It was now discovered that mother had, for years, locked herself into her room alone. She used the bedroom as a base of operations, calling the bars, as stated before, to track down her husband. In its way, the room had become a refuge, offering sanctuary. Mother said that she didn't talk to anyone about what was "really" bothering her. The seriousness of the daughter's suicide attempt, however, provided the leverage necessary to get beyond the mother's defensive position. It was then discovered that mother had been thinking about leaving her husband. Time and again she had pushed John to put the family home up for sale as a way to escape what she felt was a "trapped" existence. Finally he agreed. But the house never sold, and mother began to feel more and more a prisoner of circumstance, remaining isolated and using her room as an escape. In some way, Debbie must have sensed that mother was, in this way, "running." Dramatic current transitions had masked a long-standing structural core in which mother had been the one who wanted to run. Father's drinking had maintained mother's connection to the family. To the degree that father was irresponsible and drunk, mother had to be responsible, there, and functional. Now it was clear how much she had resented what she felt was parenting by alcoholic conscription. Debbie's abusive behavior and running away represented abuse and desire to run away at many levels throughout the system. A more detailed history-taking would not have revealed this information in the first session. The family had not permitted access to mother's strongly felt need to leave until pressed by circumstances. Instead, they had presented as a family that needed only to resolve transitional issues.

Debbie's suicide attempt and past running could now be understood differently. They were desperate attempts to hold and connect mother to the family before she could leave or isolate herself further. The systemic complement was that father, at this point, was still an unproven quantity. He had not been sober enough, there enough, or strong enough to pull mother from the solitary confines of her room. Her presence there had been previously masked by her need to track down her drunken husband. Now her isolation and desire to flee were masked by the need to study for college. Yet, if one were to use a social check-list, one could argue that, on the surface, mother looked good. Father also met the appropriate criteria for a father who was "there." He had stopped drinking for nine months. He was working full-time. He participated in decisions. He had accommodated his wife by attempting to sell the house, and he spent time with the children. But these things had not occurred long enough, with sufficient intensity or frequency, to emotionally graft into the family's experience in such a way as to create a new structure. In its own way, the suicide attempt provided the intensity with which to begin this grafting process.

Debbie's running away had begun to take shape against two structures functioning simultaneously. The one pattern was the fluid, transitional structure brought about by the rapid changes occurring in the family's life. The other, the core structure, had been overshadowed by the current changes happening in and around the family. This core structure—that of mother's isolation, lack of connectedness to the family, and wish to flee—had not been fully addressed by the first intervention. The ritual wedding had been a shotgun wedding, a marriage without romance.

To redress this, the therapist met with mother and father alone and urged them to begin talking to each other. "Otherwise your daughter will continue to jeopardize herself as a way of getting you two to resolve some of these issues between you." Mother began to tell father how angry she was with him, blaming him for the family's inability to get out of the neighborhood. Father quickly began to argue his position, but was blocked by the therapist. Mother then went on to say that she felt the family was holding her back. She could not go on living in her "petty" neighborhood. Father, with the therapist's support, was able to listen to his wife. For a moment, a new structure had been created. Courtship had begun.

The task then assigned was for father to sit with mother in the bedroom for a few minutes a day, so they could talk. It was to be father's job to keep the kids out. He was to become her gatekeeper and her confidant. He had to create a boundary between mother's world and outside pressures. At the same time, he had to convince her that he could indeed listen to be there for her. Now the parents were able to resume their executive functioning with revalued currency. They both told Debbie that suicide was not an option. The session went on for several hours. Debbie had to convince her parents that she did not need hospitalization now but would request it if things got bad. The process of the parents' staying together in the session proved vital as a way of demonstrating their commitment to the children, regardless of their marital situation. The family stabilized, and treatment was again underway. The clinician had to accept the possibility that, in the future, mother might, in fact, run away. But, for the moment, the family structure had stabilized enough to fulfill the daughter's needs.

From the above case study, we can see that new information yielded by structural interventions revealed increasing layers of complexity. In cases with runaways, sometimes the press of symptom and circumstance can detour even the most vigilant eye. By dislocating one structure, another is unfolded. Families can be quite careful about masking these deeper, structural issues, giving clinicians cause to consider the possible systemic consequences of interventions. This last case has been presented in the spirit of sharing such an instance; the case offers one clinician's-eye view of the family in all its vicissitudes. We offer it to our fellow clinicians in the hope that it will serve to improve the clarity of foresight and crystallize the certainties of hindsight.

SUMMARY

This chapter describes a structural/developmental approach to the treatment of adolescent runaways which centralizes the family as the unit of treatment. Emphasis throughout has been on examining the issues of generational hierarchy, conflict avoidance, and the triangulation of the runaway by the parental dyad. We have tried to understand these issues intimately and in a dynamic context; that is, to understand the interplay *between* forces in a family, not just the forces themselves. We believe that, in attempting to understand the complementary nature of these relationships, we gain an understanding of the patterns that lead to a runaway event, as well as of the patterns operating in all families. It is recognized that the model proposed does not address all clinical situations. Rather, this work is offered as a new map of old territory that we hope fellow researchers and clinicians will challenge, build upon, and change.

REFERENCES

Brennan, T., Huizinga, D., & Elliot, D. S. *The social psychology of runaways*, Lexington, MA: D. C. Heath, 1978.

Haley, J. *Uncommon therapy: The psychiatric technique of Milton H. Ericson*. New York: Ballantine, 1973.

Langdell, J. I. Teenagers who run away from home. *Medical Aspects of Human Sexuality*, 1983, **17**(6), 28ff.

Minuchin, S. *Families and family therapy*. Cambridge: Harvard University Press, 1974.

Mirkin, M. P., Raskin, P. A., & Antogini, F. C. Parenting, protecting, and preserving: Mission of the female adolescent runaway. *Family Process*, 1984, **23**(1), 63–74.

Montalvo, B., & Gutierrez, M. A perspective for the use of the cultural dimension in family therapy. In C. Falicov (Ed.), *Cultural perspectives in family therapy*. Rockville, MD: Aspen Systems Corporation, 1983.

Perzel, J. F., & Lamon, S. *Enmeshment within families of polydrug abusers*. In M. D. Stanton, T. Todd, and associates, *The Family Therapy of drug abuse and addiction*. New York: Guilford, 1982.

Sharts-Engel, N., & Lau, A. Damien. Nursing care for the adolescent urban nomad. *Maternal Child Nursing*, 1983, **8**, 74–77.

Stierlin, H. A family perspective on adolescent runaways. *Archives of General Psychiatry*, 1973, **29**, 56–62.

Von Glasersfeld, E. The concepts of adaptation and viability in a radical constructivist theory of knowledge. In I. Sigel, R. Gulinskoff, & D. Brodzinsky (Eds.), *New directions in Piagetian theory and their application to education*. Hillsdale, NJ: Erlbaum, 1980.

Whitaker, C. W. The hinderance of theory in clinical work. In P. J. Guerin (Ed.), *Family therapy: Theory and practice*. New York: Gardner Press, 1976.

Wood, B., & Talmon, M. Family boundaries in transition: A search for alternatives. *Family Process*, 1983, **22**, 347–357.

22

*Adolescents, Families, and Cultural Transition: A Treatment Model**

JUDITH LANDAU-STANTON, M.D.

C hange is a natural feature of our world, affecting its physical properties, geography and inhabitants. It is a topic that for years has occupied the minds of poets, songwriters and sociologists, among others. While the rate of change may vary from era to era, change is nonetheless a constant facet of human and societal development.

Although in many ways inevitable, societal change has rarely occurred without challenge from a segment of those affected. Within a given society, there usually are groups who cling to the safety of pre-existing traditions and norms rather than accept the risk and loss of security accompanying the new or the unknown. That such groups emerge is probably in the nature of human social and political organization.

As a society is composed of subgroups which assume different positions (e.g., "pro" and "con") vis-à-vis an evolving process of change, so is an extended family made up of such subgroups. In a sense,

the family often isomorphically reflects forces within the larger society; i.e., it is a microcosm of the larger society. When such a family experiences major upheaval—for instance, when one of its contingents moves to a new environment or culture—the intra-system conflict is intensified much as it would be if the same were to occur within a larger social group. Under the stress of moving "forward," the creaks and groans of the slowly advancing social organism become amplified, and the organism may begin to lose its coordination. This asynchrony of either rates or directions of change among the subsystems inevitably leads to conflict. Since the con-

*Portions of the text have been published previously in "Therapy with Families in Cultural Transition," in M. McGoldrick, J. K. Pearce, and J. Giordano (Eds.), *Ethnicity and Family Therapy*, New York: Guilford, 1982, and are used here with permission. Appreciation is extended to M. Duncan Stanton, Ph.D., for editorial input on this chapter.

flict arises from difficulties in negotiating transitions, we have called it *transitional conflict* (Landau, 1981; 1982; in press). At such points of transitional conflict, intervention (i.e., "repair" or "readjustment") may be indicated.

THE DEVELOPMENTAL PERSPECTIVE

The implications of change for individual mental health have long been recognized by students of human psychology. In great part, the connection between the two has been drawn by those working in the field of human development. They have come to recognize that the processes of change and development are inextricably linked.

Among the first to identify the connection between change, development and mental health was Sigmund Freud. In particular, he stressed the importance of early childhood development in later emotional adaptation (Jones, 1953). Subsequently, Piaget (1958) pointed out the relevance of childhood cognitive processes for adult functioning. Erikson (1950) further expanded these notions and, in his description of the "Eight Stages of Man," outlined the important points of transition from childhood through old age—a life-cycle formulation. Kubler-Ross (1975) then carried such ideas to their end point in her work on death, terming it "the final stage of growth."

Broadening the development perspective to include a *family* view of the life cycle occurred somewhat later than most of the individually oriented approaches to this topic. The first such work was sociologically based and presented by Reuben Hill and Evelyn Duvall to the National Conference of Family Life in May 1948, (Carter & McGoldrick, 1980). Subsequently, Scherz (1970) drew a comparison between the developmental tasks of the individual and those of the family. She noted that, much as the individual encounters tasks in developmental sequences that overlap and are frequently accompanied by stress, the family also moves through parallel sequential tasks and stress points.

The first explicit application of the family life-cycle paradigm to clinical operations was outlined by Haley (1973) in his book *Uncommon Therapy*, which married the techniques of Milton Erikson to a family life-cycle framework. Later, Sluzki (1979), writing on family migration, linked sound sociological thinking with the clinical implications for families undergoing changes in cultural context. Overall, then, one arm of the psychotherapy field has progressed from a focus on the individual, through a focus on the nuclear and extended family, to an ecosystemic (Auerswald, 1968) and family-in-cultural-context focus.

CULTURAL TRANSITION

"Culture may be defined as the system of social institutions, ideologies, and values that characterize a particular social domain in its adaptation to the environment. It is also implicit in the concept that these traditions and beliefs are systematically transmitted to succeeding generations." (Hamburg, 1975, p. 387)

The rapidity of change in our modern world—and more specifically the threat of cultural migration—commonly leads to an increased intensity of cultural emphasis in a threatened group. It has frequently been surmised that the enormous cultural strength and constancy of the Jews and the Poles emerged from the necessity for them to return to the security of their traditional culture when dangers threatened their group existence.

The threat to the group varies greatly according to the pattern of cultural transition. Where the migration is within the same country, the change may be limited to the loss of family support systems and the alteration of the level of urbanization. When outside influences are responsible for altering an existing culture within the home country, there is more likely to be a certain amount of group and family support as the changes impinge on the community as a whole (Landau, 1982). When, on the other hand, a new country is chosen, an entirely new value system and language may have to be contended with, as well as the loss of family support systems and the change in urbanization levels.

Migration may involve many families from a particular country, region, or culture, or it may be an isolated experience for a single family; more frequently it falls between the two extremes (Sluzki, 1979). The resources needed for handling the transition process are obviously vastly different in each case. It is, therefore, useful to ascertain the transitional history of the migrant group before drawing conclusions as to the stresses affecting any individual family. A working knowledge of the group's developmental history and social and cultural norms will help the therapist avoid misinterpreting the family process—such as viewing a family-environment conflict as primarily arising from conflicts within the nuclear family.

The period of time through which change occurs is perhaps the most crucial factor affecting adaptation. Where change occurs over many generations, the adjustment may be scarcely noticeable and may, in fact, be too gradual to be seen in the space of one lifetime, as in the case of rural Africa (Landau & Griffiths, 1981). By contrast, families undergoing cultural migration may face the stresses of both rapid industrialization and urbanization. These are often accompanied by attitudinal changes, mass media inundation, alteration in dependency patterns, gender-role confusion, and increasing occupational demands, in addition to the pressures inherent in entering a new culture.

The factors determining the facility with which each family resolves issues of transition are both intrinsic and extrinsic to the family unit. If the resources of the family itself and the support systems of the community around it are adequate, and more particularly if the other families in that social group are at a similar stage, problems of acculturation are more likely to be satisfactorily resolved—the family adapts positively (Landau, Griffiths & Mason, 1981). If, on the other hand, such resources are not available, the family may encounter a severe crisis—a transitional conflict. If unresolved, this conflict may lead to symptomatology.

Factors Affecting Cultural Transition

Some important factors affecting cultural transition include the following:

REASONS FOR MIGRATION AND REALIZATION OF GOALS

Cultural migration occurs for diverse reasons—for instance, to escape political harassment or the dangers of war. It may be a fleeing from famine and overpopulation or the founding of a penal colony. It may serve in the search for personal fulfilment and betterment of family fortunes. It may even result from a search for diamonds or gold or the glory of pioneering and the excitement of adventure. Or the move may be an attempt to resolve continuing family problems. A major consideration in the adjustment of the family to migration is the extent to which its original expectations compare with the reality.

AVAILABILITY OF SUPPORT SYSTEMS IN THE COMMUNITY AND FAMILY OF ORIGIN

The support systems in the community play an important role in determining the facility with which each family resolves transitional issues. If other families in the social group are at a similar stage of transition, the problems are more likely to be satisfactorily resolved. The attitude of the family of origin and its health and resources are also major determinants in the system's adaptation.

THE STRUCTURE OF THE FAMILY

The structure of the family is an important factor in its adaptation to the new environment. The natural development of the family as a sociological unit follows a pattern from extended to nuclear family and from nuclear family to newly emergent family forms beyond the nuclear family, such as single parent, blended family, etc. (Landau & Griffiths, 1981). Migration moves the family along this pathway at a more precipitate rate than factors such as urbanization and industrialization. An individual, or a small nuclear unit, moving away from a close traditional extended family into a new culture where nuclear independence is expected, is likely to feel severely threatened. There is a sudden lack of extended-family support at a time when it is most needed. The new isolated unit is also, for the first time, responsible for making and maintaining its own set of rules, which, in view of the new situation and its strange demands, needs to be different from those previously maintained and administered by the hierarchy of the extended family (Landau, et al., 1981).

Degree of Harmony Between Cultures

The relative stress of migration is in part determined both by the country and culture of origin and by the country and culture of adoption. A decision to emigrate from the Far East is likely to be taken by an entire nuclear family, frequently accompanied by one or more members of the extended family. On the other hand, an immigrant from the Western world—usually a male—is far more likely to move alone, followed at most by his immediate family if he has acquired one or, if a bachelor, by creating a nuclear family in the country of adoption. An immigrant from the Middle East may choose either of these alternatives but, if emigrating alone, he often retains far closer links with his family and country of origin than his Western counterpart.

As an example, a Hindu family leaving India in search of greater opportunities in the United States or Great Britain will experience a dramatic transition from the security of a close traditional extended family to the isolation of a nuclear family. It will also be confronted by the totally foreign values of a country with vastly different culture, language, religion, and life-style.

In contrast, the young Anglo-Saxon bachelor emigrating from Great Britain to Australia or South Africa may have only minor difficulty in finding a group with whom he can identify. His problems with language relate to accent only; his religion is no hindrance to the adjustment process; and his family of origin is more likely to accept his decision without question or

threat of permanent mourning. In addition, his facilities for revisiting Great Britain are great, and the stress of cultural migration slight.

When, however, a young Greek or Portuguese decides to leave his homeland in search of financial improvement and educational opportunities for his children, the bereavement is intense. He may well decide to emigrate alone, send for his wife and children later, when possible, and spend the rest of his life in sad exile supporting both his family in the homeland and his nuclear family in the country of adoption. In addition, he may face his own difficulties in the process of adaptation as well as the misery of not being accepted by the citizens of his new home.

Incorporation of Transition as a Developmental Stage: Health of System vs. Dysfunction

Severe crises frequently result from the lack of resolution of transitional issues. The family's healthy adaptation to transitions may be viewed as a successful negotiation of a developmental stage of the family's growth in society, and unresolved transitional conflict may be regarded as leading to dysfunction in the same sense that the unresolved stages of a family's life cycle may result in dysfunction in the system.

Changes Associated with Cultural Transition

The visible markers of a family's ethnic background are its language, religion, education, life-style, and appearance. A family in cultural transition must often confront change in all of these areas.

Language

This is an important vehicle of culture and tradition and therefore a major factor in the adaptation to a new cultural environment. The average youth living in a new culture regards dropping the vernacular as modern and westernized. There are many immigrant families of three or four generations in which the older generations are unable to communicate with the youth because they have no language in common. This leads inevitably to severe transgenerational conflict and the threatened disruption of family integrity and bonding. Unfortunately, it is not uncommon for the first- and second-generation youth to equate the speaking of the traditional language with "lack of education." This increases the transgenerational conflict and also, in some instances, leads to peer-group conflict—on the one side, by those who despise all things traditional and, on the other, by those who regard the aspiration to the new country's ideals as shameful and disloyal to their own identity. For immigrants who do their best to assimilate there frequently remain the problems of non-acceptance because of strange accents or foreign word-order usage.

RELIGION

Religious practices exert a strong influence on families in cultural migration, the older generations tending to adhere to the traditional and the youth forced to choose between identification with families or with peers. In some groups—such as Muslim, Jewish, and Greek Orthodox—schools are provided for religious education after ordinary school hours. Failure to attend results in severe conflict with parents and religious peers. Attendance, however, may result in the children being excluded from extracurricular sports and ordinary social activities with nonsectarian peers. These problems often lead to poor religious identification and severe transgenerational conflict.

EDUCATION

Schooling is a factor that frequently provokes further stress in families in cultural migration. It is not uncommon for the parents of an immigrant family to learn to rely heavily on the better education and adaptation of their offspring, resulting in enormous stress on the functional boundaries of the family. Further transgenerational problems are induced by the parents' feeling of inferiority vis à vis their offspring and peers. The education of the children

is often a major reason for the migration itself, and the parents are left feeling confused and ambivalent with the results. The children in turn may be ashamed of their parents' deficiencies, and problems are multiplied.

LIFE STYLE

Major adjustments in life style are frequently necessary and generally take a couple of generations to be adequately resolved. Migrants are prepared for the confrontation with a new language but are rarely aware of the enormous adjustments that are necessary in their daily living. The type of employment available in the adoptive region may be entirely different from that previously experienced. It may, at best, only appear strange because of the new environment and the foreign colleagues' attitudes. A man who is used to leisurely work in Mediterranean olive groves or vineyards needs to make an enormous adjustment to the long hours and customer demands of a busy café. A move from a socialist work-environment to a capitalist system may create great adjustment difficulties.

Apart from the enormous adjustments that may be necessary on the part of the breadwinner(s), the changes in daily living affect every member of the family. Leisure activities and mode of social contact are likely to be very different; an Italian or Greek family used to sitting in the village square in the evening is likely to become progressively more isolated in a Western city. Transgenerational conflict is easily precipitated by the differential rate at which the younger and older groups adopt new behavioral standards and customs.

It may be clear from the above that many variables determine whether the transition is negotiated with relative ease or with extreme difficulty. The following contrasting cases[1] may illustrate:

---

[1]The author was the therapist in all the cases described in this chapter. She formerly lived in South Africa, which accounts for the South African locale of some of the cases.

Case A. Mr. James Clark,[2] aged twenty-eight years, decided to emigrate from Great Britain where his family had resided for many generations. He was convinced that, for a steamfitter, South Africa offered better work opportunities and a higher standard of living. He, his wife Anne, and their two sons—Michael, aged five years, and John, aged three years—had lived in a different city from both families of origin for some years. Contact had been limited to letters and phone calls to celebrate major events or to discuss family illness. Visits had been occasional. Both sets of parents were very pleased with the young couple's drive and ambition and encouraged the venture.

On arrival in South Africa the family rapidly found friends and neighbors with whom they could communicate and identify. The only obvious difference between them and their new companions was that of accent. Mr. Clarke was easily accepted at work, as his attitudes were very similar to those of his colleagues, and he was more than happy to join them at the local pub on a Friday night. The Clarkes accompanied their neighbors to the local branch of the Anglican church and within a few months regarded themselves as well settled. They made plans to save for a future trip "home" and were very satisfied with their new position, as were both families of origin.

Case B. For Mr. da Costa, the move from Portugal to South Africa was not nearly as easy. At the age of thirty-two he decided to emigrate in search of financial improvement and educational opportunities for his children, hoping at the same time to be able to offer his parents better support than he had been able to manage in Portugal. He arrived in Capetown with a smattering of English, less education than most South Africans of equivalent socioeconomic position, and very little idea of what to expect in his new country. It had been his first parting from a very close, traditional, extended family and he was desperately lonely as well as feeling very guilty about his parents' opposition to his decision and their prolonged mourning caused by his departure and the imminent loss of their grandchildren.

After a year had elapsed he had saved sufficient money to send for his wife and four children ranging from eleven to three years. Far from life becoming easier, his problems seem to intensify. Mrs. da Costa showed no

[2]The names of all families have been changed to maintain confidentiality.

enthusiasm for learning English, wouldn't go shopping alone, and was desperately homesick. The children, on the other hand, rapidly learned the language and how to operate the local currency, and within a short time were trying to teach their mother how to behave in her new environment. They were ashamed of her and her unacceptability to their new friends.

Mr. da Costa's response to his children's reactions was to increase discipline and restrict their contact with their peers as he felt they were being adversely influenced. He emphasized the importance of their education and drove them to achieve good positions in their classes. As the rebellion of the children increased, so did the confusion about the correct standards of behavior, and the family system became severely dysfunctional. Both Mr. and Mrs. da Costa missed their large extended family desperately and felt overwhelmed by the enormity of the problems that they were forced to tackle without assistance.

Adolescents in Cultural Transition

There are many areas where transitional conflict plays a major role in the problems confronting the nuclear family. Transgenerational communication difficulties between couples and their elderly parents must be seen in the light of transitional conflict. In the face of rapid sociological and family change, this has become a problem of increasing magnitude. The perennial area of transgenerational conflict is naturally that of adolescence. As Erikson (1975) notes:

"Adolescence has always been seen as a stage of transition from an alternatively invigorating and enslaving sense of an overdefined past to a future as yet to be identified—and to be identified with. It seems to serve the function of committing the growing person to the possible achievements and the comprehensive ideals of a viable or developing civilization" (p. 175).

The broader transitional issues, therefore, should not be disregarded in the face of the obvious personal transitional tasks confronting the adolescent. If one examines the multifaceted problems of the nuclear family, it becomes self-evident that the sociological transitional process plays a major role. Adolescents facing their own (intensive) developmental issues are particularly vulnerable to the stress of cultural transition and the most likely to progress asynchronously vis à vis their families, which results in severe transitional conflict.

Family Reactions Associated with Transitional Conflict

As noted earlier, when the stresses are extreme and the support systems and health of the family insufficient, the family may become dysfunctional. When family members adjust at different rates, the system is severely stressed and transitional conflict may occur; this can be manifested in several forms.

ISOLATION

Isolation is a paramount risk of the migrant family. Fear of the new situation and a longing for the safe and familiar may cause the family to remain separate from its new environment. Differences in language, education, religion, and life style accentuate the difficulties of adjustment, and where a large, close, extended family has been left behind, the stress of isolation may lead to severe problems of acculturation. Isolation may also be perpetuated by the well-established cultural groups in the adopted country, which often see the new family as "strange" and therefore one to be excluded.

ENMESHMENT

The threat of the new culture, fear that the family's youth will be lost to it, and the family's unacceptability in its new environment may lead the system to fortify its boundaries with the outside world. The family that continues to impose strict traditional values on its members, and retains its religion and language, is forced to strengthen family bonds in an attempt to cope with the unprecedented stress confronting it. Thus, if problems arise, the family is not in a position to make use of the helping facilities of its new community, nor is it able to adapt to new demands. Under stress the family closes ranks and becomes progressively more enmeshed.

DISENGAGEMENT

In certain instances, individuals in the family become isolated as they no longer accept the family's values and life-style. This leaves them very vulnerable in their new environment. In other cases, the whole family is immobilized, which precipitates the loosening of boundaries to the point of disengagement, ultimately increasing the vulnerability of all its members.

TRANSITIONAL CONFLICT: DIFFERENTIAL RATES OF ADJUSTMENT OF FAMILY MEMBERS

The most significant transitional stress occurs when a family member or several members move more rapidly than the others along the transitional pathway. They adapt to the new environment, while others remain resistant to the process of change and struggle to retain the traditional culture at all costs. The resultant conflict of direction precipitates severe problems within the family system. *Recognition of transitional conflict is the key to helping families in cultural transition.* For example, severe sibling rivalry may, on careful assessment, be found to be based on adaptation conflicts. When one spouse is an immigrant or has immigrant parents, the presentation of marital difficulties may signal adaptational stress. The attitudes of an immigrant grandparent may be in serious conflict with those of an adolescent grandchild, who presents the symptom of behavioral disturbance or drug addiction. The resultant conflict may eventuate severe problems within the family. Such transitional conflict is rarely presented directly, and very thorough investigative methods must be employed.

Case C. As an example, Andreas Papadopoulos, aged fourteen, experienced severe schooling difficulties, and the family was referred for therapy. At the initial home visit it was apparent that his parents and maternal grandparents were rigidly traditional, as were his three older sisters. His brother, eighteen-year-old Philotheos, however, spoke excellent English and had made a reasonable adjustment to the new way of life, except that he and his parents argued continually. Mr. and Mrs. Papadopoulos, threatened by the potential loss of their older son, had responded by attempting to close the family's boundaries; they refused to allow friends to visit the house, as they were bitterly opposed to outside influences. They rigidly enforced Greek tradition and religion.

Andreas was caught in an impossible bind. In order to please his parents he had to achieve well at school, but to do this he had to adapt to the new culture and make friends with his peers, thereby risking alienation from his parents. He had to choose between conflict with his grandparents, parents, and sisters, or with his peers and much admired older brother. Each member of the family was caught in the transitional conflict of the system.

TRANSITIONAL THERAPY WITH FAMILIES IN CULTURAL TRANSITION

The range of cultures confronting the family therapist is vast, and the challenge of acquiring a working knowledge of each group's developmental history and norms is overwhelming. An attempt by any therapist to understand the values, traditions, and language of all immigrant groups, though ideal, is far from practical. Consequently, the therapist may be aided by conceptual schemata and operational principles that allow him or her to be as effective as possible across a wide range of families and ethnic groups. In essence, a therapist can proceed by combining these concepts and principles with the specific cultural information provided by a given family. It is assumed that the family knows more about itself and its culture than the therapist ever could. The therapeutic system is therefore composed of two subsystems of "experts"—the family (on its culture), and the therapist (on the theory and means for bringing about change). The remainder of this chapter will deal with the melding of these two areas of expertise.

There have been several approaches to developing a "culture-free" family therapy. The members of the Milan grop (Selvini-Palazzoli, Boscolo, Cecchin, and Prata) have devised a form of therapy that they believe cuts across cultural differences through recognition of elements universal to family systems (G. Cecchin, personal communication, November 1980). Andolfi (1979), too, uses the technique of a common therapeutic language as a tool. Our own approach takes its direction from a combined assessment of both (a) the relevant migration and acculturation stresses on the family, and (b) the presence of the kind of typical transitional problems described above.

The therapeutic methods presented below were developed more or less independently. However, the techniques, principles, and thinking often include what we later learned were structural, strategic, and experiential features (Landau, in press).

Analysis of the System

Upon encountering a symptomatic adolescent and his or her family, it is important to *establish whether transitional conflict is occurring and also whether this is relevant to the problems presented to the therapist*. Not all immigrant adolescents and their families are in need of therapy, and the therapist must take care not to overinterpret the cultural phenomena present. Many families negotiate the acculturation process with minimal difficulty if the factors affecting adaptation are favorable. On the other hand, *many families experience differential rates of transition among their subsystems, inevitably leading to transitional conflict. In the latter, therapy is usually indicated*.

The transitional techniques outlined below—transitional mapping, link therapy, and transitional sculpting (previously termed "dual sculpting"; Landau, 1982)—may be used either as the total focus of therapy or as part of an overall therapeutic plan. Further elucidation of these techniques will be found in Landau (in press). They are used for both diagnostic and therapeutic purposes. In treating families and systems the distinction between diagnosis and treatment is blurred. Any intervention has diagnostic value as the therapist observes the response to it. Any diagnostic action, by its nature, conveys a message from therapist to family and is therefore an intervention (Haley, 1970).

Transitional Mapping

Mapping has become a relatively standard practice in both individual and family therapy. It is extremely useful both as a positive reframing of the problem and as a method for assessing cultural transition. Sluzki (1979), working with migrant families, states categorically that "in the course of the first interview, the therapist should establish which phase of the process of migration the family is currently in and how they have dealt with the vicissitudes of previous phases" (p. 389). *A comprehensive map should extend beyond that of the individual's and family's life cycles to include the transitional position of the multigenerational family within its social and cultural context.* This differential map should include the position of each individual, and of the family as a whole, with respect to life-cycle stages, cultural origin, family form, and current status relative to other family members and the community. (A more detailed explanation of the technique, with illustrations, appears in Landau, 1982, and Landau, in press). Factors aiding or hindering adaptation should be considered, as should the rates of adaptation of family members and the system as a whole. *Whenever differential rates of adaptation are found, the influence of transitional conflict may be presumed, and appropriate therapy instituted.*

Case D. Mrs. Como, aged 29, was referred by her general practitioner for treatment of a severe depression. The family map elicited from Mr. and Mrs. Como and their ten-year-old son Reno at the initial family interview revealed that the family move had been instigated by Mr. Como, who had persuaded his wife that there was more opportunity for motor mechanics in South Africa than in Italy. He had adapted extremely well to the move and was anxious for his wife to become more independent both of him and of her own family.

Mrs. Como's family of origin was a traditional one, of close, extended patriarchal structure. Mrs. Como's emigration was the first rupture in her family's stable pattern. The general practitioner had noticed that Mrs. Como was most depressed when her mother from Italy visited her in South Africa and when Mrs. Como visited Italy. Her parents' response to her depression had been an immediate invitation for the young family to return home.

During the initial interview there were signs of marital conflict. Further evidence of dysfunction in the system was the recent change in Reno. His marks at school had deteriorated, and he had lost interest in sports activities. His position on the map had changed: where previously he had been adjusting well to his new environment, he was now spending more and more time with his parents; he was not speaking English to his father unless ordered to do so; and he was almost spending no leisure time with his peers. Mrs. Como's only social contacts were at the Italian Club. The family was becoming progressively more enmeshed.

The mapping showed that Mrs. Como was trying, unsuccessfully, to negotiate *both* separation from her traditional extended family *and* acculturation, while Mr. Como had successfully negotiated the transition already. Reno, too, was caught in the system's transitional conflict, which had caused decompensation at multiple levels evidenced by the changes mentioned above.

Link Therapy

It is commonly the experience of migrant families to move from close traditional extended families into new situations where nuclear independence is either expected or made inevitable by geographic isolation. As noted earlier, when some members acculturate more rapidly than others, transitional conflict develops. Under such circumstances, a therapist faces two dilemmas: (1) whether to attempt to reverse the direction of transition, or pressure the extended family into accepting the inevitability of the transition; and (2) whether to take control of the family's direction, or allow the family to determine its own direction.

Traditional extended families tend to resolve their own emotional difficulties themselves through prescriptions dictated by their culture—usually without recourse to outside agencies (Landau & Griffiths, 1981). A therapeutic decision to work with the more traditional members of the system, therefore, would imply acceptance of their set of values and lead ultimately to abdication by the therapist. Conversely, a decision to work with the most acculturated member would indicate acceptance of the new set of values. The choice of which family members to involve in therapy can, therefore, determine artificially the transitional direction taken by the therapy. It is thus necessary to establish methods of selection that will avoid such artificial momentum to the direction of resolution but that will enable *the family* to resolve the transitional conflict, thereby facilitating further growth and development.

In our initial work we tried network therapy as devised by Ross V. Speck in the mid-1960s (Speck & Attneave, 1973). We found, however, that it frequently failed in the face of resistance from the rigid, senior members of the hierarchical, extended family. An additional problem in working with these families was that many of them came from a lower-income group and could not afford therapy. There was, therefore, a real need to use brief, strategic intervention wherever possible.

It became apparent to us that a single family member could be used to provide the *link* between the family therapist and the rigid structure of the extended family, since extended families commonly deny the therapist adequate entry (Landau, 1981). This method allows us to avoid the issue of defining therapy as "family therapy," in that the whole family does not have to be present at one time. For example, many Greek, Indian, African, and Iranian parents cannot tolerate discussion in the presence of their children, which defies the typical mode of conventional family therapy. By using link therapy families who would not otherwise become involved in therapy can be treated. It is also an expedient form of therapy, using only one therapist and, for the greater part of the therapy, only one family member.

Link therapy involves the *training and coaching of a family member to function as a therapist to his or her own family system* (Landau, 1981; Landau, in press). After initial family assessment, this family member (link therapist) is selected and goes back alone into the family to initiate interventions with the continued guidance and supervision of the family therapist. The link therapist is coached to assist the family in resolving its transitional conflict in a direction of the link therapist's choice.

SELECTION OF THE LINK THERAPIST

The link therapist needs to be both acceptable to and effective with the family, as well as available and amenable to the family therapist. In a patriarchal system the most effective link would obviously be a man of some seniority, such as an uncle or older son.[3]

The therapist should avoid the temptation to select the most acculturated member of the family whose life-style and values most closely approach the therapist's. Selection of either the most traditional or the most acculturated member would give artificial momentum to the direction of resolution for the transitional conflict. However, the person initially seeking therapy is usually either an acculturated or an entrenched traditional member. In each case the motivation is clear, and agreement to work with either would predetermine the transitional direction taken. Instead, we have found that the most effective link therapist is a family member whose position has not yet been resolved, one who, caught in the system's transitional conflict, is himself in the process of cultural transition. He is generally not the complainant and may even be a peripheral family member.

Since our initial use of the link technique in transitional extended families, we have

[3]The link therapist is hereafter referred to by male pronouns, because a male is most commonly selected for this role, in accordance with what is most acceptable, culturally, for a given family.

used it successfully for other transitional situations, one of the prime areas being adolescence. Here the adolescent functions as link. By investing him or her with a specific role in the therapy, one stabilizes the adolescent's typically mercurial view of self as alternating between omnipotence and impotence. By allowing and encouraging him or her to be the link, one avoids suspicion of the coalition between therapist and parent or parents, that he so readily presumes to be present. Other instances in which it is a useful adjunct is in cases of transgenerational conflict, marital conflict, and in transitional nuclear families where therapy with other family members is not appropriate or where they are not available.

Negotiation and Logistics of the Contract

The initial negotiation occurs during the first consultation session or home visit when the link therapist is selected. The therapist explains to the family that there seem to be many difficulties because family members appear to want the family to go in different directions. Some members may want only the traditional language spoken, while others opt for only the new one; some may want to live in nuclear units, while others are trying to keep the extended family together. The areas of conflict are simplified in order to illustrate the directional discrepancy to the family.

The link therapist is invited to attend an appointment with the family therapist in order to talk about what is happening in his family and to determine whether the therapist might be able to assist him in helping the family sort out its difficulties. It is usually a great relief to the link therapist to feel that he is regarded as competent, an aspect stressed during the initial invitation.

Arrangements for payment are worked out by having the link therapist ask his family, "How shall we pay for this?" Allowing him to negotiate the issue with his family is further confirmation of his competence. In private practice, fees may be covered by medical insurance. Where the

family does not fall into this category, the link therapist decides how the clinic fee (usually nominal) will be met.

During the first link session a contract is negotiated for the link therapist to attend four to six sessions with the family therapist over a period of six to eight weeks. Preceding each appointment with the family therapist, the link therapist is encouraged to conduct a weekly session, of at least one to two hours, in the family's home. Arrangements are also made for a family interview three to six months later.

Coaching of the Link Therapist

Coaching commences during the first session with the link therapist. The object of coaching is to supervise the link therapist's work with the family. He needs to be encouraged to decide the direction of resolution of the family's transitional conflict. For him to do this, he needs to feel that he is invested with sufficient authority to create change. There is an ambivalent message implicit in this that needs to be reconciled before work can commence.

The coach must work out how to supervise, while still investing the link therapist with confidence and authority. We have found that the most effective method is to take the one-down position, using a lot of gentle humor to make the process enjoyable and to diminish the therapist's authority. Positive encouragement and reframing are used liberally in order to elevate the link therapist. Discussion and supervision are kept as simple and clear as possible.

Case E. The following excerpts from first and second link-sessions are taken from a case discussed briefly in an earlier paper (Landau, 1981).

The Naidoos, an Indian South African family, were referred to a university clinic by a local social welfare agency as a multi-problem, low-income family. Many of the family members had been treated on and off for a number of years by the agency and various other clinics. The eleven Naidoo children ranged in age from twenty-four to four years old. The three oldest were all married sons living with their wives in the family home.

The fourth was a married daughter, the only one living away. Following her were four girls (ages eighteen, sixteen, fourteen, and twelve), a boy of nine, a girl of six, and a boy four.

The major presenting problems were the serious acting-out behavior of the adolescent daughters, one of whom (the sixteen-year-old) had recently produced an illegitimate child. In addition, the daughters-in-law had severe ongoing problems with their mother-in-law, which resulted in their frequent desertion of the family home, with or without their husbands. A further finding was that Mr. Naidoo's authority had been usurped by his wife, and he relied on severe asthma attacks to retain some modicum of control.

The initial family assessment session was held in the home. Over two dozen family members were present, including both parents, nine of the eleven children, several daughters-in-law, a number of grandchildren, and some cousins. The multiplicity and severity of the problems, the checkered therapeutic history, and the complex logistics that were required to gather this clan together on a regular basis indicated that link therapy might be an appropriate option.

The third son, Ganesh (aged twenty-two) had been absent from the initial interview and also appeared to have the least difficulty moving in and out of the traditional extended-family home. He was the only son with steady, gainful employment. He had never needed therapy. As the most transitional and most peripheral member, he was invited, with the family's consent, to be the link therapist.

At the first link session, discussion revolved around the family difficulties:

THERAPIST: What have the problems been in the family?

GANESH: I've had no problems.

THERAPIST: This is the main reason I wanted to meet you. It seems that the rest of the family has had much difficulty and that you haven't, so I thought maybe you would be prepared to help me help the other members of the family. How would you feel about doing that?

GANESH: Okay.

Ganesh then discussed his feelings about being the brother with the greatest strength and the one best able to control his wife. However, he sounded daunted by the magnitude of the family's problems.

GANESH: Too many problems, too many! It's difficult to stay calm, because everyone shouts and swears and there is too much corruption because of my mother letting the girls do just what they want.

THERAPIST: Who is the boss of the house?

GANESH: The head of the house is my father.

THERAPIST: And does he manage?

GANESH: I don't think so.

THERAPIST: Can your father tell your mother what to do?

GANESH: No, she never listens. (*Chuckles.*)

THERAPIST: How would you like to change things in the family?

GANESH: Married ones should live separately.

Ganesh then outlined his ideas and goals. He wanted the family to progress to a point where there was looser bonding of the extended and nuclear units (the constellation most frequently found enroute to nuclearization).

THERAPIST: How can we best help the rest of the family?

GANESH: We have regular meetings and discuss like now, and I go back to them and help my father stop the women from winning all the time.

At the second link-interview, two weeks later, Ganesh explained:

GANESH: I spoke to my father and saw that it wouldn't work, so I called my uncle down and we chatted. I told him of all the carrying on at home and of the corruption. He has a lot of strength and he said that he would help me run the house the right way.

THERAPIST: How are you going to tell the rest of the family?

GANESH: My uncle told them, and my father is very glad because my mother will listen to him.

THERAPIST: Do you think that things in the family will work out?

GANESH: Of course. My uncle gave them all lectures about how to behave, especially the girls. My mother is scared of my uncle, and she was silent as soon as he came. She listened to every word.

THERAPIST: So you are happy about things now?

GANESH: Yes, things are coming straight now.

To the therapist's amazement, Ganesh had elected to call in a traditional authority figure to reestablish the hierarchy of the extended family. Ganesh canceled all further link meetings, and at a follow-up home visit three months later the therapist was told that there were no further problems. It was difficult to believe that there was no further dysfunction of the system. What was evident, however, was that the return of the family to its traditional extended form prevented the necessity for outside intervention, as problems were once more resolved according to strict traditional prescription within the boundaries of the family system.

Case F. The course of therapy was very different with the Casalviere family. They had been referred for treatment by the school psychologist because of the children's bad behavior. Ten-year-old Fabrizio was acting out at school. He was "untidy, rude, and constantly getting into fights." His father had given the teachers permission to discipline the boy as necessary, but they were not able to achieve much change in his behavior. In addition, Felice, fourteen years old, was refusing to speak Italian and becoming very insolent to her parents and grandparents.

At the initial family interview, it was discovered that Luigi Casalviere, an engineer, aged thirty-six, and his wife Tiziana, a housewife, aged thirty-four, had immigrated to South Africa with their three children, including Fabbiola, aged eight, five years previously. Luigi's parents remained in Italy but Tiziana's parents, Mr. and Mrs. Girone, had joined the family in South Africa eleven months before the referral. The additional member of the household was Luigi's brother, Aldo, a thirty-year-old bachelor who had arrived shortly after his brother.

The interview was very strained, with Mr. Girone keeping tight control of all that was said. He kept reiterating that "everything's fine in this house," and made the therapist feel like an unwelcome intruder. Aldo was very polite and obviously intent on not upsetting Mr. Girone. Luigi, on the other hand, made some hard comments about his son, Fabrizio, and seemed less awed by the situation.

Luigi had apparently made a large circle of friends, which he shared with Aldo and with whom he was spending increasing amounts of time away from home. His job was going well, and he couldn't see that there were any problems apart from his children's behavior. Tiziana was relatively silent but looked especially unhappy when Luigi's friends were discussed. She also remarked that the children were forgetting both their Italian and their religion, and that their respect for their grandparents had deteriorated. The latter was stated with an accusing look at her husband. It was evident that the traditional members of the family would sabotage therapy, if given the chance, so the link technique was selected.

Aldo was the most suitable link therapist; he was acceptable to the traditional members of the family, ready to work with the therapist, and in the process of making decisions about his transitional position. The family agreed, rather reluctantly, to allow him to attend the first link session one week later if something could be done about the children.

During the first session Aldo expressed his doubts about carrying any weight with Mr. and Mrs. Girone, but he felt competent to talk to the younger members of the family.

ALDO: The kids are good kids, they listen to their uncle most of the time, and my brother—well, he's okay. But her parents—everything old is good; they don't want to hear.

THERAPIST: I don't know. They seemed pretty fond of you when I saw you all together.

ALDO: Mmm.

The therapist encouraged him to look at how well he got on with the old people, how they shared a sense of humor, and how they all lost patience with Luigi at times. Aldo gradually became aware that he might have some ability to guide their opinions, certainly far more than the therapist—who shared a good laugh with him about that!

Aldo felt that the solution to the family's confusion and conflict was for everybody to learn English better, "but not forget to speak Italian ever," and for Luigi to "make more fuss of Tiziana and take her out more with his friends—She doesn't know them and makes a big noise all the time. If they go out more, she won't be hearing her mother all the time and then she won't give Luigi such a hard time." He also felt that the children should spend more time with their school-mates and be more involved in sports.

Aldo undertook to spend at least two hours a week discussing the plans with the family. With some gentle guidance he agreed that he should work with Tiziana and her parents before "interfering" in his brother's marriage. He decided to encourage Mr. and Ms. Girone to get out of the house more and planned to take them to the Italian Club.

At the fifth link-session, seven weeks after the first consultation, Aldo reported that the situation at home had improved considerably. Tiziana was even speaking English to the children on occasion, and Aldo felt that she was not so much under her father's control. Aldo still felt that Luigi ought to take his wife out more and that they were not getting along well enough. He felt, however, that he would like to continue working without the therapist's supervision, and an arrangement was made for a family meeting three months later. The therapist felt that if resolution of the cultural transitional conflict continued and there were still problems in Luigi's marriage, conventional marital therapy could be considered.

The second family consultation was markedly different from the first. Mr. Girone allowed Aldo to say almost as much as himself, and there appeared to be far less tension (possibly also because the therapist was no longer a total stranger). The most significant change was Tiziana's bright appearance and her active participation in the session. Aldo felt that no further help was required at that stage, but he promised to contact the therapist if he felt it was needed in the future.

The school reported a noticeable change for the better in Fabrizio's behavior, and the parents stated that the problems with Felice and Fabrizio had abated. At telephone follow-up six months later, the school principal stated that all the children were doing fine and that there had been no further difficulties.

The link therapists in transitional families generally elect to move the family along the natural direction of cultural transition, but this is not inevitable. Some choose to return the family to its traditional form, as did Ganesh. *Where this occurs, resolution of conflict tends to be temporary and is superseded by further crises of cultural transition until the*

natural direction is pursued (Landau, 1981). When the natural direction is followed, as in the case of the Casalviere family, the successful resolution of problems is far more likely to result.

Link therapy may be used in any situation of cultural transition where access to the family as a whole is not feasible or appropriate. It may be used for adolescent difficulties within a culturally transitional family, for a child with problems at school, or for any other instance of cultural transgenerational conflict. In one family where the traditional family members remained in Germany, the son-in-law was sent to do the link work on an intensive basis. He achieved satisfactory resolution of the directional conflict, and the South African part of the family system improved.

We might wonder how this approach differs from that developed by Bowen (1978). The two approaches are similar in that both employ the coaching of one person and both relate to the total family system. One difference is that the Bowen method emphasizes the dynamics within the multigenerational family system, while the link approach stresses a broader system involving the multigenerational family in its socioanthropological context. There are three major operational distinctions, however:

(1) The Bowen approach aims at differentiating the individual from his family system, whereas the link-therapy technique is more *problem-focused* and trains a family member to be the therapist in his own family system.

(2) The tendency with the Bowen approach is to work with the index patient or the person appearing for therapy with a complaint either about him- or herself or about other family members. In contrast, link therapy involves scanning the family system and *selecting a change-agent*. This change-agent is rarely the presenting person. Thus an intermediate step is inserted into the process, whereby the therapist attempts to analyze (e.g., map) the total system, in order to determine both where the members and subsystems lie along the transitional pathway and who might be the most appropriate link therapist. Incidentally, this method also avoids the family's *de facto* self-selection process of

nominating a symptomatic member, or a member most "upset" by the problem; the decision where (and with whom) to intervene is removed from the family, along with its possibly homeostatic—or "no change" —trappings, and is instead made by the therapist.

(3) Link therapy is a much more concentrated paradigm, aimed at rapid resolution and change over a *brief period of time*. A Bowen therapist might meet for sessions monthly or even yearly, whereas the link model usually involves four to six sessions over a period of six to eight weeks, with a follow-up session three to six months later.

Transitional Sculpting

The technique of transitional (or "dual") sculpting was developed for use in families where members in transitional conflict are amenable to and available for therapy. Should the families of, for example, a married couple (i.e., the two sculptors) not be amenable to, or available for, the session—as frequently happens in cases of severe cultural conflict—students, colleagues, or clinic staff may be used to simulate family members.

Transitional sculpting has grown out of the original sculpting technique pioneered and developed by such therapists as David Kantor, Fred and Bunny Duhl, Peggy Papp, and Virginia Satir (Duhl, Kantor, & Duhl, 1973). Hoffman (1981) summarizes the use of sculpting as follows:

> . . . to elicit major coalition formations and homeostatic sequences, so that old patterns can be perceived and played out differently . . . It can also be used by members of a family in therapy as a geospatial metaphor for various aspects of a relationship system: closeness/distance; splits and alignments; the experience of being one up to one down in reference to another. (p. 250)

Transitional sculpting differs from other sculpting in that we use a sculptor from each of the two families (or the two parts of the family) in cultural conflict and assist them in negotiating a joining of the two. Recognition is given to the larger system of the family in its cultural community. The method is thus an invaluable tool for working with families in cultural transition.

In the case of a couple in marital therapy, each member of the couple would sculpt his and her family of origin. In the case of intergenerational conflict, either a member from each generation might sculpt his or her view of the family, or, with an identified marital problem, the two parents might be the sculptors. In other words, with adolescent-parent conflict, the adolescent and a parent could be the sculptors, or both parents might sculpt. Table 22.1 outlines the various steps.

In transitional sculpting one of the two family members selected as sculptors chooses to sculpt first while the other watches. The sculpting may be either in tableau form (as though posed for a family photograph), or in action—according to the preference of the sculptor. The initial sculpting is nonverbal and as true to life as possible. Once the sculpture is complete, the therapist suggests that the sculptor move into fantasy and alter the sculpture according to his or her own personal desires. The therapist as mentor encourages as much change as possible at this stage. When real family members are used, their reactions to both the original sculpture and the changes are quietly discussed. The procedure is then reversed, with the first sculptor becoming the observer and the previous observer sculpting his or her own family or subsystem (or own view of the same family).

When both sculptors have completed realistic and fantasy sculptings, they are asked to reassemble their original sculptures. Each sculptor in turn is then asked to move into the other's sculpture in the position or role of the original sculptor to experience the feeling created by the other. After discussing their reactions, they are encouraged to make alterations with which they feel comfortable. Each then returns to his or her own sculpture to experience the changes brought about, and again their reactions are discussed. Each is usually able to go much further in fantasy in the other's sculpture than in his or her own, and a depth of experience and insight not found in individual sculpting results.

It is frequently useful at this stage to ask the two sculptors to sculpt, without words, their position relative to each other. Brief discussions may follow, but the positioning itself is nonverbal and the opportunity for negotiation is not given at this stage.

The final stage of the actual transitional sculpting then begins, when the sculptors are asked to negotiate the joining of their two original sculptures. If appropriate, they are given permission to exclude peripheral members of their families. Often a great deal can be achieved during this final phase.

As the sculptors struggle to impose the transitional directions of their choice and become ultimately aware of the opposing forces, they often achieve a profound level of insight. Family members then learn to accommodate and compromise and are also given the opportunity to be creative.

Because the technique of transitional sculpting is a very powerful tool, attention must be paid to the debriefing period, which is critical. Participants are encouraged to discuss and share their experiences of the session. We have found it useful to have audiovisual recordings for this purpose. We have also found it necessary that the initial discussion about the sculpting experience occur during the same therapy session as the sculpting, although it naturally continues beyond this into subsequent sessions.

Case G Eight-year-old Basil Wald was doing very badly at school, and his father was requested to visit the school. Mr. Wald, an accountant, aged thirty-three, whose parents were Jewish immigrants from Central Europe, was alarmed to hear that Basil's behavior was intolerable to teachers and pupils alike, that he was distractible during lessons, violent during breaks, and would have to be removed from the school if matters did not rapidly improve. The school counselor referred Basil and his parents to the family therapist.

At the first family consultation, attended by Mr. and Mrs. Wald and their two sons, Basil and Julian (aged 3 months), it became evident that the family was on the point of dissolution. There had been an underlying, scarcely suppressed, marital strife for many years, which had come to a head with the birth of Julian.[4] Mr. Wald regarded his wife, a dedicated physiotherapist, aged thirty, as far too independent, a hopeless cook (particularly when compared with his mother, whose main purpose in life was baking and cooking for the family), a careless mother,

TABLE 22.1.
The Procedure of Transitional Sculpting: Sculptors A and B

1. *A* sculpts	true to life; then according to fantasy	*B* observes
2. *B* sculpts	true to life; then according to fantasy	*A* observes
3. *A* moves into *B*'s sculpture	true to life; then according to *A*'s fantasy	*B* observes
B moves into *A*'s sculpture	true to life; then according to *B*'s fantasy	*A* observes
4. *A* and *B* sculpt their own positions relative to each other		
5. *A* and *B* create	**the transitional sculpt:** reassemble original sculptures and negotiate joining of the two	

and an undemonstrative wife, who chose to share nothing of her life, verbal or practical, with her husband. Mrs. Wald, the daughter of Irish immigrants, felt that there were no further sacrifices she could make for her husband and his family. Despite her conversion to Judaism she had never felt accepted by her husband's family. She failed to understand his need for her to give up her job and could not bear his continual demands for public displays of affection and the verbalization of every minor situation. It was evident to the therapist that Basil's behavioral disturbance was symptomatic of a stressed parental subsystem and a decision was taken to commence work on the marriage.

Since Basil's problems were the only topic of common interest currently shared by his parents, structural intervention seemed appropriate. However, on the transitional map the cultural conflict was readily apparent, and it was felt that this needed to be resolved before therapy could proceed further. The cultures of Mr. and Mrs. Wald's parents were very different, as were the needs of the couple, neither of whom seemed aware of the origins of their difficulties. As the therapist felt that the transitional conflict was primary to the problems that the family was experiencing, a decision was made to use transitional sculpting.

Since neither of the families of Mr. or Mrs. Wald could be appropriately included in the therapy session, a group of family therapy trainees was invited to participate in the sculpting. The therapist chose to exclude the children from the session, as the major business was between the parents.

Mr. Wald was invited to be the first sculptor. He was instructed to select people from the group to represent the members of this three-generational family of origin and to arrange them as he saw them in relation to each other, making use of space and movement wherever possible, but not speaking other than to inform the therapist of the identity of each member. Mr. Wald arranged his surrogate family in a busy domestic scene

[4]While the identified patient in this case is not an adolescent, the nuclear and extended family dynamics, and the critical life-cycle event (birth of a new baby), could very easily have occurred in the family of an adolescent (although with the latter, the presenting problem would more likely be an acting-out syndrome, such as running away or violence). As will be shown, the age of the index patient is frequently not central to the theoretical and operational features of the treatment.

with his mother actively involved in food preparation in the kitchen; his father reading the newspaper but observing the family's activities over the top of it from time to time; and he and his siblings sitting comfortably around the dining room table, each busily involved in some separate activity but with intermittent, marked interest in each other. His youngest sister moved repeatedly to the kitchen to participate in mother's activities. Mr. Wald placed his grandparents in a nearby room.

The therapist then asked Mr. Wald to move into fantasy and to alter the family in any way he wanted, pretending that any change was feasible. Mr. Wald's only alteration of the scene was to ensure that his older brother took a greater interest in his (Mr. Wald's) writing, discussing it with him at regular intervals. Despite considerable encouragement from the therapist, he was unable to introduce further changes.

Mrs. Wald, when asked to experience her husband's family as he had arranged it, felt severely constricted and immediately moved both the paternal grandparents, who had been sitting quietly in what appeared to be the living room, away from the sculpture. She informed the therapist that they had both been dead for a considerable time and decided that it was high time they were truly buried, as she felt that their influence over the family was iniquitous. The paternal grandparents had died prior to her husband's birth. She further separated the children, moving the married members of the family away. Her last move was to seat her mother-in-law on a chair near her father-in-law.

When Mr. Wald was asked how he felt about his wife's fantasy, he appeared delighted with the burial of his grandparents but found it extremely difficult to accept the disruption of the sibling generation. He also enjoyed the proximity of his mother and father and expressed surprise that he had felt unable to institute this necessary change. Mrs. Wald was able by her fantasy to help Mr. Wald create changes that he would never had considered.

Mrs. Wald then proceeded to choose and arrange her own family members. The scene was one of amazing activity. Her father paced restlessly up and down, two of her brothers rushed in and out of the tableau with alarming speed, and her mother repeatedly turned toward her father in supplication and then away in despair. Her younger sister lay on the carpet, apparently engrossed in a book, and Mrs. Wald sat at a table involved with her sewing.

When asked to move into fantasy, Mrs. Wald brought one brother back into the family and banished the other. She placed her father firmly in a chair with the newspaper and seated her mother nearby. She tried tentatively to make them touch but was unable to sustain the contact and returned her father's hand to his newspaper.

Mr. Wald, given free reign with his wife's family, reintroduced the missing brother and formed a cozy domestic scene with which Mrs. Wald felt extremely uncomfortable.

The couple was then asked to show the therapist, nonverbally, where they now were in relation to each other. Not surprisingly, they placed themselves at opposite ends of the room and, despite Mrs. Wald's attempts to reach her husband, they remained distant from each other. The therapist realized that her hypothesis that the couple had never really negotiated a marriage was correct. She then requested that the couple, using words where necessary, attempt to negotiate the joining of their two families of origin. They each made vain attempts to introduce their fathers and gave up; they had more success with their mothers, and none at all in a joint arrangement of the family.

The situation was gently interpreted during the session, and the interpretation was continued in the debriefing process. Mr. and Mrs. Wald spent two more sessions working through the video material with the therapist. After considerable debate, they decided they were prepared to put in the work necessary for the continuation of the marriage and committed themselves to marital therapy.

During the ensuing six months, structural family therapy (Minuchin, 1974) was employed in order to stabilize the intergenerational boundary. This was accompanied by marital therapy for the couple. The situation improved remarkably. Basil's behavior at school continued to settle, and his marks became progressively better. The therapist considered using Mr. Wald as a link therapist with his family of origin, but this proved unnecessary as the family opened its ranks to accept Mrs. Wald once the marital situation had improved.

SUMMARY

We have examined some of the specific effects of migration on the family system. It will be evident from the discussion that the larger system of the family in its community must be considered and that a knowledge of culture, tradition, and ethnicity is vital in understanding adolescents and families in cultural transition.

We have used case studies to illustrate the necessity for careful examination of families in order to locate their phase of cultural transition and the presence of conflict. Cultural conflict is usually most intense between parents who retain their traditional values and their children who move more quickly to the values of the new culture. It is all too easy for the therapist to presume that the new or dominant culture of a society must be right for everybody and that the nuclear family structure, or the therapist's own, is the only correct paradigm. Families should be allowed and encouraged to make their own choices, facilitated by the therapist where intervention is appropriate.

The key to treating families in cultural transition is to recognize that their problems arise because different family subsystems adapt at different rates. This notion underlines the framework presented here—a framework that cuts across many dimensions of family functioning, transcends ethnic boundaries, and provides a blueprint for systemic change. The particular therapeutic mode used—for example, link therapy or transitional sculpting—is less important than adherence to this conceptual paradigm. Transitional therapy clarifies the differential rates of adaptation and facilitates the family's resolution of transitional conflict.

REFERENCES

Andolfi, M. *Family therapy: An interactional approach.* New York: Plenum, 1979.

Auerswald, E. H. Interdisciplinary versus ecological approach. *Family Process*, 1968, **7**, 202–215.

Bowen, M. *Family therapy in clinical practice.* New York: Jason Aronson, 1978.

Carter, E. A., & McGoldrick, M. (Eds.). *The family life cycle.* New York: Gardner Press, 1980.

Duhl, F. J., Kantor, D., & Duhl, B. S. Learning, space and action in family therapy: A primer of sculpture. In D. Bloch (Ed.), *Techniques of family psychotherapy.* New York:

Grune & Stratton, 1973.

Erikson, E. H. *Childhood and society*. New York: Norton, 1950.

Erikson, E. H. *Life history and the historical moment*. New York: Norton, 1975.

Haley, J. Approaches to family therapy. *International Journal of Psychiatry*, 1970, **9**, 223–242.

Haley, J. *Uncommon therapy*. New York: Norton, 1973.

Hamburg, B. A. Social change and the problems of youth. In S. Arieti (Ed.), *American handbook of psychiatry* (2nd ed.). New York: Basic Books, 1975.

Hoffman, L. *Foundations of family therapy*. New York: Basic Books, 1981.

Jones, E. *The life and work of Sigmund Freud*. London: Hogarth, 1953.

Kubler-Ross, E. *Death: The final stage of growth*. Englewood Cliffs, NJ: Prentice-Hall, 1975.

Landau, J. Link therapy as a family therapy technique for transitional extended families. *Psychotherapeia*, 1981, **7**(4), 382–390.

Landau, J. Therapy with families in cultural transition. In M. McGoldrick, J. K. Pearce, & J. Giordano (Eds.). *Ethnicity and family therapy*. New York: Guilford, 1982.

Landau, J. *The family in transition: Theory and practice*. New York: Guilford, in press.

Landau, J., & Griffiths, J. A. The South African family in transition: Therapeutic and training implications. *Journal of Marital and Family Therapy*, 1981, **7**(3), 339–344.

Landau, J., Griffiths, J. A., & Mason, J. The extended family in transition: Clinical implications. *Psychotherapeia*, 1981, **7**(4), 370–381. Republished in F. Kaslow (Ed.), *The international book of family therapy*. New York: Brunner/Mazel, 1982.

Minuchin, S. *Families and family therapy*. Cambridge, MA: Harvard University Press, 1974.

Piaget, J. *The growth of logical thinking from childhood to adolescence*. (A. Parsons & S. Seagrin, trans.). New York: Basic Books, 1958.

Scherz, F. H. Theory and practice of family therapy. In R. W. Roberts & R. H. Nee (Eds.), *Theories of social casework*. Chicago: University of Chicago Press, 1970.

Sluzki, C. E. Migration and family conflict. *Family Process*, 1979, **18**(4), 379–390.

Speck, R. V., & Attneave, C. L. *Family networks*. New York: Pantheon, 1973.

Selected Bibliography

compiled by CYNTHIA GUILE ANDRIAN, Ph.D.

NOTE: For sources on family therapy in general, the reader is advised to consult works such as the first three items:

Guerin, P. J. *Family therapy: Theory and practice.* New York: Gardner Press, 1976.

Hoffman, L. *Foundations of family therapy.* New York: Basic Books, 1981.

Nichols, M. P. *Family therapy: Concepts and methods.* New York: Gardner Press, 1984.

* * *

Ackerman, N. J. The family with adolescents. In E. A. Carter & M. McGoldrick (Eds.), *The family life cycle: A framework for family therapy.* New York: Gardner Press, 1980. Identifies adolescence as a landmark phase within the life cycle, with resulting implications for treatment.

Barnhill, L. R. (Ed.). *Clinical approaches to family violence.* Rockville, MD: Aspen, 1982. Presents a variety of perspectives, including an informative chapter on adolescents who are violent within the family.

Haley, J. *Uncommon therapy: The psychiatric techniques of Milton H. Erickson, M.D.* New York: Norton, 1973. Includes classic illustrations of Erickson's techniques in dealing with problems at each stage of the life cycle. Very readable.

Haley, J. *Leaving home: The therapy of disturbed young people.* New York: McGraw-Hill, 1980. Thorough explication of a practical approach to therapy for a variety of problems in the late adolescent life-stage. Valuable case histories.

Hatton, C. L., & Valente, S. M. *Suicide: Assessment and intervention* (2nd ed.). Norwalk, CT: Appleton-Century-Crofts, 1984. Practical handbook covering a considerable variety of issues revolving around suicide. Includes useful chapters focusing on adolescents.

Howells, J. G. Family group therapy. In J. G. Howells (Ed.), *Modern perspectives in adolescent psychiatry.* New York: Brunner/Mazel, 1971. Good introduction, providing brief overview of family isssues, details of techniques, and therapist characteristics.

Kaufman, E., & Kaufmann, P. *Family therapy of drug and alcohol abuse.* New York: Gardner Press, 1979. Contains excellent exploration of family interactions customarily found when an adolescent is abusing drugs or alcohol.

Lansky, M. R. (Ed.). *Family therapy and major psychopathology.* New York: Grune & Stratton, 1981. Includes chapters applying family therapy to specific disturbances of adolescence. Important examination of the use of family therapy with hospitalized patients.

Madanes, C. *Strategic family therapy.* San Francisco: Jossey-Bass, 1981. For the therapist, clearly detailed and theoretically backed techniques for correcting power imbalances in families displaying milder and more severe problems of adolescence. Case histories provide helpful illustrations.

Minuchin, S., Rosman, B. L., & Baker, L. *Psychosomatic families: Anorexia nervosa in context*. Cambridge, MA: Harvard University Press, 1978. Benchmark family analysis of anorexia nervosa. Presents therapy techniques and informative case studies.

Napier, A. Y., & Whitaker, C. A. *The family crucible*. New York: Harper & Row, 1978. Classic, extremely readable account of the therapy done with the family of a rebellious, suicidal adolescent.

Papp, P. *Family therapy: Full-length case studies*. New York: Gardner Press, 1977. Readable case histories, many involving families with problem adolescents.

Parmelee, D. X. The adolescent and the young adult. In L. I. Sederer (Ed.), *Inpatient psychiatric disorders and treatment*. Baltimore: Williams & Williams, 1983. Practical discussion of a program model for inpatient adolescents.

Sager, C. J., Brown, H. S., Crohn, H., Engel, T., Rodstein, E., & Walker, L. *Treating the remarried family*. New York: Brunner/Mazel, 1983. Several chapters highlight issues that concern adolescents. The appendix contains guidelines for examining relationships in remarried families.

Schaefer, C. E., Briesmeister, J. M., & Fitton, M. E. *Family therapy techniques for problem behaviors of children and teenagers*. San Francisco: Jossey-Bass, 1984. Useful reference work. Detailed abstracts of the family therapy literature present practical information for interventions, which are organized by disorder.

Schomer, J. Family therapy. In B. B. Wolman, J. Egan, & A. O. Ross (Eds.), *Handbook of treatment of mental disorders in childhood and adolescence*. Englewood Cliffs, NJ: Prentice-Hall, 1978. Brief, introductory-level chapter locating family therapy within the context of traditional approaches. Oriented toward therapists not committed to a systems approach.

Shapiro, R. C. Adolescents in family therapy.

In J. R. Novello (Ed.), *The short course in adolescent psychiatry*. New York: Brunner/Mazel, 1979. Good introduction to the application of Bion's analytic group theory to family therapy.

Sholevar, G. P., Benson, R. M., & Blinder, B. J. (Eds.). *Emotional disorders in children and adolescents: Medical and psychological approaches to treatment*. New York: Spectrum, 1980. Excellent overview chapters of psychodynamic and systemic family therapy. Application of family therapy to specific problems of adolescence.

Stanton, M. D., Todd, T. C., & Associates. *The family therapy of drug abuse and addiction*. New York: Guilford, 1982. Highlights distinctions and similarities between adolescent and adult abusers, within a coherent framework of theory and research.

Stierlin, H. *Psychoanalysis and family therapy: Selected papers*. New York: Jason Aronson, 1977. Contains chapters on adolescents in a family therapy approach developed from a psychoanalytic perspective.

Sugar, M. (Ed.). *The adolescent in group and family therapy*. New York: Brunner/Mazel, 1975. Basic introduction.

Sullivan, H. S. *The interpersonal theory of psychiatry*. New York: Norton, 1953. Valuable early contribution, which laid the groundwork for the development of much of family therapy today. A standard work on adolescent development.

Visher, E. B., & Visher, J. S. *Stepfamilies: A guide to working with stepparents and stepchildren*. New York: Brunner/Mazel, 1979. Introductory work deals with children's issues relevant to divorce and remarriage. Provides some basic guidelines for interventions with stepchildren.

Woody, J. D., & Woody, R. H. (Eds.). *Sexual issues in family therapy*. Rockville, MD: Aspen, 1983. Covers the gamut of sexual issues, including adolescents' involvement with heterosexuality, homosexuality, and incest. Good introductory work for this subject area.

Author Index

Subject Index